P9-BTN-866

SUBSIDIA BIBLICA

14/I

subsidia biblica - 14/I

PAUL JOÜON, S.J.

A Grammar of Biblical Hebrew

Translated and Revised
by
T. MURAOKA

Volume I

Part One: Orthography and Phonetics
Part Two: Morphology

Reprint of First Edition, with Corrections

EDITRICE PONTIFICIO ISTITUTO BIBLICO — ROMA 2000

This is a translation and revision of *Grammaire de l'Hébreu biblique* by Paul Joüon, S.J., originally published by the Pontifical Biblical Institute in 1923 and subsequently and frequently reprinted with no substantial change.

Firs Edition, 1991
Reprint of First Edition, with Corrections, 1993
Second Reprint, 1996
Third Reprint, 2000

ISBN 88-7653-595-0

Editrice Pontificio Istituto Biblico
Piazza della Pilotta 35 — 00187 Roma, Italia

To Professor James Barr, FBA
Regius Professor of Hebrew, Oxford University
1978 — 89
in recognition of his outstanding scholarship
and warmth of friendship

PREFACE TO THE ORIGINAL FRENCH EDITION

The progress in biblical studies in our time has led to the general recognition, particularly among Catholics, of the need of deeper understanding of the "sacred language." The advancement in Semitic philology, on the other hand, makes it necessary to study Hebrew in a more scientific manner as has been the case for a long time with other dead languages such as Greek and Latin. It is with a view to meeting the need of a sufficiently complete grammar of scientific character, a need often expressed by our students, initially of the Oriental Faculty of the University of St Joseph in Beirut, and subsequently of the Pontifical Biblical Institute in Rome, that we have decided to undertake such a task. What was required was an intermediate grammar bridging the gap between the best of elementary grammars and the monumental works such as *Lehrgebäude* by E. König.

With regard to both the scope of the present work and the mode of presentation, we have had in mind the ever-growing group of students who feel it necessary to go beyond the stage of purely factual(1) knowledge and wish to develop their ability to resolve the numerous grammatical difficulties of the massoretic text instead of merely bypassing them. They will find here not only all the fundamental concepts, but also most of the details of minor importance. As for the many minute details and anomalies which can make the study of Hebrew such a discouraging undertaking, we have had to set a limit. Besides, what is important for the student is not so much to know a great number of details as to be able to identify an unusual form and to decide whether it is explicable or, having no comparable form, it is anomalous or incorrect. But where it was found that a detail, even the most trivial, could throw some light on some obscure matter, we did not hesitate to note it. One will find here many a point of detail not dealt with by E. Kautzsch; on the other hand, some details given by this grammarian have been deliberately left out.

(1) Of course, the factual knowledge of the forms and the words is the essential basis for any advanced study. One must ensure that one has a precise knowledge of the basics: writing system, pronunciation, paradigms, basic vocabulary. Although this grammar, we believe, is easily usable by any mature student with an average philological grounding, some may find it useful to make a quick survey of the elementary notions of philology. It is for this reason that J.P. Touzard has

prefaced his *Grammaire hébraïque abrégée* (Paris, 1911) with an accelerated introduction to "Premiers éléments" designed as a quick guide for beginners.

By avoiding an excess of details, we have been able to allot more space to explanation. Even those who are only marginally inclined towards a scientific approach would find that a form well explained and understood remains longer in their memory. A solid introduction to phonetics enables one to recover a forgotten form more easily and accurately and provides a safeguard against erroneous vocalisations. Logical explanation is an especially indispensable aid to memory for those who take up the study of Hebrew at a mature age.

A Semitic language like Hebrew creates the impression of a totally new world. The phonetic inventory has entities strange to our languages; the morphology and syntax have features which are completely different from ours. In order truly to appreciate the system and nature of Hebrew one needs to lay aside one's own phonetic(1) and grammatical habits as well as certain notions peculiar to our languages. Right from the start, the nature of the Hebrew vowels, their quality(2) and quantity are described in a way which is considerably different from the teaching method found in most grammars. On very many points, for instance, in the very important matter of *tenses*, we have departed from certain widely accepted views, because a serious examination has shown us that they were not accurate enough. In any case one would hardly expect a book of this kind to be a mere collection of factual details and contain very little that is new(3). Only rarely have we been able to mention dissenting opinions about controversial issues. Even less frequently, due to the nature of the book, have we been able to engage in a discussion. As for the bibliography, apart from the general reference works mentioned in the *Introduction*, we could provide references only for the more important matters, and even then only to works which are really useful(4).

(1) And this not just in theory, but also in practice. The student must, right from the beginning, discipline himself to aim at the exact pronunciation of consonants and vowels with their correct timbre, length and tone, and watch for syllable boundaries, etc. He must also, from the beginning, accord distinct prominence to the mil'el tone, which is systematically marked in this book despite the typographical difficulty.

(2) The vital importance of the quality of the Hebrew vowels necessitated the use of phonetic symbols for their transliteration.

(3) Some of these new points have been treated by us in *Mélanges de la Faculté Orientale de Beyrouth* and *Biblica*; reference to these publications will be made on occasion for the benefit of the reader who might wish to know more about an explanation proposed by us.

(4) The bibliography given by Kautzsch, which was quite full, is recorded in an almost exhaustive fashion in the grammar as revised by Bergsträsser (I. Theil, 1918).

Faced with an enormous number of grammatical explanations, we quite often had to be content, if we were to be honest, with probabilities and not much more. The reader will no doubt be surprised to see words such as *probable*, *probably* (*prob.*), *perhaps* (*perh.*) recurring so often, words which are not usually found in a grammarian's vocabulary. But, without trying to sound pedantic, we did not wish to leave the reader with the impression that all explanations are equally certain.

Although we have no blind faith in the vocalisation of the massoretic text, we have become convinced that, all in all, it faithfully reflects the linguistic reality and therefore provides a solid grammatical basis to work on. This conservative attitude however has not prevented us from indicating what has appeared to us to be arbitrary, suspect or incorrect. The reader will soon see that the study of the massoretic text can only be undertaken critically; it is not meant for immature minds.

Despite our efforts not to drown the reader in a sea of endless details, the very nature of the language and of the massoretic text compelled us to mention a considerable number of minute details(1). The student need not be alarmed by this. He would be well advised to read quickly the entire grammar once in order to gain a general overview of the language. Then he can come back for in-depth study with attention to details. In the longer paragraphs, those on irregular verbs, for example, the most important aspects are grouped towards the beginning, and the details and anomalies are relegated to the end. Obviously not all details should be memorised, especially in the preliminary study. The student will no doubt encounter them in his reading of the biblical text, when he can examine them in accordance with his progress, and with greater interest.

(1) Needless to say, all lexicological details must be sought in good dictionaries.

Phonetics, which is a necessary introduction to Morphology, presents a practical difficulty for the beginner, who is supposed to be not yet acquainted with the forms. The author, on the other hand, is likely to say, under Phonetics, things which he will have to repeat under Morphology. Consequently we have dealt with phonetics as briefly as possible.

For pedagogical reasons many examples cited in Phonetics and Morphology are taken from the paradigms; some forms, even when not marked with an asterisk (*), may therefore not be found in the biblical text. The same is true of some nouns cited in the absolute state, verbs cited for the third person sg. m. etc.

In Phonetics and Morphology we have not translated all the words cited there, particularly those which occur frequently(1). In certain cases we have resorted to Latin in order to bring out a nuance more accurately.

(1) The study of vocabulary must naturally go hand in hand with that of grammar. The student can, for instance, learn words grouped according to various criteria (meaning or form). As soon as he can read an easy text, he would be well advised to learn a few verses which may be of some special interest to him on account of the words used or the syntax involved.

Sometimes we have quoted, for the sake of comparison, Arabic, Aramaic and Syriac, for we believe that students will appreciate the necessity of at least an elementary acquaintance with these languages if they want to understand Hebrew fully.

The Syntax, a section often rather neglected in Hebrew grammars, has been given the attention to which it is entitled(1). We have endeavoured to facilitate its study by giving plenty of examples *in extenso* and with translation(2) instead of merely multiplying biblical references. Only rarely have we aimed at giving an exhaustive list of passages in which a phenomenon is attested; but we have indicated the relative degree of frequency(3).

(1) Some observations on *style*, which is closely bound up with syntax, have been proffered occasionally.

(2) It is hardly necessary to state that the translations offered are of strictly grammatical character, aiming at literalness. Towards the end of the Syntax, we have, as a pedagogical device, left out the vocalisation of a small number of words which occur so frequently that the student can be assumed to be familiar with them.

(3) A good number of examples are not found in any Syntax. For certain texts, e.g. the book of Ruth, the abundance of quoted examples amounts almost to a philological commentary.

In general we have avoided adducing examples which are textcritically problematic(1): discussion of them would have exceeded the bounds of this grammar, and it is really best left to philological commentaries.

(1) Indicated by the reverse question mark ؟.

With regard to the terminology, we have generally retained the traditional terms, except where these could give rise to a wrong notion. The terms which make part of the current vocabulary of Hebrew grammar, e.g. *Qal*, *Nifal*, *Piel*, *Hifil* are written in the simplest manner, like English words. The same applies to the traditional terms we use in Syntax to indicate the tenses, for example, *qatal* for the perfect, *yiqtol* for the future (cf. § 111 *b*).

In the Paradigms, which, for the benefit of the student, form a separate fascicule together with Indices, one will find some innovations of a pedagogical nature. Under the verbs, immediately after the Perfect we have placed the Future, this second tense being necessary and sufficient for the purpose of characterising a conjugation. Then follows the Imperative, the characteristic vowel of which is the same as that of the future. At the end one will find the nominal-verbal forms: infinitives and participles.

As the two infinitives often present difficulties for the beginner, we have prefixed the infinitive construct with the preposition לְ, which will never be found before the infinitive absolute.

In a synoptic paradigm of the verbs (Paradigm 16), one will find, under the four forms of Qal, Nifal, Hifil, and Hofal, the irregular verbs which can easily give rise to confusion.

I wish to express here my sincere thanks to Rev. Fr. Joseph Neyrand, S.J., a professor at the Pontifical Biblical Institute, who has kindly read the proofs of this grammar and whose very keen observations have been a great benefit to me.

PREFACE TO THE ENGLISH EDITION

Since its publication in 1923 Paul Joüon's *Grammaire de l'hébreu biblique* has been generally recognised as one of the finest grammars of Biblical Hebrew. Two of its obvious strengths are the clarity and lucidity of exposition, characteristic of many a work in French, and the splendid section, allocated nearly half the pages of the book, on syntax, a compartment of grammar often sadly relegated to ancillary status in Hebrew grammars. This latter aspect is important also in view of the dominant position syntax has come to occupy in contemporary general linguistics. In spite of this widely acclaimed position, Joüon's grammar, which, apart from those of Gesenius—Kautzsch and König, is the only modern and comprehensive Biblical Hebrew grammar of substantial size(1), has sometimes been unduly neglected. Even scholars who one would have thought would be better read have failed to do justice to Joüon by putting forward a particular idea on one or another aspect of Hebrew grammar as if they were the first to do so. At the other extreme, there are those whose discussion of some point of Hebrew grammar have telltale signs of their acquaintance with the position held by Joüon, but no acknowledgment of their indebtedness to this Jesuit scholar. One possible reason for this may be the fact that the grammar is in French.

(1) The size of the French edition is pp. xii + 542 + 79* (paradigms and indices).

In the preface to the original edition the author refers to progress in Semitic philology. The need he felt over sixty years ago to write a Hebrew grammar in the light of fruit of the science of Semitic philology is equally shared by us today. Since 1923 Semitic philology in general and Hebrew philology in particular have progressed significantly, and new directions of inquiry have been opened up. These advances are results of the discovery of previously unknown languages such as Ugaritic and Eblaite, the discovery of further written remains of languages which were known in Joüon's days, investigations undertaken in totally new areas and subjects, and the impact of new directions taken in the constantly evolving field of general linguistics. Whilst no Hebrew grammar comparable in scope to Joüon's has yet appeared, even the comparatively narrow discipline of Hebrew philology has hardly been dormant: a good number of important monographs and a rich crop of valuable, original articles and reviews have appeared. Thus it seems amply justified to attempt to bring this splendid grammar up to date and also to make it available in a language more widely read and understood at the present time. Such an updating must be considered essential as well as desirable, even though Joüon's grammar has honourably stood the test of time. Indeed, as the judicious reader will observe, many important features which Joüon could only reconstruct for proto-Hebrew on the basis of chronologically later Classical Arabic have now been borne out by El Amarna glosses and Ugaritic. In quite a few matters he was ahead of his time(1).

(1) On this last point, see, for example, his application of what has become known in modern linguistics as the transformational-generative approach in his discussion in § 125 *v*, *w*, and again the fundamental distinction he makes between historical and descriptive approaches in his assessment of Bauer and Leander's grammar. I further suppose that Joüon was one of the first, if indeed not the very first Hebraist, to quote Saussure in a meaningful way (§ 122 *b*).

The edition presented here is thus an English translation and revision of the French original(1). With the exception of the Preface to the original French edition, which is presented intact in English garb, there is hardly a paragraph which has been left unrevised. A revision may take the form of a new footnote, a rewriting of the body of the text to some degree, an occasional deletion of a whole paragraph or insertion of a whole new paragraph(2). In the interests of clarity of presentation and ease of comprehension from the point of view of the reader it has been decided not to mark the revisions externally or typographically.

(1) In fact the translation is based on what was published in 1947 and is styled on the title page as "Deuxième édition anastatique corrigée."
(2) Sometimes an inserted new paragraph can be recognised by double letters such as § 2 *fa* indicating a subparagraph, but not always. Deletions of whole paragraphs are extremely rare.

For the purpose of revision and updating we like to believe that we have read as extensively as possible in monographs and articles published in periodicals and Festschriften which have appeared since about 1920, including what has been published in Modern Hebrew. These days serious Hebraists or Semitists can ignore works written in that language only to their own detriment. The only genre of secondary literature that has not been covered is the huge and ever-increasing number of Old Testament commentaries.

In the Preface Joüon sets out some of the more important principles which guided him as he wrote his grammar. Without necessarily going over the same ground, we deem it necessary to restate some general lines we have pursued in our task of updating and revision.

a. The grammar is essentially descriptive in its approach and conception, or to put it differently, its approach is synchronic, and not diachronic or historical. Unlike Bauer and Leander's incomplete grammar, we do not aim to recover and reconstruct a grammar and structure of Hebrew as it may have been in the earliest recoverable phase, which is by definition decidedly pre-massoretic. We present the structure of the Hebrew that can be recovered from the Hebrew text of the Old Testament as fixed by the Tiberian scholars in the latter half of the first millennium A.D.(1) Whilst we are fully aware of the difficulties and the measure of artificiality necessarily entailed by the adoption of such an approach, we also believe that the Tiberian form of Hebrew provides the most comprehensive and solid basis to work from. This descriptive approach, however, does not prevent us from taking into account data other than what is available in the Tiberian tradition. On the contrary, there is no doubt that data available not only in non-biblical Hebrew documents such as early epigraphic materials, Dead Sea documents, the so-called "Mishnaic" Hebrew or even some later phases of the language, traditions distinct from the Tiberian, but also cognate languages and dialects, both ancient and modern, can often shed valuable light on various questions besetting Biblical Hebrew philology.

In making occasional references to pre-massoretic data in our description, we are aware that there lies a long history behind the Tiberian massoretic traidtion on which we can speak only hesitantly. Such qualifying terms as 'primitive,' 'original,' and 'etymological(ly),' which will be encountered rather frequently, especially in the sections on phonology and morphology, must be taken rather loosely: to attempt to do full justice to the complexity of the task of historical reconstruction would take us too far afield.

(1) As a result, our transliteration of Hebrew (and Biblical Aramaic) forms does not distinguish between a historically long *i* and a short *i*, hence הִסְתִּיר *histir*, not *histîr* or *histīr*.

b. Joüon does not say which text or edition of the Hebrew Bible he chose for his grammar. In the present English edition occasional reference is made to the Codex Leningradensis B 19a as printed in K.Elliger and W. Rudolph (eds), *Biblia Hebraica Stuttgartensia* (Stuttgart, 1967-77), and the "Adi" edition of the same manuscript as prepared by A. Dotan (Tel Aviv, 1973) has also been consulted, but no systematic checking of all quotations in these two editions has been undertaken. As a consequence, there will be found not a few discrepancies between this grammar and BHS in respect of, for instance, Qre/Ktiv. We have occasionally consulted a photographic reproduction (Makor: Jerusalem) of the Leningrad Codex and the Cairo Codex of the Prophets as well as the Aleppo Codex.

c. In the provision of bibliographical information, especially in footnotes, we tend to be somewhat more liberal than Joüon was, though exhaustiveness is not aimed at. We believe this is justified in the absence of a truly comprehensive, up-to-date and advanced grammar of Biblical Hebrew(1).

(1) In the meantime the reader may also consult a rather extensive, classified but not exhaustive (for instance, not a single work in Modern Hebrew listed), bibliography appended to Waltke—O'Connor, *BH Syntax*, pp. 695-716. A recent work by N.M. Waldman [for details, see below, § 2 *e*, n.] is in a way more comprehensive, but even the bibliography appended at the end of the volume appears to be rather selective and less comprehensive, especially when it comes to works in European languages on Biblical Hebrew.

d. The number of examples, both from within the Old Testament and from outside of it, has been increased to no small measure.

e. Partly for a technical reason, the use of *metheg* or *ga'ya* has been considerably curtailed, restricted to a small number of categories where it serves a useful purpose such as חָֽכְמָה *she is wise* as distinct from חָכְמָה *wisdom* (see § 14).

f. The vocalisation has been reduced a little further than in the original edition.

g. For biblical references, Joüon followed Stier and Theile Polyglot (reproduced in Vigouroux Polyglot) but the inaccessibility to us of either polyglot meant that we have not been able to quote from them passages which we have added, for we have followed *Biblia Hebraica Stuttgartensia* in this matter. It is hoped that this inconsistency will not cause the user of this grammar too great an inconvenience.

h. Joüon had a valid reason for using Latin in trying to bring out subtleties of Hebrew which he apparently felt could be better reproduced in it than in French. However, as it can no longer be assumed that Hebrew students are conversant in Latin, we have decided to discontinue that practice in most cases.

Finally, it is a most pleasant duty to put on record my sentiments of gratitude to various organisations and individuals who have contributed to the completion of this volume: a) the Faculty of Arts of the University of Melbourne through its Research and Graduate Studies Committee which made considerable grants of funds towards the acquisition of necessary computer equipment and research materials and the employment of research assistants and relief teachers, b) the former Department of Middle Eastern Studies of the same university, and its successor, Department of Classical and Near Eastern Studies, for its generous provision of secretarial and other material resources, c) the Institute for Advanced Studies of the Hebrew University of Jerusalem, which allowed and enabled me to spend on this project a fair portion of the time whilst I was there as Research Fellow during the academic year 1987-88, d) various libraries, notably the Baillieu Library of this university, the National and Hebrew University Library, the library of the W.F. Albright Institute for Archaeological Research in Jerusalem, the library of the École Biblique in the same city, the Joint Theological Library at Ormond College, Melbourne University, e) Mr Patrick Delsocorro for his draft translation of a substantial portion of the French original and his revision of my draft translation of the remainder, as well as some bibliographical research, f) Dr R.G. Jenkins, a colleague in the Department, for his most valuable assistance in computerising the printing of the volume, g) Fr J. Swetnam, S.J., of the Pontifical Biblical Institute for his unfailing support and encouragement since I first approached the Institute's Press, h) Fr A. Gianto of the same Institute for his careful reading of a manuscript of this grammar, i) the Gregorian University Press for the excellent technical execution of this publication, j) Messrs. Bryan Hewson and Nigel Statham, both postgraduate students of this Department, for execution of some tedious wordprocessing, especially the latter for his careful attention to the English of this grammar, k) Ms J. Aarts, Senior Secretary of the Department for performing an enormous amount of clerical work with uncommon patience, and last, but not least, l) my family who have had to put up with their husband and father being absent from home countless evenings.

It is our fervent hope that this grammar will help maintain and foster interest in the grammar of Classical Hebrew amongst Hebraists, Semitists, and Bible scholars, and also contribute towards a better understanding of the Hebrew Bible.

Takamitsu Muraoka

October, 1990.

Department of Classical and Near Eastern Studies,
The University of Melbourne,
Parkville, Victoria 3052, AUSTRALIA.

Preface to the corrected second printing

It is gratifying that after less than two years we should be preparing a second printing of our grammar. Partly for technical reasons and partly for the fact that the time following the publication of the original edition in mid-1991 has been barely sufficient for reviewers to assess it, the present edition is primarily concerned with corrections of typographical errors - alas no longer the human printer's fault, but our own mechanical printer's - and minor alterations and improvements which we have been able to undertake without drastically altering the general appearance. This task has been considerably facilitated by the preprint reviews very kindly made available to us by Prof. F.I. Andersen, Prof. J. Blau, and Dr M.S. Smith as well as four(!) sets of corrections and suggestions sent by Fr. R. Althann of the Pontifical Biblical Institute, to each of whom we are sincerely indebted for their kindness and care with which they have read the grammar. Last but not least we owe a great debt of thanks to Dr R.G. Jenkins of Melbourne University for generously giving of his precious time to print the pages concerned.

Takamitsu Muraoka

December, 1992

Vakgroep Hebreeuwse, Aramese, en Ugaritische Talen en Culturen,
Fakulteit der Letteren,
Rijksuniversiteit te Leiden,
Leiden, HOLLAND.

TABLE OF CONTENTS

INTRODUCTION

PART ONE: ORTHOGRAPHY AND PHONETICS

[Phonetics]

PART TWO: MORPHOLOGY

CHAPTER I: THE DEFINITE ARTICLE AND THE PRONOUN

CHAPTER II: VERB

CHAPTER III: THE NOUN

CHAPTER IV: PARTICLES

PART THREE: SYNTAX

CHAPTER I: TENSES AND MOODS

CHAPTER II: THE CASES

CHAPTER III: PREPOSITIONS

CHAPTER IV: THE NOUN

CHAPTER V: THE PRONOUN

CHAPTER VI: AGREEMENT

CHAPTER VII: CLAUSES

CLAUSES IN GENERAL

PARTICULAR CLAUSES

CHAPTER VIII: CONJUNCTION *WAW*

PARADIGMS AND INDICES

ABBREVIATIONS

A) Biblical books

Gn	Genesis	Na	Nahum
Ex	Exodus	Hab	Habakkuk
Lv	Leviticus	Zeph	Zephaniah
Nu	Numbers	Hg	Haggai
Dt	Deuteronomy	Zech	Zechariah
Josh	Joshua	Mal	Malachi
Jdg	Judges	Ps	Psalms
1Sm	1Samuel	Pr	Proverbs
2Sm	2Samuel	Job	Job
1Kg	1Kings	Ct	Canticle of Canticles
2Kg	2Kings	Ru	Ruth
Is	Isaiah	Lam	Lamentations
Jer	Jeremiah	Ec	Ecclesiastes
Ez	Ezekiel	Esth	Esther
Ho	Hosea	Dn	Daniel
Jl	Joel	Ezr	Ezra
Am	Amos	Ne	Nehemiah
Ob	Obadiah	1Ch	1Chronicles
Jon	Jonah	2Ch	2Chronicles
Mi	Micah		

B) General, and works often quoted

abs.: absolute

AC: Ancient Canaanite

acc.: accusative

adj.: adjective

adv.: adverb

AF: F.I. Andersen and A.D. Forbes, *Spelling in the Hebrew Bible* (Rome, 1986).

AJSL: *American Journal of Semitic Languages and Literatures*

Akk.: Akkadian

Andersen, *Verbless*: F.I. Andersen, *The Hebrew Verbless Clause in the Pentateuch* (Nashville/New York, 1970).

——, *Sentence*: F.I. Andersen, *The Sentence in Biblical Hebrew* (The Hague/ Paris, 1974).

apoc.: apocopated

Arb.: Arabic

Arm.: Aramaic

BA: Biblical Aramaic

Barr, *Spellings*: J. Barr, *The Variable Spellings of the Hebrew Bible* (Oxford, 1989).

Barth, *Nominalbildung*: J. Barth, *Die Nominalbildung in den semitischen Sprachen* (Leipzig, ^{2}1894).

BASOR: *Bulletin of the American Schools of Oriental Research*

Baumgartner, *Lexikon*: W. Baumgartner, B. Hartmann, and E.Y. Kutscher, *Hebräisches und aramäisches Lexikon zum Alten Testament* (Leiden, ^{3}1967-).

BDB: F. Brown, S.R. Driver, Ch.A. Briggs, *A Hebrew and English Lexicon of the Old Testament* etc. (Oxford, 1907).

Bendavid: A. Bendavid, *Biblical Hebrew and Mishnaic Hebrew*, 2 vols. [Heb] (Tel Aviv, ^{2}1967-71).

Ben-Ḥayyim, *LOT*: *The Literary and Oral Tradition of Hebrew and Aramaic amongst the Samaritans*, 5 vols. [Heb] (Jerusalem, 1957-77).

Berg.: G. Bergsträsser, *Hebräische Grammatik*, I (Leipzig, 1918); II (Leipzig, 1929).

BH: Biblical Hebrew

BHK: R. Kittel and P. Kahle (eds), *Biblia Hebraica* (Stuttgart, ^{3}1937).

BHS: K. Elliger and W. Rudolph (eds), *Biblia Hebraica Stuttgartensia* (Stuttgart, 1967-77).

Bib: *Biblica*

BL: H. Bauer and P. Leander, *Historische Grammatik der hebräischen Sprache des alten Testamentes* (Halle, 1922; repr. Hildesheim, 1962).

Blau, *Heb. Phonology and Morphology*: J. Blau, *Hebrew Phonology and Morphology* [Heb] (Tel Aviv, 1972).

——, *Grammar*: *A Grammar of Biblical Hebrew* (Wiesbaden, 1976).

BO: *Bibliotheca Orientalis*

Böttcher: F. Böttcher, *Ausführliches Lehrbuch der hebräischen Sprache*, ed. F. Mühlau, 2 vols. (Leipzig, 1866-68).

Brock., *GvG*: C. Brockelmann, *Grundriss der vergleichenden Grammatik der semitischen Sprachen*, 2 vols. (Berlin, 1908-13; repr. Hildesheim, 1961).

———, *Syntax*: *Hebräische Syntax* (Neukirchen-Vluyn, 1956).

Brønno, *Studien*: E. Brønno, *Studien über hebräische Morphologie und Vokalismus auf Grundlage der mercatischen Fragmente der zweiten Kolumne der Hexapla des Origenes* (Leipzig, 1943).

BSL: *Bulletin de la Société de Linguistique de Paris*

BSOAS: *Bulletin of the School of Oriental and African Studies, London University*

C: consonant

Codex C: Codex Cairo of the Prophets (Makor facsimile ed., Jerusalem, 1971).

Codex L: Codex Leningradensis B19a.

cohort.: cohortative

com.: common (gender)

comp.: compare

contr.: contrast

cp.: compare

cst.: construct

dat.: dative

Davidson, *Syntax*: A.B. Davidson, *Hebrew Syntax* (Edinburgh, 31912).

Driver, *Notes*: S.R. Driver, *Notes on the Hebrew Text and the Topography of the Books of Samuel* (Oxford, 21913).

———, *Tenses*: S.R. Driver, *A Treatise on the Use of the Tenses in Hebrew and some other Syntactical Questions* (Oxford, 31892).

DSS: Dead Sea Scrolls

EA: J.A. Knudtzon, *Die El-Amarna-Tafeln* (Leipzig, 1907-15).

EB: E.L. Sukenik et al. (eds.), *Encyclopaedia Biblica. Thesaurus rerum biblicarum alphabetico ordine digestus*, 3rd impression [Heb] (Jerusalem, 1965-82).

EBH: Early Biblical Hebrew

ed., eds: editor, editors

Ehrlich, *Randglossen*: A.B. Ehrlich, *Randglossen zur hebräischen Bibel. Textkritisches, sprachlices und sachliches*, 7 vols. (Leipzig, 1908).

EJ: *Encyclopaedia Judaica*, 16 vols. (Jerusalem, 1971-72).

Engl.: English

ESA: Epigraphic South Arabian

Eth.: Ethiopic, i.e. Geʿez

exx.: examples

f.: future, feminine

fem.: feminine

Fr.: French

Friedrich—Röllig: J. Friedrich and W. Röllig, *Phönizisch-punische Grammatik* (Rome, ²1970).

Fschr.: Festschrift

Germ.: German

GK: *Gesenius' Hebrew Grammar as Edited and Enlarged by the Late E. Kautzsch.* Second English ed. revised by A.E. Cowley (Oxford, 1910).

GLECS: *Comptes rendus des séances du groupe linguistique d'études chamito-sémitiques*

Gordon, *UT*: C.H. Gordon, *Ugaritic Textbook* (Rome, 1965).

HAR: *Hebrew Annual Review*

Harris, *Development*: Z.S. Harris, *Development of the Canaanite Dialects. An Investigation in Linguistic History* (New Haven, 1939).

Heb: Hebrew [in a reference to a work written in Modern Hebrew]

HUCA: *Hebrew Union College Annual*

Huehnergard, *Ugr. Vocabulary*: J. Huehnergard, *Ugaritic Vocabulary in Syllabic Transcription* (Atlanta, 1987).

Ibn Janaḥ, *Riqmah*: M. Wilensky and D. Tené (eds), ספר הרקמה לר' יונה אבן ג'נאח, 2 vols. (Jerusalem, 1964).

IEJ: *Israel Exploration Journal*

impv.: imperative

IOS: *Israel Oriental Studies*

Ital.: Italian

JA: *Journal Asiatique*

JANESCU: *The Journal of the Ancient Near Eastern Society of Columbia University*

JAOS: *Journal of the American Oriental Society*

JBL: *Journal of Biblical Literature*

JNES: *Journal of Near Eastern Studies*

JNWSL: *Journal of Northwest Semitic Languages*

JPOS: *The Journal of the Palestine Oriental Society*

JQR: *Jewish Quarterly Review*

JSS: *Journal of Semitic Studies*

JThSt: *Journal of Theological Studies*

juss.: jussive

K: Ktiv (as in Gn 3.23K)

KB³: L. Koehler, W. Baumgartner et al., *Hebräisches und aramäisches Lexikon zum alten Testament* (Leiden, ³1967-).

Khan, *Syntax*: G.A. Khan, *Studies in Semitic Syntax* (Oxford, 1988).

König: E. König, *Historisch-kritisches Lehrgebäude der hebräischen Sprache*, 3 vols. [vol. 3, *Syntax*] (Leipzig, 1881-97). [2.345 = vol. 2, p. 345.]

Kropat, *Syntax*: A. Kropat, *Die Syntax des Autors der Chronik verglichen mit der seiner Quellen* (Giessen, 1909).

Kutscher, *Isaiah*: E.Y. Kutscher, *The Language and Linguistic Background of the Isaiah Scroll (IQ Isaᵃ)* (Leiden, 1974), tr. from the Heb. ed. (Jerusalem, 1959).

——, *History*: *A History of the Hebrew Language* (Jerusalem/Leiden, 1982).

L: Codex L., i.e. Codex Leningradensis B19ᵃ

Lambert: M. Lambert, *Traité de la grammaire hébraïque* (Paris, 1931-38) [reprinted with corrections and some additional materials prepared by G.E. Weil (Hildesheim, 1972)].

LBH: Late Biblical Hebrew

Leš: *Lešonenu*

Levi, *Inkongruenz*: J. Levi, *Die Inkongruenz im biblischen Hebräisch* (Wiesbaden, 1987).

LXX: Septuagint

m.: masculine

Macuch, *Gram.*: R. Macuch, *Grammatik des samaritanischen Hebräisch* (Berlin, 1969).

MedH: Mediaeval Hebrew

Meyer: R. Meyer, *Hebräische Grammatik*, 4 vols. (Berlin, 1966-72).

MH: Mishnaic Hebrew

ModH: Modern Hebrew

Morag, *Vocalization*: Morag, Sh., *The Vocalization Systems of Arabic, Hebrew, and Aramaic* ('s-Gravenhage, 1962).

——, *Yemenite*: *The Hebrew Language Tradition of the Yemenite Jews* [Heb]

(Jerusalem, 1963).

Moscati: S. Moscati (ed.), A. Spitaler, E. Ullendorff, and W. von Soden, *An Introduction to the Comparative Grammar of the Semitic Languages. Phonology and Morphology* (Wiesbaden, 1964).

Muraoka, *Emphatic*: T. Muraoka, *Emphatic Words and Structures in Biblical Hebrew* (Jerusalem/Leiden, 1985).

MUSJ: *Mélanges de l'Université Saint-Joseph de Beyrouth* (also known as *M. de la Faculté orientale de Beyrouth*)

n.: footnote. In Indexes, spelled N in upper case.

Nid: indeterminate noun

Nöldeke, *Neue Beiträge*: Th. Nöldeke, *Neue Beiträge zur semitischen Sprachwissenschaft* (Strassburg, 1910).

Obs.: Observation

OLZ: *Orientalistische Literaturzeitung*

Or: *Orientalia*

Or Suec: *Orientalia Suecana*

OT: Old Testament

OudSt: *Oudtestamentische Studiën*

P: Pause, pausal

parall.: parallel

partic.: participle

PEQ: *Palestine Exploration Quarterly*

perf.: perfect

perh.: perhaps

pers.: person

Pesh.: Peshitta

pf.: perfect

Phoen.: Phoenician

pl.: plural

plur.: plural

poet.: poetic

Polzin: R. Polzin, *Late Biblical Hebrew: Toward an Historical Typology of Biblical Hebrew Prose* (Missoula, 1976).

pred.: predicative

prob.: probably

Proceedings: *Proceedings of the International Conference on Semitic Studies*

Held in Jerusalem, 19-23 July 1965 (Jerusalem, 1969).

pron.: pronoun

PS: Proto-Semitic

ptc.: participle

Q: Qre (as in Gn 3.23Q)

QH: Qumran Hebrew

Qimron, *Hebrew of DSS*: E. Qimron, *The Hebrew of the Dead Sea Scrolls* (Atlanta, 1986).

R: radical, root letter as in R1 = first radical.

Rabin, *Syntax*: Rabin, C. (as edited by S. Shkolnikov), *A Syntax of Biblical Hebrew* (= תחביר לשון המקרא) [Heb] (Jerusalem, 1964).

RB: *Revue Biblique*

RÉJ: *Revue des Études Juives*

Samar.: Samaritan (Pentateuch)

sbd: somebody

Schramm, *Graphemes*: G.M. Schramm, *The Graphemes of Tiberian Hebrew* (Berkeley and Los Angeles, 1964).

Sec.: Secunda, i.e. the second column in the Hexapla compiled by Origen, quoted in the main from G. Mercati, *Psalterii Hexapli Reliquiae. I. Codex rescriptus Bybliothecae Ambrosianae 0.39 Supp. phototypice expressus et transcriptus* (Rome, 1958).

Segert, *Gram. of Phoen. and Pun.*: S. Segert, *A Grammar of Phoenician and Punic* (München, 1976).

sg.: singular

SH: Samaritan Hebrew

sing.: singular

Sivan: D. Sivan, *Grammatical Analysis and Glossary of the Northwest Semitic Vocables in Akkadian Texts of the 15th-13th C.B.C. from Canaan and Syria* (Neukirchen-Vluyn, 1984).

Sperber, *Hist. Gram.*: A. Sperber, *A Historical Grammar of Biblical Hebrew* (Leiden, 1966).

sq.: sequens, sequentes (= "following")

st.: status

sth: something

subj.: subject

subst.: substantive, substantival

suf.: suffix, suffixed
s.v.: sub voce
Syr.: Syriac
UF: *Ugarit-Forschungen*
Ugr.: Ugaritic
usu.: usually
V: vowel
var.: variant reading
vs.: versus *or* verse
VT: *Vetus Testamentum*
Vulg.: Vulgate
Waltke—O'Connor, *BH Syntax*: B.K. Waltke and M. O'Connor, *An Introduction to Biblical Hebrew Syntax* (Winona Lake, 1990).
Wright, *Arabic Grammar*: W. Wright—W. Robertson Smith—M.J. de Goeje, *A Grammar of the Arabic Language*, 2 vols. (Cambridge, ^{3}1896-98).
Y.: Yahweh
Yeivin, *Babylonian*: I. Yeivin, *The Hebrew Language Tradition as Reflected in the Babylonian Vocalization* [Heb] (Jerusalem, 1985).
ZA: *Zeitschrift für Assyriologie und verwandte Gebiete*
ZAH: *Zeitschrift für Althebraistik*
ZAW: *Zeitschrift für die alttestamentliche Wissenschaft*
ZDMG: *Zeitschrift der deutschen morgenländischen Gesellschaft*

CONVENTIONAL SYMBOLS

An inverted question mark ¿ indicates that the form or the text is doubtful.

An asterisk * signifies that the form is not attested([1]).

The symbol > signifies that a form *changes* to another form, for example, § 17 *b*; or that it is *more frequent*, for example, Paradigm 2: *Hofal*.

The symbol < signifies that a form has *evolved* from another form.

The double slash // signifies a parallel passage.

The cross † signifies that the list is complete.

The x indicates the frequency of a particular form.

The stress position is marked in transliterations either as in /bay'tå/ with a single quotation mark after the stressed syllable or as in /báytå/; in Hebrew with ˂ as in בַּ֫יְתָה.

(1) In Paradigm 4, the asterisk has a different function (see the note there).

INTRODUCTION

§ 1. Hebrew grammar defined

Hebrew grammar as it is generally understood and as it is envisaged *a*
in this book is the grammar of the language of the traditional biblical text in the form in which it was established by the Jewish scholars of the Tiberian schools around the seventh century A.D. The Tiberian scholars are believed, presumably indirectly through their Babylonian counterparts, to have come under the influence of Syriac grammarians in their concern about the preservation and transmission of the reading tradition of the sacred texts(1).

(1) See Sh. Morag, *Leš* 38 (1974) 52f., and on the work of native Syriac scholars, see J.B. Segal, *The Diacritical Point and the Accents in Syriac* (London, 1953).

It might make some sense to distinguish Naqdanim who invented or were directly involved in the forging of the pointing system from "Massoretic scholars" who studied and wrote on questions arising from the text thus pointed: see below, § 16 *a*. The distinction is a useful one, even though actual biblical (and related) manuscripts do attest to diversity of linguistic realities and traditions even amongst manuscripts using the Simple Tiberian pointing system. See the way a chain of massoretic scholars are named and characterised by an anonymous early mediaeval scholar: K. Levy, *Zur masoretischen Grammatik: Texte und Untersuchungen* (Stuttgart, 1936), p. 10.

At this period the consonantal text was provided with numerous sym- *b*
bols indicating first and foremost the vocalisation(1), but also some modifications in the pronunciation of the consonants, syllable division, stress, the link between the words themselves, pauses, and modulation. These symbols, especially the vowel signs, consist mainly of *points* (נְקֻדָּה), and therefore one often speaks of *pointing* or *punctuation* of the consonantal text, and the inventors of the system are called *Naqdanim* (*punctatores*). The pronunciation thus determined by the Naqdanim with extremely meticulous care is the carefully executed, solemn, musical pronunciation in use in the religious services in the synagogues of their time. This pronunciation, which is accompanied by a certain measure of elegance and deliberate affectation, no doubt has

some features which are somewhat artificial, but there is no good reason to cast doubt on its authenticity as a whole. The Naqdanim wished faithfully to record the contemporary pronunciation, when the tradition was endangered, and one may believe that they were successful in their task. The internal coherence of the system and comparison of it with the cognate languages testify in favour of the vocalisers.

The details of Hebrew grammar, and particularly of the morphology, are based on the vocalisation recorded by the Naqdanim, and its reliability is presumed(2).

(1) Beside the Tiberian system of punctuation or vocalisation there also existed others such as the Palestinian, Babylonian, and Samaritan, each possessing its own set of signs of different shapes and representing a distinct phonological system. Furthermore, there are biblical manuscripts which are furnished with the Tiberian punctuation signs, the phonological system of which is, however, Palestinian. See BL, §§ 6-9; Morag, *Vocalization Systems*, pp. xx-xxx; idem, "Niqqud," *EB*, vol. 5 (Jerusalem, 1968), cols. 837-57; Yeivin, *Babylonian Tradition*. Of the three, the Tiberian system is the best-known, the latest, and the most meticulous one, and, more importantly, there does not exist any manuscript preserving the entire Old Testament in any of the other three systems (the Samaritan for obvious reasons: on this system, see Z. Ben-Ḥayyim, *LOT*, vol. 5, pp. 29-37).

(2) On the desirability and feasibility or otherwise of writing a complete BH grammar solely on the basis of the consonantal text, see J. Barr, *Comparative Philology and the Text of the OT* (Oxford, 1968), pp. 188-222, esp. 194-207; Ben-Ḥayyim, *LOT*, vol. 5, pp. 3f.

§ 2. Hebrew: its place among the Semitic languages(1)

a Hebrew belongs to the language family which since 1781(2) has been called Semitic (cf. Gn 10.21-31). These languages can be divided, according to their geographical distribution as outlined in § *b* - *i* below:

(1) T. Nöldeke, *Die semitischen Sprachen. Eine Skizze* (Leipzig, [2]1899); Brock., *GvG*, I, pp. 1-34; M. Lidzbarski, *Handbuch der nordsemitischen Epigraphik nebst ausgewählten Inschriften* (Weimar, 1898); G.A. Cooke, *A Textbook of North-Semitic Inscriptions* (Oxford, 1903); G. Bergsträsser (tr. P.T. Daniels), *Introduction to the Semitic Languages. Text Specimens and Grammatical Sketches* (Winona Lake, 1983); B. Spuler (ed.), *Handbuch der Orientalistik*, III. Semitistik (Leiden, 1953-54); H.J. Polotsky, "Semitics," pp. 99-111 in E.A. Speiser (ed.), *The World History of the Jewish People*, first series, vol. 1 (New Brunswick, 1964); E.A. Speiser, "Amorites and Canaanites," ib., pp. 162-69; H.L. Ginsberg, "The North-West Semitic languages," B. Mazar (ed.), ib., first series, vol. 2 (Tel Aviv, 1970), pp. 102-24; G. Garbini, *Le lingue semiti-*

che. Studi di storia linguistica (Napoli, ²1984). W.R. Garr's book, *Dialect Geography of Syria-Palestine, 1000-586 B.C.E.* (Philadelphia, 1985), is an attempt to classify Northwest Semitic dialects of the period specified by applying the method of dialect geography, on which see also C. Rabin, "The origin of the subdivisions of Semitic," D.W. Thomas and W.D. McHardy (eds), *Hebrew and Semitic Studies* [Fschr. G.R. Driver] (Oxford, 1963), pp. 104-15.

The following survey is almost exclusively concerned with ancient Semitic languages, whilst this century has witnessed considerable attention directed to modern idioms, those of Arabic, Aramaic, and Ethiopic. They are all capable of shedding light on Biblical Hebrew to varying degrees. Modern Hebrew is *sui generis* because of the special circumstances under which it evolved as a modern idiom.

(2) Following A.S. Schlözer in J.G. Eichhorn, *Repertorium für biblische und morgenländische Literatur* VIII (Leipzig, 1781), p. 161.

In addition to geographical classification, there is also a typological one based on isoglosses, namely shared linguistic features, such as consonantism, internal passive, broken plural, tense system, case system, etc. This mode of classification, however, is extremely complicated, and has ever been a hotly debated issue. The addition of newly discovered languages to the Semitic family, such as Ugaritic and Eblaite, not to speak of Amorite and Ammonite(1), has further complicated the matter. Whilst a warning is justly and frequently sounded against drawing too sharp a line between Northeast and Northwest Semitic language-groups, such a division seems to have been a tangible reality at least from about the beginning of the first millennium B.C. *aa*

(1) See J.C. Greenfield, "Amurrite, Ugaritic and Canaanite," in *Proceedings*, pp. 92-101. On Eblaite, see I.J. Gelb, "Thoughts about Ibla," *Syro-Mesopotamian Studies* 1/1 (Malibu, 1977); L. Cagni (ed.), *La lingua di Ebla. Atti del Convegno internazionale* (Napoli, 1981) and P. Fronzaroli (ed.), *Studies on the Language of Ebla* (Firenze, 1984); B.W.W. Dombrowski, "'Eblaitic' = The earliest known dialect of Akkadian," *ZDMG* 138 (1988) 211-36.

On Ammonite, which is now, contrary to its earlier North Arabic classification, generally regarded as Canaanite, see K.P. Jackson, *The Ammonite Language of the Iron Age* (Chico, 1983), a work which is, however, severely criticised by E. Lipiński, who also provides important additional bibliography: *BO* 43 (1986) 448-50. See also W.E. Aufrecht, "The Ammonite Language of the Iron Age," *BASOR* 266 (1987) 85-95. Essential is W.E. Aufrecht, *A Corpus of Ammonite Inscriptions* (Lewiston/Queenston/Lampeter, 1989).

North-East group (Babylonia, Assyria): *Akkadian* (a modern generic term, as opposed to *Sumerian*, a non-Semitic language also spoken in *b*

Babylonia). *Akkadian* comprises two dialects, *Babylonian* and *Assyrian.* We have cuneiform documents in Akkadian from the second half of the third millennium B.C. down to the beginning of the Christian era(1).

(1) There is an earlier stage, Old Akkadian, though it is not certain that Babylonian and Assyrian are direct linear descendants of it. The standard grammar is W. von Soden, *Grundriss der akkadischen Grammatik* (Rome, 1952) with *Ergänzungsheft* (Rome, 1969); for a dictionary one has idem, *Akkadisches Handwörterbuch* (Wiesbaden, 1965-81) and the on-going *The Assyrian Dictionary of the Oriental Institute of the University of Chicago* (Chicago, 1956-).

c **North-West group**(1) (Mesopotamia, Syria): *Aramaic, Hebrew, Phoenician.*

(1) On the concept of Northwest Semitic and Hebrew as its major representative, see Harris, *Development*, esp. pp. 8-10, and Garr, op. cit. [§ 2 *a*]. For a dictionary (currently under revision) covering epigraphic materials in Northwest Semitic languages, see Ch.-F. Jean and J. Hoftijzer, *Dictionnaire des inscriptions sémitiques de l'ouest* (Leiden, 1965).

d *Aramaic*(1), initially spoken, as it seems, by the tribes of the Syrian desert, gradually spread into the adjacent regions to the east and to the west. In the Persian period, it replaced Hebrew in Palestine. The oldest(2) Aramaic document known to date is the bilingual (Assyrian-Aramaic) inscription from Tell Fekheriye, which probably dates from the ninth century B.C.(3).

The Aramaic dialects of the subsequent periods can be divided into Eastern (in some post-Christian representatives of which the preformative of the third person in the Future is *n*) and Western (which have *y* like all other Semitic languages). The principal Eastern Aramaic dialects are Syriac, originally a dialect of Edessa (which can be further subdivided into Eastern or Nestorian Syriac, and Western or Jacobite Syriac), the Jewish dialect of the Babylonian Talmud, and *Mandaean.* To Western Aramaic belong the later dialects of the Palestinian Targum and the Jerusalem Talmud, and also *Samaritan, Palmyrene* (inscriptions of the first to third centuries A.D.), *Nabataean* (inscriptions of the first century A.D.), Christian Palestinian Aramaic, and a modern dialect of Maʿlula in the Anti-Lebanon(4).

In the Persian period there developed a standard literary form of Aramaic which was in use throughout the Persian Empire, hence its name 'Reichsaramäisch' or 'Imperial Aramaic'(5). There are however indications that already during this period there existed dialectal variations. This standard literary idiom attested as the language of the papyri of the Jewish colony of Elephantine (5th cent.), that of some chapters of Ezra (4.8—6.18; 7.12-26) and Daniel (2.4—7.28), lived on down to the turn of the Christian era, for it is basically this form of Aramaic that we find in some literary writings from the Judaean Desert and the Targum Onkelos.

(1) Cf. J.-B. Chabot, *Les langues et les littératures araméennes* (Paris, 1910), and F. Rosenthal, *Die aramaistische Forschung seit Theodor Nöldeke's Veröffentlichungen* (Leiden, 1939); idem, "Aramaic studies during the past thirty years," *JNES* (1978) 81-91.

(2) With the possible exception of the extremely short Tell Halaf inscription, which may date to the 10th cent. B.C.

(3) For an edition of Old Aramaic inscriptions, see H. Donner and W. Röllig, *Kanaanäische und aramäische Inschriften*, 3 vols. (Wiesbaden, ^{2}1966-69); F. Rosenthal (ed.), *An Aramaic Handbook*, in two parts (Wiesbaden, 1967); J.C.L. Gibson, *Textbook of Syrian Semitic Inscriptions*, vol. 2: *Aramaic Inscriptions Including Inscriptions in the Dialect of Zenjirli* (Oxford, 1975). For a grammar, S. Segert, *Altaramäische Grammatik mit Bibliographie, Chrestomathie und Glossar* (Leipzig, 1975, ^{3}1986).

(4) As additional reference works published since the major survey by Rosenthal (1939) [n. 1 above], note F. Rosenthal, *A Grammar of Bibl. Aram.* (Wiesbaden, 1961); R. Degen, *Altaramäische Grammatik der Inschriften des 10.-8. Jh. v. Chr.* (Wiesbaden, 1969); E.S. Drower & R. Macuch, *A Mandaic Dictionary* (Oxford, 1963); J.N. Epstein, *A Grammar of Babylonian Aramaic* [Heb.] (Jerusalem, 1960); R. Macuch, *Grammatik des samaritanischen Aramäisch* (Berlin, 1982); idem, *Handbook of Classical and Modern Madaic* (Berlin, 1965); T. Muraoka, *Classical Syriac for Hebraists* (Wiesbaden, 1987); M. Sokoloff, *A Dict. of Jewish Palestinian Aram. of the Byzantine Period* (Ramat-Gan, 1990).

(5) See J.C. Greenfield, "Standard Literary Aramaic," in A. Caquot and D. Cohen (eds), *Actes du premier congrès international de linguistique sémitique et chamito-sémitique. Paris 16-19 juillet 1969* (The Hague/Paris, 1974), pp. 280-89.

Hebrew(1) is a development of the language spoken in Canaan before the e
arrival of the Israelites(2). The ancient language of Canaan(3) is known, among other things, through *glosses* of the Babylonian letters found at Tell el Amarna (Upper Egypt). These letters, which date from around 1400, are written in the diplomatic language of the time, Babylonian, and addressed to the Egyptian government, by scribes of the land of Canaan who sometimes use words or forms of their native language. Other important sources of information include Ugaritic, Ugaritic words transcribed in the Akkadian cuneiform script with indication of vowels, Amorite personal names, and a small number of transcriptions of Canaa-

nite names in hieroglyphic Egyptian(4). Outside the biblical texts, Old Hebrew is represented by a considerable body of epigraphical materials such as the famous Gezer agricultural calendar (10th cent.), Samaria ostraca (early 8th cent.), the Siloam inscription (ca. 700), over one hundred ostraca from Arad in the Negev (mostly from the end of the 6th cent. B.C.), and 22 Lachish ostraca (from about the same period as the Arad ostraca). The inscription of Mesha, King of Moab (cf. 2Kg 3. 4) (ca. 850), is in a language which does not differ from Hebrew except in minor details(5).

(1) An excellent survey of recent studies of Hebrew may be found in C. Rabin, "Hebrew" in T.A. Sebeok (ed.), *Current Trends in Linguistics*, vol. 6 (The Hague/Paris, 1970), pp. 304-46. See also N.M. Waldman, *The Recent Study of Hebrew: A Survey of the Literature with Selected Bibliography* (Cincinnnati/Winona Lake, 1989), which covers wider ground than strictly Hebrew and its grammar.

(2) For a rebuttal of H. Bauer's thesis that Biblical Hebrew is a mixed language composed of East Semitic Canaanite and West Semitic Aramaic (*Zur Frage der Sprachmischung im Hebräischen: Eine Erwiderung* [Halle, 1924] and endorsed by G.R. Driver in his *Problems of the Hebrew Verbal System* (Edinburgh, 1936), see G. Bergsträsser in *OLZ* 26 (1923) 253-60, 477-81, B. Landsberger, *OLZ* 29 (1926) 967-76, Z.S. Harris, *Development*, p. 11, and Kutscher, *History*, p. 24.

(3) This phase of the language, which may be called Old Canaanite or Ancient Canaanite (AC) has been the subject of a series of recent studies by scholars such as W.L. Moran, A.F. Rainey, D. Sivan, S. Izre'el, and J. Huehnergard. However, there was probably not total overlap between AC and what might be called proto-Hebrew. The danger of equating the two is illustrated by the generally postulated Qal passive in the latter, i.e. *qutila* or *qut(t)ala*, vs. the AC (El-Amarna) *qatil(a)*, on which latter see Sivan, pp. 169f.

(4) See W.L. Moran, "The Hebrew language in its Northwest Semitic background" in G.E. Wright (ed.), *The Bible and the Ancient Near East. Essays in Honor of W.F. Albright* (Garden City, NY, 1961), pp. 54-72.

(5) For recent editions of these inscriptional materials, see Donner and Röllig, op. cit. [§ *d* above, n. 3]; Gibson, op. cit. [ib.], vol. 1, *Hebrew and Moabite Inscriptions* (Oxford, 1971); A. Lemaire, *Inscriptions hébraïques. Tome I: Les ostraca* (Paris, 1977); D. Pardee, *Handbook of Ancient Hebrew Letters: A Study Edition* (Chico, 1982). On the Moabite language, see S. Segert, "Die Sprache der moabitischen Königsinschrift," *Archiv Orientální* 29 (1961) 197-267; F.I. Andersen, "Moabite Syntax," *Or* 35 (1966) 81-120.

f *Phoenician*, which is represented by the inscription of King Kilamuwa (9th cent.) and by fairly numerous inscriptions later than the fifth cent., is closely related to Hebrew. The *Punic* dialect of Carthage and her colonies is related to Phoenician(1).

(1) The standard grammars are those by Z.S. Harris, *A Gram. of the Phoenician Lan-*

guage (New Haven, 1936); Friedrich-Röllig (1970); A. van den Branden, *Grammaire phénicienne* (Beyrouth, 1969); Segert, *A Gram. of Phoen. and Pun.* (München, 1976), with an extensive bibliography and a chrestomathy.

Ugaritic, mentioned above (§ *fe*), which is a language documented from the middle of the 14th to the end of the 13th cent. B.C., is best considered a separate North West Semitic language alongside Hebrew, Phoenician and Aramaic(1). Historically speaking, Ugarit was outside the area known as Canaan. The language used in the ancient city of Ugarit (Ras Shamra today) on the North Western coast of Syria and recorded on clay tablets in a cuneiform alphabet is of fundamental importance for the understanding of the prehistory of Hebrew and Biblical literature and culture in general. *fa*

(1) This is a newly discovered Semitic language. The attempt to classify it along the traditional lines has run into serious difficulties, because it shares bundles of significant isoglosses with diverse Semitic languages. See A. Goetze, "Is Ugaritic a Canaanite language?", *Language* 17 (1941) 127-38; Harris, *Development*, pp. 10f; Friedrich—Röllig, p. 1; J. Cantineau, "La langue de Ras-Shamra," *Semitica* 3 (1950) 21-34, esp. p. 34. For a similar and cautiously worded formulation by C.H. Gordon, see his *UT*, pp. 144-46. Greenfield (along with H.L. Ginsberg) emphasises the affinity between Ugr. and Can.: *Proceedings*, esp. 97-100.

Southern group (Arabia, Ethiopia): *Arabic*, *Ethiopic*. *g*

In Northern *Arabic* we have an inscription of King Mar'ulqais (A.D. 328). As a consequence of the Islamic conquests, Arabic spread to Syria, Babylonia, and Mesopotamia, where it gradually supplanted the Aramaic dialects, and to Egypt, Northern Africa, and finally even to Spain. *h*

The chief dialects of Southern Arabic are Minaean (or: Minaic), Qatabanic, Hadrami, and Sabaean (or: Sabaic)(1).

(1) M. Höfner, *Altsüdarabische Grammatik* (Leipzig, 1943); A.F.L. Beeston, *Sabaic Grammar* (Manchester, 1984).

Ethiopic or *Ge'ez* is the language of a people who emigrated from South Arabia to Ethiopia. The oldest monument in this language is the inscription of King 'Ezana of Aksum (4th cent. A.D.)(1). *i*

(1) A.J. Drewes, *Inscriptions de l'Éthiopie antique* (Leiden, 1962); idem, *Le Recueil des inscriptions d'Éthiopie des périodes pré-aksoumite et aksoumite* (Paris, 1991-).

Characteristics of the Semitic languages. The Semitic languages have *j* certain characteristic features which set them apart from other language families. Among those characteristics, which are found specifically in Hebrew, one may mention the following: 1) the existence of certain guttural sounds, *ḥ* ח and *ʿ* ע in Hebrew; 2) the existence of emphatic consonants, *ṭ* ט, *ṣ* צ, and *q* ק in Hebrew; 3) the roots are mostly purely consonantal and triliteral; the consonantal skeleton of the word expresses the general notion, whereas the vowels express the various modalities which determine this notion(1).

(1) For a discussion of the question of the extent to which speakers of Semitic languages were or are aware of consonantal roots as an entity morphologically distinct from discontinuous vowel morphemes (infixes and suffixes), see J.H. Greenberg, "The patterning of root morphemes in Semitic," *Word* 6 (1950) 162-81, where it was demonstrated that, in Semitic languages, two consecutive consonants cannot be homorganic, a constraint which holds for all 1-2 and 2-3 positions in the Semitic root, except for identical consonants in the 2-3 position. See also J. Kuryłowicz, *Studies in Semitic Grammar and Metrics* (Warszawa, 1972), pp. 17-24. (On an application of the method to Hebrew, see K. Koskinen, "Kompatibilität in den dreikonsonantigen hebräischen Wurzeln," *ZDMG* 114 [1964] 16-58.) The fact that such a constraint operates irrespective of the presence of vowels superimposed on the root is proof of the reality of root. (A similar idea, though not fully developed, had already been hinted at by Lambert in his *Traité*, § 161.) See also M. Cohen in A. Meillet and M. Cohen, *Les langues du monde* (Paris [2]1952), pp. 85-98; E. Ullendorff, "What is a Semitic language," *Or* 28 (1958) 66-75, and D. Cohen, "Qu'est-ce qu'une langue sémitique?," *GLECS* 23 (1973-79) 431-61; G. Bergsträsser, *Einführung in die semitischen Sprachen* (München, 1928), pp. 3-19 [= *Introduction to the Sem. Languages*, tr. P.T. Daniels [Winona Lake, 1983], pp. 2-24); B. Spuler, "Der semitische Sprachtypus," *Handbuch der Orientalistik*, 3.1 (Leiden, 1953-54), pp. 3-25.

k **Affinity of the Semitic group with other languages**(1)

Ancient Egyptian, from which Coptic is descended, shares certain features with the Semitic languages. It is assumed that the former has the same origin as the latter, but that, having diverged from them at a very early time and having been subjected to foreign influences, it has undergone an evolution entirely its own, resulting in a fundamental change of its character.

Even less close is the relationship of the Semitic languages with the modern Hamitic languages such as Berber and the Cushitic languages (Bischari, Saho, ʿAfar, Somali).

The suggestion of a remote relationship between the Semitic languages and the Indo-European languages is extremely problematic. Even the best recent works on the subject, particularly those by H. Möller(2), have not adduced convincing proof of an affinity(3).

(1) For a general, typological description of the Hamito-Semitic language group, see I.M. Diakonoff in "Hamito-Semitic languages," *Encyclopaedia Britannica* ([15]1974), vol. 8, pp. 589-98. See also S.J. Lieberman, "The Afro-Asiatic background of the Semitic N-stem: Towards the origins of the stem-afformatives of the Semitic and Afro-Asiatic verb," *BO* 43 (1986), 577-628, which illustrates how Hebrew could be placed in a wider linguistic context; and D. Cohen, *Les Langues chamito-sémitiques* (Paris, 1988). On some methodological questions, see W. von Soden, "Zum Methode der semitisch-hamitischen Sprachvergleichung," *JSS* 10 (1965) 159-77. See also I.M. Diakonoff, *Afrasian Languages* (Moscow, 1988), and H.J. Polotsky, in E.A. Speiser (ed.), *The World History of the Jewish People*, First series, vol. 1 (New Brunswick, 1964), pp. 121-23.

(2) *Semitisch und Indogermanisch*, I Teil: Konsonanten (Kopenhagen, 1907); *Vergleichendes indogerm.-sem. Wörterbuch* (Göttingen, 1911).

(3) See esp. A. Meillet in *Revue critique* 1 (1910) 313. More recently, see L. Brunner, *Die gemeinsamen Wurzeln des semitischen und indogermanischen Wortschatzes* (Bern/München, 1979); S. Levin, *The Indo-European and Semitic Languages* (Albany, 1971).

§ 3. History of Biblical Hebrew(1)

Although our biblical texts span a good many centuries, the language in which they are written presents an astonishing degree of uniformity. But this uniformity is not manifested to the same degree in all aspects of the language: morphology, syntax, vocabulary, and phraseology. The variations in vocabulary and phraseology between one period and another, and one writer and another are the most significant. The variations in syntax are in general the least significant. Nevertheless, the differences appear quite noticeable when one compares texts separated by a long period of time. Thus the syntax of the post-exilic historical books such as Ezra, Nehemiah, and Chronicles differs appreciably from that of Samuel and Kings(2). a

It is in the area of morphology that the uniformity of the biblical text is most apparent. It is also necessary to distinguish here between the consonantal element and the vocalic element. Given the very nature of Semitic morphology in which the consonants are comparable to a frame constituting a stable element, whilst the vowels are a variable element, the vowels must have changed more rapidly over the centuries than the consonants. Since the text which has come down to us enables us to establish only a few consonantal changes and very few vocalic changes, it is quite likely that the consonantal text was more or less standardised in the course of the centuries, and it is certain that the various parts of the consonantal text, whichever century they date from, were given a uniform vocalisation. The Naqdanim of the seventh century have imposed the synagogue pronunciation of their time on the oldest texts as well as on those for which alone it was, for the most part, valid, namely the latest texts.

In addition to the uniform consonantal text and the vocalisation imposed by the scribes and the Naqdanim respectively, there is an element of uniformity which derives from the desire of the authors themselves. In as much as the language of the late biblical books resembles very much that of the earliest, yet differs to the same extent from that of the Mishnah (2nd cent. A.D.), one must conclude that the Hebrew of the Mishnah(3) reflects the language spoken in rabbinic schools and among some sections of the Palestinian Jewish population at the time of its composition, whilst the late biblical writers generally tried to imitate, to a certain extent, the model sacred and classical alike of the early books. The imitation, however imperfect, prevents us somewhat from regarding Biblical Hebrew of the later stage as reflecting the contemporary spoken idiom.

All this goes to show how difficult it is to trace the development of Biblical Hebrew. The difficulty becomes greater still when one remembers that we do not know the even approximate date of composition or redaction of some writings(4).

(1) Cf. W. Chomsky, *Hebrew: the Eternal Language* (Philadelphia, 1964); C. Rabin, *A Short History of the Hebrew Language* (Jerusalem, n.d.); M. Hadas-Lebel, *Histoire de la langue hébraïque des origines à l'époque de la Mishna* (Paris, 1981); Kutscher, *History*.
(2) See Kropat, *Syntax*; Polzin (1976); A. Hurvitz, *A Linguistic Study of the Relationship between the Priestly Source and the Book of Ezekiel* (Paris, 1982).

Contrary to the prevailing view that the priestly source reflects the exilic and post-exilic period, recent studies tend to underline the archaic nature of the Hebrew used in the source: e.g., M. Paran, *Forms of the Priestly Style in the Pentateuch. Patterns, Linguistic Usages, Syntactic Structures* [Heb] (Jerusalem, 1989); J. Milgrom, *Numbers* במדבר [The JPS Torah Commentary](Philadelphia/New York, 1990), pp. xxxii-xxxv.
(3) The language of the Mishnah in a broad sense is also that of other related rabbinic literature, Tosefta, Midrashim, and more importantly, recently found writings from Qumran and the Wilderness of Judaea. On Mishnaic Hebrew in general, see E.Y. Kutscher, in *EJ*, vol. 16, cols. 1590-1607.

(4) It would also be extremely interesting to know what language was spoken by the Israelites at the time of the exodus after staying several centuries in Egypt, and what languages they spoke on entering Canaan. On this last point, one may refer to Bauer and Leander (pp. 23f.), who opt for Aramaic, which was, according to them, nothing but a dialect of Arabic. But the arguments put forward by them are not convincing. See § 2 *e*, n. 2.

Therefore we shall be content with distinguishing two main periods *b*
in the history of the Hebrew language: the pre-exilic and post-exilic periods(1). The pre-exilic period is the golden age of the language; it is, so to speak, the period of *Classical* Hebrew. During the post-exilic period the language changes, partly under the influence of Aramaic, which becomes more and more the everyday idiom of Jews. The most advanced stage of post-exilic Hebrew is represented by the language of Ecclesiastes, Esther, Ezra, Nehemiah, and Chronicles(2).

(1) On the evolution of "Classical BH," see C. Rabin, "The emergence of Classical Hebrew," in A. Malamat (ed.), *The Age of Monarchies: Culture and Society. The World History of the Jewish People*, vol. 4.2 (Jerusalem, 1979), pp. 71-78.

(2) The student ought to study these books only after having acquired a sufficient knowledge of good classical prose. However, for those whose first encounter with Hebrew was through Modern Hebrew, these late books would look more familiar and thus serve as a useful bridge to Classical Biblical Hebrew. Such students may consult H.B. Rosén, *A Textbook of Israeli Hebrew* (Chicago, 1962), pp. 307ff.

In addition to the differences between forms of Hebrew of different *c*
periods due to the evolution of the language over the centuries, the language must have presented dialectal peculiarities within the various regions in which it was spoken(1). Differences in language must have existed, for instance, between the northern kingdom and the southern kingdom. But the data at our disposal hardly enable us to pinpoint those differences sufficiently to speak of a northern dialect and a southern dialect.

(1) From the account in Jdg 12.6 it emerges that the Ephraimites pronounced the sibilant of שִׁבֹּלֶת differently from the people of Gilead.

A difference of another order and of paramount importance in grammar *d*
is that between the language of poetry and that of prose. In Hebrew poetry a good number of words occur which are typical of it, and of those words, a remarkably large number are found in Aramaic, e.g., אֱנוֹשׁ "man" for אָדָם, אֹרַח "road" for דֶּרֶךְ, אָתָה "come" for בּוֹא, מִלָּה "word" for

דָּבָר, חָזָה "see" for רָאָה. Poetry, whether for effect or on metrical grounds, often uses rare, anomalous or archaic forms. Thus one finds in poetry the archaic long forms of the prepositions אֱלֵי = אֶל; עֲדֵי = עַד; עֲלֵי = עַל (§ 103 *m*); the endings ִי־, וֹ of the noun (§ 93 *l, r*); the pronominal suffixes מוֹ, ־ָמוֹ, ־ֵמוֹ (§ 61 *i*). Poetry exercises a great deal of freedom in the area of syntax, and particularly the use of tenses. One could indeed be in dire straits if one attempted to deal with certain questions of syntax solely on the basis of poetic texts(1). It is, no doubt, for reasons of aesthetics or brevity that poetry makes far less use than prose of the definite article, the relative particle אֲשֶׁר, and the particle of the accusative אֵת.

(1) The grammar, especially the syntax, is based mainly on classical prose texts, and good narrative texts in particular. For attempts to tackle the grammar of poetic Hebrew, see D. Michel, *Tempora und Satzstellung in den Psalmen* (Bonn, 1960); M. O'Connor, *Hebrew Verse Structure* (Winona Lake, ID, 1980), and R. Sappan, *The Typical Features of the Syntax of Biblical Poetry in its Classical Period* [Heb] (Jerusalem, 1981).

§ 4. **History of Hebrew grammar**(1)

a The earliest works on Hebrew grammar appeared in the tenth century, under the influence of Arabic grammar, with Saadia Gaon of Fayyum (d. 942). The principal Jewish grammarians whose works we possess are Ḥayyuj (ca. 1000), Abu'l Walid Merwan Ibn Janaḥ (ca. 1030), Abraham Ibn Ezra (d. 1167), David Qimḥi [= Radaq] (d. ca. 1235), his father Joseph and brother Moshe. These Jewish scholars were aided in their task by their knowledge of Aramaic and Arabic.

(1) W. Bacher, *Hebräische Sprachwissenschaft vom 10. bis zum 16. Jahrhundert* (Trier, 1892); idem, "Die Anfänge der hebräischen Grammatik," *ZDMG* 49 (1895) 1-62, 335-92 [also as a monograph: Leipzig, 1895]; D. Tené and J. Barr, "Hebrew linguistic literature," *EJ*, vol. 16, cols. 1352-1401.

b The first grammar published by a Christian is that of John Reuchlin, *De rudimentis hebraicis* (Pforzheim, 1506). A good number of technical terms used in Hebrew grammar have their origin in his writings. A Jewish scholar by the name of Elias Levita (d. 1549) made notable contributions to the dissemination of the knowledge of Hebrew amongst Christian scholars through his writings and instruction. John Buxtorf

(d. 1629) and his successors still follow closely the grammatical theory developed by the Jews. In the eighteenth century, A. Schultens (d. 1750) put to good use his knowledge of Arabic in order to explain, and deepen the understanding of, Hebrew. But it was in the nineteenth century that Hebrew grammar was transformed, taking an increasingly scientific approach.

W. Gesenius (d. 1842) was the forerunner of this movement. His grammar went through many editions. After numerous and thoroughgoing revisions, it became a veritable *vade mecum* for Old Testament commentators, most of whom made constant reference to it. E. Rödiger (14th-21st ed) and E. Kautzsch (22nd-28th eds) constantly improved Gesenius' work. The last editions produced by Kautzsch contain a vast amount of data in a rather compact volume. The grammatical theory is rather conservative; the presentation is generally clear and accurate; and the bibliography is almost complete up to the date of the last edition. After the death of Kautzsch in 1910 the 29th edition was published by G. Bergsträsser, who has radically altered the work of his predecessor. This is in fact an entirely new work in which even the order of the matters dealt with differs considerably from its predecessor; it is a work of much greater erudition, far more critical, and gives much more attention to the historical development of the language(1). c

H. Ewald (d. 1875) attempted to establish laws which could provide rational explanation for grammatical facts. His grammar (*Ausführliches Lehrbuch der hebr. Sprache*, 8th [and last] ed., Göttingen, 1870) is still useful, especially in the area of syntax.

J. Olshausen (d. 1882), in his *Lehrbuch der hebr. Sprache* (Braunschweig, 1861), which only deals with phonetics and morphology, seeks to explain the forms of Hebrew by means of primitive Semitic, generally represented by Arabic.

F. Böttcher (d. 1863) in his *Ausführliches Lehrbuch der hebräischen Sprache*, edited by F. Mühlau, 2 vols. (Leipzig, 1866-68), was also able to handle only phonetics and morphology (the latter incomplete; cf. vol. 2, p. VI). However, this work is the most complete inventory of forms, and therefore highly useful.

B. Stade (d. 1906) also published only in the areas of phonetics and morphology (*Lehrbuch der hebr. Grammatik* [Leipzig, 1879]). His morphology of the verb contains a well-nigh complete inventory of the forms of the perfect, future and imperative, classified according to person. This mode of presentation is convenient for research and comparison of forms.

E. König wrote a comprehensive grammar *Lehrgebäude der hebr. Sprache* in three volumes: vol. 1 (Leipzig, 1881), on the pronoun and the verb; vol. 2 (Leipzig, 1895), on the noun, the particles, morphology in general and phonetics; and vol. 3 (Leipzig, 1897), on syntax. His work is often more complete than his predecessors'; on many a point he cites and discusses divergent opinions. It is a valuable storehouse of data.

H. Bauer and P. Leander have brought out their *Historische Grammatik der hebräischen Sprache* (Halle, 1922). This work is not only a historical grammar, as is indicated by the title, but also a descriptive one. In the historical part, hypothesis plays a significant role; the descriptive part, e.g., the section on noun formation, is rich and very meticulous. The authors, availing themselves of many works of detail and the important synthesis of comparative Semitic grammar by Brockelmann, have attempted to raise Hebrew grammar to the plane of scientific perfection attained by the Indo-European linguistics. The grammar remains incomplete, lacking syntax.

M. Lambert's *Traité de la grammaire hébraïque* (Paris, 1931-38), recently reprinted with some supplementary materials(2), is a comprehensive grammar. In contrast to Joüon's grammar in the original French edition, the originality of Lambert's is apparent more in morphology than in syntax. The author has published numerous articles on aspects of Hebrew grammar in *Revue d'études juives* and *Journal Asiatique*.

Useful and original is C. Brockelmann's *Hebräische Syntax* (Neukirchen, 1956), which is based largely on vol. 2 of the same author's monumental *Grundriss der vergleichenden Grammatik der semitischen Sprachen* (Berlin, 1908-13).

Another recent comprehensive grammar is R. Meyer's *Hebräische Grammatik*, 4 vols. (Berlin, 1966-72), in Sammlung Göschen, in which he attempts to take into account recent advances in the study of Ugaritic, Qumran Hebrew, non-Massoretic traditions of Hebrew pronunciation and the like.

(1) Cf. P. Joüon in *Bib* 1 (1920) 111.

(2) Edited by G.E. Weil and published by Dr H.A. Gerstenberg: Hildesheim, 1972.

d Apart from these comprehensive works of major importance, one must also mention as particularly useful *Hebrew Syntax* by A.B. Davidson (Edinburgh, ^{3}1912) and the excellent book by S.R. Driver, *A Treatise on the Use of the Tenses in Hebrew and some other Syntactical Questions* (Oxford, ^{3}1892). One should also mention the stylistics of König (*Stilistik, Rhetorik, Poetik* [Leipzig, 1900]), which is a useful supplement to his grammar. In addition, the past two decades have witnessed the publication of a number of important monographs dealing with specific questions of Hebrew syntax such as F.I. Andersen's *The Hebrew Verbless Clause in the Pentateuch* (1970); idem, *The Sentence* (1974); T. Muraoka, *Emphatic Words and Structures in Biblical Hebrew* (1985); B. Waltke and M. O'Connor, *An Introduction to Biblical Hebrew Syntax* (1989).

e Lexicography made significant progress during the nineteenth and twentieth centuries, but much remains to be done. The *Thesaurus linguae hebraicae* of W. Gesenius (published between 1829 and 1858), though many parts of it are outdated, still remains a storehouse where one can find many valuable things some of which have been wrongly discarded. The German editions of Gesenius' dictionary have been gradually and thoroughly revised by successive editors. The last (16th) edition, prepared by F. Buhl, dates from 1915: *W. Gesenius' hebr. und aram. Handwörterbuch*(1). This dictionary is particularly useful for the abundance of literature cited, its etymological section, and its suggested textual emendations. On these matters the *Oxford Lexicon* of Brown, Driver and Briggs (*A Hebrew and English Lexicon of the Old Testament*, 1906) is inferior. On the other hand, the latter is often more exhaustive and careful. Its specifically grammatical sections treated by S.R. Driver, notably the particles, are excellent. One inconvenient deficiency is its lack of an English-Hebrew index(2). The arrangement of words by roots, which are in fact sometimes disputable (cf. § 34 *b*) or arbitrary, is also less practical than the purely alphabetical arrangement of Gesenius-Buhl. The dictionary by König (*Hebr. und aram. Wörterbuch* [Leipzig, ^{2}1910]), though far less comprehensive than the last mentioned works, is helpful in its many cross-references to the grammar by the same author. L. Koehler and W. Baumgartner's *Lexicon in veteris testamenti libros* (Leiden, 1958) is a useful, modern tool, highly acclaimed for its Aramaic section compiled by Baumgartner, but in terms of general lexicography is inferior to Brown-Driver-Briggs, commonly referred to as 'BDB'(3). Finally, mention may be made of E. Ben-

Yehudah, *Thesaurus totius hebraitatis et veteris et recentioris* (1908-58)(4); F. Zorell, *Lexicon hebraicum et aramaicum veteris testamenti* [in Latin] (Rome, 1968)(5) and a still incomplete אוצר לשון המקרא (Jerusalem, 1957ff.) by S.E. Loewenstamm, J. Blau, and M.Z. Kaddari, which also serves as a concordance.

(1) 17th ed. (photomechanical reproduction of the 16th), 1920. The first fascicule of a thorougly revised 18th edition (by H. Donner and R. Meyer) made its appearance in 1987.

(2) The dictionaries of Gesenius and Köhler-Baumgartner mentioned above both contain a German-Hebrew index. There is also available a useful index: *Index to Brown, Driver & Briggs' Hebrew Lexicon*, compiled by B. Einspahr (Moody Press: Chicago, 1976).

(3) A revised edition entitled *Hebräisches und aramäisches Lexikon zum alten Testament* to which various people have made contributions is currently in progress, four fascicules having appeared so far (Leiden, 1967-). Unlike its predecessor, which has entries in English and German throughout, the revised edition is entirely in German. Despite some notable advances beyond its immediate predecessor and BDB, the last-mentioned can still claim many strengths by comparison.

(4) As the title indicates, the dictionary covers the whole gamut of the history of Hebrew, enabling even those primarily interested in Biblical Hebrew to see BH words in historical perspective. Following the death of the author the work was brought to completion by N.H. Tur-Sinai (Torczyner), who added innumerable footnotes.

(5) The Aramaic part was published by E. Vogt as *Lexicon linguae aramaicae veteris testamenti documentis antiquis illustratum* [in Latin] (Rome, 1971).

f The classical and comprehensive Hebrew concordance is that of S. Mandelkern, *Veteris Testamenti Concordantiae hebraicae atque chaldaicae* (Leipzig, 1896)(1). Two more recent additions are: G. Lisowsky, *Konkordanz zum hebräischen alten Testament* etc. [based on Biblia Hebraica as edited by P. Kahle - R. Kittel and printed from the compiler's handwritten copy] (Stuttgart, 1958) and A. Even-Shoshan, *A New Concordance of the Bible* [available in various formats] (Jerusalem, [4]1981). Both are extremely useful, the latter in particular in that it provides a wealth of information presented in ways which greatly facilitate semantic and lexical studies of the Old Testament languages(2). However, neither has rendered Mandelkern's concordance redundant, since Lisowsky's does not include the so-called function words such as prepositions, pronouns, and neither gives the actual text for all occurrences of common words and forms, merely giving references, albeit exhaustively(3).

(1) Reprinted with additions and corrections by F. Margolin and M.H. Goshen-Gottstein

(Shocken: Tel Aviv/Jerusalem, ^{5}1962).

(2) Lisowsky's work excludes the Aramaic portions of the OT.

(3) In addition there are available computer-generated databases and concordances based on them, e.g. F.I. Andersen and A. Dean Forbes, *A Linguistic Concordance of Ruth and Jonah: Hebrew Vocabulary and Idiom. The Computer Bible*, vol. IX (1976).

Comparative table of alphabets

1 Mēšaʿ (ca.850)	2 Samaritan	3 Egyptian papyri (5-3 cent)	4 Square: Petersburg (916-7)	5 Rabbinic
𐤀	ࠀ	𐡀	א	א
𐤁	ࠁ	𐡁	ב	ב
𐤂	ࠂ	𐡂	ג	ג
𐤃	ࠃ	𐡃	ד	ד
𐤄	ࠄ	𐡄	ה	ה
𐤅	ࠅ	𐡅	ו	ו
𐤆	ࠆ	𐡆	ז	ז
𐤇	ࠇ	𐡇	ח	ח
𐤈	ࠈ	𐡈	ט	ט
𐤉	ࠉ	𐡉	י	י
𐤊	ࠊ	𐡊	כ ך	כ ך
𐤋	ࠋ	𐡋	ל	ל
𐤌	ࠌ	𐡌	מ ם	מ ם
𐤍	ࠍ	𐡍	נ ן	נ ן
𐤎	ࠎ	𐡎	ס	ס
𐤏	ࠏ	𐡏	ע	ע
𐤐	ࠐ	𐡐	פ ף	פ ף
𐤑	ࠑ	𐡑	צ ץ	צ ץ
𐤒	ࠒ	𐡒	ק	ק
𐤓	ࠓ	𐡓	ר	ר
𐤔	ࠔ	𐡔	ש	ש
𐤕	ࠕ	𐡕	ת	ת

PART ONE

—

ORTHOGRAPHY AND PHONETICS

—

§ 5. Consonants: script and pronunciation

a The phonemes(1) can be divided into consonants and vowels. But it needs to be noted that this division is not adequate; certain vowels (*i* and *u* in Hebrew) can become consonantal (*y* י, *w* ו)(2), and certain consonants can become vocalic (no example in Hebrew).

(1) On a definition of 'phoneme,' see below, § *gb*.

(2) See also § 21 *c* (furtive pataḥ).

b The Hebrew **alphabet**, like the majority of Semitic alphabets(1), consists of consonant letters only(2). The characters of our printed Bibles as well as those of all known manuscripts(3) have a shape similar to a square, hence the name *square script* כְּתָב מְרֻבָּע. This script, which emerged in about the third century B.C., is a development of the *Aramaic* script, and was adopted gradually by Jews together with the Aramaic language (§ 3 *b*) after the return of the Babylonian exiles. This new script, sometimes called Jewish script, replaced the ancient script called *Hebrew script* (כְּתָב עִבְרִי), which is used, for instance, in the Gezer calendar, the Siloam inscription and the stele of Mesha (§ 2 *e*)(4). The old script, called Paleo-Hebrew, was kept alive to a limited extent in some Dead Sea writings such as Pentateuch fragments and on Jewish coins of the Hellenistic-Roman era, and continued to be used, but appreciably modified, by the Samaritans after their separation from the Jews, whenever it took place. The *rabbinic* script or *Rashi* script(5) is a modification of the square script. It is used especially in rabbinic bibles for the commentaries printed in the margins.

(1) On the development of the Hebrew alphabet and its ancestors, and the Aramaic and Samaritan scripts, see respectively, J. Naveh, *Early History of the Alphabet* (Jerusalem and Leiden, ^{2}1987), idem, *The Development of the Aramaic Script* (Jerusalem, 1970), and J.D. Purvis, *The Samaritan Pentateuch and the Origin of the Samaritan Sect* (Cambridge,

MA, 1968). See also S. Birnbaum, *The Hebrew Scripts*, 2 vols. (Leiden, 1971-72); G.R. Driver, *Semitic Writing: From Pictograph to Alphabet* (London, ^{2}1976), and B. Sass, *The Genesis of the Alphabet and its Development in the Second Millennium B.C.* (Wiesbaden, 1988).

(2) On the supposedly originally syllabic character of Semitic alphabets, see M. Lambert, "L'origine de l'alphabet," *JA*, 11ème série, 11 (1918) 563-65; I.J. Gelb, *A History of Writing* (Chicago, 1952), pp. 147-53.

(3) Except a small number of fragmentary Qumran biblical manuscripts. The oldest dated complete manuscript is the Cairo codex of the Prophets (895). The Wilderness of Judaea, including Qumran caves, has produced a vast number of biblical manuscripts, mostly fragmentary, dating probably from the late 3rd cent. B.C. onwards. The Nash papyrus found in 1902, which contains Ex 20.2ff. (Decalogue) and Dt 5.6ff., 6.4f. probably dates from around A.D. 100.

(4) The letters in the modern script which resemble one another and are thus likely to cause confusion are not the same as those which resembled one another in the ancient script. In order to understand some emendations of the text we need to take this into account. See the comparative table of the alphabets on p. 18.

(5) So called not because Rashi invented this script, but because right from the beginning of Jewish printing (1475) his commentaries on the Bible and the Talmud were printed in this script.

c The letters of the Hebrew alphabet are 22 in number, or 23, if one takes into account the diacritical point of ש(1).

(1) The names of the letters are based on the system of acrophony, i.e. the first sound of the name of a given letter of the alphabet is that indicated by the letter: e.g. the seventh letter ז [za'yin]. For details, see Driver, *Semitic Writing* [§ *b*, n. 1 above], pp. 152-71. The order of the letters of the alphabet is ancient, as is attested by the so-called acrostic poems such as Ps 119, Lam 1-4, Ben Sira 51; indeed, as the Ugaritic materials show, it goes back as far as the 14th century B.C. Lambert (p. 10) thinks that the actual sequence of the letters was, at least partly, determined by visual similarities of letter shape (Alef, Bet, Gimel, Dalet in Paleo-Hebrew) and partly by semantic similarities of letter names, e.g., Yod and Kaf.

Numerical value	Name		Transliteration	Pronunciation	Phonetic description
1	Alef	א	'	hamza ʾ of Arabic (§ j)	voiceless guttural
2	Bet	בּ	b	English b (§ o)	voiced labial plosive
		בֿ	v	English v (§ o)	voiced labial fricative
3	Gimel	גּ	g	English hard g (§ o)	voiced palatal plosive
		גֿ	ḡ	Mod. Gk γ (§ o)	voiced palatal fricative
4	Dalet	דּ	d	English d (§ o)	voiced dental plosive
		דֿ	ḏ	Engl. soft th as in this (§ o)	voiced dental fricative
5	He	ה	h	English h (§ j)	voiceless guttural
6	Waw	ו	w	English w (§ 7 d)	vocalic bilabial glide
7	Zayin	ז	z	English z	voiced dental sibilant
8	Ḥet	ח	ḥ	ح (§ k)	voiceless guttural
9	Ṭet	ט	ṭ	ط (§ i)	voiceless dental plosive velar
10	Yod	י	y	English y (§ 7 d)	vocalic palatal glide
20	Kaf	כּ	k	English k (§ o)	voiceless palatal plosive
		כֿ	ḵ	Mod. Gk χ (§ o), خ	voiceless palatal fricative
30	Lamed	ל	l	Engl. "clear" l (§ 5gb)	voiced lingual
40	Mem	מ	m	English m	voiced bilabial nasal
50	Nun	נ	n	English n	voiced dental nasal

60	Sameḫ	ס	*s*	English *s* (§ *m*)	voiceless sibilant
70	‘Ayin	ע	‘	ع (§ *k*)	voiced guttural
80	Pe	פּ	*p*	French *p* (§ *o*, n. 5)	voiceless bilabial plosive
		פֿ	*f*	English *f* (§ *o*)	voiceless bilabial fricative
90	Tzadé	צ	*ṣ*	ص (§ *m*)	voiceless velar sibilant
100	Qof	ק	*q*	ق (§ *i*)	voiceless velar plosive
200	Resh	ר	*r*	Italian, Arabic *r* (§ *n*)	voiced lingual
	Sin	שׂ	*ś*	(?) (§ *m*)	voiceless sibilant
300					
	Shin	שׁ	*š*	English *sh* (§ *m*)	voiceless sibilant
400	Taw	תּ	*t*	French *t* (§ *o*, n. 5)	voiceless dental plosive
		תֿ	*ṯ*	Engl. *th* as in *thin*, Mod. Gk θ (§ *o*)	voiceless dental fricative

d **Final letters.** Five letters have a special form at the end of a word(1). These five letters are contained in the mnemonic word כמנפץ *kamnappeṣ* "like the one who shatters." The non-final and final pairs are: כ and ך; מ and ם; נ and ן; פ and ף; צ and ץ. When the word-final form of the letter Mem is written, the end of the stroke on the top left is written so as to join its beginning, thus forming a closed shape. When writing the word-final form of the remaining four letters, the end of the stroke is extended downwards, instead of being turned towards the left.

(1) All word-final forms, except that for Mem, are historically older than their corresponding non-word-final shapes.

e **Extendible letters.** Hebrew is written from right to left. At the end of a line, a word is not split(1). To avoid blanks, some letters, namely, א, ה, ל, ם, ת are widened.

(1) In inscriptions, words are often broken up at the end of a line.

f **Numerical values**(1). 1-9 = א-ט; 10-90 = י-צ; 100-400 = ק-ת; 500 is expressed by 400 + 100 = תק; similarly for 600-800; 900 is expressed by 400 + 400 + 100 = תתק. (For 500-900 one also makes use of the word-final letters: 500 ך, 600 ם, 700 ן, 800 ף, 900 ץ). For the thousands one uses the letters used for the units with two dots written above, e.g. א̈ = 1000. The number 15 logically is יה, but since this combination of letters represents the abbreviated divine name יהוה, 15 is expressed by 9 + 6 = טו. Likewise 16 logically is יו, but since this sequence of letters represents the divine name as it appears in proper nouns (e.g., יוֹאָב "Yahweh <is> father"), 16 is expressed by 9 + 7 = טז.

(1) See the Table of the Alphabet on p. 18. The use of letters as numbers dates back at least to the second century B.C. See Driver, *Semitic Writing* [§ *b*, n. 1 above], p. 270.

g **Abbreviations**(1). As an indication of abbreviation one uses a symbol similar to an "apostrophe" at the end or a double quotation mark between two letters, e.g., פְּלֹנִי = פ' "so and so," וְגוֹמֵר = וגו' "and one who completes = et cetera," רש"י Rashi (Rabbi Shlomo Yitzhaqi), תנ"ך (pronounced *tanach* = תּוֹרָה, נְבִיאִים, כְּתוּבִים "Law - Prophets - Writings" (= the Hebrew Bible). One writes, for example, פ"ן verbs, namely verbs the first radical of which (represented by פ, the first radical of the verb פעל) is Nun(2); cf. § 40 *c*.

(1) See esp. the dictionary of abbreviations of Händler in G. Dalman, *Aramäisch-neuhebräisches Wörterbuch* (Leipzig, [2]1905). Abraham Even-Shoshan's dictionary, הַמִּלּוֹן הֶחָדָשׁ (Jerusalem, 1976), lists all common abbreviations incorporated in the dictionary in alphabetical order. On the question of abbreviation, see Driver, op. cit. [§ *b* above, n. 1], pp. 270f.

(2) Pronounce as *oo* (as in *book*) the Semitic vowel transliterated by *u*.

ga Naturally we only have indirect sources of information about the pronunciation of Classical Hebrew. Among the more important of them are:

1. The Jewish traditions: Ashkenazi, Sephardi, and Yemenite(1).
2. The pronunciation of living Semitic languages, esp. Arabic, Ethiopic and Aramaic.
3. Internal considerations.
4. Transliteration and transcription of Hebrew words and names, esp. in Greek and Latin, e.g. the second column of the Hexapla, Je-

rome, and the Septuagint; there are some inherent difficulties arising from the nature of the phonemic inventories of these classical, non-Semitic languages.

5. Transliterations in Akkadian, Ugaritic, and Egyptian, though here again similar problems arise.

(1) Contributions by Israeli scholars are prominent in this field, e.g. H. Yalon, Sh. Morag, I. Yeivin, and I. Eldar. Note also the ongoing series עדה ולשון under the editorship of Morag.

gb Modern linguistics insists on an important distinction between phone and phoneme. A phone is a sound heard or articulated in actual speech, and as such it is a physical entity which can be measured and recorded by mechanical devices. A classification of consonants as labial, dental, etc. and of vowels as front, back, mid, high, etc. accords with such an approach. By contrast, a phoneme is what is *perceived* to be a particular phonetic entity, and thus by definition it is an abstraction, something like the common denominator of countless phones, namely actual sounds which share certain essential features. Even one and the same speaker—and of course, different speakers of a given language—pronounces a given phoneme in numerous variations, which however are normally perceived as one phoneme, without creating any serious problem of communication. For instance, standard English has two distinct kinds of /l/ phoneme, sometimes called 'dark *l*' as in *keel* and 'clear *l*' as in *leek*. They are so different in sound that if a native French or German speaker, for example, pronounced *keel* with the 'clear *l*,' he or she would give away his or her non-English origin, but the native English speaker would still discern without difficulty the meaning of the word. The choice between these two kinds of *l*, technically called 'allophone,' is conditioned by their respective positions within a word: clear *l* occurs before a vowel, whilst dark *l* occurs before a consonant or at the end of a word. In other words they are positional variants. Moreover, phonemes distinguish meanings. To take two examples from Hebrew, the semantic difference between נִשְׁחַת *he was ruined, corrupted* and נִשְׁחַט *he was slaughtered* is expressed solely by means of a phonemic contrast between ת and ט. Although the phonetic difference between them may sound to us rather marginal, they are nonetheless two distinct phonemes. By contrast, the presence or absence of dagesh in the Taw in

תַּעֲשֶׂה and לֹא־תַעֲשֶׂה has no bearing on the meaning of the verb form, so that they are two allophones of the /t/ phoneme. In dealing with ancient languages, it is naturally easier to deal with phonemes than phones.

h **Classification of the consonants**(1). The consonantal phonemes may conveniently be classified as follows:

Labials: ב ו מ פ (mnemonic word: בּוּמַף *bumaf*)
Dentals: ד ת ט (velar)
Palatals: ג כ י
Velars: ט (dental), צ (sibilant), ק
Gutturals: א ה ח ע
Sibilants: ז ס צ (velar), שׂ שׁ
Linguals: ל ר
Nasals: נ מ

(1) For a description of the traditional pronunciations of the Hebrew consonants, see Schramm, *Graphemes*, pp. 15-24.

i **Velars or emphatics**. The three consonants *ṭ* ט, *ṣ* צ, *q* ק(1) are called *emphatic* in relation to the three corresponding consonants *t* ת, *s* ס, *k* כ. The former are articulated in the region farther back in the mouth called the soft palate, and with greater tension of the articulatory organs than is the case for the latter. Their values, which have no equivalents in our languages, are precisely those of the corresponding emphatic sounds in Arabic ط ,ص, ق. For צ see § *m*.

(1) ק is transliterated by the character *q*, which is graphically similar, or by *ḳ* (with a point below as with the other velars).

The precise nature of the so-called "emphatic" consonants in Ancient Hebrew, and all the dead Semitic language for that matter, is an unręsolved question: for a well-balanced exposé of the question, see J. Cantineau in *Semitica* 4 (1951-52) 91-93, where he inclines towards the modern Ethiopic type of articulation which is characterised by glottal stoppage followed by forceful emission of air like a piston. See also I. Garbell in *BSL* 50 (1954) 234. Laufer, an experimental phonetician, notes that, in Modern Hebrew and Arabic, the articulation of all these consonants is characterised by the secondary feature of pharyngealisation: A. Laufer, "Descriptions of the emphatic sounds in Hebrew and in Arabic" [in Heb], M. Bar-Asher (ed.), *Language Studies* II-III (Jerusalem, 1987), pp. 423-38. On other varieties, see I.M. Diakonoff in *Encyclopaedia Britannica* ([15]1974), vol. 8, p. 591a, and Berg., § 6, n.

j **Gutturals.** The gutturals are sometimes further classified into laryngals (ʾ and *h*) and pharyngals (*ḥ* and ʿ). **Alef** א (when it is pronounced)(1) is a voiceless guttural stop. In order to produce this sound one must abruptly stop the emission of the vowel by sudden closure of the glottis(2). This is the sound one sometimes hears in the German word *ja'* pronounced with some emotion (in place of *jā*) or after the prefix *ge* as in *geatmet*. One may also hear it in the pronunciation of the *tt* in a word like *better* in the north of England. For example: יֶאְשַׁם *he will make himself guilty*. א is conventionally transliterated by the symbol /'/ (the smooth breathing of Greek).

He ה is the voiceless guttural fricative, which one has in English and German *Hand*. This sound does not exist in French.

(1) In practice, in Hebrew as we know it, א is not pronounced except under certain conditions in the middle of a word as detailed in § 24 *b*. In Contemporary Israeli Hebrew it is hardly audible at the beginning of a word.

(2) The glottis is the slit which separates the vocal cords. W. Vycichl suggests that Alef may originally have been a voiced fricative laryngal: *GLECS* 18-23 (1973-79) 495-97.

k *Ḥet* is a voiceless guttural which does not exist in our languages. It exactly corresponds to *ḥ* ح in Arabic as in *Muḥammad*. In comparison with ה, one can say that this is a ה produced with forcible constriction of the larynx. It has been rather fittingly described as a *guttural hiss* (Gismondi).

Comparison of various Semitic languages shows that the symbol ח corresponds to two distinct sounds represented in Arabic by ح *ḥ* and خ *ḫ*(1). *ḫ* is the voiceless velar spirant, which one hears in the Swiss pronunciation of, e.g. German *nach* or Scottish *loch*. It is highly probable that formerly ח had in some words the value of *ḥ*, and in others that of *ḫ*. But at the time of the Naqdanim ח represented the single sound *ḥ*. If the symbol ח had had two values, the Naqdanim, who were so careful to note the minutest nuances, such as the twofold pronunciation of *begadkefat* (§ *o*), would not have failed to indicate them. The existence of the value *ḫ* for ח at the time when the Kaf rafé כ *ḵ* (= *ḫ*) existed is most unlikely, because the two sounds are too close to each other. *ḵ* is, in effect, the voiceless palatal spirant, which one hears, e.g., in Modern Greek χάρις or in German *nach* in the standard pronunciation (as against the Swiss variety). Certain details of the vocalisation indicate the sound *ḥ*, and preclude the value *ḫ*; thus *pataḥ furtive*, e.g., in טָבוּחַ (cf. Arb. *ṭ-b-ḫ*) *slaughtered*; likewise *auxiliary pataḥ*, e.g. in the type שָׁלַחַתְּ "you (f.sg.) have sent" (§ 70 *f*), for in order to pronounce *šålạḥt there would be no need of an auxiliary vowel any more than there would be to pronounce אַל־תֵּשְׁתְּ *'ạl tẹšt* "don't drink." Furthermore, a doubling of the sound *ḵ* (כ) is totally foreign to Hebrew; it would be the same for its analogue *ḫ*. But, ח, whilst rejecting, as do all the gutturals, genuine gemination, does permit virtual gemination (or weak gemination); it sometimes even permits spontaneous gemination (§§ 20 *a,c*)(2). Hence ח presupposes the value *ḥ* (3).

(1) Cf. J.W. Wevers, "Ḥeth in Classical Heb." in J.W. Wevers and D.B. Redford (eds), *Essays on the Ancient Semitic World* (Toronto, 1970), pp. 101-12. The distinction between the two consonants in question is observed in transcriptions in Egyptian of Canaanite names and loan words in the middle of the second millennium B.C. The same applies to the distinction between /'/ and /ḡ/; see below § *l*.

(2) Even in cases where ח corresponds to an original *ḫ*, e.g. in אַחִים *brothers* (cf. Arb. *'aḫ*).

(3) For a recent discussion on a possible date for the merging of *ḫ* with *ḥ* on the one hand, and *ḡ* with ʿ on the other, see a summary by Z. Zevit in his *Matres Lectionis in Ancient Hebrew Epigraphs* (Cambridge, MA, 1980), p. 5, n. 22.

'ayin ע is a voiced guttural which does not exist in our languages. *l*
It is exactly the sound of ع ʿ in Arabic as in *ʿAyn* "eye." This sound has been compared with "the guttural noise made by a camel being loaded with its pack saddle" (C. Huart, *Littérature arabe* [Paris, 1902], p. 139)(1). Comparison with other languages reveals that the symbol ע corresponds to two appreciably distinct Semitic sounds represented in Arabic by ع ʿ and غ *ḡh*(2). This last consonant is a voiced velar fricative; it is a fricative corresponding to velar *ḡ* (this *ḡ* itself being the voiced counterpart of the voiceless *q* ק). It is highly probable that ע once had the value of ع ʿ in some words, and the value of غ *ḡh* in others. But at the time of the Naqdanim, ע represented the single sound ʿ. If the symbol ע had had two values, the Naqdanim, so careful to record even the minutest phonetic details, would not have failed to indicate them. The existence of the sound غ *ḡh* at the time when the Gimel rafé (ג *ḡ*) existed is rather unlikely. The two sounds are too close to each other. *ḡ* is in effect the voiced palatal fricative, which one hears, for example, in Modern Greek γάλα. Certain details of vocalisation indicate the sound ʿ, and preclude the sound *ḡh*: thus the *furtive pataḥ*, for example, in שָׁמוּעַ "heard"; likewise the auxiliary *pataḥ* in the type שָׁמַ֫עַתְּ "you (f.sg.) have heard" (§ 70 *f*). The conventional transliteration of ע is /ʿ/ (the rough breathing in Greek).

(1) The onomatopoeia أُعْ أُعْ *u' u'* imitates the sound of vomiting; cf. Wright, *Arabic Grammar*, I, p. 295.

(2) In spite of a long series of writings by R. Růžička the existence of Ghain in Proto-Semitic as a genuine Semitic phoneme is universally accepted. See a summary of the debate in Moscati, § 8.45. Transliterations of names in the Septuagint such as Γαζα for עַזָּה attests to *ġ*, although the Septuagint evidence is not consistent: cf. G. Lisowsky, *Die Transkription der hebraeischen Eigennamen des Pentateuch in der Septuaginta*, diss. Basel, 1940, pp. 122f, and A. Murtonen, *Hebrew in its West Semitic Setting*, Part 1, Section A (Leiden, 1986), p. 5, n. 6; p. 171 on item 1185; p. 177, on item 1258; and p. 179 on item 1274. See also § *k*, n. 1 above.

la Whilst there are signs of a gradual weakening of the gutturals—note, e.g. לָבִיא for לְהָבִיא (§ 54 *b*), and ת for את (nota accusativi) in the Bar Kokhba letters—there is no question of a general confusion of the gutturals like that observable in the SH tradition(1).

(1) See Kutscher, *History*, pp. 18-21, and on the SH pronunciation, Ben-Ḥayyim, *LOT*, vol. 5, pp. 25-29, and Macuch, *Gram.*, pp. 132-36.

m **Sibilants.** צ *ṣ* is a voiced velar sibilant, and the emphatic counterpart of ס *s* (§ *m*). It is commonly pronounced as /ts/, an affricate stop, though the practice is sometimes condemned as wrong. In any event, this /ts/ pronounced as in Engl. *cats* or Germ. *Zeit* must be considered a single phoneme, that is to say, not /t/ + /s/(1).

שׂ is currently pronounced *s* like ס(2) by all Jews and has been so from time immemorial(3). שׁ is the alveolar, which is heard in Engl. *shoe* and Germ. *Schuh*. Between *s* and *š* there is an intermediate sound (e.g. Polish *ś*, Spanish *s*, and the final *s* in Portugese). It is possible that some intermediate sound existed in Hebrew. However Sin may have sounded in Early Hebrew, it is clear that, for Hebrew, Sin and Shin were two distinct phonemes, as evidenced by a neat and consistent correspondence between those sounds and their equivalents in other Semitic languages, e.g. Arabic. See below § *q*. The reason why *š* and *ś* are expressed by the same character ש is that the language or languages for which the Phoenician alphabet had been invented had ceased to make such a distinction by the time the Hebrews had borrowed it. In Early Hebrew and Aramaic, it appears, *ś* did not sound sufficiently distinct from *š* to prompt the addition of a separate written symbol, but later the former approximated to *s* as is evidenced by the occurrence side by side of words such as סְבָךְ *thicket* and שְׂבָכָה *network*. Hebrew and South Arabian, both Ancient Epigraphic and Modern, are the only two Semitic languages which seem to have this phoneme(4). On the other hand, it is rather doubtful that the symbol שׂ with the diacritical point was intended to indicate this sound. At the time of its introduction the symbol שׂ probably indicated *s*. This would be an etymological spelling used for cases where an earlier *š* (or *ś*) had become *s*. Many biblical words are found spelled now with ס, and now with שׂ: for example, one finds סוּג *retreat* nearly always, but שׂוּג once only; one ordinarily finds כַּ֫עַס *irritation*, but also כַּ֫עַשׂ three times (cf. Gesenius, *Thesaurus*, *sub* ס). Whilst in Post-biblical Hebrew שׂ is often replaced by ס(5), in Early Hebrew the two sounds were clearly kept apart: √ סכל *to be foolish* vs. √ שׂכל *to be intelligent*.

(1) See R.C. Steiner, *Affricated ṣade in the Semitic Languages* (New York, 1982), which makes a plausible case for the affricate pronunciation (= /ts/) for early Semitic. But J. Cantineau refers to Codex Vaticanus of Lamentations (LXX), where this letter is transcribed with Σ and T one on top of the other: *BSL* 46 (1950) 88, and see also M. Cohen, *Nouvelles études d'éthiopien méridional* (Paris, 1939), pp. 26f.

(2) Thus הִשְׂכִּיל *he acted prudently* and הִסְכִּיל *he acted foolishly* (§ 54 *d*) are pronounced in the same way: *hiskil*. As to whether the pronunciation of שׂ as /s/ is due to Aramaic influence or not, see W. Diem, *ZDMG* 124 (1974) 221-52 as against J. Blau, *HAR* 1 (1977) 100-8.

(3) The Samaritans have only one symbol ש, which they pronounce *š*: see Ben-Ḥayyim, *LOT*, vol. 5, p. 24; Macuch, *Gram.*, pp. 84f.

(4) This is widely believed to have been a lateralised sibilant, as it is in Mod. South Arabian dialects. See J. Cantineau in *Semitica*, 4 (1951-52) 86f., R.C. Steiner, *The Case for Fricative-laterals in Proto-Semitic* (New Haven, 1977), and A.F.L. Beeston, *Sabaic Grammar* (Manchester, 1984). p. 9. There is some evidence to suggest that Old Akkadian also had a similar phoneme. For a summary of the discussion of the problem, see Moscati, § 8.29.

(5) See J. Blau, *On Pseudo-corrections in some Semitic Languages* (Jerusalem, 1970), pp. 114-25. Occasional substitution of ס for שׂ may result in possible *double entendre*: see Ibn Ezra on Ho 8.4 הֵשִׂ֫ירוּ "they appointed someone king" as well as "they deposed him."

Linguals. ר is a lingual like ל. It consists of one or more vibrations of the tongue as in the Arabic *r*, the Italian and Spanish *r*(1). n
One must be very careful not to prounounce ר like the fricative guttural of the contemporary German and French which one hears in many parts of France, especially in the cities(2). The fact that ר is to some extent treated like a guttural does not allow us to consider it to be

guttural (cf. § 23).

(1) Cf. *MUSJ* 5 (1911) 383-88.

(2) But cf. M.H. Goshen-Gottstein, in *Leš* 16 (1949) 209-11, and I. Eldar, ib. 48-49 (1983-85) 22-34.

o **Begadkefat.** The six consonants contained in the mnemonic word בְּגַד- כְּפַת have a twofold pronunciation: *plosive* and *fricative* or *spirant*(1). The plosives have the value of the corresponding consonants in English, i.e. *b*, *g* (hard as in *get*), *d*, *k*, *p*, *t*. In order to indicate the plosive sound, one places inside the letter a point called a *dagesh*(2). The fricatives have the corresponding *spirantised* or *continuous* sounds resulting from partial regressive assimilation to the preceding vowel. In order to indicate the fricative sound, a horizontal stroke called *rafé*(3) is written over the letter concerned; that, at any rate, is how it is marked in the manuscripts. But in the printed editions of the Bible, the absence of *dagesh* is a sufficient indication that the consonant is *rafé*. The following are the spirantised sounds:

בֿ *ḇ*, *bh* like β in Mod. Gk., almost like the Engl. *v*(4)
גֿ *ḡ*, *gh* like γ in Mod. Gk. in γάλα (cf. § *l*)
דֿ *ḏ*, *dh* like δ in Mod. Gk. (*th* in Engl. *this*)
כֿ *ḵ*, *kh* like χ in Mod. Gk. χάρις (cf. § *k*)
פֿ *p̄*, *ph* like φ in Mod. Gk. = Engl. *f*(5)
תֿ *ṯ*, *th* like θ in Mod. Gk. = *th* in Engl. *thing*)(6)

The correct reading of Hebrew requires the accurate pronunciation of these six fricatives(7).

(1) Berg. I, § 6 m postulates the 4th cent. B.C. as the earliest date for the onset of this twofold pronunciation. Cf. also N.H. Torczyner (Tur-Sinai) in *Leš* 8 (1937) 297-306.

Kahle once hypothesised that this double pronunciation was an academic invention of the Massoretic scholars, since only the fricative sounds were known, for example, to Origen and Jerome: P.E. Kahle, *The Cairo Geniza* (Oxford, 21959), pp. 179-84. For a convincing rebuttal of the theory, see Z. Ben-Ḥayyim, *Studies in the Traditions of the Hebrew Language* (Barcelona/Madrid, 1954), pp. 15ff. and also E. Brønno, in *JSS* 13 (1968) 195-99. How these spirants were pronounced amongst a Karaite group is shown by the use of ذ for ד, خ for כ, and ث for ת in certain early mediaeval Hebrew texts transcribed with the Arabic alphabet: see G. Khan, *JSS* 32 (1987) 33f., 44.

On a tradition which recognises a twofold pronunciation of Resh as well, see E.J. Revell, "The nature of Resh in Tiberian Heb.," *Association for Jewish Studies Review*

6 (1981) 125-36. and I. Eldar. "The twofold pronunciation of Tiberian Resh." *Lcš* 48-49 (1985) 21-34.

(2) דָּגֵשׁ, Aramaic participle. "piercing." according to Kahle. in BL. p. 119. The plosive or instantaneous consonant is also called by the ancients *dagesh* or קָשֶׁה "hard."

(3) רָפֶה, Aramaic participle, "relaxed." The spirant consonant is also called by the ancients רַךְ "soft."

(4) Pronounced in some communities as a voiced bilabial fricative [β]: see Schramm, *Graphemes*, p. 15, and Sh. Morag in *EJ*, vol. 13, col. 1131.

(5) Lambert (§ 25) notes the possibility of the existence of an aspirated *p* with a puff like the English syllable-initial *p* as in *pot* as against *spot*, since Ps 25 and 34, both acrostic psalms, have an extra verse beginning with Peh added at the end, as is also mentioned by Jerome and Saadia. Cf. Berg., I, § 6 i. This was most likely true of /k/ and /t/ as well; see J. Cantineau, *Semitica* 4 (1951-52) 90, and BL, § 10 q. Thus one is probably dealing with three phonetic triads: /p/ (plosive)-/p'/-/f/ (spirant or fricative); /k/-/ḫ/-/q/(emphatic); /t/-/t'/-/ṭ/.

(6) A well-known variety is /s/ in the Ashkenazi tradition.

(7) Currently only the Yemenite community and the Aramaic speaking community of Zakho in Iraqi Kurdistan have preserved this distinction in full: Sh. Morag, in *EJ*, vol. 13, col. 1131.

Whilst the use of a stroke above or below the letters of the alphabet or the addition of an *h* makes for neat and transparent representation, our transliteration system (see the table on pp. 21f.) differs for a number of reasons.

On the *dagesh*, cf. § 10. On the rules pertaining to the spirantisation of the *begadkefat*, cf. § 19; let us be content here with giving the following general rule: Every vocalic element, even a minimal one (e.g. a "so-called" vocalic shewa) turns the following *begadkefat* into a fricative. *p*

Phonologically speaking, the six sets of phones discussed above (§ *o*) are allophones, i.e. sets of two phonetically conditioned variations of what can be conceived of as a single phoneme[1]. This means that, counting Sin and Shin as two separate phonemes, Ancient Hebrew possessed 23 consonantal phonemes, and that the Hebrew alphabet was phonemic in principle, whilst in the Tiberian tradition it possessed 29 consonantal phones. Of the postulated 27 Proto-Semitic consonantal phonemes (excluding *w* and *y*), 21 (or 20 if שׂ and ס were pronounced in identical manner) have been preserved in Hebrew (77 or 74%), whilst four of the lost phonemes have survived as allophones in the Tiberian tradition. *q*

(1) There are however some signs of incipient phonematisation of the fricatives, e.g. לָקַחַת as infinitive *to take* as against לָקַחַתְּ *you* (f.sg.) *took*: despite the preceding

/a/ vowel, the plosive תּ in לָקַחַתְּ can be explained as due to the analogy of 2m.sg. לָקַחְתָּ, 2pl. לְקַחְתֶּם/ן, and 1sg. לָקַחְתִּי. Similarly אַתְּ vs. אַתָּה (§ 39*a*, n. 4). A word-final long consonant has got simplified where there is no such influence of analogy: so אֱמֶת (< *'*amitt* < *'*amint*), אַחַת (< *'*aḥatt* < *'*aḥadt*). Note also וַיְדַבֵּר as against וַתְּדַבֵּר: the dagesh of the Taw in the latter is most likely lene; and /'alfē/, pl. cst. of /'elef/ vs. the somewhat doubtful /*'alpē/, du. cst. of the same word as reconstructed by Z.S. Harris. This last contrast was unsuccessfully rebutted by H.B. Rosén in *JNES* 20 (1961) 124-26, where another pair [qirbi] *my inside* and [qirvi] *approach* (impv. f.sg.) is mentioned, though rejected by Rosén. See also Schramm, *Graphemes*, pp. 56-58, and our observation below (§ 18 *m*, n.). On the other hand, a full discussion of the question must take into account pairs of forms called by Cantineau "variantes facultatives," namely non-obligatory variants such as רִשְׁפֵּי / רִשְׁפֵי: J. Cantineau, *BSL* 46 (1950) 101f.

r The following table showing the normal correspondence of consonants between Hebrew, Aramaic[1], Syriac, Arabic, and Proto-Semitic (PS) may be found of some interest:[2]

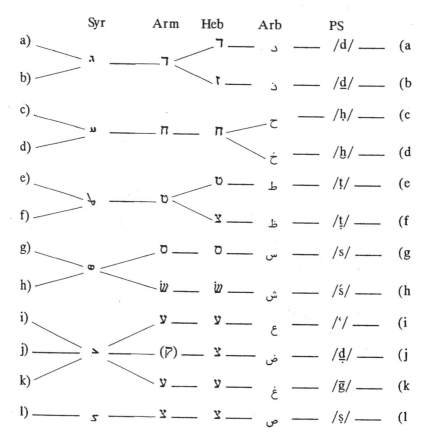

	Syr	Arm	Heb	Arb	PS	
a)	ܕ	ד	ד	د	/d/	(a
b)	ܕ	ד	ז	ذ	/ḏ/	(b
c)	ܚ	ח	ח	ح	/ḥ/	(c
d)	ܚ	ח	ח	خ	/ḫ/	(d
e)	ܛ	ט	ט	ط	/ṭ/	(e
f)	ܛ	ט	צ	ظ	/ṯ̣/	(f
g)	ܣ	ס	ס	س	/s/	(g
h)	ܣ	שׂ	שׂ	ش	/ś/	(h
i)	ܥ	ע	ע	ع	/ʿ/	(i
j)	ܥ	(ק)	צ	ض	/ḏ̣/	(j
k)	ܥ	ע	ע	غ	/ḡ/	(k
l)	ܨ	צ	צ	ص	/ṣ/	(l

m)	ܫ	ש	שׁ	س	/š/	(m
n)	ܬ	ת	ת	ت	/t/	(n
o)	ܬ	ת	שׁ	ث	/ṯ/	(o

Examples:

a) *debbā*	ܕܶܒܳܐ	דִּבָּא	דֹּב	دُبّ	"bear"
b) *drā'ā*	ܕܪܳܥܳܐ	דְּרָעָא	זְרֹעַ	ذِرَاع	"arm"
c) *ḥakkim*	ܚܰܟܺܝܡ	חַכִּים	חָכָם	حَكِيم	"wise"
d) *ḥamrā*	ܚܰܡܪܳܐ	חַמְרָא	חֶמֶר	خَمْر	"wine"
e) *ṭabbāḥā*	ܛܰܒܳܚܳܐ	טַבָּחָא	טַבָּח	طَبَّاخ	"cook"
f) *ṭellālā*	ܛܶܠܳܠܳܐ	טלל	צֵל	ظِلّ	"shade"
g) (*s-g-d*)	ܣܓܶܕ	סגד	סגד	سجد	"prostrate"
h) *'sar*	ܥܣܰܪ	עֲשַׂר	עֶשֶׂר	عَشْر	"ten"
i) *'aynā*	ܥܰܝܢܳܐ	עַיְנָא	עַיִן	عَيْن	"eye"
j) *'ar'ā*	ܐܰܪܥܳܐ	אֲרַקָא/אַרְעָא	אֶרֶץ	أَرْض	"earth"
k) *tar'ā*	ܬܰܪܥܳܐ	תַּרְעָא	שַׁעַר	ثَغْر	"gate"; Arb. "opening"
l) *ṣev'ā*	ܨܶܒܥܳܐ	אֶצְבְּעָא	אֶצְבַּע	إِصْبَع	"finger"
m) *šmayyā*	ܫܡܰܝܳܐ	שְׁמַיָּא	שָׁמַיִם	سَمَاء	"sky"
n) *kṯāvā*	ܟܬܳܒܳܐ	כְּתָבָא	כְּתָב	كِتَاب	"document"
o) *tlāṯ*	ܬܠܳܬ	תְּלָת	שָׁלֹשׁ	ثَلَاث	"three"

(1) Biblical Aramaic is meant here.

(2) Most cases of straight one-to-one correspondence such as /l/, /m/, /n/ are not given here. For a complete table, see Moscati, pp. 43-45. (Note that the line for /k/ is missing from the second table in § 8.60.)

In present-day Israeli Hebrew the twofold articulation of Begadkefat s is maintained only for ב, כ, and פ: בּ = [b], ב = [v]; כּ = [k], כ = [ḫ] (as in German *doch*); פּ = [p], פ = [f]. ג, ד, and ת are pronounced [g, d, t] irrespective of the presence or absence of the dagesh point. Furthermore, Ayin and Het are not universally articulated as described above, the former being treated like Alef, and the latter like Kaf rafé, i.e. *ḫ*. ט, צ, and ק are pronounced like *t*, *ts* (as in *cats*), and *k* respectively. Finally, consonantal Waw is pronounced [v]: so מָוֶת [mávet].

§ 6. The vowels: their symbols and pronunciation

a Essentially the Hebrew vowels differ from one another in *timbre* (or *quality*). Two vowels having the same timbre can, however, differ in respect of *quantity*, namely in respect of the time required for their articulation. The timbre and the *quantity* of vowels must be rigorously kept apart. In the Tiberian Hebrew, the latter has no phonemic status. Let us first examine the *timbre* of the Hebrew vowels.

b The natural scale of the principal **timbres** is as follows:

í ì ẹ ę ą ạ ǫ ọ ù ú

It will be noted that there are, for each vowel, a *close* and an *open* variety(1).

The vowels *i* and *u* are the most close (*i* being a close back variety, and *u*(2) a close front vowel), and the vowel *a* is the most open(3).

The generally recognised Proto-Semitic vowel-scale contains only the three vowels *i*, *a*, *u*. These are still the only three vowels notated in the Arabic vocalisation.

The scale of the Hebrew vowels notated by the Naqdanim of Tiberias consisted of seven timbres indicated by the following signs(4):

i	*ẹ*	*ę*	*ą*	*ǫ*	*ọ*	*u*
◌ִ	◌ֵ	◌ֶ	◌ַ	◌ָ	◌ֹ	◌ֻ
ḥireq	*ṣeré*	*seghol*	*pataḥ*	*qameṣ*	*ḥolem*(5)	*qibbuṣ*(6)

In this scale *ą* is a central vowel.

These seven timbres can be grouped, in accordance with their genetic relationship with the three primitive vowels of Proto-Semitic, as follows:

1st Group **a**: *ą*

2nd Group **i**: *i*, *ẹ*, *ę*

3rd Group **u**: *u*, *ọ*, *ǫ*(7)

(1) In the articulation of a close vowel the aperture between the most raised part of

the tongue and the roof of the mouth is narrow, whereas in the articulation of an open vowel this aperture is wider.

(2) The transliteration *u* represents the vowel *oo* of *book*.

(3) For typographical reasons, we use here *í*, *ú* for the closed varieties and *ì*, *ù* for the open varieties. The difference between the two varieties of *i* and *u* is much less discernible than is the case with the other vowels, *a*, *e*, and *o*.

On the Hebrew names of the vowel signs and their origins, see Kahle in BL, § 7i-m, A. Dotan, *EJ*, vol. 16, cols. 1448f., and Lambert, § 34 including n. 3. The latter makes an interesting observation that the fact that seghol alone refers to its shape, the shape of a cluster of grapes, points to the secondary origin of the sign, and indeed the foreign origin of the names of all the Tiberian vowel signs. This is interesting in view of the fact that the Babylonian system has a single sign, pataḥ (called *pittaḥ'* in the Babylonian massorah), representing both the Tiberian pataḥ and seghol.

(4) For a modern linguistic attempt to interpret the various vocalisation systems of Hebrew, see Morag, *Vocalization Systems*, pp. 22-29.

(5) The ḥolem, the only vowel written above the letter, can be omitted, for economy's sake, when it comes too close to the diacritical point of שׁ and שׂ. Thus we may write מֹשֶׁה *mošę* "Moses" (or מֹשֶׁה), נְשֹׂא *nśo'* "to carry" (or נְשֹׂא). A quiescent, i.e. unpronounced א takes the ḥolem of the preceding consonant on its top right-hand side: רֹאשׁ *ro(')š* "head," חַטֹּאת or חַטֹּאות "sins of" (but this usage is not always observed).

(6) The vowel *u*, when historically or etymologically long, is often written וּ (*shureq*), e.g. כָּתוּב *written*. Saadia knows of seven vowels only, and makes no distinction between *shureq* and *qibbuṣ*, as stressed by Ben-Ḥayyim, *Lešonenu* 18 (1953) 92, n. 1. If the Naqdanim had been aware of any phonetic difference between the two, they could have pointed the striking כּוּלָּם "all of them" Jer 31.34 with qibbuṣ instead of shureq and have given כֻּלָּם as Qre instead of merely noting that this is the only case in the Bible of this particular form spelled plene. Nor is one justified in interpreting a not uncommon defective spelling such as יָקֻם Gn 27.31 as evidence that the Naqdanim pronounced the form any differently from the standard יָקוּם. In this case they could only note in the margin that this is the only case in the Bible in which this particular form is spelled defectively.

(7) The presence of a bewilderingly large number of transliteration methods needs to be briefly mentioned. The maximalist extreme attempts to reproduce, with the Latin alphabet and a range of diacritics, every graphic symbol used in written Hebrew. Thus כָּתַב can be rendered, for instance, *kåtab*. Variations between *scriptio plena* and *scr. defectiva* can also be reproduced: e.g., לוֹא *lô'* vs. לֹא *lō'*. The minimalist extreme, currently used, for instance, in the *Journal of Jewish Studies*, roughly approximates the current Israeli pronunciation. Sometimes one and the same graphic symbol in a fully vocalised Hebrew text is transliterated in different ways. Quite a few systems falling between the two extremes are also in use. Each system has its own reasons, merits and demerits. A reasonable compromise for use by those who are familiar with the contemporary Israeli pronunciation is suggested in Muraoka, *Emphatic*, p. x: we would substitute *ḫ* for *x*. Cf. W. Weinberg, "Towards a world standard in the trans-

literation of Hebrew," *Proceedings of the Fifth World Congress of Jewish Studies*, 4. 137-51.

c These seven timbres are known to us through the tradition, the ancient descriptions, and comparison with cognate languages. They have their precise counterparts in many languages, e.g. Italian, which has, like Hebrew, only one *a* (open), but two *e*'s and *o*'s, and Contemporary French, which has taken to the extreme the distinction between the open and close vowels.

The graphic notation of seven timbres is an indication of the finely tuned ear of the Naqdanim and the perfection of their system(1). One may assume that this system contains all the vowels that existed around the seventh century in Tiberias.

This system expresses only the *timbres*; it ignores quantity and the etymological prehistory of the vowels(2), although it is generally agreed that at an earlier stage of Hebrew the vowel length had phonemic status and even as late as the time of Origen and Jerome it was perceived to be a significant feature of Hebrew vowels (see below § *e* [3]). Thus ֹ (often written וֹ) very often represents a primitive long *a*, e.g. טוֹב *good* (from the original *ṭāb*). Thus ָ often represents an original short *a*, e.g. *šålọm* שָׁלוֹם *peace* (from **šalām*). Likewise ֶ fairly frequently represents an original short *a*, e.g. *'ęḥåd* אֶחָד *one* (for **'aḥad*), *hę'årim* הֶעָרִים *the cities* (for **ha'arim*), *yęḏḇęm* יֶדְכֶם *your hand* (for **yadkęm*).

(1) The Tiberian system probably imitates that of the East Syrians, which also comprises seven vowels, whilst that of the West Syrians has only five. Cf. Berg., I. § 9 c. In addition to the Tiberian system, there were also in use two others: the Palestinian and the Babylonian, both characterised by the position of the vowel signs above the letters, hence called the supralinear system as against the sublinear Tiberian system.. Each system represents a phonetic / phonological system of its own. See Morag, *Vocalization Systems*. On the Babylonian system, see Yeivin, *Babylonian Tradition*, and on the Palestinian system, E.J. Revell, "Studies in the Palestinian Vocalization of Heb.," in J.W. Wevers & D.B. Redford, *Essays on the Ancient Semitic World* (Toronto, 1970), pp. 51-100; idem, *Hebrew Texts with Palestinian Vocalization* (Toronto, 1970); idem, *Biblical Texts with Palest. Pointing and their Accents* (Missoula, 1977); Y. Yahalom in *Leš* 34 (1969-70) 25-60. The Samaritan system is rather poorly developed: see Z.B. Ḥayyim, "The Samaritan vowel system and its graphic representation," *Archiv Orientální* 22 (1954) 513-30, and idem, *LOT*, vol. 5. pp. 4-7.

(2) This however does not mean that the vowel system represented by the Tiberian symbols is completely phonemic; seghol, for instance, can at times be interpreted as

an allophone of pataḥ; see Sh. Morag, *Yemenite*, p. 119. See also idem, *Vocalization Systems*, p. 22, n. 17.

The only quantitative vowel distinction one can legitimately postulate for the Tiberian pronunciation is that between three of the seven ordinary full vowels and the corresponding three short vowels called ḥaṭefs: ◌ֲ ḥaṭef pataḥ, ◌ֱ ḥaṭef seghol, and ◌ֳ ḥaṭef qameṣ (§ 9). However, they are allophones of *shewa*, the zero vowel(1). d

As far as Tiberian Hebrew is concerned, there is no phonetic difference between יָדֶךָ (pausal, singular) *your hand* and יָדֶיךָ (dual) *your hands*, or between יָדֵנוּ *our hand* (sg.) and יָדֵינוּ *our hands* (du.). Both vowels are found in identical phonetic environment: an open, stressed penultimate syllable(2). It is wrong to assume that a semantic distinction must necessarily be expressed by a phonetic one. Ambiguity is a common feature of any language(3).

The absence of long *i* or *u* is demonstrated by the fact that the so-called compensatory lengthening produces ◌ֵ and ◌ֹ from *i* and *u* respectively. Thus מְבָרֵךְ (vs. מְגַדֵּל), but בֵּרַךְ (vs. גִּדֵּל) and מְבֹרָךְ (vs. מְגֻדָּל): the qameṣ in מְבָרֵךְ is agreed to go back to an earlier long vowel, /ā/. See also above under § *b*, n. 6.

(1) In some cases, however, the opposition between two ḥaṭefs is significant: e.g. אֲנִי "I" but אֳנִי "ships"; עֲנִי "Answer!" (imperative, f.sg.) but עֳנִי "poverty." Likewise BA אֱמַר "Say!" (imper.) as against אֲמַר "he said" (perf.), but both גְּלִי and גֱּלִי mean "it was revealed."

(2) The change ◌ֵ > ◌ֶ is possibly assimilatory, under the influence of the following open or mid vowel ◌ָ.

(3) The variant reading יָדֵינוּ at Josh 2.24 furnishes indirect evidence for the phonetic identity between יָדֵנוּ and יָדֵינוּ, since the correctness of the singular form in this idiom נָתַן יַד־ is assured, for instance, by a case such as Josh 21.42 נָתַן יהוה בְּיָדָם. Another case of glaring ambiguity in the Tiberian vocalisation system is the absence of number distinction in certain forms of BA noun declension as in /'ẹlåhåḵ/, which can signify either *your god* or *your gods*. Note also an analogous picture emerging from the Secunda: e.g., σεμαχ שִׁמְךָ Ps 31.4 and ηναχ עֵינֶיךָ 31.23; for a discussion, see Brønno, *Morphologie*, pp. 199f.

OBSERVATIONS. 1. The distinction of five long vowels, ā, ē, ī, ō, ū, and five short vowels *a*, *e*, *i*, *o*, *u*, which was first(1) introduced in its classic form by Joseph Qimḥi (12th cent.) and generally accepted down to our times, is a radical alteration of the Tiberian vowel system. He was probably influenced in this by the Romance dialect he spoke e himself or by Latin, or even by Arabic (which distinguishes three long ā, ī, ū, on the one hand, and three short *a*, *i*, *u* on the other).

2. The questions concerning the timbre and quantity of the Tiberian vowels had hardly been addressed before the end of the nineteenth century. See in particular H. Grimme, *Grundzüge der hebräischen Akzent- und Vokallehre* (Freiburg, 1896), pp. 32ff.; C. Sarauw, *Über Akzent und Silbenbildung in den älteren semitischen Sprachen* (København, 1939); H. Birkeland, "Akzent und Vokalismus im Althebräischen," *Skrifter utgitt av det Norske Videnskaps-Akademi i Oslo*, II, Hist.-Fils. Klasse, no. 3 (Oslo, 1940); J. Blau, *Grammar*, §§ 3.3 - 3.7.1.

3. In addition to phonetic length, i.e. length which can be measured by some mechanical device, one can also speak of phonological length. For instance, one can regard ֵ of the adjective כָּבֵד as long, since it is not subject to the vowel deletion rule as in, say, the m.pl. כְּבֵדִים, whereas the vowel notated by the same sign would be phonologically short in the verb כָּבֵד, as is evident from, say, the Qal pf. 3pl. כָּבְדוּ.

Analogously, if pataḥ is to be regarded as phonologically short, paradigmatic analogy requires that ṣeré and ḥolem are to be so considered: יִלְבַּשׁ as against יִשְׁמֹר and יִתֵּן; שָׁמַר as against קָטֹן and כָּבֵד; שַׁעַר as against קֹדֶשׁ and סֵפֶר(2). And indeed the second column of the Hexapla tends to use ο and ε in these cases. On the other hand, it does sometimes use ω and η for ḥolem (e.g. Qal participle νωσηρ for נוֹצֵר at Ps 31.24) and ṣeré respectively (e.g. עֵשָׂו Ησαυ, קֵדָר Κηδαρ), suggesting that *phonetically* they were, in the tradition underlying the transcription, pronounced as long vowels in these particular forms(3).

(1) According to Ben-Ḥayyim (*Leš* 18 [1953] 95) Qimhi had predecessors in this notion.

(2) That Joüon had a similar insight can be seen in § 28 *d-e* of the French original of this grammar, although his position there runs counter to his view of four-scale vowel length (§ 6 *f* in the original French edition).

(3) Brønno, *Studien*, pp. 250f., 258, 453f. and J. Blau, *IOS* 8 (1978) 94. The loss of distinctive vowel-length in Greek, incidentally, may be placed most probably in about the 2-3 cent. A.D.: S. Allen, *Vox Graeca. The Pronunciation of Classical Greek* (Cambridge, [3]1987), p. 94. We are assuming that by the time of Origen a whole series of vowels such as ι, η, ει, υ had not yet quite converged into a single phoneme. There is no suggestion here that every ḥolem and ṣeré is notated by Origen with ω and η respectively. The picture is more complicated: see Brønno, *Morphologie*, pp. 248-62, 360-64.

f Whilst this is not a historical grammar, it can be helpful to have some understanding of how the Tiberian Hebrew vowel system relates to its hypothetical Proto-Hebrew or Proto-Semitic. Thus the variation between the absolute form דָּם and its construct form דַּם־ can be said to reflect a pre-Tiberian contrast in vowel length /ā/ and /a/. Likewise the qameṣ of כָּתַב can be explained as reflecting a pre-Tiberian pre-stress lengthening of an earlier short /a/. Again, the ḥolem in טוֹב and אֱלֹהִים can be traced back to an earlier long /ā/ (as preserved in Arm. טָב, and Arm. אֱלָהּ or Arb. /'ilāh/(1). It is for this reason that we shall have occasion below to speak about short or long vowels in hypothetical "primitive" or "original" forms. One can also observe that a long vowel causes an original *i* to drop out: **ṣirār* > צְרוֹר *bag*; on the other hand, **'inab* > עֵנָב *grapes*. Likewise **ruḥāb* > רְחוֹב *square* (Brock., *GvG*, I, p. 351), but **šu'ar* > שֵׂעָר *horrible* (cf. § 30). The forms appearing in this grammar with an asterisk are such reconstructed primitive or original forms. It is widely believed that Proto-Hebrew / Semitic had three short vowels (*a*, *i*, *u*), their long counterparts (ā, ī, ū), and two diphthongs (*ay*, *aw*). The relationship between these eight primitive vowels and the seven Tiberian vowels may be shown as in the chart below (§ *i*).

Furthermore, the transition from quantitative to qualitative distinction in the Hebrew vowels appears to have taken place relatively late. Transliteration of Hebrew in the Septuagint and the second column of Origen's Hexapla as well as explicit statements by St Jerome (4th cent.) all point to quantitative distinction(2). Cf. § *e* above towards the end.

(1) On a plausible reconstruction of the history of stress shifts in Hebrew, see Blau, *Grammar*, § 9.

(2) There is no telling when such a shift took place: the 9th cent. is argued for by T. Harviainen, *On the Vocalism of the Closed Unstressed Syllables in Hebrew: A Study Based on the Evidence Provided by the Transcriptions of St. Jerome and Palestinian Punctuations* (Helsinki, 1977), pp. 104-9.

The pronunciation of the two vowels ◌ִ *i* and ◌ֻ *u*(1), which are diametrically opposed in terms of the position of tongue in their articulation, presents no difficulty. *g*

The vowel ◌ֵ ẹ is a close e, as in Fr. *pré*, *blé*, *désir*, Ital. *nero*. This sound is close to *i*, representing the first degree of alteration of the latter in respect of openness. Thus the original *ʿinab becomes ʿẹnåv עֵנָב *grapes*(2).

The vowel ֶ ę is an open *e* as in Fr. *près, règle, terrain, miel*, Ital. *mięle*. This sound lies between ֵ and ַ; phonetically it belongs to the i group. From the point of view of pronunciation there is no difference between the ֶ originating from *a*, e.g. in אֶחָד *'äḥåḏ* = *'ęḥåḏ* and the ֶ originating from *i* or *ẹ*, e.g. in *bęn* בֶּן *son of* (from בֵּן, בֶּן). Where it originates from *a*, the ֶ may be transliterated ä.

The vowel *ą* ַ is an open *a*, akin to the vowel ֶ ę, with which it frequently alternates(3).

The vowel ָ (ǫ) is an open *o*, as in Fr. *sort, pomme, bonne*, Ital. *buǫna*, Engl. *doll* (comp., e.g., *all* spelled with a like-sounding *å*). The vowel ָ originates from either an original short *u* or an original short *a*. Where it originates from an *a* one may indicate it (conventionally) as ָֽ with a *metheg* (§ 14) and transliterate it etymologically with *å*. But phonetically, in terms of timbre, *å* has merged with ǫ in the Tiberian tradition(4). (For details, see § *j*).

The vowel ֹ ọ is a close *o* like in Fr. *dos, rose*, Ital. *croce*. This sound is close to *u*, of which it is the first degree of modification in terms of openness. Thus the original **kul* becomes *kọl* כֹּל *all*(5).

One sees that in the Tiberian vowel system the most close vowels *i* and *u* are symmetrical, and likewise the close vowels ẹ and ọ, and the open vowels ę and ǫ(6).

(1) According to Saadia, this vowel was accompanied by lip-rounding: see *JQR* NS 42 (1951-52) 303 in S.L. Skoss's translation of Saadia's *Kutub al-Lughah*.

(2) Compare the Italian ẹ stemming from the Latin *i*, e.g. in *vẹrgine, vẹndico, sẹno, capẹllo* (*capillus*; contrast *cappęllo* derived from *cappa*).

(3) In the Babylonian pronunciation *ą* has become *ä* (= ę); cf. BL, p. 100. The Babylonian vocalisation system has a single vowel sign corresponding to both the Tiberian pataḥ and seghol. We shall see (§ *i*) that in the Tiberian pronunciation the alteration has, in contrast, affected the close *ạ*, which has become *å* (= ǫ). The symmetry of the two phenomena is remarkable.

(4) If we wish to adhere to the Tiberian tradition we should pronounce all ָ's with the same timbre ǫ. Many Jews pronounce ָֽ derived from an original *a* as *a* (and in practice like ַ *ą*). The origin of this pronunciation can hardly be an etymological consideration or a pedagogical concern. It is an aspect of a non-Tiberian, probably Babylonian, pronunciation within the Tiberian tradition. The differentiation of ָ into two timbres ǫ and *a*, contrary to the Tiberian system, is considered by many modern grammarians to be wrong. Ibn Ezra († 1167) was already aware that the pronun-

ciation of ◌ָ as *a* is suspect. (Cf. W. Bacher, *Abraham Ibn Esra als Grammatiker* [Budapest, 1881], p. 37). See on this question J. Derenbourg in *JA*, 6th series, 13 (1869) 513ff.; Bergsträsser, I, § 10 *a*; BL, p. 100. Can we expect that the *scientific* pronunciation may ultimately prevail over the erroneous pronunciation which has become traditional? This is doubtful, especially because the double pronunciation of ◌ָ has the pedagogical advantage of compelling the beginner to recognise immediately whether ◌ָ derives from *u* or *a*. In this grammar we shall transliterate ◌ָ phonetically by *ǫ*, etymologically by *ǫ* or *å*, as the necessary case may be. When not transliterating, we will simply write *a* for *å* in accordance with the accepted practice, e.g., *qameṣ*, *ḥaṭef* in the grammatical terms instead of *qåmeṣ*, *ḥåṭẹp*.

How that sign in the Babylonian vocalisation system which corresponds to the Tiberian qameṣ was pronounced is a moot point. E.Y. Kutscher (*JSS* 11 [1966] 224) inclines to the opinion that it was [ā], but Sh. Morag, *Yemenite*, pp. 102-5 believes it was [å]. Ben-Ḥayyim deduces from Saadia's treatise on the vowels that in the Babylonian tradition as well the qameṣ was pronounced [å]: see *Lešonenu*... *Leš* 18 (1953) 91.

(5) Compare the Italian *ọ* derived from Lat. *u*, e.g. in *mọlti*, *mōglic*, *sọpra*, *vọlto* (from *vultus*; contrast *vǫlto* from *volgere*), *cọlto* (from *cultus*; contrast *cǫlto* from *cogliere*).

(6) On the traditional pronunciation of Hebrew vowels in various communities, see G.M. Schramm, *Graphemes*, pp. 24-29, and Sh. Morag in *EJ*, vol. 13, cols. 1135-43.

Contemporary Israeli pronunciation has a vowel system in which length is not phonemically significant, and it consists of the five vowels /a, i, u, e, o/. Thus h

- ◌ָ (qameṣ), ◌ַ (pataḥ), and ◌ֲ (ḥaṭef pataḥ) = /a/ (central, open as in Engl. *cup*)
- ◌ִ (ḥireq) with Yod or not = /i/ (front, close as in Engl. *hit*)
- ◌ֻ (shureq) and וּ (qibbuṣ) = /u/ (back, close as in Engl. *put*)
- ◌ֵ (ṣeré), ◌ֶ (seghol), and ◌ֱ (ḥaṭef seghol) = /e/ (front, mid as in Engl. *pen*)
- ◌ֹ (ḥolem), ◌ָ (qameṣ qaṭan), and ◌ֳ (ḥaṭef qameṣ) = /o/ (back, mid as in Engl. *law*, but more open and shorter)(1).

(1) On the shewa, see below § 8.

Hebrew vowels in relation to the original vowels. i

It is recognised that Proto-Semitic had three long vowels, ā, ī, ū, three short vowels *a*, *i*, *u*, and two diphthongs *ay*, and *aw*. When one examines their evolution in Hebrew, it appears that the long vowels had a close sound in comparison to the corresponding short vowels.

The table below shows the usual principal changes(1) of the Proto-Semitic vowels into Hebrew vowels.

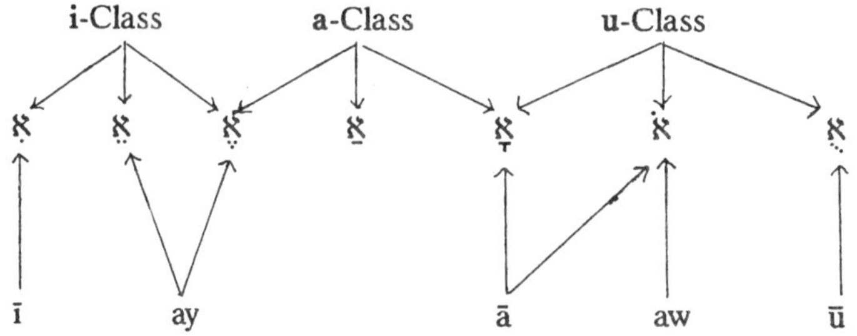

The following are examples illustrating the evolution of the Proto-Semitic vowels to the corresponding Hebrew vowels with the indication enclosed within the square brackets as to in which type of syllable—open or close, stressed or unstressed—they may be found:

/ā/ > אָ (rare): כְּתָב "a writing" (Aramaising) < /*kitāb/ [closed and stressed]

> אֹ : טוֹב (in BA still טָב); כֹּתֵב Qal ptc., cf. Arb. /kātib/(2) [open; closed and stressed]

/ī/ > אִ : יָדִין "he will judge" < /*yadīn/; דִּ֫ינִי /di'ni/ imperative, f.sg. "Judge!" [open; closed and stressed]

/ū/ > אוּ : יָקוּם "he will arise" < /*yaqūm/—this is a standard spelling, not יָקֻם; ק֫וּמוּ /qu'mu/ "Arise!," impv. m.pl. [open; closed and stressed].

/a/ > אֶ : מֶ֫לֶךְ "a king" < /*malk/ ; הֶעָרִים "the cities"; וַיֹּ֫אמֶר /wąyyọ'mẹr/ [open; closed and unstressed]

אַ : כָּתַב "he wrote" < /*kataba/; מַלְכִּי "my king"; נַ֫עַל "a shoe" [closed; open and stressed]

אָ : דָּבָר "a word" < /*dabar/; קָ֫מָה /qå'må/ "she arose"; [open; closed and stressed]

/i/ > אִ : מִן "from" [closed and unstressed]

אֵ : יָקֵם "May he raise!" < /*yaqim/; סֵ֫פֶר /sẹ'fẹr/ < /*sifr/; לֵבָב /lẹvåv/ "a heart" [open; closed and stressed]

אֶ : קֶ֫בֶר "a grave" < /*qibr/; חֶלְקִי "my portion" [closed and unstressed; open and stressed]

/u/ > אָ : כָּל־ "all of," cst. of כֹּל < /*kull/; וַיָּ֫קָם /wąyyå'qǫm/ "and he arose" < /*wayya'qum/ [closed and unstressed]

אֹ : כֹּל "all"; יָקֹם "May he arise!" < /*ya'qum/; קֹ֫דֶשׁ /qọ'dẹš/ "sanctity" < /*qudš/; קְרֹבָה "near" f.sg. < /*qaruba/

[open; closed and stressed]
אָ : כֻּלָּם "all of them" [closed and unstressed]
/ay/ > אֵ : בֵּית־ "the house of" < /*bayt/; סוּסֵ֫ינוּ /susẹ'nu/ "our horses"
אֶ : סוּסֶ֫יךָ "your (m.sg.) horses" [open and stressed]
/aw/ אֹ : מוֹת־ "the death of" < /*mawt/

In sum, as regards **timbre**, the originally **long** ī and ū are preserved in Hebrew as *i* and *u* respectively. But ā has generally become ọ, rarely å. The originally **short** vowels *a*, *i*, *u* are often preserved(3) in an unstressed closed syllable, and ordinarily in an unstressed sharp syllable(4). But in a stressed closed syllable (often) and in an open syllable, their timbre is changed; they become *å* (= ǫ), ẹ, ọ respectively(5).

One may note that the change from ā to ọ and that from ą to ǫ (å) are parallel: each of the two original vowels becomes closer by two degrees. On the other hand, the two original symmetrical vowels, *i* and *u*, become open by one degree, when they change to open ẹ and ọ respectively, but by two degrees when they become ę and ǫ respectively(6).

(1) The table, which is an only slightly modified version of that which is given by Lambert (§ 129), is meant to give only a general idea. Details are complicated in the extreme: see also § 29.

(2) The change is as early as the 14th cent. B.C.: see EA *a-nu-ki* = Heb. אָנֹכִי (§ 39 *a*). See also Harris, *Development*, pp. 43-5.

(3) *u* much less frequently than *a* or *i*; thus in the nominal pattern **qutl* we usually have קָטְלִי, e.g. קָדְשִׁי; in the verbal pattern *yuqtal* we have יָקְטַל rather than יֻקְטַל. According to E.Y. Kutscher, Palestinian substandard Hebrew, i.e. excluding the reading tradition of BH, often attests, between the period of the LXX and Jerome, to the change PS /i/ > /e/ and /u/ > /o/: E.Z. Melammed (ed.), *Studies in Memory of B. de Vriez* (Jerusalem, 1969), p. 226.

(4) A syllable is called sharp when it closes with a double identical consonant as in כֻּלָּם /kullåm/.

(5) The secondary character of /ọ/ derived from either /*ā/ or /*u/ appears to be reflected in the fact that "the plene spelling of /ū/ has taken hold more extensively (about 80 %) than the plene spelling of /ō/ (46.5 %)" (AF, p. 311).

(6) On the behaviour of vowels in closed unstressed syllables in the Palestinian (as distinct from the Tiberian) tradition, cf. T. Harviainen, op. cit. [§ *f* above, n.].

On the vowel ָ in particular. This vowel, which because of its twofold origin presents special difficulties, warrants some further com- *j* ments (cf. *g*). The sign ָ is a transformation of the original sign ַׁ composed of the stroke of pataḥ and the point of ḥolem(1). This sign is a rather felicitous one for the sound ọ, which lies between ạ and ọ(2).

As for its origin, the vowel ָ derives from a primitive vowel *u*(3) (the so-called qameṣ qaṭan or ḥaṭuf) as well as from a primitive vowel *a* as in כָּתַב (the so-called qameṣ gadol or raḥav)(4). In the latter case one conventionally writes it as ָֽ as is sometimes done in biblical manuscripts, and transliterates it with *å* to indicate that it derives from an original *a*. The symbol ָ expresses a single timbre ọ despite its twofold origin, exactly as the symbol ֶ, despite its twofold origin, expresses the single timbre ẹ It is inconceivable that the Tiberian graphic system, which is so precise as to distinguish two nuances of the vowel *e* and two nuances of the vowel *o*, could have indicated by a single symbol two vowels so mutually different as *o* and *a*. It seems to be temerarious to accuse the Naqdanim of an error in such an important matter. A number of phonetic phenomena suggest that *å* really sounded like ọ in the pronunciation of the Naqdanim. Thus, in the case of the euphonic dagesh (§ 18 *i*), e.g. לְכָה־נָּא *lḵånnå*, the first *å* in this position, a sharp unaccented syllable, must have had the nuance of open ọ. A close variety such as ạ is rather unnatural in this position just like the close vowels ẹ and ọ. If one says לְכָה־נָּא, as one says נַכֶּה־בּוֹ and מַה־זֶּה, it is because ָ is a variety of open vowel (ọ) such as ֶ ẹ and ַ ạ (cf. § 18 *i*). See further the law of harmonisation as exemplified by אֶחָד (§ 29 *f*). More details pointing to the same direction will be adduced in the section on phonetics and morphology (§§ 6 *l* 1; 7 *b* n.; 9 *d* 2; 32 *c*; 88 B *g*; C *f*).

(1) Already Abraham Ibn Ezra made the same observation: *Sefer ṣaḥot* (ed. C. del Valle Rodriguez [Salamanca, 1977]), p. 115, and this is confirmed by some good biblical manuscripts such as Codex Leningradensis B 19a, the Aleppo Codex, and the Cairo Codex of the Prophets.

(2) Compare the three vowels ִ, ֵ, and ֶ of the i class with one, two or three dots.

(3) In the Babylonian tradition, /u/ is the usual equivalent of this type of qameṣ: see Yeivin, *Babylonian Tradition*, p. 375.

(4) Thus כָּל־ "the totality of" from **kul*, כֹּל (root כלל) = *kọl*, cf. כֻּלָּם; but כָּל "he has measured" (Is 40.12†) = *kål* (root כיל or כול).

k The change from original *a* to ọ has a parallel in Western Aramaic, i.e., in the very region where Hebrew was spoken. In Western Aramaic, original ā has become ọ̄ (written ָ in BA, - <originally ο μικρόν> in Western Syriac)(1). The change from *a* to *o*, whether ǫ or ọ, is a phenomenon found in many languages and dialects; comp. e.g. Engl. *what* = [wǫt], with an ǫ in *not* [nǫt], and also note how the two words are pronounced in the standard American English.

The transition from primitive ą to Heb. ǫ must have passed through the intermediate stage of ạ(2).

On the variety of realisations of the ָ originating from *a*, see A. Idelsohn, "Die gegenwärtige Aussprache des Hebräischen bei Juden und Samaritanern," *Monatschrift für Geschichte und Wissenschaft des Judentums*, 75 (1913) 527-45, 697-721, and Sh. Morag, *Yemenite*, pp. 100-6, and idem, in *EJ*, vol. 13, cols. 1135f.

(1) Thus the primitive **lā* "no" becomes *lå* (= *lọ̄*): BA לָא, Syr. (in contrast, *lọ* לֹא in Hebrew).

(2) The ǫ derived from *a* could originally have been velar. Velar ǫ is the vowel which is homogeneous with the velar ק, i.e. that vowel which is perceived when we try to pronounce ק without any definite vowel.

Practical observations on the two kinds of ָ. The sound ָ, which *l*
originates from *u*, is called קָמֶץ חָטוּף *shortened* (literally, *snatched*) *qameṣ*. The ָ, which originates from *a*, is called קָמֶץ רָחָב *broad qameṣ*.

The vowel ǫ, therefore, is not usually found except in an unstressed closed syllable; *å* is found in the other types of syllable, namely in stressed closed syllables and in open syllables, whether stressed or unstressed. E.g. אָכְלָה *'ǫḇ-lå* "food," וַיָּקָם *wąyyå'qǫm*, חָנֵּנִי *ḥǫnnẹ'ni* "have pity on me."

The exceptions are not numerous; the more important are the following:

1) Alongside the form קֳדָשִׁים(1) one also has קָדָשִׁים, both pronounced traditionally [qodašim](the latter as [qa-] by Sephardis) with ǫ in an open syllable. This unusual spelling suggests that the symbol ָ represents the sound ǫ alone. Likewise one has שָׁרָשִׁים(2) for שֳׁרָשִׁים*; cf. § 96 Ag(3).

2) The plural of בַּיִת "house" is בָּתִּים *bắt-tim* (§ 98 *f*) with *å* in an unstressed closed syllable(4).

3) The pausal form of שָׁכֹלְתִּי *šåḇọl'ti* "I have lost children" is שָׁכָלְתִּי *šåḇǫl'ti*, i.e. with an ǫ for ọ (see more examples in § 32 *c*).

Another way of identifying qameṣ qaṭan is to try and see whether a given qameṣ can be considered an inflectional variant of either *u* or ọ (ḥolem). If the base form has either of these two vowels, the qameṣ appearing in a form modified in the course of inflection would normally be qameṣ qaṭan. Thus וַיָּקָם related to יָקֹם or יָקוּם; כָּל־ related to כֹּל; קָדְשׁוֹ related to קֹדֶשׁ; לְחָק־לָךְ as against לְחֹק לָךְ.

(1) Plural of קֹדֶשׁ *qo'dęš* "sanctity." קֳ occurs with the article and in קֳדָשָׁיו (except in 2Ch 15.18). (2) Plural of שֹׁרֶשׁ *šo'ręš* "root."

(3) The word דָּרְבוֹן* "goad" is read *dǫ-rwon*. But BL, p. 500, presuppose *då-*. Unfortunately the etymology is obscure. It is one of those very rare cases where the origin of the qameṣ escapes us.

(4) The Codex L. does not seem to have a case of the form with metheg.

m In one type of form, the qameṣ intended is indirectly indicated by the pointing. The third person feminine Perfect is קָֽטְלָה *qå-ṭlå* "she has killed," derived from the primitive **qaṭalat*. The *metheg* of the qameṣ indicates here the syllable boundary: *qå*. In contrast, the type קָטְלָה without a metheg is *qǫṭ-lå* "kill," i.e. the imperative קְטֹל with a paragogic ־ָה (§ 48 *d*) (the vowel *o* has been shifted on to the ק, becoming *ǫ*), e.g. אָכְלָה "Eat!"

n ־ָֽ before ḥaṭef qameṣ (־ֳ) is an *ǫ* despite the metheg, except in cases where ־ָֽ represents the vowel *å* of the article (הָ), e.g. פָּֽעֳלִי *pǫʕǫli* "my deed" from פֹּעַל, נָֽעֳמִי *Nǫʕǫmi* (female name) from נֹעַם "sweetness." But the form בָּֽאֳנִיָּה is equivocal: it represents either *bǫ'ʕǫniyyå* "in a boat" without the article or *bå-'ʕǫniyyå* "in the boat" with the article (§ 35 *e*).

§ 7. Consonants (matres lectionis) indicating the timbre or the quantity of vowels

a Some consonant letters indicate, albeit imperfectly, certain vowels. They are ו, י, ה and occasionally א. They are called matres lectionis (sg. mater lectionis), which is a mediaeval Latin translation of אִמּוֹת הַקְּרִיאָה; they are also termed quiescentes, i.e. not pronounced (as against mobiles, i.e. pronounced)(1).

(1) Andersen and Forbes (1986), and Barr, *Spellings* (1988) are interesting and important studies of the whole question of the use of *matres lectionis*. This traditional term conceivably meant "helping letters" added to an unpointed text comparable to a mother helping her child.

See also W. Weinberg, "The history of Hebrew plene spelling," *HUCA* 46 (1975) 457-87;

47 (1976) 237-80; 48 (1977) 301-33; 49 (1978) 311-38; 50 (1979) 289-337 [now published as a monograph of the same title (Cincinnati, 1985)].

The *matres lectionis* as indicators of timbre. The reasons for which a certain vowel is indicated by a certain consonant letter may be phonetic, etymological or practical in nature, according to individual cases. *b*

The vowels *u* and *i* (generally as historically long vowels) are naturally indicated by the letters representing the corresponding vocalic consonants, ו, י, e.g. קוּם = קוּם, דִּין = דין.

The vowels *o̩*, *e̩*, *ȩ* are also often indicated by ו and י; first, in cases of contraction (*aw* > *ō̩*; *ay* > *ē̩*, *ȩ̄*, e.g. יוֹם = יום (from /*yawm/), בֵּית = בית (cst. st. from בַּ֫יִת), and subsequently in some other cases as well.

Word-final vowel *o̩* is sometimes indicated by ה. This orthography came into existence where *o̩* derives from *ahu*; thus כֻּלֹּה = כלה (as frequent as כֻּלּוֹ ; cf. § 94 *h*)([1]). Some cases of word-final *å* may represent subsequent analogical extension of this orthographic principle: e.g. פֹּה, כֹּה, שְׁלֹמֹה, שִׁילֹה; יְרִיחֹה 1Kg 16.34, פַּרְעֹה; שׂוֹכֹה Josh 15.35 (2Ch 11.7 שׂוֹכוֹ)([2]).

Word-final vowel *å* is indicated by ה. This orthography must have come into existence in the abs. st. of nouns ending in *at*, the old pausal form of which was probably *ah* (with *h* pronounced as in Classical Arabic), e.g. מַלְכָּה = מלכה([3]).

Word-final vowel *e* (*e̩*, *ȩ*) is indicated by ה. This orthography can have come about under the influence of future forms with the third person suffix such as יִגְלֶ֫הָ, יִגְלֵהוּ, and nominal forms such as שָׂדֶ֫הָ, שָׂדֵהוּ. Examples: יִגְלֶה, גְּלֵה; שָׂדֶה, שְׂדֵה.

The historically short *u* is also spelled with Waw rather frequently when followed by gemination: e.g. עֲרוּמִּים. Examples may be found in AF, pp. 96-98.

In sum, ו can indicate the vowels *u*, *o̩*([4]);

> י can indicate the vowels *i*, *e̩*, *ȩ*;
>
> word-final ה can indicate the vowels *å*, *e̩*, *ȩ*; or also somewhat rarely *o̩*.

א can be quiescent when combined with any vowel; but in fact it often represents an etymological orthography, e.g. ראשׁ "head" (cf. Arb.

ra's with a pronounced Alef). On the negative לֹא or לוֹא, see § 102 *j*.

Non-etymological א is occasionally found in forms with the vowel ָ, e.g. קָאם (Ho 10.14 for קָם, § 80 *k*), שֵׁנָא "sleep" (Ps 127.2, an Aramaic orthography for שֵׁנָה); 1Ch 6.65 רָאמוֹת (// Josh 21.38 רָמוֹת)(5).

The addition of otiose Alef after a final vowel as in נָקִיא Jon 1.14; רִבּוֹא Ezr 2.64; אֵפוֹא was eventually to become a characteristic feature of both Qumran Hebrew and Aramaic orthography. It is also common in Arabic.

The particle נָא (§ 105 *c*) is written with א, perhaps in order better to distinguish it from the ending נָה of the f.pl. of the future and the imperative.

(1) This orthographical practice is now amply attested in early Hebrew epigraphical materials: e.g. Lachish 3.12 אתה *it* (m.sg.); Yavneh-Yam line 2 עבדה *his servant*. Indeed, it is more archaic than the spelling with Waw.

(2) On ה in another sense than "his," e.g. פַּרְעֹה, cf. AF, pp. 184-86.

(3) Final vowel *å* is sometimes not represented by ה. E.g., Ktiv אַתְּ for אַתָּה *you* occurs five times. We often find ןָ for נָה, the fem. pl. ending of the future, e.g. תִּקְטֹלְןָ (§ 44 *d*); the 2nd m.sg. perfect ending is regularly תָּ, e.g. קָטַלְתָּ (but in the verb נָתַן *to give* the spelling נָתַתָּה is more common, § 42 *f*). Cf. Blau, *Heb. Phonology and Morphology*, pp. 54f., and Z. Zevit, *Matres Lectionis in Ancient Hebrew Epigraphs* (Cambridge, MA, 1980), p. 33, n.

(4) In some rather rare cases ו seems to be *mater lectionis* of the sound *o*: אֶשְׁקוֹטָה Is 18.4; לִשְׁאָול־לוֹ 1Ch 18.10. In the Mishnah and Talmud, we sometimes find ו as an indication of ָ (whether *å* or *ǫ*, which presupposes the common vowel sound *ǫ*). Cf. S. Krauss, *ZDMG*, 67 (1913) 738, line 30, and Sh. Morag, *Yemenite*, p. 102.

(5) More examples may be found in AF, pp. 82-84.

c **The *matres lectionis* as indicators of historical vowel quantity.** The *matres lectionis* not only indicate certain timbres, albeit imperfectly, but they also indicate etymologically long vowels, again imperfectly. Unlike the Arabic script, the Hebrew script does not use quiescent letters exclusively to indicate all such long vowels. Certain long vowels often are not represented by any *mater lectionis* (*scriptio defectiva* כְּתִיב חָסֵר), and conversely, historically short vowels sometimes are indicated by a *mater lectionis*, although the *scriptio plena* (כְּתִיב מָלֵא) is uncalled for. ו is used in order to indicate the etymologically long vowels וּ and וֹ, whereas י is employed to indicate the etymologically long vowels יֵ and יֶ(1). The absence of a *mater lectionis* for the vowel *å* can probably be explained by the fact that *å* is only rarely long (e.g.

in כְּתָב from **kitāb*, § 96 D *d*), since primitive ā usually became ọ̄ in Hebrew.

Certain common forms are often written defectively; thus one generally writes שָׁלֹשׁ *šå lọš* "three" despite the undoubtedly historically long ọ; likewise the active Qal participle, e.g. קֹטֵל (from **qāṭil*)(2). Often, as a measure of economy, the *mater lectionis* is omitted when a ו or י occurs in the same word. Thus גּוֹיִם "peoples" is almost always written for גּוֹיִים, מִצְוֹת *miṣwọt* "commandments" for מִצְווֹת, and לְוִיִּם for לְוִיִּים, but חַיִּים. אֱלוֹהַּ "God" is the regular spelling for the singular, but always אֱלֹהִים for the plural. מַחְסוֹר "lack" is always spelled plene except in two cases where there is a ו in the form: מַחְסֹרוֹ Dt 15.8 and וּמַחְסֹרְךָ Pr 6.11.

By contrast, certain etymologically short vowels occasionally have a *mater lectionis*; thus the future of the type יִקְטֹל, where the ọ was originally short (derived from a *u*), is quite often written with ו (cf. BL, p. 302); likewise, but rarely, the form קְטֹל (imperative and infinitive construct).

Short *o* or *u* is fairly frequently indicated by means of ו before a geminated consonant: e.g. הוּכָּה Ps 102.5; יוּלָּד Job 5.7; כּוּלָּם Jer 31.33(3).

The *scriptio plena* tends to become more frequent in the later books. The Dead Sea Scrolls are an eloquent testimony to this trend(4). It is highly developed in postbiblical writings and thus makes up for the absence of vowel signs. It is often said that the *matres lectionis* were first used in word-final positions, and subsequently spread to word-medial positions. But a recently discovered Assyrian-Aramaic bilingual inscription which probably dates to the 9th cent. B.C. and so is the earliest Aramaic writing yet known provides ample instances of word-medial Yods and Waws(5), and not always for long vowels. But how arbitrary BH orthography can be in this regard may be illustrated by 1Sm 12.17 יִתֵּן קֹלוֹת וּמָטָר // vs. 18 יִתֵּן יהוה קֹלֹת וּמָטָר, cf. 1Q M 6,12 קולות.

(1) The seghol in such forms as יָדֶיךָ can only be said to have been long at a pre-Tiberian stage once the original plural noun ending /-ay/ had systematically changed to /-ē/.

(2) קוֹטֵל 1040 x as against קֹטֵל 4269 x according to AF, p. 129.

(3) Berg., I, § 7 e. For a full listing, see AF, pp. 95-98. The last instance cited above (כּוּלָּם), however, is the only case of the word spelled plene when a pronoun is attached to it.

(4) See Qimron, *Hebrew of DSS*, pp. 17f.

(5) See T. Muraoka, in *Abr-Nahrain* 22 (1983-84) 83-87. Another recently discovered Aramaic inscription, also datable to the 9th cent. B.C., has זי, the relative pronoun, as the only instance of a vowel letter, which is not surprising: see I. Ephal and J. Naveh, "Hazael's booty inscriptions," *IEJ* 39 (1989) 192-200. See also G. Sarfatti, *Maarav* 3 (1982) 58-65.

d N.B. When a ו and a י are not used as *mater lectionis*, they are pronounced. This is true in the following cases where the preceding vowel is heterogeneous: וַ, וָ, וֵ, וֶ; יַ, יָ, וֹי, וּי. In these combinations the ו and י probably(1) have a consonantal value, e.g. יַ = *ạy*, and not *ại*, וָ = *åw* and not *åu*. In the sequence יו ָ suffix for the 3rd pers. m.sg. of a plural noun the י is quiescent, e.g. סוּסָיו "his horses," pronounced *susåw*.

(1) In favour of this view, see § 19 *d*.

§ 8. Shewa

a The sign ְ *shewa*(1) indicates the absence of a vowel, comparable to the Arabic *sukūn*. One cannot fail to notice its graphic resemblance to the symbol marking the end of a verse, *sof pasuq*: the latter signifies the absence of a sound at the end of a verse, whilst the former marks the absence of a vowel after a consonant as in שָׁמַ֫רְתִּי. Whereas it is common practice to speak of two kinds of *shewa*, namely vocalic (*mobile*) shewa(2) and silent (*quiescens*) shewa(3), we believe that the shewa is essentially an indication for zero vowel. The vocalic shewa is said to indicate a hurried, murmering vowel, usually transliterated with either ᵉ or ə, something like *a* in Engl. *about*(4). From the diachronic, historical point of view, the vocal shewa appears where there once occurred a vowel which was subsequently deleted in the wake of stress shift. In some cases one can easily recover the original vowel, but in other cases it is only through comparison with cognate langugaes that a plausible, original vowel can be postulated: e.g. כָּתְבוּ from כָּתַב, but כְּתָב *a document*, with which one can compare Arb. *kitāb*. Whilst one is fully aware that this apparent ambiguity of the shewa symbol has been recognised as a major issue of Hebrew grammar since one of the earliest scientific treatises on Hebrew grammar(5), namely *Diqduqé haṭṭᵉʿamim*, it is intrinsically inconceivable and highly unlikely that scholars who manifest such a high degree of sensitivity to subtle phonetic nuances as the Naqdanim could have allowed such a margin of ambiguity(6).

(1) שְׁוָא *šwå*, according to BH שָׁוְא "nothing." The shewa indicates either *nothing* in the strict sense of the word or *nothing* in the figurative sense, i.e. *almost nothing*. This etymology, if correct, masks the ironic complexity of the phenomenon: shewa is the central issue, for instance, of the reputed Massoretic treatise דִּקְדּוּקֵי הַטְּעָמִים usually ascribed to Aharon Ben Asher: A. Dotan, *The Diqduqé hattĕʻamim of Ahăron ben Mošе ben Ašér* etc. (Jerusalem, 1967), pp. 30f. For an alternative etymology linking the Hebrew term to Syr. *šwayyå*, see A. Dotan in *Leš*, 19 (1954) 13-30, esp. 15-17, and also Lambert, § 38, n. 2: according to this view, the Hebrew symbol was called shewa, because its important function is to mark syllable divisions, just as the Syriac sign called *šwayyå*, which means "sameness" (with reference to its form consisting of two identical dots), marks logical divisions within a sentence. Note again that *sof pasuq* stands where there occurs larger sense division of an utterance. Interestingly enough, Saadia's Arabic term for 'shewa' is /jazm/, "cutting off, apocopation," a technical term used also for the Arabic jussive. He then goes on to discuss /ḥaraka sākina/ "resting vowel" on the one hand and /ḥaraka mutaḥarrika/ "moving vowel" on the other. See S.L. Skoss, *Saadia Gaon: The Earliest Hebrew Grammarian* (Philadelphia, 1955), p. 30.

(2) This is a Latin equivalent of the Heb. נָע, which is a translation, in turn, of Arb. /mutaḥarrik/, "moving, i.e. vocalic."

(3) Heb. נָח = Arb. /sākin/ "resting."

(4) This is of Sephardic origin, and does not belong to the genuine Tiberian tradition: A. Dotan, *Diqduqé hattĕʻamim* [n. 1 above], p. 35. The rules laid down by Massoretic grammarians for the pronunciation of vocalic shewa are: a) a full vowel, before gutturals, similar to that of the gutturals concerned, e.g. בְּאֵר roughly = /bę'ęr/. b) /i/ before Yod, and c) /a/ elsewhere. It is difficult to accept this traditional view (so explicitly Kimhi, ספר מכלול, p. 137a and reflected precisely in the Yemenite pronunciation of BH, see Morag, *EJ*, vol. 13, col. 1138) that shewa mobile before a consonant other than a guttural or Yod had the quality of /a/, presumably short /ă/, thus equivalent to ֲ, for surely, if this were so, the inventors of the vowel signs would have used ֲ in such cases. There are indeed occasional examples of ֲ for shewa mobile, albeit with considerable variation and fluctuation between manuscripts: e.g. וּזֲהַב Gn 2.12 (more examples in § 9 *c*). Also according to BHK, it occurs in 22 out of about 1,000 cases of identical consonants, e.g. שָׁנֲנוּ Ps 140.4; מִלֲלַי גִּלֲלַי Ne 12.36: Dotan, op. cit., p. 36. Such a ḥatef, however, was not really necessary if a gaʻya (metheg) was present, but it was added nonetheless as an extra help for the less knowledgeable reader: Dotan, op. cit., p. 231. In sum, on a synchronic level, shewa was intended by the Naqdanim as a sign for zero vowel phoneme, whereas the composite shewas were its allophones. Equally allophonic were the various phonetic realisations of shewa mobile as laid down in early grammatical treatises as outlined above.

Mediaeval grammatical treatises vacillate between full plain pataḥ and ḥaṭef pataḥ as the basic phonetic realisation of shewa mobile; according to some this depends on the presence or absence of ga'ya with the shewa. See Morag, *Yemenite*, pp. 160-65.

On a 10th(?) century anonymous exposition of the nature of the Tiberian shewa, see K. Levy, op. cit. [§ 1 *a*, n.].

(5) For the phonetic interpretation of shewa by Massoretic scholars and mediaeval grammarians, see N. Allony, "Shewa mobile and quiescent in the Middle Ages," *Leš* 12 (1943-44) 61-74, 13 (1944-45) 28-45, and Morag, *Yemenite*, pp. 160-66.

(6) Cf. also BL, p. 168, n. 3: "... Bei der geradezu minutiösen Sorgfalt, mit der die für den gottesdienstlichen Vortrag bestimmte Aussprache hier bezeichnet wird, ist es schwer glaubhaft, dass zwei so verschiedene Dinge wie Murmelvokal und gänzliche Vokallosigkeit nicht auseinander gehalten worden wären." A similar sentiment is expressed by A. Jepsen: see his "Zur Aussprache der tiberiensischen Punktation," *Wissenschaftliche Zeitschrift der Universität Greifswald*, I (1951/52), Gesellschafts- und sprachwissenschaftliche Reihe, Nr. 1, pp. 1-5, esp. pp. 2f. Harviainen thinks that the use of shewa may have been a compromise designed to allow for a range of phonetic realisations: T. Harviainen, op. cit. [§ 6 *f*, n.], pp. 227f. In one of the earliest expositions of the Tiberian pronunciation, *Kitāb al-muṣawwitāt*, attributed by some to Moshe Ben Asher, the shewa is considered as a set of mere allophones of the seven vowels: see Sh. Morag, in M. Bar-Asher (ed.), *Massorot: Studies in Language Traditions I* [Heb] (Jerusalem, 1984), pp. 47f.

Also in the old Babylonian tradition the distinction between the two kinds of shewa is somewhat doubtful; see Yeivin, *Babylonian Tradition*, pp. 398, 404. Rabin concedes that shewa mobile is to be regarded as allophonic, and admits that in the Tiberian scholars' pronunciation the phonetic value of shewa, whether mobile or quiescens, was most likely zero, i.e. = quiescens: C. Rabin, *The Phonetics of Biblical Hebrew* [Heb] (Jerusalem, 1970), pp. 24-26. See also A. Jepsen, art. cit., pp. 1-5, esp. 2-4; I. Garbell, "On the phonological status of shewa and hataphs," *Proceedings of the Second World Congress of Jewish Studies* (1957), Section: Hebrew Language [Heb], p. 12; idem, in *Leš* 23 (1959) 152-55; M.L. Margolis, *AJSL* 26 (1910) 62-70, and W. Chomsky, *D. Kimhi's Heb. Gram.* (New York, 1952), pp. 34f., n. 19. Saadia, loc. cit. [§ 6 *b*, n.], recognises seven vowels, which do not include shewa, although he does discuss the traditional distinction between shewa mobile and shewa quiescens (see Skoss, op. cit. [n. 1 above], pp. 30-34). Note further that, in the Secunda, in 184 out of 270 cases of shewa mobile, the Greek transcription has no corresponding vowel indication: Brønno, *Studien*, pp. 322-41.

b Five rules formulated by Elias Levitas (15th cent.) for identifying a shewa mobile are:

1) At the beginning of a word, e.g. כְּתַבְתֶּם
2) Second of two adjacent shewas, e.g. יִכְתְּבוּ
3) After a "large" vowel, e.g. כֹּתְבִים

4) Under a dageshed consonant, e.g., דִּבְּרָה

5) Under the first of two identical consonants, e.g. רוֹמְמוּ.

That these are not absolute rules is apparent from the fact that even in the 15th cent. (Almoli) there was a dispute about whether shewa preceded by a "long" vowel as in שָׁמְרוּ is quiescent or mobile, though it was generally considered quiescent(1).

(1) For a discussion see Sh. Morag in J.A. Emerton and S.C. Reif (eds), *Interpreting the Hebrew Bible: Essays in Honour of E.I.R. Rosenthal* (Cambridge, 1982), pp. 184f. According to G. Khan, the shewa was generally quiescent even after a "long" vowel, as can be seen from massoretico-grammatical treatises, and analysis of the so-called "accents" and Karaite manuscripts: *JSS* 32 (1987) 54-56. See also Yeivin, op. cit. [§ 14 *a*, n.], §§ 377-86.

One must beware of the rather common circular argument that, since a simple shewa followed by a plosive must be quiescent, therefore the Bet in שַׁרְבִיט must be preceded by a vocal shewa(1). c

(1) A similar questionable circular argument is sometimes employed in interpreting the dagesh in forms such as וַתִּכָּבֵד. We suggest that this should be analysed as /wąṯhąbbęḏ/, and not /wąttḥąbbęḏ/: see § 5 *q*, n.

The shewa attached to a final consonant as in the 2nd person f.sg. קָטַלְתְּ /qåṭąlt/ (where the shewa represents an old short *i*); וַיַּשְׁקְ /wąyyąšq/ *and he gave water* (apocopated future Hifil of שׁקה); וַיִּשְׁבְּ /wąyyišb/ *and he took captive* (apoc. fut. Qal of שׁבה); אַל־תֵּשְׁתְּ *Don't drink!* (apoc. fut. Qal of שׁתה); אַתְּ /'ątt/ (possibly /'ąt/) *you* fem. (for *'*atti*) should not be considered exceptions to the above rule, but rather special cases of § *b* (2). Cf. also the type שָׁלַחַתְּ /šålą'ḥąt/ *you* (f.sg.) *have sent*(1). d

(1) In the Samaritan tradition of Hebrew pronunciation the word-final consonantal clusters of the three types mentioned add a short /i/ at the end, which may not be secondary but primitive; see R. Macuch, *Gram.*, §§ 43c (p. 196), 62a, 64c. On the other hand, segholate nouns show a syllable structure similar to the Tiberian one with an anaptyptic vowel between the last two radicals. Does this short /i/ go back to an original long /i/, as is assumed by some (e.g. P.-E. Dion, *La langue de Ya'udi* [Waterloo, 1974], pp. 187f.) for Old Aramaic jussives of Lamed-Yod verbs? Cf. the proper nouns יַחְדִּיאֵל and יַעֲשִׂיאֵל (Berg., II, § 30 r [p. 169]).

As indicated in § *c* above, a fricative Begadkefat sometimes occurs in the middle of a word following a simple shewa and a historically short vowel, chiefly pataḥ, seghol, and qameṣ qaṭan: e.g. מַלְכֵי pl.cst. *kings of* as against מַלְכִּי *my king*. As a Begadkefat in such a position is e normally pronounced as plosive, receiving a dagesh point (dagesh lene), such a shewa as in מַלְכֵי has often been wrongly interpreted as vocalic, being accorded a special term, shewa medium. However, even if we allowed the conventional distinction between silent and vocal shewa, it is scarcely possible to conceive of yet another variety of short vowel. The simplest explanation for this kind of shewa must be that a vowel which originally followed such a stop(1) must have been deleted when the law regulating the automatic alternation between the plosive and fricative articulations of the stops had ceased to operate: cf. § 96 A *b*(2).

(1) For an attempt to explain cases of "shewa medium" which do not stand for a historical short vowel such as אֶתְכֶם, see Meyer, I, pp. 62f.

(2) For a most detailed and balanced exposé of the nature of shewa medium, see Berg., I, § 21 q-t,v. See also Z. Ben Ḥayyim in *Leš* 11 (1941) 83-93. Lambert, § 39, n. 1, is in favour of the vocalic nature of the shewa medium. See further literature in Morag, art. cit. [§ *b* above, n. 1], p. 168, n. 45.

f In the contemporary Israeli pronunciation there is no phonemic distinction between silent shewa and vocal shewa pronounced *e*, the latter of which is a positional and non-obligatory allophone. Thus [gdolim] is perfectly normal and acceptable alongside [gedolim] for גְּדוֹלִים(1). So is יִשְׁמְרוּ [yišmru] alongside [yišmeru]. Moreover, *e* is heard as a rule at morpheme boundaries, e.g. מְדַבֵּר [medaber]; יְדַבֵּר [yedaber]; בְּסֵפֶר [beséfer] *in a book*; וְגָדוֹל [vegadol] *and large*.

(1) The phonetic environments in which vocal shewa may be heard are specified in H.B. Rosén, *A Textbook of Israeli Hebrew* (Chicago, 1962), p. 4. On a whole range of phonetic phenomena whereby the contemporary Israeli pronunciation deviates from the classical rules, see W. Weinberg, "Spoken Israeli Hebrew: Trends in the departures from classical phonology," *JSS* 11 (1966) 40-68.

§ 9. Nuanced or ḥaṭef shewas

a The three signs ֲ, ֱ, and ֳ (§ 6 *e*) are called *ḥaṭef* (Arm. חֲטַף *snatching, carrying off, abbreviating*[1]), or also *compound shewas*(2). We call them here *nuanced* shewas as against unnuanced, i.e. simple shewa. These are extremely short vowels; therefore one may call them *semi-vowels* as against full vowels. The three nuanced shewas(3) often occur with gutturals; the relevant rules will be given later when we discuss the gutturals (§ 21 *f-i*).

(1) Since the name is most probably derived from חֲטָפָא of the Babylonian massoretic terminology, the original pronounciation was more likely חֲטַף: see A. Dotan in *Leš* 19 (1954) 21.
(2) See I. Yeivin, "Quantitative modifications of ḥaṭef vowels," *Leš* 44 (1980) 163-84.
(3) On a unique ḥaṭef ḥireq occurring occasionally in the Aleppo Codex of the OT, see I. Yeivin, *The Aleppo Codex of the Bible. A Study of its Vocalization and Accentuation* (Jerusalem, 1968), p. 21.

It is not uncommon for a nuanced shewa rather than a plain shewa to appear with a non-guttural. One cannot give precise rules for this phenomenon, as manuscripts often fluctuate in this regard(1). *b*

With non-gutturals, if it is necessary to have a vowel slightly stronger than a simple shewa, the vowel chosen is hardly ever ֱ, no doubt because it is felt too weak, but generally ֲ, unless there is a special reason, such as etymology or vowel harmony, for choosing ֳ. It follows, therefore, that this ֲ or ֳ does not necessarily represent a primitive vowel *a* or *u*; e.g. one finds אֲסוֹבֲבָה from סוֹבֵב, אֶשֳּׁקָה from אֶשַּׁק(2).

(1) It is remarkable that the Hebrew usage on this point should show a very marked analogy with that of Biblical Aramaic (cf. E. Kautzsch, *Grammatik des Biblisch-Aramäischen* [Leipzig, 1884], p. 36). It is quite possible that we have here Aramaic influencing Hebrew vocalisation.
(2) Cf. F.R. Blake, "The Heb. ḫatephs" in C. Adler and A. Ember (eds), *Oriental Studies* [Fschr. P. Haupt] (Baltimore/Leipzig, 1926), pp. 329-43. Incidentally, the cohortative form mentioned above, which occurs only at 1Kg 19.20, is pointed in Cod. L and A as אֶשְּׁקָה; Cod. C seems to have אֶשֲּׁקָה.

Principal cases where one finds ֲ (ḥaṭef pataḥ): *c*

1) Generally under a consonant which is then repeated, e.g. in the conjugation of ע"ע verbs: סוֹבֲבוּ, גָּלֲלוּ. But note, e.g., יְבָרֶכְךָ *he will bless you* Gn 27.10, and הִנְנוּ, הִנְנִי (but הִנֶּנּוּ, הִנֵּנִי in pause)(1).

2) Usually with an **internal** consonant which has lost its gemination, e.g. וַתְּאַלֲצֵהוּ *and she pressed him* Jud 16.16 (Piel).

3) With כ, ר, in certain forms, after an etymologically long vowel, before the stress, e.g. תֹּאכֲלֶנָּה Gn 3.17; בָּרֲכִי Ps 103.1.

4) With a sibilant after וּ *and*, e.g. וּזֲהַב *and the gold of* ... Gn 2.12; וּשֲׁמָע *and listen* Nu 23.18; וּשֲׁבֵה *and take captives* Jdg 5.12.

5) Miscellaneous: וַתִּהֲלַךְ Ex 9.23; כִּנֲרוֹת Josh 11.2; וּלֲהַבְדִּיל Gn 1.18; רֻטֲפַשׁ Job 33.25; הַצֲפַרְדְּעִים Ex 8.5 (usually הַצְ׳); אֶכְתֲּבֶנָּה Jer 31.32; וָאֶשְׁקֲלָה Ezr 8.26.

(1) According to *Diqduqé haṭṭeʿamim*, para. 5 (ed. Dotan [§ 8 *a*, n.], pp. 115f., 190-

92), when there is no ga'ya (or metheg) before the first identical consonant, the two consonants are pronounced without any breakage in between, that is to say, as a purely geminated consonant: e.g., הִנְנוּ Jer 3.22, even with ב rafé as in רִבְבוֹת אֶפְרַיִם Dt 33.17 (as against רִבְבוֹת אַלְפֵי Nu 10.36).

d Principal cases where one finds ֳ (ḥaṭef qameṣ)(1):

1) For some etymological reason, e.g. קָדְקֳדוֹ *the crown of his head* from **qudqud* > קָדְקֹד; קֳדָשִׁים from **qudš* > קֹדֶשׁ (alongside קָדָשִׁים *qǫ-ḏåšim*, § 6 *l*).

2) For the sake of harmony: occasionally before a guttural or a velar with *å*, e.g. וְנִקְרֳאָה *and she will be called* Esth 2.14 (not in Codex L.); אֶשְּׁקֳה־נָּא *I would like to kiss* 1Kg 19.20 (not in Codex L., but apparently so in Codex C.). This ֳ can probably be explained by the fact that ָ was pronounced *ǫ*.

(1) Mediaeval grammarians knew of no distinction between qameṣ ḥaṭef and the so-called qameṣ qaṭan. Both were called qameṣ ḥaṭef. See W. Chomsky, *David Kimhi's Hebrew Grammar* (New York, 1952), p. 34, and also I. Yeivin in *Lešˇ* 44 (1980) 175.

§ 10. Dagesh

a Dagesh with a *begadkefat* (§ 5 *o*), e.g. in פּ, is an equivocal sign(1). It may indicate either that the begadkefat is a plosive, e.g. in יִשְׁפֹּט *yiš-pǫṭ* "he will judge" or it may indicate that it is long, i.e. geminated or doubled, as well as plosive, e.g. in יִפֹּל *yippǫl* "he will fall" (for *יִנְפֹּל, from נָפַל). In all other consonants, dagesh is not ambiguous: it signifies that the consonant concerned is geminated, e.g. in קִטֵּל *qiṭṭel*. The dagesh which indicates the gemination of the consonant is called *dagesh forte*(2); from the point of view of its function, one can call it the dagesh of *doubling*. The dagesh which, in the *begadkefat*, indicates the plosive or instantaneous sound is called *dagesh lene*(3); from the point of view of its function, one may call it the dagesh of *simple plosion*. With the *begadkefat* the dagesh forte is one of *prolonged plosion*. In the Hebrew vocalised by the Naqdanim, it is often claimed, there is no doubled fricative, e.g. *ff*: thus אַפּוֹ *his nose* is necessarily *'ąppǫ* (root: אנף), but there is no absolute reason why a form such as לְבָבוֹת should not have been meant to be pronounced with geminated /v/, whilst the orthography presumably represents an earlier stage in which the first /b/ was followed by a vowel of some sort or other(4).

(1) Early Massoretic scholars made no distinction between dagesh forte and lene: I. Yeivin in M. Bar-Asher et al. (eds), *Hebrew Language Studies Presented to Prof. Z. Ben-Ḥayyim* [Heb] (Jerusalem, 1983), p. 305.
(2) דָּגֵשׁ חָזָק *strong dagesh*, also called ד' כָּבֵד *heavy dagesh*.
(3) *Soft dagesh*, a free translation of דָּגֵשׁ רָפֶה, also called *light dagesh* (ד' קַל).
(4) See above, § 9 *c*, n.

On the quantity of consonants, cf. § 18 *a*; on the spirantisation of the *begadkefat*, cf. § 19. *b*

Contemporary Israeli Hebrew does not recognise dagesh forte: הַדָּבָר *the word* is therefore pronounced [hadavar]. *c*

§ 11. **Mappiq**

In printed bibles the point called *mappiq* is found only in word-final ה to indicate that it is not quiescent, but must be pronounced, e.g. אַרְצָהּ *'ạrṣåh' her land* (as opposed to אַרְצָה *'ạr'ṣå to the land*); סוּסָהּ *her horse* (as opposed to סוּסָה *a mare*); קָטְלָהּ *to kill her* and *Kill her* (as opposed to קָטְלָה *Kill*, Imperative with a paragogic ה, § 48 *d*). *a*

The הּ occurs in the following roots: גבהּ *to be high*, מהמהּ (הִתְמַהְמַהּ) *to hesitate*, נגהּ *to shine*, תמהּ *to be surprised*.

The word מַפִּיק, from Arm. נְפַק *to go out*, signifies *to make go out*, i.e. *to make pronounce* the consonant; cf. the Syr. *mhaggyånå'* sign. *b*

§ 12. **Rafé**

Rafé is a horizontal stroke over a consonant letter(1). This stroke expresses the opposite of a *point*, namely of dagesh (forte or lene) [§ 10], and of mappiq [§ 11]. Therefore, it has, according to the circumstances, three values: 1) in contrast to dagesh forte, it indicates that the consonant is not doubled, e.g. one finds in manuscripts such forms as עִוְרִים *blind people* in order to avoid the pronunciation *'iwwrīm* (cf. § 18 *m* 4); 2) in contrast to dagesh lene, it expressly indicates that the *begadkefat* is fricative, e.g. מַלְכֵי (cf. § 5 *o*); 3) in contrast to mappiq, it indicates that a final ה is not pronounced, e.g. *a*

לָהּ *lå*, not *låh* (§ 25 *a*).

(1) Most current editions of the Hebrew OT omit the sign for technical reasons.

b On the meaning of the word **rafé**, cf. § 5 *o*.

§ 13. **Maqqef**

a The *maqqef*(1) is a small stroke, similar to our dash, indicating that two words form an extremely closely knit group. The two words linked by a maqqef form a phonetic unit: the first word has lost its main stress and can now have only a secondary stress, in other words, it becomes proclitic(2). The unity indicated by maqqef is generally closer than that indicated by a conjunctive accent.

Maqqef can link two, three or even four words, e.g. אֶת־כָּל־אֲשֶׁר־לוֹ Gn 25.5.

(1) מַקֵּף, from Arm. נְקַף, means, strictly speaking, *encircling*; here one usually understands it as meaning *linking*. The first word is described as זָרִיז *rapid, hurrying* in the language of the Massorah (*RB* 13 [1904] 536).

(2) Compare the proclitics in Greek, which lose their own accent when closely dependent on the following word: ὁ, ἡ etc.; ἐν, εἰς, οὐ etc.

b The use of maqqef does not have hard and fast rules.

It is used especially after monosyllabic words(1). Thus, among nouns the following are used with a maqqef: בֶּן־ *son* (almost always) and בַּת־ *daughter* (usually). In contrast, one rarely has a maqqef with אֵם *mother*, שֵׁם and שֶׁם *name*, and never with אָב (st. cst. אֲבִי) *father*. In the st. cst. כָּל־ is more frequent than כֹּל *all*.

The following particles are nearly always provided with a maqqef: אַל־ *not*, אֶל־ *towards*, אִם־ *if*, מִן־ *from*, פֶּן־ *lest*, עַד־ *until*, עַל־ *on*, עִם־ *with*. The two particles spelled both אֵת, one of which is a preposition meaning "with" and the other the accusative-marker, occur quite often with a maqqef (אֶת־)(2).

The particle ־נָא *please* (§ 105 *c*) is nearly always preceded by a maqqef, thus rendering the preceding word proclitic.

(1) Cf. I. Yeivin, "Syntactical and musical influence on the use of maqqef with short words," *Leš* 23 (1959) 35-48.

(2) אֶת־: three exceptions אֵת—Ps 47.5, 60.2, Pr 3.12, on which see Dotan, op. cit. [§ 8 *a*, n.], p. 118.

c The word that precedes a maqqef, becoming proclitic, tends to have a rather shorter vowel. Thus שֵׁם (st.abs. and cst.), כֹּל (st. abs. and cst.) become שֶׁם־ , כָּל־(1); the infinitive קְטֹל becomes קְטָל־ ; יָד *hand* יַד־; מָה *what?* מַה־.

The word יָם *sea* (root: ימם, cf. יָמָּה [§ 93 *d*], pl. יַמִּים) has a remarkable peculiarity. The qameṣ is retained(2) in יָם־, e.g. יָם־כִּנֶּרֶת *the Sea of Genesareth*, except in יַם־סוּף *the sea of reeds, the Red Sea.*

Observation. A noun in st. abs. can be followed by a maqqef, e.g. לְחָק־לְךָ *as an ordinance for you* Ex 12.24 (without maqqef, חֹק); גֵּר־יָתוֹם וְאַלְמָנָה *the foreigner, the orphan and the widow* Dt 27.19. Similarly, one may have the infinitive absolute, e.g. הַכֵּר־פָּנִים *to recognise the face* Pr 28.21 (cf. § 123 *b*). d

(1) כָּל without maqqef and with qameṣ: Ps 35.10, 87.7, Is 40.12, Pr 19.7: see Dotan, op. cit. [§ 8 *a*], p. 119.

(2) Under the influence of מ; cf. the adjective תָּם (root תמם), always with qameṣ.

§ 14. Metheg

Metheg (מֶתֶג *bridle*) has, as indicated by the name, the function of restraining the pronunciation(1). It is a small perpendicular stroke usually placed to the left of a vowel in order to ensure its precise pronunciation, or, to put it negatively, to prevent a rapid or accelerated pronunciation. But just as the accents often indicate the place of the principal or secondary stress (§ 15 *d*), although this is not their primary function, so the metheg often indicates the secondary stress(2). In some cases it will be found indicating syllabic division as well. The fact that metheg forms part of the accent system, and is generally used only in manuscripts in which the accent signs are used, but not in those which show only vowel signs(3) seems to suggest that it was not primarily designed to indicate the nature of the vowel *per se* to which it is attached. Thus it is rather doubtful that the metheg in a star example such as חָֽכְמָה (pf. 3f.s.) Zech 9.2 was meant to indicate that the first qameṣ is to be pronounced differently from that under the same consonant in חָכְמָה as a substantive meaning *wisdom*(4), nor is it certain that the metheg was invested, by design, with the added function of marking the conventional differentiation between shewa mobile a and shewa quiescens.

As neither manuscripts nor grammarians are in accord regarding the use of metheg, it will suffice to give here some concrete examples and indicate the most common uses([5]).

(1) Cf. I. Yeivin (tr. and ed. E.J. Revell), *Introduction to the Tiberian Massorah* (Missoula, 1980), pp. 240-64, and "Meteg," *EB*, vol. 5 (Jerusalem, 1968), cols. 641-43. Manuscripts differ considerably in the placement or non-placement of metheg: one of the more notable differences between the massoretic schools of Ben Asher and Ben Naphtali consists therein, as has been shown in L. Lipschütz (ed.), *Kitāb al-khilaf: Mishael Ben Uzziel's Treatise on the Differences between Ben Asher and Ben Naphtali* (Jerusalem, 1965).

(2) It is probably because of this fact that metheg is called by some grammarians *ga'ya* גַּעְיָה "lowing, lifting of voice." Actually, *ga'ya* is the older of the two names: Yeivin, op. cit., p. 241.

(3) Yeivin, op. cit., p. 242.

(4) Cf. Ps 86.2 שָׁמְרָה, *Preserve*, a long imperative, and 16.1 שָׁמְרֵנִי *Preserve me*.

(5) Outside of the biblical text, the metheg is often left unprinted, except in those cases where it is useful in distinguishing a form. We should particularly note it in cases where it serves to distinguish ָ, e.g. יִלְבָּשְׁךָ *he will dress you*, in contrast to, say, יִקְטָלְךָ *he will kill you*, which is without metheg.

b   **Examples:** In קָטְלָה /qå-ṭlå/ *she killed* (§ *c* 1) the metheg here is found marking the syllable boundary. It further indicates a secondary stress: qå`-ṭlå'. _ In וְקָטַלְתִּי (§ 43 *a*), the metheg signals that the qameṣ should be pronounced accurately; it further indicates the position of the secondary stress: w-qå`ṭalti' (§ *c* 2). Likewise in אָנֹכִי (§ 39 *a*).

c   **Principal uses:** The metheg is placed([1])

1) with a historically long vowel followed by a shewa and a stressed syllable, e.g. קָטְלָה, יִירְאוּ or (*defectively*) יִרְאוּ *they will fear* (in contrast to יִרְאוּ /yir-'u/ *they will see*); Pr 4.16 יִישָׁנוּ *they sleep*, but Ne 13.21 תִּשְׁנוּ *you do again*. As has become obvious, this metheg can be diacritical.

2) With the vowel of the second open syllable before the stress, e.g. הָאָדָם, הָעַמִּים, וְקָטַלְתִּי, הֶחָכָם (with the vowel of the third open syllable before the stress if the second syllable is closed, e.g. הָאָרְבָּעִים)([2]). Likewise with the vowel of the second open syllable before a vowel having a metheg, e.g. שָׁבְעֹתֵיכֶם šå`vu'o'tehem'([3]). Exception: וְ *and* does not take a metheg, e.g. וּבָנִים; probably because this

u is originally short(4). In this use, metheg, apart from protecting the vowel as usual, also marks the secondary stress.

3) With the vowel which precedes a ḥaṭef, e.g. יַֽעֲמֹד; likewise in cases where a ḥaṭef becomes a full vowel, e.g. יַֽעַמְדוּ (§ 22 *c*).

4) With the vowel of the first closed syllable of the verbs הָיָה *to be* and חָיָה *to live* in order to ensure accurate pronunciation, e.g. יִֽהְיֶה *yih-yẹ he will be*; in the forms וַיְהִי, וַיְחִי only before a maqqef or when they have the accent *pashṭa*.

5) In the particle אָֽנָּה, אָֽנָּא: *Ah!, For goodness' sake* (§ 105 *c*).

6) With the pataḥ of the article before a consonant with virtual gemination and a shewa, e.g. הַֽמְכַסֶּה *hąm*(*m*)*ḥąssẹ the one who conceals* Lv 3.3; except before י, e.g. הַיְלָדִים. Likewise with the pataḥ of the interrogative adverb הֲ, e.g. הַֽמְכַסֶּה אֲנִי Gn 18.17.

7) With an etymologically long vowel before a maqqef in order to prevent it from being shortened, e.g. שָֽׁת־לִי Gn 4.25 *šåṯ-li*; כֹּל־ Ps 138.2 (not כָּל־, but so in Cod. L and A); אֵֽת־ Job 41.26 (not אֶת־).

(1) On two kinds of metheg, see further literature in Berg., I, p. 71, which in the main follows S. Baer, "Die Metheg-Setzung," *Archiv für wissenschaftliche Erforschung des Alten Testaments*, I (1867-69) 56-67, 194-207: Baer's study needs to be used critically and cautiously.

(2) So in Nu 33.38; 1Ch 26.31. We may formulate one general practical rule (encompassing both 1 and 2): metheg is added to the vowel of the first open syllable (or so considered here) removed from the stress at least by a mobile shewa, e.g. מֽוֹאֲבִיָּה, אֹֽרְחֹתָיו, דְּֽלִיּוֹתָיו.

(3) Not according to Codex L. in the sole occurrence of the form in Nu 28.26.

(4) With the mediaeval poets וּ is short; cf. S.D. Luzzatto, *Grammatica della lingua ebraica* (Padova, 1853), p. 584. Likewise we write, e.g. וּבְנֵי without metheg, contrary to 1; but with metheg, e.g. וְֽזָהָב, § 9 *c* 4.

§ 15. **Accents**(1)

Every Hebrew word, when it is not proclitic, namely not closely dependent on the following word, has a **tonic** or stressed vowel which is pronounced more loudly and emphatically relative to the other vowels of the word. When a word is somewhat long, it can also have a secondary stress, and even two if it is very long as in, e.g. שְֽׁבֻעֹֽתֵיכֶם (cf. § 14 *c* 2) where the secondary stress is indicated by the metheg. The position of the stress, primary or secondary, is generally indicated *a* by signs called **accents** (טְעָמִים, literally *tastes* or נְגִינוֹת *melodies*).

(1) In order to avoid confusion, the term *accent* is reserved here for graphic symbols (and neumes expressed by these symbols), which usually indicate the place of the stress; the term *stress* is applied to the phonetic elevation of the voice, although, strictly speaking, the Hebrew stress, unlike that in ancient Greek and Latin, refers rather to more forceful articulation than higher musical pitch, the latter being a secondary element as in Modern Greek, Vulgar Latin, Greek, English, Italian etc. That the Hebrew stress is essentially a prominence of intensity or force of articulation is manifest in its effects on the vocalisation. In contrast, the contemporary Israeli pronunciation of Hebrew is characterised by a musical pitch accent. For the same reason we prefer the term "stress" to "tone," likewise "pre-stress" to "pretonic" and so on.

b In the state of Hebrew as recorded by the Naqdanim, the primary stress occurs only on the ultima, i.e. the last syllable most commonly by far, or on the penultima, i.e. the second last syllable. The Hebrew stress, in its evolution, tends towards the end of the word(1). The penultimate stress is called מִלְּעֵיל *mil'el* (from Aramaic מִן + לְ + עֵיל = *desuper*, "from above," i.e. towards the beginning of the word); the stress on the ultima is called מִלְּרַע *mil'ra* (from Arm. מִן + לְ + אֲרַע, "on the earth," *deorsum*, "from below," i.e. towards the end of the word)(2).

In this grammar the stress is marked by the conventional sign ˂ (in major pause by athnaḥ ˄), e.g. וַיָּקָם *wąyyå'-qǫm* (mil'el), וַיָּקֹם *wąyyåqǫm'* (mil'ra, in major pause)(3).

On the rules relative to the position of the stress, cf. § 31.

(1) For an attempt to show how the stress system as we have it in the Tiberian tradition may be understood *vis-à-vis* a reconstructed prehistory of it, see Blau, *Grammar*, §§ 9.1 - 9.3.5, with a slight modification in idem, *IOS* 9 (1979) 49-54. The most important element in this reconstruction is the postulated general penultimate stress as originally canvassed by M. Lambert as early as 1890 in his article, "L'accent tonique en hébreu," *RÉJ* 20 (1890) 73-77. See also J. Cantineau, "De la place de l'accent de mot en hébreu et en araméen biblique," *Bulletin de l'Institut Oriental Français, Damas*, I (1931) 81-98.

(2) On the various uses of the two terms at an early stage, especially as a diacritical device distinguishing pairs of homographs and homonyms as exemplified in *Ochla we-Ochla*, see A. Dotan, "The beginnings of Masoretic vowel notation," H.M. Orlinsky (ed.), *Masoretic Studies I* (Missoula, 1974), pp. 21-34, esp. 23-25. Dotan justly stresses that there is so far no evidence among Hebrew manuscripts attesting to the sometimes alleged use of dots above and below words comparable to their diacritical use in Syriac manuscripts.

(3) As the *mil'ra* accent is decidedly more common, it is generally left unmarked for economy's sake, e.g. בָּנוּ is considered to represent בָּנ֫וּ.

The position of the stress is extremely important; it is sometimes phonemic, i.e. distinguishes meaning. Compare, e.g., בָּנ֫וּ *they built* from בָּנָה and בָּ֫נוּ *in us*, קָ֫מָה *she arose* and קָמָ֫ה *arising* (f. participle, § 80 *j*), וְקָטַ֫לְתִּי *and I have killed* and וְקָטַלְתִּ֫י *and I shall kill* (with the inversive Waw), ק֫וּמִי *Arise!* fem. and קוּמִ֫י *my arising* (infinitive), תַּ֫מָּה *she is perfect* and תַּמָּ֫ה *perfect* (f. adj.). c

Our Hebrew Bible has two systems of accents: 1) the ordinary or prose system used in 21 books; 2) the system used in the three poetic books אִיּוֹב Job, מִשְׁלֵי Proverbs, and תְּהִלִּים Psalms (mnemonic word אֱמֶת *truth*). d

The accentuation presupposes that the biblical text had previously been divided into **verses** (פְּסוּקִים). Although an attempt was apparently made to achieve verses of approximately equal length, some have turned out rather short (but never less than three words). The division into verses does not always accord with logic; thus the apodosis is sometimes separated from its protasis in order to avoid too long a verse (Dt 19.16-17; 1Kg 3.11-12; 21.20-21; Ru 1.12-13). e

The origin of the accents is obscure(1). Their main purpose is to regulate the musical modulation or recitation of the Bible. The accents are principally *neumes* or groups of notes. As some of these *neumes* possess a *pausal* character (§ 32), it sometimes happens that the signs marking them indicate the *caesuras* or the divisions of the sentence into units. Finally, the neume signs (pausal or not) are in general placed on the stressed syllable of the word, so that the accents usually mark the position of the stress.

The accents that mark the caesuras (major, intermediate, or minor pauses) are called *disjunctive*, for in effect they separate a word from the following word, as do our punctuation marks (. ; ,). The other accents, in contrast, unite a word with the following and are called *conjunctive*.

(1) The invention of the accent signs is believed to have preceded that of the vowel signs; see Sh. Morag, *Leš* 38 (1974) 50, 52f.

The few accents, disjunctive or conjunctive, which are not placed on a stressed syllable are either *prepositive*, i.e. always positioned at f the beginning of the word, or *postpositive*, i.e. always positioned at the end of the word. In contrast to the *prepositive* or *postpositive* accents, those which are placed *on* a stressed syllable can be called *impositive*. Some manuscripts repeat a prepositive or postpositive accent on the stressed syllable; in the standard editions this does not happen except for the postpositive accent called *pashṭa* (disjunctive, cf. § *g*: A 8 *a*), which is repeated if the stress is mil'el, e.g. הַמַּ֙יִם֙ *the water* Gn 1.7: the accent, being postpositive, is written on the last letter of the word; here the *pashṭa* has been repeated on the stressed syllable *ma*, *hạmmạ'yim*(1). The stress position in words having a prepositive or postpositive accent other than pashṭa cannot be determined except through a knowledge of grammar.

(1) When a mil'ra word has pashṭa, the sign ֙, which is positioned at the far left of the word (e.g. לָא֑וֹר֙ Gn 1.5), has no chance of being confused with the graphically similar impositive conjunctive accent *azla* (e.g. וְר֨וּחַ 1Kg 18.12, § *g*: A 18).

g A. Accents of the standard system (of the twenty-one books)

Disjunctive accents

1 ֽ *silluq* (opposed to *metheg*, § 14) on the last word of the verse before (:) *sọf påsuq* "end of the verse," Gn 1.1 הָאָֽרֶץ.

2 ֑ *atnaḥ* in the middle of the verse, Gn 1.1 אֱלֹהִ֑ים.

3a **postp.** ֒ *sgoltå* at the fourth or fifth caesura before the *atnaḥ*, Gn 1.7 הָֽרָקִיעַ֒.

3b ֓ major *shalshelet* (with a vertical stroke on the left), very rare (7 times) for *segoltå*, at the beginning of a sentence, Gn 19.16 וַיִּתְמַהְמָ֓הּ ׀.

4a ֔ *zåqẹf qåṭọn* Gn 1.14 הַשָּׁמַ֔יִם.

4b ֕ *zåqẹf gåḏọl*, instead of *zåqẹf qåṭọn* if the preceding accent is not conjunctive, Gn 1.14 לְהַבְדִּ֕יל.

5 ֖ *ṭifḥå* (or *ṭarḥå*) Gn 1.1 בְּרֵאשִׁ֖ית; sometimes in place of the *atnaḥ*, especially in short verses, Gn 3.21 ע֖וֹר (compare with *m'ayyelå*, a conjunctive accent, no. 21).

6 ֗ *rvia'*, Gn 1.2 וְהָאָ֗רֶץ.

7 **postp.** ֮ *zarqå*, Gn 1.7 אֱלֹהִים֮.

8a **postp.** ֙ *pashṭå*, Gn 1.5 לָאוֹר֙ (cf. § *f*) (to be contrasted with the conjunctive *azlå*, no. 18).

8b **prep.** ֚ *ytiv* (comp. with the conjunctive *mhuppåḥ*, no. 15, which is not prepositive) in place of *pashṭå*, in monosyllabic words or in words having the stress on the first syllable if the preceding accent is not conjunctive, Gn 1.11 עֵ֫שֶׂב.

9 ֛ *tvir*, Gn 1.8 אֱלֹהִ֛ים.

10a ֜ *gẹrẹsh*, Gn 1.9 הַמַּ֜יִם.

10b ֞ *gråshayim* (or *gẹrshayim*), double *gẹrẹsh*, rare (16 x) for *gẹrẹsh* if the stress is on the ultima and if the conjunctive accent *azlå* (no. 18) does not precede, Gn 1.11 פְּרִ֞י.

11a ֡ *påzer*, Gn 1.21 הָֽרֹמֶ֡שֶׂת.

11b ֟ *påzer gådọl* or *qarnẹ fårå* "horns of a cow," rare (16 x), Esth 7.9 הָמָ֟ן.

12 **prep.** ֠ *tlishå gdọlå*, Zech 4.5 וַיַּ֠עַן (contrast with the conjunctive *tlishå qṭannå*, no. 19).

13 ׀֣ *lgarme* "for itself": this is the conjunctive accent *munaḥ*, no. 14 with a vertical stroke on the left, Is 39.2 וְאֵ֣ת ׀.

Conjunctive accents

14 ֣ *munaḥ* (contrast with the disjunctive *lgarme*, no. 13), Gn 1. בָּרָ֣א.

15 ֤ *mhuppåḵ* (contrast with the disjunctive prep. *ytiv*, no. 8 *b*), Gn 1.7 בֵּ֤ין.

16a ֥ *mērḵå*, Gn 1.1 אֵ֥ת.

16b ֦ *mērḵå kfulå*, double *mērḵå*, Gn 27.25 ל֦וֹ.

17 ֧ *dargå*, Gn 1.4 וַיַּ֧רְא.

18 ֨ *azlå*, 1Kg 18.12 וְר֨וּחַ; also called *qadmå* when it is associated with the disjunctive *gẹrẹsh*, Gn 1.9 יִקָּו֨וּ הַמַּ֜יִם (contrast with the disjunctive, postpositive *pashṭå*, no. 8*a*).

19 **postp.** ֩ *tlishå qṭannå*, Gn 1.29 הִנֵּה֩ (contrast with the disjunctive prepositive *tlishå gdọlå*, no. 12).

20 ֪ *galgal* "wheel" or *yẹraḥ* "moon," rare (16 x) like *påzer gådọl* (no. 11 *b* to which it is related), Esth 7.9 עָשָׂ֪ה.

21 ֖ *m'ayylå*: this is the *ṭifḥå* (no. 5) used to mark the secondary stress in words or groups which have *silluq* (no. 1) or *atnaḥ* (no. 2), Nu 28.26 שָׁבֻעֹתֵיכֶ֑ם, Gn 8.18 וַיֵּצֵא־נֹ֑חַ.

B. Accents of the poetic system (of the three אֱמֶת books, § *d*) *h*

Disjunctive accents

1 ֽ *silluq* (cf. A 1 in the table of the accents of the standard system).
2 ֥֫ *ʿọlẹh wyọrẹd* "ascending and descending," stronger than *atnaḥ*.
3 ֑ *atnaḥ* (cf. A 2), less strong than *ʿọlẹh wyọrẹd*.
4 ֗ *rviaʿ gådọl* (cf. A 6).
5 ֗֜ *rviaʿ mugråsh*, i.e. *rviaʿ* with *gẹrẹsh* (cf. A 10 *a*).
6 ׀֓ major *shalshelet* (comp. 19 and cf. A 3 *b*).
7 **postp.** ֘ *ṣinnọr* (*zarqå*, cf. A 7). (The *ṣinnọrit* [no. 20], which has the same form ֘, is placed on an open syllable before *mērḇå* [no. 12] or *mhuppåḵ* [no. 17]).
8 ֗ *rviaʿ qåṭọn* before *ʿọlẹh wyọrẹd*.
9 **prep.** ֭ *dḥi* or *ṭifḥå* (prepositive) (cf. A 5) (comp. the conjunctive accent, no. 15).
10 ֡ *påzer* (cf. A 11 *a*).
11a ׀֤ *mhuppåḵ lgarme*, i.e. *mhuppåḵ* (no. 17) with a vertical stroke on the left.
11*b* ׀֨ *azlå lgarme*, i.e. *azlå* (no. 18) with a vertical stroke to the left.

Conjunctive accents

12 ֥ *mērḇå* (cf. A 16 *a*).
13 ֣ *munaḥ* (cf. A 14).
14 ֬ *ʿilluy* or upper *munaḥ*.
15 ֖ *ṭarḥå* (comp. the prepositive, disjunctive *dḥi*, no. 9).
16 ֪ *galgal* or *yẹraḥ* (cf. A 20).
17 ֤ *mhuppåḵ* (comp. no. 11 *a* and cf. A 15).
18 ֨ *azlå* (comp. no. 11 *b* and cf. A 18).
19 ֓ minor *shalshelet* (comp. no. 6).
[20 ֘ *ṣinnọrit* comp. no. 7].

i The **ordinary use** of the standard system of accents. A verse ends with *silluq*, followed by *sọf påsuq*; this constitutes the major break. The verse is divided by *atnaḥ* into two halves, which can be of unequal length. Each half, depending on its length, is then further divided, each part being subdivided (dichotomy) by the following accents: *segoltå* ֒, *zaqef* ֔, and *rviaʿ* ֗, whose descending value is graphically apparent. Moreover, the two major accents, namely *silluq* and *atnaḥ*, and the three sub-dividers (*sgoltå*, *zaqef*, *rvia‘*) are each preceded, if need be, by a weak disjunctive accent, which is, so to speak, its precursor:

1 *silluq* —ֽ and 2 *atnaḥ* —֑ have as their	**precursor**		5 —֖ *ṭifḥå*
3 *segoltå* —֒ (and *shalshelet* ׀—֓)	=	=	7 —֮ *zarqå* (rather rare)
4 *zåqef* —֔ —֕	=	=	8 —֙ *pašṭå* [—֚ *ytiv*]
5 *ṭifḥå* —֖	=	=	9 —֛ *tvir*]
			10 —֜ *gęręš* [—֞ *gråshayim*]
6 *rvia‘* —֗	=	=	11 —֡ *påzer* [—֟ *påzer gådǫl*]
			12 —֠ *tlishå gdǫlå*

Example: Is 39.2. In this long verse, it was necessary to use all *j*
the disjunctive accents, even *segoltå*. Below we indicate the relative importance of the disjunctive accents by an appropriate number of vertical strokes |||| for *silluq* and *atnaḥ*, which is practically equivalent to the former, ||| for *segoltå*, || for *zaqef*, | for *rvia‘*; the accent *ṭifḥå*, precursor of *silluq* and *atnaḥ*, is indicated by //, and all the other precursor accents, practically of equal value, are indicated by /.

וַיִּשְׂמַח עֲלֵיהֶם / חִזְקִיָּהוּ ||| וַיַּרְאֵם אֶת־בֵּית נְכֹתֹה / אֶת־הַכֶּסֶף / וְאֶת־

הַזָּהָב וְאֶת־הַבְּשָׂמִים / וְאֵת | הַשֶּׁמֶן הַטּוֹב | וְאֵת / כָּל־בֵּית כֵּלָיו ||

וְאֵת/ כָּל־אֲשֶׁר נִמְצָא // בְּאוֹצְרֹתָיו |||| לֹא־הָיָה דָבָר | אֲשֶׁר לֹא־הֶרְאָם

חִזְקִיָּהוּ / בְּבֵיתוֹ // בְּכָל־מֶמְשַׁלְתּוֹ:||||

As one can see, the verse is divided into two halves of rather disproportionate length, separated by *atnaḥ* —֑. The first half is subdivided by *sgoltå* —֒: the first part, which precedes the *segoltå*, is not divided any further, for it is short; however, the second part, from the *sgoltå* to the *atnaḥ*, is subdivided by *zåqef* —֔ into two portions the first of which is subdivided in turn by *rvia‘*. The second half of the verse from the *atnaḥ* to the *silluq*, being rather short, is not subdivided except once by *rvia'* —. Furthermore, before the *atnaḥ* and *silluq* one has a *ṭifḥå* as precursor which itself has a precursor, *tvir* —. Likewise *sgoltå* has its precursor in *zarqå* —, the *zåqef* has its precursor in *pashṭå* —; the first *rvia'* has *påzer* —, *tlishå gdọlå* —, and *gẹrẹsh* — for precursors. The choice of these various disjunctive accents as well as that of the conjunctive accents which precede them is governed by rules of logic and syntax; many anomalies have something to do with music.

k A knowledge of the accents is sometimes important for grammar and also for interpretation. Thus in the verse cited above the ב of בְּאֽוֹצְרֹתָ֑יו has no *rafé*, because the preceding vowel is separated from it by a disjunctive accent. In Ru 2.14 the accentuation suggests the following breakdown of the verse: "and Boaz said to her at meal-time, 'Come here...,'" and not "and Boaz said to her, 'At meal-time, come here...'."

In Is 40.3 קוֹל֙ קוֹרֵ֔א בַּמִּדְבָּ֕ר the accentuation suggests the following break in the verse: *The voice of one who cries: In the desert* ..., which is in accordance with the rule that of two similar accents the first is always the stronger (cf. Delitzsch *ad loc.*)(1). This rule also clearly appears in Ru 3.9, where the first *zåqef* has led to the pausal vocalisation אֲמָתֶ֔ךָ, but not the second *zåqef* (אֲמָֽתְךָ֔)(2).

(1) This differs from the usual understanding of the LXX version φωνὴ βοῶντος ἐν τῇ ἐρήμῳ Ἑτοιμάσατε . . . , and cf. Jn 1.23 ἐγὼ φωνὴ βοῶντος ἐν τῇ ἐρήμῳ.

(2) Important implications of the Massoretic accentuation for the interpretation of the Biblical text are illustrated in Yeivin, op. cit. [§ 14 *a*, n.], pp. 218-28. Cf. also M. Aronoff, "Orthography and linguistic theory: the syntactic basis of Masoretic Hebrew punctuation," *Language* 61 (1985) 28-72.

l The accents are most useful in determining where the stress lies, because all the accents which are neither prepositive nor postpositive indicate the stress position directly, and the postpositive *pashṭå* indicates it indirectly (§ *f*). The reader of the sacred text therefore should, right from the beginning, always place the stress where the accents indicate. In actual pronunciation it would be convenient to indicate the *mil'el* stress clearly and the *mil'ra* stress less clearly.

m *Påseq* (פָּסֵק, an Aramaic participle meaning "separating") is a vertical stroke placed on the left of a word. This sign is graphically similar to the vertical stroke of some accents such as *lgarme*, major *shal-*

shelet. Paseq was introduced at a late period and in a manner less coherent than other accents, as a result of which its use is not very clear. In most of about 480 examples found in our editions(1), this sign serves as a bumper which prevents two words being brought into too close a relation under certain circumstances, e.g. when the same consonant appears both at the beginning and at the end of a word as in Jer 51.37 בָּבֶל | לְגַלִּים | מְעוֹן. But quite a few instances of it do not seem to fit this definition, and several hypotheses of varying degrees of likelihood have been put forward to account for these: e.g., that paseq is a diacritical symbol, or that it indicates an ancient abbreviation, or the insertion of a short gloss.

(1) The list is found in Wickes, *Accentuation of Prose Books* (cf. § *n*), pp. 120ff.

n On accents there are two fundamental works: W. Wickes, *A Treatise on the Accentuation of the Three so-called Poetical Books of the Old Testament* (Oxford, 1881) and *A Treatise on the Accentuation of the Twenty-one so-called Prose Books of the Old Testament* (Oxford, 1887). Also consult the entry 'Accents' by Max L. Margolis in *Jewish Encyclopedia*; J. Derenbourg, "Quelques observations sur l'accentuation," *JA* 2 (1870) 519-28); P. Kahle, "Zur Geschichte der hebr. Accente," *ZDMG* 55 (1901) 167-94; I. Yeivin, op. cit. [§ 14 a, n.]; A. Dotan, "Masorah," in *EJ*, vol. 16, cols. 1433-68.

o Although nothing is known of intonation, two considerations strongly suggest that the declarative and interrogative utterances must have had different intonation patterns: 1) the two are not differentiated in word-order, and 2) not all Yes/No questions are marked by the special interrogative particle /ha/ (§ 161 *b*).

§ 16. The massoretic text and the massorah(1)

a The Hebrew text in our Bible editions, with all of its details, is commonly called the *massoretic* text(2). In reality certain particulars of our text antedate the massoretes, whilst some others postdate them. The work of the massoretes is later than that of the *Naqdanim* and presupposes it. The massoretes completed their work over the period of the 8th to the 10th centuries; the textus receptus is generally that of Ben Asher (10th cent.), which has been preferred to that of his rival Ben

Naftali.

(1) For a brief introduction on the OT text and the work of massoretes, see E. Würthwein, *Der Text des Alten Testaments: Eine Einführung in die Biblia Hebraica* (Stuttgart, [5]1988), a useful handbook for the user of Biblia Hebraica Stuttgartensia. An English translation by E.F. Rhodes, *The Text of the Old Testament. An Introduction to the Biblia Hebraica* (London, 1980) is based on the fourth German edition of 1972.

(2) *Massorah* represents the late form מַסּוֹרָה or מָסוֹרָה for מַסֹּרֶת *tradition* derived from MH מָסַר *to transmit*. The word has nothing in common with מָסֹרֶת of Ez 20.37† *chain* for מַאֲסֹרֶת.

b **Divisions of the text.** From the grammatical point of view, the most important division is that into *verses* (פְּסוּקִים, § 15 *e*). The division into *chapters*, introduced by the Christians into the Vulgate in the 13th century, has been accepted by the Jews (פֶּרֶק or קַפִּיטוּלִי). It was Rabbi Nathan who has used it for the first time, for his Concordance, towards 1440.

c The Pentateuch, in view of its recitation in the synagogue service, is divided into 54 *sections* (פָּרָשָׁה). A section is said to be *open* (פְּתוּחָה) when the following section must begin at the start of the following line, thus leaving some space at the end of the open section; it is said to be *closed* (סְתוּמָה) when the following section need not begin at the very start of the following line. These *major sections* are indicated by פפפ (e.g. Ex 30.11) or ססס (e.g. Ex 38.21). They are subdivided into *minor sections* by פ or ס (e.g. Gn 1.6; 3.16).

d Observations of various kinds compiled by the massoretes may be found either in the margin of every page (*Masora marginalis*) or at the end of each book or of the entire Bible (*Masora finalis*). The standard editions provide only part of these notes. (See H. Hyvernat, "Petite introduction à l'étude de la Massore," *RB* 9 [1902] 551-61; 10 [1903] 529-49; 11 [1904] 521-46; 12 [1905] 203-34)(1). The words of this technical terminology are Post-Biblical Hebrew or Aramaic; they are often written as abbreviations.

אוֹת *letter*; אֶלָּא *except, if not*; אֶמְצַע *middle*; אַתְנָח סוֹף פָּסוּק = אס״ף e.g., Ez 17.15 קמץ בלא אס״ף i.e. "one has a qameṣ here although there is no *atnaḥ* or *sof pasuq*."

ב׳ (as a numerical sign) *two*, e.g. ב׳ טְעָמִים *two accents*; בָּתַר *after*; דָּגוּשׁ, f. דְּגוּשָׁה *which has a dagesh* (or a *mappiq*); דַּף *leaf, page*;

זְעֵיר, f. זְעֵירָא *small*;
חוֹל *profane*; חוּץ *outside of*; חָסֵר *deficiens, defectivus* (cf. § 7 *c*);
טַעַם *accent*; יַתִּיר *abundans, excessive*;
כָּאן *here*; כְּתִיב (§ *e*); לֵית = ל׳ (from לָא אִית) *there is not, non est*;
מָלֵא *full*; *plene scriptus* (§ 7 *c*); מִקְרָא *the Bible*; מִקְצָת *part*;
נוּסְחָא אַחֲרִינָא = נ״א *another version*; pl. נוּסְחָן אַחֲרִינָן *other versions*;
נָח, f. נָחָה *quiescent* (i.e. not pronounced); נִקּוּד *point*; נָקוּד *pointed*;
סְפָרִים אֲחֵרִים = ס״א *other books* or *copies*; סְבִיר *conjecture*;
סִימָן (σημεῖον) *symbol, mnemonic word*; סְכוּם *counted, number*;
סוֹף פָּסוּק *end of verse*;
פִּסְקָא *separation, interval* (in many cases it indicates a lacuna);
קְרֵי = ק׳ (§ *e*); קודם or better קֳדָם *before*; קָמוּץ, f. קְמוּצָה *which has a qameṣ*; קָמֵץ בְּזָקֵף (§ 32 *f*); רַבָּתִי, רַבְּתָא *large*;
תֵּיבָה *word* (as consising of letters); תִּקּוּן *correction*; תְּרֵי *two*.

(1) The following are essential tools for a study of the Massorah: C.D. Ginsburg, *The Massorah Compiled from Manuscripts, Alphabetically and Lexically Arranged*, 4 vols. (London, 1880-1905; repr. New York, 1975); G.E. Weil, *Massorah Gedolah juxta codicem Leningradensem B 19a*, vol. I (Rome, 1971).

e **Qre-ktiv.** The most important massoretic notes are those which relate to *Qre* and *Ktiv*. The קְרֵי (Aramaic passive participle: *lectum*, or here *legendum*) is the reading which, according to the massoretes, must be read; the כְּתִיב (Arm. passive ptc.: *scriptum*) is the reading which emerges from the consonantal text. The Qre is indicated by a small circle above the word, referring to a marginal note where the consonants to be read are indicated; the vowels of the Qre are those of the text. The Ktiv is represented only by the consonants of the text, whereas the vowels are not indicated, and need to be reconstructed from the form of the word and the context. Thus in Ru 3.3 one finds וְשַׂמְתְּי and in the margin ושמת ק׳, i.e. the Qre is וְשַׂמְתְּ, the normal form of the second pers. f., whilst the Ktiv is וְשַׂמְתְּי, an archaic form. Where a word of the text must not be read, its vocalisation is left out and a note is appended, saying כתיב ולא קרי *written, but not read*, e.g. Ru 3.12 אם. Conversely, if a word must be added in the reading, the vowels of that word are found written in the text, the consonants being indicated in a note, e.g. in Ru 3.17 one finds אָמַר _ .. and the note אלי קרי ולא כתיב "אֵלַי must be read, though it is not written."

The *Qre-Ktiv* is always concerned with the consonantal text; it represents two variants of the consonantal text. Very often the Qre gives a reading preferable to that of the Ktiv, but there are cases where the Ktiv is as good as or even better than the Qre. The fact is that the Qre does not always pretend to give the best reading in itself, but the best among the manuscripts(1). Frequently the Ktiv preserves archaic forms(2).

(1) Indeed the manuscripts vary considerably; the total number of Qre/ktiv pairs moves between 800 and 1,500.

(2) The LXX sometimes agrees with K, sometimes with Q; no clear picture emerges from Dead Sea MSS, either. On the whole question of Qre/ktiv, see I. Yeivin, *Introduction* [op. cit., § 14 *a*, n.], pp. 56-61; idem, entry "Qre uxtiv," *EB*, vol. 7 (Jerusalem, 1976), cols. 262-65; R. Gordis, *The Biblical Text in the Making: A Study of the Kethib-Qere* (Philadelphia, 1937).

f **Qre perpetuum.** For some common words which must be read differently than indicated by the consonantal text, one finds that, for the sake of economy, the marginal note indicating the consonants of the Qre is omitted. This applies to the following words:

1) the divine name יְהוָה: the Qre is אֲדֹנָי *the Lord*, whilst the Ktiv is probably(1) יַהְוֶה (according to ancient witnesses). [One may note that in the word יְהוָה one has an unusual simple shewa instead of ḥaṭef pataḥ of אֲדֹנָי]. If the name יהוה is already preceded by the word אֲדֹנָי, יְהוִה is written[2]): the Qre is אֱלֹהִים. Of course the vocalisation of particles etc. before יהוה presupposes the pronunciation of the Qre אֲדֹנָי: thus the preposition מִן becomes מֵ' before the guttural, e.g. מֵיהוה = מֵאֲדֹנָי (§ 103 *d*). Likewise, for instance, instead of לָמָּה one spells לָ֫מָּה יהוה, namely לָ֫מָּה אֲדֹנָי (§ 37 *d*).

2) The pronoun of the 3rd pers. sg.f. הִוא in the Pentateuch: the Qre is הִיא, the Ktiv הוּא (§ 39 *c*).

3) The feminine substantive נַעֲרָ *girl* in the Pentateuch (instead of the normal נַעֲרָה, which one finds only in Dt 22.19). This is probably an orthographical oddity (like הִוא): it is not found in the Samaritan Pentateuch. It seems rather unlikely that נַ֫עַר was ever used in the sense of *girl*, for one would expect נְעָרִים in the plural; yet one finds in fact נְעָרוֹת (cf. Gn 24.61; Ex 2.5).

4) For יְרוּשָׁלַ֫ם the Qre is probably יְרוּשָׁלַ֫יִם, the Ktiv probably יְרוּשָׁלֵם

Jerusalem(3).

5) The proper noun *Yiśśåḇår* is written יִשָּׂשכָר to ensure the pronunciation יִשָּׂכָר (Gn 30.18 etc.), whilst Ben Naphtali read the first sibilant as שְׂ with shewa and the second as שָׂ with qameṣ.

6) For שְׁנֵים, שְׁתֵּים *two*, cf. § 100 *c* and *g*.

(1) In our translations, we have used *Yahweh*, a form widely accepted by scholars, instead of the traditional *Jehovah*.

In Codex L. the usual form is יְהוָה, based on the Aramaic שְׁמָא *the name*, i.e. the Divine Name, but rarely יְהֹוָה (e.g. Ex 3.2).

(2) There are considerable variations between manuscripts in this regard: אֲדֹנָי יְהֹוִה (e.g. Ez 5.5 in Cod. L and A, but אדני יְהוִה in Cod. C); אדני יֱהוִה (e.g. Gn 15.2,8 in Cod. L), though they all agree in adding ḥireq under the Waw.

(3) In five cases the name of the city is spelled plene with Yod: Jer 26.18; Esth 2.6; 1Ch 3.5; 2Ch 25.1, 32.9.

Lectiones mixtae. Some forms have a strange vocalisation which suggests that the vocalisers wanted to indicate thereby two possible vocalisations(1). Thus the vocalisation of יִרַדֹּף Ps 7.6 indicates that one can read it either as Qal יִרְדֹּף or Piel יְרַדֵּף. This hypothesis of *lectiones mixtae* allows us to explain in a plausible manner some forms the vocalisation of which is otherwise unjustifiable(2). *g*

(1) Cf. E. Kautzsch, *Hebr. Gramm.*[27] (p. V; this important observation has disappeared from the 28th ed.); König, I, p. 160; Berg., I, § 4 *b*.

(2) Cf. § 75 *g* תְּהַלַּךְ, § 89 *j* וְיִלַּדְתְּ, § 91 *b* כִּכְּרִים.

It remains to point out certain **minor peculiarities** of our massoretic text, the significance of which is not always apparent, and which for that reason are partly neglected by the editors. *h*

1) *external points* placed over some consonants, e.g. Gn 16.5 over the second yod of וּבֵינֶיךָ, or over entire words, e.g. Gn 33.4. These points all seem to require deletion of the letter or letters so marked, as is the case with Dead Sea manuscripts(1).

2) The *majuscule letters*, e.g. Gn 1.1, Ct 1.1, Lv 11.42 (ו indicating the middle point of the Pentateuch), and *minuscule letters*, e.g. Gn 2.4.

3) The *suspended letters*, e.g. Jdg 18.30, Ps 80.14 (ע indicating the middle point of the Psalms).

4) Finally some letters written in an unusual manner for some obscure reason.

(1) See M. Martin, *The Scribal Character of the Dead Sea Manuscripts* (Louvain, 1958),

vol. 1, pp. 154-60.

[PHONETICS]

§ 17. Changes occurring to consonants

a **Consonant added** at the beginning of a word: *prosthetic Alef*. An initial Alef (not pronounced in reality) with its vowel is sometimes added in order to facilitate the pronunciation: e.g. אֶתְמוֹל *yesterday* (five times) alongside תְּמוֹל (23 x), אֶזְרוֹעַ *arm* (2 x) alongside the usual זְרוֹעַ(1). The same phonetic phenomenon is observable in our own languages, e.g. in Vulgar Latin *iscientia, istare, estatio, Estephanus*; Engl. *especially, esquire, estate*; Fr. *esprit, espérer*. Very rarely one has an Alef forming an open half-syllable, e.g. אֲבַטִּחִים *melons* (Ar. *biṭṭīḫ*); cf. § 88 L *a*.

(1) The initial vowel ę was probably adopted because ę was felt to be the weakest vowel in this position; cf. § 9 *c* on ֱ as a very weak *ḥaṭef*; § 21 *i* on ֱ as weaker than ֲ, and § 68 *a*, n. Then one could perhaps explain the ḥaṭef pataḥ of אֲמַרְכֶם, אֲכָל־מִמֶּנּוּ, אֲכָלְכֶם with a maqqef as due to the secondary stress which comes on it (see also the pair אֱלֵי *towards* and אֲלֵיכֶם *towards you*), but there are exceptions such as Ex 18.12 לֶאֱכָל־לֶחֶם etc. On the likelihood that the initial Alef was not actually pronounced, see K. Levy [§ 1 *a*, n.], p. כז (p. 24*).

b **Metathesis**. In the *Hithpael* conjugation, the /t/ is interchanged with an immediately following sibilant, e.g. /*hit-šammẹr/ > הִשְׁתַּמֵּר *to guard oneself*. Thus one avoids the clusters *ts, tš*, and *tṣ*, which already were not allowable in Proto-Semitic (cf. § 53 *e*).

However, in view of the existence of infixed *t* conjugations in various Semitic languages, even in an idiom as close to Hebrew as Moabite, it is not impossible that what happens in Hitpael is not genuine metathesis, namely a universal phonetic phenomenon, but a conditioned residue of an earlier *t*-infixed conjugation. Note also the absence of such metathesis outside of the verb conjugation in general, its confinement to the Hitpael in particular, and the existence of roots such as נתשׁ, תֵּשַׁע *nine*, Arm. כתשׁ.

From a lexicographical point of view one can sometimes observe metathesis. For example, alongside the usual כֶּבֶשׂ *lamb* (107 x) and כִּבְשָׂה

(female) lamb (8 x) one encounters כֶּ֫שֶׂב (13 x) and כִּשְׂבָּה (1 x); and alongside שִׂמְלָה *dress* (30 x) one finds שַׂלְמָה (16 x).

Consonant dropped. The phenomenon is frequent in Hebrew, whether at the beginning (*aphaeresis*), in the middle (*syncope*), or at the end of a word (*apocope*). The consonants which can be dropped are notably the two vocalic consonants, /w/ and /y/, the two weak gutturals, /'/ and /h/, as well as /n/ (which in Hebrew tends to assimilate), and rarely /l/. *c*

Aphaeresis. An initial consonant *w*, *y*, *n*, *l*, or ' without a full vowel can drop out: e.g. in the פ"י verbs, Impv. שֵׁב; in the פ"נ verbs, Impv. גַּשׁ; in the verb לָקַח *to take*, Impv. קַח; in place of the usual אֲנַ֫חְנוּ *we* we have נַ֫חְנוּ six times. *d*

Syncope. *h* (usually intervocalic, diachronically at least) is ordinarily syncopated in the causative conjugations in the future and the participle, e.g. יַקְטִיל for *יְהַקְטִיל (§ 54 *a*). Likewise in the reflexive (Hitpael), in the third person suffix pronouns (*hu*, *hęm*, *hęn*, thus בָּנוּ, בָּם for בָּהֶם, יַקְטְלֵם, קִבְּצָן, and in the theophoric element -יְהוֹ as in יוֹנָתָן for יְהוֹנָתָן. The ה of the definite article is syncopated after the prepositions ב, כ, and ל, e.g. לַמֶּ֫לֶךְ for *לְהַמֶּ֫לֶךְ (§ 35 *e*). *e*

' is quite often syncopated, but is generally retained in the spelling in certain forms, e.g. לִקְרַאת *towards* for *לִקְרַ֫אַת; מוּם *defect* for *מְאוּם (2 x מאום)(1).

(1) Cf. Kutscher, *Isaiah*, pp. 498-500.

Apocope. Apocope is frequent in the verbal and nominal forms of the ל"ה roots, e.g. וַיַּ֫עַן *and he answered* (Root: ענה) for וַיַּעֲנֶה (1 x); לְמַ֫עַן *on account of* for *לְמַעֲנֶה. *f*

Diachronically speaking, the feminine singular suffix /t/ or /at/ also belongs here, though it is still retained in the construct and related forms: e.g. מַלְכַּת *queen of* and שְׁמָרַ֫תּוּ (< שְׁמָרַתְהוּ) *she kept him.*

Assimilation. The consonant *n* without a vowel tends to assimilate to the following consonant, which is then doubled, e.g. the *n* of the preposition מִן; thus מִן + שָׁם > מִשָּׁם *from there*, מִן + זֶה > מִזֶּה *from this, from here*. The phenomenon is regularly observed in verbal and nominal forms of פ"נ roots, e.g. יִגַּשׁ for *יִנְגַּשׁ from נגשׁ (for details, cf. § 72)(1). *g*

Assimilation does not take place in verbs with an *n* as the third radical, e.g. שָׁכַ֫נְתְּ *you have inhabited*; תֶּאֱמַ֫נָּה for תֶּאֱמַנְנָה; תֵּעָגֵ֫נָה for

תְּעַנֵּנָּה; נָתַתָּה *you have given* is an exception (no doubt due to the initial נ).

The ת of the preformative הִתְ assimilates to a following dental, e.g. /*mitdạbbẹr/ > מִדַּבֵּר; /*hitṭạmmå'/ > הִטַּמָּא. It also partially assimilates to the emphatic *ṣ*, i.e. it becomes an emphatic *ṭ*, e.g., /*hitṣạddẹq/ becomes (with possible metathesis, § *b*) הִצְטַדֵּק (cf. § 53 *e*).

l is assimilated in the verb לָקַח, e.g. יִקַּח (§ 72 *j*).

d is assimilated in אַחַת *one* (f.), from /*'aḥadt/ (§ 100 *b*).

h is assimilated to the preceding *t* or *n*: e.g. *שְׁלָחַתְהוּ > שְׁלָחַתּוּ *she sent him* (§ 62 *d*) and *אֵינֶנְהוּ > אֵינֶנּוּ (§ 61 *f*).

(1) For עֵז *goat*, the root ענז, which does not appear in Hebrew, can be inferred only on the basis of comparison with cognate languages, e.g. Arab. *'anz*; cf. § 96 A *o*.

§ 18. Doubling of consonants

a **Doubling** or **prolongation of** consonants. Although the differences in the time required to articulate a consonant are much less perceptible than in the case of vowels, one can easily distinguish at least two quantities of a consonant. When a consonant is prolonged, the implosion and explosion are separated by a noticeable interval, creating the impression of a double consonant(1). A long or doubled consonant is usually transcribed by repeating the letter concerned(2), e.g. אַפּוֹ /'ap-pọ/, but this has the disadvantage that it can give rise to the mistaken belief that the consonant is repeated, when in fact one is dealing with a single consonant. It would be logical to indicate a long consonant in the same way as a long vowel, namely by means of a macron, i.e. a horizontal stroke over the letter concerned, e.g. *'ạp̄ọ* or the use of a colon as in *'ạp:ọ*. But in fact we do not know what the precise meaning of dagesh forte was. In conclusion we may say that phonetically we are not dealing with full repetition of a consonant, whereas morphophonemically the phenomenon is equivalent to a cluster of consonants in the middle of a word with no vowel intervening, as can be shown by comparison of a Piel form, say, יִסֵּר *he chastised* with a related Pilpel form such as טִלְטֵל *he hurled*.

(1) P.J. Rousselot, *Principes de phonétique expérimentale* (Paris, 1902), p. 993; P.E. Passy, *Petite phonétique comparée des principales langues européennes* (Leipzig, [2]1912),

§ 144ff. See also J. Cantineau in *BSL* 46 (1950) 105f. This widely practised mode of pronouncing dageshed consonants is analogous to the articulation of Italian *Boccaccio* or Japanese *Hokkaido*. Plosives or stops cannot be doubled or lengthened in the same way as, say, sibilants, liquids or nasals can.

(2) The English double-letter as in *sitting* is an orthographic device to indicate the shortness of the preceding vowel in contrast to, e.g. *siting*. So Germ. *Haffen* "lakes" (the pl.dat. of *Haff*) vs. *Hafen* "harbour," and Dutch *bomen* "trees" vs. *bommen* "bombs."

The gemination is phonemic as can be shown by such contrasting minimal pairs as מִלָּה *word* vs. מִילָה *circumcision*, מִנִּי *from* (poetic) vs. מִינִי *my kind*, עֻלָּהּ *her yoke* vs. עוּלָהּ *her sucking child*. aa

In addition to this genuine gemination indicated by dagesh forte, Hebrew also has **virtual** gemination, which may be better called *semi-gemination* or *weak gemination*(1), e.g. in שִׁחֵת *he has corrupted* (Piel of שחת), הַיְלָדִים *the children*. In these examples the morphological rule would require doubling: /*šiḥ-ḥeṯ/, /*hą̄y-ylå̄ḏim/. In fact, gemination in the ordinary sense of the term has not taken place, but the vowel is what one would expect if it did take place, namely the occurrence of a vowel which is characteristic of a sharp syllable. It is generally supposed that gemination did exist at an earlier stage, and that this gave rise to the vowels characteristic of sharp syllables, but that subsequently the gemination was suspended, without change to those vowels, and in spite even of the fact that the syllable now appears to be open. According to this explanation, gemination is now non-existent, though its force is still there. But if gemination is now non-existent, one must now have a vowel characteristic of open syllables, e.g. שֵׁחֵת*(2). If the vowel typical of sharp syllables has been retained, there must indeed be a certain gemination, some kind of lengthening of the consonant(3). This seems to have been much more frequently the case in cases of spontaneous virtual gemination of a guttural (e.g. אַחִים, § 20 *c*), where one can hardly postulate an earlier genuine gemination(4). The consonant only slightly lengthened is not really long, since then one should have a dagesh in the guttural; it could not be short either, for then the syllable would be open and the vowel would be one appropriate for open syllables; therefore the consonant concerned must be intermediate in length. In order graphically to indi- b cate this phenomenon one could transcribe, e.g. /hạylå<u>d</u>im/ or /hạy^{ye}-lå<u>d</u>im/.

(1) Cf. E. Gismondi, *Linguae hebraicae grammatica*², § 16 "mitior reduplicatio."

(2) This argument presupposes that there is a close relationship between vowel and syllable (cf. § 28 *a*).

(3) For the case of a final consonant, cf. § *l*.

(4) But cf. § 98 *b* 2.

From Biblical Aramaic, in which there is virtual gemination as in Hebrew, it emerges that this gemination was not null, but a semi-gemination, a length of intermediate degree. As a matter of fact, this virtual gemination, like the strong gemination, can be resolved into *n* + consonant. Just as יִדַּע* and מַדַּע* are resolved into יִנְדַּע and מַנְדַּע respectively, a form such as לְהֶעָלָה *to make enter* (Hafel inf. of עלל) can be resolved into לְהַנְעָלָה (Dn 4.3).

c **Strong gemination** (indicated by dagesh forte) can be *essential* or *euphonic* (§ *h*)(1). Essential gemination occurs in the following cases:

1) when a consonant is followed *immediately* by the same consonant, e.g. /nåtạn/ + /nu/ = נָתַ֫נּוּ (between the two *n*'s there is no vocalic element); /kårạt/ + /ti/ = כָּרַ֫תִּי (§ 42 *e*).

2) when there is assimilation as in יִתֵּן for /yintẹn/.

3) when gemination is required by the very nature of the form: thus in Piel verb forms such as קִטֵּל, קֻטַּל, הִתְקַטֵּל; in associated noun forms like קַטָּל, קִטּוֹל, קַטִּיל etc.

4) in the case of *spontaneous* gemination of a (non-guttural) consonant (§ *d*).

(1) These ancient terms (*dagesh necessarium, d. euphonicum*), which are retained here, are rather unsatisfactory: *necessary* here is in no way an antonym of *optional*, and among the *necessary* dageshs, all (except the third, which is organic), are due to *euphony*. In some manuscripts one finds still further kinds of dagesh of later invention which one can call *emphatic* (cf. S.D. Luzzatto, *Prolegomeni ad una grammatica ragionata della lingua ebraica* [Padova, 1836], pp. 197f.).

d **Spontaneous gemination** of a (non-guttural) consonant. This gemination is called *spontaneous* because it appears not to have any extrinsic cause, unlike doubling due to assimilation, or any intrinsic cause as in the case of the doubling in the intensive forms(1).

(1) D. Sivan, "Problematic lengthening in North West Semitic spellings of the middle of the second millennium B.C.E.," *UF* 18 (1986) 301-12 discusses consonant lengthening which is not grammatically conditioned in Akkadian of Syria-Palestine. However, the factors occasioning such a lengthening appear to be different in BH.

Spontaneous gemination regularly takes place with the non-final consonant (with the exception of the gutturals and ר), which follows a primitive short vowel /u/. Thus an adjective of the primitive pattern /*'agul/ (Heb. עָגֹל) *round* becomes in the fem. עֲגֻלָּה (and not עֲגֹלָה*)(1), in the pl. עֲגֻלִּים; likewise אָדֹם *red*, אֲדֻמָּה; עָמֹק *deep*, עֲמֻקָּה. So it is that the passive form of the Qal, which originally was /*qutal/, became in Hebrew קֻטַּל, a form which has the same shape as the passive Piel form קֻטַּל (§ 58 *a*). e

If the non-final consonant is a guttural or ר, which cannot be doubled, the short /u/ becomes /ọ/ in an open syllable as in /*gabuh/ (Heb. גָּבֹהַּ) *high* changing in the fem. to גְּבֹהָה.

It can be seen that /ọ/ cannot be maintained in an open syllable except before a guttural or ר. (But a secondarily restored /ọ/ is attested, e.g. in יִקְטֹלוּ in pause, and even in יִקְטֹלוּן before a pause, § 32 *d*)(2). It follows from this that a ֵ in an open syllable before a non-guttural consonant was historically long, e.g. קֹטֵל (*qātil* form); מְחֹלָה *dance* from the root חול.

(1) The Phoenician name of the Etruscan city of Caere (today Cerveteri located to the south of Lake Bracciano about 50km to the NW of Rome) is transliterated Ἄγυλλα, Lat. Agylla (= *the round-shaped*). Gemination, therefore, must have also existed in Phoenician.

(2) Certain adjectives of the pattern קָטוֹל, e.g. גָּדוֹל *large* were originally of the pattern *qatul*; the *ọ* was secondarily lengthened for particular reasons (cf. § 88 D *c*).

Spontaneous gemination occurs quite frequently after the vowel *a* as in גָּמָל *camel*, pl. גְּמַלִּים(1); עַקְרָב *scorpion*, pl. עַקְרַבִּים; שָׁפָן *jerboa*, pl. שְׁפַנִּים; many nouns of the pattern מַקְטָל, e.g. מַעֲמַקִּים *deep places*, § 96 C *b*. Note the adjective קָטָן *small*, קְטַנִּים, קְטַנָּה; the parallel form קָטֹן has no feminine or plural (§ 99 *d*). One can also observe spontaneous gemination in monosyllabic nouns with a final vowel such as הֲדַס *myrtle*, pl. הֲדַסִּים; זְמַן* *time*, pl. זְמַנִּים; אֲגַם *marshland*, pl. אֲגַמִּים. f

(1) *Camēlus* (κάμηλος) is sometimes written, in a post-classical period, *camellus* (cf. Ital. *cammello* with two spontaneous geminations!).

Spontaneous gemination is attested rather infrequently after the vowel *i*, e.g. in אִסָּר *obligation* (of the *qitāl* pattern); with suf. g

אֶסָּרָה(1). It also occurs after a secondary *i* (stemming from *a*) in the formation קִטָּלוֹן (from *qatalān*), e.g. זִכָּרוֹן *remembrance*, cst. זִכְרוֹן (§ 88 M *b*).

On the virtual spontaneous gemination of the guttural ח, see § 20 *c*.

(1) Here also belong forms such as Jdg 5.7 חָדֵ֫לּוּ and the demonstrative pron. pl. אֵ֫לֶּה. Most cases of spontaneous doubling can, it seems, be accounted for by assuming that originally a stress preceded the consonant now doubled: so Lambert, § 74.

h Amongst the **euphonic** geminations, one may distinguish especially the **conjunctive** gemination (or conjunctive dagesh) and the **dirimens** or **separating** gemination (or dagesh)(§ *k*). The conjunctive dagesh is caused by the close or very close juncture of two words(1). One must distinguish two cases, that of *dḥiq* and that of *mẹrạḥiq* (§ *j*).

(1) This is a sandhi phenomenon, unique in that Dagesh occurs word-initially, whilst the normal dagesh forte appears after a vowel.

There is some doubt whether this is a genuine gemination or not: see Berg., I, § 10 *o*, *p*, and N.H. Tur-Sinai, *The Language and the Book*, the *Language* vol. [Heb] (Jerusalem, 1954), p. 173. The former, however, seems to go too far in saying that the begadkefat with such a dagesh is not meant to be pronounced hard. Cf. Ps 30.10 מַה־בֶּצַע transcribed μεββεσε in the Secunda of the Hexapla.

i *Dḥiq* (Aram. דְּחִיק), i.e. *compressed* (the vowel is, so to speak, *compressed* between the two words). The necessary conditions for a *dḥiq* to occur are as follows:

1) The final vowel of the first word must be either ֶ (in fact always with the *mater lectionis* ה) or ָ /å/ following a shewa "mobile" (in fact always with ה).

2) The stress of the first word must be mil'ra, but it disappears on account of the very close juncture with the following word, which is marked by maqqef or, more rarely, by a conjunctive accent.

3) The stress of the second word must be on the first syllable. Examples: לְכָה־נָּא /lḫån-nå'/ *come then*; נַכֶּה־בּוֹ /nạkkẹb-bọ'/ *we shall strike him* (Nu 22.6).

In words lacking primary stress such as לְכָה, נַכֶּה the qameṣ in this position must have an open variety, /ọ/, like the /ẹ/, which receives the same treatment (cf. § 6 *j*). The phenomenon does not take place with the close vowels /ẹ/(1) and /ọ/, and would not do so with a close variety of *a*, i.e. /ạ/.

Observations. 1) With זֶה gemination takes place irrespective of the stress, e.g. וְזֶה־פִּרְיָהּ "and behold its fruit" Nu 13.27 (the stress is on the second syllable). Therefore this case does not strictly belong here.

2) The case of מַה־ (with pataḥ) does not belong here; cf. § 37 *c*.

3) The details of the rules and exceptions are complicated; cf. S. Baer, *De primarum vocabulorum literarum dagessatione*, in his edition of *Liber Proverbiorum* (Leipzig, 1880), pp. vii-xv. Likewise for the *mẹrạḥiq*.

(1) Thus one always finds הִנֵּה־נָא (e.g. Gn 19.8), with one exception, in הִנֶּה־נָּא Gn 19.2 (var.: a conjunctive accent instead of maqqef). This example shows clearly the disinclination towards the euphonic gemination following the close vowel *ẹ*.

Mẹrạḥiq (abbreviated from Aram. אָתֵי מֵרַחִיק *coming from afar*), i.e. j
the stress coming from afar (for the stress of the first word is mil'el). The conditions required for *mẹrạḥiq* to occur are as follows:

1) The final vowel of the first word must be either ֶ (in fact always with the *mater lectionis* ה) or ָ /å/ (here with or without ה)(1).

2) The stress of the first word must be mil'el, whether by nature or by accident, namely because of the receding stress by virtue of the law of *nsiga*(2). The link with the following word must be close, but not too close; and also there is usually no maqqef, but merely a conjunctive accent.

3) The stress in the second word must be on the first syllable. Examples: חָפַצְתָּ בָּהּ /ḥåfạ'ṣtåb-båh'/ *you like it* Dt 21.14; הָיְתָה לּוֹ *she was his* 1Kg 2.15 (nsiga); עֹשֶׂה פְּרִי *fruit-bearing* Gn 1.11 (nsiga); שָׁבִיתָ שֶּׁבִי *you captured prisoners* Ps 68.19 (שֶׁבִי, a pausal form of שְׁבִי); לָמָּה זֶּה *why then?* (17 times without maqqef, 7 x with one). Qameṣ in this position must be an open variety, like seghol (cf. § *i*).

Observations 1) The principal difference between these two cases of euphonic dagesh is found in the stress of the first word. In the case of *dḥiq* the stress ought to be mil'ra, but it disappears; in the case of *mẹrạḥiq* it *is* or *becomes* mil'el.

2) The fact that qameṣ, though shortened, retains its affinity with /ọ/ instead of becoming /ạ/ (as in, e.g. עָם, עַם, עַמִּי; מָה, מַה־), shows that the phenomenon is of secondary origin(3).

(1) Exceptionally after /u/, e.g. Gn 19.14 קוּמוּ צְּאוּ; for more examples, see Lambert, § 78, n. 4, though not all the cases mentioned there are attested to in BHS.

(2) Cf. § 31 *c*. According to this law, the first recedes in order to avoid the coming

together of two stresses.

(3) A phenomenon analogous to the euphonic gemination of Hebrew can be adduced from a number of languages, e.g. the vernacular Arabic of Syria-Palestine: *qultu'llọ* (for *qult*[*u*] + *lọ*) "I said to him"; in contemporary French *tu l'as* is often pronounced *tu ll'as* (on the analogy of *il l'a*) cf. § 35 *b* n.

k **Dagesh dirimens** (or **separating** dagesh). Consonants within a word sometimes occur with this euphonic dagesh.

The gemination, together with the resultant shewa, produces something like a *separation* between the syllables. Thus, instead of עִנְבֵי*, which would be the expected form for the pl. cst. of עֵנָב *grapes*, one finds עִנְּבֵי, Lv 25.5; Dt 32.32. Likewise one has עִקְּבֵי Gn 49.17, pl. cst. of עָקֵב *a heel*. Cf. also 1Sm 1.6 הַרְּעִמָהּ.

Dagesh dirimens occurs especially with the liquid consonants *l*, *m*, *n*, with the sibilants, with the velar *q*, and especially before *b*, *p*, *r*. In contrast, one very often omits dagesh with these consonants; cf. § *m* 3. It is rare with the begadkefat where its purpose *can* be to avoid the fricative pronunciation, which would otherwise ensue, e.g. סֻבְּכוֹ (var. סֻבְכוֹ) Jer 4.7.

l **Omission of dagesh forte.**

A) A dagesh forte which would be required by a consonant is omitted, if this consonant is word-final. Thus in the future Qal of the verb סָבַב *to encircle*, we find יָסֹבּוּ, but in the singular, יָסֹב; in the fut. Hif-il יָסֵבּוּ, but יָסֵב; in the fut. Qal of the verb קַל *to be light* (from the root קלל) we find יֵקַלּוּ, but, in the singular, יֵקַל; in the case of the substantive derived from the root עמם we find עַמִּי *my people*, but עַם, and, with a disjunctive accent, עָם(1).

The vowels ◌ַ and ◌ֶ (esp. ◌ַ), which often occur in this position, indicate at least a tendency of the consonant towards gemination or slight lengthening (cf. § *b*). This would account for the fact that the vowels ◌ַ and ◌ֶ are retained in place of ◌ָ and ◌ֵ, which one would expect, e.g. in עַם alongside עָם (with a disjunctive accent) and הָעָם; צַו apocopated Impv. from צַוֵּה (as against, e.g. אֱלָיו, עָנָו); the words such as מְעַט (pl. מְעַטִּים); בַּת from **bint*, § 98 *d* (as against, e.g. אָב); אֱמֶת from *'*amint*; כַּרְמֶל, with suf. כַּרְמִלּוֹ.

(1) On the dagesh forte in אַתְּ *'at* (§ 8 *d*, n.) and נָתַתְּ *nātat*, see § 39 *a*, n. 4.

m B) A dagesh forte which would have been demanded by a consonant followed by shewa "mobile" is often omitted, no doubt because in some cases there was a disinclination to make a long consonant depend on such a weak vowel. This is therefore a case of semi-gemination or weak gemination (§ *b*).

The suspension of strong gemination, in other words, the shortening of the long consonant into an intermediate one before a shewa, occurs especially in the following cases:

1) Mainly in an initial י: *a*) always in the Future after the strong Waw (וַ), e.g. וַיְקַטֵּל (§ 47 *a*), וַיְהִי; *b*) in the nouns after the definite article, e.g. הַיְלָדִים, so long as the second consonant is not ה or ע, e.g. הַיְהוּדִים, הַיְעֵפִים (§ 35 *c*).

2) Regularly with an initial מ of the Piel and Pual participle after the definite article, e.g. הַמְבַקֵּשׁ (perhaps in order to avoid two dagesh's) (§ 35 *c*).

3) Often in the liquids ל, מ, and נ, the sibilants, and the velar ק. (However, in these same consonants one often finds *dagesh dirimens*, cf. § *k*). Examples: הִנְנִי (in pause הִנֵּנִי); הַלֲלוּ (for the ḥaṭef pataḥ, cf. § 9 *c*); מִלְמַעְלָה *from above* (but מִלְמַטָּה *from below*); בִּקְשָׁה etc. (often with this verb בִּקֵּשׁ; even after an initial omission of the dagesh in הַמְבַקְשִׁים, Ex 4.19; Jer 11.21); יִשְׂאוּ (Fut. of נָשָׂא *to carry*); כִּסְאִי from כִּסֵּא *throne*; הַצְפַרְדְּעִים Ex 7.29; הַשְׁפַתַּיִם Ez 40.43.

4) In the Waw, e.g. עִוְרִים (sg. עִוֵּר *blind*)(1).

(1) Thus only *ṭ* and the Begadkefat sounds do not allow of the omission of gemination under any circumstances. This is further possible evidence for the case that the apparent dagesh forte with these plosives may in reality be dagesh lene, at least under the phonetic conditions in which the remaining sounds may give up dagesh, and that this points to the first stage of phonematisation of the six fricatives. See above § 5 *q*, n.

§ 19. Spirantisation of the consonants begadkefat

The twofold pronunciation of the *begadkefat* has been mentioned in a
§ 5 *o*; we have spoken about the *soft dagesh*, a sign of the plosive pronunciation, § 10, and about the *rafé*, a sign of the spirantised or fricative pronunciation, § 12(1).

(1) On this complex issue, cf. W. von Soden, "Die Spirantisierung von Verschlusslauten im Akkadischen: Ein Vorbericht," *JNES* 27 (1968) 214-20.

b **The law of the begadkefat.** A *begadkefat* consonant retains its primary plosive value if it is not preceded by any vocalic element; it becomes spirantised or fricative (1) if it is preceded by a vowel, whether full or ḥaṭef, (2) if the initial consonant of a word has a simple shewa (e.g. כְּתֹב *Write!*), (3) if it follows a word-medial consonant with a shewa which has resulted from the deletion of a vowel in the course of inflection (e.g. כָּתְבוּ < כָּתַב; יִכְתְּבוּ < יִכְתֹּב)(1).

In addition, there are some important categories of spirantisation, which may be explained in terms of morphological pressure or inflectional influence. These are cases where a *begadkefat* consonant is spirantised despite an immediately preceding simple shewa. Thus the cst. of נְדָבָה is נִדְבַת with [v]; 2m.pl. Imperative כִּתְבוּ with [v], derivable from כְּתֹב; the inf. cst. with a proclitic בּ, בִּנְפֹל with [f]; the 2nd person pronominal suffix always with [ḫ] as in דְּבַרְכֶם *your word*, probably influenced by a form such as אָבִיךָ *your father* or אֲבֹתֶיךָ *your fathers* (pl. noun), or with a verb, יִשְׁמָרְךָ [yišmọrḫå] *he will keep you*; the plural of so-called segholate nouns as in מַלְכֵי *kings of* (§ 96 A *b*), possibly influenced by מְלָכִים(2).

This law is based on the natural tendency towards inertia. The plosive emission of a begadkefat requires at its onset the closure of the organs of speech, whilst the spirant emission carries with it a measure of aperture. On the other hand, the emission of any vowel leads to an appreciable opening up of the organs of speech. After a vowel, the organs which have the open position necessarily have less effort to make in order to take the position of less opening required by a spirant than the position of closure required by a plosive(3).

(1) The shewa in the last two categories is the so-called "shewa mobile." On a seeming exception to (1), see § 100 *c*.

(2) This is a synchronic description. A diachronic approach might lead to a different interpretation.

(3) Cf. E. Sievers, *Metrische Studien* (Leipzig, 1901), vol. I, p. 15, n. 1.

c At the beginning of a word a begadkefat is plosive if the word is at the very beginning of an utterance or if the preceding word ends in a consonant. If the preceding word ends in a vowel it becomes spirant if there is a juncture, but it is plosive if there is a separation (a disjunctive accent). Compare, e.g. וַיְהִי־כֵן Gn 1.7 and וַיְהִי כַּאֲשֶׁר Jdg 11.5

(*zåqef gådọl*).

The quiescent א, ה, ו, and י do not, of course, prevent spirantisa- *d*
tion. But ו and י, when pronounced (cf. § 7 *d*), generally do prevent spirantisation, which proves their consonantal character, e.g. יָדָיו תְּבִיאֶינָה Lv 7.30; עָלַי פִּיהֶם Ps 22.14. Similarly within a word, e.g. שָׁלַוְתִּי Job 3.26.

Exception. Spirantisation does not take place in the initial begad- *e*
kefat of the groups בב, בפ, כב after a vowel, e.g. וַיְהִי בְּבוֹאָהּ Jdg 1.14. Two similar or analogous spirants are thus avoided.

In certain cases the plosive realisation of the begadkefat conso- *f*
nants is built into a morphological or lexical pattern. Thus a begadkefat as R2 (= second root letter) in the Qal future is always plosive if preceded by a simple shewa: e.g. יִכְתֹּב. Likewise in singular segholate nouns with a pronominal suffix: e.g. מַלְכִּי *my king* (but מַלְכֵיהֶם *their kings*).

At the end of a word-form, unlike דִּבַּרְכֶם mentioned above (§ *b*), the Taw of the second person Past ending is always pronounced hard if preceded by a shewa: e.g. כָּתַבְתְּ(1).

(1) On seeming exceptions such as שָׁלַחַתְּ, see § 5 *q*, n.

§ 20. The guttural consonants (and ר) and gemination

The gutturals א, ה, ח, and ע (§ 5 *j-l*) were no doubt capable of ge- *a*
mination, namely doubled, at some stage, in Hebrew as in Semitic in general and as is still the case in Arabic. But at the stage of the history of Hebrew which concerns us the gutturals are never geminated(1). But like the non-guttural consonants they are capable of a weak gemination or *virtual* doubling (§ 18 *b*). This weak gemination is the vestige of an earlier full gemination, except in the case of the spontaneous gemination of ח (§ *c*). The lingual consonant ר can have neither full gemination (except in a very small number of cases, § 23 *a*) nor weak gemination(2).

A form with original full gemination of the guttural can, in Hebrew as we know it, either retain weak gemination, e.g. in the future Pi. יְבַעֵר *it will consume*, or not retain any gemination at all, as in the Pi. infinitive בָּעֵר. The reason why virtual gemination is found at times, but no gemination at all at other times, as illustrated by the above-given two examples, is not clear. In the type יֵעָמֵד (Nif. future of first guttural verbs) one never finds virtual gemination (§ 68 *c*).

The tendency of the gutturals to virtual gemination is rather uneven. It is strong for ח, fairly so for ה, weak for ע, very weak for א, and nil for ר. The order of aptitude for gemination is then ח > ה > ע > א > ר.

(1) The dot in Alef in וַיָּבִיאּוּ in Gn 43.26; Ezr 8.18; תָּבִיאּוּ in Lv 23.17, and רֻאּוּ in Job 33.21 does not indicate doubling, but informs the reader that it is not a vowel letter, a practice known in biblical manuscripts with the Palestinian pointing system: cf. I. Yeivin, "Alef with a dagesh in the Bible" [in Heb.] in Y. Avishur & J. Blau (eds), *Studies in Bible and the Ancient Near East* [Fschr S.E. Loewenstamm] (Jerusalem, 1978), pp. 223-27.

(2) The Yemenite and Babylonian traditions did know of the gemination of ר; see Yeivin, *Babylonian Tradition*, pp. 351-55, and for the literature, ib., p. 355.

b When there is virtual gemination, the syllable is deemed closed, and its vowels are those typical of closed sharp syllables, e.g. in יְבַעֵר as in יְקַטֵּל. When there is no virtual gemination, the syllable is open, and its vowels are those typical of open syllables(1), namely ָ, ֵ, and ֹ. Examples with ר: in the Piel conjugation of the verb *to bless* one has, e.g. יְבָרֵךְ, בֵּרַךְ (pausal בֵּרֵךְ), בֹּרַךְ (cf. § 18 *e*).

(1) Therefore there is no place for talking of a *compensatory* lengthening of the vowel. Cf. § 6 *d*. In purely phonetic terms, however, the tradition preserved in the Secunda attests to long vowels in these forms, e.g. νηερθ נֵאַרְתָּה Ps 89.40; ηρφου חֵרְפוּ 89.52. For a discussion, see Brønno, *Morphologie*, pp. 68-70.

c **Spontaneous gemination of ח.** Like the non-guttural consonants (§ 18 *d*), the guttural ח occasionally receives spontaneous, virtual gemination. This property can hardly be explained in terms of weakening of full gemination, because it takes place in words in which the guttural does not require gemination. It is a secondary phenomenon, and is explicable in terms of the nature of the sound *ḥ* (§ 5 *k*). This gemination occurs:

1) in the plural of אָח *brother* (Arb. *'aḫ*) in st. abs. אַחִים *'aḥḥim* and with the light suffixes, e.g. אַחִי (P. אָחִי), אֶחָיו (for the ֶ, cf. § 29 *f*); cf. § 98 *b*.

2) in the singular of the numeral adjective אֶחָד *one*, f. אַחַת, which is of the pattern *qatal* (but pl. אֲחָדִים). Comp. Arb. *'aḥad*. Cf. § 100 *b*.

3) in the singular of the adjective אַחֵר *other*, which is of the pattern *qatil* (√ אחר), f. אַחֶרֶת (but pl. אֲחֵרִים, אֲחֵרוֹת).

4) in the preposition אַחַר *after* (§ 103 *n*), properly speaking st. cst. of a substantive of a pattern the st.abs. of which does not exist: √ اخر (but the preposition with the form of the st.cst.pl. is אַחֲרֵי).

5) in the noun מִבְטָח *confidence* with suffixes, e.g. מִבְטַחִי ; cf. § 96 C *b*.

§ 21. Influence of the guttural consonants on the vowels

The influence of the gutturals on vowels is considerable. The gutturals favour the vowel ַ, which is *homogeneous* to them; they tend to select it or approximate other vowels to the sound *a*. The degree of attraction by the gutturals of the vowel ַ is, in descending order, ע > ח > ה > א. a

The vowel ַ often supplants a primitive vowel *i* or *u* before a guttural closing a stressed syllable. Thus the future of the action verb שָׁלַח *to send* is, in context, יִשְׁלַח (instead of /*yišluḥ/); the Piel future is, in context, יְשַׁלַּח (instead of /*yešalliḥ/, P. יְשַׁלֵּחַ). The st. cst. of /*mizbiḥ/ is מִזְבַּח (abs. מִזְבֵּחַ *altar*). b

The vowel ַ **slips in furtively** before a guttural closing a stressed final syllable, after the vowels /ọ, i, u/, which are heterogeneous to gutturals and can never be supplanted, and also after the vowel /ẹ/, which, in certain circumstances, cannot be supplanted(1). This ַ, picturesquely called *furtive pataḥ*(2), is an extremely short /ạ/; it is used, in the context just described, as a consonant, i.e. it forms a centering diphthong with the preceding vowel, e.g. רוּחַ *spirit*(3); inf. cst. שְׁלֹחַ; שִׂיחַ. c

(1) There is no trace of this secondary vowel in the Secunda. Furthermore, א, which has become silent at the end of a word, never takes furtive pataḥ.

(2) In good ancient manuscripts this sign is written between the vowel and the final guttural or slightly to the left of the guttural.

(3) Brock., *GvG*, I, p. 198; BL, p. 169. In Spoken Arabic this same phenomenon exists, e.g. in the very same word /rūḥ/ *spirit*, and in *Go away!* in the vernacular, which is pronounced /rūạḥ/.

Before a guttural which closes an unstressed syllable (or considered closed), the primitive vowels *i* and *u* become in Hebrew ẹ and ọ, i.e. d they approach the sound ḁ (**partial assimilation**), e.g. /*yi'-šam/ > יֶאְשַׁם *he will render himself guilty*, /*yiḥ-zaq/ > יֶחְזַק *he will be strong*, /*mu'-mad/ > מָעֳמָד *positioned*(1); also וַיָּ֫נַח for either וַיָּ֫נַח* (Qal) or וַיַּ֫נַח* (Hifil) (§ 80 *k*); נֶחְמָד Nifal (§ 68 *c*).

Observation. Of course, a guttural has no influence on the vocalisation of a preceding syllable; thus a preceding shewa is not modified, e.g., שְׁחַט, שִׁלְחָה, פְּעָלִים (plural of פֹּ֫עַל), וְהָאָ֫רֶץ.

(1) Hofal participle. Contrast מָקְטָל, which is more frequent than מֻקְטָל (§ 57 *a*).

e **After a guttural** the influence of the guttural is much less.

In stressed closed syllables one often finds ◌ַ for primitive *i* and *u*, e.g. יִשְׁחַט *he will slaughter* for /*yišḥuṭ/, יִשְׁחֹט*; וַיָּ֫עַד for וַיָּ֫עֶד* (inverted Hif. future of עוד) *and he testified*.

In unstressed closed syllables ◌ֶ is quite often found for ◌ִ, e.g. in Hif. perfect of ל"ה verbs הֶגְלָה occurs alongside הִגְלָה; in nouns, e.g. חֶלְקִי (from חֵ֫לֶק *part*), עֶזְרִי (from עֵ֫זֶר *help*, variant feminine form עֶזְרָה); in verbs, e.g. חֶשְׂפִּי *strip* in Is 47.2 (with an anomalous dagesh); הִגָּיוֹן, cst. הֶגְיוֹן.

f After a guttural one has a *ḥaṭef* in those cases where a non-guttural consonant would have shewa, e.g. שָׁחֲטוּ: קָטְלוּ; עֲמֹד: קְטֹל.

Within a word the ḥaṭef is ordinarily ◌ֲ.

The simple shewa is retained after a guttural in a stressed syllable, e.g. שָׁמַ֫עְתָּ, whilst in an unstressed syllable, it changes to a ḥaṭef, so נַעֲרִי for /*nḁ'ri/, יֶאֱסֹף for /yę'sọf/, but יַחְשֹׁב (§ 68 *e*).

g At the beginning of a word, after ה, ח, or ע, one finds ◌ֲ for a primitive *a* and *i*, occasionally ◌ֱ for a primitive *i*, and ◌ֳ for a primitive *u*. Examples: חֲמוֹר *donkey* (from **ḥimār*, so still in Arb.); הֱקִימֹ֫תָ alongside 'הֲ from הֵקִים; חֳלִי *disease*, עֳנִי *poverty* (pattern *qutl*).

h At the beginning of a word, after א one has ◌ֲ for a primitive *a*; ◌ֱ for a primitive *i*; ◌ֳ for a primitive *u*. Examples: אֲבִי, st.cst. of אָב *father*; אֱלוֹהַּ, pl. אֱלֹהִים (Arb. /'ilāh/); אֳנִי *vessel* (pattern *qutl*). Note also אֱ in אֱנוֹשׁ *man* (from /*'unāš/ > /*'unọš/, whence, through dissimilation, /*'inọš/ > אֱנוֹשׁ, § 29 *h*).

However, in the primitive patterns *qiṭāl* (Heb. קְטוֹל) and *qiṭūl* (Heb. קְטוּל) אֵ is generally found in place of אֱ, even in the st. cst., e.g. אֵזוֹר *girdle*, אֵבוּס *manger* (cf. § 30 *d*).

i When, in the course of inflection, ◌ֱ moves away from the stress, it generally becomes ֲ, e.g. אֱדוֹם, אֲדוֹמִי; the preposition אֶל, in poetry אֱלֵי, אֲלֵיכֶם. Likewise the sequence ֶ ֱ generally becomes ַ ֲ, e.g. הֶעֱבַרְתִּי Zech 3.4, but וְהַעֲבַרְתִּי Jer 15.14(1).

The phenomenon must be considered as a case of reinforcement: the ḥaṭef is slightly reinforced in order to counterbalance the stress (cf. P. Joüon in *MUSJ* 5 [1911] 374).

(1) Examples such as the last two should not be considered in isolation; the /ha-/, therefore, is a rather unlikely vestige of the widely assumed, primitive form of Hifil, i.e. **haqtal* (§ 54 *a*).

On the change from ַ to ֶ before a guttural followed by a qameṣ, cf. § 29 *f*. *j*

On the preference of pataḥ to seghol as the second vowel of mil'el nouns, see § 88C *c*, *d*, *h*, *j*. *k*

§ 22. **Auxiliary ḥaṭef after a guttural**

A guttural can be followed by a simple shewa, exactly like a non-guttural; e.g. in Qal future we find יֶחְזַק as one has יִכְבַּד. But very often, in place of a shewa, one finds an extremely short auxiliary vowel, normally a ḥaṭef, of the same timbre as the full vowel; thus, instead of the very rare יֶחְזַק, one ordinarily has יֶחֱזַק. The aim of this auxiliary ḥaṭef is to facilitate the transition from the guttural to the following consonant. This very short vowel is spread over the two contiguous syllables, as a result of which syllable division becomes impossible (cf. § 27 *a*); thus יַעֲמֹד may graphically be represented as /yaʿəmoḏ/(1). *a*

(1) These ḥaṭefs are not, as Kahle thought, an artificial invention of Tiberian scholars' born out of their desire to revive the proper consonantal pronunciation of the gutturals: Sh. Morag in *Tarbiz* 26 (1957) 11f.

The use of the ḥaṭef is not governed by strict rules; there are plenty of variations and inconsistencies. One might note the following points: *b*

1) The auxiliary ḥaṭef occurs only after an unstressed vowel.

2) The auxiliary ḥaṭef is more frequent than the simple shewa.

3) א and ע readily take the ḥaṭef; ה and ח readily go without it.

4) The following consonant may or may not favour the use of the ḥaṭef; indeed the difficulty of transition from the guttural to a following consonant depends on the nature of the latter.

Practical examples are found in the conjugation of first-guttural verbs (§ 68) and second-guttural segholate nouns, e.g. נַעֲרוֹ *his youth*, but לַחְמִי *my bread* (§ 96 A *i*), פָּעֳלוֹ *his work* (§ 96 A *j*).

c **Change from ḥaṭef to full vowel.** When, in the course of the inflection and concomitant lengthening of a word, the vowel which comes after a ḥaṭef must become shewa, the ḥaṭef becomes a full vowel, e.g. יַעֲמֹד, but יַעַמְדוּ. More examples: נַעֲרוֹ but נַעַרְךָ; פָּעֳלוֹ but פָּעָלְךָ (cp. § 65 *c* and 96 A *j*: auxiliary ֳ without a guttural). For the metheg cf. § 14 *c* 3.

As the auxiliary ḥaṭef is not always used, this auxiliary vowel is not always used either; thus alongside the usual יֶחֶזְקוּ one finds יֶחְזְקוּ in Is 28.22.

d There occurs a secondary suppression of ḥaṭef occasionally after the preposition לְ, e.g. לַחְפֹּר in place of *לַחֲפֹר (§ 68 *e*); very rarely after בְּ: בְּעְזֹר 1Ch 15.26 (var. עֱ), very rarely after וְ: וַעְצֹר Job 4.2. See also, with the verbs הָיָה and חָיָה, forms like לִהְיוֹת (§ 79 *s*).

§ 23. The consonant ר compared with the gutturals

a The lingual consonant ר is treated in part like the gutturals, though it is not guttural in articulation (§ 5 *n*).

Like the gutturals, ר does not lend itself to gemination. It never has virtual gemination(1). As for the full gemination indicated by the dagesh, ר does allow it very rarely, though never after the definite article. One always (3 times in fact) finds הַרְּאִיתֶם(2) *have you seen?* 1Sm 10.24; 17.25; 2Kg 6.32†; מָרַּת /mǫrrạṭ/ *bitterness of* Pr 14.10; לֹא־כָרַּת שָׁרֵּךְ *your umbilical cord was not cut* Ez 16.4; שֶׁרֹּאשִׁי *that my head* Ct 5.2; sometimes after a euphonic dagesh (*dḥiq* or *mẹrạḥiq*), in some editions.

(1) Cf. Σαρρα = שָׂרָה; Γομορρα = עֲמֹרָה.

(2) Cf. SH forms such as /ar'rå/ *he showed*; Ben-Ḥayyim, *LOT*, vol. 5, p. 119. ר following the interrogative הֲ is not treated like the gutturals; thus one says הֲרָאִיתָ *did you see?* (§ 102 *n*).

b Like the gutturals, final ר favours the vowel ַ(1). Examples: וַיָּסַר from סוּר *to turn* for Qal *וַיָּסָר and for Hif. *וַיָּסֵר (§ 80 *k*); וַיַּרְא from

רָאָה *to see* (Qal future יִרְאֶה), which can be easily confused with Hif. (apoc. fut. of יַרְאֶה); וַיָּ֫צַר *and he besieged* from צוּר, for וַיָּ֫צֻר*, a form which can be easily confused with וַיָּ֫צַר *and he pressed hard*, Hif. of צַר, root צרר, Hif. הֵצַר, יָצַר. But with ־ one finds וַיֵּ֫צֶר *and it was narrow*, § 82 *b*; וַיֹּ֫אמֶר, § 73 *d*. In nouns we find ־ֶ, e.g. בֹּ֫קֶר, אֹ֫מֶר etc.

(1) In Syriac final *r* and even final *l* sometimes attract the vowel *a*.

§ 24. The guttural א

Alef is the weakest of the gutturals. In the period of the history *a* of Hebrew we are concerned with, it is very often no longer pronounced; sometimes it is not even written. (On the pronunciation of א, see § 5 *j*; on א as *mater lectionis*, § 7 *b*).

Alef is actually pronounced in a syllable that is closed in one way *b* or other, namely: 1) in a properly closed syllable, e.g. יֶאְשַׁם /yę'-šạm/ *he will make himself guilty* (the syllable is closed as in יִכְבַּד; 2) in semi-closed syllables, e.g. יֶאֱהַב, הַבְרָאָה (§ 22 *a*); 3) in virtually closed syllables, i.e. after virtual gemination (§ 20 *a*), e.g. נִאֵף *he has committed adultery*.

Alef, when it is a word-medial or final radical, is pronounced when followed by a vowel: e.g. כִּסֵּא = [kisse] *chair*, but כִּסְאִי = [kis'i] *my chair*, and שָׁאַל [šå'ạl] *he asked*. Morphophonemically it makes some sense to analyse a form such as מָצָא *he found* as /måså'/, resulting in a neat picture of the paradigm vis-à-vis, say, מָצְאוּ /måṣ'u/ *they found*.

Everywhere else Alef is not pronounced. Silent Alef occurs either *c* after the vowel of a syllable which it once closed, e.g. מָצָא from /*maṣa'/ (Alef *quiescens*), or before the vowel of a syllable of which it was once the first constituent(1), e.g. אָמַר from /*'åmar/, now pronounced /åmạr/, as if the vowel were the first sound of the sequence.

(1) In this case the א has become a mere prop for a vowel, like the Arabic Alif without hamza. It would be rather strange if, in the stage of the language when Alef was no longer pronounced at the end of a word, where it is easy to pronounce, it should have been pronounced at the beginning of a word or a syllable where it is more difficult to pronounce. But many authors give to Alef at the beginning of a word or a syllable a consonantal value, even at the latest stage of the language.

The /a/ preceding a vowelless /'/ has undergone two different deve- *d* lopments. On the one hand, it has developed into /ā/, subsequently /ọ/, which is common Semitic phenomenon, as is the case in רֹאשׁ *head* from /ra'š/ > /rāš/ > רֹאשׁ (§ 98 *f*) and in צֹאן *small cattle* from /ṣa'n/ (cf. Arb. /ra's/ and /ḍa'n/). One also finds מֹאזְנַ֫יִם *scales* (in Arb. with the root /wazana/), מוֹסֵר *link* from /ma'sir/ (א omitted in writing)(1); cf. § 88 L *h*. One must note further the /ọ/ of אֹכַל (Fut. 1st pers.): the primitive sequence /'a'/ has become in Common Semitic /'ā/, whence Heb. /'ọ/ (cf. § 73 *b*).

On the other hand, after this typically Canaanite phonetic change had ceased to operate, /a/ became /ā/, then /å/, as in /maṣa'/ > /māṣā'/ > /måṣå/.

(1) For a classification and a listing of graphically omitted etymological Alef's, see AF, pp. 85-88.

e **Contractions.** Through its quiescence א occasions contractions, e.g. *לֶאֱמֹר > לֵאמֹר, *לֶאֱלֹהִים > לֵאלֹהִים (§ 103 *b*). In view of וְאָצַלְתִּ֫י Nu 11.17 and no unmistakable example of a Hifil of this verb, וַיָּ֫אצֶל ib. 11.25Q must be considered an *i* impf. (*pace* Berg., II, §§ 14 h, 31 h). In certain forms of the word אָדוֹן after בְּ, כְּ, לְ, and וְ the vowel ֲ is retained in open syllables, e.g. לַאדֹנִי, לַאדֹנָי (§ 103 *b*). Note also וַאעַנֶּה 1Kg 11.39; וַיַּאת Is 41.25; מַשַּׁאת Dt 24.10. וָאַבֶּדְךָ Ez 28.16 for וָאֲאַבֶּדְךָ is slightly different.

f **Transposition of vowels.** Through its quiescence א sometimes occasions a transposition of vowels, e.g. מָאתַ֫יִם *200* for *מְאָתַ֫יִם (from מֵאָה); הָראוּבֵנִי *the Reubenite* from רְאוּבֵן; מְלָאכָה *work* for *מַלְאָכָה; שְׂמֹאל (שְׂמֹאוֹל) from /*śim-'āl/.

On the vocalisation of the initial א, cf. § 21 *h*.

fa The syncope of /'/ after a vowelless consonant, which is standard in Late Aramaic, is not as common as in Qumran orthography, on which see Qimron, *Hebrew of DSS*, p. 25. A case such as Ez 28.16 מָלוּ *they filled* is most likely a different phenomenon, namely the merging of ל"א with ל"ה verbs; see Kutscher, *Isaiah*, p. 343. See also § 17 *e*.

Note also רָאשִׁים for /*r'āšim/. An Alef such as this can be elided graphically as well: תוֹמִם Gn 25.24; אֲחַטֶּ֫נָּה ib. 31.39; לַהְשׁוֹת 2Kg 19.25 (// לְהַשְׁאוֹת Is 37.26, but לשאוות in 1Q Is[a]).

§ 25. **The guttural ה**

ה is a rather weak guttural; often it is not pronounced. *a*

ה within a word is always pronounced. Word-final ה is generally quiescent. Therefore, when it is irregularly pronounced, it is marked by a mappiq (§ 11 *a*), e.g. גָּבֹהַּ /gåvọ^{a}h/ *high*, לָהּ /låh/ *to her*. The massorah demands that the ה of this last word in Nu 32.42; Zech 5.11, and Ru 2.14 (§ 103 *f*) not be pronounced; in these verses לָהֿ is spelled with a rafé for the sake of greater clarity (§ 12 *a*). Other examples of the fem. suffix ה ָ without a mappiq: with the verb, § 61 *i*; with the noun, § 94 *h*. Note the theophoric element יָה as in יְשַׁעְיָה for יְשַׁעְיָהוּ and יִרְמְיָה for יִרְמְיָהוּ.

On the syncope of ה, cf. § 17 *e*. *b*

With the perf. 3f. one has קְטָלַתְהוּ and, by syncope of ה and gemination of ת, קְטָלַתּוּ and קְטָלַתָּה (cf. § 62 *d*). *c*

The ה of the pronominal suffix 3m. disappears in many forms, e.g. /*lahu/ > /law/ > לוֹ; /pīhu/ > פִּיו (/piw/).

§ 26. **Semi-vocalic consonants ו and י**

The semi-vocalic consonants ו and י often lose their consonantal character, frequently coalescing with a preceding vowel, and sometimes dropping out completely. *a*

The sequence /uw/ becomes /u/, e.g. /*huwšab/ > הוּשַׁב. The group /iy/ becomes /i/, e.g. /*yiyraš/ > יִירַשׁ; with the prepositions בְּ, כְּ, לְ, and מִן, and the conjunction וְ one finds, e.g., with יְמֵי *days of*: בִּימֵי, כִּימֵי, לִימֵי, מִימֵי, and וִימֵי (cf. § 103 *b*). *b*

The word-final cluster /iy/ may become ה ֶ, e.g. /šmōniy/ > שְׁמֹנֶה (cf. Arb. /ṯamān^{in}/) *eight*; גֵּאֶה *proud* (*qittil* pattern); cf. Barth, *Nominalbildung*, pp. XXXff.

The groups /aw/ and /ay/ may be either retained or simplified(1) respectively into /ọ/ and /ẹ/ (less frequently /ę/). *c*

In the st.abs. occurs מָוֶת, but יוֹם, שׁוֹט, צוֹם (according to the st. cst., § 96 A *l*); in the st.cst. מוֹת, יוֹם, etc.(2).

In the st.abs. we find בַּיִת with a paragogic ה, בַּיְתָה; in the st.cst. בֵּית(3).

The negative particle אַ֫יִן becomes אֵין when closely linked to the following word (§ 160 *h*).

The substantive /śaday/, poet. שָׂדַי, becomes abs. שָׂדֶה, cst. שְׂדֵה. Before the suffixes, the form of the pl. noun /susay/ becomes סוּסֵי in סוּסֵ֫ינוּ etc., but סוּסֶי in סוּסֶ֫יךָ, סוּסֶ֫יהָ, § 94 *d*.

On the pronunciation of the sequences /aw/, /ay/ etc., cf. § 7 *d*.

(1) In contrast to the contraction observable in the northern dialect (Samaria ostraca ין for יַ֫יִן) and Ammonite (same word).

(2) One should note the absence of contraction in עַוְלָה *injustice* (no doubt in order to avoid confusion with עוֹלָה *burnt-offering*) and in שַׁוְעָה *a cry for help* (for שַׁוְעָה* from שִׁוַּע *to cry for help*); cf. also § 79 *a* שָׁלַ֫וְתִּי.

(3) Note the absence of contraction in לַ֫יְלָה *night*, § 93 *g*, n.

d At the end of a word, for example, /w/ and /y/ after a consonant become /u/ and /i/ respectively; e.g. /wąyyištą'ḥw/, an apocopated form of יִשְׁתַּחֲוֶה *he will worship* becomes וַיִּשְׁתַּ֫חוּ /wąyyištą'ḥu/ (§ 79 *t*); /śa'ḥw/ *swimming* becomes שָׂ֫חוּ (Ez 47.5); /pa'ty/ *simple, unsophisticated* becomes פֶּ֫תִי.

Note that this short *u* and this short *i* are necessarily written *plene*.

e The conjunction וְ before a labial and any consonant other than /y/ with a plain shewa becomes וּ, i.e. the simple vowel *u* (cf. § 14 *c* 2), e.g. וּמֶ֫לֶךְ (cf. § 104 *c*)(1).

Word-initial יְ, properly *yi*, seems to have been prounounced simply as *i*, at least in certain schools, and so in Contemporary Israeli Hebrew. Thus the proper noun יִשַׁי is written אִישַׁי in 1Ch 2.13. According to Qimḥi יִקְטֹל is pronounced [iqṭol](2).

(1) Not *ū* or *'u*, according to a 10th (?) century massoretic scholar: K. Levy, op. cit. [§ 1 *a*, n.], p. 24*.

(2) For examples of a word-initial /'/ > /y/, see C.D. Isbell, "Initial 'Alef-Yod interchange and selected biblical passages," *JNES* 37 (1978) 227-36.

f A word-initial primitive *w* is replaced by *y*(1), e.g. **walad* > יָלַד *to give birth* (§ 75 *a*), as a result of which one does not find words beginning with a ו, except for the conjunction וְ, the common וָו *hook*, two isolated and suspect words, וָזָר and וָלָד, as well as several proper nouns. Moreover, the original Waw can still be recognised in some verb forms (§ 75 *a*).

The verbs with a primitive *w* as the third radical have been absorbed by those with a primitive *y* as their third radical (§ 79 *a*).

Alongside the normal but very rare form קֻוָּם (from קוּם) one has the rare form קִיֵּם (§ 80 *h*).

(1) This had already occurred in Ugaritic.

Within a word the doubling of /w/ or /y/ is sometimes avoided by substituting the adjacent consonant for it: /znunim/ for /*znuwwim/; /plili/ for /*pliyyi/; /*'ariri/ for /*'ariyyi/ ; see also § 80 *h*(1). *g*

(1) See Lambert, § 111.

§ 27. **On the syllable**

In Hebrew, as in some other languages, the division into syllables is not always possible(1). When it is possible, the syllables are normal, but when it is not, one can only speak of improper or abnormal syllables. *a*

(1) On this important phenomenon of phonetics, see especially O. Jespersen, *Elementarbuch der Phonetik* (Leipzig/Berlin, 1912), p. 153, and *Lehrbuch der Phonetik* (Leipzig/Berlin, [2]1913), pp. 201-3, where he adduces useful examples from German, some of which have their analogue in Hebrew.

A **normal** syllable is either *open* or *closed*. *b*

The *open* syllable ends with a vowel: in קָֽטְלָה /qå-ṭlå/ *she killed*, /qå/ and /ṭlå/ are open syllables.

The closed syllable ends with a consonant or consonants: in אָכְלָה /'ọḇ-lå/ *food*, מַלְכִּי /mąl-ki/ *my king*, the syllables /'ọḇ/ and /mąl/ are closed.

When the consonant which closes the syllable is doubled, the syllable is said to be *sharp*, e.g. עַמִּי /'am-mi/, אִמִּי, חֻקִּי; לָ֫מָּה, יָסֹ֫בּוּ, יָסֹ֫בּוּ.

The **abnormal** syllables in Hebrew are syllables *incompletely closed*. One can distinguish: *c*

1) the *semi-closed* syllable(1). This may be found in the case of auxiliary ḥaṭef (§ 22 *a*), e.g. יַֽעֲמֹד /yą'ₐmọḏ/; in the case of a full auxiliary vowel replacing an auxiliary ḥaṭef (§ 22 *c*), e.g. יַֽעַמְדוּ /yą'ąmḏu/; and finally in the case of the auxiliary vowel of segholated forms, e.g. סֵ֫פֶר /sẹ'fẹr/ (properly speaking, /sẹ'f^e^r/, § 96 A *b*), וַיִּ֫גֶל /wąyyi'g^e^l/ (an apocopated form of יִגְלֶה, § 79 *i*)(2).

2) the *virtually closed* syllable. This is a simple variant of the semi-closed syllable similar to what we have in cases of virtual gemination, e.g. יְבַעֵר (§ 20 *a*), אַחִים (spontaneous gemination, § 20 *c*).

(1) This term is preferable to *half-open*, for the vowels are those of closed syllables.
(2) In these forms the last vowel was originally very short; however, the final vowel marked with the same vowel sign must have been slightly longer in forms like וַיֵּשֶׁב (from the future יֵשֵׁב) where the ֶ is not auxiliary (syllabification: *way-yę'-šęv*).

d **Observations** 1) In the laws of rhythm, one takes into account full syllables only; thus in יוֹרְדֵי בוֹר Ps 28.1 the first word is counted as disyllabic (cf. § 31 *c*). Likewise, one ignores the auxiliary vowels; e.g. in נַעַמְדָה יָּחַד Is 50.8 the first word is counted as disyllabic (cf. § 22 *c*).

2) A syllable is considered always to begin with a consonant (or consonants), and this is reflected in the Hebrew writing system. But phonetically the syllable occasionally begins with a vowel; this is often the case with א, e.g. in words such as אָמַר, where the Alef is not pronounced (§ 24 *c*), in the case of initial Waw (§ 26 *e*), and perhaps of initial Yod (§ 26 *e*).

da 3) A syllable may begin with a cluster of two consonants, the first bearing a shewa, whether simple or compound: e.g. סְפָרִים /sfå-rim/; אֲרָצוֹת /'ªråṣọt/(1).

(1) To early Mediaeval Hebrew grammarians shewa as in דְּרָכִים or ḥaṭef's did not have the same syllabic status as full vowels: thus the Hebrew word mentioned was segmented into דְּךָ and כִים, though this does not necessarily mean that such a shewa was considered "quiescent." (Y.P. Gumpertz, *The Pronunciations of our Language: Studies in Phonetics* [Heb] (Jerusalem, 1953), pp. 131-41, and D. Kimḥi, מכלול, [ed. I. Rittenberg] (Lyck, 1862), p. 136b.

db 4) A syllable may close with two different consonants, the last being more often than not a plosive: וַיֵּשְׁתְּ *and he drank*; יֹלַדְתְּ [partic.] (*she will*) *bear*; וַיֵּבְךְּ *and he wept*; וַיִּשְׁבְּ *and he took captive*; נֵרְדְּ *nard*; קֹשְׁטְ *truth*. On אַתְּ and forms such as כָּתַבְתְּ (pf. 2f.s.), cf. § 18 *l*, n. 1. Where an identical consonant was originally doubled at the end of a word, it is simplified: so לֵב but לִבִּי, חֹק but חֻקִּי. This also suggests that אַתְּ = /'ạt/ rather than /'ạtt/, and that נָתַתְּ = /nåṯạt/ rather than /nåṯạtt/, let alone /nåṯạ'ttə/.

§ 28. Vowels in relation to various types of syllable

There are rules governing relationships between vowel type and syllable type(1). Certain vowels are impossible or exceptional in certain positions. We shall give a practical table of the most common relationships, which should enable the student to avoid certain glaring errors in vocalisation. The vowels ִי, וּ, ִ (i.e. /i/ spelled without Yod as *mater lectionis*), and ֻ cause no difficulty: the last two occur only in unstressed closed syllables, e.g. יְקֻטַּל, יִקְטֹל. a

(1) Cf. contemporary French in which, for example, *e* in a closed syllable is always an open *ę*. The academic orthography *événement* presupposes the pronunciation of the silent *e* and the syllabification *é-vé-ne-ment*; in fact, since the silent *e* is no longer pronounced, the word becomes phonetically *é-vèn-ment*.

A. 1) In an **open** *unstressed* syllable one can have the following vowels: b

Historically long וּ, ֵי, and ֹ: e.g. קֹטֵל, תְּקִימֶ֫ינָה, תְּקוּמֶ֫ינָה (from /*qāṭil/), אֱלֹהִים (from /*'ilāhīm/).

ָ, ֵ, and ֹ: שָׁלוֹם, עֵנָב, גְּבֹהָה (but ֹ only before a guttural; § 18 *d*).

ַ, ֶ, and ָ: only in special cases, e.g. with the interrogative ה (§ 102 *n*): הַאֵלֵךְ *shall I go?*, הֶחָכָם *is he wise?*; very rarely ָ, e.g. קָֽדָשִׁים (§ 6 *l*).

ḥaṭef: אֲנִי, אֱנוֹשׁ, אֳנִי *ships*.

2) In an **open** *stressed* syllable one can have the following vowels: Historically long וּ, ֵי, and וֹ: נָקֹ֫ומָה, יָקִ֫ימוּ, יָקֻ֫ומוּ.

ָ, and ֵ: סוּסֵ֫נוּ, יְקַטְלֵ֫הוּ; לָ֫נוּ, קְטָלָ֫נוּ, וְקָטַלְתָּ֫, אַתָּה.

ַ and ֶ: only in special cases, e.g. יִקְטְלֶ֫הָ, קְטָלַ֫נִי; never ָ (nor ִ or ֻ).

B. 1) In a **closed** *unstressed* syllable one can have the following vowels: c

ַ, ֶ and ָ (only): חָנֵּ֫נִי, וַיָּ֫קָם, קָדְשִׁי, חֶלְקִי, מַלְכִּי.

2) In a non-final **closed** *stressed* syllable one can have the following vowels:

ָ, ֵ, and ֹ: תִּקְטֹ֫לְנָה, תַּקְטֵ֫לְנָה, לָ֫מָּה, יָ֫מָּה.

normally ַ: תְּכַבֵּ֫דְנָה; rarely ֶ and only in a sharp syllable, e.g. in the suffixes ֶ֫נּוּ, ֶ֫נִּי etc.; never ָ (nor ִ or ֻ).

3) In a final *stressed* **closed** syllable one can have the following

vowels:

Historically long וּ, ִי, and וֹ: קָטוֹל, יָקִים, יָקוּם.
ָה, ֵ, and ֹ: קָטֹן, כָּבֵד, דָּבָר.
often ֵ: קְטַל, קָטֵל (form of liaison); rather infrequently ֶ: אֱמֶת, דִּבֶּר, כַּרְמֶל, בָּבֶל; suffixes כֶם, כֶן; תֶם, תֶן; never ָ (or ַ or ֶ).

§ 29. **Vowel changes**

a Vowel changes, whether from primitive vowels (§ 6 *i*) or within Hebrew, are a prominent characteristic of Hebrew (and Aramaic). This fluidity is, moreover, rather uneven, conditioned by vowel quantity and syllable type. Vowel changes and deletions are often due to stress shift (§ 30).

aa Two important laws capable of accounting for alternation between /a/ and /i/ at either a diachronic or synchronic level are often mentioned. The first, Philippi's law(1), states that /i/ in a closed stressed syllable changes to /a/: e.g. /*bint/ (as in Classical Arabic) > בַּת (but with the original vowel retained when suffixed, בִּתִּי etc.). The second, the law of attenuation, purports to account for the opposite phenomenon: /a/ in a closed, but *unstressed* syllable changes to /i/: e.g. /*haqtal/ > /*hiqtal/ > (on the analogy of the future) /hiqtil/, which is the standard and basic Hifil pattern. Neither law is free from exceptions or difficulties(2).

(1) So named after F.W.M. Philippi, *ZDMG* 32 (1878) 42. On a reconstructed chronology of Philippi's law, see J. Blau in *Proceedings of the Ninth World Congress of Jewish Studies*, Division D, vol. 1 (Jerusalem, 1986), pp. 1-4, and Blau, *Grammar*, § 9. Cf. also T.O. Lambdin, "Philippi's law reconsidered," A. Kort and S. Morshcauser (eds), *Biblical and Related Studies* [Fschr. S. Iwry] (Winona Lake, 1985), pp. 135-45.
(2) See the succinct survey in Harviainen, op. cit. [§ 6 *f*, n.], pp. 16-21.

b The originally **long** vowels /ọ/ (derived from /ā/ or /aw/), /u/, and /i/ are generally quite stable(1), but /ọ/ in a syllable which has become unstressed, often weakens to /u/. The latter phenomenon is a regular one in the conjugation of the Nifal נָקוֹם of ע"ו verbs in the Perf.: the /ọ/ becomes /u/ when it has lost the principal or secondary stress: נָקוֹמָה, נְקוֹמֹתֶם, but נְקוּמֹתִי (§ 80 *l*)(2). One may occasionally observe the same alternation in certain doublets: מָנוֹחַ *rest* and מְנוּחָה, מָלוֹן *a place where one spends a night* and מְלוּנָה; מָנוֹס *flight* (with suf. מְנוּסִי)

and מְנוּסָה[3].

(1) See § 89 *i* for an exception in the case of *ọ*, and § 89 *f* for an exception in the case of *i*.

(2) This could have been influenced by the same change which is frequent in cases such as יָסֹ֫בּוּ, תְּסֻבֶּ֫ינָה; חֹק, חֻקִּי.

(3) In certain words for which there is no similar doublet, e.g. תְּבוּנָה *understanding*, the *u* seems to derive from an *ọ* (and therefore from a primitive *ā*); cf. P. Joüon in *Bib* 1 (1920) 369. See also words like מוּסָר, § 88 L *e*.

The vowel ָ, on losing stress, normally becomes ַ: דָּבָר, cst.st. דְּבַר; c
דָּם *blood*, cst.st. דַּם־.

The vowel ֹ, on losing stress, normally becomes ָ or (particularly in a sharp syllable) ֻ: כֹּל, כָּל־, כֻּלָּם; יָסֹב, וַיָּ֫סָב; יָסֹ֫בּוּ, תְּסֻבֶּ֫ינָה; חֹק, חֻקִּי.

The vowel ֵ, on losing stress, normally becomes ֶ or (especially in a sharp syllable) ִ: אֵת, אֶת־; יָסֵב, וַיָּ֫סֶב; יָסֵ֫בּוּ, תְּסִבֶּ֫ינָה; אֵם, אִמִּי.

The weakening of ֵ to ִ has occasionally been felt excessive; then ֵ d
simply becomes ַ. Thus, in Piel, קִטֵּל is the normal and pausal form, whereas קִטַּל is a secondary form of liaison (§ 52 *c*). In the quiescent פ״א verbs, יֹאכֵל is the pausal form, and יֹאכַל the contextual form (§ 73 *d*). In the inflection of the type זָקֵן the st.cst. is זְקַן (§ 96 B *d*)[1], a change in which one can observe Philippi's law (§ *aa*) at work. Similarly, in a stressed closed penultimate syllable, one often finds ַ for ֵ: כָּבֵד, כָּבַ֫דְתָּ; קִטֵּל, קִטַּ֫לְתָּ, and in Hifil הִקְטַ֫לְתָּ (for **hiqtilta*, הִקְטֶ֫לְתָּ*). The behaviour of the f.pl. future ending *ẹlnå*, however, is problematic: *ẹlnå* remains in the Hifil תַּקְטֵ֫לְנָה (in order to preserve somehow the characteristic *i*); *ẹlnå* generally remains in Piel, whereas in Hitpael one generally finds *ạlnå*; *ạlnå* is always found in the Nifal, even in pause (i.e. as in the passive conjugations Pual and Hofal, and perhaps on the analogy of these conjugations); in the Qal of פ״ו verbs one always has *ạlnå*: תֵּשַׁ֫בְנָה. In the imperative one finds only לֵ֫כְנָה† (in spite of תֵּלַ֫כְנָה) and Pi. לַמֵּ֫דְנָה (Stade, § 612). The abnormal form *ẹlnå* occurs once in וַתְּהַלֶּ֫לְנָה Ez 13.19.

(1) However ֵ can become ַ, e.g. הֵפֵר, הֵפַר (§ 32 *c*).

The vowel ַ can be weakened to either ִ or ֶ (§ *g*). e
The first degree of attenuation of ַ to ִ is frequent[1]. It occurs:

1) in the segholate nouns of מֶ֫לֶךְ type (cf. מַלְכִּי) and verb יִ֫גֶל (apocopated from יִגְלֶה) where the stressed ֶ for ַ is due to the influence of the auxiliary ֶ, § 96 A *b*,

2) probably in the majority of forms /mẹqṭål/ and /mẹqṭlå/ before a non-guttural, e.g. מֶרְכָּבָה *chariot*, מֶמְשָׁלָה *rule*(2),

3) in certain isolated cases the most notable of which is יֶדְכֶם *your* (m.pl.) *hand* from יָד, cst. יַד. (Likewise in BA one has יְדְהֹם *their hand* Ezr 5.8).

(1) In the Babylonian pronunciation *ą* became *ä* (= *ẹ*), § 6 *g*, n.

(2) Before a guttural ֶ probably derives from the partial assimilation of an original *i* to the guttural (§ 21 *d*), e.g. in מֶחֱזָה *window* (contrast מַחֲזֶה *vision*).

f Furthermore, ַ regularly becomes ֶ before a **guttural followed by a qameṣ** or by ḥaṭef qameṣ. Examples: אַחִים but אֶחָיו, אַחַי but אֶחָ֑י (§ 20 *c*); בַּחֶ֫רֶב but בֶּחָ֑רֶב; יִתְנַחֵם* but יִתְנֶחָ֑ם *he will repent*; הֶחָכָם *the sage* and *Is he wise?*; הַחֹ֫דֶשׁ but הֶחֳדָשִׁים (§ 34 *d*).

If the qameṣ is "short" (i.e. in unstressed closed syllables), the ַ will remain, e.g. הַחָכְמָה *wisdom*. The reason for this exception is not clear.

The change from ַ to ֶ can hardly be considered here as attenuation. The two timbres /ẹ/ and /ọ/ are two symmetrical open vowels in the vowel scale of Hebrew (§ 6 *b*): indeed they are separated by one degree from the central vowel /ạ/. The law in question therefore can be explained in terms of a tendency to *vowel harmony*.

This vowel sequence /ẹ — ọ/(1) is very much favoured and is found outside of the bounds of the law cited here. Thus:

A) **Before gutturals**: 1) יִקְטְלֵהוּ but יִקְטְלֶהָ; 2) one has יַחֲבֹשׁ *he will bind*, וַיַּחֲבָשׁ־, but יֶחְבָּ֑שׁ Job 5.18† (where one has /ọ/, stemming from /u/ in pause, § 32 *c*); in two closely linked words, e.g. מֶה עָשִׂיתִי (for מָה [§ 37 *c*]), דְּעֶה חָכְמָה (for דְּעָה; before a short qameṣ!) Pr 24.14 *Know wisdom!*.

B) **Before non-gutturals**: 1) סוּסֵ֫נוּ, but סוּסֶךָ; 2) סוּסֵ֫ינוּ, סוּסֵיכֶם but סוּסֶ֫יךָ; 3) פְּרִי, פִּרְיִי, but פֶּרְיְךָ; 4) פַּדָּן (a proper noun) but פַּדֶּ֫נָה(2).

(1) In discussing this vowel sequence, we transcribe the qameṣ derived from *a*, namely *å*, in a purely phonetic manner: *ọ*, for the reason that we wish to draw attention to a phonetic phenomenon.

(2) See also §§ 68 *e*, 79 *q*, 88 L *g*, 93 *c*, 94 *c,d,h*, 96 A *q*, B *f*.

g The second degree of attenuation from ַ to ִ (the law of attenuation; § *aa*) is likewise very frequent.

A primitive /a/ has become ִ in the perfects נִקְטַל, הִקְטִיל (but fut. יַקְטִיל), קִטֵּל (in a sharp syllable, but fut. יְקַטֵּל); in the Qal future of action verbs יִקְטֹל (§ 41 *e*), in the cst.pl. of the type דִּבְרֵי (from דָּבָר) for /davrẹ/ (§ 96 B *b*)(1).

The attenuation from ַ to ִ occurs frequently in declension of nouns: 1) in the types צִדְקִי alongside מַלְכִּי, בִּגְדֵי alongside מַלְכֵי, נִסְכֵּי alongside כַּסְפֵּי, כִּבְשָׂה alongside כַּבְשָׂה (thus one finds the fem. infinitive קִטְלָה alongside קַטְלָה, § 49 *d*)(2); in the declension of the type מַרְבֵּץ, cst. מִרְבַּץ (dissimilation; cf. § 96 C *c*); 3) in the form דִּמְכֶם *your* (m.pl.) *blood*. (Likewise in Targumic Aramaic one has דִּמְכוֹן; cf. G. Dalman, *Grammatik des jüdisch-palästinischen Aramäisch* etc. [Leipzig, ^{2}1905], p. 202); 4) in some nouns of *qall* pattern, e.g. פַּת - פִּתִּים; מַס - מִסִּים, but not in שַׂק - שַׂקִּים nor in adjectives as in רַב - רַבִּים; דַּל - דַּלִּים.

(1) An alternative (widely accepted) explanation for this last example and its likes is to say that the /i/ is a helping vowel designed to resolve word-initial consonantal clusters, namely /*dvrẹ/> /divrẹ/, including clusters of which the initial consonant is a proclitic as in /*ld̲vårim/> /lid̲vårim/. But see § 96 B *b*, and the relevant footnote. The notion of "helping vowel" is mediaeval, being known already to Lambert (§§ 39, 3; 118), and is fully expounded and applied to various grammatical categories by J. Cantineau in his "La voyelle de secours *i* dans les langues sémitiques," *Semitica* 2 (1949) 51-67, which is a penetrating critique of M. Bravmann, "Über *i* als Hilfsvokal im Wortinnern: eine Untersuchung zum Verhältnis von Akzent und Vokal im Semitischen," *Monde Oriental* 32 (1938) 1-102. Cantineau rejects Bravmann's account of phonetic processes involved, but agrees that helping vowels of various kinds, chiefly /i/, arose to resolve word-initial consonantal clusters which resulted from the loss of vowels in word-initial open syllables.

(2) There is no absolute certainty, however, that the underlying vowel in these forms is really /a/: evidence from cognate languages is often contradictory (e.g. Syr. /kespå/) and there are internal fluctuations as well (e.g. נֶסֶךְ as well as נֵסֶךְ). Cf. § 88C *a**.

Dissimilation. Certain vowels cannot be explained except in terms of a tendency to avoid a sequence of two vowels of identical or similar timbre. *h*

The first vowel in רִאשׁוֹן (from רֹאשׁ) is due to dissimilation; analogously חִיצוֹן from חוּץ, תִּיכוֹן from cst. תּוֹךְ, אֱנוֹשׁ (§ 21 *h*), יֵשׁוּעַ for *יוֹשׁוּעַ from יְהוֹשׁוּעַ (proper noun).

The second vowel is dissimilated in לוּלֵא (4 times; לוּלֵי 10 times) *if . . . not* from לוּ + לֹא; and in the type אֹכֶל of the future of quiescent פ"א verbs, for /'ọḇọl/ (§ 73 *c*).

§ 30. Loss of vowels

a Vowels, whether primitive or Hebrew, often disappear by virtue of the energic character or shift of the stress. The elided vowel leaves a slight trace in the form of a shewa or one of its substitutes, namely the ḥaṭefs. Thus the word דָּבָר becomes דְּבַר in the construct state in which the principal stress disappears, and דְּבָרִים in the pl.abs. in which the stress shifts on to /im/.

b Originally **long** vowels and contracted vowels are not lost; for example, in the type מֵיטִיב for /mayṭib/, the two vowels concerned remain throughout the inflection: cst. מֵיטִיב, pl. מֵיטִיבִים, cst. מֵיטִיבֵי.

In the alternations of the fut. indicative יָקוּם, fut. jussive יָקֹם, inverted fut. וַיָּקָם, one has to do with different forms in that the primitive form of the indicative had a long vowel and the primitive form of the jussive a short vowel.

c The primitive **short** vowels in **closed syllables** are protected by the very nature of the syllable; they can change their timbre, but are not lost, e.g. /*qudši/ > קָדְשִׁי.

d The primitive **short** vowels in **open syllables** are liable to be lost. The following principal facts may be observed:

A) In the **mil'ra disyllabic** words:

1) the initial vowel remains if the second is a primitive short one, e.g. /*qatal/ > קָטַל; /*dabar/ > דָּבָר; /*'inab/ > עֵנָב; /*'ilay/ > אֵלַי *towards me*.

2) If the second vowel was originally long, the initial primitive vowel /a/ remains(1), the primitive /i/ and /u/ are lost, e.g. with initial /a/: /*qaṭāl/ > קָטוֹל (inf. abs.), /*šalām/ > שָׁלוֹם, /*qaṭūl/ > קָטוּל (pass. ptc.); with initial /i/: /*zirā'/ (Arb. /ḏirā'/) > זְרוֹעַ; /ṣirār/ > צְרוֹר (§ 6 *f*), /*ḥimār/ (still so in Arb.) > חֲמוֹר (with ḥaṭef pataḥ under the guttural, § 21 *g*) [but in the primitive forms /qiṭāl/ and /qiṭūl/ which have א as the first radical, the /i/ does not fall, but becomes ֱ, e.g. אֱזוֹר, אֱבוּס (§ 21 *h*)]; with initial /u/: /*lubūš/ >

לְבוּשׁ *clothes* (opposed to passive participle לָבוּשׁ *clothed*); /*gubūl/ > גְּבוּל *frontier.*

(1) Qameṣ is especially stable before the stress (*prestress qameṣ*).

B) **In mil'ra words of more than two syllables:** e

Generally the prestress vowel remains unaffected and the ante-prestress vowel, namely the one removed two places from the stress, drops out, e.g. /*ṣadaqat/ > צְדָקָה; /*ḥakamat/ > חֲכָמָה *a wise woman*; /*zaqinat/ > זְקֵנָה *an old woman*; /*qaṭaltẹm/ > קְטַלְתֶּם.

But in the perfect (without suffixes) the ante-prestress vowel remains and the prestress vowel drops out, e.g. /qaṭalat/ > קָטְלָה; /*qaṭalū/ > קָטְלוּ; /*ḥakamat/ > חָכְמָה *she is wise*; /zaqinat/ > זָקְנָה *she is old*. The difference in treatment of a primitive form such as /ḥakamat/ depending upon whether it is verbal or nominal form is probably explicable in terms of a difference in the placement of the stress at an earlier stage of the language. The verbal form חָכְמָה would reflect a stage /ḥa'kamat/ anterior to a stage /ḥaka'mat/ represented by the pausal form חָכָמָה* (cf. § 95 *c*).

The prestress vowel /a/ remains in certain forms, e.g. פָּרָשִׁים as plural of פָּרָשׁ *horse*, § 96 B *b*; שָׁבֻעוֹת, sg. שָׁבוּעַ *week*, § 96 D *b*; גָּלוּתִי *my exile*, § 88 M *j*; מָעֻזִּי *my refuge*, § 88 L *e*; מָגִנִּי *my shield*, § 88 L *h*. Special mention must be made of the pronoun אָנֹכִי (§ 39 *a*) and the forms of the perfect with the inversive Waw וְקָטַלְתָּ, וְקָטַלְתִּי (§ 43 *a*)(1).

(1) Generally speaking, the abnormal stability of the vowels ָ, ֵ, and ֻ is not an infallible indication of their primitive length.

C) **In mil'el words of more than two syllables,** one may note the following points of practical value: f

In the perfect with suffixes prestress /a/ is retained, e.g.: /qaṭala'ni/ > קְטָלַנִי; /i/ drops out in the Piel, e.g. קִטְּלַנִי, but is retained in the Qal, e.g. שְׁכֵחַנִי *he forgot me* (§ 61 *e*).

In the future with suffixes, prestress /a/ is retained, but /i/ and /u/ are dropped, e.g. יִלְבָּשֵׁנִי (from /yilbaš/ > יִלְבַּשׁ), but יִתְּנֵנִי (from /yittin/ > יִתֵּן), יִקְטְלֵנִי (from /yiqṭul/ > יִקְטֹל).

Observation. In the future, prestress /a/ is dropped as are the vowels /i/ and /u/, e.g. יִלְבְּשׁוּ, יִמְצְאוּ; יִתְּנוּ, יִמְצָאוּ; יִקְטְלוּ.

D) The treatment of the **vowel ְ in inflections** calls for separate consideration. g

In the absolute state ֳ is generally retained, but in the construct state it is generally dropped. Thus /*mi'at/ > מֵאָה *hundred*, cst. מְאַת, pl. abs. מֵאוֹת (the cst.st. would be מְאוֹת*); שֵׁם, שֵׁמוֹת, cst. שְׁמוֹת. ֳ is retained in the cst.st. in certain words: in words such as אֵזוֹר (§ 21 *h*); in זֵעַת *sweat of*, נֵכַר *the foreignness* (abstract) *of*, מַהְפֵּכַת *catastrophe of*, תַּרְדֵּמַת *deep sleep of*, בְּרֵכַת *a pool of*, עֲרֵמַת *a heap of*, etc.

In the verb conjugation we find the imperative of the type יָשַׁב: שֵׁב, שְׁבִי, שְׁבוּ. In the participle of the type קֹטֵל one finds קֹטְלָה or קֹטֵלָה or (mostly) קֹטֶלֶת; pl. קֹטְלִים (§ 50 *g*).

In the participle of the type מֵקִים one finds, e.g., cst. מֵשִׁיב (Ru 4.15); מְשִׁיבָה*, pl. מְשִׁיבִים.

In the participle of the type מֵסֵב: one finds, e.g. מֵרַע *acting wrongly*; pl. מְרֵעִים (contrast the participle מֵיטִיב with a stable /ẹ/, § *b*).

In the adjective of the type קָטֵל we find, e.g., אִלֵּם *dumb*, pl. אִלְּמִים.

§ 31. Stress: its position and shift

a The fundamental points concerning the stress have been presented in the section on accents (§ 15 *a-c*). The position of the stress, we have seen, can, in the majority of cases, be determined from the accents. The morphology may also provide a clue. Generally speaking, the position of the stress depends on the nature of the syllables. One can formulate the following two *negative* rules concerning closed syllables:

1) A closed penultimate syllable cannot have the stress unless the last syllable is open: e.g. one has קָטַ֫לְתָּ, but קְטַלְתֶּ֫ם.

2) Conversely a final closed syllable cannot lack a stress unless the penultimate syllable is open; e.g. one finds וַיָּ֫קָם, וַיָּקָם, but וַיִּקְטֹ֫ל וַיִּקְטֹל.

b The different forms taken by a word when inflected as well as some other considerations can cause a shift of stress either backwards (*receding* stress) or forwards (*advancing* stress); cf. § 15 *b*.

Often, when a word is lengthened, the new syllable receives the stress, e.g. דָּבָ֫ר, pl. דְּבָרִ֫ים: the stress *advances*, i.e. is shifted forwards on to /im/. In pause it is also thrown forwards in the case of the inverted future: וַיָּ֫קָם, but וַיָּקֹ֫ם (§ 32 e).

In the perfect the stress is mil'el in קָטַ֫לְתָּ, קָטַ֫לְתִּי, but it *advances* in the forms with the inversive Waw וְקָטַלְתָּ֫, וְקָטַלְתִּ֫י; in pause it *recedes* וְקָטָ֫לְתָּ (§ 32 *e*).

On the other hand, in the inverted future the stress *recedes* as much as possible (cf. § *a*): for example, we find יֵלֵךְ, but וַיֵּ֫לֶךְ. In the pause the stress *advances* in certain cases (§ 32 *e*).

Furthermore, the stress can *recede* for a rhythmical reason, that is to say, in order to avoid a coming together of two stressed syllables, which happens when two words are joined by a conjunctive accent, the first with the stress on its final syllable and the second with the stress on its first syllable[1]. *c*

The *receding* of the stress for a rhythmic reason is called נְסִיגָה *retreat* or נָסוֹג אָחוֹר[2], namely, stress *moving away backwards*.

In order for the *nsiga* to occur, it is necessary, in addition to the two negative rules given in § *a* being satisfied, that, if the last syllable is closed, it should not have an originally long vowel. E.g.: קָרָא לָ֫יְלָה Gn 1.5; מַשְׁכִּ֫ימֵי קוּם Ps 127.2; תֹּ֫אכַל לֶחֶם Gn 3.19; but לְמֵשִׁיב נֶ֫פֶשׁ Ru 4.15 (with an originally long *i*).

Furthermore, the heavy suffixes -כֶם, -כֶן; -הֶם, -הֶן always retain the stress. But the verbal afformatives -תֶם and -תֶן may give it up, e.g. הֱיִ֫יתֶם לֹא (Q= לוֹ) Job 6.21.

In the application of the *nsiga*, as in the case of the other rhythmical laws, it needs to be borne in mind that only full vowels count (§ 27 *d*). Thus one finds י֫וֹרְדֵי בוֹר Ps 28.1 (/yọ/ is regarded as a penultimate syllable). Likewise, one says, for example, בֹּ֫צֵעַ בָּצַע Pr 1.19 (the furtive pataḥ does not count).

(1) Therefore there is no clash when the accent is disjunctive, e.g. וְיָשַׁבְתָּ֫ שָׁם 1Kg 2.36; nor when there is a maqqef, for then the first word becomes proclitic.

(2) נָסוֹג Nifal ptc. of סוג.

Anomalous cases. One finds a *nsiga* in cases like אַ֫חַר כֵּן 1Sm 10.5, וְכִחֶשׁ בּוֹ Job 8.18, in a virtually closed syllable; וַיַּ֫חֲזֶק בּוֹ Ex 4.4 in a semi-closed syllable. *d*

In contrast, the *nsiga* is not found in some cases where it is expected, e.g. הָיְתָה תֹ֫הוּ Gn 1.2.

§ 32. **Pause**

a The pause is a halt, a noticeable break after a word in the course of recitation, and especially at the end of a verse. This break involves a certain amount of preliminary or preparatory protraction, which one can compare to the slowing down of a runner who prepares to stop. The pronunciation of a word in pause is slow, full, and emphatic.

As a result of this protraction, 1) the stressed vowel, whatever its timbre may be, can be assumed to have been originally longer than it would have been in context, and 2) some deleted vowels resurface, as a result of which the pausal forms are often forms which are primitive or closer to the primitive state, and generally the vowel thus restored carries the stress(1).

Moreover, it is likely that, in pause, apart from the quantitative difference, there often took place a change of vowel timbre, often involving a change of quantity. Finally, in certain cases, there occurred a shift of stress.

(1) For an attempt to reinterpret Hebrew phonology and morphology, starting from pausal forms and formulating a series of sandhi rules, see H.B. Rosén, "La position descriptive et comparative des formes contextuelles en hébreu," in A. Caquot and D. Cohen (eds), *Actes du premier congrès international de linguistique sémitique et chamito-sémitique. Paris 16-19 juillet 1969* (The Hague/Paris, 1974), pp. 246-55.

b **Purely quantitative change.** It cannot be determined with certainty whether the vowel /ọ/ in pausal שָׁ֑לוֹם or יִקְטֹ֑ל is any longer than its contextual, i.e. non-pausal counterpart. In any case, the Naqdanim did not invent any separate vowel sign. If they were aware of some quantitative difference, they did not consider it significant enough for special marking.

It needs to be noted that ַ often remains unchanged in pause, especially in monosyllabic words: thus one always has אַרְבַּ֑ע, בַּ֑ת; in the future, before the afformative -נָה, e.g. תִּכְבַּ֑דְנָה.

ֶ remains in pause as in אֱמֶ֑ת (§ 18 *l*), כַּרְמֶ֑ל; it remains unchanged notably in certain nouns of the segholate type מֶ֫לֶךְ, e.g. in the noun מֶ֑לֶךְ itself (§ 96 A *c*).

Change of vowels. c
ַ very often becomes ָ, e.g. קָטַל, קָטָל; קָטַלְתָּ, קָטָלְתָּ; יִכְבַּד, יִכְבָּד; מַ֫יִם, מָ֫יִם; נַ֫עַר, נָ֫עַר.
ֶ becomes ָ in the majority of the nouns of the type מֶ֫לֶךְ, e.g. קֶ֫שֶׁר, קָ֫שֶׁר (§ 96 A *c*); but also סֵ֫תֶר from סָ֫תֶר, and נֶ֫גַע from נָ֫גַע with its נִגְעוֹ (§ 96 A *e*). The Pf. דִּבֶּר becomes דִּבָּר.
ֵ sometimes becomes ֶ, e.g. יִגְמַל, יִגְמֹל; הֵפֵר, הֵפַר; וַיֵּלֶךְ, וַיֵּלַךְ.
The Hitpael with ֵ takes ֵ in an intermediate pause, and ָ in a major pause, e.g. יִתְיַצֵּב, יִתְיַצֵּב, יִתְיַצָּב (§ 53 *c*); יִתְנֶחָם (§ 29 *f*).
ְ becomes ָ (here /ǫ/) in certain words, e.g. שִׁכַּ֫לְתִּי, שָׁכָ֫לְתִּי Gn 43.14 (§ 6 *l*); יַחֲבֹשׁ, יֶחְבָּשׁ Job 5.18 (§ 29 *f*); יִטְרֹף, יִטְרָף Gn 49.27; יִשֹּׁךְ, יִשָּׁךְ Dt 23.20; Pr 23.32; עָז Gn 49.3 (actually with silluq). In Is 7.11, instead of the normal pausal form שְׁאוֹלָה Gn 42.38, one finds, in an intermediate pause, שְׁאָ֫לָה /š'ǫ'lå/, probably for the sake of assonance with לְמָ֫עְלָה /lmå''lå/ (phonetically /mǫ/)(1).
ַ becomes ֶ in the formula לְעוֹלָם וָעֶד *for ever and ever* (for עַד).

(1) This phenomenon, like many others, presupposes for the symbol ָ a single timbre /ǫ/.

Restoration of vowels. Normal cases: Pf.: קָֽטְלָה, קָטָ֫לָה; מָֽלְאָה, מָלֵ֫אָה; d
יִקְטְלוּן, יִקְטֹ֫לוּן; Fut.: יִקְטְלוּ, יִקְטֹ֫לוּ; יִתְּנוּ, יִתֵּ֫נוּ; יִכְבְּדוּ, יִכְבָּ֫דוּ; קְטַנָּה, קְטַנָּה; יִקְטֹלוּן (/o/ before a pause is retained).
אֲנִי, אָ֫נִי; פְּרִי, פֶּ֫רִי; חֲצִי, חֵ֫צִי (the primitive form is /ḥiṣy/); דַּרְכְּךָ, דַּרְכֶּ֫ךָ; בְּךָ, בָּ֫ךְ; לְךָ, לָ֫ךְ; אֹתְךָ, אֹתָ֫ךְ (in the last three examples, however, with the concomitant loss of the original, final vowel).
Stress shift. The stress *recedes* in, e.g. אָנֹכִ֫י, אָנֹ֫כִי; in the inverted Pf.: וְקָטַלְתִּ֫י; וְקָטָ֫לְתִּי. e
The stress *advances* in the inverted Fut. in cases like: וַיָּ֫קָם, וַיָּקֹ֫ם; וַיֹּ֫אמֶר, וַיֹּאמַ֫ר; וַיֵּ֫לֶךְ, וַיֵּלַ֫ךְ.
The pauses(1) that produce the above-mentioned effects are the major pauses, namely the pause at the end of a verse marked by the accent silluq and the pause in the middle of a verse marked by the accent athnaḥ. However, some accents indicating an intermediate pause can have some of the effects produced by the major ones. Such is the case especially with the accent zaqef, with which ַ often becomes ָ (hence the frequent massoretic note קָמֵץ בְּזָקֵף, e.g. Gn 11.3 ; § 16 *d*). On a special f

case of אֲנִי, see § 39 a.

One and the same word may have three different forms: a contextual form, a form in intermediate pause, and a form in major pause, e.g. אַתָּה you with /ă/, אַתָּ֫ה with mil'ra stress and /ă/, אָ֫תָּה with /å/ (§ 39 a). Likewise one has עַתָּה, עַתָּ֫ה, עָ֫תָּה now. See also the triple form of יִתְיַצֵּב (§ c).

(1) There are phenomena which are explicable in terms of *prepause*: a syllable preceding a pausal syllable (§ d) or a word preceding a pausal word (e.g., § 104 d).

The retention of the vowel in יִקְטְלוּן or further secondary lengthening in תְּדַבֵּרוּן in forms with the paragogic Nun (§ 44 e) is different from the restoration or modification of vowels in pausal forms in that the vowels restored or modified are stressed, which is not the case with the extended future forms.

g   The slowing-down which precedes the pause accounts for the fact that in certain cases longer forms are preferred in pause. Thus in the פ"נ verbs in pause, the assimilation of the נ is often omitted, e.g. יִנְצֹרוּ (§ 72 b). The Future endings וּן and ־יִן with a paragogic נ are found especially in pause (§ 44 e-f). See also § 62 c, e.

§ 33. Hiatus

a   We shall mention here this rhythmic phenomenon which displays some analogy with the pause(1). When a mil'el word ending with a vowel is followed by a word beginning with one of the gutturals א, ה, and ע, the stress becomes mil'ra. The phenomenon is attested especially with לָ֫מָה, which becomes לָמָ֫ה (without gemination), e.g. לָמָ֫ה אַתֶּם 2Sm 19.11 (§ 37 d). הָ֫בָה becomes in Gn 29.21† הָבָ֫ה אֶת־אִשְׁתִּי; likewise the imperatives שׁ֫וּבָה, ק֫וּמָה, ס֫וּרָה, e.g. סוּרָ֫ה אֵלַי Jdg 4.18; קוּמָ֫ה יהוה Nu 10.35 (where יהוה = אֲדֹנָי). Contrary to the normal accentuation one also finds, for instance, רָבֹ֫ו עָלֶ֫יהָ Gn 26.22; שָׂמֹ֫ו אֹתִי Gn 40.15; זָדֹ֫ו עֲלֵיהֶם Ex 18.11; שַׁתָּ֫ה עֲוֺנֹתֵ֫ינוּ Ps 90.8; וּבָאתָ֫ אַתָּה Zech 6.10 (cf. § 43 b); וְהִבְדִּילָ֫ה הַפָּרֹ֫כֶת Ex 26.33; וְהֵבִיאָ֫ה אוֹתָם Lv 15.29.

Before a guttural, a longer form seems to be preferred; cf. § 78 i, 79 m.

(1) For want of a better term, we call this phenomenon *hiatus*: there is a link between the stressed final vowel and the initial guttural (except ה, no doubt due to the particular nature of this guttural, cf. § 5 k, 20 c).

PART TWO

MORPHOLOGY

§ 34. General Observations

a The *root* is the simplest element of a word. It can be obtained by eliminating all derivational and inflectional elements, that is to say, not only all the vowels, but also certain consonants, chiefly the seven consonants ה א מ נ ת י ו known as "he'emantic" (from the mnemonic word[1] הֶאֱמַנְתִּיו). Thus in the word הִתְקַדְּשׁוּ *they sanctified themselves* the root is composed of the consonantal group קדשׁ which expresses the notion of sanctity; not included in the root therefore are the vowels, the gemination of ד (which indicates that the action is factitive, § 52 *d*), the sequence הִתְ (which indicates the reflexive, § 53 *a*), the final וּ (which marks the third person plural)(2). Thus the great majority of Hebrew words and word-forms consist of two elements, namely root consonants and pattern, the latter consisting in turn of vowels or consonantal affixes, or both, both of which are discontinuous morphemes(3).

For the sake of convenience one usually cites the root in the form of the third person sg.m. of the perfect, e.g. קָטַל *he killed*, which, in the regular verb and in part of the irregular verbs, represents the consonants of the root, only two vowels being added.

The majority of the currently known Hebrew roots are triliteral. Triliterality is such an integral part of the language that, in certain cases where it did not exist or no longer exist, it has been reinstated(4).

Hebrew has some quadriliteral roots, though many of them are of secondary origin (cf. § 60 and 88 K).

On the other hand, some roots are biliteral, at least in a sense (cf. ע"ע and ע"ו verbs).

(1) It would mean "I believed him," but הֶאֱמִין is always construed with a preposition.
(2) See the preformatives of the nominal forms in § 88 L, and the afformatives in § 88 M.
(3) For a lucid, theoretical, and general-Semitistic exposition of the matter, see J. Cantineau, "La notion de 'schème' et son altération dans diverses langues sémitiques," *Semitica* 3 (1950) 73-83. This was of course the doctrine implicit among mediaeval Arab grammarians and, in their wake, Jewish grammarians. Whereas a root thus conceived is obviously an abstraction, it is nonetheless a linguistic and psychological reality, which can account for the essentially consonantal character of the early Phoenician and cognate alphabets and orthographies. See now also D. Cohen, "Remarques sur la dérivation nominale par affixes dans quelques langues sémitiques," in his *Études de linguistique sémitique et arabe* (The Hague/Paris, 1970), pp. 31-48 [originally in *Semitica* 14 (1964) 73-93]; whilst agreeing with Cantineau in principle, Cohen demonstrates that some words can best be conceived of as possessing another component, an added morpheme.
(4) There also exist a considerable number of bi-consonantal words of common usage which must have formed part of the vocabulary since the very beginning of the history of the language such as אָב, יָד, דָּם, בֵּן as well as a series of monoconsonantal particles, e.g. בּ, לְ, כּ, ו. For an earlier attempt to argue for original, universal biconsonantism, see S.T.H. Hurwitz, *Root-determinatives in Semitic Speech: A Contribution to Semitic Philology* (New York, 1913). It has also been pointed out that a number of seemingly triconsonantal roots share an identical sequence of two consonants with an identifiable semantic content, e.g. קצב, קצע, קצף, קצץ, קצר with -קצ meaning "to cut off" or פרד, פרר, פרס, פרשׂ with -פר "to separate." Thus it appears that the predominance of triconsonantal roots most likely represents a historically late stage of development involving partial accommodation of originally biconsonantal roots. Nonetheless, it is wrong to say that all present triconsonantal roots can be ultimately reduced to biconsonantal roots. Nöldeke has shown how primitive mono- or biconsonantal roots underwent a process of conforming to the dominant triconsonantal pattern: e.g., ים > יום and יָמָּה; מ > מֵימֵי, pl. cst. of מַ֫יִם; פֶּה > pl. פִּיפִיּוֹת. See Th. Nöldeke, "Zweiradikalige Substantive," in his *Neue Beiträge zur semitischen Sprachwissenschaft* (Strassburg, 1910), pp. 109-78. See also Berg., II, § 1 *d-g*, Moscati, § 11.5-11.9, G.J. Botterweck, *Der Triliteralismus im Semitischen* (Bonn, 1952), and M. Lambert, "De la formation des racines trilitères fortes," in G.A. Kohut (ed.), *Semitic Studies in Memory of Alexander Kohut* (Berlin, 1897), pp. 354-62.

b One can determine the root of most words with confidence. However, there are a fair number the root of which is not so apparent. Thus lexicographers occasionally hesitate when they come to certain ע"ו or ע"י verbs; this is so, for instance, in the case of the word עֵדוּת *ordinance*, which could be derived from the root יעד or (more probably) from the root עוד.

The root of several words is unknown, e.g. מַקֵּל *staff*, עַל אֹדוֹת *concerning*.

The roots of some words can be rendered unrecognisable by the operation of the phonetic laws or analogy. In such cases there is an apparent root and a real root (according to other authorities, a secondary and a primary root). Thus Hitpael הִתְיַצֵּב appears to belong to a root יצב, whilst its true root is נצב (§ 77 *b*). The substantive תְּקוּפָה *cycle* seems to belong to a root קוף, but in truth this word relates to the Hifil הִקִּיף *to encircle* of the root נקף. Likewise תְּשׁוּעָה *victory* relates to the Hifil הוֹשִׁיעַ *to save* of the root ישׁע(1).

(1) These words were formed on the analogy of words of the pattern *taqtul* of ע"ו roots, § 88 L *s*.

c The same root can have verbal and nominal forms. If a noun is derived from a verb, it is called *deverbal*, whilst a verb derived from a noun is called *denominative*.

d The parts of speech are the pronoun (with the definite article included), the verb, the noun (substantive and adjective), and the particles (adverb, preposition, conjunction, and interjection).

CHAPTER I: THE DEFINITE ARTICLE AND THE PRONOUN

§ 35. The Definite Article

a The Hebrew definite article is an old demonstrative(1) and still retains, in some cases, a weak demonstrative force (cf. § 137 *f*). We therefore have decided to treat it under the same heading as the demonstrative pronoun. In meaning, the Hebrew definite article corresponds almost to the definite article in English.

(1) Likewise the article of the Romance languages has its origin in a Latin demonstrative pronoun, e.g. French *le* from Lat. *illum*.

b The normal form of the article is ·הַ, i.e. the consonant ה followed by the vowel ḁ, which adds some force to the following consonant, tending to produce gemination, e.g. הַסּוּס *hassus* "the horse"(1).

The primitive form of the Hebrew pronoun is simply a forceful (short) *ha* like the וַ of the inverted future וַיִּקְטֹל, § 47 *a*(2).

The tendency of the vowel of the article to effect the gemination of the following consonant is not always observed.

(1) See E. Ullendorff, who also adopts the gemination hypothesis in his "The true form of the definite article in Arabic and other Semitic languages," in G. Makdisi (ed.), *Arabic and Semitic Studies in Honour of Hamilton A.R. Gibb* (Leiden, 1965), pp. 631-37 [= E. Ullendorff, *Is Biblical Hebrew a Language?* etc. (Wiesbaden, 1977), pp. 165-71], and Phoenician evidence like אבבנם *the sons*, עמקם *the place* (Friedrich-Röllig, § 117). The evidence in Origen's Secunda is clear, e.g. 29.3 αχχαβωδ הַכָּבוֹד, 30.1 αββαιθ הַבַּיִת: see Brønno, *Studien*, pp. 203-5. See further T.O. Lambdin, "The junctural origin of the West Semitic definite article," in H. Goedicke (ed.), *Near Eastern Studies in Honor of William Foxwell Albright* (Baltimore/London, 1971), pp. 315-33. Berg. (II, § 5 *e*) maintains that the original form cannot have been /hal-/.
(2) This phenomenon of adding force (cf. *dḥiq*, § 18 *i*) exists especially in Italian: *a punto* becomes *appun'to*, *a lato* > *alla'to*, *a fine* > *affi'ne*; *a Roma* pronounced *arro'ma*; *da vero* > *davve'ro*; *da mi* > *dam'mi*; *va te ne* > *vatte'ne*; *si signore* > *sis-signo're*; in Tuscan dialect *a casa* > *accasa*; cf. § 18 *j*, n.

c **A non-guttural consonant followed by shewa** is often ungeminated (§ 18 *m*), e.g. הַלְוִיִּם *the Levites* (for the metheg, cf. § 14 *c* 6). One should take special note of the following two cases:

1) The dagesh is normally omitted from י, e.g. הַיְלָדִים *the children*, הַיְשׁוּעָה *the succour, the victory* (as opposed to הַתְּשׁוּעָה of the same meaning); exceptions occur when the gutturals ה or ע follow, e.g. הַיְּהוּדִים *the Jews*, הַיְּעֵפִים *the weary*.

2) The dagesh is often(1) omitted from the preformative מ of the participle Piel and Pual, e.g. הַמְכַסֶּה LXX: τὸ κατακαλύπτον, *that which conceals* (Lv 3.3; the same form occurs in Gn 18.17, with the interrogative ה: *Surely I shall not hide?*, § 102 *m*). Before ה or ע, one ordinarily has the dagesh, e.g. הַמְּעָרָה *the cave*, הַמְּהוּמָה *the disturbance*.

(1) Cf. A. Dotan, *Diqduqé haṭṭĕʽamim* [§ 8 *a*, n.], p. 364.

d A **guttural** consonant (and ר) cannot have strong gemination, but it is, with the exception of א and ר, capable of virtual or weak gemination. The capacity of the gutturals for receiving virtual gemination after the definite article is in descending order as follows: ח > ה > ע (cf. § 20 *a*). After the article, א never suffers virtual gemination, nor does ר, of course (likewise after מָה). When virtual gemination takes place, the vowel is ַ; but this ַ is nuanced as ֶ if the guttural is followed by qameṣ, i.e. /å/ or ḥaṭef qameṣ (§ 29 *f*).

ח almost always has virtual gemination, e.g. הַחֹ֫דֶשׁ *the month*, הֶחֳדָשִׁים *the months*; הַחָכְמָה *the wisdom*, הֶחָכָם *the wise man*; הַחֶ֫רֶב *the sword*, הֶחָ֑רֶב; הַחַי *the living* (always except in Gn 6.19 where הָחַי occurs without any apparent reason!).

ה generally allows virtual gemination, e.g. הַהֵיכָל *the temple*; הַהוּא *that* (the same form occurs in Nu 23.19† with the rhetorical interrogative ה: *num ipse?* [Did he really ... ?]), הַהִיא *that* (f.); הֶהָרִים *the mountains*.

Notable exception: accented הָ֫ can never have virtual gemination, e.g. הָהָר *the mountain*.

Other exceptions: e.g. הָהֵם *those*, and its less frequent variant הָהֵ֫מָּה; f. הָהֵ֫נָּה (1Sm 17.28†)(1).

ע generally does not allow virtual gemination, e.g. הָעָם *the people*, הָעַמִּים *the peoples*; הָעִיר *the city*; הָעֶ֫רֶב *the evening*, הָעָ֑רֶב.

Noteworthy exception: unstressed עָ- requires virtual gemination, e.g. הֶעָרִים *the cities* (perhaps on the the analogy of הֶהָרִים).

Other exceptions: e.g. הַעִוְרִים *the blind* (with a ו rafé, § 18 *m* 4), הַעֹזְבִים *they who abandon* Pr 2.13, הַעֹ֫זֶבֶת Pr 2.17 etc.

Observation. Where the gutturals ה and ע have ָ, they are treated in an analogous manner: stressed ה and ע are not capable of virtual gemination, e.g. הָהָר, הָעָם , whilst unstressed -הָ and -עָ effect virtual gemination, e.g. הֶהָרִים, הֶעָרִים. In brief, הָ and עָ cannot have both the stress and virtual gemination, but they have either one or the other.

(1) Note the asymmetry: sg. הַהוּא, הַהִיא, but pl. הָהֵם etc.

e The consonant ה of the definite article is syncopated following the prepositions בְּ, כְּ, לְ, e.g. לַמֶּלֶךְ for לְהַמֶּלֶךְ* (cf. § 17 *e*); בַּיָּמִים הָהֵם *in those days*, בָּעֵת הַהִיא *at that time*; בַּחֶרֶב *with the sword*, בְּחֶרֶב.

In those cases where the first consonant of the noun has a ḥaṭef, one has forms such as כָּאֲרִי *like the lion* (as opposed to כַּאֲרִי [§ 103 *b*], without the definite article, *like a lion*). There are two situations where the spelling is materially identical both with and without the article:

1) when a ֲ follows a guttural which takes virtual gemination; e.g. בַּחֲלוֹם can signify either *in the dream* or *in a dream* (cf. בַּחֲלוֹמִי).

2) with ֳ, e.g. בָּאֳנִיָּה can be either for /bå'ʕniyyå/ *in the ship* or for /bǫ-'ʕniyyå/ *in a ship* (cf. § 6 *n*).

Observation. ה is sometimes not syncopated, e.g. לְהָעָם 2Ch 10.7; לְהַגְּדוּד 25.10; such examples are found especially in late biblical books. One distinguishes between כַּיּוֹם *in the first place*, e.g. Gn 25.3 and כְּהַיּוֹם *immediately* 1Sm 9.13, Ne 5.11†; alongside כַּיּוֹם הַזֶּה *as (it still is) today* one sometimes finds כְּהַיּוֹם הַזֶּה with the same meaning.

f **Nouns the vowel of which is modified under the influence of the article.** Under the influence of the ָ of the article the following four words with a guttural as their first radical take ָ under the guttural: הַר, עַם (עָם with a disjunctive accent), אֲרוֹן *ark* (cf. Arb. *'irān*), and אֶרֶץ become הָהָר, הָעָם, הָאָרוֹן, and הָאָרֶץ respectively. The word חַג *festival* becomes חָג even in a minor pause. With the article one always finds הֶחָג, in fact always in a minor pause. The word פַּר (rarely פָּר) *young bull* always becomes הַפָּר with the article.

g **Observation.** 1) Before the article, the form of the interrogative pronoun is מָה (§ 37 *c*).

2) Before the article, the form of the preposition מִן generally remains unaltered (§ 103 *d*).

§ 36. Demonstrative pronoun

a Hebrew has, strictly speaking, only one demonstrative pronoun, and thus makes no distinction between the demonstrative for the near object (*hic, this*) and one for the remote object (*ille, that*).

The ordinary forms of the demonstrative pronoun are: sg.m. זֶה; f. זֹאת; pl.com. אֵ֫לֶּה.

The plural form has no relation whatsoever with those for the singular. On the contrary, the singular forms seem to derive from a primitive form *zā* with *anceps* vowel. The short form *ză* could not be maintained in Hebrew except by being modified to *ze* (like מָה, § 37 *b*). The long form *zā* occurs in the rare feminine forms זֹה, זֹו and the standard fem. זֹאת= *zā* + *t* of the feminine. The א of זֹאת may be etymological rather than a mere *mater lectionis*(1).

(1) See T. Muraoka, *Abr-Nahrain* 22 (1983-84) 93f.

b Rare forms: sg.f. זֹה (8 x, out of which 6 x are in Ec); זֹו (2 x), which is a regular MH form; com.pl. אֵל (8 x) in the Pentateuch, and always with the article, הָאֵל(1), except once without the article in 1Ch 20.8.

The poetic form זוּ, for both genders and both numbers, is used chiefly as a relative pronoun.

There is, furthermore, a *reinforced demonstrative*: m. הַלָּזֶה or הַלָּז(2) (particularly with a strong disjunctive accent); f. הַלֵּ֫זוּ (Ez 36.35); e.g. הָאִישׁ הַלָּזֶה *this person here* Gn 24.65.

(1) Comp. הָהֵם, which is more frequent than הָהֵ֫מָּה, § 35 *d*.
(2) Fem. in 2Kg 4.25.

c The demonstrative pronoun זֶה *this* etc. after a determined noun becomes demonstrative adjective, and as such takes the definite article, e.g. הָאִישׁ הַזֶּה *this man* (§ 137 *e*).

The pronouns of the third person, הוּא, הִיא; הֵ֫מָּה, הֵם; הֵ֫נָּה *he, she; they* (m.); *they* (f.) mean, strictly speaking, *the same*, but have virtually acquired a weak demonstrative sense, e.g. בַּיָּמִים הָהֵם *in the same days* = *in those days* (cf. § 35 *e*).

The article has sometimes preserved a weak demonstrative force (cf. § 137 *f* I).

§ 37. Interrogative pronoun

a One form serves for people of both genders and both numbers: מִי *who?*(1). מִי is used as subject מִי בָא *who is coming?*, as predicate מִי הָאִישׁ *who is this man?*, as accusative אֶת־מִי *whom?*, as genitive בַּת־מִי *whose daughter?*, with a preposition לְמִי *to whom?*, מִמִּי *from whom?*.

(1) The Yod of מִי was probably consonantal in origin as in AC *miya* (Sivan, pp. 129f.), Ugr. *my*, and Ph. מי.

b For things(1) one uses מה (with varied vocalisations), also as subject, predicate, accusative, genitive, and with a preposition.

The primitive form is *mă̄* with an anceps vowel (comp. *ză̄*, § 36 *a*; in Arabic one has the long form in *mā* and the short one *ma* in *li'ma*). In Hebrew the long form *mā* has become מוֹ, which occurs in the poetic form כְּמוֹ *like* and in the forms of כ with suffixes, e.g. כָּמוֹנִי, § 103 *g*, also occasionally בְּמוֹ for -בְּ, and לְמוֹ for לְ(2). The short form *ma* has become in Hebrew מָה, מֶה, -מַה.

Without stress, -מַה is the usual form.

In comparison with the vocalisation of the article (and that of the interrogative particle הֲ) the vocalisation of מה is rather complicated. The fact is that מה is not only proclitic (like the article), but also enclitic (or ex-enclitic), and even independent (non-clitic). Therefore there are three cases to be considered in accordance with the threefold role of מה: I proclitic, II enclitic, III independent.

(1) This is the only instance in Semitic of personal - impersonal contrast expressed by vowel alternation. The *a* - *i* relationship is reversed in Akkadian: *mannu* "who?" - *minu* "what?." Cf. G. Garbini, *Lingue semitiche* (Napoli, 1972), p. 33.
(2) The addition of /-m/ is well attested in Ugr.: see Gordon, *UT*, § 10.2.

c **I Proclitic** מה (generally with maqqef, occasionally with a conjunctive accent). The normal vocalisation is *i* מַה, namely a short *ą* with reduplication of the following consonant. The frequent gemination of the following consonant may be accounted for by postulating /mah/ as the original form as in Ugaritic *mh* with consonantal *h*, the gemination arising from the assimilation of /h/(1). This vowel adds some force, like the vowel of the article (§ 35 *b*) and that of וַ in the inverted future וַיִּקְטֹל (§ 47 a), e.g. מַה־יָּפִית *how beautiful you are!* Ct 7.7;

מַה־זֹּאת; מַה־זֶּה (מַזֶּה once in Ex 4.2K); מַה־לָּכֶם (מַלָּכֶם once in Is 3.15K).

Before a **guttural** the vocalisation is rather similar to that of the article (§ 35 *d*).

ח always shows virtual gemination, e.g. מַה חַטָּאתִי *what is my sin?* Gn 31.36.

ה generally shows virtual gemination, e.g. מַה־הוּא (comp. הַהוּא). Remarkable exception: the ה of the article shows no virtual gemination, e.g. מָה־הַמַּעֲשֶׂה *What is the deed?* Gn 44.15 (a unique exception is Ec 2.12 מֶה הָאָדָם).

Other exceptions: e.g. מָה־הֵמָּה, מָה־הֵם (comp. הָהֵמָּה, הָהֵם).

ע generally does not display virtual gemination, e.g. מָה עִמָּדִי *what do I have?* Gn 31.32.

Remarkable exception: עָ does show virtual gemination, e.g. מֶה עָשִׂיתִי *what have I done?*

After מה, א never shows virtual gemination nor, of course, ר (as is the case with the article).

Observation. In cases of virtual gemination, if the guttural has a qameṣ, ַ becomes ֶ (cf. the law of vowel harmony, § 29 *f*), e.g. מֶה חָטָאתִי *what sin have I committed?* 1Kg 18.9; ... מֶה חֳרִי *what means the heat of... ?* Dt 29.23.

Moreover, one sometimes finds מֶה even when the vowel which follows the guttural is not qameṣ.

(1) Cf. J. Blau and S.E. Loewenstamm, *UF* 2 (1970) 31f. See also G. Khan, "The pronunciation of ־מה before *dageš* in the medieval Tiberian Hebrew reading tradition," *JSS* 34 (1989) 433-41.

II Enclitic (or ex-enclitic) מה occurs after a preposition (particularly בְּ and כְּ). מה is enclitic when it has no stress, ex-enclitic when it has resumed stress. *d*

In general we find מֶה in context: בַּמֶּה(1), כַּמֶּה, יַ֫עַן מֶה (with the accent *rvia'*, Hg 1.9). מָה is used before a guttural or in a major pause, e.g. בַּמָּה 1Kg 22.21; בַּמָּה אֵדַע *With what would I know?* Gn 15.8.

With ל we find: 1) לָ֫מֶה, three times only (1Sm 1.8). This isolated form, though well attested and the analogue of the Arabic *li'ma*, appears to be the first form (with mil'el accent) in which מה remains enclitic(²).

2) לָ֫מָּה, usually, but before the gutturals א, ה or ע the form לָמָה is found (§ 33), e.g. לָמָה אַתֶּם 2Sm 19.11; לָמָה יהוה Jdg 21.3.

(1) Contrast the vocalisation of, e.g. בָּזֶה, § 103 c.
(2) Cf. P. Joüon in *Bib* 1 (1920) 363.

e **III Independent מה** (rather rare)

1) before a word, ordinarily with a disjunctive accent, one generally has the intermediate form מֶה, e.g. מֶה קּוֹל 1Sm 4.14 (accent: *tvir*).

2) after a word, actually always in pause, one has מָה, e.g. וְנַ֫חְנוּ מָ֫ה *and as for us, what are we?* Ex 16.7.

f In **summary**, one finds:

מָה 1) as a proclitic before a guttural without virtual gemination;
    2) after a preposition before a guttural or in major pause, and in לָמָה לָ֫מָּה;
    3) independent, after a word (rather rare).

מֶה 1) as proclitic before a guttural with virtual gemination followed by a qameṣ;
    2) after a preposition, in the usual fashion;
    3) independent before a word (rather rare).

מַה־ as proclitic before a non-guttural consonant, and before a guttural with virtual gemination (not followed by a qameṣ).

§ 38. Relative pronoun

The following two words, which do not seem to have had anything in common originally(¹), are employed as relative pronouns: אֲשֶׁר(²) and שֶׁ. The relative שֶׁ, which is found mostly in late books of the OT, must have existed in Hebrew at all times in the vernacular(³); its antiquity is assured by its Akk. counterpart *ša* and the occurrence of שׁ in the Song of Deborah (Jdg 5.7). In the literary idiom שׁ was supplanted almost completely by אֲשֶׁר prior to the exile. After the exile it appears fairly frequently(⁴). In the post-biblical period (Mishna) it completely replaced the written אֲשֶׁר(⁵).

In place of שֶׁ very rarely one finds שַׁ, and שָׁ (once, in Jdg 6.17 before א)(⁶). The short vowel, which requires gemination of the following consonant(7), is retained in all positions, e.g. שֶׁאֵין, שֶׁאֲנִי, שֶׁעַל, שֶׁרֹאשִׁי Ct 5.2 (§ 23 *a*).

We also find זוּ(8), זֶה and the article used as relative pronouns (cf. § 145 *c-d*).

(1) Cf. P. Joüon in *MUSJ* 6 (1913) 129.

(2) The etymology of the word is probably a noun meaning "place," cf. Akk. *ašru* (cst. *ašar*), Arb. *'iṯr*, Syr. *'aṯar*, Eth. *'ašar*. See D. Cohen, *Dictionnaire des racines sémitiques ou attestées dans les langues sémitiques* (Paris/The Hague, 1970-76), p. 37b.

(3) See G. Bergsträsser, *ZAW* 29 (1909) 40-56.

(4) See the detailed statistics in BDB, s.v. •שֶׁ; König, II, p. 322. It is not irrelevant to point out the error of BL, § 32 *b*, according to which •שׁ is common in Ezra (in fact it occurs only once in this book) and in Chronicles (twice). For a full list of the occurrences (136 x) of -שֶׁ, see Even-Shoshan, *A New Concordance* [§ 4 *f*], s.v., and Y. Peretz, *The Relative Clause* [Heb] (Tel Aviv, 1967), p. 127.

(5) N.H. Tur-Sinai (Torcyner) holds that אשׁר was in common, not only literary, use in the Biblical period, as can be seen in the Lachish (and now in Arad letters, and Ammonite); see a note by Tur-Sinai in E. Ben-Yehudah, *Thesaurus* [§ 4 *e*], vol. 7, col. 6779, n. 2. Cf. also B.A. Levine in *Eretz Israel* 18 (1985) 147-52. J.R. Davila holds that שׁ is typical of Northern Hebrew: *Maarav* 5-6 (1990) 82f.

(6) The variant vocalisations of the shorter form are: •שַׁ Gn 6.3(?), Jdg 5.7*bis*, Job 19.29(?), Ct 1.7†; שְׁ Ec 3.18 שְׁהֵם, and similarly at 2.22 (in some manuscripts including ed. Dotan, cf. Sh. Morag, *JAOS* 94 [1974] 308f.). No compensatory lengthening takes place except in Jdg 6.17 שָׁאַתָּה. The shewa with Shin is common in the Babylonian tradition: E. Porath, *Mishnaic Hebrew as Vocalised in the Early Manuscripts of the Babylonian Jews* [Heb] (Jerusalem, 1938), pp. 149f., and Yeivin, *Babylonian Tradition*, pp. 1158-62. See also Sh. Morag in *The Annual of the Shocken Institute for Jewish Studies*, The Jewish Theological Seminary of America, vol. 2, [in Heb] (Jerusalem, 1969-74), pp. 118f.

(7) The lengthening of the consonant following שׁ is also attested in Phoenician in Latin transcriptions (Segert, *Gram. of Phoen. and Pun.*, § 51.42), MH (M.H. Segal, *A Grammar of Mishnaic Hebrew* [Heb] [Tel Aviv, 1936], § 89), and SH (Ben-Ḥayyim, *LOT*, vol. 5, p. 243).

(8) Cf. Ugr. *d*, which, in syllabic transliteration, appears as *du-ù*.

§ 39. Personal pronoun
(Paradigm 1).

A. Separate pronouns

First pers. *Singular* (of common gender). The primitive Hebrew form a is *'anā'ki > אָנֹ֫כִי (pausal form)(1). In context the stress becomes mil'ra; but the vowel ָ, now being found two syllables away from the stress, is retained (§ 30 *e*): אָנֹכִ֫י.

Another form, which one finds especially in the later books and which, in post-biblical Hebrew(2), ousted אָנֹכִי, is אֲנִי(3), אָ֫נִי in pause (even minor), and sometimes even with a conjunctive accent, e.g. always in חַי אָ֫נִי *I am alive!* (for emphasis).

First pers. *Plural* (common). The primary form נַ֫חְנוּ is very rare (5 x; once in a Lachish letter [4.10]); otherwise the secondary form אֲנַ֫חְנוּ is used, the א of which is probably due to the analogy with the singular אֲנִי (cf. Brock., *GvG*, I, p. 299). In pause we find אֲנָ֫חְנוּ. The post-stress *u* was originally short (cp. Arb. *naḥ'nu*). Note אנו once as Ktiv in Jer 42.6, which is the normal form in MH.

Second pers. *Sing. masc.* The primitive form *'an'ta* remains mil'el in intermediate pause אָ֫תָּה, e.g. Gn 3.19, and in major pause אָ֫תָּה (§ 32 *f*). In context, according to the general tendency of Hebrew, the stress is mil'ra: אַתָּ֫ה(4).

Second pers. *Sing. fem.* The primitive mil'el form *'an'tī* becomes אַתְּ with the deletion of the post-stress vowel; the pausal form is אָתְּ. The form אַתִּי*(5) is found only as Ktiv (7 times).

Second pers. *Pl. masc.* The primitive form *'*antumu* has not survived: the *u* has been replaced by the *i* of the feminine, giving the form *'*antim*, which has then become אַתֶּם (with a seghol![6]) (cf. Brock., *GvG*, I, p. 302)(7).

Second pers. *Pl. fem.* The primitive form *'*antinna*, claimed to be still found in the unique (and suspect) form אַתֵּ֫נָּה Ez 13.20, is not admitted in Cod. L, A, or C. Elsewhere one has אַתֵּ֫נָה (3 x), without dagesh in the נ. Finally the post-stress vowel can drop out, giving אַתֵּן Ez 34.31† (var. אַתֶּן).

Third pers. *Sing. masc.*: Primitive form **hū'a*; Heb. הוּא. Compare הואה, which frequently occurs in some Qumran manuscripts.

Third pers. *Sing. fem.*: Primitive form **šī'a*; Heb. הִיא. The *š* of the feminine is found in Akkadian, Eblaite, Minaean, and in Mehri (Brock., *GvG*, I, p. 303). In Hebrew the *š* has been replaced by the *h* of the masculine(8).

Third pers. *Pl. masc.*: Primitive form **humu*; Heb. הֵם, הֵ֫מָּה. The most frequent form is הֵ֫מָּה (272 x as against הֵם 191 x)(9), but with the article it is usually הָהֵם, הָהֵמָּה attested only 12 times. The two vowels of the primitive feminine *šinna have been transferred on to the Hebrew masculine הֵמָּה.

Third pers. *Pl. fem.*: Primitive form *šinna; Heb. הֵנָּה(10). The ה is due to the analogy of the masculine form. The curtailed form, הֵן, standard in MH, does not occur in BH except as a bound morpheme as in לָהֶן, בָּהֶן.

Observation. One might note that the final ָה occurs in the plural in three forms: 3rd f. הֵנָּה (only form); 3rd m. הֵמָּה (the more frequent form); 2nd f. אַתֵּנָה (the more frequent form—4 x : 1 x). The longer forms are very much prominent in QH.(11)

(1) Cf. Ugr. *a-na-ku*, and Amarna Canaanite, which also attests to *a-nu-ki* (EA 287.66,69).

(2) See Polzin, pp. 126f. For statistics showing the distribution pattern of the two forms among various OT books, see BDB, s.v. אָנֹכִי. For a discussion of some questions arising from the coexistence of the two forms, see K. Aartun, *UF* 3 (1971) 1-7; H.B. Rosén, "'*nky* et '*ny*: Essai de grammaire, interprétation et traduction," *Mélanges A. Neher* (Paris, 1975), pp. 253-72; and A. Schoors in *Hebrew Studies* 30 (1989) 71f.

(3) The ḥaṭef of אֲנִי is abnormal; in a prestress syllable the full vowel ָ would be expected. Perhaps the ḥaṭef is due to the overuse of the form, or to the influence of the Aramaic אֲנָה (BL, pp. 248f.), or to the influence of אֲנַחְנוּ (in which the א, in its turn, is due to the analogy of אֲנִי).

(4) The spelling אַתְּ (Ktiv) occurs five times.

See Ps 89.39 אַתָּה in Secunda αθ, cf. 18.41 נָתַתָּה ναθαθ, which is, incidentally, another indication of the nascent phonematisation of בגדכפת. Those who want to interpret אַתְּ as /'att/ or /'attə/ would have to explain why Qal inf. cst. תֵּת has not come down to us as *תֵּתְּ (< תֵּתְ < *תִּנְתְּ), whereas אַתְּ can be attributed to the analogy of the other second person forms. See also Ben-Ḥayyim, *LOT*, vol. 5, p. 168, n. 4.

According to AF (p. 135): "The normalization [= Ktiv] achieves consistency, but the survival of apparently fem. vocalization of clearly masc. forms (Nu 11.15; Dt 5.24; Ez 28.14) suggests that אַתְּ was a variant masc. form."

(5) With regard to stress, *אַתְּי must be treated like אַתָּה; compare the old 2nd f. form קָטַלְתִּי, § 42 *f*. However, the short form אַתְּ [att] or [at] (see § 8 *d*, n. and § 27 *db*) is attested three times as masculine: Nu 11.15; Dt 5.27; Ez 28.14.

(6) The seghol may be a residue of the earlier penultimate stress: see A. Dotan in M. Bar-Asher et al. (eds), *Hebrew Language Studies* [Fschr. Z. Ben-Ḥayyim] [Heb] (Jerusalem, 1983), p. 160.

(7) QH אתמה; cf. SH /attimma/(reading tradition, not the written consonantal Samaritan Pentateuch with אתם). See Ben-Ḥayyim, *LOT*, vol. 5, p. 167.

(8) The forms הואה and היאה, which occur frequently in QH (and Aramaic) alongside הוא, הו on the one hand, and הי on the other, probably attest to this Proto-Hebrew form and /hi'a/, or /huwa/ and /hiya/—ultimately traceable back to /huwat/ and

/hiyat/, Sh. Morag, *VT* 38 (1988) 157—respectively, which makes the Massoretic spellings הוּא and הִיא instances of defective spelling, the Alef representing a vestige of its ancient consonantal value, dissimilated from *w* and *y* respectively. AC *ù-wa* (= *huwa*; Sivan, p. 126), Ugr. *hw* (= /huwa/) and *hy* (= /hiya/) also point in the same direction. See a discussion by E.Y. Kutscher, *Isaiah*, pp. 433-40 and Qimron, *Hebrew of DSS*, pp. 57f. The former, however, considers it equally likely that the long forms are a secondary, analogical development based on *hemma* and *henna*. The ending /-t/ is preserved in Ugr. *hmt*, Phoen. 3ms האת, pl. המת, and Ethiopic 3ms. *we'etu* and f. *ye'eti*. On Ugr. *hw*, see Huehnergard, *Ugr. Vocabulary*, pp. 86, 293.

(9) Note also the alternation of the two forms in two adjacent verses (Lv 11.27f.).

(10) To be distinguished from the adverb הֵנָּה *hither, here* (with movement, Lat. *huc*).

(11) See Qimron, *Hebrew of DSS*, p. 58.

b On the pronouns of the third person preceded by the article הַהוּא, הַהִיא; הָהֵם, הָהֵמָּה, הָהֵנָּה, see § 36 *d*.

c **The feminine Ktiv הוא in the Pentateuch.** In the consonantal text of the Pentateuch (but not in the Samaritan Pentateuch) we find the spelling הוא not only for the masculine, but almost always (11 exceptions) for the feminine, for which the Naqdanim write הִוא (Qre perpetuum, § 16 *f* 2), e.g. הָאָרֶץ הַהִוא Gn 2.12. This rather strange phenomenon, it seems, may be explained fairly plausibly as derived from a certain late recension of the Pentateuch. With many writers we may assume that the primitive spelling was הא both for the masculine, which probably was still *hū'a* and for the feminine, which probably was *hī'a*(1). When these forms became *hū* and *hī* respectively in Hebrew, the spelling הא was found insufficiently clear. A scribe, one may suppose, could have wished to indicate the long vowels *ū* and *ī* by means of the *matres lectionis* in respect of both timbre and quantity. Now for several centuries, especially during the period of Hebrew inscriptions in square script from the first to the fourth centuries, the form of the letter י was nearly identical with that of the letter ו(2). A scribe, under such conditions, wanting to add a ו or a י in the sequence הא found himself actually adding a character which could, to all intents and purposes, pass for a ו. Later, when the shape of ו was unequivocally distinct from that of י, one would not dare, out of respect for this manuscript, modify the spelling of the הוא sequence in cases where the sense indicated the feminine(3).

(1) We find הא in the Moabite inscription of Mesha (9th cent.) for the masculine, and for the feminine in Phoenician (except in late Vulgar Punic, which shows הי).

(2) However, in the manuscripts which were used by the LXX translators, ו and י had an almost identical shape; cf. Driver, *Notes*, p. lxiv.
(3) The Samaritan Pentateuch regularly has היא where the MT has הִוא.

B. Suffix pronouns

d

The pronouns can be suffixed to a verb, e.g. קְטָלַ֫נִי *he killed me* (a verbal suffix in the accusative, § 61) or to a noun, e.g. סוּסִי, literally *the horse of me* = *my horse* (nominal suffix in the genitive, § 94). Moreover particles, especially prepositions, can take suffixes, e.g. לִ֫י *to me*, הִנְנִי *here I am*. The forms of the suffix pronouns are mostly traceable to those of the separate pronouns.

CHAPTER II: VERB

§ 40. General observations and classification

a **Conjugations.** The Hebrew verb comprises a number of *conjugations*(1) (בִּנְיָנִים *buildings*): a *simple* conjugation, called *Qal* (קַל = *light*) and a number of *derived* or *augmented* conjugations. The *simple* conjugation is well named because, in comparison with the others, its form is the simplest and the action which it expresses is equally simple, e.g. קָטַל *he killed*(2). The *derived* or *augmented* conjugations have an expanded form in relation to the simple conjugation, and the action which they express has an added objective modality: an aspect of causality, e.g. הִקְטִיל *he made kill.*

Furthermore, the conjugation of the simple, intensive (?) or causative action can be in one of the three **voices**: active, passive, and reflexive, e.g. הָקְטַל *he was made to kill.*

The table of the actual conjugations may be presented in the following fashion by using the traditional designations and by taking as examples the perfects of the uncommon verb קטל(3) adopted as paradigm:

VOICE	ACTIVE	PASSIVE	REFLEXIVE
Simple action	Qal קָטַל *he killed*	Cf. § 58 *a*	Nif'ạl נִקְטַל *he killed himself*; *he was killed*
Intensive(?) action	Pi"ẹl קִטֵּל *he killed intensely*(?)	Pu"ạl קֻטַּל *he was killed intensely*(?)	Hiṯpạ"ẹl הִתְקַטֵּל *he killed himself intensely*(?)
Causative action	Hif'il הִקְטִיל *he made kill*	Họf'ạl הָקְטַל *one has caused him to kill*(4)	

(1) This term, used here for want of a better one, is taken, as one can see, in a sense rather different from that which it has in English grammar. For a general and

structural discussion, cf. M.H. Goshen-Gottstein, "The system of verbal stems in the classical Semitic languages," *Proceedings*, pp. 70-91.

(2) When we simply want to designate a verb, we often translate the form of the perfect 3rd pers. by the infinitive, e.g. קָטַל *to kill*. It is common practice to designate a Hebrew verb by the 3rd pers. m.sg. of Qal, except ע"ו and ע"י verbs which one designates by the infinitive construct (cf. § 80 *c*, n.).

(3) The verb קְטַל, common in Aramaic (and in Arabic *qatala*, with the original non-emphatic *t*), occurs only three times in Hebrew (in poetic texts, Ps 139.19; Job 13.15, 24.14). הָרַג is the usual word for *to kill*, and רָצַח for *to commit a homicide*.

(4) Strictly speaking: *he has been caused to kill*.

Tenses and moods. Corresponding to what we call **tenses** Hebrew has two forms which we, for want of a better alternative (cf. § 111 *b*), shall call **perfect** and **future**, e.g. in the simple conjugation: perfect קָטַל *he killed, he has killed*; future יִקְטֹל *he will kill*. *b*

From the point of view of **moods**, the perfect קָטַל and future יִקְטֹל are **indicative**. The future can have, in a great number of words, two variations corresponding to two volitive nuances, namely the **jussive** mood, for example, יִקְטֹל *may he make* (someone) *kill!* and (in the first person) the **cohortative** mood, e.g. אֶקְטְלָה *I want to kill*. The **imperative** constitutes the volitive mood of the second person, e.g. קְטֹל *Kill!*

Besides these temporal and modal forms there are two *atemporal* and *amodal* (and also impersonal) forms, which partake of the nature of both verb and noun: the **infinitive** and the **participle**. The infinitive is an action noun with the force of a verb; one distinguishes two forms of it, namely the **infinitive absolute** and the **infinitive construct**. The **participle** partakes of the nature of both verb and adjective; it designates the *agent*, the one who performs the action (active participle) or the *patient*, the one who suffers the action (passive participle).

In the simple conjugation, Qal, we have so far spoken of *action* only. But, in fact, apart from **verbs of action** or **active verbs**(1) such as קָטַל *he killed*, there are **verbs of state** or **stative verbs** expressing a state or quality, e.g. כָּבֵד *he is heavy, he was heavy* (§ 41 *b*)(2).

(1) We use *active verb*, *active perfect*, *active future* in the sense of *action verb*, etc., and not in the sense of verb in the *active voice* (cf. § *a*).

(2) The *transitivity* and *intransitivity* are syntactic phenomena, which do not affect the vocalisation of verbs.

Verb classes. The majority of verbs are triliteral. According to the *c* state of the root, verbs are said to be either **strong** or **weak. Strong** verbs have three unchangeable root consonants. The strong verb presents some peculiarities of vocalisation when one (or more) radical is guttural. **Weak** verbs present within their root a *weak* consonantal (or vocalic) element. In order to designate these verbs one uses the letters of the verb פָּעַל (poetical) *to do* (an old paradigm[1] originating in Arabic grammar). The פ represents the first element, the ע the second, and the ל the third element of the root. Thus a פ"ן verb is one whose first letter is Nun. The other weak verbs are similarly designated: פ"א, פ"י, ל"א, ל"ה, ע"ו, ע"י (cf. § 71). The designation ע"ע verbs is given to the *geminate* verbs, the second radical of which is repeated, e.g. סָבַב *he encircled*.

(1) Hence the conventional terms for designating the conjugations, *Nif'al*, *Hif'il* etc.

d We shall first deal with the regular strong verb, beginning with the Qal conjugation. In order to avoid repetitions, we shall give *on the first occasion* what would apply to an entire category of forms (conjugations or verb classes)(1).

(1) The student therefore would do well first to go rapidly over the principal forms or the details which would not be repeated subsequently.

§ 41. **Qal conjugation**

a The Qal conjugation comprises **action verbs** and **stative verbs** (§ 40 *b*).

The **action verbs** are of the form **qatal* > קָטַל, קָטָֽל, e.g. נָתַן *to give*, יָשַׁב *to sit*, אָכַל *to eat*.

In the future the second vowel is generally **u* > ֹ in strong verbs. The vowel **i* > ֵ is found in יִתֵּן (§ 72 *i*), in the type יֵשֵׁב (§ 75 *c*), in the type יֹאכַל (here by dissimilation, cf. § 73 *c*)(1). As for the first vowel (the vowel of the preformative), cf. § *e*.

Action verbs express a transitive or intransitive action. Some verbs can also express a reflexive action, e.g. רָחַץ *to wash* and *to wash oneself*, *to take a bath* (likewise in Latin *lavare*), סוּךְ *to pour*, *anoint* and *to anoint oneself*; מָשַׁח *to anoint* and *to anoint oneself* (Am 6.6); טָבַל *to dip* and *to dip oneself*. In certain cases the reflexive sense seems to derive from ellipsis, e.g. הָפַךְ *to turn* and *to turn oneself*

(Jdg 20.39 etc.), סָעַד *to sustain* and *to sustain oneself* (1Kg 13.7†, namely *to sustain one's heart* לֵב).

Certain action verbs are denominative, e.g. לָבַן *to manufacture bricks* (לְבֵנָה), מָלַח (1 x) *to season with salt* (מֶלַח), שָׁבַר *to purchase grain* (שֶׁבֶר), אָהַל (2 x) *to pitch a tent* (אֹהֶל)(2).

(1) According to J. Barth, ֵ as stem vowel occurs in regular verbs as well: *ZDMG* 43 (1889) 177.

(2) For an attempt to classify Qal verbs in terms of the stem vowel mutation ('Ablaut') in the perfect and future on the one hand, and semantic categories on the other, see Waltke—O'Connor, *BH Syntax*, pp. 367-71 (§ 22.3). See also J. Aro, *Die Vokalisierung des Grundstammes im semitischen Verbum* (Helsinki, 1964), pp. 108-38.

The **stative verbs**, which are "conjugated adjectives"(1), have two forms, a more frequent form **qatil* (cf. Akk. *paris*), e.g. כָּבֵד *he is heavy*, and a less frequent form **qatul* (cf. Akk. *maruṣ*), e.g. קָטֹן *he is small*. To these two forms of the perfect correspond a single form of the future with a second vowel *a*: יִכְבַּד *he will be heavy*, יִקְטַן *he will be small*. As for the first vowel (that of the prefix), cf. § e. b

At the earliest stage all stative verbs must have expressed what, from the point of view of the Semites, was conceived as a state or an attribute rather than as an action. But numerous stative verbs actually express what for us would really be an action, e.g. שָׁמַע, שָׁמֵעַ *to hear*. Certain verbs, in addition to having purely stative meaning, e.g. *he is heavy* (כָּבֵד), have nuances which come close to the notion of action, like *he becomes heavy, he grows heavy*. In general terms one could say that the stative verbs tend to become action verbs whether in terms of meaning or in terms of vocalisation(2). The encroachment of the active on the stative is due to evolution of meaning, to the fact that the action verbs are altogether the most numerous, and occasionally due to particular phonetic laws.

Some verbs whose perfect bears a vowel characteristic of stative verbs show, in the fut., a vowel typical of action verbs: שָׁכֵן, שָׁכַן, fut. יִשְׁכֹּן *to inhabit*; חָפֵץ, f. יַחְפֹּץ *to like, desire*; נָבֵל, f. יִבֹּל *to wither*; עָמֵל*, עָמַל־, f. יַעֲמֹל *to become weary*; מֵת, f. יָמוּת *to die*; שָׁמֵם*, f. יִשֹּׁם *to be stupefied, desolate*.

In the perfect the vowel ֵ of stative verbs has often been replaced by the vowel ַ of action verbs: 1) especially in context, e.g. שָׁכַן, but שָׁכֵן; 2) quite often even in pause, e.g. חָזָק *to be strong*(3); 3) in two verbs the stem vowel can be ◌ֶ as in שְׁאֶלְתֶּם (1Sm 12.13) or ◌ִ as in וִירִשְׁתֶּם (Dt 4.1), esp. with object suffixes as in וִירִשְׁתָּהּ (Dt 17.14), שְׁאִלְתִּיו (1Sm 1.20), both before or after a sibilant, but יְלִדְתִּיךָ Ps 2.7. Occasionally the vowel ◌ֵ has not been able to maintain itself except before a suffix, e.g. שְׁאֵלְךָ but שָׁאַל, שָׁאֵל; גְּדֵלַנִי (Job 31.18 ?), but גָּדַל(4).

(1) H. Bauer, *Die Tempora im Semitischen* (Leipzig, 1910), p. 33.

(2) Cf. P. Joüon, "Verbes actifs et verbes statifs," *MUSJ* 5 (1911) 356ff. For the view that stative verbs are equally "verbal," see K. Aartun, *UF* 7 (1975) 1-11. See also E. Rubinstein, "Adjectival verbs in Biblical Hebrew," *IOS* 9 (1979) 55-76, esp. 60-64 on the difficulty in choosing between the static and dynamic aspects. The only certain thing that can be said is that the use of the adjectival verb is obligatory for expression of dynamism.

(3) Here perhaps under the influence of ק; but the verbal adjective is חָזֵק. Comp. רָחַק *to be remote*, despite the adjective רָחוֹק; verbal adj. רָחֵק (once).

(4) In these two verbs the *a* was probably suggested by the ל of the closed syllable.

c A verb which is strictly stative cannot have a participle, but only a verbal adjective, e.g. חָזֵק, יָרֵא *fearful*. But in reality, as a consequence of the evolution of the stative towards the active, stative verbs often have participles, e.g. אֹהֵב *loving*; שֹׂנֵא *hating*. Sometimes there exist both a participle and a verbal adjective, e.g. שֹׁכֵן *inhabiting* (Lat. habitans) vs. שָׁכֵן *inhabitant* (Lat. habitator), *neighbour*.

d In practice, a stative verb can be identified most surely by the vowel *a* of the future (provided that this *a* is not due to any phonetic cause, e.g. a guttural); in certain verb classes, by the vowel *i* or *ẹ* of the preformative (cf. § *e*); less frequently by the vowel *ẹ* of the perfect (which has often been replaced by *a*).

There are some other secondary traits, e.g. the existence of a verbal adjective (types כָּבֵד and קָטֹן), the existence of an infinitive with ◌ָה (as a matter of fact, the infinitives קַטְלָה, קִטְלָה, קָטְלָה hardly occur except in stative verbs, § 49 *d*).

e **The vowel of the future preformative in action** verbs and **stative** verbs. The view that the vowel of the future preformative was originally *a* in action verbs, and *i* in stative verbs is rather plausible(1). In Hebrew these vowels do appear when the syllable is open, i.e.: in ע"ע verbs: action יָסֹב, stative יֵקַל (§ 82 *b*); in ע"ו verbs: action יָקוּם, יָשִׁיר, stative יֵבוֹשׁ (for **yibāš*, § 80 *b*). In closed syllables, the primitive vowel *a* of action verbs has been attenuated to *i* in accordance with a rather widespread tendency (§ 29 *g*); **yaqtul* has become יִקְטֹל, with *i* as in stative verbs, e.g. יִכְבַּד. However, even in closed (and semi-closed) syllables, the primitive vowels may turn up: 1) in first-guttural verbs, e.g. action יַעֲמֹד, stative יֶחֱזַק, יֶחְזַק (§ 21 *d*), and יַחֲרֹשׁ *he will plough* vs. יֶחֱרַשׁ *he will be silent*; 2) in פ״י verbs (in syllables originally closed), e.g. action יֵשֵׁב (for *yayšib*), stative יִירַשׁ (for *yiyraš*), cf. § 75 *b*, *c*.

(1) First formulated by Barth (hence Barth's law) as *yaqtul*, *yaqtil*, but *yiqtal*: J. Barth, *ZDMG* 48 (1894) 4-6. Subsequently, it was noted by Ginsberg that the law also applies to Ugaritic, and hence it is now usually called Barth-Ginsberg's law: H.L. Ginsberg, *Or* 8 (1939) 319-22. The law is applicable to Eblaite and El-Amarna Canaanite as well: H-P. Müller, *Bib* 65 (1984) 152 and A.F. Rainey, *Eretz Israel* 14 (1978) 8*-13*, but not to Amorite, which is about 700 years younger than Eblaite; see H.B. Huffmon, *Amorite Personal Names in the Mari Texts: A Structural and Lexical Study* (Baltimore, 1965), p. 64. The universal *ya-* in Arabic may be a result of levelling.

Note that, in the future, action verbs may show either *i* or *u* as stem vowel; cf. §44 *c*.

A list of the most common **stative verbs** grouped according to mean- *f*
ing(1):

I Attributes

Pf. טוֹב, f. יִיטַב (root יטב), inf.cst. טוֹב; defective verb, § 85 *a*, *to be good*; adj. טוֹב.

רַע, f. יֵרַע *to be evil*; adj. רַע.

גָּדֵל*, גָּדַל (1 x), גְּדֵלַנִי (Job 31.18 ?) *to be great*; adj. גָּדוֹל (*qatul* form, § 88 D *c*).

קָטֹן *to be small*; adj. קָטֹן and קָטָן, § 18 *f*.

גָּבַהּ *to be high*; adj. גָּבֹהַּ.

שָׁפֵל *to be low*; adj. שָׁפָל.

חָזַק, חָזֵק *to be strong*; adj. חָזָק (verbal adj. חָזֵק 2 x).

דַּל, f. יִדַּל *to be weak*; adj. דַּל.

כָּבֵד*, כָּבַד (1 x) *to be heavy*; adj. כָּבֵד.

קַל, f. יֵקַל *to be light*; adj. קַל.

רָחֵק, רָחַק *to be far*; adj. רָחוֹק (*qatul* form, § 88 D *c*).

קָרֵב*, קָרַב, קָרְבָה *to be near*; adj. קָרוֹב (*qatul* form, § 88 D *c*).

נָגַשׁ*, f. יִגַּשׁ *to approach* (§ 72 *g*; defective verb, § 85 *b*).

דָּבֵק, דָּבַק *to cling*.

טָהֵר *to be pure*; adj. טָהוֹר (*qatul* form, § 88 D *c*).

טָמֵא *to be impure*; adj. טָמֵא.
מָלֵא *to be full*; adj. מָלֵא(2).

II Mental states

אָהֵב, אָהַב, f. יֶאֱהַב *to love.*
חָפֵץ, f. יַחְפֹּץ (§ *b*), *to love, desire.*
שָׂנֵא *to hate.*
יָרֵא, f. יִירָא *to fear.*
יָגֹר, f. יָגוּר (root גּוּר), *to dread*(3); defective verb, § 85 *a.*
חָרֵד f. יֶחֱרַד *to tremble.*
פָּחַד, *to tremble.*
שָׁכֵחַ*, שָׁכַח, שָׁכֵחוּ *to forget.*

III Physical states

לָבֵשׁ, לָבַשׁ *to be clothed.*
שָׂבֵעַ*, שָׂבַע, שָׂבֵעוּ *to be sated*; adj. שָׂבֵעַ.
רָעֵב *to be hungry*; adj. רָעֵב.
צָמֵא *to be thirsty*; adj. צָמֵא.
יָשֵׁן*, f. יִישַׁן *to sleep.*
שָׁכַב, שָׁכֵב *to be lying, to lie down*; inf. שְׁכַב, § 49 *c.*
שָׁכֹל *to lose one's children, to be/become childless.*

IV Miscellaneous

יָכֹל, f. יוּכַל (but probably fut. Hofal, § 75 *i*) *can, to be able to.*
לָמַד *to learn, to accustom oneself.*
מֵת, f. יָמוּת (§ *b*) *to die.*
שָׁאַל, שָׁאֵל, שְׁאֵלְךָ *to ask*(4).
שָׁכַן, שָׁכֵן, f. יִשְׁכֹּן (§ *b*) *to inhabit.*
שָׁמַע, שָׁמֵעַ *to hear, listen.*

(1) The future is in *a* unless proof of the contrary can be given.
(2) The antonym *to be empty* does not occur; adj. רֵק.
(3) The fut. *he fears* יָגוּר is treated as an action verb (cf. Dt 32.27, Ho 10.5, Job 41.17); cf. § *b.*
(4) Comp. שְׁאֵלָה and שְׁאֵלָתִי *request*, § 97 B *d.*

§ 42. Inflection of the Qal Perfect

The inflection of the Qal Perfect (and other Perfects) occurs through the addition of afformatives, in the majority of which one easily recognises the separate personal pronouns. In the third person, the pronoun is understood; the feminine is marked by *å* for **at* (as in nouns): קָטְלָה; the plural by *u*: קָטְלוּ. The form of the perfect seems to have been initially used with stative verbs, e.g. כָּבַ֫דְתָּ = כָּבֵד + אַתָּה: *heavy-you* = *you are heavy*(1). Similarly, in order to express an action we find, with a form such as **qatal*, קָטַ֫לְתָּ *killer-you*, whence the past meaning: "you are one who has killed," *you have killed*. a

(1) The genesis of the perfect is clearly recognisable in the Akkadian stative and the Amarna Canaanite; on the latter, see F.M. Th. Böhl, *Die Sprache der Amarnabriefe* (Leipzig, 1909), pp. 42-48.

The perfect of action verbs is always of the type **qatal*, which normally becomes קָטָל (pausal form) as in nouns, e.g. **dabar* becomes דָּבָר *word* (in pause and context). In context the form is קָטַל with ַ(1). This second vowel *a* of **qatal* is dropped in open syllables: קָטְלָה, קָטְלוּ, but reappears in pause: קָטָ֫לָה, קָטָ֫לוּ. The first vowel *a* drops in open syllables two places away from the stress as in קְטַלְתֶּם, קְטַלְתֶּן, the heavy afformatives of which carry the stress (§ 30 *e*). b

(1) Compare the ַ of the construct state of nouns, e.g. דְּבַר (§ 95 *d*).

The stative perfect of the type כָּבֵד equally loses its ֵ in כָּבְדָה and כָּבְדוּ. In closed syllables ֵ normally becomes ַ (§ 29 *d*), e.g. כָּבַ֫דְתָּ, כְּבַדְתֶּם. (One also finds קָטֵל, קָטֵ֫לְתָּ; הִקְטִיל, הִקְטַ֫לְתָּ). c

The stative perfect of the rare type קָטֹן equally loses its ֹ in קָטְנָה, קָטְנוּ. In stressed closed syllables ֹ is maintained, e.g. קָטֹ֫נְתָּ; it changes to ָ in unstressed syllables קְטָנְתֶּם, וְיָכָ֫לְתָּ *and you will be able to*, יְכָלְתִּיו *I overpowered him*.

Instead of ַ one sometimes finds ִ (ֶ in one instance) in unstressed closed syllables. Thus from the stative verb יָרַשׁ *to inherit* (for יָרֵשׁ*) one finds, e.g. וִירִשְׁתֶּם Dt 4.1 etc., where the *i* is perhaps due to the influence of the primitive vowel and of the sibilant; from the stative verb שָׁאַל *to ask* (for שָׁאֵל*) שְׁאִלְתִּיו 1Sm 1.20 etc., שְׁאִלְתֶּם 1Sm 12.13; 25.5; Job 21.29. (Cf. the weakening of *a* to ִ, § 29 *e* and to ֶ, § 29 *g*). d

The coming-together of the afformative ת with a ת as a radical pro- e duces a contraction (§ 18 *c*), e.g. כָּרַ֫תִּי *I have cut* Ex 34.27 (כָּרַת); נָתַ֫נּוּ *we have given* Gn 34.16 (נָתַן) is a mere graphic shorthand.

f **Observations on individual endings**

3rd sg.m. The primitive form was *qatala* with *a* at the end as in Arabic and Ethiopic and as is still preserved in suffixed forms such as קְטָלַ֫נִי *he killed me.*

3rd sg.f. The primitive form is *qatalat*. The ת is preserved before object suffixes (§ 62 *a*) and in ל"ה verbs (§ 79 *d*). One finds other forms with ת: וְנִשְׁכַּ֫חַת צֹר(1) *and Tyre will be forgotten* Is 23.15; אָזְלַת יָד *the strength is gone* Dt 32.36 (nsiga); וְשָׁבַת לַנָּשִׂיא *and it will return to the prince* Ez 46.17 (verb שׁוּב; perhaps ?)(2).

2nd sg.m. The primitive form is *qatalta* with a short final *a*(3). In קָטַ֫לְתָּ the post-stress *å* was originally short, which can have influenced the orthography without ה in contrast to אַתָּה (§ 39 *a*). The spelling with ה is common in נָתַ֫תָּה (much more frequent than נָתַ֫תָּ[4]; a sort of compensation for the graphic abbreviation arising from the contraction), and often in ל"ה verbs, e.g. רָאִ֫יתָה(5). One finds it also sporadically for no apparent reason, e.g. in Gn 21.23; 2Sm 2.26; 2Kg 9.3 (after four forms without ה). Likewise in Hifil, e.g. 2Kg 9.7.

On the form וְקָטַלְתָּ֫, cf. § 43.

2nd sg.f. The primitive form is *qatalti* with a short *i*. The ancient form קָטַ֫לְתִּי occurs sporadically as Ktiv, for example, Ru 3.3,4 (in the middle of קָטַ֫לְתְּ forms), especially and remarkably in Jeremiah and Ezekiel(6). In the Samaritan Pentateuch one finds תי or ת (see the edition by von Gall, p. lxviii, which prefers תי). The post-stress short vowel has been weakened to shewa: קָטַ֫לְתְּ *qåṭalt*, which is the usual form. But the *i* reappears before suffixes (§ 62 *a*)(7).

1st sg.com. The primitive Semitic form is *qatalku*; the *k* has become *t* under the influence of *t* of the second person; *u* has become *i* on the analogy of the separate pronoun and the suffix of the first person. One sometimes finds the spelling קָטַ֫לְתְּ without י, ordinarily in Ktiv, e.g. Ps 140.13. Already El Amarna glosses attest to the ending *-ti* as in *ba-ni-ti* "I built."

On the form וְקָטַלְתִּ֫י, cf. § 43.

3rd pl.com. The primitive form is *qatalū*. One finds קָטְלוּן three times with a *paragogic Nun,* which is suspect or faulty: Dt 8.3,16; Is 26.16. On the *paragogic Nun* of the future, cf. § 44 *e*.

For the feminine, primitive Semitic had a form *qatalā*, which normally would have produced, in Hebrew, קָטְלוֹ*. One finds in our text some קָטְלָה forms, which have a plural feminine subject, e.g. בָּנוֹת צָעֲדָה Gn 49.22; יָדֵ֫ינוּ שָׁפְכָה Dt 21.7 (Qre-Ktiv). But these examples(8), which occur mainly as Ktiv, are really 3rd sg.f. forms (so already Ibn Ezra ad Gn 49.22; cf. § 150 *h*). In some cases it could involve a misspelling of ה for ו, possibly under the influence of Aramaic(9), which has preserved the form *qatalā* (which in turn has become קְטַ֫לָה)(10).

2nd pl.m. The primitive form *qataltumu* has become *qataltim* > קְטַלְתֶּם on the analogy of the feminine (as in the separate pronoun, § 39 *a*). The *u* is preserved before suffixes (§ 62 *a*). The unique עֲשִׂיתֶן (2m.pl.) Ez 33.26 also occurs very cccasionally in MH.

2nd pl.f. The primitive form *qataltinna* has become קְטַלְתֶּן, a form used very infrequently; comp. אַתֶּן, § 39 *a*.

1st pl.com. The primitive form is *qatalna*. Hebrew has replaced *na* by *nu* on the analogy of the separate and suffix pronoun.

(1) There is nsiga; the form is segholised. In BA one finds also הִשְׁתְּכַ֫חַת *was found* Dn 5.14 and (perhaps with nsiga) 5.11,12, 6.5,23. Kutscher (*Isaiah*, p. 191) thinks that this phenomenon may be an Aramaism.

(2) For an explanation of these examples, see E.Y. Kutscher, *History*, p. 39.

(3) In the Tel Amarna letters one always finds *ta*; cf. P. Dhorme, *RB* 22 (1913) 388ff. The *a* is long according to Brock., *GvG*, I, p. 572 and others.

(4) נָתַ֫תָּ 27 x and נָתַ֫תָּה 65 x: AF, p. 180. *Pace* AF, this is hardly a case of a Massoretic imposition of uniformity, for there is not a single case of the masculine נָתַתְּ, whereas we find three examples of masc. אַתְּ alongside Q אַתָּ (5 x)(see § 39 *a*). On the vowelless ending /-t/ alongside /-tå/ attested in abundance in the Greek and Latin transliterations, see Brønno, *Morphologie*, pp. 19-21, and Sperber, *Hist. Gram.*, p. 177.

(5) For a listing of examples of the spelling תָּה- and (כָה-), see Barr, *Spellings*, pp. 125-27. Barr thinks that the long spelling is earlier.

(6) On the situation in 1QIs^a, cf. Kutscher, *Isaiah*, pp. 25, 188-90 (Aramaic influence), but *pace* Harris (*Development*, p. 75) it is hardly dialectal.

(7) Comp. the old form of the 2nd f. pronoun אַתִּי* alongside אַתְּ, § 39 *a*. SH has consistently preserved the archaic ending /-ti/ (Ben-Ḥayyim, *LOT*, vol. 5, p. 74, and Macuch, *Gram.*, p. 261).

(8) All possible examples are listed by Berg., II, § 4 b.

(9) As regards examples in 1QIs^a, see Kutscher, *Isaiah*, pp. 191f.

(10) On this question, see Mayer Lambert, *Une Série de qeré ketib* (Paris, 1891), in which he admits the existence in Hebrew of a 3rd pl. fem. with ָה.

§ 43. Inverted perfect וְקָטַלְתִּי

a With Waw inversive of the perfect the mil'el stress tends to turn mil'ra; but in many cases this tendency is not realised. In the 1st pers.pl. in which the stress *could* advance, it never does, although the phonetic reason for this is not apparent(1).

In the 3rd pers.f. of ע״ע verbs (§ 82 *g*) and ע״ו verbs (§ 80 *j*) the stress can advance, e.g. וְקָמָה, וְרַבָּה.

In the 1st pers.sg. and the 2nd pers.m.sg., the stress **normally advances**, e.g. וְקָטַלְתָּ, וְקָטַלְתִּי(2). (In these forms the ante-prestress qameṣ is maintained, § 30 *e*).

Exceptions: 1) In pause the stress does not advance: וְקָטָלְתָּ, וְקָטָלְתִּי.

(1) All this possibly under the influence of the position of stress in the corresponding separate 1st and 2nd pers. personal pronouns. This may account for the irregular retention of the qameṣ in the contextual form אָנֹכִי, though the influence of the shorter form אֲנִי may also be responsible for the mil'ra form וְקָטַלְתִּי. This implies that the stress in these forms has not arisen as a result of the general shift to the ultima stress.

(2) The inversive Waw of the perfect has the weak vocalisation (in contrast to the inversive Waw of the future, § 47), namely shewa or its substitutes: i.e. וּ before a labial and וַ before ḥaṭef pataḥ, e.g. וַהֲקִמֹתָ (cf. § 104 *c*). For the meaning of the inverted perfect, cf. § 119; here we can be content with the commonest translation, that of the future, e.g. *and I shall kill*.

b 2) In ל״א and ל״ה verbs the stress often does not advance. In this matter one can hardly formulate hard and fast rules. One can nevertheless note that ָא and ִי tend to retain the stress more than ֵא and ֵי respectively. Moreover, it is necessary to distinguish between various conjugations, because the Qal conjugation deserves special treatment. Having said this, we can make the following observations(1):

ל״א **verbs**: In Qal, the vowel ָ of action verbs and ֵ of stative verbs retain the stress: וּבָאתִי, וְיָצָאתָ; וְיָרֵאתָ. In the other conjugations ֵ loses its stress: וּמִלֵּאתָ, וְהֵבֵאתִי, וְהוֹצֵאתִי.

ל״ה **verbs**: In Qal, the vowel ִי retains its stress, e.g. וְעָשִׂיתָ (89 examples), וְעָשִׂיתִי (20 x); וְהָיִיתָ, וְהָיִיתִי. In the other conjugations, ִי generally retains the stress, but ֵי loses it; thus one finds וְהַעֲלִיתָ in Dt 27.6; Jdg 6.26; Jer 38.10, but וְהַעֲלֵיתָ in Ex 40.4.

Observation. Before the guttural א the form tends to be mil'ra (cf.

§ 33). Thus instead of וּבָ֫אתָ one finds וּבָאתָ֫ before א, e.g. Zech 6.10; instead of וְהִשְׁקִ֫יתָ Dt 11.10 one finds וְהִשְׁקִיתָ֫ אֶת־ Nu 20.8; Jer 35.2.

(1) When the penultimate is a closed syllable, the stress shifts to the ultima, and the same tendency exists where both the penultimate and the antepenultimate are naturally long. See C.H. Gordon, "The accentual shift in the perfect with a Waw consecutive," *JBL* 57 (1938) 319-25, and J. Blau, *IOS* 1 (1971) 15-18. F.R. Blake justly points to a major category of exceptions to Gordon's rule, namely וְהִקְטִ֫ילוּ and וְהִקְטִ֫ילָה: *JBL* 63 (1944) 285, n. 29. Cf. also E.J. Revell, "Stress and the '*Waw* consecutive' in BH," *JAOS* 104 (1984) 437-44.

§ 44. Inflection of Qal Future

The inflection of the Qal Future (and of other conjugations) consists of preformatives marking the person and (in five cases) by sufformatives marking the gender and the number. As the perfect can be morphologically described as the 'sufformative tense,' the future can be described as the 'preformative tense.' The preformatives א and נ of the first person, and ת of the second person are also attested in the corresponding separate pronouns; in contrast, the preformatives י and ת of the third person are difficult to explain. The sufformative וּ of the second and third person pl.m. is the same as in קָטְלוּ. For the fem. sing. one has the sufformative ִי- in the second person; for the fem. plural נָה, in the second and third persons. *a*

In contrast to the perfect, which has a nominal base and looks like a 'conjugated' adjective or substantive, the future is formed on a verbal base (e.g. קְטֹל) which generally recurs in the imperative. The future is therefore an essentially verbal form in origin like the imperative.

First vowel (that of the preformative). In the Qal conjugation of regular verbs as we have it now, the vowel is ִ in verbs of action and in stative verbs alike, e.g. יִקְטֹל, יִתֵּן; יִכְבַּד. But, as we stated in § 41 *e*, the original vowel in action verbs was probably *a*. In the first person singular one has אֶקְטֹל, אֶכְבַּד with the vowel seghol(1). *b*

(1) The explanation of this vowel is controversial. If א, as we believe, was no longer pronounced, seghol would have been the initial vowel as in the case of the prosthetic Alef (§ 17 *a*). If יִקְטֹל was pronounced *iqṭol* (§ 26 *e*), the pronunciation *ẹqṭọl* (with silent א) would have been distinct from the former.

Second vowel. As we saw (§ 41 *a*), the second vowel of action verbs *c* is generally *u > ◌ֹ, sometimes *i > ◌ֵ; always ◌ַ in stative verbs (§ 41 *b*).

These vowels can drop out in open syllables and in fact do so, e.g. יִקְטְלוּ, יִתְּנוּ, יִכְבְּדוּ; but they are maintained in pause: יִקְטֹ֫לוּ, יִתֵּ֫נוּ, יִכְבָּ֫דוּ (§ 32 *d*). Since the *o* reflects here an originally short *u*, the fairly frequent(1) plene spelling יִקְטוֹל with ו is striking, except in those cases where there may have been a secondary lengthening.

The following three cases with וּ must be considered abnormal or faulty: יִשְׁפּוּט֫וּ הֵם Ex 18.26; לֹא תַעֲבוּרִי מִזֶּה Ru 2.8; תִּשְׁמוּרֵם Pr 14.3. If these forms are genuine, one can perhaps explain them as follows: in prepause and in pause a full vowel may have been preferred, and here, with a labial, *u* may have been preferred over *ọ*.

(1) יִקְטֹל : יִקְטוֹל = 1356 : 125, and for פ״נ verbs, 192 : 44: AF, pp. 194f.

d **Observations on certain persons.**

In the f.pl., the third and second persons have the same form: תִּקְטֹ֫לְנָה. This form, as second person, is extremely rare (so is the 2nd pl.f. of the perfect קְטַלְתֶּן). In תִּקְטֹ֫לְנָה the third person has a twofold indication of the feminine. The ת is here of secondary origin and originates with the 3rd sg.f. תִּקְטֹל. The original form must have been *יִקְטֹ֫לְנָה (with י as in Arabic, Western Aramaic, etc.); this appears only three times: Gn 30.38; 1Sm 6.12; Dn 8.22. The /-nā/ form, including that of the imperative, has completely disappeared from MH, and already in BH the masculine /-u/ form often doubles for the feminine (§ 150 *a*,*c*).

Instead of the ordinary spelling נָה we often(1) find ןָ, especially in the Pentateuch and notably after Waw inversive, e.g. Gn 19.33,36(2).

(1) In 41 out of 342 cases: AF, p. 103, 180.

(2) Barr (*Spellings*, p. 130), on the basis of the spelling variation and the two striking cases, Gn 4.23 שְׁמַ֫עַן and Ex 2.20 קְרֶ֫אןָ, both f.pl. imperative, concludes that the short spelling possibly represents a variant pronunciation ending with /-n/ (so already Berg., II, § 5 *a*).

da Occasionally /tiqṭlu/ occurs for 3f.pl., with /t/ indicating the f.sg. and /u/ the pl. morpheme respectively: Ez 37.7 תִּקְרְבוּ and Job 19.15 תַּחְשְׁבֻנִי, both with a f.pl. subject.

e Added to the sufformative וּ of the 3rd pers. pl.m. and 2nd pl.m. יִקְטְלוּ, תִּקְטְלוּ we often find a ן called **paragogic Nun**, i.e. added Nun. In reality the ן belongs to primitive forms and is found in Ugaritic,

Arabic, Aramaic, etc. The total of 305 examples are pretty widely spread in the Old Testament; one finds them especially in Deuteronomy (56), Isaiah (37), Job (23), and Psalm 104 (15)(1). The reasons for the presence of a form with וּן can be the antiquity of a text, a deliberate archaism, Aramaic influence, and metre. But the usual reason seems to be preference for a fuller and more emphatic form. This explains why one finds forms with וּן especially in pause (in major and intermediate pauses). In pause, the preceding vowel is retained and occasionally given secondary lengthening, e.g. יִקְטֹלוּן (cf. § 32 *d*), יְלַקֵּטוּן Ps 104. 28, תִּדְבָּקוּן Dt 13.5, יִלְמָדוּן Dt 4.10. But these forms are sometimes found in context as well, e.g. יִקְצֹרוּן Ru 2.9 (pashṭa).

When the meaning demands the jussive, one very rarely finds the form with וּן(2), e.g. יִכְרְעוּן Job 31.10; בַּל־יֶחֱזָיוּן Is 26.11.

The fact that no long form occurs with the prohibitive אַל and extremely rarely (only 9 times: Dt 1.22, 4.11 [2 x], 5.20, Jdg 8.1, Is 41.5, Ez 44.8, Am 6.3) with the inversive Waw accords with the general assumption that the short form represents the original jussive(3).

These extended forms are stressed on the last syllable, and their stress position agrees with that of the assumed primitive form such as /yaqtulū'na/.

(1) Driver, *Notes* ad 1Sm 2.15 (p. 30). It is true, as Lambert notes (§ 703), that the long forms are more common in older books: they are absent from Lam, Ec, Esth, Dn, Ezr, Ne; the Chronicler has only two, due to the influence of his source (2Ch 6.26 // 1Kg 8.35; 2Ch 7.19 //1Kg 9.6), and normally substitutes (under the Aramaic influence according to Kutscher, *Isaiah*, p. 193) the short form for the long one (2Ch 6.29,33 //1Kg 8.38,43; 2Ch 11.4 //1Kg 12.24). However, the antiquity alone cannot account for all the examples.

(2) In BA as in Early Aramaic generally, where we always find ון in the indicative, the ן is eliminated where the sense requires the jussive. The position of Ya'di (Samalian) (8th cent. B.C.) in North West Syria is unique, showing the /-ū/ ending in both the indicative and the jussive: see P.-E. Dion, *La Langue de Ya'udi* (Waterloo, 1974), pp. 184-86.

(3) Cf. J. Hoftijzer, *The Function and Use of the Imperfect Forms with Nun paragogicum in Classical Hebrew* (Assen/Maastricht, 1985), pp. 2-4.

Similarly, to the sufformative ִי- of the second pers. sg.f. one sometimes adds a **paragogic Nun**. There are not many examples, e.g. *f*
תַּעֲשִׂין Ru 3.4; תֵּדְעִין 3.18; תִּדְבָּקִין 2.21; תִּדְבָּקִין 2.8 (ṭifḥa). This ן, which is equally primitive and occurs in Arabic and Aramaic, is used

under the same conditions as those described above, and must be interpreted in the same fashion.

§ 45. Cohortative אֶקְטְלָה

a The cohortative is the volitive mood of the first person(1): אֶקְטְלָה, נִקְטְלָה. It is formed by adding a **paragogic** (= added) ָה, the origin of which will be explained in the syntax section, § 116 *b*, n. The sufformative ָה is treated like the sufformatives ִי and וּ; hence it takes the stress in context, and the preceding, originally short vowel is dropped, e.g. נְנַתְּקָה Ps 2.3 (from נְנַתֵּק), נִשְׁכְּבָה Jer 3.25 (from נִשְׁכַּב); in pause the preceding vowel reappears and takes the stress, e.g. אֶשְׁמֹרָה Ps 59.10; אֶחְכָּמָה Ec 7.23. A preceding, originally long vowel is naturally maintained and retains its stress, e.g. אָקוּמָה, אַקְטִילָה, although the non-extended form without the energic Nun is, as a rule, used if the suffixed verb is intended as jussive in force or joined to the inversive Waw: thus אַל תְּשַׁלְּחֵהוּ *Don't send him* or וַתְּשַׁלְּחֵהוּ *and she sent him*, and not אַל תְּשַׁלְּחֶנּוּ or וַתְּשַׁלְּחֶנּוּ (§ 61 *f*).

(1) Only rarely do we find in the 3rd person the ה of the cohortative; the three examples in Is 5.19 יָחִישָׁה *may he hasten!*, תָּבוֹאָה *let it come!*, and Job 11.17 תָּעֻפָה (if not תָּעֻפָה) *may it fly away!*, all occur instead of the normal jussive. Cf. also Ez 23.16Q, 20 וַתַּעְגְּבָה.

b As we shall see in Syntax (§ 114, 116), the cohortative has a *direct* use, e.g. *May I kill!*, *I wish to kill!*, and an *indirect* or subordinated use (with ו), e.g. *in order that I may kill* (וְאֶקְטְלָה). It is the same with the jussive.

The volitive nuance of the cohortative can be reinforced by the affective particle נָא, e.g. אָסֻרָה־נָּא Ex 3.3 (dḥiq, § 18 *i*) *I* (therefore) *wish to advance* (§ 105 *c*).

The imperative also can have the paragogic ָה, § 48 *d*.

§ 46. Jussive יִקְטֹל

a The jussive is the volitive mood of the third person; it is also used in some cases as the volitive of the second person (§ 114 *g*, in place of the imperative, which is the volitive proper of the second person), and very rarely as the volitive of the first person (the volitive proper of which is the cohortative). The jussive tends to take a form shorter than that of the indicative, but not always. Thus in the regular verb type, the Qal future יִקְטֹל cannot be shortened; it is the same with many other futures except Hifil future יַקְטִיל, which has an originally long vowel. This long vowel *ī* was shortened to *i* > ֵ; hence in practice one has יַקְטֵל *may he cause* (somebody) *to kill!* and תַּקְטֵל *may she cause* (somebody) *to kill!* One sees that the jussive form can appear only in certain futures, and within these futures only in certain forms, and furthermore, the jussive of these forms no longer appears if they are suffixed(1).

(1) This is a probable explanation of the tendency of the language to substitute the indicative for the jussive form where the latter could have been used, e.g. in ל"ה verbs. Cf. § 114 *g*, n.

b The distinct jussive form is found particularly in certain weak verb classes, namely ע"ו and ע"י. In ל"ה verbs the shortening amounts to apocope (§ 17 *f*), e.g. the indicative יִגְלֶה becoming in the jussive יִ֫גֶל.

Very rarely the jussive has the paragogic ן (§ 44 *e*).

§ 47. Inverted Future וַיִּקְטֹל

a The inverted future, e.g. וַיִּקְטֹל *and he killed*, has a strong Waw, that is to say, a Waw which has vowel *a* that adds some force (like that of the definite article [§ 35 *b*] and that of the interrogative pronoun מָה [§ 37 *c*]) to the following consonant, which, as a consequence, is doubled. The doubling is omitted in, e.g. וַיְקַטֵּל (§ 18 *m*)(1).

With the Waw inversive the verb form undergoes two changes in accordance with the phonetic laws: 1) the final vowel reflects earlier shortening as in the jussive (§ 46 *a*); 2) the stress recedes, and as a consequence, the post-stress vowel becomes short. These changes may occur only if the first syllable is open, and the last closed, and the first vowel is qameṣ, ṣere or ḥiriq, although a notable exception is וַתֵּ֫רֶא *and she saw*. Sometimes one observes the first change, sometimes the second, and sometimes neither. Examples: וַיִּקְטֹל (the vowel cannot be shortened here any more than in the jussive; the stress cannot recede, § 31 *a*); וַיַּקְטֵל (the vowel of יַקְטִיל is shortened as in the jussive; the stress cannot recede —/*yaqṭīl'/ > /*yaqṭil'/ > /yạqṭẹl/); וַיָּ֫קָם (the vowel of יָקוּם was shortened as in the jussive יָקֹ֫ם—/*yaqū'mu/ > /*ya'qum/ > /yå'qọm/; but in pause the stress is mil'ra, and the ḥolem indicates earlier secondary lengthening of short *u*); וַיָּ֫קָם (the stress recedes); וַתְּגָ֫רֶשׁ Josh 24.12 (Piel); וַיְ֫בָרֶךְ (with the omission of gemination in יְ)(2).

(1) Despite the absence of the pataḥ following the Waw in the second column of Origen's Hexapla and the Samaritan pronunciation of Hebrew, it must be considered primitive, whilst the gemination of the following consonant may be regarded as a device to preserve this primitive vowel; see a discussion by Z. Ben-Ḥayyim, in Sh. Warses et al. (eds), *Sefer Dov Sadan* [Heb] (Tel Aviv, 1977), p. 81, and Blau, *Heb. Phonology and Morphology*, p. 217. Gordon's proposal (*UT*, § 12.9) to compare Ugr. *wn* (= /wan/ ?) founders in view of examples such as *wn. ymġy* "and now he arrives" and *wn ʿ[n]* "and he answered."

(2) The prohibitive negative אַל also tends to push the stress back, e.g. אַל־תָּ֫שֶׁב 1Kg 2.20 (compare וַתָּ֫שָׁב), אַל־תָּ֫שֶׁת Ex 23.1, but אַל־יָ֫נַע 2Kg 23.18 (guttural), § 80 *k*, n.

b In certain cases where the stress, in accordance with the general phonetic laws (§ 31 *a*), can recede, it does not. One may note the following cases:

1) In the Qal future of פ"ו and פ"י verbs with *a*: וַיִּ֫יטַב, וַיִּ֫ירַשׁ.

2) In forms with final Alef: וַיָּ֫בֹא, וַיָּ֫בֵא; וַיֵּ֫צֵא, וַיֹּ֫צֵא; וַיִּ֫ירָא.

3) In the Nifal, the stress does not generally recede, e.g. וַיִּוָּלֵד.

But there are a good number of exceptions; thus one always has וַיִּלָּ֫חֶם, and וַיִּנָּ֫חֶם seven times (twice mil'ra). Note the forms with stressed ָ, frequently even in pause, וַיִּשָּׁ֫בַע, וַיִּשָּׁ֫מַע, וַיִּוָּ֫דַע, וַיִּוָּ֫עַץ, וַתֵּעָ֫צַר. Alongside וַיֵּאָסֵף Nu 11.30; Jdg 20.11℘ one always has the mil'el form in the formula וַיֵּאָ֫סֶף אֶל־עַמָּיו *and he was reunited with his kinsfolk* (always at the end of a verse: Gn 25.8,17; 35.29; 49.33; Dt 32.50℘).

For the Piel of second guttural verbs, cf. § 69 *d*.

c In ל"ה verbs the shortening results in apocope, as in the jussive (§ 46 *b*), e.g. וַיִּ֫גֶל, יִגְלֶה.

d In the **1st pers. sing.** there are many peculiarities. Before the guttural Alef, which cannot be doubled, the *a* in open syllables following the Waw is ָ, e.g. וָאֶקְטֹל. The stress does not recede (e.g. וָאָקוּם)(1). In the Pentateuch and very often in the Prophets, cases of this kind are written without *mater lectionis*, e.g. וָאָקֻם, וָאָקֻם. The preponderance of full spelling in these forms in late books suggests that in early BH the 1st person was no different from the other persons in this respect (Berg., II, § 5 d).

Apart from the normal form וָאֶקְטֹל, there is a secondary form וָאֶקְטְלָה with **paragogic** ־ָה (as in the cohortative, § 45) having precisely the same meaning as וָאֶקְטֹל *and I have killed*, and in which, as a consequence, ־ָה has no semantic value. The form וָאֶקְטְלָה occurs especially in certain late books, in particular Daniel, Ezra and Nehemiah(2). The ־ָה of the inverted future וָאֶקְטְלָה is no doubt due to the analogy of the ־ָה of the indirect cohortative וְאֶקְטְלָה *in order that I may kill*; its existence is probably due to some consideration of rhythm.

(1) For ל"ה verbs, cf. § 79 *m*, n.

(2) For details, see Kropat, *Syntax*, p. 75. QH almost exclusively uses forms with the paragogic /-ā/; Qimron, *Hebrew of DSS*, p. 44. For a full list of וָאֶקְטְלָה forms, see Berg., II, § 5 f.

In the **1st pers. plur.** the ordinary form is the norm, e.g. וַנִּקְטֹל, e
וַנָּקָם. One also finds some rare forms with the paragogic ־ָה. Böttcher (vol. 2, p. 199) cites six examples: Gn 41.11; 43.21; Ps 90.10; Ezr 8.23 (וַנָּצוּמָה וַנְּבַקְשָׁה); 8.31. The ־ָה of וַנִּקְטְלָה is probably due to the analogy of the indirect cohortative וְנִקְטְלָה *in order that we may kill.*

§ 48. **Imperative**

The imperative is the volitive mode of the second person. The in- a
flection of the imperative consists of the sufformatives ־ִי, וּ and נָה of the future. The theme of the imperative is that of the future, e.g. קְטֹל *Kill!* as in תִּקְטֹל *you will kill.*

Generally speaking, when in a future the form of the jussive differs from that of the indicative, the imperative, being a volitive mood, takes the vowel of the jussive, also a volitive mood. For example, in the regular verb, Hifil, we find imperative הַקְטֵל with the ֵ of the jussive יַקְטֵל; likewise in ע"ו verbs we find הָקֵם as in יָקֵם. But in Qal of ע"ו verbs, alongside the jussive יָקֹם we find (abnormally) the imperative קוּם (§ 80 *c*). If one agrees, along with some modern philologists, that the imperative preceded the future, one must say that the jussive is an imperative in the second and third persons.

The vowel of the imperative is mostly identical with that of the future (jussive), e.g. קְטֹל as in יִקְטֹל, קְרַב as in יִקְרַב, תֵּן as in יִתֵּן. The exceptions seem to be very rare(1).

In the derived conjugations, the imperative also resembles the future as far as the vocalisation is concerned: Nifal הִקָּטֵל as in יִקָּטֵל, Piel קַטֵּל as in יְקַטֵּל, Hifil הַקְטֵל as in jussive יַקְטֵל, Hitpael הִתְקַטֵּל as in יִתְקַטֵּל.

In the passive conjugations proper, i.e. Pual and Hofal, the imperative does not exist(2). One may note two exceptions: הָשְׁכְּבָה Ez 32.19 which probably means *Lie!, be in a lying position!* (cf. מֻשְׁכָּב *whom they have laid; lying* 2Kg 4.32§); הָפְנוּ (?) Jer 49.8, which could mean *Be turned around!*

(1) In strong verbs I can only find סְעָד־ Jdg 19.8 (cf. vs. 5) despite the future יִסְעַד.

(2) So also in genuine passive Nifals. Thus an example such as Gn 42.16 הֵאָסְרוּ is striking; cf. § 114 *o*.

b In קְטֹל, כְּבַד, and תֵּן the vowel, as in the corresponding futures (§ 44 *c*), drops out before the sufformatives ־ִי, ־וּ, and ־ָה (§ *d*), e.g. קִטְלִי; but is retained in pause, e.g. גְּזֹרוּ 1Kg 3.26; שְׁמָעוּ; תֵּנִי Is 43.6. The ǫ being originally short, the orthography קְטוֹל, which one finds occasionally, must be considered unusual(1).

(1) קְטֹל : קְטוֹל = 874 : 202, including inf. cst., but not לֵאמֹר (945 x) vs. לֵאמוֹר (3 x; Gn 48.20; Jer 18.5, 33.19); AF, p. 195.

c **Observations on the inflection.**

In the type כְּבַד, the primitive fem. form was **kabdī* etc., whence כִּבְדִי by attenuation of *a* to *i*(1). The *a* has not been preserved except in second-guttural verbs, e.g. שַׁחֲטִי.

In the type קְטֹל the expected symmetrical form is קָטְלִי with ǫ. We always find this form with ǫ before object suffixes, e.g. קָטְלֵנִי (§ 64 *a*) and most frequently with the paragogic ־ָה, e.g. קָטְלָה (§ *d*). On the other hand, with the sufformatives ־ִי and ־וּ, the form with ǫ is rather rare, e.g. מָלְכִי Jdg 9.10; מָשְׁכוּ Ez 32.20; indeed the ordinary forms are קִטְלִי, קִטְלוּ (similar to כִּבְדִי, כִּבְדוּ). The replacement of קָטְלִי and קָטְלוּ by קִטְלִי and קִטְלוּ is difficult to explain; perhaps it is due to the analogy of the types כִּבְדִי and כִּבְדוּ respectively.

(1) The shewa is "medium," and consequently the begadkefat is rafé (§ 19 *f*). Like-

wise, of course, in the imperatives of the type קְטֹל, e.g. מָלְכִי. The original form seems to be *qutl, which became *qtul > קְטֹל. The shewa may be a vestige of the vowel shifted forward. Others admit a primitive form *qutul, as in Akkadian. Cp. also AC (= EA 252.25) *nu-pu-ul-mi*, if it means "Fall!"

d **Imperative with paragogic ָה.** In the sing. masc. we often find a form augmented by the paragogic ָה, which is emphatic in origin, but in practice does not often seem to add any particular nuance, though it often seems to carry an honorific one, being addressed to God (Ps 5.2), father (Gn 27.19), prophet (Nu 22.6), and priest (1Sm 14.18), and sometimes reinforced by נָא (Gn 27.19)(1). With the type קְטֹל the form is usually קָטְלָה (§ *c*), rarely קְטֹלָה, e.g. מִכְרָה Gn 25.31 (with a guttural, e.g. עֶרְכָה Job 33.5; אֶסְפָה Nu 11.16). In the type כְּבַד one naturally finds כִּבְדָה, e.g. שִׁכְבָה, שִׁמְעָה; exception קָרְבָה Ps 69.19 despite קְרַב(2).

This sufformative ָה is treated like the sufformatives ִי and וּ (§§ *b,c*); thus the pausal forms are קְטֹ֫לָה, כְּבָ֫דָה, לֵ֫כָה.

The preference for the form with ָה seems usually to be purely in the interests of euphony(3). Furthermore, its usage is very inconsistent; thus one has תְּנָה 23 times and תֵּן 16 times; לֵךְ, however, is much more frequent than לְכָה (written 3 times לְךָ). One always has חוּשָׁה *hasten!* (8 x, ouf of which 7 are in Ps), הַגִּישָׁה *present!* (5 x), עוּרָה *wake up!* (6 x, in Ps), הִשָּׁבְעָה *swear!* (5 x), הַקְשִׁיבָה *lend an ear!*, *listen!* (9 x; הַקְשֵׁב once in Job 33.31).

Since the nuance added by ָה is virtually non-discernible, the emotive particle נָא (cf. § 45 *b*) is added, if greater emphasis is required, e.g. לֶךְ־נָא Gn 27.9; לְכָה־נָּא Nu 23.27 *go then!*, *please, go!* (cf. § 105 *c*).

(1) See Lambert, § 719, n. 1.

(2) Here again the shewa is "medium" (cf. § *c*, n.).

(3) For this reason perhaps it is frequent in poetry: see M. Tsevat, *A Study of the Language of the Biblical Psalms* (Philadelphia, 1955), p. 25, and n. 255.

§ 49. **Infinitive**

a The infinitive (§ 40 *b*) is called *absolute* or *construct*(1) depending on its form and syntactic usage (§§ 123-24).

In the **Qal conjugation**, the two infinitives are rigorously distinguished: inf. abs. קָטוֹל, inf. cst. קְטֹל(2). These two forms, which now have a certain resemblancc, originally had no connection whatsoever. The inf. abs. is a nominal form **qatāl*, normally developed into קָטוֹל (with an originally long ọ; very often[3] spelled defectively as קָטֹל). The inf. cst. קְטֹל, like the imperative קְטֹל, comes from **qtul*(4) (the ọ is a deletable or variable vowel; the occasional spelling קְטוֹל is therefore unusual)(5). Thus it happens that currently the two forms have, in final syllable, the same vowel ọ, originally long in קָטוֹל and deletable in קְטֹל. Furthermore, considering the opposition between קָ and קְ, the two infinitives seem to have the same relation as that between, for example, abs. גָּדוֹל *great* and cst. ־גְּדוֹל. The old grammar, and perhaps even the linguistic consciousness, seems to have admitted this relation as real, hence the names *infinitive absolute* and *infinitive construct*(6).

(1) When we say (e.g. in this grammar) *infinitive*, without any qualification, the reference is to the infinitive construct, which is the usual infinitive, the infinitive absolute being used only in very special cases.

(2) In the paradigms, in order better to distinguish between the two infinitives, we prefix the preposition (לְ) to the infinitive construct, e.g. (לִ)קְטֹל, (לָ)קוּם.

(3) Usage is rather varied; thus we have הָלוֹךְ 34 times, הָלֹךְ 12 times; in contrast, יָדוֹעַ twice and יָדֹעַ 11 times. GK (§ 45 *a*) claims erroneously that the spelling קָטֹל occurs "sometimes" (likewise BL, p. 317). According to AF, p. 193, the frequencies of קָטוֹל : קָטֹל are 245 : 179, inclusive apparently of relatively few non-Qal abs. inf.'s. See also Barr, *Spellings*, pp. 109-12.

(4) *Pace* Sivan, pp. 167f., the AC form could not have been *qatālu*. If a suffixed pattern such as קְטָלֵנִי is to be considered to have preserved the archaic shape, as is often the case, then the inf. cst. pattern must have resembled that of the imperative; otherwise one would be hard put to account for the difference between the inf. cst. קְטֹל and the inf. abs. קָטוֹל.

(5) See § 48 *b*, n. 1.

(6) Strangely, the two infinitives have uses which correspond rather closely, syntactically speaking, to those of their names. The infinitive absolute is used in an *absolute* fashion, like a noun in the absolute state, whereas the infinitive construct can be *construed* with a noun or a pronoun, like a noun in the construct state.

b In the **derived conjugations** the infinitive absolute seems to be a secondary formation. Hence the distinction between the two infinitives is not as rigorously maintained as in Qal. Furthermore, the form of the infinitive construct can often be employed as infinitive absolute, e.g.

in Nifal הִקָּטֵל, Piel קַטֵּל. Sometimes the inf. abs. differs from the inf. cst. only by a secondary modification; thus in the Hifil of regular verbs one has cst. הַקְטִיל, abs. הַקְטֵל; in the Piel of third guttural verbs: cst. שַׁלַּח (light form), abs. שַׁלֵּחַ (heavy form)(1).

The infinitives with ọ (with ọ, no doubt etymologically long, on the analogy of קָטוֹל) are hardly found except in Nifal: types נִקְטֹל (נִקְטוֹל) and הִקָּטֹל.

In the purely passive conjugations (Pual and Hofal) the two infinitives are rare. In Hofal the inf. abs. הָקְטֵל is remarkable for its hybrid character: it is the inf. abs. of the Hifil הַקְטֵל *passivised* by the shift of the first vowel ַ to ָ.

The inf. abs. is relatively rare in LBH (Polzin, pp. 43f.), and in QH, and virtually extinct in MH.

(1) Just as we find, in the participle, e.g., abs. שֹׁלֵחַ, cst. שֹׁלַח.

The vowel of the infinitive construct. In general the infinitive c
cst. has the same vowel as the future. This is the case in all the derived conjugations, e.g. הַקְטִיל like יַקְטִיל. In Qal one has קְטֹל like יִקְטֹל. But futures with *a* have, rather infrequently, an inf. with *a*, e.g. שְׁכַב (stative; this is the principal example)(1); ordinarily we find the inf. in ọ. Thus in second-guttural verbs one has שְׁחֹט despite יִשְׁחַט; in third-guttural verbs שְׁלֹחַ despite יִשְׁלַח; in ל"א verbs one has מְצֹא despite יִמְצָא. Almost all the stative verbs with *a* in the future, therefore, have an infinitive with ọ, e.g. שְׂנֹא, שְׁאֹל, שְׁמֹעַ, שְׂבֹעַ; חֹם, תֹּם, רֹב. The vowel ọ is hardly a reflection of the inf. abs., but rather attests to the conformity to the dominant inf. cst. pattern.

Thus the form קְטֹל is on the way to becoming *the* form of the infinitive construct(2).

(1) With the exception of שְׁכַב, the infinitives with *a* do not occur except with a suffix or in close juncture with the following word.
(2) Partly perhaps on account of the supposed relationship between קְטֹל and קָטוֹל.

BH possesses a series of verbal nouns of various patterns which can ca
also function as infinitives(1). These may be then called pseudo-infinitives. They are discussed in § *d, e*. It is not true to say that they are late or due to Aramaic influence. An interesting passage is Hb 3.13 יָצָאתָ לְיֵשַׁע עַמֶּךָ לְיֵשַׁע אֶת־מְשִׁיחֶךָ, where יֵשַׁע functions both times in

the manner of the inf. cst., though in its first occurrence it is more like a verbal noun because of the absence of אֶת.

(1) H.M. Orlinsky, "Notes on the Qal infinitive construct and the verbal noun in Biblical Hebrew," *JAOS* 67 (1947) 107-26.

d Qal infinitive constructs with feminine ending ָה.

One sometimes also finds in the Qal of certain verbs (in fact, almost solely of stative verbs) an infinitive with a feminine ending ָה of the types קַטְלָה (from which by attenuation) קִטְלָה, and קָטְלָה (or קָ'), alongside the ordinary infinitive.

The most common examples are: יִרְאָה *to fear* (also substantive: *fear*) alongside יְרֹא (only twice); אַהֲבָה *to love* (also substantive: *love*), and לֶאֱהֹב once only in Ec 3.8. [By way of contrast, the inf. of the antonym *to hate* is ordinarily שְׂנֹא, e.g. 2Sm 19.7 (where it is put opposite אַהֲבָה); the fem. (cst.) form occurs only twice, and that in two cases where the subject of the action is in the genitive (§ 124 *g*): בְּשִׂנְאַת יהוה אֹתָנוּ Dt 1.27; מִשִּׂנְאָתוֹ אוֹתָם 9.28]. Note also מָשְׁחָה Ex 29.29; חֶמְלָה Ez 16.5. The form לִקְרַאת (always in cst. st.) *to meet*, hence with a prepositional value *before*, *in front of* (from the verb קָרָא = קָרָה *to meet*, § 78 *k*) is used like a substantive. On Piel fem. inf. see § 52 *c*.

e We also find some rare infinitives with a preformative מ (like the inf. מִקְטַל in Aramaic). These Aramaising infinitives appear to be of later origin. Examples: לְמִקְרָא הָעֵדָה Nu 10.2 *to convene the assembly* (everywhere else מִקְרָא is a substantive: *assembly*, *convocation*); מַסַּע 10.2 (Dt 10.11†; the pataḥ as characteristic of the infinitive [cf. § 95 *d*]; the substantive would be מַסָּע*); מַשָּׂא Nu 4.24; 2Ch 20.25; 35.3. Sometimes the form מִקְטָל has a rather substantival sense, e.g. מַשֹּׂא פָנִים וּמִקַּח־שֹׁחַד 2Ch 19.7 *partiality and taking of bribes*; מִשְׁלוֹחַ מָנוֹת Esth 9.19 *sending of portions* (here *miqtāl* form).

f Infinitives קְטֹל, שְׁכַב **with the prepositions** בְּ, כְּ, לְ. When the second radical is a begadkefat, it usually remains rafé after בְּ and כְּ, e.g. בִּנְפֹל Job 4.13; כִּנְפֹל 2Sm 3.34; there are some exceptions. However, after לְ it becomes plosive, e.g. לִנְפֹּל Ps 118.13; לִשְׁכַּב Gn 34.7; there are some exceptions. With לְ, which is far more frequent(1) before the infinitive than בְּ and כְּ, and which often has a very weak meaning or even no meaning at all, the form may have been felt to constitute a closer unit(2). Compare the לַחְפֹּר type with a first-guttural verb, § 68 *e*; just as this form with quiescent shewa could have been influenced by the future יַחְפֹּר, the inf. לִקְטֹל with quiescent shewa (instead of shewa "medium") could have been influenced by the future יִקְטֹל. Note also the parallelism between יָקוּם and לָקוּם as against בְּקוּם, and forms such as לִיתֵּן, לוֹמַר, לֵרֵד typical of MH.

(1) Same relative frequency as לֵאמֹר and בֶּאֱמֹר, § 103 *b*.

(2) Note that with a substantive like cst. דְּבַר we always have בְּדַבֵּר, כְּדַבֵּר, לְדַבֵּר, § 103 *b*. In Late Aramaic dialects the Lamed has become an integral part of the infinitive, so that it hardly occurs without Lamed.

§ 50. **Participle and verbal adjective**

The participle is either active or passive (§ 40 *b*). The active participle is found in the active and reflexive conjugations. The passive participle occurs in the passive conjugations. Furthermore, in the conjugation Qal, stative verbs can have a verbal adjective (§ 41 *c*). a

Qal. The **verbal adjective** has the forms *qatil* and *qatul*, e.g. כָּבֵד, b
קָטֹן. It is these forms that produced the stative perfects, which are nothing but "conjugated adjectives." The nominal form *qatal*, from which the perfect of action קָטַל has developed, is not found used as a verbal adjective except in ע"ו verbs and in the Nifal, e.g. קָם *arising*, where it has supplanted the genuine participle (§ 80 *d*), and נֶחְמָד *desirable*. The verbal adjective of the קָטֹן type is very rare; one finds יָגֹר *afraid*, בּוֹשׁ *ashamed*, אוֹר *shining*, יָכֹל *able*. The verbal adjective of כָּבֵד type is however rather frequent, e.g. יָשֵׁן *asleep*, יָרֵא *afraid*. But it has often been replaced by the active participle, e.g. אֹהֵב *loving*, שֹׂנֵא *hating* (§ 41 *c*). Compare Ps 9.18 שְׁכֵחֵי אֱלֹהִים and 50.22 שֹׁכְחֵי אֱלוֹהַּ, both "forgetful of God"(1).

(1) Note examples of alternation between MT *qāṭēl* and 1Q Is[a] *qōṭēl*: Kutscher, *Isaiah*, pp. 340f.

The **active participle** has the primitive form *qātil*, a simple extension of the form *qatil* by lengthening of the first vowel, whence *qōṭēl*, often(1) written defectively קֹטֵל (§ 7 *c*). For the conjugation, cf. § *g*. c

The **passive participle** has the primitive form *qatūl*, a simple extension of the form *qatul* by lengthening of the second vowel, whence קָטוּל(2).

(1) קֹטֵל : קוֹטֵל = 4269 : 1040 (AF, p. 193).
(2) The form קָטוּל is the only surviving passive in Qal. There are vestiges of an ancient Qal passive participle *qutal* > קֻטָּל, § 58 *b*. The defective spelling of the type קָטֻל is rather common: 271/1089, i.e., 25%: AF, p. 202.

d **Participium tantum.** Quite often a verb otherwise not attested in Qal has a participle קֹטֵל, e.g. דֹּבֵר *speaking* (39 times, with the sense of מְדַבֵּר also 39 times); קֹוֶה *hoping* (the participle of Piel קַוֵּה does not exist); חֹכֶה once *hoping*, like מְחַכֶּה 3 x; כֹּסֶה 1 x *covering* and passive כָּסוּי 1 x *covered*, like מְכֻסֶּה, מְכַסֶּה; passive participle בָּרוּךְ *blessed* (Pual מְבֹרָךְ only 6 x) probably on the analogy of the antonym אָרוּר *cursed*.

e Some קָטוּל participles have an active sense or a sense close to that of the active: אָחוּז in Ct 3.8 אֲחֻזֵי חֶ֫רֶב *holding a sword, armed with a sword*; זָכוּר Ps 103.14† *(he) remembers*; 1Ch 5.18 לְמוּדֵי מִלְחָמָה *well-versed in matters of war*(1). In Aramaic there are a good number of קְטִיל passive participles used with the active sense, e.g. דְּכִיר and אֲחִיד, which correspond to the above-quoted examples, which are probably Aramaisms. One has יָדוּעַ in Dt 1.13, 15 in the sense of *an expert, a connoisseur*.

(1) This probably has something to do with the fact that a genuine passive participle usually indicates a state arising from a previous action, rather than an ongoing action looked at in its passive aspect. Thus אָחוּז = *having seized, caught hold of* > *holding*. The term 'perfect participle' may be suggested. See § 121 *o*.

f **Derived conjugations.** In the derived conjugations (except Nifal) the participle is formed with the preformative מ. The vowel of the מ is that of the preformative of the future, e.g. מַקְטִיל like יַקְטִיל. There are two exceptions among the irregular verbs: in ע"ע verbs one has מֵסֵב despite יָסֵב; in ע"וי verbs one has מֵקִים despite יָקִים (in these two forms מֵ arose on the analogy of מֵיטִיב, § 76 *c*). For the other vowels, the participle is also modelled on the future, e.g. מְקַטֵּל like יְקַטֵּל.

The old form of Nifal, which also had the preformative מ, has been replaced by the form נִקְטָל. This is the form of the Perfect נִקְטַל, with ָ due to the nominal character of the participle (comp., e.g., the nouns מִדְבָּר, דָּבָר). In Nifal one therefore has essentially the same form in the participle and in the perfect as in the Qal of stative verbs, and perhaps on the analogy of these verbs.

Inflection of participles. Examples: קֹטֵל, קֹטְלִים (§ 30 *g*); קֹטְלָה or קֹטֵלָה and (mostly) קֹטֶלֶת (§ 97 C a); —נִקְטָל, נִקְטָלִים; נִקְטָלָה and (mostly) נִקְטֶלֶת; —מַקְטִיל, מַקְטִילִים; מַקְטִילָה and (mostly) מַקְטֶלֶת (cf. § 89 *g*)(1). *g*

(1) The form with the distinctive morpheme /t/ is far more numerous than that with /-ā/; Böttcher, II, § 993. According to Lambert (§ 787), the segholate form is commoner for the genuine participle, and the other for participles used adjectivally or substantivally.

§ 51. Nifal conjugation

Nifal is the reflexive conjugation of simple action (§ 40 *a*). The **characteristic** of Nifal is a נ which expresses the notion of reflexivity. After a preformative, and hence in the future, imperative, and infinitive, the נ is assimilated to the following consonant; these forms are therefore characterised by the **doubling of the first radical.** *a*

Perfect. The primitive form is *naqtal*(1). The first *a* is weakened to *i*, hence נִקְטַל (§ 29 *g*)(2). But this *a* is retained in the type **nawšab* > נוֹשַׁב (§ 75 *a*) and, in open syllables, in the types נָסַב (§ 82 *c*) and נָקוֹם (§ 80 *f*).

Future. The primitive form is *yanqatil*(3), whence *yinqatil* by attenuation of *a* to *i*, and then יִקָּטֵל.

Imperative. The preformative is ה: הִקָּטֵל. The same form is found in the **infinitive construct.** In the **infinitive absolute** the form of the inf. cst. הִקָּטֵל is used, or this same form with the final vowel *ọ*, הִקָּטֹל, or the form נִקְטֹל fashioned after the perfect (§ 49 *b*).

The **participle** as we now have it, and which has supplanted a primitive form with preformative מ, has the form of the perfect, but with ָ due to the nominal character of the participle: נִקְטָל (§ 50 *f*). Inflection, § 50 *g*.

(1) Note Ugr. /napṭarū/: Huehnergard, *Ugr. Voc.*, p. 321.

(2) This weakening may have begun in forms such as **naqtaltem'*, away from the stress.

(3) Note EA 250.33 *yi-in₄-na-pí-iš* "it shall be done."

Observations concerning various forms. *b*

Future. In the 1st pers. sg., alongside אֶקָּטֵל we also find אִקָּטֵל frequently, with *i*, which is normal in sharp syllables, and אֶקָּטְלָה always; the *i* is also the rule in פ"ו verbs of the type אִוָּשֵׁב (§ 75 a, n.).

The second vowel of the impf. sometimes turns up as /a/, esp. in pause (most likely as a result of Philippi's law): e.g. Gn 21.8 וַיִּגָּמַל, Ex 31.17 וַיִּנָּפַשׁ, but in context in Ez 32.28 תִּשָּׁבַר (because of Resh?, cf. Yeivin, *Babylonian Tradition*, p. 504)(1). The Babylonian tradition, in fact, prefers /a/: Yeivin, ib., and there are some traces of it in SH, see Ben-Ḥayyim, *LOT*, vol. 5, pp. 84f.

In the fem. pl. the ending is always ־ַ֫לְנָה (§ 29 *d*).

For the inverted future, cf. § 47 *b*.

Imperative. הִשָּׁ֫מֶר always occurs with the mil'el stress, no doubt on the analogy of the common הִשָּׁ֫מֶר לְךָ, in which there is a nsiga.

Infinitive construct(2). There are some forms the ה of which is syncopated after a preposition, e.g. לֵרָאוֹת *in order to appear* Is 1.12 (for לְהֵרָאוֹת), בֵּעָטֵף Lam 2.11. But in the two examples cited here, as also almost everywhere else, the vocalisation may be faulty. Thus in Is 1.12 one can read Qal לִרְאוֹת, and in Lam 2.11 one is probably to read Qal בַּעֲטֹף *languishing* as in Ps 61.3 (a similar observation for Hifil, § 54 *b*).

Infinitive absolute. In the regular verb the most frequent form is הִקָּטֹל (a form of the inf. cst.); it is employed for reason of assonance in cases like אִם הִפָּקֵד יִפָּקֵד *if he should happen to be missing* 1Kg 20.39; cf. Nu 15.31; Dt 4.26; 1Sm 27.1. In contrast, the form נִקְטֹל (§ 49 *b*) is affiliated to the perfect in 1Sm 20.6 נִשְׁאֹל נִשְׁאַל *he earnestly asked to be allowed* (comp. § 81 *e* and cf. § 123 *p*).

(1) More examples in Berg., II, § 16 g.
(2) See § 54 *b*, n.

c **Meaning**(1). The principal meaning, **reflexive**, is often preserved. Thus נִשְׁמַר almost always means *to guard oneself*, נִקַּם almost always *to revenge oneself*; נִשְׁעַן almost always *to support oneself*; נֶחֱנַק* *to strangle oneself* (once). Other Nifals also have at the same time the passive meaning, e.g. נִסְתַּר *to hide oneself* and *to be hidden*; נִגְאַל *to redeem oneself* and *to be redeemed*.

Nifal toleratívum. In some cases the meaning is that of *to allow* something *to happen* to oneself, generally with a notion of effective action, e.g. נִדְרַשׁ *to allow oneself to be asked*, and that effectively, hence practically = *to answer* (speaking of God); נִזְהַר *to allow oneself* *to be warned*, and that effectively, hence practically = *to take note of the warning*; נוֹסַר *to allow oneself to be chastised, to chastise oneself*; נֶעְתַּר *to allow oneself to be entreated* (effectively), *to grant an entreaty*(2).

Nifal can have the force of the Greek **middle** voice, e.g. נִשְׁאַל *to ask for oneself*; the **reciprocal** sense, e.g. נוֹעַץ *to consult each other, to deliberate*; נוֹעַד *to meet each other* (at an appointed time and place); נִלְחַם *to fight*; נִדְבַּר *to converse with each other*.

Very often Nifal assumes a purely **passive** sense, e.g. נוֹלַד *to be born*; נִקְבַּר *to be buried*. (For the passive of Qal, cf. § 58)(3).

Although Nifal is, strictly speaking, the reflexive (and often the passive) of Qal, one also finds it as the reflexive (or passive) of the Hifil(4) and also of the Piel (whose proper reflexive is Hitpael); thus. Nifal נִחַם in the sense of *to console oneself* is the reflexive of Piel נִחַם *to console*; נִזְהַר *to allow oneself to be warned*, the reflexive of הִזְהִיר *to warn*.

The majority of the meanings of the Nifal are naturally shared by Hitpael, which is the reflexive conjugation of Piel.

(1) See M. Lambert, "L'emploi du *nifal* en hébreu," *RÉJ* 41 (1900) 196-214.

(2) Compare the Hifil of *consent*, e.g. הִשְׁאִיל *to lend* (§ 54 *d*).

(3) When Nifal has a passive sense, its participle overlaps with the passive participle of Qal, e.g. נָתוּן (3 x) and נִתָּן (3 x) *given*. But a differentiation in meaning is possible: at a grammatical level, נִתָּן usually indicates a process, נָתוּן a result, except at Dt 28.31,32, whereas at a lexical level, קָרוּא = *invited, called, elected*, נִקְרָא = *named* (2 x), *read* (1 x).

(4) E.g. Ne 6.1 נִשְׁמַע לְ *it was made to be heard by* = *they reported to him* (not: *it was heard by*). Alternatively this is a case of impersonal passive, § 152 *fa*.

§ 52. Piel conjugation

In terms of the identification of function, Piel is the most elusive of the Hebrew(1) conjugations. Whatever its precise function or functions may be, one can say at least that it is the active pattern corresponding to the passive Pual and reflexive Hitpael. The formal and prominent **characteristic** of Piel is the doubling of the second radical. Traditionally it has been considered intensive in meaning. It is to be a doubted whether there is a direct link between this assumed function and the doubling of the second radical.

It will be convenient to begin exposition of the forms with the future.

Future. The primitive form is *yaqattil*(2), which has normally become יְקַטֵּל. (The ante-prestress vowel drops out, § 30 *e*).

Perfect. Unlike the primitive Semitic form *qattal*(3), still preserved in Classical Arabic, the perfect appears to have changed in Early Hebrew to *qattil*(4), the change of the second /a/ to /i/ deriving from the future(5). Subsequently, the first /a/ has been attenuated to /i/ (§ 29 *g*)(6). Thus the historical Hebrew Piel form קִטֵּל has not preserved either of the two earliest /a/ vowels, resulting however in a clear opposition between the perfect and the rest of the paradigm. (Compare the perfect of Hifil, § 54 *a*).

The **imperative** קַטֵּל has the vowels of the future. The same form occurs in the **inf. cst.**(7) The **inf. abs.** mostly uses the form of the inf. cst. קַטֵּל, but rarely with the final vowel *ọ* קַטֹּל (this *ọ* was probably long, § 49 *b*).

The **participle** has the vowels of the future: מְקַטֵּל(8).

(1) The same difficulty exists with the corresponding pattern in all other cognate Semitic languages, including modern living languages.

(2) As testified by Ugr. (Gordon, *UT*, § 9.35), and unlike *yuqattil*, which is preserved in Arabic and Akkadian and considered by many as the primitive form. It is quite conceivable that *yaqattil* had been preceded by *yuqattil*. The vowel of the 1st sg. /'ă/ could be due to the influence of the following vowel, namely that of R1. But the participle was most likely *muqattil* (so in Ugr. and AC): the preservation of the /u/ can be attributed to the preceding labial.

(3) For the theory that Early Hebrew may have possessed an alternative pattern *qittil* (and *hiqtil* for Hifil), see J. Blaù in *HUCA* 42 (1971) 152-58, though Blau discusses only the perfect tense, thus not allowing for the possibility of mutual influence between the pf. and impf. On the whole the evidence for the hypothesised vowel sequence /i-i/ appears to be weaker than that for /a-a/: in any event the hypothesis is claimed to have only partial application, for הוֹשִׁיב, for instance, can only have developed from /hawšib/. Bergsträsser's account of the first /a/ to /i/ (Berg., II, § 17 i) is not convincing.

(4) Ugr. has /šallima/ "it paid/delivered" (as in Aramaic): Huehnergard, *Ugr. Vocabulary*, p. 321. SH has preserved the primitive first /a/: Ben-Ḥayyim, *LOT*, vol. 5, p. 81, and Macuch, *Gram.*, p. 283. On Ps 89.45 μαγαρθ (MT מִגַּרְתָּה) in the Secunda, see Brønno, *Studien*, pp. 65f.: the form is best interpreted as Qal.

(5) On ◌ֵ/◌ֶ as the second vowel of Proto-Heb. Piel, see E. Qimron in *Leš* 50 (1986) 80. Likewise in Hifil the second vowel of the perfect is due to the analogy of the future.

(6) Perhaps this weakening started in forms such as *qattaltem', away from the stress. The pataḥ is preserved only in נַשַּׁנִי he made me forget, for the sake of assonance with מְנַשֶּׁה, in the folk-etymology of this name, Gn 41.51; it is probably an archaic form.
(7) EA attests to ḫal-li-iq "to destroy" (250.7,37,55) as the inf. cst.
(8) See n. 2 above.

A general observation. The genuine gemination is quite often reduced to virtual gemination when the consonant has shewa (§ 18 *m*), e.g. בִּקְשָׁה and often in the verb בִּקֵּשׁ (but always בַּקְּשׁוּ in the impv.); it is always so reduced in הַלְלוּ *praise*. b

Observations on various forms. c

Perfect 3rd pers. m. sg. Although ֵ is secondary, קִטֵּל is the proper form of Piel and also its pausal form(1). One very often finds the form קִטַּל(2), the pataḥ of which is not the primitive *a*, but an attenuation of ṣeré (§ 29 *d*). The form קִטֶּל, a lighter form, is used mostly with the conjunctive accent and when קִטֶּל־ loses the stress (before maqqef), and only rarely with a disjunctive accent. Thus, with a conjunctive accent, we find בֵּרַךְ always; with a weak disjunctive accent we find בֵּרַךְ twice and בֵּרֵךְ twice; the pausal form (which does not occur) would have been בֵּרֵ֑ךְ. The fact that the vowel alternation in question is almost totally confined to the perfect(3) may suggest, however, that one is not dealing here with a purely phonetic phenomenon; analogy of Qal or Nifal, or that of the first and second persons in the perfect may be responsible. The fairly common Hitpaal (§ 53 *b*) needs to be viewed separately.

In three verbs(4) we find the vowel ֶ: דִּבֶּר *he spoke*, כִּפֶּר *he expiated*, וְכִבֶּס *and he will wash* (11 times, but twice כִּבֵּס!). These anomalies are difficult to explain. In pause one finds דִּבֵּ֑ר and כִּבֵּ֑ס (2Sm 19.25†).

In the conjugation one also finds ַ (Philippi's law, § 29 *aa*, *d*), which is no more primitive than in קִטֵּל, e.g. קִטַּ֫לְתָּ(5).

Future. In the 1st pers. sg. in place of אֲ we very occasionally find אֱ, e.g. in אֱזָרֶה *I will disperse* Lv 26.33; Ez 5.12; 12.14† (before qameṣ, cf. § 29 *f*); this ֱ becomes ֲ in וָאֲסָעֲרֵם Zech 7.14 (cp. § 21 *h*)(6).

In the fem. plur. the ending is usually ־ֵּ֫לְנָה(§ 29 *d*), e.g. תְּדַבֵּ֫רְנָה (in context and in pause). ־ַ֫לְנָה is found in three pausal forms due to various other considerations (Ho 4.13,14; Is 3.16; 13.18). The abnormal form ◌ֶ֫לְנָה Ez 13.19 is found once.

Imperative. The ◌ֵ of קַטֵּל is changed to ◌ַ in פַּלַּג Ps 55.10; קָרַב Ez 37.17.

The **inf. construct** with a feminine ending ◌ָה (cf. § 149 *d*) occurs in יַסְּרָה Lv 26.18; זַמְּרָה Ps 147.1; with a suf. in צַדֶּקְתֵּךְ Ez 16.52.

The **inf. absolute** קַטֹּל is rare. The form of the inf. cst., קַטֵּל, is most often used instead, e.g. 2Kg 2.11 הוֹלְכִים הָלוֹךְ וְדַבֵּר. In 2Sm 12.14 the *a* has been weakened to *i* for the sake of assonance: נִאֵץ נִאַ֫צְתָּ.

Participle. The form מָאֵן (always in the phrase אִם־מָאֵן אַתָּה. Ex 7.27; 9.2; 10.4; Jer 38.21) is in origin a haplography for מְמָאֵן*. The vocalisation מֵאֲנִים Jer 13.10 seems to be faulty (usually 'מָ). Cf. Brock., *GvG*, I, pp. 264ff.(7) Zeph 1.14 מַהֵר looks like a similar case, though it is not preceded by a word ending in Mem.

(1) Compare the form with a suffix קַטֶּלְךָ.

(2) Dictionaries often give Piels with the vowel ◌ֵ, which, in fact, they do not have in our texts. An important study on this question is C. Rabin's "The vocalization of the third singular perfect of *Piʿēl* in Tiberian Hebrew," *Leš* 32 (1967) 12-26. In the Babylonian tradition the vowel in question is normally /a/, not /ẹ/: Yeivin, *Babylonian Tradition*, p. 514. One of the rarer conjugations, Pa'lel (§ 59 *b*) may also belong here: so S. Har-Zahav, *Leš* 2 (1930) 161.

(3) The vowel /a/ is far more widespread in the Babylonian tradition: see Yeivin, *Babylonian Tradition*, pp. 519, 525-27, 535, 537-41.

(4) For an attempt to explain the three exceptions, see J. Blau in *HUCA* 42 (1971) 155f., though his explanation postulates /i/ as the second original vowel of Pi. pf. (§ *a*, n. 3 above). Note in this connection that the second column of the Hexapla regularly shows ε as the second vowel of Pi. and Hi. in the first and second persons as well: Brønno, *Studien*, pp. 88f.

(5) The tradition preserved in the Secunda, however, differs in this regard: κ.σσες קִצֵּץ Ps 46.10, but חִלַּ֫לְתָּ ελλελθ ib. 89.40. Likewise in Hifil: εσθερθα הִסְתַּ֫רְתָּ Ps 30.8 vs. εελικ הֶחֱלִיק 36.3. For a discussion see Brønno, *Morphologie*, pp. 66-68. The evidence of the Secunda regarding Hitpael is not unequivocal: for data, see Brønno, op. cit., pp. 107f.

(6) The vowel *e* with the prefix of Pi. impf. 1st sg. is standard in the Babylonian tradition: Yeivin, *Babylonian Tradition*, p. 522. Cf. also Secunda, Ps 18.30 אֲדַלֶּג־ εδαλλεγ; 89.36 אֲכַזֵּב εχαζεβ.

(7) Whilst Ben-Ḥayyim (*LOT*, vol. 5, p. 14) argues that these are Qal participles, neither verb is used in Qal elsewhere.

d **Meaning.** As briefly indicated in § *a* above, the question how the function of Piel in relation to other conjugations, notably Qal, should be defined still remains one of the major challenges facing Hebrew and Semitic linguistics(1). In the present state of our knowledge, we can only point to a number of fairly distinct meaning categories into which some verbs seem to fit. Others, an uncomfortably large number, still defy such categorisation(2). Nor can we suggest, without doing violence to all the evidence available, a single notion or meaning category which can be said to underlie all those "nuances."

Factitive(3). This type of Piel corresponds to Qal of intransitive action or state, and one can often postulate an underlying adjective or resultative participle: from אָבַד *to perish, disappear*: אִבֵּד *to make someone perish, disappear*; from קָדַשׁ *to be holy*: קִדֵּשׁ *to sanctify*; from גָּדַל *to be great*: גִּדֵּל *to make great, raise (a child)*; *to provoke*: *anger* כִּעֵס (twice), *jealousy* קִנֵּא (once): *to leave*: נִקָּה *to leave unpunished*, חִיָּה *to leave to survive* (= *not to kill*): *to keep* זִכָּה *to keep pure*, *סִתֵּר (once) *to keep hidden*. Pi. לִמֵּד *to teach* probably has to do with its Qal's original intransitive status (note its fut. יִלְמַד). בֵּרֵךְ *to bless* may belong here (cf. בָּרוּךְ *blessed*), or alternatively under **declarative**, or even **denominative** (*to pronounce a blessing* [בְּרָכָה] *upon*).

Declarative-estimative force: *to declare innocent* נִקָּה, *to decl. clean* טִהַר, *to decl. unclean* טִמֵּא. This may be subsumed under **factitive** in the sense that, whilst the **factitive** denotes the generation of a state or quality actually and physically, the **declarative-estimative** does so mentally or verbally.

Pluralising. The action denoted by some Piel verbs involves either multiple subjects or objects(4). *Numerous subjects*, e.g. *שִׁאֵל *to ask* 2Sm 20.18†; *לִקֵּק *to lick* Jdg 7.6; *numerous objects*, e.g. שִׁלַּח *to dispatch* Jdg 20.6; קִבֵּר *to inter* 1Kg 11.15; קִצֵּץ *to chop* Jdg 1.6. The so-called frequentative may belong here(5): it has to do with the frequency of an action, e.g. *צִחֵק *to mock at* (Qal: *to laugh*); *שִׁאֵל *to beg* (once; Qal *to ask*); שִׁבֵּר *to break into pieces* (Qal: *to break*); *סִפֵּר *to recount* (Qal: *to count*); פִּתַּח *to untie* (Qal: *to open*).

Denominative. The following examples are denominative in the sense that there lies behind each of them a related, and assuredly more primitive, noun: דִּבֵּר *to speak* (vs. דָּבָר); כִּהֵן *to act as priest* (כֹּהֵן); אִלֵּם *to bind sheaves* (אֲלֻמָּה). Unlike the **factitive** and the **declarative-estimative** this is not a grammatical, but lexical category. Somewhat different are denominative Piels which have a *privative*, i.e. depriving or removing force, e.g. דִּשֵּׁן *to remove fat* (i.e. the fatty ashes = דֶּשֶׁן from the altar); שֵׁרֵשׁ *to uproot* (from שֹׁרֶשׁ; in contrast, הִשְׁרִישׁ is *to strike root*); חִטֵּא *to remove sin* (from חֵטְא; compare the privative Hitpael הִתְחַטֵּא *to purify oneself from sin*); in contrast, הֶחֱטִיא is *to make someone sin*; סֵעֵף *to lop off boughs*; Jer 50.17 עִצֵּם *to gnaw at bones*; Josh 10.19 זִנֵּב *to cut off the tail*; and possibly Ct 4.9 לִבֵּב *to capture the heart*.

Adverbial Piel (as against Hifil) is rare, e.g. שִׁחֵת *to act wickedly, sin* (probably by ellipsis of the object, like הִשְׁחִית, § 54 *d*); עִוֵּל* *to act in an iniquitous manner* (twice); מִהַר in the sense of *to act quickly* (whence the adverb מַהֵר *quickly*, § 102 *e*). For Pual, the passive of Piel, see § 56.

(1) A fresh and fruitful approach to the question has been inaugurated in modern times by A. Goetze, "The so-called intensive of the Semitic languages," *JAOS* 62 (1942) 1-8, in which the author, drawing upon Akkadian evidence, challenged the traditional characterisation of the Piel as intensive. Some of his insights were subsequently applied with particular regard to BH by E. Jenni, *Das hebräische Pi'el: Syntaktisch-semasiologische Untersuchung einer Verbalform im Alten Testament* (Zurich, 1968); cf. also S.A. Ryder II, *The D-Stem in Western Semitic* (The Hague, 1974), F. Leemhuis, "Sibawaihi's treatment of the D stem," *JSS* 18 (1973) 238-56, and a review article by M.H. Goshen-Gottstein in *BO* 42 (1985) 279-83.

(2) For an attempt to see how some studies since Goetze's above-mentioned trail-blazing article can be made to apply to BH, see Waltke—O'Connor, *BH Syntax*, pp. 396-417.

(3) From Lat. *facere* "to make." This is to be distinguished from the notion of "causative": "to make him holy" as against "to make him walk."

One normally associates 'causative' with Hifil, and indeed some verbs, such as אִבֵּד and קִדֵּשׁ, do occur in both Piel and Hifil with scarcely discernible difference in meaning or nuance. Despite their extended discussion, Waltke and O'Connor (*BH Syntax*, pp. 435-41), in our estimation, have not demonstrated any meaningful difference between the members of these and other pairs. It is only rarely possible to distinguish between Piel and Hifil thus used, e.g. Is 29.13 בְּפִיו וּבִשְׂפָתָיו כִּבְּדוּנִי as against 1Kg 12.10 אָבִיךָ הִכְבִּיד אֶת־עֻלֵּנוּ, but 1Sm 6.6 כַּאֲשֶׁר כִּבְּדוּ מִצְרַיִם וּפַרְעֹה אֶת־לִבָּם, and חיה Pi. and Hi. are often interchangeable; see E. Rubinstein in *IOS* 9 (1979) 67f.

(4) Here some would see evidence of the often assumed essential or direct link between form (*signifiant*) and meaning (*signifié*), which of course flies in the face of the universally acknowledged, essentially arbitrary nature of linguistic signs.

(5) Lambert (§ 649) compares Ct 2.8 דִּלֵּג with Zeph 1.9 Qal דָּלַג. See also J. Zlotniq, "Piel," *Lĕš* 2 (1930) 22-34.

§ 53. Hitpael conjugation

Hitpael is the reflexive conjugation associated with Piel (§ 40 *a*). The two **characteristics** of Hitpael are the doubling of the second radical as in Piel (§ 52 *a*) and a ת which expresses the reflexive notion (like the נ of Nifal, § 51 *a*)(1). *a*

It is convenient to begin the exposition of the forms with the future.

Future: The Hebrew form is *yitqaṭṭel* יִתְקַטֵּל (like Piel יְקַטֵּל).

Perfect: The group *iṯ*, composed of the vowel of the preformative and the characteristic *ṯ* goes over to the perfect, in which the vowel must necessarily be preceded by a consonant. This consonant is ה (instead of א)(2) as in the imperative and the inf. cst. Nifal (§ 51 *a*), hence הִת. The rest of the form is due to the analogy of the future, hence הִתְקַטֵּל. The sequence הִת is also found in the **imperative** and the **infinitive** הִתְקַטֵּל. In the **participle** one finds מִתְקַטֵּל with the vowels of the future.

(1) The corresponding form in Arabic is *tafaʻʻala*, and not *'iftaʻala* (with an infixed *t*), as is justly noted by Abu'l Walīd against his contemporary grammarians.

The infix *t* is an almost universal Semitic phenomenon, attested in Moabite, Ugr., Old Phoen., Amorite, and Old Aramaic; on Amorite, see H.B. Huffmon, *Amorite Personal Names* [§ 41 *a*, n.], pp. 81f. In Moabite and Phoen., however, there is no telling whether the second radical is geminated or not, whereas Ugr. appears to have had a genuine *t*-infix pattern corresponding to Qal, so-called Gt, on which see Huehnergard, *Ugr. Vocabulary*, pp. 320f. On a survey of the infixed *t*-conjugation in BH, see A.M.L. Boyle, *Infix-*t *Forms in BH*, Diss. Ph.D. [Boston] 1969. On possible vestiges of the *t*-infixed Hifil, see J. Blau in *VT* 7 (1957) 385-88.

(2) We have א in אֶתְחַבַּר 2Ch 20.35 (with exceptional final pataḥ).

General observations. Apart from the ordinary type in *ẹ*, which alone we have only spoken about so far, there exists a secondary and rare type which has the vowel *a* in the perfect, future and imperative. The form **hitpaal** occurs in 7 verbs, three of which are ל"א verbs: הִתְאַנַּף *to get angry*, הִתְאַפַּק *to restrain oneself*, הִתְנַפַּל *to precipitate oneself*, הִתְעַנַּג *to give oneself up to effeminacy*, הִתְחַטָּא *to remove one's own sin*, הִטַּמָּא (§ e) *to render oneself impure*, הִתְפַּלָּא *to show oneself as astonishing* (?). The form Hitpaal is standard in the Babylonian tradition of BH(1) and Aramaic; in Hebrew, where it is rare, it is probably due to *Aramaising*(2). *b*

(1) Yeivin, *Babylonian Tradition*, p. 550.

(2) In Aramaic the form *hitpaal* is probably a secondarily *passivised* reflexive form; cf. P. Joüon in *Bib* 1 (1920) 354ff.

c The **pausal forms of the type in ẹ** in the perfect, future, and imperative take the vowel *a*, namely ַ in intermediate pause, and ָ֑ in major pause (§ 32 *c*), e.g. יִתְיַצֵּב *he will station himself* becomes יִתְיַצָּ֑ב 1Sm 3.10 (with zaqef), יִתְיַצָּֽב Job 41.2; likewise יִתְנַשֵּׂא becomes יִתְנַשָּׂ֑א Nu 23.24. This pausal vowel *a* is not primitive; it stems from the Hitpaal type, and replaces in pause the proper vowel *ẹ* by virtue of its greater sonority.

d **Comparison with Piel.** In the perfect of the Piel, the first primitive vowel *a* has been attenuated to *i*: קִטֵּל; it has been preserved in Hitpael: הִתְקַטֵּל. In the perfect of the Piel the vowel *a* of the form of juncture קִטֵּל has evolved from ֶ; in the type הִתְקַטֵּל the *a* is pausal, and stems from the type הִתְקַטַּל.

e The ת is subject to *metathesis* before a *sibilant*, e.g. *hiṯ-šąmmẹr* becomes הִשְׁתַּמֵּר (§ 17 *b*).

The ת becomes **assimilated** to a following **dental**, e.g. **mit-dąbbẹr* becomes מְדַבֵּר, but מִתְדַּפְּקִים Jdg 18.22; **hit-ṭąmmå'* becomes הִטַּמָּא. It becomes partially assimilated to the emphatic צ, namely becomes emphatic *ṭ*, e.g. **hit-ṣąddẹq* becomes, with metathesis, הִצְטַדֵּק (§ 17 *g*). Sometimes the ת becomes assimilated to נ, e.g. הִנַּבֵּא alongside הִתְנַבֵּא; to כ, e.g. תִּכַּסֶּה Pr 26.26; to שׁ Ec 7.16 תִּשּׁוֹמֵם.

f **Observations on various forms.**

In the inflection of the **perfect** we find ַ as in Piel, e.g. הִתְקַטַּ֫לְתָּ like קִטַּ֫לְתָּ (Philippi's law, § 29 *aa*). We find some forms such as וְהִתְגַּדִּלְתִּ֫י Ez 38.23 with attenuation of *a* to *i* in an unstressed closed syllable.

Future. In the plur. fem. the ending is usually ַ֫לְנָה, e.g. תִּתְהַלַּ֫כְנָה (§ 29 *d*). The **inf. cst.** has the Aramaic ending in Dn 11.23 הִתְחַבְּרוּת (§ 88 M *j*). The anomalous form Ex 2.4 וַתֵּתַצַּב is usually corrected in the light of ותתיצב in the Samaritan Pentateuch to וַתִּתְיַצַּב; it may be a mixed form arising from וַתִּתְיַצַּב and וַתֵּעָמֵד (Nifal) of similar meaning.

g **Detailed observations.**

In the verb פָּקַד *to muster* etc. one has a form הִתְפָּקֵד *to be mustered, to have a census taken of* without the doubling of the ק, e.g. Jdg 20.

15, 17; 21.9. According to some, this form could be a Hitpael where the gemination may have been omitted on account of the nature of the ק, but one may object that Piel of this root is very rare (only Is 13.4). According to others, one could be dealing with a reflexive of Qal here (e.g., Brock., *GvG* I, p. 529)(1). One thus finds four times הָתְפָּקְדוּ, which is the form הִתְפָּקְדוּ secondarily *passivised* through the change of the first vowel *i* to *u* (ọ); but this strange form is all the more suspect especially as it has the same meaning *to be passed in review* (Nu 1.47; 2.33; 26.62; 1Kg 20.27). Finally, one may be dealing with a T-conjugation of Pā‘ēl, which corresponds to the sixth conjugation in Arabic *tafā‘ala*(2).

(1) According to some the place-names אֶשְׁתָּאוֹל and אֶשְׁתְּמוֹעַ are, also of same pattern with metathesis.
(2) M.H. Goshen-Gottstein in *Proceedings*, p. 86, n. 75.

Rather rarely the Hitpael form is secondarily passivised into Hotpaal: inf. הֻכַּבֵּס *to be washed* (without the reflexive nuance) Lv 13.55, 56; הֻטַּמָּאָה Dt 24.4, properly *one made her defile herself*, but perhaps simply *she was defiled*; הֻדַּשְׁנָה for הֻדַּשְּׁנָה Is 34.6 *it got fat*. h

Meaning. The basic meaning is the **reflexive** of Piel(1), e.g. הִתְקַדֵּשׁ *to sanctify oneself* (קִדֵּשׁ *to sanctify*). Generally speaking, Hitpael can have the diverse meanings of the Nifal together with the nuances proper to Piel. Thus it can have the sense of the Greek **middle**, e.g. הִתְפָּרֵק *to tear something off oneself* Ex 32.3. It can develop into a pure **passive**, e.g. הִשְׁתַּכַּח *to be forgotten*. It sometimes has the nuance of *to disguise oneself as* or *to show oneself* (truly or falsely) *to be such and such*, e.g. הִתְחַלָּה *to pretend illness* 2Sm 13.5,6; 14.2 הִתְאַבֵּל *feign to be a mourner*; 19.4 הִתְגַּנֵּב *to behave like a thief* (גַּנָּב); Pr 13.7 "there is one who pretends to be rich (מִתְעַשֵּׁר), yet has nothing, there is another who pretends to be poor (מִתְרוֹשֵׁשׁ), yet has great riches." See also Is 10.15; Pr 25.6. i

In a few examples the conjugation seems to have the meaning of "to ask for": הִתְפַּלֵּל *to ask for justice* (פְּלִילָה or פְּלִילִים); הִתְחַנֵּן *to ask for mercy* (חֲנִינָה or תַּחֲנוּנִים)(2).

As a denominative, it can have the **privative** sense like the Piel (§ 52 *d*), e.g. הִתְחַטֵּא *to remove sin from oneself* (comp. חִטֵּא *to remove sin*).

(1) An 'iterative' or durative nuance has been claimed for a verb such as הִתְהַלֵּךְ: see E.A. Speiser, "The durative hithpa'el: A *tan* form," *JAOS* 75 (1955) 118-21.

(2) See S. Yeivin in *Lešonénu* 2 (1929-30) 49, where he refers to the tenth form in Arabic: /'istasqā/ *to ask for drink, to pray for rain*; /'istaǧfara/ *to ask for pardon*.

§ 54. Hifil conjugation

a The Hifil is the active conjugation of causative action (§ 40 *a*). The **characteristic** of Hifil is a ה, which usually drops after a preformative, thus in the future and the participle (§ *b*).

It will be convenient to begin the exposition of the forms with the future.

Future. The primal Hebrew form is **yhaqtil* (with a short *i*), whence, by syncope of the ה (§ 17 *e*), **yaqtil*(1).

This short *i* is preserved in the **jussive** and the **imperative**, where it usually becomes ֵ. But in the **indicative** (except in תַּקְטֵלְנָה) the *i* became long (יַקְטִיל), probably on the analogy of the Hifil of ע"ו verbs, e.g. יָקִים (§ 80 *g*). Exception: in the type יָסֵב for **yasibb*, the *i* was not lengthened because of the tendency of the final consonant of ע"ע verbs to gemination (cf. § 18 *l*).

Perfect. The primitive form *haqtal* has not preserved in Hebrew either of the two *a*'s. (Consider the perfect of Piel, § 52 *a*).

The first *a* has weakened to *i* (§ 29 *g*)(2). But the *a* has been preserved in the types *hawšib*, *hayṭib*, which have become הוֹשִׁיב (§ 75 a), הֵיטִיב (§ 76 *c*); see, in Nifal, the type *nawšab* > נוֹשַׁב (§ 51 *a*)(3).

The second *a* became *i* on the analogy of the future, hence **hiqtil*. This *i* was lengthened (and retained the stress) in the third person הִקְטִיל, הִקְטִילָה, הִקְטִילוּ, on the analogy of the future forms of יַקְטִיל, יַקְטִילוּ. Exception: in the type הֵסֵב for **hisibb*, the *i* was not lengthened. In the remaining persons the *i* (ֵ) became *a* (Philippi's law, § 29 aa), e.g. הִקְטַלְתָּ.

The **imperative** הַקְטֵל has the vowel of the future jussive יַקְטֵל (§ 48 *a*).

The **infinitive** cst. הַקְטִיל has the vowel of the future (§ 49 *c*).

The **infinitive abs.** הַקְטֵל is a secondary modification of the infinitive construct (§ 49 *b*).

The **participle** מַקְטִיל has the vowels of the future (cf. § 50 *f*).

(1) The prefix vowel of the impf. was /a/ in Amorite: see Huffmon, *Amorite Personal Names* [§ 41 *a*, n.], pp. 66-69.

(2) Already in El Amarna we find /hi-/: 256.7 *ḫi-iḫ-bé-e* "he hid." Perhaps this weakening began in forms such as **haqtaltem'*, away from the stress. The pataḥ is found preserved in וְהַרְאֵיתִי Na 3.5, and also in SH (Ben-Ḥayyim, *LOT*, vol. 5, p. 80, though Macuch, *Gram.*, pp. 287f., indicates /-æ-/). For 'הֶ, cf. § *c*.

(3) J. Blau postulates **hiqtil* (ultimately < **huqtul*) as coexisting with *haqtal* (*HUCA* 42 [1971] 152-58).

General observations. The **syncope** of ה, as we have said, is usually observed in the future and participle. In the **future**, however, one finds some examples with ה, perhaps partly under the influence of Aramaic, e.g. יְהוֹשִׁיעַ 1Sm 17.47; Ps 116.6 (in pause), יְהוֹדֶה Ne 11.17 etc.; יְהֵילִילוּ Is 52.5. *b*

In the **infinitive** the ה after a preposition is maintained, e.g. לְהַקְטִיל. In several examples the ה is syncopated, e.g. לַקְטִיל; but in the majority of cases the vocalisation is suspect, e.g. לַסְתִּר Is 29.15 can be vocalised as Piel לְסַתֵּר; לַצְבּוֹת and לַנְפִּל Nu 5.22 can be vocalised as Qal לִצְבּוֹת and לִנְפֹּל; לַנְחֹת Ex 13.21 must be vocalised as Qal לִנְחֹת (a similar note on the Nifal in § 51 *b*). The vocalisation, however, is assured in לַאֲדִיב 1Sm 2.33; לַחֲטִיא Ec 5.5; לַעֲבִיר 2Sm 19.19. See also לַשְׁבִּית Am 8.4; לָבִיא 2Ch 31.10; לשחית 1QpHb 4.13(1).

(1) On the inf. cst., G. Rendsburg, "*Laqtîl* infinitives: Yiph'il or Hiph'il?", *Or* 51 (1982) 231-38, rejects Dahood's and Segert's suggestion that Yiph'il existed in BH as well as in Phoenician, but argues that the alleged Yiph'ils in BH and the Nif. imperatives without /h/ are cases of the syncope of the consonant aided by the analogy of the fut. as in MH. But since BH does not attest to such typically MH forms as לֵלֵךְ, they are merely cases of the syncope.

Observations on various forms. *c*

Perfect. Instead of 'הִ one has, e.g. הֶכְלַמְנוּם *we discomfited them* 1Sm 25.7, without any apparent reason. One finds 'הֶ many times in ל"ה verbs, e.g. הֶגְלָה (§ 79 *q*).

Future. In some rare examples the originally long *i* seems to drop out in the inflection, e.g. וַיַּדְבְּקוּ 1Sm 14.22; there is probably *lectio mixta* (§ 16 *g*) giving the choice between Hifil and Qal, or more likely a secondary development based on וַיַּדְבֵּק. Comp. § 63 *c*.

In the fem. pl. the ending is always ֵ֫לְנָה (§ 29 *d*).

Imperative. Instead of הַקְטֵל we find, rarely, the abnormal spelling הַקְטֵיל, e.g. 2Kg 8.6; the rare vocalisation הַקְטִיל, e.g. הוֹפִיעַ Ps 94.1, is possibly an error for הַקְטֵיל.

The *i* for *e* occurs in both the fut. and imprv. when a vowel ending is added: e.g. הַקְטִ֫ילִי; הַאֲכִ֫ילֵהוּ *Feed him!*; יַקְטִ֫ילוּ, which therefore can be either future or jussive, הוֹשִׁ֫יעָה with a paragogic ā. The *i* is almost always accented. Further, in some abnormal cases: וַיַּחְשִׁךְ Ps 105.28; וַנַּעֲמִיד Ne 4.3, whilst *i* is almost the rule in 1st sg.(1), and in ל"א verbs(2).

Inf. cst. Instead of הַקְטִיל one sometimes finds הִקְטִיל, e.g. Nu 21.35 הִשְׁאִיר; Dt 7.24 הִשְׁמִדְךָ (cf. 28.48; Josh 11.14, and contrast Josh 23.15; 11.20 etc.); but this *i* is suspect(3).

The infinitive construct has the Aramaic ending in Ez 24.26 לְהַשְׁמָעוּת (§ 88 M *j*).

Inf. abs. The spelling הַקְטֵיל instead of הַקְטֵל occurs fairly frequently. This spelling suggests that the ẹ was originally long or tended to become so.

Participle. On the inflection, cf. § 50 *g*.

(1) Berg., II, § 5 d, notes that these are often spelled defectively: e.g. וָאָבִא Ex 19.4, וָאַשְׁלִךְ Dt 9.21.

(2) Lambert, § 819: e.g. וַיּוֹצִא Dt 4.20.

(3) If this were authentic, it would have to be explained as a weakening of *a*. We always (7 x) find עַד־בִּלְתִּי הִשְׁאִיר (with maqqef; the *a*, away from the stress, could easily have been weakened; the *i* could also have been triggered by the sibilant and by the adjacent *i*'s) Nu 21.35, Dt 3.3, Josh 8.22, 10.33, 11.8, 2Kg 10.11†. Some grammarians erroneously see in these forms perfects in the third person. Cf. König, 1, pp. 212, 276; *Syntax*, §§ 385 *l*, 401 *v*; Driver, ad Dt 3.3, 7.24 (*ICC*). However, the pf. is rather plausible in 2Sm 22.1 (// Ps 18.1) בְּיוֹם הִצִּיל יהוה *on the day when Y. rescued* with an asyndetic relative clause (§ 158 *a*).

Abul Walid (R. Ibn Janaḥ), in his *Riqmah* (ed. Wilensky—Téné [Jerusalem, 1964], § 31 [30]), refers to הֶחֱזִיקִי Jer 31.32 and הִדְרִיכָה 51.33, both as inf. (csts) and likewise הִצִּיל Is 31.5 (// גָּנוֹן) and הִמְלִיט (// פָּסֹחַ).

d **Meaning.** The basic meaning is that of **causation**, e.g. הוֹצִיא *to make go out* (יָצָא *to go out*); הֶאֱכִיל *to make eat, give* something *to eat, to feed* (אָכַל *to eat*); הִפִּיל *to make fall* (נָפַל *to fall*); הֶרְאָה *to make see, show* (רָאָה *to see*); הֵמַר *to make bitter* (מַר *bitter* and *it is bitter*). But *to make* do such and such action in the sense of *to order* something to be done is not a meaning of the conjugation; הִקְטִיל must not therefore be translated *he ordered to kill*. To convey this idea קָטַל(1) is used. Thus Qal בָּנָה *to build* is used for *to make build*, הָרַג *to kill* for *to make kill*, עָשָׂה *to do* for *make do* (all these verbs without a causative form); likewise Hifil הִכָּה *to hit* may also be employed for *to make to hit* Dt 25.2.

Quite often the meaning is **intransitive causative**, or **ingressive**, that is to say, the action remains with the subject itself, constituting an intransitive counterpart of the **factitive** Piel (§ 52 *d*), e.g. הִשְׁמִין *to become fat*; הֶאְדִּים *to become red*; הֶחְשִׁיךְ *to become dark*; הֶאֱרִיךְ *to become long*; הֶחֱרִישׁ *to fall silent*; הִשְׁקִיט *to be quiet*; הִלְבִּין *to become* (but also *make*) *white*; הֵקִיץ *to wake up* (always intransitive); הִזְקִין *to grow old*.

Sometimes what results is a **mode** of action (**adverbial Hifil**), e.g. הֵיטִיב *to act well*; הִשְׁחִית *to act badly* (likewise שִׁחֵת, § 52 *d*); הֵרַע *to act wickedly*; הִשְׂכִּיל *to act prudently*; הִסְכִּיל *to act foolishly* (cf. § 124 *n*); הִרְבָּה *to do much* (§ 141 *h*); הִמְעִיט *to do little*.

Associated with the causative meaning is that of the **declarative-estimative**, e.g. הִצְדִּיק *to pronounce just*; הִרְשִׁיעַ *to declare guilty*; הֵקַל *to despise (to consider someone insignificant)*; הֶעֱרִיץ* *to fear (to consider someone strong)*(2).

A rather special meaning is that of **conceding** the thing expressed by the root, e.g. הִשְׁאִיל *to agree to a request, to grant something asked/ requested*(3), hence *to lend* (שָׁאַל *to ask / request, borrow*). Corresponding to the Qal *to borrow* לָוָה and עָבַט we find the Hifil *to lend* הִלְוָה*, הֶעֱבִיט*.

In many Hifil **denominatives** the noun from which the verbal form is derived is either the object or the effect of the action, e.g. הִשְׁרִישׁ *to put down roots* (from שֹׁרֶשׁ; but שֵׁרֵשׁ = *to pull up roots* § 52 *d*); הִקְרִין *to grow, have horns* (קֶרֶן); הִפְרִיס *to have a cloven hoof* (פַּרְסָה); הִמְטִיר *to produce rain, to make rain* (מָטָר) and הִגְשִׁים 1 x (גֶּשֶׁם). There are some Hifil denominatives of nouns of time or place, e.g. הֶעֱרִיב* *to do something in the evening* (עֶרֶב); הֵימִין *to go to right* (יָמִין *the right side*); הִשְׂמְאִיל *to go left* (שְׂמֹאל *the left side*; quadriliteral root, § 60).

(1) However, a case like Is 29.21 מַחֲטִיאֵי אָדָם *make a man an offender* does involve a forced action, possibly imposed against someone's will; perh. also הִבְרִיךְ *to make (a camel) kneel down*, and Am 2.12 וַתַּשְׁקוּ אֶת־הַנְּזִרִים יָיִן (note צִוִּיתֶם in the same verse; cf.

Ibn Ezra ad loc.).
(2) Cf. W.T. Classen, "The declarative-estimative Hiph'il," *JNWSL* 2 (1972) 5-16.
(3) Compare the *Nifal tolerativum*, § 51 *c*.

J. Margain seems to exaggerate slightly the notion of "tolerative" Hifil (and Piel): *GLECS* 18-23 (1973-79) 23-31. Thus Jdg 16.19 וַתְּיַשְּׁנֵהוּ *elle le laissa s'endormir sur ses genoux* is too weak. "She got him to sleep on her knees" would rightly underline the active role (Margain's 'stratagème') that Delilah played. It is not as if she acceded to his request to sleep as he did, nor of course was she so tactless as to force him to put his head on her knees. In cases of the Hifil of genuine causative force, the primary notion is that the subject of such Hifil verbs is the leading character, the first cause in a figurative sense.

e The **intransitive** sense of certain Hifil verbs can appear strange. Sometimes this sense stems from the ellipsis of the object, e.g. הִקְשִׁיב *to listen*, i.e. *to incline (the ear)*; הֵשִׁיב *to reply / answer*, i.e. *to make (the word* דָּבָר*) return*. The same explanation may hold for certain adverbial Hifils, e.g. הֵיטִיב *to make (the action* מַעֲלָל*) good = to act nicely;* הִשְׁחִית *to make (the action* עֲלִילָה*) bad = to act badly* (§ *d*).

f In some other cases where the sense is not that of Hifil but of Qal, there may be a secondary or **pseudo-Hifil**(1), for especially in the case of Qal future verbs with *i*, the form, which would resemble Hifil, could easily pass over to the Hifil form. There is probably pseudo-Hifil in the following verbs: קִיא *to vomit* (§ 81 *c*), קִיץ *to wake up* (§ 76 *d*), רִיב *to dispute*, שִׂים *to place*; בדל and פרד *to separate*; טָמַן *to hide*, יָסַף *to add* (§ 75*f*), יָרָה *to throw* (§ 75 *f*), ישׁע *to save*, כלם *to abuse / insult*, נדח *to repel*, נָחָה *to lead*, נצב *to station*, סתר *to conceal*, קהל *to assemble*, רנן *to give out cries of joy*, שׁקה *to water*.

(1) The use of Hif. for Qal became more frequent in the late biblical books, QH, and MH (M. Moreshet in *Sefer Bar-Ilan* 13 [1976] 249-81; see also Qimron, *Hebrew of DSS*, p. 49). For earlier literature on this question, see J. Barth in *ZDMG* 43 (1889) 179ff. and H. Yalon, *Pirqe lashon* [Heb] (Jerusalem, 1971), pp. 43-55.

§ 55. The Passive conjugations

a Hebrew has a passive conjugation for Piel קִטֵּל and Hifil הִקְטִיל. For Qal it once had a conjugation (**qutal*), which in the perfect was confused with Pual, and in the future was confused with Hofal, as will be explained in § 58 *a*.

b **Formation.** In the passive conjugations (including also the passive of Qal) the first vowel in the perfect and the future is the primitive vowel *u*: **quṭal*, **yuqṭal* (§ 58 *a*); קֻטַּל, יְקֻטַּל; הָקְטַל(הָ), יָקְטַל(יָ).

The second vowel in the future is the primitive vowel *a*, as in stative verbs, and probably on the analogy of these verbs.

The second vowel in the perfect was originally *i* (compare *qutila*, *quttila*, *'uqtila* in Arabic), as in the stative verbs of the first group, and probably on the analogy of these verbs. In Hebrew, this vowel *i* has been supplanted by the vowel *a* on the analogy of the future, e.g. **quttil* has been replaced by קֻטַּל on the analogy of יְקֻטַּל.

These passive conjugations, as we can see, are contrasted with their active counterparts by means of vowel change, unlike Nifal and Hitpael, both of which, in addition to their original reflexive force, serve also as passive conjugations. For this reason, the term 'internal passive' is sometimes applied to these purely passive conjugations.

Compared with some non-Semitic languages such as English, Hebrew makes a rather sparing use of passive constructions. About 40% of Puals and an even lower percentage of Hofals in BH are participles denoting a state rather than an action(1).

(1) E. Jenni in *Proceedings of the Fifth World Congress of Jewish Studies* (Jerusalem, 1973), p. 66.

§ 56. **Pual conjugation**

For its formation, cf. § 55. *a*

The first vowel is almost always *u*, which is normal in a sharp syllable. Sometimes this *u* is nuanced as *ọ* under the influence of certain consonants, e.g. מְאָדָּם *coloured red* (always, e.g. Ex 25.5); בָּרַת (§ 23 *a*); כָּלּוּ Ps 72.20.

The inf. cst., which is not attested(1), would be קֻטַּל. *b*

As inf. absolute we find only גֻּנֹּב in Gn 40.15.

Certain forms which have the appearance of a Pual perfect belong in reality to the Qal passive, e.g. אֻכַּל (§ 58 *a*).

Likewise, some forms which resemble the Pual participle without מ *c*
belong in reality to the Qal passive, e.g. אֻכָּל (§ 58 *b*).

The Pual is the passive of the Piel in meaning.

(1) In Lv 14.43 we should read the inf. cst. חַלֵּץ (Ehrlich, *Randglossen*, ad loc.).

§ 57. **Hofal conjugation**

a For its formation, cf. § 55.

The ה is syncopated as in the Hifil (§ 54 *b*).

The first vowel, originally *u*, is maintained in sharp syllables, hence in those verbs in which the second radical is doubled as in פ"ן verbs, e.g. הֻגַּשׁ. It is quite often preserved in participles under the influence of the labial מ, hence מֻקְטָל, which is more frequent than מָקְטָל. Otherwise, in closed syllables we normally find *ǫ*: הָקְטַל, יָקְטַל rather than הֻקְטַל, יֻקְטַל. The choice of the vowel is rather arbitrary; thus in the perfect of the verb שׁלך we find וְהֻשְׁלַךְ Dn 8.11; הֻשְׁלָכָה Ez 19.12; וְהֻשְׁלְכוּ Jer 22.28; הָשְׁלַכְתָּ Is 14.19; הָשְׁלַכְתִּי Ps 22.11.

b The inf. cst. is of the type הָקְטַל, but is not attested by any regular verb.

The inf. abs. הָקְטֵל has a hybrid character: it is the inf. abs. of Hifil הַקְטֵל, *passivised* by the change of the first vowel ַ to ָ (§ 49 *b*), e.g. הָחְתֵּל Ez 16.4; הֻגֵּד Josh 9.24.

On the imperative, cf. § 48 *a*.

c Certain forms, which resemble Hofal future, in fact belong to the Qal passive, e.g. יֻתַּן (§ 58 *a*).

The Hofal is the passive of the Hifil in meaning: הָקְטַל accordingly should normally mean *he was made to kill* = *one had him kill*.

§ 58. **Passive Qal**

a In Proto-Semitic, as in Arabic still, the passive of a simple action was of the type: pf. *qutil(a)*(1), fut. *yuqtal(u)*.

Future. In Hebrew the primitive form has remained יֻקְטַל(יָ). This form is formally similar to that which the future Hofal has taken with the syncope of its ה: יֻקְטַל for *יְהֻקְטַל(2).

Perfect. In Hebrew the primitive form *qutil* has become *qutal* with *a* as the second vowel on the analogy of the future, as in the other passive conjugations (§ 55 *b*). Now a *u* in an open syllable is not maintained; the syllable therefore must become closed, which occurs through secondary gemination of the (non-guttural) consonant, cf. § 18 *e*; *qutal* therefore must become *quttal*. This form is formally similar to the Pual perfect קֻטַּל.

Thus it happens that now, in the perfect, the passive in Qal is identical with Pual, and in the future, with Hofal. That is why the ancient grammarians consider all קֻטַּל forms as Pual and all יֻקְטַל forms as Hofal. But these forms *per se* could just as well be Qal passive forms. Therefore, in each case, one must examine the particular reasons for which the form can, or cannot, be a passive of Qal. If a given קֻטַּל form does not have an active Piel, whilst it does have a Qal, and if the meaning of the form concerned is not that of passive Piel, then the form will have to be regarded as passive Qal. Likewise, if a given יֻקְטַל form does not have an active Hifil, whilst it does have a Qal, and if the meaning of the form is not that of passive Hifil, then the form will have to be regarded as Qal passive.

Thus לֻקַּח *he was taken* and יֻקַּח *he will be taken* (§ 72 *j*) are most probably Qal passives, for the meaning is not that of the passive of Piel, but that of the passive of a simple action; this verb does not have Piel and Hifil forms, whilst it does have a Qal. Likewise the perfect יֻלַּד *he was born* is passive Qal(3): the meaning is that of the passive of Qal, not of Piel which signifies *to deliver* (as a midwife, § 52 *d*)(4). Similarly also the future יֻתַּן(5) *he will be given* (§ 72 *i*): the meaning is that of the Qal passive, and the verb has no Hifil; likewise the perfect אֻכַּל *it was eaten*: it has no Piel. Also יֻקַּם has no known Hifil. There are a good number of more or less plausible examples of Qal passive which one would find indicated in modern dictionaries as Puals or Hofals.

(1) Cf. Brock., *GvG*, 1, p. 537.

(2) Likewise in Arabic the Qal future *yaqtul* and the future of the causative *yuqtil* have in the passive the same form *yuqtal*.

(3) Compare in Arabic the perfect *wulida* "he was born."

(4) Cf. P. Joüon in *Bib* 1 (1920) 539ff.

(5) In the Tell el Amarna letters one finds three times *yu-da-an* or its variations with suffixes "it be given." The passive Qal was already known to Ibn Jikatilla (10th c.) and Samuel ha-Nagid (11th c.): see W. Bacher, *Abraham Ibn Esra als Grammatiker* (Budapest, 1881), p. 99; W. Chomsky, *D. Kimhi's Heb. Grammar* (New York, 1952), p. 103, n. 146.

Corresponding to the perfect passive Qal קֻטַּל there is a **participle** *b*

קֻטָּל, just as there is a participle נִקְטָל corresponding to the perfect נִקְטַל. Thus one has אֻכָּל *eaten, consumed*, Ex 3.2, corresponding to the perfect אֻכַּל; יוּלָּד (for יֻלָּד) *born*, Jdg 13.8 corresponding to the perfect יֻלַּד; לֻקָּח *taken* 2Kg 2.10 corresponding to the perfect לֻקַּח (cf. § 56 *c*).

c Some **infinitives** also seem to belong to the passive Qal, thus הֻלֶּדֶת *to be born, birth* (cf. P. Joüon in *Bib* 1 [1920] 360), and possibly שִׂים *to be put* (*ib.* 362) 2Sm 14.7; Job 20.4.

d The passive Qal, some vestiges of which still remain(1), as we have seen, disappeared little by little from the linguistic consciousness of Hebrew for the phonetic reasons indicated and also because Nifal, having gradually assumed the passive meaning, had made it well-nigh redundant.

(1) The existence of passive Qal in Ugaritic is a distinct possibility: Gordon, *UT* (§ 9.31).

§ 59. **Rare conjugations**

a Apart from the ordinary conjugations enumerated above, Hebrew possesses a number of rather rare conjugations, most of which are associated with the Piel.

1) The most frequent is the conjugation *pọẹl*(1), which represents diverse forms. In strong verbs, *pọẹl* is properly *pọ‘ẹl*; passive *pọ‘ạl*; reflexive *hitpọ‘ẹl*. The primitive forms of the active are pf. *qātal(a)*, fut. *yuqātil(u)*. In the future the form usually becomes יְקוֹטֵל; the perfect קוֹטֵל is due to the analogy of the future, as so often is the case in Hebrew. The form *qātala* with lengthening(2) of the first vowel, like *qattala* with lengthening of the second consonant, is considered by many authorities to express a certain nuance of intensity(3). Example: מְשֹׁפְטִי *exercising judgement towards me* Job 9.15(?); שֹׁרֵשׁ *to take root* Is 40.24; מְאֹסְפָיו 62.9 (but 'מְאַ in Cod. L and C); תְּרָצְחוּ Ps 62.4 (despite the dagesh in the צ); מְלָוֹשְׁנִי 101.5.

In ע"ו verbs, where it is common, the form *pọẹl* is properly *pọlẹl*, e.g. קוֹמֵם *to raise*. The origin of this form is controversial (§ 80 *h*).

In ע"ע verbs, where it is seemingly infrequent (§82 *e*), the form *pọẹl* is properly *pọ‘ẹ‘*, e.g. סוֹבֵב *to encircle*. The origin of this form is controversial (§ 82 *e*).

(1) We use this imprecise transliteration for the forms with *ọ* as the first vowel and *ẹ* as the second.
(2) See H. Fleisch, *Les verbes à allongement vocalique interne sémitique* (Paris, 1944).
(3) On an attempt to apply to these cases some functions conventionally attributed to the third conjugation in Arabic (fāʿala), conative, for instance, see Sh. Morag, art. cit. [§ 38, n. 6], pp. 120-25.

2) The form *pạʿlẹl*(1) (or with attenuation of *a* to *i*: *piʿlẹl*) has the passive form *puʿlạl*. Examples: שַׁאֲנַן *to be quiet* (from the adj. שַׁאֲנָן), רַעֲנַן *to be verdant* (from the adj. רַעֲנָן); passive אֻמְלַל *to fade*. b

(1) On the old interpretation of הִשְׁתַּחֲוָה *to worship, to prostrate oneself* as hitpaʿlel, see § 59 *g*.

3) The form *pilpẹl* with repetition of the first and last consonants occurs in ע"ו verbs in which it is properly a *pilpẹl*, and in ע"ע verbs in which it is properly *piʿpẹʿ*. In many cases it is difficult to choose between these two classes of verbs. The passive is *pulpạl* and the reflexive *hiṯpạlpẹl*. Examples: גִּלְגֵּל *to roll* (tr.); הִתְגַּלְגֵּל *to roll* (intr.) (from גלל); טִלְטֵל *to throw* (from טול); the frequent כִּלְכֵּל *to sustain somebody*, passive כָּלְכַּל (prob. from כיל); הִתְמַהְמַהּ *to hesitate* (root?)(1). c

(1) Most verbs of this group as well as of the group in the following paragraph showing repetition of two consonants signify repetition of an action, often in quick succession. See I. Eitan, *JPOS* 1 (1920-21) 174-77 and I. Yannay, "Augmented verbs in Bib. Heb.," *HUCA* 45 (1974) 71-95.

4) The very rare form *pʿạlʿạl* occurs in סְחַרְחַר *to palpitate* Ps 38.11 (imitative harmony); passive חֳמַרְמַר *to be effervescent* Lam 1.20; 2.11; *to become red* (a different root; Job 16.16). Likewise Ps 45.3 יָפְיָפִיתָ *you are more beautiful* (than anybody); Ho 4.18 אָהֲבוּ הֵבוּ *they did not care about anything but love;* cf. Is 61.1 פְּקַח־קוֹחַ *great liberation.*(1) d

(1) See I. Eitan, *JPOS* 1 (1920-21) 176.

5) Furthermore one finds some isolated forms which are probably denominative, e.g. תְּתַחֲרֶה *you become excited, argue* Jer 12.5 is a denominative of תַּחֲרָה*, which appears in Ben Sira 31.29; 40.5; תִּרְגַּלְתִּי *I led the way* Ho 11.3. e

The form of MH *Niṯpạʿʿẹl* for the reflexive of Piel, a hybrid form f with the נ of Nifal added to Hitpael, may be found in Ez 23.48 וְנִוַּסְּרוּ (for וְנִתְוַסְּרוּ?) *and they will submit themselves to chastisement* (but this can be vocalised as Nifal וְנוֹסְרוּ) and in Dt 21.8 וְנִכַּפֵּר (for וְנִתְכַּפֵּר?) *and it will be expiated* (but probably faulty for וִיכֻפַּר)(1).

(1) Cf. SH forms such as /wniššåmmådti/; Ben-Ḥayyim, *LOT*, vol. 5, pp. 85f.

g In the light of Ugr. *tštḥwy* "she prostrates herself," what used to be considered *hiṯpaʿlel*, represented almost entirely by the frequent הִשְׁתַּחֲוָה *to worship, to prostrate oneself*, is most likely a Hištafʿel of √ חוו(1).

(1) In Ugr. the causative conjugation is characterised by /š/, not /h/ or /ʾ/. But cf. J.A. Emerton, in *OudSt* 20 (1977) 41-55. On plausible vestiges of the ancient causative Shafel attested in some cognates such as Akkadian and Ugaritic, see J.A. Soggin, *Annali dell'Istituto Orientale di Napoli*, NS 15 (1965) 17-30; C. Rabin, *Eretz Israel* 9 (1969) 148-58; L. Wächter, *ZAW* 83 (1971) 380-89.

h נוּלְּדוּ 1Ch 3.5, 20.8 is an example of Nufal(1).

(1) First identified as such by H. Yalon, *Introduction to the Pointing of the Mishnah* [Heb] (Jerusalem, 1964), pp. 152-59. See also Sh. Morag, art. cit. [§ 38, n.], pp. 126-28, I. Shivtiel in *Quntresim l-ʿinyne halašon haʿivrit*, 2 (1948) 212, and Yeivin, *Babylonian Tradition*, pp. 608f.

§ 60. Quadriliteral verbs

Quadriliteral verbs are very few in number. One finds, on the analogy of the Piel: the type תִּרְגֵּם* *to translate*, יְתַרְגֵּם*, passive מְתֻרְגָּם. E.g. יְכַרְסְמֶנָּה *it devours it* Ps 80.14; מְכֻרְבָּל *clothed* 1Ch 15.27; —on the analogy of the Hifil: הִשְׂמְאִיל* *to go left*, יַשְׂמְאִיל and (with the syncope of א) inf. הַשְׂמֹאל*, הַשְׂמִיל; מַשְׂמְאל (cf. § 54 *d*).

§ 61. Verb with object suffixes
(Paradigm 3).

a The personal pronoun object of a verb, which would be in the accusative in Latin, can be expressed in two ways. Either one may use the particle אֵת called the *exponent of the accusative* (*nota accusativi*) which receives personal suffixes (§ 103 *k*), e.g. קָטַל אֹתוֹ *he killed him*; or, more frequently, the suffixes are attached to the verb form itself, e.g. קְטָלוֹ *he killed him*. Certain syntactic circumstances condition the use of אֵת (§ 125 *e* ff.). In the perfect, with the suffix of the second pers. pl. we almost always find את (קְטַלְנוּכֶם is the only example with the 1st pers. pl. suf.[1]). Often the choice is arbitrary, for no apparent reason; thus we find וַיַּכֵּם *and he hit them* 15 times and וַיַּךְ אוֹתָם only three times (Jdg 15.8; 1Sm 5.6; 2Kg 25.21)(2).

(1) A combination attested only once in Ps 118.26 בֵּרַכְנוּכֶם.

(2) On the choice between the synthetic and analytic constructions, in addition to the literature quoted in Muraoka, *Emphatic*, p. 152, see also Polzin, pp. 28-31, and E.Z. Melammed in *ʿoz l-David* (Jerusalem, 1964), pp. 568-84 [now in idem, *Meḥqarim bamiqra' b-tirgumav uvimfaršav* (Jerusalem, 1984), pp. 200-216. Bendavid (1.71) believes that the synthesis, which is the rule in MH, is more typical of LBH. In Moabite, את occurs only with a substantive, whereas a pronominal object is always directly attached to the verb.

Whereas in French (and English) a **reflexive** action, e.g. *he sanctified himself*, is rendered by an object pronoun (§ 146 *k*), Hebrew uses reflexive forms of the verb: *Nifal, Hitpael*, e.g. here הִתְקַדֵּשׁ. Some verbs in Qal can have the reflexive meaning (§ 41 *a*); likewise, e.g. Piel כִּסָּה *to clothe oneself* Gn 38.14 (cf. Ehrlich, *Randglossen*, ad loc.). Note also the use of נֶפֶשׁ with a suffix: § 146 *k*. *b*

The form of the verbal suffixes varies according to whether the verb form ends in a vowel or a consonant (cf. Paradigms 1 and 3). From the point of view of the stress, the *heavy* suffixes כֶם, הֶם (כֶן, הֶן) always carry the stress; the suffixes נִי, נוּ, הוּ and הָ never carry the stress; ךָ preceded by a vowel does not carry the stress, but if preceded by a shewa, it does carry the stress (exception: the type קְטַלְתְּךָ, § *d*). *c*

A verb form ending in a consonant is joined by a **linking vowel** to a suffix beginning with a consonant. In the **perfect** this vowel is *a* (either ָ or ַ), e.g. קְטָלָנוּ, קְטָלַנִי, but קְטָלַנִי. This *a* probably comes from ל״ה verbs, e.g. גָּלָנוּ(1); according to others, this may be the final *a* which one finds in Arabic perfect *qatala*. *d*

In the **future** and other tenses(2) the linking vowel is *e* (either ֵ or ֶ), e.g. יִקְטְלֵהוּ, but יִקְטְלֶהָ (§ 29 *f*). This *e* originates from ל״ה verbs, e.g. יִגְלֵהוּ, יִגְלֶהָ.

Exceptions: Before the suffixes כֶם and ךָ there is no linking vowel, but only a shewa, and the כ, whether of the singular or plural suffix, is always rafé: e.g. יִקְטָלְכֶם, קְטַלְכֶם(3), יַלְבִּשְׁכֶם; יִקְטָלְךָ; קְטָלְךָ(4),

קְטָלַתְךָ; קְטָלְךָ; שְׁאֵלְךָ, אֲהֵבְךָ; יְבָרֶכְךָ.

Before ךָ, in pause, there is a linking vowel, generally ֶ, e.g. קְטָלֶךָ, יִקְטְלֶךָ (in the perfect the anticipated form קְטָלָךְ is rare). This ֶ probably originated in the future of ל״ה verbs: יִגְלֶךָ (similarly in nouns one finds, e.g. שְׁמֶךָ, § 94 *c*).

(1) In support of this view one can adduce the analogy of the future where the vowel of juncture is derived from the ל״ה verbs (cf. below), and not from an original final vowel. Other cases of vowels being derived from ל״ה verbs may be found in § *f*, and see the references in § 94 *b*, n.

(2) The vowel of juncture allows the proper form to be distinguished in the case of the imperative with *a* (before a guttural), e.g. שָׁלְחֵנִי *send me* (opp. שְׁלָחַנִי *he sent me*).

(3)(4) Instead of ֶ, in this position, we sometimes find ֵ, e.g. in the future, אֹסִפְךָ 1Sm 15.6 (cf. Driver, *Notes*, ad loc.), Is 25.1, Ps 30.2, 145.1; in the participle Ex 31.13; in the infinitive, Is 1.15. Comp. amongst the nouns, e.g. שִׁמְךָ Ps 145.1.

e **Deletion of a vowel** before a suffix, in the future (and imperative), in open syllables. The primitive vowels *u* and *i* drop out, e.g. יִקְטֹל, יִקְטְלֵנִי; יְקַטֵּל, יְקַטְּלֵנִי; יִתֵּן, יִתְּנֵנִי; תֵּן, תְּנֵהוּ; however, the primitive vowel *a* is maintained, e.g. יִלְבַּשׁ, יִלְבָּשֵׁנִי. In the perfect the primitive vowel *i* is deleted in Piel, e.g. קִטֵּל, קִטְּלַנִי; it is maintained in (stative) Qal, e.g. שְׁכֵחַנִי (by necessity) (cf. § 30 *f*).

f **Suffixes with energic נ.** In the future (and imperative) we also find a series of suffixes with a נ called *energic* or *epenthetic* (*inserted*) *Nun*. This נ, originally, probably indicated a certain energic meaning (as in Arabic)(1). But it now carries no semantic value; its energic force is merely phonetic. The usual forms are ֶנּוּ, ֶנָּה, ֶךָּ.

The origin of the seghol is disputed. It may have originated in the forms with ָ by a tendency towards vowel harmony (cf. § 29 *f*); it may then have spread to other forms (cf. BL, p. 216), e.g. *innå* may have become *ęnnå*(2). But, in our opinion, this ֶ derives from ל״ה verbs, e.g. יִלְוֶנּוּ, יִרְאֶנָּה, אֶרְאֶךָּ (§ 79 *k*) on the model of יִלְוֶה etc.

The use of the forms without *energic* נ is typical of the future joined to the inversive Waw, and also the jussive, whether preceded by the prohibitive אַל or not. Typically, therefore, one would have תִּשְׁמְרֶנּוּ but וַתִּשְׁמְרֵהוּ(3).

This rule does not seem to apply to the cohortative(4). Even allowing for possibly erroneous pointing (e.g. 1Sm 9.26 קוּמָה וַאֲשַׁלְּחֶךָּ, in which one expects וַאֲשַׁלֵּחֲךָ), one cannot explain away cases such as 2Kg

6.28,29 וְנֹאכְלֶנּוּ ... תְּנִי and Jer 48.2 לְכוּ וְנַכְרִיתֶנָּה, though we do find instances such as Jer 18.18 לְכוּ וְנַכֵּהוּ ... וְאַל־נַקְשִׁיבָה. In poetry the distinction may be reduced to stylistic variation, e.g. Is 26.5 יַשְׁפִּילֶנָּה יַשְׁפִּילָהּ. The conditioning factor appears to be the presence or absence of a vowel after the third radical(5).

Only rarely do we encounter free-standing energic forms: Ex 1.10 כִּי־תִקְרֶאנָה מִלְחָמָה *should a war break out*; as a substitute for the preterital (short) yiqtol in poetry such as תִּשְׁלַחְנָה Jdg 5.26.

(1) In Arabic the emphatic future ends with *anna* or *an*. In Hebrew the forms can be more easily explained by supposing a simple *n*: *ẹnhu* > *ẹnnu*, *ẹnhå* > *ẹnnå*, and *ẹnkå* > *ẹkkå*. Incidentally, the derivation of *ẹkkå* from *ẹnkå* rather than from *ankå* accords with the tradition reflected in the Secunda of the Hexapla, e.g. Ps 30.10 הֲיוֹדְךָ αἰωδεχχα; Brønno, *Studien*, pp. 196f.

(2) In BA we have *inn*, e.g. יִתְּנִנַּהּ *he will give it* (= Heb. יִתְּנֶנָּה).

(3) A fundamental study on this question is M. Lambert, "De l'emploi des suffixes pronominaux avec noun et sans noun au futur et à l'impératif," *RÉJ* 46 (1903) 178-93. See also T. Muraoka, "The *Nun energicum* and the prefix conjugation in BH," *Annual of the Japanese Biblical Institute*, 1 (1975) 63-71; J. Blau, *Eretz Israel* 14 (1978) 125-31; E. Qimron, *JQR* 77 (1986-87) 159f. The pausal form ־ֶךָּ occurs even with the perfect (Dt 24.13), the infinitive (Dt 4.36, 23.5, Job 33.32), and the participle (Dt 8.5; 12.14,28; Job 5.1).

(4) *Pace* H.L. Ginsberg, p. 113 of an article cited in § 2*a*.

(5) See R. Hetzron in *Orientalia Suecana* 18 (1969) 101-27, and Garr, *Dialect Geography* [§ 2 *a*, n.], p. 111.

Rare forms with נּ. In the 1st pers. sg. one has the forms ־ֶנְּנִי and ־ֵנְּנִי, which are rare. In the 1st pers. pl. ־ֵנּוּ is dubious. In the 2nd pers. one has, rarely, the spelling ־ֶכָּה, especially in יַכֶּכָּה(1). g

(1) See Barr, *Spellings*, pp. 116f.; for an explanation of the form, see above, § 42 *f*.

In elevated or poetic style, one finds, rarely (and almost always in pause), forms with נ (without assimilation), e.g. אֲרֹמְמֶנְהוּ Ex 15.2; Dt 32.10 (in context); Jer 5.22 (in pause); אֶתְּקֶנְךָ Jer 22.24(?). The form יְכַבְּדָנְנִי (with ־ָ) Ps 50.23 is unique. h

Rare forms with suffixes(1). **Sing.** *2nd m.*: ־ָכָה (rare spelling for ־ְךָ)(2); ־ָךְ Is 55.5; *2nd f.*: ־ָךְ (for ־ֵךְ) rarely, mainly in pause, e.g. Is 60.9; 54.6; ־ְכִי Ps 103.4; ־ֵכִי Ps 137.6; *3rd m.*: ־ֹה Ex 32.25; Nu 23.8; *3rd f.*: ־ָה (without mappiq, § 25 *a*) Ex 2.3; Jer 44.19; Am 1.11 (nsiga). **Plur.** *3rd m.*: the forms in מוֹ are poetic; in Ex 15.5 one has מוּ in יְכַסְיֻמוּ (perhaps for assonance or a dialectal form[3]). i

(1) Compare the rare forms of suffixes attached to nouns, § 94 *h*.

(2) See Barr, *Spellings*, p. 127. Barr thinks that the long spelling is earlier (ib., p. 125).

(3) μου occurs thrice in the Secunda: 49.12 בָּתֵּ֫ימוֹ βηθαμου; 28.8, 49.14 לָמוֹ λαμου; but 35.16 שִׁנֵּ֫ימוֹ σεννημω.

§ 62. Perfect with suffixes
(Paradigm 3).

a For the linking vowel *a*, cf. § 61 *d*; on the loss of the vowel *i*(ֵ), § 61 *e*.

Before the suffixes, certain persons in the perfect have a form more like the **primitive form** (§ 42 *f*). We find *3rd f.sg.* קְטָלַת (primitive form: *qatalat*); *2nd f.sg.* קְטַלְתִּי(1) (primitive form: *qatalti*); *2nd m.pl.*(2) קְטַלְתּוּ (primitive form: *qataltumu*).

(1) Thus the 2nd pers. f. was confused with the current form of the 1st pers., hence equivocal forms such as קְטַלְתִּ֫יהוּ *you* (f.) *killed him*, *I killed him*; קְטַלְתִּ֫יהָ; קְטַלְתִּים. On the continuation in post-BH phases of the syntagm pf. 2m.pl. + obj. suf., see E. Qimron, *JQR* 78 (1987) 49-55.

(2) This form also serves for the feminine. In any case, the combination is extremely rare: Nu 20.5, 21.5 הֶעֱלִ֫יתֻנוּ; Zech 7.5 צַמְתֻּנִי. Normally the analytic construction is preferred: e.g. Josh 4.3 וְהַעֲבַרְתֶּם אוֹתָם עִמָּכֶם וְהִנַּחְתֶּם אוֹתָם.

b Verb forms, with the addition of suffixes, are subject to modifications in the **arrangement of vowels**. Thus in the *3rd pers. f.sg.*, קָֽטְלָה becomes קְטָלַת. The new arrangement of vowels is perhaps due to the analogy of nouns with suffixes; compare, e.g. קְטָֽלְךָ *he killed you* and דְּבָֽרְךָ *your word*. The vowels protected by their position or by their length naturally retain their position; consequently it happens that in Hifil, in all persons, the vowel arrangement remains unaltered.

c **Observations on some persons.**

3rd masc. sing. In context, we find קְטָלַ֫נִי with ַ in open stressed syllables, against the general norm (§ 28 *b*), in pause קְטָלָ֑נִי (compare קָטַל and קָטָ֑ל). In Gn 30.6; Ps 118.18 we find ַ֫נִי (perhaps for emphasis before a divine name). With the *3rd pers.m.sg.* suffix the earlier form קְטָלָ֫הוּ is found only once in the strong verb, Jer 20.15 (in pause);

otherwise we always find the form קְטָלוֹ with syncope and contraction of *ahu* to *ọ* (compare, in the *2nd pers. m.* קְטַלְתָּהוּ and קְטַלְתּוֹ), § *e*.

3rd fem. sing. The verb form קְטָלַ֫ת is treated in a very special fashion: 1) it always carries the stress; 2) before a suffix beginning with a consonant it does not receive the linking vowel; 3) before the other suffixes, we find קְטָלָ֫תֶךְ ,קְטָלָ֫תַם: the final *a̧* of the verb form becomes *å* in open syllables, retaining the stress, and the post-stress vowel is shortened. Thus we have קְטָלַ֫תְנִי, קְטָלָ֫תְנִי; קְטָלַ֫תְךְ, קְטָלָ֫תְךְ; קְטָלַ֫תְהוּ and (with *tt* for *th*) קְטָלַ֫תּוּ; קְטָלַ֫תְהָ, hence קְטָלַ֫תָּה; קְטָלַ֫תְנוּ. *d*

2nd masc. sing. In context we also find here קְטַלְתַּ֫נִי, in pause קְטַלְתָּ֫נִי. With the *3rd pers.m.sg.* suffix the earlier form קְטַלְתָּ֫הוּ occurs only once in the strong verb, Ez 43.20 (in pause); elsewhere we always find the form קְטַלְתּוֹ (comp. the *3rd pers.m.sg.*, § *c*). *e*

2nd fem. sing. With the *3rd pers.m.sg.* suffix we only find the non-syncopated form קְטַלְתִּ֫יהוּ (twice). We find in pause הִשְׁבַּעְתָּ֫נוּ Josh 2.17,20; Ct 5.9 with ָ, difficult to explain; likewise יְלִדְתָּ֫נוּ Jer 2.27. *f*

1st sing. The form, קְטַלְתִּיו, with syncope of ה, is more common than קְטַלְתִּ֫יהוּ. The reason for the choice is not very clear; compare, e.g. 2Sm 7.10 and 1Ch 17.9 (parallels)(1). *g*

(1) In QH the fuller form is the rule, though ה may not have been pronounced: Qimron, *Hebrew of DSS*, p. 60.

The plural ending /-u/ attached to an object suffix is spelled both defectively (312 x), e.g. Lv 17.5 וֶהֱבִיאֻם and fully (511 x), e.g. Is 14.2 וֶהֱבִיאוּם: AF, p. 201. *h*

§ 63. **Future with suffixes**
(Paradigm 3).

On the linking vowel *e*, cf. § 61 *d*; on the loss of the vowel, cf. § 61 *e*; on the suffixes with נּ, cf. § 61 *f*, and with נ, cf. § 61 *h*. Instead of the form תִּקְטֹ֫לְנָה, תִּקְטְלוּ is used: Jer 2.19; Job 19.15; Ct 1.6. Instead of the **linking vowel** *e* we sometimes find *a* (as in the perfect); thus ַ֫נִי occurs many times, e.g. Gn 19.19; 29.32; Ex 33.20, ֶ֫נִי sometimes, e.g. Gn 27.19 (§ 61 *g*). With other suffixes: וַיַּכִּירָהּ Gn 37.33; *a*

יְלְבָּשָׁם Ex 29.30.

b One finds תָּעָבְדֵם in major pause in Ex 20.5 and Dt 5.9; and in intermediate pause (zaqef) in Ex 23.24; also נָעָבְדֵם in major pause in Dt 13.3. It seems that the intention here was to avoid the form anticipated in pause תַּעֲבֹדֵם*. The ọ has shifted to the beginning of the word with the nuance of ọ (comp. imperative קְטֹל, קָטְלֵם)(1).

Note also יָחְנְךָ Gn 43.29, Is 30.19; יְחָבְרְךָ Ps 94.20; תְּאָכְלֵהוּ Job 20.26. Especially noteworthy are cases with ָ with the second radical: יֶהְדָּפֶנּוּ Nu 35.20; יִגָּפֶנּוּ 1Sm 26.10(2).

(1) *Pace* Berg., II, § 14 g, these are certainly no Hofals. In the Babylonian tradition, the /o/ of the impf. is also retained, e.g. תֹּטַבְּלֵנִי: for more examples, see P. Kahle, *Masoreten des Ostens* (Leipzig, 1913), p. 185.

(2) Eight more listed in Berg., II, § 14 *g*, though not all are attested in BHS, and most are found in major pause. Similar forms (such as ידורשהו and ידרושהו) are common in Dead Sea Hebrew documents; see Qimron, *Hebrew of DSS*, pp. 51-53 with full data in Qimron's dissertation *A Grammar of the Heb. Lang. of the Dead Sea Scrolls* [in Heb.] (Jerusalem, 1976), pp. 161-75 and further relevant data in I. Yeivin, "The forms יקטולני and יקוטלנו in the Dead Sea Scrolls in the light of the Babylonian tradition of punctuation" [in Heb.], in B. Uffenheimer (ed.), *Bible and Jewish History. Studies in Bible and Jewish History Dedicated to the Memory of Jacob Liver* (Tel Aviv, 1971), pp. 256-76, and idem, 469-72. Our examples quoted above (תָּעָבְדֵם etc.) have apparently escaped Qimron's notice. Whilst it is clear that the Hebrew of the DSS possessed an organic system of its own distinct from that of the Tiberian Hebrew, one can still maintain that some marginal features of the Tiberian system have been transformed into major components of the Qumran Hebrew system and that the vowel following the first radical did start as a helping vowel; Qimron offers no explanation for its origin. Qimron's description of the mode of suffixation with infinitives and imperatives is, as far as the Tiberian tradition is concerned, somewhat inaccurate: no instance of imperatival קטולני is attested; Qimron is not concerned with /a/ imperatives such as שְׁלחני. The question would be irrelevant for unpointed Qumran Hebrew anyway. It also upsets the "three-fold parallelism" between the impf., inf., and impv. which, for Qimron, is the major principle accounting for all the relevant data of Qumran Hebrew, including a case such as וישׁומעוני.

These Qumran forms in no way support the theory of the existence in BH of the Akkadian type present tense /yiparras/ argued for by O. Rössler, "Eine bisher unbekannte Tempusform im Althebräischen," *ZDMG* 111 (1961) 445-51; idem, "Die Präfixkonjugation Qal der Verba Iae Nun im Althebräischen und das Problem der sogenannten Tempora," *ZAW* 74 (1962) 125-41; R. Meyer, "Spuren eines westsemitischen Präsens-Futur in den Texten von Chirbet Qumran," *Von Ugarit nach Qumran*, BZAW 77 (²1961), pp. 118-28; H.B. Rosén in *Proceedings*, pp. 214, 227f. For a refutation of the theory, see A. Bloch, "Zur Nachweisbarkeit einer hebräischen Entsprechung der akkadischen Verbalform *iparras*," *ZDMG* 113 (1963) 41-50; T.L. Fenton, "The absence of a verbal formation

**yaqattal* from Ugaritic and North-West Semitic," *JSS* 15 (1970) 31-41, and concerning the misinterpretation of Samaritan data, Ben-Ḥayyim, in Sh. Warses et al. (eds), *Sefer Dov Sadan* (Tel Aviv, 1977), pp. 84f.

c In Hifil, the originally long *ī* occasionally (though secondarily, § 54 *a*) drops out before a suffix: יַעְשְׁרֶנּוּ 1Sm 17.25; תַּעְשְׁרֶנָּה Ps 65.10. Comp. § 54 *c*.

d The remark made in § 62 *h* equally applies to the future ending in /-u/: e.g. Josh 11.8 וַיַּכֻּם as against 10.39 וַיַּכּוּם.

e The futures with the paragogic Nun can also take object suffixes: e.g. Ho 5.15 יְשַׁחֲרֻנְנִי; Job 19.2 תְּדַכְּאוּנַנִי; Jer 5.22 יַעַבְרֻנְהוּ: more examples in Berg., II, § 5 g.

§ 64. **Imperative with suffixes**
(Paradigm 3).

a On the linking vowel *e*, as in the future, cf. § 61 *d*; on the loss of the vowel, cf. § 61 *e*; on suffixes with נ, cf. § 61 *f*. In place of the form קְטֹלְנָה we find קִטְלוּ. The form of the *m.sg.* קְטֹל becomes קָטְל, e.g. קָטְלֵנִי; a begadkefat as the third radical is pronounced as a fricative as in forms such as כָּתְבֵם Pr 3.3; 7.3.

The form with *a*, e.g. לְבַשׁ would probably have become, e.g. לְבָשֵׁנִי* (comp. fut. יִלְבָּשֵׁנִי). But there are no examples, so it seems, except in the 2nd- and 3rd-guttural verbs, e.g. אֱהָבֶהָ Pr 4.6; שְׁלָחֵנִי Is 6.8; קְרָאֶנָּה Jer 36.15; קָחֶנּוּ 1Sm 16.11.

The forms קִטְלִי and קִטְלוּ before suffixes are retained.

b Rarely, as in the future (§ 63 *a*), the linking vowel is *a*, e.g. כָּתְבָהּ Is 30.8.

In Hifil in the *2nd pers.sg.m.*, the verb form before suffixes is הַקְטִיל, not הַקְטֵל (as, when inflected, we get הַקְטִילִי, הַקְטִילוּ), e.g. הַקְרִיבֵהוּ Mal 1.8.

§ 65. **Infinitive with suffixes**
(Paradigm 3).

a In the infinitive (construct), which is a verbal noun, the verbal or objectival (accusative) suffixes have almost entirely been **replaced by**

the nominal or subjectival (genitive) **suffixes**. It is solely in the 1st pers. that the verbal suffix has been preserved, e.g. קָטְלֵנִי *to kill me* (in contrast to קָטְלִי *my act of killing*). Moreover, even in the 1st pers. one finds the nominal suffix instead of the verbal one in יַבְּמִי *to marry me* Dt 25.7; תִּתִּי *to allow me* Nu 22.13; עָצְבִּי *to afflict me* 1Ch 4.10 (§ *b*). In the other persons we find the nominal suffix instead of the verbal one, e.g. בִּקְעָם *to cleave them* 2Ch 32.1 as in Am 1.13 *their act of cleaving*; הַכֹּתוֹ 1Sm 20.33 *to strike him* (cf. § 124 *i*).

b The form of the inf. cst. קְטֹל becomes קָטְל; a begadkefat as the third radical is pronounced as a fricative, e.g. כָּתְבוֹ Jer 45.1; and rarely as a plosive, e.g. עָצְבִּי 1Ch 4.10 (§ *a*). Sometimes the infinitive קְטֹל becomes קִטְל (comp. the inflection of the imperative קְטֹל, קִטְלִי), e.g. בִּגְדוֹ (1) *his act of betraying* Ex 21.8; מִכְרָם Am 2.6 (alongside מָכְרָהּ Ex 21.8); נִפְלוֹ 2Sm 1.10 (alongside נָפְלוֹ 1Sm 29.3); always שִׁבְרִי Lv 26.26; Ez 30.18; 34.27†; שִׂטְנוֹ Zech 3.1)(2).

The only suffixed example of the infinitive with *a* is found in שִׁכְבָהּ Gn 19.33, 35 side by side with שָׁכְבְּךָ Dt 6.7; 11.19 and שָׁכְבוֹ Ru 3.4. Cf. also § 69 *b*, 70 *d*.

(1) We find forms from בֶּגֶד, בֶּגֶד *garment* with *i*: בִּגְדֵי, בִּגְדוֹ, בִּגְדִי etc. Indeed the *i* vowel of the suffixed inf. cst. is possibly due to the analogy of the related *i* segholate nouns such as בֶּגֶד, מֶכֶר: Lambert, p. 310, n. 1, and H.M. Orlinsky, in *JAOS* 67 (1947) 109,111, and note AC *pí-iṭ-[rú]*, Sivan, p. 168.

(2) As regards a possible morphosyntactic distinction between the two forms, the statistics are: *qtol*- 22 x (suf. = subj., 13; = obj., 9) and *qotl*- 38 x (suf. = subj. 34, = obj., 4). So Bendavid's observation that *qtol*- is used in the main for the objectival suf., and *qotl*- for the subjectival suf. (2. 497f., so already Abul Walid, *Riqmah* [ed. Wilensky—Téné , p. 203]) is not entirely substantiated. See also §63 *b*, n. 2. The *qtol*-pattern is thus used optionally where the suffix begins with a consonant. Thus for the 2f.sg., and forms with the paragogic ָה, only the *qotl*-pattern appears. (One should not give too much weight to the unique רדופי Ps 38.21K.) This partial morphological distribution is phonetically conditioned, i.e. it depends on whether the suffix begins with a consonant or a vowel. A helping vowel is inserted in similar morphological environments in some Arabic dialects; see J. Cantineau in *Semitica* 2 (1949) 56.

c Before the suffixes ךָ and כֶם, one occasionally finds קְטָל with transposition of the vowel, instead of קָטְל, no doubt in order to facilitate the pronunciation, e.g. אֲכָלְךָ Gn 2.17. Another way in which the pronunciation is facilitated is the addition of an auxiliary *ǫ* to the second(1) consonant, e.g. קָרָבְכֶם *qǫrǫvḇęm* Dt 20.2; מָאָסְכֶם Is 30.12

(comp., e.g. פָּעָלְךָ *your action*, § 22 *c*; קְטָבְךָ, § 96 A *j*). Cf. also מֹצַאֲכֶם Gn 32.20.

(1) It is also possible to regard the first vowel as auxiliary; so also Yeivin, art. cit. [§ 63 *b*, n. 2], p. 265. From the data gathered by Yeivin one can see that all the examples with /o/ after a second radical are suffixed with a 2nd pers. pronoun.

Very rarely does one find the suffix of the infinitive with **energic Nun**, in ֶ֫ךָּ: Dt 4.36; 23.5; Job 33.32. *d*

§ 66. **Participle with suffixes**

The participle, which is a verbal noun, always takes, in the plural, a nominal suffix: קֹטְלַי *those who kill me*. In the singular, we usually find a nominal suffix: קֹטְלִי *one who kills me*, rather rarely a verbal suffix: קֹטְלֵ֫נִי, e.g. עֹשֵׂ֫נִי *he who made me* Job 31.15. With the article a verbal suffix necessarily occurs: הַמְאַזְּרֵ֫נִי *the one who girdles me* Ps 18.33. Cf. § 121 *k*. *a*

In Is 47.10 one has the abnormal form רֹאָ֫נִי (compare § 63 *a*). *b*

Very rarely we find the suffix of the participle with **energic Nun** in ֶ֫ךָּ: Dt 8.5; 12.14,28; Job 5.1. Compare the inflection of אֹיֵב, § 96 C *c*.

§ 67. **Guttural verbs**

The guttural verbs are those the root of which has a guttural in their first, second or third radical, namely ח, ע, or a pronounced א or ה. The lingual ר is treated to some extent like these gutturals (§ 23). The guttural verbs do not differ from the regular verbs, as far as the consonants are concerned, except in the inability of the guttural to allow genuine gemination. However, the vocalisation of the guttural verbs is extremely unique; it is regulated by the principles given in the section Phonetics on the gutturals (§§ 20ff.).

§ 68. **First-guttural verbs**
(Paradigm 4: עָמַד *to stand*)

The following **phonetic laws** are applicable here: *a*

1) **After an initial guttural**, instead of shewa, we find ḥaṭef pataḥ, e.g. impv. עֲמֹד. However א does not produce ḥaṭef pataḥ; rather it usually receives ḥaṭef seghol(1), e.g. impv. אֱמֹר (§ 73 *c*), אֱזֹר, but pf. 2m.pl. אֲמַרְתֶּם, and inf. cst. with a suf. אֲכָלְךָ.

2) **Before a guttural**: in open syllables *i* becomes ֶ, e.g. Nif. fut. **yi-ʿåmẹd* > יֵעָמֵד. In closed (or semi-closed) syllables, *i* > ֶ, e.g. **yiḥ-zaq* > יֶחֱזַק; *u* > ָ, e.g. **muʿmad* > מָעֳמָד (comp. מָקְטָל, which is less frequent than מֻקְטָל; cf. § 21 *d*).

3) Often one has auxiliary ḥaṭef (§ 22 *b*), which becomes a full vowel when the word is lengthened, e.g. יַעֲמֹד, יַעַמְדוּ (§ 22 *c*).

(1) Since this is the weakest vowel, Alef is not pronounced; cf. § 17 *a*, n. Comp. below, § *b* (end) אֶעֱמֹד. עֱנוּ *sing* (Nu 21.17, Ps 147.7†) is distinguished from עֲנוּ *answer* (1Sm 12.3†).

b **Qal.** In the future, the distinction between active and stative verbs appears in both vowels, e.g. *yąʿmud* > יַעֲמֹד; *yiḥzaq* > יֶחֱזַק (§ 41 *e*)(1).

But in ל"ה verbs(2) the vowel of the preformative mostly depends on the nature of the guttural. Before ה and ח it is ֶ; before ע it is ַ, e.g. יֶהְגֶּה, יֶחְסֶה; יַעֲלֶה, יַעֲשֶׂה; exceptions: יִהְיֶה, יִחְיֶה (§ 79 *s*).

In active פ"א verbs, therefore, with *ọ* as the second vowel, the vowel of the preformative is ֶ, e.g. יֶאֱזֹר, יֶאֱסֹר, יֶאֱרֹב, perhaps on the analogy of the imperative, e.g. אֱזֹר(3).

In the 1st pers.sg. we find אֶ (not אַ): אֶעֱמֹד, אֶעֱלֶה, אֶעֱשֶׂה.

(1) Other stative verbs: אָהֵב (הַ) *to love*, יֶאֱהַב; אָשֵׁם (שַׁ) *to become guilty*, יֶאְשַׁם; חָסֵר *to lack*, יֶחְסַר.

(2) Occasionally also with a non-ל"ה verb: Ps 29.9 (BHS) וַיֶּחֱשֹׂף.

(3) In the nominal forms we have, e.g. מַאֲרָב *ambush*.

c **Nifal.** The perfect נֶעֱמַד is a development from the secondary form *niʿmąd* = נִקְטַל; but in the inf. absolute we find נַעֲמוֹד. Otherwise, ַ is rare(1). In ל"ה verbs there are some perfects with ַ, e.g. נַעֲשָׂה.

In the future, in fact, there is no example of virtual gemination: one always finds the type יֵעָמֵד .

(1) Cf. Ps 28.7 Secunda ουναζερθι (MT וְנֶעֱזָרְתִּי).

d **Hifil.** The perfect הֶעֱמִיד has developed from the secondary form *hiʿmīd* = הִקְטִיל.

e **Further observations.**

In the **Qal imperative** the *i*, which follows the guttural in unstressed closed syllables, shows a slight tendency to become *ẹ*; e.g. one has אִסְפוּ but אֶסְפָה (perhaps under the influence of ָ, cf. § 29 *f*); עִרְכוּ but עֶרְכָה; חֶשְׂפִּי (cf. § 21 *e*). With a second-guttural we find, e.g. אֱהֱבוּ, אֱחֱזוּ.

In the **Qal inf. cst.**, alongside the normal type לַעֲמֹד the type לַחְפֹּר (comp. לִנְפֹּל, § 49 *f*) occasionally occurs. Nearly all the examples are with ח: לַחְשֹׁב (always, 4 times), לַחְצֹב (always, twice), לַחְשֹׂף Hg 2.16; לַחְתּוֹת (from חתה) Is 30.14; לַחְסוֹת Is 30.2 (but לַחֲסוֹת Ps 118.8, 9; Ru 2.12). Generally speaking, ח easily dispenses with ḥaṭef, § 22 *b*. Compare the corresponding futures יַחְפֹּר, יַחְשֹׁב, and יַחְצֹב, which could have influenced these forms(1). Cf. § 22 *d*.

(1) Similarly: יֶאְשַׁם, יַאְדִּיר, יַאְדִּימוּ; הַחְכִּים; יִהְיֶה.

The **alternation** between ֱ ֶ and ֲ ַ is frequent, as the sound *ẹ* tends to become *a̧* under the influence of the guttural. Thus we find in Qal, e.g. יֶאֱסֹף, תַּאַסְפִי; however, in Nifal we find, e.g. נַעֲשָׂה, נֶעֶשְׂתָה, נַעֲשָׂתָה. In Hifil perfect(1) ֱ ֶ of the 1st and 2nd persons regularly become ֲ ַ after Waw inversive, even if the stress does not advance, e.g. הֶאֱבַדְתָּ Job 14.19, but וְהַאֲבַדְתִּי Lv 23.30 and often; הֶעֱבַדְתִּיךָ Is 43.23, but וְהַעֲבַדְתִּיךָ Jer 17.4. Cf. אֱדוֹם, from which the gentilic אֲדוֹמִי is derived(2). *f*

In Hifil, in some forms with ע, the 1st syllable is open, hence ֱ; the ע normally takes ֲ, e.g. הֶעֱבַרְתָּ Josh 7.7 (in place of הֶעֱבַרְתָּ). This weakening, which brings about an abnormal syllable division, probably has the aim of ensuring the exact pronunciation of ע. Likewise, in Hofal one has ֲ ָ for ֳ ָ in, e.g. הֹעֲלָה Jdg 6.28; 2Ch 20.34 (for a similar phenomenon in nouns, see § 96 A *j*). Further examples showing the influence of the advancing stress are: וַתֶּאֱרַכְנָה // יַאַרְכוּ; יֶחְדַּל // וַיֶּחְדְּלוּ; יַחְפְּרוּ // תַּחְפְּרוּ; וַיֶּאֱסֹר // וַיַּאַסְרֻהוּ (Berg., II, § 21 c).

On the vocalisation of the irregular verbs הָיָה and חָיָה, cf. § 79 *s*.

(1) Cf. Driver, *Notes* ad 1Sm 15.18.

(2) This seems to be part of a general phonetic pattern caused by the forward shift of stress, which also affects forms such as אֵסוּר vs. אֲסֻרִים; אֱמֶת vs. אֲמִתּוֹ; אֵבוּס vs. אֲבוּסֶךָ (but אֵמֻן vs. אֱמוּנִים); חֶדְרוֹ vs. חֲדָרַי; הֶבְלִי vs. הֲבָלַי. This alternation is more common in the Babylonian tradition: Yeivin, *Babylonian Tradition*, pp. 385f.

§ 69. Second-guttural verbs
(Paradigm 5: שָׁחַט *to slaughter*)

a The following **phonetic laws** apply here:

1) In place of the shewa of the corresponding forms of the regular verb we find ◌ֲ (§ 21 *f*), e.g. שָׁחֲטוּ (comp. קָטְלוּ), יִשְׁחֲטוּ (comp. יִקְטְלוּ), יְשָׁחֲטוּ (comp. יְקָטְלוּ).

2) After gutturals, in stressed closed syllables, the vowel *a* tends to replace the primitive or normal vowel (§ 21 *e*). Because of this tendency, the future and the imperative of action verbs usually take *a*, like those of stative verbs(1), e.g. יִשְׁחַט, שְׁחַט (for יִשְׁחֹט*, שְׁחֹט*). But the inf. cst. retains the vowel *ọ* (likewise in 3rd-guttural verbs such as שְׁלֹחַ and almost all stative verbs, § 49 *c*), e.g. שְׁחֹט, but with a suffix also with *a*, e.g. שַׁחֲטָם, מַעֲלָם, and סַעֲדָם.

3) In Piel, Pual and Hitpael, ר never(2) receives virtual doubling, e.g. in the verb ברך of Paradigm 5, we find Piel בֵּרֵךְ (בֵּרַךְ, § 52 *c*), יְבָרֵךְ; Pual בֹּרַךְ.

א receives virtual doubling in a few verbs only: נִאֵף *to commit adultery*, נִאֵץ *to insult, despise*, and שֵׁאֵל *to practise beggary*(3).

The gutturals ח, ה and even ע (§ 20 *a*) usually receive virtual doubling, e.g. שִׁחֵת *to corrupt*; נִחַם(4) *to console*; נִהַג *to lead*; בִּעֵר *to consume*, fut. יְבַעֵר, but inf. cst. בָּעֵר.

(1) Stative verbs: אָהֵב (הָ), *to love*, יֶאֱהַב; רָחַק *to be far*; טָהֵר *to be pure*; רָעֵב *to be hungry*; שָׁאַל (אָ) *to ask*, שְׁאֶלְךָ.

(2) In כָּרַּת Ez 16.4 (§ 23 *a*) there is a genuine gemination.

(3) Some fluctuation is to be noted: e.g. נִאֵר vs. נֵאַרְתָּה, יְנָאֲפוּ vs. תְּנָאַפְנָה; שִׁאֲלוּ vs. יְשָׁאֲלוּ.

(4) This Piel with *a* is found to have the same vowels as Nifal נִחַם, *to change one's mind, to regret* (§ 72 *b*).

b **Detailed observations.**

Qal. Examples of the **future** in *ọ*: יִנְהֹם *it will roar*, יֶאֱחֹז *he will seize* (rare; alongside יֹאחֵז, § 73 *f*). **Imperatives** in *ọ*: only נְעֹל *Lock!* 2Sm 13.17; אֱחֹז Ex 4.4; 2Sm 2.21; fem. אֶחֱזִי Ru 3.15 (with *ọ* shortened to very short *ǫ*); plural אֶחֱזוּ Ne 7.3, אֶחֱזוּ Ct 2.15; סְעָד־ Jdg 19.8, but יִסְעָד. Note תִּמְעֹל alongside יִמְעַל.

The inf. with a suf. may have *a* after the first radical as in Jdg 13.25 לְפַעֲמוֹ; //Ez 25.6 מַחְאֲךָ...רַקְעֲךָ; 23.39 וּבְשַׁחֲטָם; Jdg 5.4 בְּצַעְדְּךָ(1).

(1) The vowel is most likely due to that of the related segholate nouns: see H.M. Orlinsky, *JAOS* 67 (1947) 112.

In the inflection of the **imperative** in *a*, e.g. שְׁחַט becomes שַׁחֲטִי, שַׁחֲטוּ, the vowel *a* shifting to the beginning of the word (cf. § 48 *c*). These forms can be confused with the Piel imperative with virtual gemination; e.g. Qal רַחֲצוּ Gn 18.4 and סַעֲדוּ Gn 18.5 could be Piel; Piel מַהֲרִי Gn 18.6 could be Qal. *c*

Piel. In the inverted future we find, where the guttural has no virtual gemination, forms such as וַתְּגָ֫רֶשׁ Josh 24.12 (§ 47 *a*), וַיְבָ֫רֶךְ. Cf. also לְצַחֶק Gn 39.14. *d*

§ 70. **Third-guttural verbs**
(Paradigm 6: שָׁלַח *to send*)

The following **phonetic law** applies here: *a*

In syllables closed by a guttural, the vowel ַ, which is homogeneous with gutturals, is introduced: 1) either forcibly replacing the primitive vowel (§ 21 *b*) or furtively slipping in between the vowel and the guttural (§ 21 *c*).

1) The primitive vowels *i* and *u* are supplanted by *ạ* in relatively **lighter** forms, namely forms of a finite verb (perfect, future, impv.) in context, the inf. cst., the participle in the construct state, e.g. יִשְׁלַח (contrast יִקְטֹל); יְשַׁלַּח (cont. יְקַטֵּל); the Hifil jussive יַשְׁלַח (cont. יַקְטֵל); the Hifil impv. הַשְׁלַח (cont. הַקְטֵל); Nif. fut. יִשָּׁלַח (cont. יִקָּטֵל); Piel inf. cst. generally שַׁלַּח (cont. קַטֵּל), participle in the cst. state שֹׁלַח (cont. קֹטֵל); cf. § *e*. *b*

Exceptions: In the Qal inf. cst. we nearly always find *ọ*, e.g. שְׁלֹחַ (likewise in second-guttural verbs like שְׁחֹט, and cf. § 49 *c*); cf. § *d* below.

2) The primitive vowel *i*, which has usually become ֵ, is retained, but undergoes the insertion of furtive pataḥ in relatively **heavier** forms, namely the forms of the finite verb in pause, the inf. abs., the participle in the absolute state, e.g. יְשַׁלֵּ֑חַ; the inf. abs. שַׁלֵּחַ; the partic. in the abs. state שֹׁלֵחַ. The primitive vowel *u* is not retained except in the inf. cst. שְׁלֹחַ(1).

A fortiori the originally long vowels ī, ū, and ọ̄ are retained, e.g. the Hifil indicative יַשְׁלִיחַ; the passive participle שָׁלוּחַ; inf. abs. שָׁלוֹחַ.

We can see that the distinctions between the light and the heavy forms are of two kinds: in the finite forms the distinction is made in terms of context vs. pause, but in the infinitive and the participle in terms of construct vs. absolute.

3) The syllable-final guttural does not take a ḥaṭef vowel, except when the verb is followed by an object suffix for 2m.sg. or 2pl. such as אֶשְׁלָחֲךָ, or in a case such as Ps 35.25 בִּלַּעֲנוּהוּ.

(1) The primitive vowel *u* is therefore not treated as the symmetrical vowel *i*. Thus the pausal form of the future of an action verb is יִשְׁלָח, not יִשְׁלֹחַ*.

c In the Qal future (and imperative) in context and in pause, action verbs fall into line with stative verbs(1): both have the vowel ◌ַ or ◌ָ.

(1) Stative verbs: גָּבַהּ *to be high*; שָׁכֵחַ*, שָׁכַח, שָׁכֵחוּ *to forget*; שָׂבֵעַ*, שָׂבַע, שָׂבֵעוּ *to be sated*; שָׁמַע, שָׁמֵעַ *to hear, listen.*

d **Detailed obsrvations.**

The **infinitive** in *a* is very rare (§ 49 c) and occurs solely in close juncture with the following word: Nu 20.3 גְּוַע; Is 58.9 שְׁלַח.

With suffixes the inf. has the vowel ◌ָ, e.g. שָׁלְחִי Nu 32.8, שָׁלְחֶךָ Gn 38.17 or ◌ְ, e.g. בִּטְחֵךְ Jer 48.7, פִּתְחִי Ez 37.13; בִּקְעָם Am 1.13; or (rarely) ◌ַ, e.g. רַקְעֲךָ Ez 25.6.

e There are some exceptions to the general rules given in § *b*. Thus one finds as Piel inf. cst. (in context): לְשַׁלֵּחַ Ex 10.4; לְפַתֵּחַ 2Ch 2.6.

f In the 2nd pers.fem.sg. of perfects one has, e.g. שָׁלַחַתְּ (for שָׁלַחְתְּ*) with an auxiliary pataḥ, which does not lead to the spirantisation of the תּ (§ 19 *f*). Thus לָקַחַתְּ *you took* is distinguished from לָקַחַת *in order to take* (prep. לְ + inf. קַחַת, § 72 *j*).

g Pausal vowels in inflected verbs: Examples: Piel: שִׁלַּח, שִׁלֵּחַ, שִׁלֵּחוּ Jdg 1.25. Qal: יִשְׁלַח, יִשְׁלָח, תִּשְׁלָחוּ 2Kg 2.16; impv. שְׁלַח, שְׁלָח*, שְׁלָחוּ.

h Forms with suffixes: Examples: יִשְׁלָחֵנִי, שָׁלְחֵנִי (*Send me!*; but שְׁלָחַנִי *he sent me*); אֶשְׁלָחֲךָ, אֲשַׁלֵּחֲךָ.

§ 71. **Weak verbs**

a Those verbs which are distinct from the normal type קָטַל not only in respect of their vocalisation, like the guttural verbs, but also in respect of consonants, are called **weak verbs**(1)(§ 40 *c*). These verbs present within their root a *weak* consonantal element, or in the case of ע"ו and ע"י verbs, a weak vocalic element.

The consonants ו, י, א, and נ are *weak*, but to different degrees. The ו is particularly weak. It cannot be maintained at the beginning of a word (§ 26 *f*): either it drops out, e.g. שֵׁב (from ושׁב*) or it is replaced by י, e.g. יָשַׁב. In the ל"ה verbs, the verbs with *w* as their primitive third radical have been absorbed by those with *y* in that position.

(1) One can see why they can be called *irregular*.

b The effects of the *weakness* of a consonant are diverse:

1) The consonant (ו or נ) may drop out, e.g. שֵׁב (from ושׁב*), גַּשׁ (from נגשׁ).

2) The consonant (ו or י) may coalesce with the preceding vowel, e.g. הוֹשִׁיב (for *hawšīb*), הֵיטִיב (for *hayṭīb*).

3) The consonant נ may be assimilated to the following consonant, e.g. יִגַּשׁ (for *yingaš*).

4) The consonant א may become quiescent, e.g. יֹאכַל, מָצָא.

c Classification of weak verbs:

1) Verbs with a weak first radical: נָגַשׁ*, אָכַל, יָשַׁב.

2) Verbs with a weak third radical: מָצָא, גָּלָה.

3) Verbs with two radical consonants between which, in the normal state of the root, there is an originally long vowel, *ū* or *ī*: קוּם, דִּין.

4) Verbs with two radical consonants the second of which, in the normal state of the root (e.g. in the impv. pl. סֹבּוּ), was originally long: סָבַב.

§ 72. פ"ן verbs

(Paradigm 7: נָגַשׁ* *to approach*)

a The *weakness* of the initial נ of these verbs has two consequences, the one peculiar to נ, namely its assimilation, and the other accidental, namely aphaeresis.

b **Assimilation** of נ without a vowel to the following consonant is extremely frequent and even standard (§ 17 *g*), e.g. *yinṣọr* > יִצֹּר.

Exceptions:

1) In pause, where the longer forms (§ 32 *g*) are favoured, the assimilation does not often take place, e.g. יִנְצֹ֫רוּ(1), יִנְקֹ֫פוּ.

2) Before a guttural there is generally no assimilation, e.g. יִנְהֹם. There is assimilation in Nifal נִחַם as in all Nifals (to avoid two נ's)(2).

3) There is no assimilation in the usual form (§ 49 *f*) of the inf. cst. of the נְפֹל type with לְ, e.g. לִנְפֹּל.

4) The verb לָקַח, which is treated as a פ"ן verb (§ *j*), appears as נִלְקַח in Nifal without assimilation (contrast נִקַּח *we shall take*, Qal future).

(1) On Rössler's drawing a wrong conclusion from a form such as this, see § 62 *b*, n. 2 above.

(2) Nifal נִחַם *to change one's mind, to repent* has the same vowels as Piel נִחַם *to console* (§ 69 *a*).

c The **aphaeresis** of נ (§ 17 *d*) is an accidental phenomenon, which is secondary and analogical and occurs only in the imperative and the inf. cst. of certain verbs which in the future have the stem vowel *a*. Thus, in these verbs we find the imperative of גַּשׁ type(1) almost always, the inf. cst. of the גֶּ֫שֶׁת type (§ *h*) quite often. The aphaeresis in the פ"ן verbs is probably on the analogy of פ"ו verbs, where it is usual. Furthermore, a form such as impv. גַּשׁ can easily have been influenced by the future יִגַּשׁ, in which the *n* disappears, then spread to the infinitive: *gaš*, hence גֶּ֫שֶׁת(2).

(1) Gn 19.9 גֶּשׁ־הָ֫לְאָה *go over there* with the vowel sequence *ę-ǫ* (cf. § 29 *f*); *e* may also have been triggered by the sibilant.

(2) The question may be asked as to why the aphaeresis does not occur in the verbs of *ǫ*-future. In the infinitive, the preponderance of the pattern קְטֹל (cf. § *h*) may account for נְפֹל; then, by analogy, the imperatival נְפֹל may have been retained.

d The aphaeretic infinitive גֶּ֫שֶׁת is formed from *gaš* and the feminine *t*, the latter having been added to re-establish the triliteralism (Barth's law of compensation)(1); then **gašt* was *segholised* into גֶּ֫שֶׁת (as in nouns such as **malk* changing to מֶ֫לֶךְ, § 96 A *b*). With a guttural we find, e.g. גַּ֫עַת (like, e.g. נַ֫עַר).

(1) Cf. *Nominalbildung*, pp. XIIff.

e In practice, according to what has just been said, in the presence of an imperative or an aphaereticinf., one would first think of a פ״ו verb (e.g. דַּע, שֵׁב; שֶׁבֶת), and only secondly of a פ״ן verb.

Detailed observations. f

In פ״ן verbs the Nifal and the Piel can be identical, e.g. נִקָּה (ל״ה verb) Nifal: *to be unpunished*, Piel: *to declare innocent*; נִחַם (§ *b* 2).

The stative verb נָגֵשׁ*, יִגַּשׁ is defective (§ 85 *b*). The Qal signifies, strictly speaking, *to be near*(1), *to approach*, the Nifal *to make oneself near, to approach*. In practice, in the perfect and in the participle the Nifal נִגַּשׁ, נִגָּשׁ is used, whilst in the other tenses (future, impv., inf. cst.) the Qal יִגַּשׁ, גַּשׁ, גֹּשִׁי, גֹּשׁוּ/גְּשׁוּ, גֶּשֶׁת is used. The forms with נ rafé are therefore avoided. g

The stative perfect נָבֵל *to wither, fall* (of flowers or leaves) is matched by the active future יִבֹּל (§ 41 *b*).

(1) This purely stative sense occurs in Job 41.8.

The type קְטֹל, which is almost the standard form of the inf. cst., has sometimes been preserved in some verbs with *a* future, either solely or side by side with the aphaeretic infinitive; thus always נְסֹעַ (5 x) *to decamp*; in action verbs, normally intransitive, נָגַע *to touch* נְגֹעַ occurs six times and גַּעַת twice; in the irregular verb נָשָׂא *to carry* (§ 78 *l*) נְשֹׂא only occurs four times alongside the usual שְׂאֵת. h

Verbs which have *a* in the fut. and whose initial Nun assimilates lack the Nun in the impv. as well. Thus גַּשׁ and נְהַג vs. נְפֹל. ha

Irregular verb נָתַן *to put, give*. This verb is remarkable for its future with *i* > ֵ, which one hardly finds except in פ״ו verbs (יֵשֵׁב type): יִתֵּן, hence impv. תֵּן(1). Likewise the form of the inf. cst. is תֵּת from **tint* (*tin* + *t*), hence *titt* (which occurs before the suffixes, e.g. תִּתִּי *my act of giving*), hence, by cancellation of the gemination, *tit* > תֵּת. The future יִתֵּן is matched by the passive יֻתַּן *it will be given*, which is a Qal passive (§ 58 *a*). i

In the perfect, the final ן assimilates to the following consonant: נָתַתִּי for *nåtanti*, נָתַתָּה (much more frequent than נָתַתָּ, § 42 *f*) etc. (contrast, e.g. שָׁכַבְתָּ, זָקַנְתִּי).

The infinitive with *o* occurs only in Nu 20.21 נְתֹן and Gn 38.9 נְתָן־.

(1) Cf. Akk. pret. *iddin* and pres. *inaddin* from *nadānu*.

Irregular verb לָקַח *to take*. This is the only פ״ל verb that is j treated like a פ"ן verb. This rather unique treatment is probably due to the following semantic analogy. In accordance with the future of the antonym *to give* יִתֵּן (with assimilation) one formed יִקַּח(1); hence in the impv. קַח, in the inf. קַחַת, לָקַחַת (contrast perf. 2f. לָקַחַתְּ, § 70 *f*).

In the Nifal נִלְקַח there is no assimilation (§ *b* 4).

The perfect לֻקַּח, the participle לֻקָּח, and the future יֻקַּח are passive Qals (§ 58 *a,b*).

(1) According to Ungnad, *Beiträge zur Assyriologie* 5 (1905) 278, followed by Brock., *GvG*, I, pp. 176, 293; cf. Berg., I, § 19 *a*, BL, § 52 *p*. There is perhaps an influence of נָשָׂא, יִשָּׂא, which also means *to take*.

k Irregular verb נָשָׂא *to carry, to take* etc.; see § 78 *l*.

On פ"ן verbs which are simultaneously ל"ה, and which have apocopated forms reduced to a single radical, cf. § 79 *i, j*.

l Comparison with **noun forms.**

The **assimilation** takes place in noun forms as in verb forms, e.g. מַטָּע *plantation*, like יִטַּע *he will plant*; מַגֵּפָה *a blow, plague*, like יִגֹּף *he will strike*; but, before a guttural, מִנְהָג *driving*, like יִנְהַג *to drive (a chariot)*.

The fact that aphaeresis does not take place in these forms demonstrates the secondary nature of the aphaeretic impv. and inf. of verbs with *a* in the future.

§ 73. פ"א verbs

(No paradigm)

a א is quiescent in the future Qal of five verbs: אָכַל *to eat*, אָמַר *to say*, אָבַד *to stray, to perish*, אָבָה *to desire*, אָפָה *to bake (bread)*(1). The reason the א in these verbs is not treated like that of any other first-guttural verb (§ 68) but becomes quiescent is no doubt their high frequency. Generally speaking, the forms which are the most often used are also the most weakened.

(1) MH has added אָגַד, אָסַר, and הָפַךְ to this list: see G. Haneman, *A Morphology of Mish. Heb. acc. to the Tradition of the Parma MS (De-Rossi 138)* (Tel Aviv, 1980) [Heb.], pp. 225-27.

b **Explanation of the future** יֹאכַל.

First vowel. The first vowel *ọ* has its origin in the 1st pers.sg. in which originally two Alefs would have occurred. The primitive form is *'a'kul* (with *a* as the first vowel of action verbs, § 41 *e*). Now, in Semitic, the sound sequence *'a'* becomes *'ā*; so *'ākul* became, in Hebrew, **'ōkul* > **'ọ̄kọl* > **'ọkọl*. Finally, this *ọ* spread to the other persons. Cf. Brock., *GvG*, I, pp. 239, 591(1).

(1) In Arabic we have in the 1st person *'ākul*, but, e.g., in the 2nd person *ta'kul*.

2nd vowel. In the verb אָכַל the second primitive vowel of the future is *u* (cf. BA יֵאכֻל, Arb. *ya'kul*), as can be seen from the imperative אֱכֹל(1) (comp. אֱמֹר). In the first person, at the stage of **'ọ̄kọl* the two vowels happened to have the same timbre; consequently the second *ọ* was dissimilated to *ẹ*, hence אֹכֵל (which is the pausal form), § 29 *h*. c

(1) For ֱ, cf. § 68 *b*. Likewise, in the infinitive we have אֱכֹל rather than אֲכֹל.

Variations of the 2nd vowel. This new vowel *ẹ*, which has replaced the primitive vowel *u* (> *ọ*) is the usual vowel in אָכַל, אָמַר, אָבַד. It can be weakened by two degrees: to ַ (minor weakening) and to ֶ (major weakening); cf. § 29 *d*. d

The vowel ֵ is not maintained except in major pause, and then not always. One has יֹאכֵל, יֹאבֵד, תֹּאמֵר (twice); but יֹאמַר, וַיֹּאמַר(1).

The major weakening from ֵ to ֶ does not happen except in וַיֹּאמֶר, probably on account of the extremely common usage of this form(2). Note, however, the form וַיֹּאכַל (no example for the verb אבד).

The minor weakening from ֵ to ַ occurs in the remaining cases: יֹאכַל, יֹאמַר, יֹאבַד.

The vowel ַ is therefore the usual vowel.

From all this it emerges that:

The stressed vowel in major pause is ֵ: exception יֹאמַר, וַיֹּאמַר.

The stressed vowel outside of major pause is ַ.

The post-stress vowel is ַ or ֶ.

(1) Except in the formulae introducing poetic discourses in the book of Job where we have וַיֹּאמַר, 3.2 etc.

(2) Comp. יֵצַר, וַיֵּצֶר *to be narrow* (צרר, § 82 *b*).

The differences in treatment of the 2nd vowel between the two futures יאכל and יאמר can be summarised by distinguishing three degrees e of pronunciation (strong, medium, weak) as follows:

Strong degree	Medium degree	Weak degree
יֹאכַ֫ל	יֹאכַל	וַיֹּ֫אכַל
יֹאמַ֫ר	יֹאמַר	וַיֹּ֫אמֶר
יֹאבֵ֫ד		יֹ֫אבַד
fem. תֹּאמַ֫ר (2 x)		
pl. תֹּאמֵ֫רוּ, יֹאמֵ֫רוּ		

f Outside of Qal, א is rarely quiescent, e.g. אֹבִ֫ידָה Jer 46.8 *I will destroy*; Nifal נֹאחֲזוּ Nu 32.30; Josh 22.9.

א is quiescent sporadically in some verbs other than those five listed in § *a*.

In the verb אָחַז *to seize*, א is often quiescent. In the 1st pers., where the ọ is more natural (cf. § *b*), we find אֹחַז; but alongside יֹאחַז we rarely find יֶאֱחֹז(1). Altogether, in this verb, א is quiescent 18 times, and pronounced 3 times.

In the stative verb אָהַב, אָהֵב, יֶאֱהַב *to love*, in the 1st pers. אֹהַב is found (once אֵהָב, § *g*).

In the verb אָסַף *to gather*, there are four examples in which א is quiescent and even omitted in the spelling, e.g. Ps 104.29 תֹּסֵף for תֹּאסֵף. These forms, both of which are suspect, resemble forms of the root יסף.

(1) For the vowel ֶ, cf. § 68 *b*.

g **Detailed observations**

1) The sequence ֱ ֶ is contracted to ֵ in לֵאמֹר (for לֶאֱמֹר) *in order to say, saying*, no doubt by virtue of the high frequency of this form (contrast, e.g. לֶאֱכֹל); cf. § 103 *b*.

The same contraction occurs in אֵהָב Pr 8.17†, תֵּאתֶה Mi 4.8; וָאֵחַר Gn 32.5.

2) Since the two verbs אָבָה and אָפָה are also ל"ה verbs, their future is יֹאבֶה, יֹאפֶה*.

Comparison with the **nominal forms**. In the nominal forms א is very rarely quiescent, e.g. מֹאזְנַ֫יִם *scales*, מוֹסֵר *bond*, from *ma'sir* (א omitted in the spelling); cf. § 88 L *h*.

§ 74. פ״י verbs in general

Verbs with י as the first radical can be subdivided into three classes: a

1) Verbs with primitive ו replaced by י in certain forms (פ״יו) (§ 75).

2) Verbs with primitive י (פ״יי). They are small in number in Hebrew as in Arabic (§ 76).

3) Finally there is a special category of פ״י verbs the צ in the second radical of which is geminated in certain forms. All these verbs (פ״יצ), not many, are probably verbs with primitive ו (§ 77).

An alternative synchronic classification which does not include פ״יצ verbs is 1) verbs which show *a* in the stem of the fut., the initial radical of which is incorporated in the prefix vowel e.g. יִינַק, and 2) those whose thematic vowel in the fut. is ē and whose R1 is lacking in the fut., impv., and inf. cst., e.g. יֵשֵׁב. But verbs such as יָרַשׁ (etymologically of the פ״ו type) sit astride the division: fut. יִירַשׁ, but inf.cst. רֶ֫שֶׁת. and impv. רַשׁ alongside רֵשׁ.

§ 75. פ״י verbs, originally פ״ו (= פ״יו)
(Paradigm 8: יָשַׁב *to sit,. remain*)

In the originally פ״ו verbs, the ו is retained in the derived conjugations, Nifal, Hifil and Hofal. In Qal, it is either replaced by י or it drops out. In Piel and Pual it is replaced by י. a

1) **Forms with ו: Nifal.** The underlying form is *nawšab* with the primitive preformative *na* (§ 51 a), hence, through contraction, נוֹשַׁב. In the future the ו is doubled: יִוָּשֵׁב(1) (like יִקָּטֵל).

Hifil. The primitive *a* of the preformative (§ 54 a) is retained, hence *hawšīb, yawšīb* > הוֹשִׁיב, יוֹשִׁיב.

Hofal. The theoretical form *huwšab* becomes הוּשַׁב with originally long ū(2).

Qal: in the futures יוֹרֶה, יוֹסֵף (§ *f*).

2) **Forms where the ו is replaced by י.** In the **Qal** conjugation, at the beginning of a word, when there is a vowel: Perfect יָשַׁב; partic. יֹשֵׁב, יָשׁוּב. Moreover, in the future יֵשֵׁב (which is probably for *yayšib*, § *c*).

In **Hitpael** one has ו or י, e.g. הִתְוַדָּה *to confess* (rather frequent), הִתְיַלֵּד *to have oneself recorded in a genealogy* (denominative of תּוֹלֵדָה) Nu 1.18. For הִתְיַצֵּב, cf. § 77 *b*.

3) **Forms with aphaeresis of** ו. In the conjugation **Qal**, at the beginning of a word, ו drops when it should have shewa: **impv.** שֵׁב (for וְשֵׁב*) and **inf. cst.** **šib*, hence with the feminine *t* (§ 72 *d*) **šibt*. This form, when segholised, would give שֵׁבֶת* (§ 89 *h*). In fact one has שֶׁ֫בֶת, perhaps on the analogy of the infinitive with *a*, e.g. רֶ֫שֶׁת from *raš-t*(3).

(1) In the 1st pers. we have אִ (not אֵ) type אִוָּשֵׁב (§ 51 *b*): אִוָּתֵר, אִוָּעֵד, אִוָּדַע etc.
(2) This *ū* penetrated ע"ו and ע"ע verbs: הוּקַם (§ 80 *h*), הוּסַב (§ 82 *d*).
(3) Generally the final ◌ֶת ◌ֶ tends to become ◌ֶ֫ת ◌ֶ֫, e.g. קְטֶ֫לֶת (= קְטֵל + ת); cf. 89 *h*. Compare the contamination of the form *qitl* by *qatl*, § 96 A *f*.

b **Active and stative verbs. Stative perfects:** יָרֵא *to fear*, יָגֹר *to dread*. In the paradigm we have cited יָרַשׁ *to inherit*, the primitive form of which is יָרֵשׁ* (comp. Arb. *wariṯa*).

In the future, the action verbs and the stative verbs differ not only in the second, but also in the first vowel (§ 41 *e*). The future of an action verb is **yayšib* > יֵשֵׁב; the stative future is **yiyraš* > יִירַשׁ.

c **Active future** יֵשֵׁב. The second vowel ◌ֵ derives from the primitive vowel *i* of the action verb future (§ 41 *a*). Apart from פ"ו verbs, the ◌ֵ is very rare (e.g. יִתֵּן).

The first vowel ◌ֵ, according to many grammarians, could come from *i* on the analogy of the vowel of R2. According to this hypothesis **yišib* would be a syncopated form lacking the first radical, like the Arabic future of פ"ו verb, *yalidu* (from *walada*)(1). It seems much more likely that this ◌ֵ comes from *ay* and was originally long for the following reasons:

1) In the stative future יִירַשׁ the first vowel *i* was originally long, since it originates from *iy*; by analogy, in the active future form, the first vowel *ẹ* must also have been originally long, and hence have had its origin in *ay*.

2) In Hebrew, generally speaking, the active future and the stative future differ, where possible, not only in respect of the second, but also in respect of the first vowel (§ 41 *e*). It is therefore normal that in the stative future **yiyraš* with the first vowel *i* is in opposition to an active future **yayšib* with the first vowel *a*(2).

3) In favour of *ay* one can invoke the parallelism of the forms יוֹסֵף (for *yawsif*) and יוֹרֶה (§ *f*), which are Qal futures in which the primitive ו has been preserved.

4) The length of the ֵ is rendered probable by the fact that it never drops out; we find, e.g. יֵדָעֲךָ *he shall know you*(3) as against יְדָעֲךָ (pf.) *he knew you* or *he knows you.*

5) Note Greek transliterations such as ιησηβ (Ps 9.8) and θηληχ (ib. 32.8) in the Secunda of the Hexapla.

Observation. With the inversive Waw יֵשֵׁב becomes וַיֵּ֫שֶׁב (likewise in the Hifil one has וַיּ֫וֹשֶׁב).

(1) However, Ugr *a-ši-ib* "let me dwell" (Huehnergard, *Ugr. Vocabulary*, p. 320) as well as forms such as *abl* = /'abil/ "I shall bring" and *atn* = /'atin/ "I shall give" (Gordon, *UT*, § 9.48) suggest that at least in Ugr. the situation was probably similar to that in Classical Arabic, though once we have *id*' = /'ida'u/(?) (S. Segert, *A Basic Gram. of the Ugaritic Language* (Los Angeles/London, 1984), § 54.54. See also J. Blau in Fschr. B. Krutzweil (Jerusalem, 1975), p. 71.

(2) A mixed form is represented by יֵיקַר or יֵקַר as against יִיקַר. Likewise רֵשׁ impv. as against רָשׁ in pause.

(3) It is remarkable that this long ֵ is never written with *mater lectionis*, except, perhaps, in Ps 138.6 where we must read יֵידַע for יְיֵדָע.

Stative future יִירַשׁ. As has been stated (§ *c*), the two vowels indicate the stative future. *d*

As for the stress, one may note that in וַיִּ֫ירַשׁ the stress does not recede (§ 47 *b*). It is the same in וַיִּ֫יטַב (§ 76 *b*); compare, e.g. וַיִּ֫חַר (from חרה, § 79 *i*).

The two Qal futures יֵשֵׁב and יִירַשׁ appear to be of secondary origin. *e*
After the preformative one would have expected a primitive ו as in נוֹשַׁב, הוֹשִׁיב, and הוּשַׁב. But a form like *yawšib* > יוֹשֵׁב* uncomfortably resembles the Hifil jussive and the Qal active participle. But the ו has been preserved in יוֹרֶה and יוֹסֵף (§ *f*).

Qal future with primitive ו of the verbs יָרָה *to throw* and יָסַף *to add.* *f*

1) The future יוֹרֶה is in fact a Qal form. Since it bears complete resemblance to Hifil, it has secondarily been considered as such, hence the participle מוֹרֶה, which is synonymous with יוֹרֶה(1).

2) The future יוֹסֵף is in fact a Qal form which is preserved in Gn 4.12; Dt 13.1; Jl 2.2; Nu 22.19† (cf. § 114 *g*). The form is similar to that of a Hifil jussive, and almost identical with that of a Hifil in-

dicative יוֹסִיף. On account of this resemblance יוֹסֵף has been *hifilised* to יוֹסִיף. Then, on the model of יוֹסִיף, were formed the perfect (rare, 6 x) הוֹסִיף, the inf. cst. הוֹסִיף (4 x), and the participle מוֹסִיף (1 x). The verb יסף is therefore quasi-defective (§ 85 *b*). The usual forms are: יָסַף in the perfect, יוֹסִיף in the future, and הוֹסִיף in the inf. cst.(2)

Forms such as מוֹרֶה, יוֹסִיף, הוֹסִיף are therefore secondary or pseudo-Hifils (§ 54 *f*; see other examples in ע"י verbs, § 81 *c*).

(1) Note 2Kg 13.17 יְרֵה וַיּוֹר (*he said,*) "*Shoot!*," *and he shot*. The change from Qal to Hifil may have been triggered by the fact that other verbs meaning *to throw* are in Hifil: הִשְׁלִיךְ and הֵטִיל (both without Qal).

(2) Cf. M. Lambert in *RÉJ* 37 (1898) 142; 33 (1896) 154.

g **Common verbs:**

Action verbs of יָשַׁב type:

יָרַד *to descend*

יָלַד *to give birth*; יֻלַּד is Qal passive (§ 58 *a*).

יָדַע *to know*. Because of the third guttural one has fut. יֵדַע(1), impv. דַּע, and inf. דַּעַת (with vowel =).

יָצָא *to go out*. This verb is neither treated as a פ"יצ nor as a ל"א, but as a פ"ו: fut. יֵצֵא; impv. צֵא; inf. צֵאת (for צֵאֶת*). For the forms of the inverted perfect, cf. § 43 *b*, and for those of the inverted future, see § 47 *b* (rare abnormal forms: וַיּוֹצֵא, impv. הוֹצִיא, § 78 *i*).

הָלַךְ *to go*. This is the only פ"ה verb which is treated like a פ"ו, an analogical development based on פ"ו verbs(2), though the conditions which led to this development are unknown. Fut. יֵלֵךְ, impv. לֵךְ, and inf. לֶכֶת. In pause, one has וַיֵּלַךְ (§ 32 *c*). The Hitpael is regular: הִתְהַלֵּךְ. One finds some strong forms, e.g. יַהֲלֹךְ Ps 58.9 etc.(3) The form תִּהֲלַךְ Ex 9.23; Ps 73.9 is perhaps a *lectio mixta* (§ 16 *g*) giving a choice between תַּהֲלֹךְ and תִּתְהַלַּךְ.

(1) Compare, in the ע"ע stative verbs, futures such as יֵקַל (*yeqal*), יֵרַע.

(2) See A. Ungnad, *Beiträge zur Assyriologie* 5 (1905) 278; M. Lambert, *RÉJ* 27 (1893), 137, n. An alternative explanation, first put forward by F. Prätorius, *ZAW* 2 (1882) 310, and followed by Brock., *GvG*, I, p. 585, Berg., I, § 16 and BL, p. 214, is inadmissible; apart from the fact that this would constitute a unique example of such a phonetic change (/*hah-/> /*hā-/), one must note the evidence now available in Ugr, in which the causative morpheme is /š/ rather than /h/; see Harris, *Development*, p. 33. Gordon's suggestion (*UT*, p. 390) that the root הלכ is a (late?) mixture of the original biconsonantal לכ and הכ (the latter attested in BA) is unlikely in view of

the Akkadian /alāku/.
(3) In the Moabite Mesha inscription one finds לך alongside אהלך (which is unlikely Piel).

Stative verbs in the manner of the יָרֵשׁ*, יָרַשׁ type: h

יָשֵׁן* *to sleep*; inf. לִישׁוֹן Ec 5.11†.

יָעֵף* *to be tired.*

יָעַץ, יָעֵץ *to counsel*, with *a* on account of the guttural.

יָרֵא *to fear* (simultaneously ל"א): fut. יִירָא, וַיִּירָא; impv. יְרָא, יִרְאוּ (=*yru*, not יִרְאוּ*); inf. יְרֹא (2 x alongside the ordinary יִרְאָה, § 49 *d*).

Stative verbs with the vowel *u* > ◌ֹ: i

יָגֹר *to dread*. The future and the imperative, יָגוּר and גּוּר, stem from the related root גור; the verb is thus defective, § 85 *a*.

יָקֹשׁ *to set a trap*, a denominative of יָקוֹשׁ *fowler*; without future.

יָכֹל *to be able*. The meaning of the root יכל seems to be that of *capacity*. Compare the related root כול (or rather כיל) *to measure* (especially in terms of *capacity*); Hifil: *to contain*.

The verbal adjective יָכֹל is not found in our massoretic text, but it must be read in Jer 38.5([1]).

The inf. cst. יְכֹלֶת is of a very rare type which one does not find elsewhere except in יְבֹשֶׁת *to be dry*, Gn 8.7 (cf. § 76 *d*).

The future יוּכַל is explicable in various ways:

1) According to some, it could be a Qal passive. But a verb expressing a *state* can hardly have a passive form, since the passive is conceivable only of an *action* incurred.

2) According to others this could be a Qal future for *yọḇạl*, which would come from *yawkal*. But 1) if this were the case, the *ọ* would be maintained as it is in יֹאכַל (§ 73 *b*), etc.; 2) in stative verbs the vowel of the preformative is *i* (§ 41 *e*).

3) The most likely view still seems to be the time-honoured and widely held one (Ewald, Olshausen, etc.) that יוּכַל is a Hofal future. The form itself indicates a Hofal, and it is wise not to look for anything else, if the meaning *he could* can be reconciled with the causative passive form. One could envisage the following semantic process: the original meaning of Hofal, *he will be made capable*, could easily, and may have weakened to *he will become capable, he will be capable*, becoming finally *he will be able to*([2]), the causative meaning may then

have gradually evaporated(3). Likewise, the Hofal יוּקַד, strictly speaking *to be set ablaze*, loses its causative sense, and comes to mean *to be in flames, to be ablaze* like Qal יֵיקָד*, יִיקַד(4).

The verb יכל is therefore defective; the perfect is Qal, whereas the future is Hofal. The normal Qal future would be יִיכַל*. We do not know why it has disappeared. In Biblical Aramaic in which the (stative) perfect is יְכִל, the stative future has likewise disappeared; it has been replaced by an active form with *u*: יִכֻּל (comp. § 41 *b*).

(1) Cf. Ehrlich, *Randglossen* ad loc. In MH יכל is found in the sense of *possible*; cf. Dalman, *Aram. Neuhebr. Wörterbuch* [§ 5 *g*, n], s. v.

(2) This is how in German *befähigt* can assume a meaning close to that of *fähig* "capable"; likewise we have *Befähigung* in the sense of capability like *Fähigkeit*.

(3) In MH, Jewish Aramaic, and Syriac, many causative passive participles are used as pure adjectives without any causative nuance, e.g. MH מְבוֹאָר *clear, evident* (originally *rendered clear, explicated*).

(4) Another plausible explanation, suggested by Blau, is to see in these forms examples of a sound shift *iwC* > *ū*: /yiwkal/> /yūḫal/, but such a shift does not appear to be widespread. See J. Blau in *IOS* 1 (1971) 3f.

j **Detailed observations.**

Future יֵשֵׁב. The ending of the fem. plural is always *ạlnå* (§ 29 *d*), but the corresponding imperative, due to the analogy of the m.sg., shows *ẹlnå*, e.g. תֵּלַכְנָה but לֵכְנָה.

Future יִירַשׁ. One often(1) finds the defective spelling יִרַשׁ, e.g. יִרְאוּ *they will fear* (with metheg indicating the syllable division *yi-r'u*; as opposed to יִרְאוּ *yir-'u* "they will see," § 14 *c* 1).

(1) In 46 out of 362 cases: AF, p. 167.

k Strong **imperatives:** יְרָא *Fear!*, pl. יִרְאוּ(1); יְצֹק *Pour!* (from the highly irregular יָצַק, which is also treated as פ״צ, § 77 *b*) alongside צַק.

In the masc. sg. we often meet the paragogic ה ָ, e.g. שְׁבָה, רְדָה (cf. § 48 *d*).

Hebrew has only the imperative of the unused verb יָהַב* *to give*. Especially in the singular we find the form הָבָה(2) (but before א, Gn 29.21 הָבָה, hiatus, § 33), once הַב, and in the plural הָבוּ; sg. f. הָבִי. In these last two forms the *a* is maintained (contrast דַּע, דְּעוּ, דְּעִי).

(1) Not יִרְאוּ like מִלְאוּ, because the א has become silent.

(2) One would have anticipated הֲבָה*. The stronger vocalisation of this imperative may

be derived from the fact that it is also used as an interjection, § 105 *e*; by analogy we also have הָבוּ, הָבִי, but mil'ra.

l **Strong infinitives:** יְסֹד *to found* in לִיסֹד (also לִיסּוֹד 2Ch 31.7 with gemination [§ 77 *a*, n. 2]: the length passes from the vowel to the consonant); יְרֹא (2 x, alongside the usual יִרְאָה, § 49 *d*); יְכֹלֶת, § *i*; יְבשׁ and יְבֹשֶׁת.

m Comparison with the **nominal forms** (cf. *a*).

1) **Forms with ו**: מוֹעֵד *appointed meeting* (יָעַד *to fix [the time, the place]*); מוֹשָׁב *dwelling*; תּוֹדָה *praise* (root: ידה, Hif. הוֹדָה *to praise*). In all these forms, *ọ* derives from *aw*.

2) **Forms in which the ו is replaced by י**. At the beginning of a word, e.g. יִרְאָה *fear* (also infinitive, § 49 *d*), יַחַד *at the same time* (adverb).

3) **Form with aphaeresis of ו** (לֵדָה type): לֵדָה *birth* (also used as infinitive); חֵמָה *heat, fury* (from the extremely rare יחם *to be in heat*, cf. Syr. *ḥemṯå*); עֵדָה(1) *appointed meeting, assembly* (cf. Syr. *'ẹḏtå*); עֵצָה *counsel*; שֵׁנָה *sleep* (cf. Syr. *šenṯå*); דֵּעָה *knowledge*; זֵעָה* *sweat*.

This form is that of the inf. of the type *šib* + *t* > שֶׁבֶת (§ *a* 3), but with the feminine ending ־ָה, e.g. *lid* + *å* = לֵדָה. One meets לֵדָה alongside לֶדֶת; דֵּעָה alongside דַּעַת. The inf. שֶׁבֶת is used as a pure substantive, e.g. 1Kg 10.19 *seat* (of the throne of Solomon).

(1) Contrast עֵדָה, fem. of עֵד *testimony* (root עוד), § 80 *s*; 97 E *b*.

§ 76. **Primitive פ"י verbs** (פ"יי)
(Paradigm 9: יטב *to be good*)

The verbs with primitive י as the first radical number only seven. They are all stative(1)(future with *a*). Examples are found only in Qal and Hifil. a

In the paradigm we have cited יטב*, the perfect of which is non-existent (§ *d*).

The primitive י is maintained in all the forms.

(1) Is it a pure coincidence, or perhaps a deliberate attempt to avoid forming action verbs with פ"י root?

Qal. Future **yiyṭab* > יִיטַב (comp. יִירַשׁ, § 75 *b*), with the first and b the second vowel of the stative future (§ 41 *e*).

As regards the stress, one should note that in וַיִּיטַ֫ב it does not recede (cf. § 75 *d*).

c **Hifil. Future** **yayṭīb* > יֵיטִיב.

Perfect **hayṭīb* (with the primitive *a*) > הֵיטִיב. This vowel *ẹ* has spread to perfects הֵקִים (§ 80 *g*) and הֵסֵב (§ 82 *d*), but by losing its original length in the process.

Participle **mayṭīb* > מֵיטִיב. This vowel *ẹ* has spread to the participles מֵקִים and מֵסֵב, but again by losing its original length.

Remark. In the verb *to be good*, the forms without י after the preformative, e.g. הֵטִיב, מֵטִיב, in themselves, belong to the verb טוֹב; in order to relate them to the root יטב it would be necessary to suppose a defective spelling. In fact, the Hifil forms are usually(1) written with י after the preformative; they therefore belong to the root יטב (§ *d* 4).

(1) In 106 out of 117 cases: AF, p. 173.

d The seven **primitive פ״י verbs.**

1) יָבֵשׁ, fut. יִיבַשׁ *to be dry* (cf. Arb. *yabisa*, fut. *yaybasu*). Inf. יְבֹשׁ (1 x) and יְבֹשֶׁת (1 x; this type also only in יְכֹ֫לֶת, § 75 *i*). The Hifil abnormally has w for *y*: הוֹבִישׁ *to dry*(1).

2) יָנַק* (cf. Syr. *yineq*, Akk. *enēqu*), fut. יִינַק *to suck*. Hifil הֵינִיק *to give a suck, to suckle*.

3) יָשַׁר, fut. יִישַׁר *to be straight* (cf. Arb. *yasira*, fut. *yaysaru*).

4) יטב* *to be good*. There is no perfect: it would be יָטַב* or יָטֹב*. It is replaced by the perfect טוֹב, טֹ֫בוּ (§ 80 *q*). Future יִיטַב. Hifil: הֵיטִיב, יֵיטִיב; less frequently הֵטִיב, יֵטִיב (§ *c*).

5) יקץ* *to wake up*. There is no perfect; it would be יָקֵץ* (cf. Arb. *yaqiẓa*). It is replaced by the Hifil perfect הֵקִיץ (root: קיץ), which is probably a pseudo-Hifil (cf. § 54 *f*). Future יִיקַץ (rarely יָקִיץ), וַיִּקַ֫ץ, and once וַיִּ֫יקֶץ Gn 9.24.

The causative action *to wake up* is expressed by הֵעִיר (עור).

6) ילל* Hifil הֵילִיל *to groan*: fut. abnormally יְיֵלִיל(2).

7) ימן* Hifil הֵימִין *to go to the right* (denominative of יָמִין *the right-hand side*).

(1) The same form הוֹבִישׁ is the metaplastic Hifil of the verb בּוֹשׁ *to be ashamed* and

means (like its Qal) *to be ashamed* (§ 80 *q*).
(2) Perhaps for יְהֵילִיל, which does indeed occur once in Is 52.5.

Comparison with the **nominal forms**. The primitive י is maintained as in verbal forms, e.g. מֵיטָב *the best part*, מִישׁוֹר *a plain*, תֵּימָן *south*, יַבָּשָׁה *dry land, firm ground*. e

§ 77. פ״צ verbs(1)
(No paradigm)

In six פ״י verbs the second radical of which is צ, the צ after a vowel is doubled in certain forms. The emphatic sibilant צ, by its very nature, easily lends itself to doubling(2). This takes place in those forms in which there occurred a long vowel before *ṣ*, e.g. in Qal fut. **yīṣaṯ* > *yiṣṣaṯ*; in Hofal fut. **yūṣa̧ʿ* > *yuṣṣa̧ʿ*; similarly in Hofal perfect(3). This, therefore, is a case of metathesis of quantity: the length has been transferred from the vowel to the *ṣ*(4). From these forms the gemination of the *ṣ* has spread to other forms, e.g. Nifal נִצַּת, Hifil יַצִּיעַ and even the nominal form מַצָּע. a

(1) In this convenient notation the צ represents the second radical. A mnemonic is פ״צ בְּקַעַ״ת גֵּר "the valley of sojourner": the verb roots concerned are יצב, יצק, יצע, יצת, יצג, and יצר.
(2) The sporadic attestation of similar gemination of other sibilants suggests that the phenomenon may have little to do with the emphatic feature of צ. Note אֶסָּרֵם Ho 10.10; וְיִסְּרֵנִי Is 8.11 (if not wrongly pointed for Pi. pf. וְיִסְּרַנִי); יִשַּׁרְנָה 1Sm 6.12; לְיִסּוֹד 2Ch 31.7 alongside לִיסֹד Is 51.16 (the former form reminds one of a MH form such as לֵישֵׁב), מוּסָּד Is 28.16, מֻסָּד *foundation* 1Kg 7.9.
(3) Cf. Brock., *GvG*, I, p. 601.
(4) Cf. BL, pp. 218, 379. Compare הִסִּית etc., § 80 *p*.

The six פ״צ verbs. N.B. The attested forms are rather few in number. The roots of two verbs, יצת and יצג, are not absolutely certain; the root of another verb, יצב, is secondary. b

1) יצב, only in Hitpael הִתְיַצֵּב *to position oneself*. The true root is נצב, which has Nifal נִצַּב(1), Hifil הִצִּיב and Hofal הֻצַּב. As these forms resemble those from the root יצב, a Hitpael הִתְיַצֵּב has been created(2).

2) יצק *to pour*. Qal fut. יִצֹּק(3); Hifil fut. יַצִּיק. There are also

forms with unlengthened צ, thus all Hofal forms הוּצַק, יוּצַק, מוּצָק. In Qal there are anomalous forms such as וַיִּצֶק(4) 1Kg 22.35.

3) יצע *to spread*. Hifil fut. יַצִּיעַ; Hofal fut. יֻצַּע. Nominal form מַצָּע (1 x) *bed*.

4) יצת *to catch fire*. The root is not absolutely certain; it could be נצת. Qal fut. יִצַּת(5); Nif. pf. נִצְּתָה (§ 85 *b*); Hif. הִצִּית, יַצִּית, but abnormally אֲצִיתֶנָּה Is 27.4.

5) יצג *to place*. The root is not absolutely certain; it could be נצג. Hifil הִצִּיג, יַצִּיג; Hofal fut. יֻצַּג.

6) יצר *to form*. Qal fut. יִצֹר: abnormal form וַיִּיצֶר, וַיִּצֶר(6); Qal passive יוּצַר.

Remark. The verb יָצָא is not treated as a פ"צ, § 75 *g*.

(1) The Nifal of the verb occurs only in the perfect and participle as in נִגַּשׁ, but unlike the latter no Qal is attested nor is it used in any other tense or mood for which Hitpael הִתְיַצֵּב is used.

(2) Cf. Brock., *GvG*, I, p. 601; BL, p. 379.

(3) Only thrice according to Codex L., whilst in the majority of cases the dagesh is wanting in צ.

(4)(6) Used intransitively: *the blood flowed*. The *i* was originally long; contrast יִגֶל, an apocopated Qal form of גָּלָה, § 79 *i*. Compare, וַיֵּצֶר from יֵצַר *it will be narrow* (root צרר, § 82 *b*). According to Yeivin, the seghol here is a neutral variant of the original /u/: *Lš* 44 (1980) 184.

(5) יִצָּתוּ (2 x) is as if from √ צתת.

§ 78. ל"א verbs

(Paradigm 10: מָצָא *to find*)

a What we have said about the guttural א in § 24 applies to the conjugation of ל"א verbs, which differ from other R3-guttural verbs(1). In the inflection of these verbs the Alef is no longer pronounced; in consequence, a syllable originally closed by א becomes open and takes the vowels of open syllables. Most of the deviations of their conjugation from that of the regular verb can be explained in terms of the phonetic laws: *a'* > ā > å, *i'* > ē > ę, and *u'* > ō > ǫ.

(1) יָצָא and יָרֵא combine features characteristic of פ"י verbs as well; see § 75.

b **Qal.** In the perfect, apart from the active form, there is a stative form with ָ. The perfect of action verbs: the primitve form **maṣa'* with two short *a*'s becomes מָצָא *to find* with two å's, in open syllable. Stative perfect: the primitive form **mali'* becomes מָלֵא *to be full* (short *i* usually becomes ֵ in open syllables)(1), and this ṣeré is retained in the 1st/2nd pers. pf. (מָלֵאתִי; מְלֵאתִי) in contrast to זָקַנְתִּי from זָקֵן.

Future. The stative future has *a*, as usual, e.g. יִמְלָא. The future of action verbs also has *a*, e.g. יִמְצָא (instead of *יִמְצֹא), perhaps on the analogy of the future **yiglay*, from which comes יִגְלֶה, § 79 *e*.

The pl.f. form with ֶאנָה (also spelled often ֶאןָ), which occurs in Qal and in the derived conjugations, is due to the analogy of ל"ה verbs, e.g. תִּמְצֶאןָ like תִּגְלֶינָה.

The imperative has the vowel of the future: מְצָא.

But the infinitive has *ọ*: מְצֹא, the form קְטֹל having become like the proper form of the infinitive, § 49 *c*.

(1) Other stative verbs are: יָרֵא *to fear*, fut. יִירָא (simultaneously פ"יו, § 75 *h*), טָמֵא *to be impure*, שָׂנֵא *to hate*, צָמֵא *to be thirsty*.

Nifal: נִמְצָא. In inflection, instead of the expected forms *נִמְצָאתָ etc., one meets with נִמְצֵאתָ etc., with ֵ, which comes from ל"ה verbs, e.g. נִגְלֵיתָ or possibly from Qal forms such as יָרֵאתָ (§ *b*). c

Piel: מִצֵּא(1). In inflection we naturally find ֵ, e.g. מִצֵּאתָ.

Hifil: הִמְצִיא When inflected, it has ֵ, e.g. הִמְצֵאתָ as in the other derived conjugations, and not ִי.

Hitpael. As in the strong verb (§ 53 *b*), we find, in addition to the standard type with ֵ, also the rare type with *a* (here ָ) in הִתְחַטָּא *to remove one's sin*, הִטַּמָּא *to render oneself impure*, הִתְפַּלָּא *to show oneself as astonishing*(?). As in the strong verb, the type with ֵ loses *a* in pause, e.g. יִתְנַשֵּׂא becomes יִתְנַשָּׂא Nu 23.24.

(1) Examples: מִלֵּא *to fill*, קִנֵּא *to be jealous*, טִמֵּא *to defile*, חִטֵּא *to remove sin*, רִפֵּא *to heal*.

General observations d

The א is silent before a consonantal ending of the pf. (תִּי, תָ, תְּ, נוּ) and impf. (נָה, ןָ) and where it ends a verb form (e.g. הִמְצִיא, but הִמְצִיאוּ /himṣí'u/). Elsewhere it is pronounced.

The fact that the א is not pronounced has certain consequences: 1) א is sometimes omitted in spelling; 2) ל"א verbs are quite often treated like ל"ה verbs, a process which, under quite likely Aramaic influence, is much farther advanced in MH: e f 1) א omitted in spelling. Examples: וַתִּשֶּׂנָה Ru 1.14 (correctly spelled in vs. 9); אָבִי 1Kg 21.29 (correctly spelled אבִיא in the same verse); יָצָתִי Job 1.21; מָלֵתִי 32.18. Some may be cases of haplography: e.g., ...הֶחֱטִי אֶת־... 2Kg 13.6; ...מֵבִי אֶל־... Jer 19.15.

g 2) ל"א verbs are quite often treated as ל"ה verbs, phonetically or graphically(1):

Forms which have the vocalisation of ל"ה: e.g. כָּלָאתִי *I held back* Ps 119.101; חוֹטֶא *sinning* Ec 2.26 etc.; חֹטְאִים 1Sm 14.33; מִלָּא *he filled* Jer 51.34; רִפֵּאתִי *I healed* 2Kg 2.21; נִפְלְאַתָה (anomalous pataḥ; comp. the pausal form נִגְלָתָה, § 79 *d*) *it was great* 2Sm 1.26 (*MUSJ* 6 [1913] 177); הִפְלָא *he made great* Dt 28.59.

Forms which have the ה typical of ל"ה verbs: e.g. אֶרְפָּה *I shall heal* Jer 3.22; רְפָה *Heal!* Ps 60.4; הֵחָבֵה *to hide* 1Kg 22.25; יְמַלֵּה *he will fill* Job 8.21.

It is difficult to say whether any of these anomalous forms really existed or if they are due to later scribal error.

(1) Sometimes, conversely, ל"ה verbs are treated as ל"א verbs, § 79 *l*.

h **Remarks on certain forms.**

On the form of the inverted perfect, cf. § 43 *b*; on that of the inverted future, § 46 *b*.

The cohortative (נִמְצָאָה, אֶמְצָאָה) is avoided (§ 114 *b*, n.)(1).

The f. sg. participle is generally of מֹצֵאת type (for מֹצֶאֶת*); more rarely one has the type מֹצְאַת (comp. inf. שְׂאֵת alongside לָשֵׂאת, § *l*, and the type בְּאֵר, § 88 C *i*). In the plural, instead of מֹצְאִים, we find, very occasionally, מֹצאם with quiescent א.

In the m. pl. participle of Nifal, instead of the normal type נִמְצָאִים, we often meet the type נִמְצְאִים; e.g. we almost always find נִמְצְאִים and נִבְאִים (cf. § 96 C *b*).

i In Hifil, in the imperative, jussive and inverted future, instead of the usual vowel ֵ, we very occasionally meet originally long *ī*. Examples: impv. הָבִיא Jer 17.18 and הוֹצִיא Is 43.8 (both before ע); וַיָּבִיא Ne 8.2 (before ע); וַיּוֹצִא Ps 105.43 (before ע); וַתַּחֲטִא 1Kg 16.2; 21.22 (before א); וַיּוֹצִא Dt 4.20; 2Kg 11.12 (before א); וַתַּחְבִא 2Kg 6.29 (before א). In these cases, the vowel *i* (which is also suspect when not accompanied by the mater lectionis י) could be explained in terms of the desire to have a longer vowel before the guttural(2). But one also finds *i* before a non-guttural: Is 36.14 jussive יַשִּׁא (written יַשִּׁיא in the parallel passages 2Kg 18.29; 2Ch 32.15); וַיַּחֲטִא 2Kg 21.11; וַיּוֹצִא Ps 78.16. In these cases the *i*, if authentic, is hard to explain.

(1) A rare example is concealed in the Ktiv at 1Sm 28.15 וָאֶקְרָאֶה.

(2) Compare the phenomenon of hiatus, § 33, and cf. § 79 *m*.

Especially irregular verbs *j*

The verb יָצָא *to go out* is not treated like a ל"א, but like a פ"יו, § 75 *g*. On the verb בּוֹא *to enter, come*, cf. § 80 *r*.

The stative verb מָלֵא means *he is full* and also *he fills* in the quasi-stative sense, as in "the water *fills* the vase." For the action in the strict sense of the term, as in "the man *fills* the vase with water," one usually uses Piel מִלֵּא. The form מְלָאוֹ Esth 7.5 *he filled it* (supposing that the text is right) supposes a perfect of the action verb מָלָא*, which may have existed (perh. under the influence of Aramaic). On the analogy of ל"ה verbs, the Qal inf. is מְלֹאת; in Piel inf. one has מַלֹּאת (5 x) alongside מַלֵּא (7 x).

Apart from the verb I קָרָא *to call, cry*, there is a verb II קָרָא *to go to meet*, which often takes the form קָרָה. To the form קָרָא is related the verbal noun לִקְרַאת *to meet up with, to go towards* (§ 49 *d*). The other nominal forms are related to קָרָה, e.g. מִקְרֶה *occurrence, fate, lot*. *k*

The verb נָשָׂא *to carry* etc. is at the same time a פ"ן verb: fut. יִשָּׂא; impv. (with aphaeresis) שָׂא. The inf. is rarely (4 x) נְשׂא (§ 72 *h*); usually one has the aphaeretic form. The primitive form **śa'* + *t* first became, by segholisation, שֶׂאֶת*, which in turn became שֵׂאת*, a form which one finds in לָשֵׂאת; without ל the form is שְׂאֵת, with the vowel at the end as in, for example, the substantive בְּאֵר *well*, § 88 C *i* (compare the type מְצֵאת alongside מְצֹאת, § *h*)(1).

(1) Note the three infinitives with ֵ: תֵּת, § 72 *i*, צֵאת, § 75 *g*, שְׂאֵת.

§ 79. ל"ה verbs
(Paradigm 11: גָּלָה *to reveal*)

The ל"ה verbs are so called because they are spelled with a final (quiescent) ה in the perfect 3rd pers. sg. m., גָּלָה; in fact, these are verbs with י as the third radical(1). Alongside ל"י verbs there once existed in Hebrew, as in Arabic, some ל"ו verbs, but these have been *a* absorbed by the ל"י verbs, as the פ"ו verbs have, in certain forms, been replaced by פ"י verbs (§ 75 *a*). As a vestige of ל"ו verbs one finds the form שָׁלַוְתִּי Job 3.26 *I am calm* (comp. שָׁלֵו *tranquil*, שַׁלְוָה *tranquility*)(2). With the contraction of diphthongs one would have expected, for example, *גָּלוֹתִי (for *gålawti*)(3).

(1) The notion that all ל"וי roots were originally biradical with a final long vowel has been put forward from time to time; for a recent and detailed exposition of the theory see W. Diem, "Die Verba und Nomina tertiae infirmae im Semitischen," *ZDMG* 127 (1977) 15-60. However, Ugr. and Phoen., neither of which was considered by Diem, strongly, however, attest to *w* or *y* as the third radical: see Gordon, *UT*, § 9.51, 52, and Segert, op. cit. [§ 75c], § 54.57; Friedrich—Röllig, § 176. For a defence of the triradical alternative, see R.M. Voigt, *Die infirmen Verbaltypen des Arabischen und das Biradikalismusproblem* (Stuttgart, 1988).

(2) Cf. 1Sm 25.18K עֲשׂוּוֹת; Is 3.16K נְטוּוֹת. In the Mesha stone, line 5, we find the future יענו *he will oppress* from a root ענו (= ענה), from which are derived עָנָו *humble*, עֲנָוָה *humility*. In contrast, the root ענה *to answer* was originally עני.

(3) The verb גָּלָה *to uncover, reveal, to go into exile* itself is probably a primitive ל"ו verb; comp. Arabic *jalā*, fut. *yajlū* "to reveal."

b The conjugation of ל"ה verbs in Hebrew is characterised by *considerable uniformity*(1). For: 1) the old ל"ו verbs have been absorbed by the ל"י verbs, as we have just stated; 2) in Qal, the distinction between action verbs and stative verbs is no longer recognisable; 3) in the derived conjugations, in all tenses (saving the inf. abs.), the final vowel is that of Qal, i.e.: all perfects have ָה, all futures have ֶה, all imperatives have ֵה, and all infs. cst. have וֹת. All participles (even passive, saving גָּלוּי) have ֶה, like גֹּלֶה.

(1) In Arabic the degree of uniformity is not very noticeable; in Aramaic far less noticeable than it is in Hebrew.

c The **primitive 3rd radical** י still appears in: 1) the passive participle גָּלוּי; 2) and in certain rare forms, especially in pause, such as the types גָּלָיוּ for the standard גָּלוּ, and יִגְלָיוּ for the standard יִגְלוּ.

The י is latent in forms such as נִגְלֵיתִי (*ẹ* for *ay*), תִּגְלֶינָה (*ę* for *ay*), גָּלִיתִי (*i* for *iy*).

The י drops out in syncopated forms, e.g. גָּלוּ for **galayu*, יִגְלוּ for **yiglayu*; in apocopated forms, e.g. יִגֶל from יִגְלֶה (= **yiglay*).

The י is quiescent at the end of a word in, e.g. **galay*, which became *gålå* and is spelled גָּלָה.

Compare in the nominal inflection forms with *e* (with latent י) שָׂדֶה, cst. שְׂדֵה; שָׂדֵהוּ, שָׂדֶהָ (§ 96 B *f*), and syncopated forms, e.g. שָׂדַי, שָׂדְךָ (and compare these with the verbal forms with the suffix ךָ: גָּלְךָ, יִגְלְךָ).

Qal conjugation d

Perfect. Certain forms come from action verbs, and others from stative verbs.

1) Forms derived from *action verbs*: 3rd sg. m. גָּלָה for **galay*(1); the י is quiescent, like א in מָצָא (comp. Arb. *rama*[*y*] *to throw*, pronounced *ramā*).

The 3rd f. is formed directly from the 3rd m.: **gala* + *t* > גָּלָת, a rare form in BH, but standard in MH and Aramaic(2). Generally an extra feminine ending ה ָ is added, hence גָּלָתָה, which is the pausal form, and the contextual form גָּלְתָה (comp. קָטָלָה and קָטְלָה).

The rare 3rd plural form גָּלְיוּ.

2) Forms derived from *stative verbs*: all forms with גָּלִית, for example, גָּלִיתָ (comp. Arb. *raḍīta* from the stative *raḍiya to be content*).

Remark. In the 3rd pl. גָּלוּ, the syncopated form does not enable us to recognise the primitive vowel (*a* and *i*).

(1) In Hebrew one would expect **gâlē*; the *a* is perhaps due to analogy with other active perfects קָטַל etc. Comp. the masc. substantive מוֹרָה *razor* from *mōray*, § 89 *b*.

(2) So Jer 13.19 הָגְלָת. It is attested in the Siloam inscription (היַת). This form with ת is obligatory before suffixes. The standard Arm. form is גְּלָת.

Future. The form יִגְלֶה probably comes from *yiglay*: יִגְלֶה is therefore e originally a form of stative verb. The rare forms like יִגְלָיוּ are additional evidence of this.

Observations. 1) In syncopated forms such as יִגְלוּ and תִּגְלִי one cannot recognise the primitive vowel.

2) The ה ֶ, derived from *ay*, is originally long.

3) On the vowel of the preformative in ל"ה verbs with a guttural as the first radical, cf. § 68 *b*.

4) In the jussive and the inverted future one fairly frequently finds the form of the indicative (§ *m*), but normally the apocopated form (§ *i*).

Imperative. Instead of open *ę* of the future, we meet closed *ẹ*: גְּלֵה. f

Inf. absolute: גָּלֹה, by analogy with קָטוֹל (cf. § *p*).

The **inf. cst.** is גְּלוֹת, a form the origin of which is not clear. Perhaps the language, considering the inf. abs. as a sort of noun in the abs. state, and the inf. cst. as a sort of noun in the cst. state (§ 49 *a*), associated גְּלוֹת with גָּלֹה, like, e.g. שְׁנַת with שָׁנָה (cf. § *p*).

Active participle גֹּלֶה(1), cst. גֹּלֵה, f. גֹּלָה; pl. גֹּלִים, f. גֹּלוֹת (cf. § *p*).

Passive participle: גָּלוּי, with pronounced י (§ *c*); cf. § *p*.

(1) From *gāliy* (= *qātil*) according to Barth (*Nominalbildung*, p. xxxi) and others. According to another explanation, it is from *gālay*.

g **Derived conjugations.** Generally, as has been stated (§ *b*), in the derived conjugations, in all tenses (except the inf. abs.), the final vowel is that of Qal. Thus the Nifal ptc. is נִגְלֶה (f. נִגְלָה); comp. גֹּלֶה (f. גֹּלָה, cf. § *p*).

h **Alternation of the vowels** ẹ **and** *i* **in the derived conjugations**(1). It is necessary to distinguish between the non-passive conjugations, Piel, Hifil, and Hitpael, and the passive conjugations, Pual and Hofal. Nifal is treated like the passive conjugations.

In the **passive** conjugations we always find ẹ̄. In Nifal, an exception is וְנִקִּיתָ Gn 24.8; moreover, in the 1st pl. we only find *i*: e.g. נִגְלִינוּ 1Sm 14.8; נִפְלִינוּ Ex 33.16).

In the **non-passive** conjugations *i can* always occur; *in fact i* occurs more often than ẹ. *i* occurs: 1) always before suffixes; 2) always in the 1st pl. ־ִינוּ; 3) always in the 2nd sg. Piel גִּלִּיתָ, גִּלִּית; 4) nearly always in the 2nd pl. ־ִיתֶם.

In Hifil and Hitpael, and in the 1st pers. sg. Piel, the variation is considerable. One can make the following observations: 1) in the 1st pers. sg. ẹ is very frequent; thus in Piel the ordinary form is גִּלֵּיתִי. Notable exceptions are: צִוִּיתִי (30 x; ẹ 5 x); קִוִּיתִי (6 x; ẹ 2 x); 2) in the 2nd sg. *i* is very frequent (in Piel it is the rule, as we have just said).

Accordingly the inflection of Piel is: 2 sg. גִּלִּיתָ, גִּלִּית; 1 sg. גִּלֵּיתִי (usual form)(2); 2 pl. גִּלִּיתֶם; 1 pl. גִּלִּינוּ.

(1) Cf. Driver, *Notes*, p. 183 (ad 1Sm 23.2), and Berg., II, § 30 o.

(2) The preponderance of ṣeré in the 1sg. is most probably due to dissimilation /-iti/ > /-ẹti/); so A. Ungnad, *Beiträge zur Assyriologie* 5 (1905) 263.

i **Apocopated forms.** In the jussive and the inverted future as well as in the imperative we often meet apocopated forms. It should be noted that, unlike in the jussive and the impf. after inversive Waw, the apocopation of ל"ה verbs occurs in the first person, both sg. and pl. as well.

Future: Qal. The form of the indicative יִגְלֶה, through the cutting off of ֶה, first becomes יִגְל (a rare form), then יִגֶל (a rather rare form). Usually one has *segholised* forms: most frequently we find יִגֶל(1), occasionally יֵגֶל. Examples: וַיִּבֶן, יִרֶב; וַיֵּרְדְּ, וַיֵּבְךְּ, וַיֵּשְׁתְּ; וַיִּשְׁבְּ; וַיִּגֶל, וַיִּבֶז, וַיִּמַח (with a 3rd-guttural), וַיִּשַׁע. The form יִגֶל is very rare in the 3rd m. (e.g. יֵרֶא), but we find וָאֵפֶן, וַנֵּפֶן, וַתֵּפֶן alongside וַיִּפֶן; יִרֶב and וַיִּרֶב alongside וַתֵּרֶב; וַתֵּכֶל alongside יִכֶל; with a second-guttural תֵּתַע(2).

With a 1st-guttural verb one normally finds ַ ַ: e.g. וַיַּעַל, וַיַּעַשׂ, וַתַּהַר, וַיַּעַן, forms similar to those of Hifil, but the *i* is retained in יִחַר, וַיִּחַן, יִחַדְּ (comp. the תּ of שָׁלַחַתְּ, § 70 *f*).

Verbs which are ל"ה and פ"ן at the same time are וַיֵּט; וַיַּז.

The verb רָאָה has the apocopated forms יֵרֶא, וַתֵּרֶא, וָאֵרֶא, but וַיַּרְא (also Hifil, 2Kg 11.4† *and he made to see = and he showed*).

Hifil. The form of the indicative יַגְלֶה, through the cutting off of ֶה, becomes יַגְל, which is sometimes segholised to יֶגֶל (like **malk* to מֶלֶךְ)(3). Examples: יַרְדְּ, וַיַּשְׁק, וַיַּרְא 2Kg 11.4† (also Qal), וַיַּט (from נָטָה); וַיַּךְ (from נכה); וַיֶּגֶל, וַיֶּפֶר, וַתֶּמֶר; with a 1st-guttural verb וַיַּעַל (also Qal).

Nifal. The form of the indicative יִגָּלֶה, by the amputation of ֶה, becomes יִגָּל, e.g. תִּגָּל Is 47.3.

Piel. Likewise יְגַלֶּה becomes יְגַל, e.g. וַיְצַו.

(1) Contrast the nominal form סֵפֶר from **sifr*, § 96 A *b*. In יִגֶל the *i* has been preserved probably under the influence of the י. Contrast the forms of פ"י (with *i*) וַיִּיקֶץ, § 76 *d*, וַיִּיצֶר, § 77 *b*.

(2) Note the *assymetry* of forms of a same tense.

(3) Note a significant distinction between Hif. יֶגֶל (< *yagl*) and Qal יִגֶל or יֵגֶל (< *yigl*). Thus in Ps 71.21 תֶּרֶב גְּדֻלָּתִי the verb is a causative Hifil.

Imperative: Hifil. The form הַגְלֵה, by the amputation of ֵה, becomes *j*
**hagl*, a form which is always segholised to הֶגֶל, e.g. הֶרֶב, הֶרֶף; with a 1st-guttural הַעַל. ל"ה verbs which are also פ"ן verbs include הַט, הַךְ.

Piel. The form גַּלֵּה, through the amputation of ֵה, becomes גַּל, e.g. צַו, גַּל. Likewise in Hitpael, one has הִתְחַל 2Sm 13.5.

k **Forms before suffixes** (Paradigm 12):

Perfect. One has גָּלַנִי (like קְטָלַנִי), but גָּלָנִי in pause, even minor; גָּלְךָ, a syncopated form like שָׁדְךָ, in pause גָּלֶךָ and גָּלָךְ. Note also גָּלָהוּ.

Future: יִגְלֵנִי comes from *yigle* + *ni* (this e, as a linking vowel, has spread to all the other verbs, § 61 *d*); יִגְלְךָ, a syncopated form, in pause יִגְלֶךָּ.

In the forms with the energic נ one has, e.g. אֶרְאֶךָּ, יִרְאֶנָּה, יִלְוֶנּוּ with ֶ in accordance with יִלְוֶה etc. (cf. § 61 *f*).

In the future and the imperative one finds, very rarely, the erroneous spelling ֵי, e.g. הַכֵּינִי *Hit me!* 1Kg 20.35,37.

Participle. Examples: מַפְרְךָ *makes you fruitful* Gn 48.4; עֹשָׂהּ *made it* Jer 33.2; מְפַתֶּיהָ (with erroneous י) *seduce her* Ho 2.16. (Compare the nominal forms in ֶה with suffixes, § 96 B *f*).

l **General observations**

Although the conjugation of ל"ה verbs tends to encroach on the domain of ל"א verbs (§ 78 *g*), one finds, on the contrary, certain ל"ה forms treated like ל"א verbs, whether graphically or phonetically. Forms spelled with א: וַיֶּחֱלֶא 2Ch 16.12; נִקְרֹא (followed by נִקְרֵיתִי) 2Sm 1.6. Forms with the vocalisation of ל"א: אָתָנוּ Jer 3.22; תִּכְלָה 1Kg 17.14 (perh. for the sake of assonance with תֶּחְסָר). Forms totally similar to ל"א are: לִירוֹא 2Ch 26.15; יַפְרִיא Ho 13.15. Cf. § 78 *j* on קרא / קרה.

m **Non-apocopated** forms of the inverted future and the jussive. The phenomenon is so frequent, especially in the 1st pers. sg.[1], that it can hardly be considered erroneous.

Sometimes the long form appears to have been preferred before a guttural[2], or with a disjunctive accent. We find וַיַּעֲשֶׂה 4 times 1Kg 16.25; 2Kg 3.2; 13.11; Ez 18.19 (all before a guttural): וַיַּעֲלֶה twice 1Kg 16.17; 18.42 (both before a guttural): וַיִּבְנֶה three times Josh 19.50; 1Kg 18.32; 2Ch 26.6 (all before a guttural): וַתַּעֲלֶה three times 1Kg 22.35; Jer 44.21 (before a guttural); 1Kg 10.29 with a disjunctive accent. Jussive: תֵּרָאֶה Gn 1.9 (before a guttural); יַעֲשֶׂה Jer 28.6 (before a guttural); יַעֲשֶׂה פַרְעֹה Gn 41.34. The long forms are particularly frequent in the books of Kings.

Note, however, that in some cases the non-apocopated form with inversive Waw actually represents an iterative, durative past (§ 113 *e*, *f*), e.g. 1Kg 10.29 וַתַּעֲלֶה וַתֵּצֵא ; 16.25 וַיַּעֲשֶׂה עָמְרִי הָרַע בְּעֵינֵי יהוה, and possibly also 1Sm 1.7 כֵּן תַּכְעִסֶנָּה וַתִּבְכֶּה וְלֹא תֹאכַל, where the energic Waw, on the analogy of the normal syntax, serves to place the events in the past.

(1) In the 1st pers. sg. there is considerable variation, e.g. וָאֶרְאֶה 20 x, וָאֵרֶא 15 x; וָאֶהְיֶה 9 x, וָאֱהִי 12 x; וָאֶעֱשֶׂה 2 x, וָאַעַשׂ 5 x; וָאֲצַוֶּה 5 x, וָאֲצַו 1 x.

In the OT there are a total of 56 cases of non-apocopated 1 sg. futures of Lamed-He verbs. Altogether there are 1,210 proper apocopated forms as against 110 non-apocopated ones none of which occurs in the Pentateuch. See H-J. Stipp, "Narrativ-Langformen 2. und 3. Person von zweiradikaligen Basen nach qalY im biblischen Hebräisch," *JNWSL* 13 (1987) 109-49.

(2) Compare the phenomenon of hiatus, § 33, and comp. § 78 *i*.

Anomalous forms **with הֵ for הֶ.** n

We find a certain number of examples(1) where the vowel ֵ occurs, as in Aramaic and perh., in part, under its influence, e.g. מַה־תַּעֲשֵׂה Josh 7.9; אַל־תַּעֲשֵׂה 2Sm 13.12; Jer 40.16 (Qre); וַנַּעֲשֵׂה Josh 9.24. In a group of texts in Leviticus we have תְּגַלֵּה in pause: 18.7*a* (7*b* תְּגַלֶּה), 12,13,14,15*a* (15*b* תְּגַלֶּה),16,17;20.19.

(1) In several cases the editions vary.

The הָ of the **cohortative** is not used in ל"ה verbs; for that the indicative form is used, e.g. אָסֻרָה־נָּא וְאֶרְאֶה *I wish to go near and see* Ex 3.3; Gn 1.26; Dt 32.20; 2Kg 14.8. Only three cohortatives with הָ occur, probably for the sake of assonance: Ps 77.4; 119.117; Is 41.23. o

For the place of the **stress** in the **inverted perfect**, cf. § 43 *b*.

Detailed observations on various forms. p

Qal: in the **inf. abs.**, we frequently meet with the spelling גָּלוֹ instead of גָּלֹה. The form גָּלוֹת (Is 22.13; 42.20; Hb 3.13) also occurs very occasionally.

In the **inf. cst.** גְּלֹה or גְּלוֹ is sometimes found instead of גְּלוֹת(1).

In the **active ptc.** גֹּלָה, גֹּלִיָּה is sometimes found in poetry alongside the syncopated fem. גֹּלָה, e.g. פֹּרִיָּה (always, 4 x); בֹּכִיָּה Lam 1.16; אֹתִיּוֹת Is 41.23.

The **passive ptc.** גָּלוּי has the regular inflection גְּלוּיָה, גְּלוּיִם, גְּלוּיוֹת.

Very occasionally the 3rd radical *w* is found for *y*, e.g. עָשׂוּ Job 41.25 (for *ʿāśuw*), עֲשׂוּוֹת (Ktiv) 1Sm 25.18.

(1) Cf. 2Kg 13.17,19 עַד־כַּלֵּה; Ezr 9.14, 2Ch 24.10, 31.1 עַד־לְכַלֵּה. Cf. N. Berggrun in *Ha-Tsofe* 18 (23.4.1943), printed now in M. Bar-Asher (ed.), *Qoveṣ ma'amarim bilšon ḥazal* I [Heb] (Jerusalem, 1972), p. 255.

q **Hifil: perfect.** Alongside the form הִגְלָה one fairly often meets with הֶגְלָה (cf. § 54 *c*); thus alongside הִשְׁקָה, הִקְשָׁה, and הִפְנָה one finds הֶרְאָה and הֶגְלָה. We find ֶ especially when the 2nd vowel is ָ (vowel sequence ẹ-ǫ, § 29 *f*), e.g. always הֶגְלָה (excepting 2Kg 24.14 וְהִגְלָה), but הִגְלֵיתָ etc.; always הֶרְאָה, but הִרְאִיתָ etc.; we find הֶרְאָנִי, but הִרְאַנִי; הֶרְאָנוּ, הֶרְאָם; הֶלְאָנִי, but also הֶלְאֵתִיךָ.

Inf. abs. The usual form is הַגְלֵה (comp. הַקְטֵל). Exception: in the verb רָבָה *to be numerous, much*, the inf. abs. is הַרְבָּה (3 x), because the form הַרְבֵּה has assumed the specialised adverbial meaning of *much, very much* (more precisely, *by making much*) (§ 102 *e*)(1).

On the Hishtafel form of the root חוה, cf. § *t*.

(1) We sometimes find the form of the inf. cst. הַגְלוֹת as inf. abs., § 123 *q*.

r **Comparison with the nominal forms** (cf. § *c*).

ל"ו forms in which ו appears: שַׁלְוָה *tranquility*, שָׁלֵו *tranquil* (comp. שָׁלַוְתִּי, § *a*); עֶרְוָה *nakedness* (more frequent than עֶרְיָה); עָנָו *humble*, עֲנָוָה *humility*; כְּסוּת *a covering*, § 88 M *j*.

ל"י forms in which י appears: אֲרִי and אַרְיֵה *lion*; שְׁבִי and שִׁבְיָה *captivity*; בְּלִי *naught* (negation); חִזָּיוֹן, cst. חֶזְיוֹן *vision*, from **ḥaz[a]yān* (*qatalān* form with or without syncope of the second *a*: cf. § 88 M *b*); בְּכִית *mourning*, § 88 M *i*.

Forms in which the י is latent: שָׂדֶה *field*, for שָׂדַי (poet.); קָצֶה *extremity* (alongside קֵץ *end* from √ קצץ).

Forms in which the י is dropped: syncopated forms—קָצָה *extremity*; תּוֹרָה *law* from *tawrayat* (√ *wry*, cf. Arm. אוֹרָיְתָא); חָזוֹן *vision*, § 88 M *b*; עָוֹן *iniquity*. Apocopated forms: רֵעַ *companion* (alongside רֵעֶה); מַעַל *above* (alongside מַעֲלֶה *ascent*); לְמַעַן *for the sake of* (alongside מַעֲנֶה *intention*); יַעַן *because*; בַּל poetic negative, לְבִלְתִּי negation of the inf. cst., § 93 *q*.

s **Irregular verbs** הָיָה *to be* and חָיָה *to live*.

These two verbs of analogous shape, which are 1st-guttural, ע"י and ל"ה verbs at the same time, are treated more or less identically.

They display numerous peculiarities:

1) The guttural has hardly ever any influence on the vowel of the preformative, e.g. יִהְיֶה, יִחְיֶה (contrast יֶחְסֶה, יֶהְגֶּה, § 68 *b*); נִהְיֶה; but

הֶחָיָה (comp. הֶגְלָה, § *q*).

2) The י of these two ע"י verbs is consonantal (cf. § 81 *a*, n.); it is not quiescent except in the apocopated forms יְהִי and יְחִי.

3) The apocopated forms יְהִי and יְחִי become in pause יֶהִי and יֶחִי (comp. בְּכִי, בֶּכִי *weeping*).

4) Instead of ְ we generally find ֱ, probably under the influence of the י which follows, e.g. הֱיֵה, הֱיִיתֶם, הֱיוֹת.

5) The prefixed particles have the vowel ְ probably under the influence of the י; the guttural takes simple shewa; e.g. לִהְיוֹת, בִּהְיוֹת, § 103 *b*, and (modelled on these forms) מִהְיוֹת, § 103 *d*, וִהְיִיתֶם, וִהְיוּ, § 104 *c*. Exception: one has וֶהְיֵה and וֶחְיֵה with ֶ probably under the influence of ֵ.

Observation. In the Qal perfect of the verb *to live*, one rarely finds (7 x) the form חָיָה(1); the usual form (24 x) is חַי, from the geminated root *ḥayay* (comp. the stative perfect תַּם)(2).

On the metheg of יִֽהְיֶה, וַֽיְהִי etc., cf. § 14 *c* 4.

(1) Except Gn 12.13 חָיְתָה, all in late books, which agrees with the pattern in MH: see G. Haneman in *In Memoriam Prof. E.Y. Kutscher* [Heb] (Ramat-Gan, 1972), pp. 1-3. Also according to G. Haneman (*ʿerḵe ha-milon he-ḥadaš l-sifrut ḥazal*, vol. 2 [Ramat-Gan, 1974], p. 25), חַי is characteristic of early BH, and חָיָה of late BH.

(2) In Syriac many forms of the verb *ḥyâ* are derived from a geminate root, e.g. fut. *neḥḥe*, Afel *'aḥḥi*.

Verb שחה: **Hištafʿel form** הִשְׁתַּחֲוָה *to bow down, to prostrate oneself, to worship.* *t*

The original root is חוו, hence ל"ו (cf. § *a*). The conjugation is *hištafʿel* (§ 59 *g*; not Hitpaʿlel). The form expresses the causative reflexive action *to bow down, to prostrate oneself*.

In the perfect the primitive form is *hištaḥwaw*. The ending has become *ay*, hence ה ָ, just as **galaw* has become **galay* > גָּלָה. The future **yištaḥwaw* has become **yištaḥway* > יִשְׁתַּחֲוֶה (3rd pl. יִשְׁתַּחֲווּ). The apocopated form is **yišta'ḥw*, in which the consonantal *w* becomes the vowel *u*: וַיִּשְׁתַּחוּ.

Observation. In 2Kg 5.18 הִשְׁתַּחֲוָיָתִי the inf. has been vocalised in Aramaic fashion (wrongly, actually, for with the suffixes the inf. takes the ending *ūt*, cf. H. Bauer—P. Leander, *Gramm. des Biblisch-Aramäischen* [Halle, 1927], p. 127; Dalman, *Gramm.* [§ 29 *g*], p. 279). After a scribe had wrongly spelled וי, this sequence was later vocalised mechanically in the Aramaic fashion. One must read (in the 3rd pers.) הִשְׁתַּחֲווֹתוֹ(1).

(1) Another Aramaic infinitive, § 80 *n*.

§ 80. ע"ו verbs
(Paradigm 13: קוּם *to arise*)

a The verbs generally called ע"ו (*Ayin Waw*) are those with two radical consonants between which, in the normal state of the root, there is a non-deletable vowel *u*, e.g. *qum* "to arise"(1). The root of these verbs does not appear in a single state, but in three states, and this, as it seems, goes back to the earliest stage of the language(2). The element intervening between the two consonants can be non-deletable *u* or *w*.

In the *normal* state of the root, the intervening element is the originally long, non-deletable vowel *u*: **yaqūm* > יָקוּם (indicative).

In the *reduced* state, the intervening element is the originally short, changeable vowel *u*: **yaqum* > יָקֹם (jussive).

In a third state, which one may call *consonantal*, the intervening element is the consonant *w*, e.g. קַוֵּם (§ *h*). In Hebrew, the consonantal state is rare in the verb; but it is frequent in nouns, e.g. עִוֵּר *blind*, מָ֫וֶת *death*, יוֹם (for **yawm*) *day* (§ *s*).

The state with the non-deletable *u* must be considered the *normal* state. In fact, it occurs, in the future, in the form of the indicative, which is the normal future, e.g. יָקוּם. Note that **yaqūm* has almost the same quantity as the future of the regular verb **yaqtul*: *ū* has a quantity well-nigh equivalent to the consonant *t* + *u*. That the state with this kind of *u* is the normal one is apparent also from the tendency of the language to retain this intervening vowel as much as possible, even at the expense of an adventitious linking vowel, e.g. in תְּקוּמֶ֫ינָה (§ *b*).

(1) Cf. Th. Nöldeke, *Syrische Grammatik* (Leipzig, 21898), § 177. Contrast the verbs with consonantal *w* as the second radical, such as רָוַח *to be spacious*; גָּוַע *to die*; צוה, צִוָּה *to order*; קוה, קִוָּה *to wait*; רוה *to soak*, רִוָּה, הִרְוָה in which the ו is treated as a strong consonant.

(2) Compare the analogous case of ע"ע verbs, § 82 *a*.

b **Qal.** The explanation of the forms will be given in the following order: future, imperative, infinitive, verbal adjective, perfect.

Future. There are active and stative forms distinguished by two different vowels (cf. § 41 *e*).

The active future is **yaqūm* > יָקוּם, with the *u* of the normal state(1).

The stative future is **yibāš*. The second vowel of the stative verbs was originally long, like the vowel ū of the action verbs. The form has normally become יֵבוֹשׁ with ọ (derived from ā)(2).

The **jussive** originally had the short vowel *u* (reduced state), e.g. **yaqum*, which usually became יָקֹם with ọ. In the inverted future this ọ becomes ǫ in post-stress position, e.g. וַיָּקָם; but in pause the vowel ọ is retained: וַיָּקֹם*.

In the fem.pl. we sometimes find a prolonged form תְּקוּמֶינָה. In order to conserve the characteristic *u* of the normal state in this form when it has a consonantal afformative, the language has resorted to a linking vowel ẹ, under the influence of ל"ה verbs (§ 79 *c*). Otherwise, in this position (i.e. closed stressed syllable), ọ must occur: תָּקֹמְנָה. In this form the normal state is sacrificed, resulting in the reduced state. Statistically this is the normal form: e.g. Ex 16.55: twice תָּשֹׁבְןָ 3rd pl.(without ה, § 44 *d*), then the long form תְּשֻׁבֶינָה 2nd pl. (cf. § *i*)(3).

(1) The defective spelling of the type יָקֻם is rather frequent (234 out of 927, i.e. 25%): AF, p. 203.

(2) יֵבוֹשׁ *he will be ashamed* is the sole certain example of stative future: וַיֵּאֹר 2Sm 2.32 is rather a Qal than a Nifal; יָבֹא is an active future (§ *r*).

(3) One is tempted to regard תְּהִימֶנָה Mi 2.12; תְּמוּטֶנָה Is 54.10; תְּמוּתֶנָה Ez 13.19; תְּעֻנֶּנָה 4.12, all spelled without Yod, as wrongly vocalised on the analogy of the ל"ה verbs, but among the latter one also occasionally finds וַתִּדְלֶנָה Ex. 2.16; וַתַּעֲלֶנָה Dn 8.8, etc.

Imperative: קוּם. The primitive form is **qum* with a short vowel (in Arabic *qum*; comp. Hifil impv. הָקֵם); therefore one would have expected קֹם* (cf. f.pl. קֹמְנָה). In fact the *u* is lengthened, perh. on the analogy of the forms קוּמִי and קוּמוּ where the *u*, in an open syllable, is etymologically long. c

The **inf. cst.** is normally קוּם(1) with the vowel of the future.

The **inf. abs.** is קוֹם with ọ on the analogy of קָטוֹל.

(1) It is according to the infinitive construct that many designate ע"ו and ע"י verbs, e.g. קוּם verb and דִּין verb. This usage is regrettable, because the infinitive (which, moreover, is as much nominal as verbal) does not always show the characteris-

tic element of the root. Thus the verb of the root שִׂים has the inf. שׂוּם (§ 81 *b*). It would be more appropriate to designate these verbs by the imperative, e.g. קוּם verb, שִׂים verb.

d The **verbal adjective** is קָם; it is used as a **participle**. In stative verbs, verbal adjectives **mit*, **buš*, which have become מֵת and בּוֹשׁ (written with ו), have been created on the analogy of the verbal adjectives *qatil* and *qatul* respectively, by assuming the characteristic vowels *i* and *u*. On the analogy of **mit* and **buš* there emerged in action verbs a form **qam* > קָם, corresponding to the adjective *qatal*, (e.g. חָכָם *wise*). This form has replaced the genuine Semitic participle preserved, for instance, in Arabic and Aramaic(1). The vowel ◌ָ is similar in nature to the vowels ◌ֵ and ◌ֹ of the symmetrical forms; they are retained, however, in the pl. cst.: מֵתֵי, קָמֵי.

The **passive participle** is קוּם with *u* on the analogy of קָטוּל. It is very rare (e.g. מוּל *circumcised*), most ע"ו (and ע"י) verbs possessing an intransitive meaning.

(1) Perhaps we are dealing with an ancient participle in בּוֹסִים Zech 10.5 with *ọ* coming from *ā*.

e **Perfect**. The stative perfects מֵת and בֹּשׁ (spelled without ו) are "conjugated" verbal adjectives מֵת and בּוֹשׁ, as in the regular verb. Furthermore, the perfect קָם is the "conjugated" verbal adjective קָם. Like the verbal adjective קָם, the perfect קָם is secondary. Here again the vowel ◌ָ cannot have been long in Proto-Hebrew. With a long ā one would expect קוֹם*, a form which probably existed once, for it is contained in Nifal נָקוֹם. If the ◌ָ were long, one would have in the inflection, e.g. קָמוֹתָ* with a linking vowel, as in Nifal and Hifil. Now one has קַמְתָּ with a short vowel, as one has מַתָּה from מֵת(1), but בֹּשְׁתָּ /bọštå/, cf. Ancient Canaanite *nu-uḫ-ti* "I was restful" (EA 147.56).

(1) The qameṣ in קָם may originally have been short; on a wide range of proposed explanations, see Berg., II, § 28 v, n. 3.

f **Nifal: Perfect** נָקוֹם. The primitive preformative **na* is preserved in open syllables (§ 51 *a*). The element קוֹם (from **qām*), which occurs in Arb. *'inqām*(*a*), is probably the old form of Qal perfect.

The **future** יָקוֹם seems to be formed on the model of the perfect, on the analogy of the Qal of פ"ן verbs, e.g. נָפַל, יִפֹּל, the perfect נָקוֹם resembling the Qal of פ"ן(1).

(1) Same explanation for ע"ע verbs, § 82 *c*.

g **Hifil**: in the **future** the primitive form is **yaqīm* > יָקִים. The long *ī* has spread to the strong verb: יַקְטִיל* (§ 54 *a*). In the **jussive**, **yaqim*, with short *i*, becomes יָקֵם; inverted future וַיָּקֶם. Likewise in the imperative we find הָקֵם (contrast קוּם with a long vowel, § *c*).

Perfect הֵקִים. The *ī* comes from the future (also in the strong verb). The vowel ֵ may be due to the analogy of הֵיטִיב where it is etymologically long (§ 76 *c*)(1).

Similarly the **participle** מֵקִים is due to the analogy of מֵיטִיב (cf. § 50 *f*).

The **Hofal** הוּקַם has *u* on the analogy of הוּשַׁב (§ 75 *a*).

(1) In the verb טוֹב the Hifil הֵטִיב is similar to Hifil הֵיטִיב of יטב except for the quantity of the vowel *ẹ* (cf. § 76 *c*). As with many suggestions invoking the principle of analogy, one might be tempted to ask why a particular form or class of forms, הֵיטִיב in this case, should trigger analogical changes or formations of the entire Hifil conjugation of ע"ו roots.

h In the *geminated* conjugation we find consonantal *w* in עִוֵּד *to entwine* Ps 119.61; elsewhere one has *y* instead of *w* as in Aramaic. The examples, rather rare and late, appear to be loans from Aramaic: קִיֵּם *to establish, to enact* (Arm. קַיֵּם) Esth 9.21 etc., Ru 4.7; Ps 119.28,106; חִיֵּב *to make debtor* Dn 1.10(1).

But the normal geminated form is *pọẹl*, more precisely *pọlẹl* in this case (§ 59 *a*), e.g. קוֹמֵם *to raise*; מוֹתֵת *to put to death, to finish off (a dying person)*; רוֹמֵם *to lift*. Passive: רוֹמַם *to be lifted*. Reflexive: הִתְבּשֵׁשׁ *to feel shame*, הִתְעוֹרֵר *to become agitated*(2).

(1) Several examples in Ben Sirah: 8.6, 30.12,23; cf. R. Smend, *Die Weisheit des Jesus Sirach* (Berlin, 1906), p. XLIV. This, קִיֵּם type, is the standard Piel/Pual/Hitpael formation in MH and Aramaic. On MH, see recently G. Haneman, *A Morphology of Mish. Heb.* [§ 73 *a*, n. 1], pp. 302f.

(2) Plene and defective spellings of these forms are evenly balanced (241: 206): AF, p. 196. See § 82 *e*.

Lambert's attempt to explain the origin of the long intensive conjugations on the basis of the phonetic law mentioned in § 26 *g* cannot be made to apply to the same conjugations common in geminate roots, unless one postulates mutual influence between the verb classes. Otherwise one would have to seek a separate explanation for geminate roots: see M. Lambert in *RÉJ* 24 (1892) 107, n. 2, cf. also J. Barth, "Die Pôlēl-

Conjugation und die Pôlāl Participien," *Semitic Studies in Memory of A. Kohut* (Berlin, 1897), pp. 83-93; J. Blau, *HUCA* 42 (1971) 148, n. 72.

i **Linking vowel.** In the Hifil future, as in the Qal future (§ *b*), one has in the fem.pl. the linking vowel ȩ so that the *i*, which is characteristic of the form, can be preserved: תְּקִימֶ֫ינָה. Otherwise, in this position (stressed closed syllable), the vowel ẹ would have to occur: תָּקֵ֫מְנָה, a form which is found, in fact, in Job 20.10 תָּשֵׁ֫בְנָה(1).

In the perfect, in the Nifal and Hifil conjugations, one also finds a linking vowel, ọ in this instance(2), which also makes it possible to maintain the vowel in the forms with a consonantal afformative. Unlike the ȩ of the future, this ọ is more likely to be traced to the early West-Semitic stative of the type *qatlāti*, which is akin to Akk. *parsāku*: *qatlāti* > *qatlōti*(3): e.g. הֲקִימ֫וֹתִי, נְקוּמוֹתֶם. In the Hifil, the vowel is sometimes given up and the form becomes, e.g. הֵקַ֫מְתִּי (comp. הִקְטַ֫לְתִּי): הֲנַ֫פְתָּ Ex 20.25 (but הֲנִיפ֫וֹתִי Job 31.21)(cf. § *m*).

Compare the linking vowel in ע"ע verbs, § 82 *f*.

(1) Note also Lv 7.30 תְּבִיאֶ֫ינָה and Mi 2.12 תְּהִימֶ֫נָה. Cf. *b* above.

(2) Spelled defectively more often than not (186: 92): AF, p. 192.

(3) Cf. P. Joüon, *MUSJ* 5 (1911) 356-62; Berg., II, 27 s; Blau, *Heb. Phonology and Morphology*, p. 191. For examples such as *al-ka-ti* "I went" in Amarna Canaanite, see A.F. Rainey, *UF* 5 (1973) 237, S. Izre'el, *IOS* 8 (1978) 31 and Sivan, p. 144. Influence from Lamed-Waw verbs is intrinsically improbable.

The short pattern without *o* seems to be the norm in MH: G. Haneman, op, cit. [§ 73*a*, n. 1], p. 290. So in ע"ע verbs: id., p. 322.

j **Stress.** The root syllable, on account of its importance, generally carries the stress, e.g. יָק֫וּמוּ, תָּק֫וּמִי. In the perfect we find קָ֫מָה (but קָמָ֫ה in the fem. ptc.) and generally קָ֫מוּ (contr. גָּל֫וּ). Sometimes we find קָמ֫וּ, e.g. Is 28.7 פָּק֫וּ (following forms of the גָּל֫וּ type); especially before a guttural ע or א, e.g. Ps 131.1 (hiatus, § 33)(1). In the inverted perfect both וְקָ֫מָה and וְקָ֫מוּ can occur.

In the inverted perfect we usually find וַהֲקִימוֹתִ֫י, וְקַמְתִּ֫י, וְקַמְתָּ֫.

The imperative ק֫וּמָה becomes קוּמָ֫ה before a guttural (§ 33).

(1) For further details, see Berg., II, § 28 e.

k **Dẹtailed observations on various conjugations**

Qal. Instead of קָם one very occasionally finds the orthography קָאם, e.g. participle (verbal adjective) לָאט *hidden* Jdg 4.21; רָאשׁ *poor* 2Sm

12.1,4. This א of the participle may be due to Aramaic, but in the perfect קָאם Ho 10.14 (§ 7 *b*) it is inexplicable. In שָׁאטִים Ez 28.24,26, שָׁאטוֹת 16.57 the vocalisers no doubt saw participles of שׁוּט *to despise*, but it probably ought to be vocalised שֹׁאֲטִים from שׁאט *to attack, harass.*

In the **future** we find the vowel ọ for *u* in the isolated form יָדוֹן Gn 6.3†(1). In the verb חוּס *to be deeply moved, to have pity*, one does not find the vowel *u* except in Jer 21.7 לֹא־יָחוּס and Is 13.18 לֹא־תָחוּס עֵינָם (both with the force of the indicative). Elsewhere one always finds לֹא תָחוֹס whether in a prohibition (where the meaning may have favoured the vowel ọ of the jussive): Dt 7.16; 13.9; 19.13,21; 25.12, or even with a purely indicative force, Ez 5.11; 7.4,9; 8.18; 9.10†(2).

The jussive יָקֻם Gn 27.31, instead of יָקֹם, is odd or faulty; likewise תָּמֻשׁ Jdg 6.18; יָסֻר Pr 9.4,16. (Comp. וָאָקֻם, § 47 *d*).

The etymologically short unstressed ָ of the inverted future becomes ַ before a guttural or ר, e.g. וַיָּנַח, וַיָּנַע(3); וַיָּסַר *and he turned aside* (a form identical with that of the Hifil, § *n*); וַיָּצַר *he laid siege* (cf. § 23 *b*). But one finds וַיָּגָר from I גּוּר *to sojourn* and from II גּוּר *to dread*. וַיָּעַף occurs 4 times (but always in a suspect context) Jdg 4.21; 1Sm 14.28,31; 2Sm 21.15; it is generally admitted that the intended form was וַיִּעַף for וַיִּיעַף *and he was exhausted* (for another explanation, see König, *Wörterbuch*, s.v. עיף).

In the 1st pers. the usual form is וָאָקֻם, i.e. without mater lectionis (§ 47 *d*).

In the **imperative** we find ọ for *u* in דּוֹשִׁי Mi 4.13 (why?).

In the **inf. cst.** we sometimes find ọ for *u*: בְּמוֹט Ps 38.17; 46.3 (in juncture); כְּנוֹחַ Nu 11.25; Josh 3.13 (in juncture), but לָנוּחַ 2Sm 21.10; כְּנוֹעַ Is 7.2 (in juncture) but לָנוּעַ (always so, 4 x); לָעוֹז Is 30.2 (perh. assonance with מָעוֹז); וּבְרוֹמָם Ez 10.17 (perh. for euphony's sake); שֹׁב Josh 2.16 (in juncture).

In contrast, the inf. cst. with ọ is normal in stative verbs (the future of which shows ọ stemming from ā): טוֹב, בּוֹשׁ (§ *q*).

(1) Possibly "he will rule, wield power"; cf. Akk. *danānu* "to be / become strong."

(2) Alongside חוּס there may have existed a root חסס corresponding to Arb. *ḥassa*, "to feel," etc., the future of which would be יָחֹס*. This future may sometimes have replaced the future יָחוּס from חוּס. We have יָחֹס in Ps 72.13 *he will have mercy* (the

vocalisation with *ọ* is probably due to defective spelling).
(3) Contrast אַל־יָנַע 2Kg 23.18 (§ 47 *a*, n.).

l **Nifal: perfect.** The *ọ* of נָקוֹם becomes *u* when it is deprived of the principal or secondary stress: thus we find נָקוֹמָה, נְקֹמוֹתֶם, but נְקוּמוֹתִי (§ 29 *b*), e.g. נְסוּגֹתִי *I have moved back, drawn back* Is 50.5.

The **participle** נָבוֹךְ* has the pl. נְבֻכִים Ex 14.3†, but נָכוֹן, נְכֹנִים.

m **Hifil: perfect.** The originally long *i* tends to be shortened to *ẹ* in anteprestress position, namely: in the 2nd pers. pl., with certain suffixes, and in the inverted perfect; but there is no hard and fast rule.

In the 2nd pers. m.pl., one finds 5 forms with *i* and 2 forms with *ẹ*, e.g. הֲפִיצוֹתֶם (2 x), הֲשֵׁבוֹתֶם (2 x); הֲקֵמֹתוֹ Ps 89.44; וַהֲקֵמֹתָ Ex 26.30; Dt 27.2†, but וַהֲקִימוֹתִי always (22 x); וַהֲשֵׁבֹתָ Dt 4.39; 30.1†, but וַהֲשִׁיבֹתִי always (10 x); וַהֲרֵמֹתָ Nu 31.28†, but וַהֲפִיצוֹתִי always (4 x). One ought to note the difference in treatment between the 1st and 2nd persons (a case of asymmetry), but Ps 89.43 הֲרִימוֹתָ (Sec. αρημωθ) and 89.44 Sec. ακιμωθω (הֲקִימֹתוֹ).

Vowel of ה. In anteprestress position the ֲ is not retained; it sometimes becomes shortened to ֱ, e.g. הֱשִׁיבוּ 1Kg 13.20,23,26†; הֱשִׁיבוֹתָ Ps 85.4; but most often we find ֲ, e.g. הֲקִימֹתִי הֲרִימֹתִי, הֲרִימֹתָ. In the 3rd position before the stress we always find ֲ, e.g. וַהֲשֵׁבֹתָ (cf. above).

Before a guttural the ֲ is lengthened to ָ (compare forms such as הַאֵלֵךְ *shall I go?* with the interrogative הֲ, § 102 *n*). The sole examples are הַעִידֹתִי *I have witnessed* Dt 4.26; 8.19; 30.19; Jer 11.7; 42.19; הַעִירוֹתִי *I have stirred up* Is 41.25; הַעִירֹתִהוּ 45.13 (cf. the same phenomenon in ע"ע verbs, § 82 *n*).

Forms **without a linking vowel** (cf. § *i*). Without a linking vowel, the form is normally הֵקַמְתִּי with ֵ, e.g. וְהֵטַלְתִּי Jer 16.13; הֵכַנּוּ 2Ch 29.19 (here by haplography for הֲכִינֹנוּ 1Ch 29.16), הֵמַתָּה (haplography for הֲמִיתוֹתָה*, cf. Brock., *GvG* I, p. 265). The *ạ* can be weakened to *i* when it loses the stress (§ 29 *g*), e.g. וַהֲמִתִּיהָ, הֲמִתֶּם etc., but וְהֵמַתָּה, וְהֵמַתִּי(1).

(1) הֵסַתָּה *she has incited* 1Kg 21.25 is inadvertently vocalised as 2nd person; vocalise הֵסַתָּה. This error can be explained in terms of the tendency of the Naqdanim to give the consonant groups the most obvious vocalisation.

n **Future.** The ֶ of the inverted future וַיָּקֶם becomes ָ before a guttural or ר, e.g. וַיָּ֫רַח, וַיָּ֫סַר *and he removed, he took away*, a form identical with that of Qal, § *k* (cf. § 23 *b*); after a guttural, וַיָּ֫עַד.

With אַל the stress recedes, e.g. אַל־תָּ֫שֶׁב 1Kg 2.20 (§ 47 *a*, n.).

In the 1st pers. the usual form is וָאָקָם, without mater lectionis (§ 47 *d*); one also finds, e.g. וָאָשִׁיב Ne 2.20, and more rarely, e.g. וָאָשֵׁב Josh 14.7.

In the **infinitive cst.** we find the Aramaic form הֲקָמָה (cf. Dn 5.20 הֲזָדָה *to become proud*) in הֲנָפָה Is 30.28 (cf. § 88 L *b*)(1).

As **inf. abs.** one finds הָכִין Ez 7.14 (if the text is correct), and הָכֵן Josh 3.17 (but // הָכִין ib. 4.3).

Contamination of ע"ו by ע"ע. These two verb classes share, in the normal state of the root, a common feature, namely the length of an element. In ע"ו there is an originally long vowel, whilst in ע"ע there is a long consonant (generally the 2nd, sometimes the 1st in Aramaising forms, § 82 *h*). The forms in the reduced state are often similar: e.g. Qal, jussive future יָקֹם and fut. יָסֹב; Hifil, jussive fut. יָקֵם and fut. יָסֵב; Hofal הוּקַם and הוּסַב. Because of these multiple resemblances, the two verb classes contaminate each other. Examples of contamination of ע"ו verbs by ע"ע verbs: בַּז Zech 4.10 (for בָּז); נָקֹ֫טּוּ Ez 6.9 (for נָקֹטוּ)(2); all the forms of Nifal of רוּם appear to stem from a root רמם, e.g. יֵרֹ֫מּוּ Ez 10.17. (For the contamination of ע"ע by ע"ו verbs, cf. § 82 *o*). *o*

(1) Another Aramaic infinitive, § 79 *t*.

(2) Job 10.1 נָקְטָה looks like a Qal of פ"ן which has been built on a Nifal of ע"ע (נָקַט*, נָקֹ֫טָּה*), displacing the normal Nifal נָקוֹט from קוט *to detest intensely*. A Qal נָקַט may have actually existed; comp. Jewish Aramaic קְנַט *to detest*.

Forms with geminated 1st radical. The existence of numerous forms of ע"ו with a geminated first radical is probably due to the influence of the Aramaising forms of the ע"ע roots, although one finds this gemination in ע"ו roots even in some tenses (Nifal perf., ptc.; Hifil pf., impv.) where it never exists in ע"ע roots. Therefore one can also call these forms *Aramaising*, though the influence is only indirect. *p*

The most important group of these forms with the geminated 1st radical occurs in the Hifil of the verb נוּחַ *to rest*. In this verb there are two Hifil's with different meanings. The 1st Hifil, הֵנִ֫יחַ, which is regular, means: 1) *to set sth down*; 2) *to give rest to* (לְ). The 2nd, הִנִּ֫יחַ, with gemination, means: 1) *to put, to place* (like נָתַן, with which it shares most meanings); 2) *to leave there*; 3) *to leave sbd in peace, to give a free hand*. Forms of the 2nd Hifil are: pf. הִנִּיחַ; fut. יַנִּיחַ, וַיַּנַּח; impv. הַנַּח, הַנִּיחוּ; inf. הַנִּיחַ; ptc. מַנִּיחַ (with the 1st vowel of the future; contr. מֵנִיחַ). In the perfect there is no linking vowel, e.g., הִנַּחְתִּי (comp. הֲנִיחוֹתִי). Hofal: הֻנַּח, מֻנָּח.

In the Hifil the verb סוּת (or סִית?) has forms with gemination side by side with standard forms: הֵסִית or הִסִּית *to incite, to provoke*; יָסִית or יַסִּית; מַסִּית.

The verb סוּג in the Hifil only has forms with gemination: יַסִּיג *to move sth back* or *push back*, מַסִּיג; Hofal הֻסַּג.

In these last two verbs the sibilant may have contributed to the lengthening as in the פ״צ verbs (§ 77 *a*), e.g. הִצִּיג, יַצִּיג. In הִנִּיחַ the differentiation of the form is perh. due to the difference in meaning. In the future יַנִּיחַ the form may have been influenced by the analogous יִתֵּן *he will put, he will place*.

In **Nifal** one finds the form נִקּוֹם (for נָקוֹם) with gemination (which perh. stems from the future יִקּוֹם) in נִמּוֹל *he was circumcised*; comp. נֵעוֹר Zech 2.17 *to wake up* (with a guttural R1). This type of Nifal has developed in MH, e.g. נִדּוֹן *he was judged*(1).

(1) In SH the doubling of the first radical is not confined to this class of verbs: Ben-Ḥayyim, *LOT*, vol. 5, p. 84 and Macuch, *Gram.*, p. 289.

q **Stative verbs.** The only stative verb with ֵ is מוּת *to die*, which, furthermore, does not have the stative form except in the verbal adjective and the participle מֵת. In the future we find the action verb form (cf. § 41 *b*) יָמוּת, hence the impv. and inf. cst. מוּת. On הֲמִתָּה etc., cf. § *m*. Some stative verbs with ָ are:

Inf. בּוֹשׁ *to feel shame*, pf. בֹּשׁ (for *buš*), verbal adjective בּוֹשׁ, fut. יֵבוֹשׁ (for *yibāš*). Alongside the regular Hifil הֵבִישׁ *to make feel shame*, there exists a metaplastic Hifil הוֹבִישׁ *to feel shame* (like Qal) similar to the Hifil הוֹבִישׁ *he dried* from יָבֵשׁ, § 76 *d*.

Inf. אוֹר* *to be light, to shine*, pf. אוֹר; fut. יֵאוֹר (Qal rather than Nifal), but תָּאֹרְנָה 1Sm 14.27; verbal adjective אוֹר.

Inf. טוֹב *to be good*, pf. טוֹב (and only 3rd pl. טֹבוּ); verbal adjective טוֹב in 1Sm 2.26 הֹלֵךְ וְגָדֵל וָטוֹב; inf. abs. טוֹב in Jdg 11.25 הֲטוֹב טוֹב אַתָּה ... אִם־נִלְחֹם נִלְחַם בָּם. The future יִיטַב belongs to the associated root יטב (§ 76 *d*).

Irregular verb בֹא, בוֹא *to enter, to come*. This is an action verb, because 1) the perfect is בָא with the vowel typical of action verbs; if it were stative we would find בֵא* (comp. מָלֵא) or בֹא*; 2) the future is יָבֹא (15 x יָבוֹא)(1), with the 1st vowel *a* of action verbs, § 41 *e*; the stative form would be יֵבוֹא* (comp. יֵבוֹשׁ for *yibāš*); 3) in Arabic the verb *bā'a* has the future with *u* of action verbs, and this despite the guttural that follows. Therefore in יָבֹא the ◌ָ does not derive from the primitive *a* of stative verbs, but from the *u* of action verbs(2). Impv. and inf. cst. also have ◌ֹ: בֹא, בוֹא(3). r

For the forms of the inverted perfect, cf. § 43 *b*, and for those of the inverted future, § 47 *b*.

Linking vowel. In the Qal future we find, very rarely, תְּבוֹאֶינָה; the usual form is תָּבֹאנָה. In the Hifil future one finds only תְּבִיאֶינָה. In the Hifil perfect the forms with a linking vowel are far less numerous than the others, e.g. הֲבִיאוֹתֶם (1 x), and הֲבֵאתֶם (10 x); the forms הֲבִיאוֹתָ and הֲבִיאוֹתִי do not occur except before suffixes.

The vowel of the ה (cf. § *m*). In anteprestress positions the ◌ֵ is maintained in the forms with no suffix, e.g. וְהֵבֵאתָ; in the forms with a suffix in the 3rd pers. sg. it is shortened to ◌ֱ, e.g. הֱבִיאַנִי; everywhere else to ◌ֲ, e.g. הֲבִיאֹתָנוּ, הֲבֵאתָנוּ.

On the anomalous forms of the imperative הָבִיא and of the inverted future וַיָּבִיא, cf. § 78 *i*.

One finds the inf. לָבִיא with syncope of the ה (cf. § 54 *b*) in Jer 39.7; 2Ch 31.10.

(1) If one counts all forms (not just 3m.sg.), the proportion is: plene 315 x and defective 805 x: AF, p. 195.

(2) The vowel of יָבוֹא is perh. due to the analogy of the jussive-imperative with *o*: see Joüon, in *Bib* 1 (1920) 357-59.

(3) The plene and defective spellings are evenly balanced: 264 vs. 275. See AF, p. 196.

Comparison with the nominal forms (cf. §§ *a-b*) s

Forms with ו: עִוֵּר *blind*, מָוֶת *death*, יוֹם (for **yawm*) *day*; מָנוֹחַ and מְנוּחָה (§ 29 *b*) *rest*; תְּעוּדָה *testimony* (from הֵעִיד *to testify*).

Forms without ו. Like קָם: זָר *foreigner*, זָרָה *prostitute*, עָב(1) *cloud*.

Like מֵת: גֵּר *foreigner, immigrant*, כֵּן (adj.) *honest*, נֵר *lamp*, עֵד *witness*, f. עֵדָה *witness, testimony*(2).

Words of *qul* type, § 88 B *f*: טוּב *the good*, צוּר *rock*.

(1) Cst. st. עַב rather than עָב (cf. König, 2, p. 75). No other example of קָם type in the cst. st.

(2) Contrast עֵדָה *assembly* from יָעַד, § 75 *m*, 97 E *b*.

§ 81. ע"י verbs
(Paradigm 14: דִּין *to judge*)

a What has been said for the explanation of ע"ו verbs holds for ע"י verbs, the verbs with two radical consonants between which, in the normal state of the root, there is an originally long vowel *ī*, e.g. *dīn* "to judge"(1). There are far fewer ע"י verbs than ע"ו verbs. One can enumerate fifteen of them, which is, actually, more than generally admitted by lexicographers, who tend to list as ע"ו those roots on which there is some doubt, or even complete ignorance, because of lack of sufficient indices. There are insufficient indices for the purpose of determining the root of, e.g. אָץ *to urge*, הֵמִיר *to exchange*, הֵנִיף *to wave*, הֵסִית *to incite*, הֵרִיעַ *to shout*. In view of the analogy of the Arabic, the root of כָּל *to measure* should rather be כִּיל, but comparison with cognate languages is not always conclusive. Thus, the Hebrew and Syriac words for *to be narrow* (צוק and *'āq* respectively) have *w*, whereas Arabic *ḍāq* has *y*. In certain cases the root ע"ו and the root ע"י seem to have coexisted, e.g. דוּשׁ and דִּישׁ *to tread*, רוּח and רִיח *to breathe*(2). It is especially in the strictly verbal forms of the future and the imperative that the root becomes manifest. Thus one must postulate the roots שִׂים(3), לִין and שִׂישׂ, despite the anomalous infinitives with *u* (§ *b*): שׂוּם *to put*, לוּן *to spend the night*, שׂוּשׂ *to rejoice* (cf. § 80 *c*, n.), and despite some isolated and perh. faulty forms. It seems necessary to postulate the roots רִיק *to be empty*, רִישׁ *to be indigent*, and זִיד *to be proud* (cf. adj. זֵידוֹן = *zayd* + *ōn*).

(1) Contrast these with verbs with consonantal *y* such as איב (pf. אָיַבְתִּי Ex 23.22, ptc. אֹיֵב *enemy*), עָיֵף*(?) *to be tired*, הָיָה, and חָיָה, § 79 *s*.

(2) Moreover, since the two vocalic consonants *w* and *y* are analogous, the transition from the one to the other is easy: thus in the Piel of ע"ו we have the קִיֵּם rather than the קוֹמֵם type (§ 80 *h*).

(3) In Syriac this verb has *y* as its second radical: pf. *sâm*, fut. *nsim*.

b **Qal: future:** יָדִין with the normal state **dīn*; jussive יָדֵן with the reduced state **din*. These forms are similar to the Hifil of both ע"י and ע"ו roots.

The **imperative** דִּין has, anomalously, the etymologically long vowel (like קוּם, § 80 *c*).

The **infinitive cst.** usually takes the vowel of the future, e.g. דִּין, שִׂית *to place*. In three verbs the infinitive has *u*(1): שׂוּם *to put* (35 x); לוּן *to spend the night* (6 x; 1 x לִין in Gn 24.23 לָנוּ לָלִין, perh. in order to avoid a second vowel sequence *å* - *u*); שׂוּשׂ *to rejoice* (1 x).

The **passive participle** is extremely rare: שִׂים(2), שׂוּם (? cf. 2Sm 13.32).

The **verbal adjective**, with the value of a **participle**, is as in ע"ו verbs, e.g. דָּן (like קָם); also לָן *spending the night*, Ne 13.21 is modelled on the מֵת type (comp. the adjectives זֵד *proud* and לֵץ *insolent*).

The normal perfect דָּן is formed from the verbal adjective as in ע"ו verbs (§ 80 *e*).

(1) Probably under the influence of some nominal form with *u*; cf. P. Joüon in *Bib* 1 (1920) 370.

(2) שִׂים as passive infinitive, § 58 *c*.

The **Nifal** is as in ע"ו verbs (§ 80 *f*), e.g. נָדוֹן, נָבוֹן. *c*

The **Hifil** is as in ע"ו verbs (§ 80 *g*), e.g. הֵבִין.

N.B. In these verbs the Hifil is sometimes secondary or only apparent (**pseudo-Hifil**, § 54 *f*), e.g. הֵקִיא *to vomit* (with the sense of Qal). Since the Qal future, e.g. יָקִיא, has the appearance of, and considered to be a Hifil, a secondary perfect הֵקִיא has been formed from this future. Other probable examples: הֵקִיץ (§ 76 *d*), הֵשִׂים, הֵרִיב.

Irregular verb בִּין. For the meaning *to comprehend* the usual and old form is הֵבִין; hence the future יָבִין is a Hifil. From this future, which has the appearance of a Qal, a secondary perfect בָּן *to comprehend* has been created, though examples of it are rather rare. Apart from this Qal perfect there is another even more secondary form בִּין (only 2 x: Dn 9.2; 10.1). It is a hybrid form modelled on the perfect הֵבִין, and inflected accordingly: Dn 9.2 בִּינֹתִי (cf. Job 33.13 רִיבוֹתָ). *d*

The Hifil הֵבִין, in addition to the meaning *to comprehend* (originally *to make a distinction, to distinguish*), has the meaning *to make understand*. The creation of these secondary perfects, בָּן and בִּין, may be due to the desire to distinguish the two meanings by reserving the sense *to make understand* for הֵבִין(1).

The forms בּוֹנֵן and הִתְבּוֹנֵן are as in ע"ו verbs, § 80 *h*.

(1) Cf. P. Joüon in *Bib* 1 (1920) 356f.

e **Observations on certain forms.** (Most of the peculiarities or anomalies occur also in ע"ו verbs).

Perfect. In לָנֶה for לָנָה Zech 5.4 there is a nsiga: the ָ has been changed to ֶ (comp. לָמֶה alongside לָמָה, § 37 d).

Future. Jussive: e.g. וַיָּשֶׂם, but וַתָּשַׁר before ר, Jdg 5.1; with אַל: אַל־תָּשֶׁת Ex 23.1; אַל־תָּשֶׂם 1Sm 9.20 (§ 47 a, n.). Both Gn 24.33Q וַיּוּשַׂם and 50.26 וַיִּישֶׂם can, from the context, be construed as passive Qal(1).

Inf. absolute. Instead of the proper form with *ọ*, e.g. רֹב Jdg 11.25, one finds the inf. cst. functioning as inf. abs. רִיב יָרִיב Jer 50.34; בִּין תָּבִין. Pr 23.1 for the sake of assonance (cp. § 51 *b* and § 123 *q*).

(1) Cf. Blau, *Heb. Phonology and Morphology*, p. 191.

f **Comparison with nominal forms**

Forms with י: דִּין *judgement*, רִיב *dispute, litigation*, שִׁיר *song*; בִּינָה *understanding*, § 88 B e.

Forms without י: שָׁר *singer*; זֵד *proud*, לֵץ *insolent*; מָדוֹן *quarrel* (√ דִּין); שָׂשׂוֹן *joy* (*sas* + afformative **ān*; this form copies *qatalān* like the verbal adjectives קָם and דָּן copying *qatal*); likewise זָדוֹן *pride*, לָצוֹן *insolence* (cf. § 88 M *b*).

§ 82. ע"ע verbs.

(Paradigm 15: סָבַב *to surround*).

a ע"ע verbs(1) or **geminate** verbs are verbs with two root consonants the second of which, in the normal state of the root, e.g. in the pl. impv. סֹבּוּ, is etymologically long. (See the similar definition of ע"ו and ע"י verbs, § 80 *a* and 81 *a* respectively). The root of these verbs does not present itself in a single state, but in three, and apparently from the earliest period at that(2). The second consonant of the root may be long, short or repeated.

In the *normal* state of the root, the second consonant is long: *s-bb*;

in the *reduced* state it is short: *s-b*; in a third state, which may be called *dissociated*(3), it is repeated: *s-b-b*.

The *s-bb* type state, with a long second consonant, must be regarded as the *normal* state. Indeed this long consonant is characteristic of this class of verbs, as for instance, a long second consonant is characteristic of the Piel form קִטֵּל. That the *s-bb* type state is the normal one is also apparent from the fact that the language tends to retain it whenever possible, even adding a linking vowel, e.g. in סַבּוֹתָ, תְּסֻבֶּינָה (§ *f*).

On the whole the *normal* state is found whenever phonetically possible, i.e. when followed by a vowel, e.g. in impv. סֹבּוּ, fut. יָסֹבּוּ; 3rd pers. f. and pl. of stative pf. תַּמָּה, תַּמּוּ. Exception: in the 3rd pers. f. and pl. of the active pf. the dissociated state is used, e.g. סָבֲבָה(4), סָבֲבוּ, probably to distinguish these from the stative verbs. In the 3rd pers. m. sg. the dissociated state סָבַב is used with active verbs, but the reduced state תַּם (< **tamma* < **tamima*; cf. § 88 B *g*, n.) is used with the stative verbs.

The *reduced* state is found when no vowel follows, e.g. יָסֹב, סֹב. The consonant, though in fact short, has a certain tendency towards lengthening (doubling).

The *dissociated* state is hardly ever found except for reasons of necessity or of usefulness. The repetition of the consonant is necessary, for instance, for forming the participles סֹבֵב, סָבוּב and the inf. abs. סָבוֹב; it is useful in that it allows the active perfect סָבַב to be distinguished from the stative perfect תַּם. Otherwise the dissociated state is quite rare (§ *k*).

(1) The symbol ע"ע means that the 2nd radical is repeated, § 40 *c*.

(2) Compare the analogous case of ע"ו verbs § 80 *a*.

(3) *dissociated*: this metaphorical term indicates that the normal long consonant *bb* seems to be dissociated into two separate elements *b-b*. We could also use the, albeit less accurate, term, *dilated* or *extended*. Compare the dissociation, again in a somewhat different sense, of the long consonant in, for example, Arm. **yidda'* > יִנְדַּע *he will know*: the phenomenon may be better called degemination.

(4) ֲ instead of ָ because of the repetition of the consonant, § 9 *c*, though this does not actually occur in this particular verb in the Leningrad Codex. As far as the perfect 3rd f.sg. and pl. are concerned, the ḥaṭef pataḥ occurs mostly with linguals: גָּלֲלוּ, דָּלֲלוּ, צָלֲלוּ, צָרֲרוּ, but כָּלְלוּ and שָׁלְלוּ. Cp. also שָׁנְנוּ Ps 64.4 and שָׁנֲנוּ Ps 140.4.

Qal: Perfect. Generally speaking, verbs of action occur in the dis- b sociated state סָבַב (from *sabab[a]) and stative verbs in the reduced state תַּם (from *tamim[a]); for exceptions, see § k.

Future. Active verbs and stative verbs differ not only in their second vowel but also in the first (cf. § 41 *e*): יָסֹב(1), יֵקַל(2). (Cf. יָרֹעַ *he will break* and יֵרַע *he will be bad*).

With Waw inversive we have, on the one hand, וַיָּסָב, but, on the other hand, וַיֵּקַל (mil'ra; comp. וַיִּירַשׁ) and וַיֵּצֶר *and it was narrow* (for the ṣeré, cp. וַיֹּאמֶר < יֹאמַר). In pause we have וַיָּסֹב.

The **imperative** סֹב has the vowel of the future.

The **inf. cst.** is usually in the reduced state סֹב, sometimes in the dissociated state סְבֹב (§ k). The vowel ọ, as in the other classes of verbs (§ 49 *c*), has affected the stative verbs, e.g. תֹּם, חֹם, רֹב (cf. § *l*).

The **inf. abs.** is in the dissociated state סָבוֹב; likewise the participles סֹבֵב and סָבוּב.

The **verbal adj.** is found in רָב 1Sm 14.19; 2Sm 15.12; חַת* or חָת* 1Sm 2.4; Jer 46.5(3).

(1) A likely example of active future with *i* as 2nd vowel is יָגֵן *he will cover* (cf. § 41 *a*). According to Barth, there are more, e.g. יָגֵל.

(2) With the Aramaising doubling **yiqal* becomes יִקַּל, e.g. יִדַּל.

(3) These must not be confused with pausal forms such as וָחָי; for details see E.J. Revell, *HAR* 5 (1981) 97-99.

c **Nifal: Perfect** נָסַב. The original preformative **na* is retained in an open syllable (§ 51 *a*). The future יִסַּב seems to have been formed on the analogy of the Qal of פ"ן verbs (e.g. נָגַשׁ*, יִגַּשׁ), the perfect נָסַב being similar to the Qal of a פ"ן. verb(1). Because of this similarity, the language has gone so far as to create Nifal perfects such as נָמֵס *it melted*, which look like the stative Qal of פ"ן verbs; hence fut. יִמַּס (similar to יִגַּשׁ) with the vowel *a* of the stative(2); cf. § *m*. The future in ọ יִסֹּב is, or could be, Nifal also, according to certain grammarians; cf. § *h* and *m*, n. Naturally in the participle the same form is found: נָמֵס, נָקֵל (fem. נְקַלָּה).

Inf. cst. הִסֵּב, הִמֵּס (ִ‑ֵ on the analogy of הִקָּטֵל).

(1) Same explanation for ע"ו verbs, § 80 *f*.

(2) The יִסֹּב and יִסַּב forms may also be Aramaising Qal futures (§ *h*); it is according to the meaning that a particular form may be said to be Qal or Nifal.

Hifil: Future יָסֵב, the originally short vowel *i* having become ֵ. d
With Waw inversive: וַיָּ֫סֶב.

Perfect. The ֵ of the future has spread to the perfect הֵסֵב: הֵחֵל *he began*, הֵפֵר *he broke* (in pause הֵפַר, § 32 *c*). But with stative verbs ַ is usually found: הֵדַק(1), הֵמַר, הֵצַר, הֵקַל, הֵרַךְ(2).

The vowel ֵ of the ה was probably used on the analogy of הֵקִים, which itself emerged on the analogy of הֵיטִיב (where *ẹ* from *ay* is long, § 80 *g*). The evolution of הֵקִים would then be symmetrical with that of the participle מֵסֵב (with ֵ as its first vowel, in spite of the future יָסֵב (§ 50 *f*), which emerged on the analogy of מֵקִים, which itself emerged on the analogy of מֵיטִיב(3).

In the **imperative**, in the **inf. cst.**, and in the **inf. abs.** we find הָסֵב.

Observation: we can see that in ע"ע verbs, because of the tendency of the final consonant towards doubling, the etymologically long vowel *ī* is never found.

The **Hofal** הוּסַב has an etymologically long *ū* on the analogy of הוּשַׁב (§ 75 *a*).

(1) Alongside the stative verb pf. דַּק, unattested fut. יֵדַק*, there is an active unattested pf. דָּקַק*, fut. יָדֹק.

(2) The presence of this *a* in the Hifil of stative verbs can be explained thus. For the adjective (also serving as verbal adjective) we have דַּק, מַר, etc. The same form is also that of the stative perfect. Finally in the stative future we again find the vowel *a*, e.g. יֵקַל. The *a* of Hifil could be due to the analogy of these forms in *a*. Thus, one must have said הֵמַר *he has caused to be bitter* on the analogy of מַר *bitter, it is bitter*, and with יֵמַר *it will be bitter* (cf. P. Joüon in *Bib* 1 [1920] 354). In some cases the presence of *a* may have been influenced by the following consonant. In contrast, E.J. Revell understands the preceding consonant to condition the choice of the vowel: *JNES* 44 (1985) 322f.

(3) It is generally claimed that הֵ is due to the analogy of הִ in הִקְטִיל. But, then, in Nifal we should find נֵסַב* on the analogy of נִקְטַל.

In the Piel conjugation we find either the *qittẹl* form סִבֵּב, or the *pọẹl* form סוֹבֵב—here strictly speaking a *pọ‘ẹ‘* form (§ 59 *a*). Passive: סוֹבַב. Reflexive: הִסְתּוֹבֵב. e

Examples of *sovev* and *histovev* types would be far more frequent than the *sibbev* type if one were to take into account the possibility of repointing (Berg., II, p. 140 [§ 27 *r*]). Note, in this connection, that in

ע"ו (§ 80 *h*) and ע"י (§ 81 *d*) roots the former predominates, and that contamination or interaction between these two root-patterns and the geminate pattern are well documented (§ 80 *o*, 82 *o*)(1).

(1) For a recent discussion on the subject, see J. Blau in *HUCA* 42 (1971) 147-51. Note, however, that, in MH, acc. to Haneman, op. cit. [§ 73*a*, n. 1], pp. 302, ·327, no single instance of the long Piel is found in the entire Mishnah in Codex Parma.

f **The linking vowel.** In the future and in the perfect, in order to preserve the normal state of the root in the forms with a consonantal afformative, a linking vowel is used (likewise with ע"ו verbs, § 80 *b*, *i*).

In the future we find the vowel ẹ, which comes from the ל"ה verbs (§ 79 *c*): תְּסֻבֶּ֫ינָה, תְּסֻבֶּ֫ינָה.

In the perfect we find the vowel ǫ (on its origin, see § 80 *i*), e.g. סַבּ֫וֹתָ.

Sometimes the normal state of the root is given up and there is no linking vowel; cf. § *j*.

g **Stress.** In forms with a linking vowel, that vowel carries the stress, e.g. סַבּ֫וֹתָ, except, of course, when there is a heavy suffix, e.g., סַבּוֹתֶ֫ם. In the inverted perfect one usually has וְסַבּוֹתִ֫י, וְסַבּ֫וֹתָ.

Otherwise, a sharp penultimate syllable generally carries the stress, e.g. fut. יָסֹ֫בּוּ; pf. קַ֫לָּה, קַ֫לּוּ (but often קַלּ֫וּ). In the inverted perfect the stress can advance, e.g. וְרַבָּ֫ה.

In the imperative, instead of normal forms such as סֹ֫בִּי and סֹ֫בּוּ, mil'ra forms are sometimes found (for no apparent reason), and with the vowel ◌ָ instead of the usual ◌ֻ, e.g. always רָנּ֫וּ (3 x), רָנִּ֫י 3 x, but רֹ֫נִּי 2 x.

Observation. The vowels ẹ and ǫ of a stressed sharp syllable usual-ly become *i* and *u* when that syllable no longer carries the stress: תְּסֻבֶּ֫ינָה, יָסֹ֫בּוּ; תְּסֻבֶּ֫ינָה, יָסֻ֫בּוּ. Exceptions: יְשָׁדֵּם Pr 11.3K; יְשָׁלּ֫וּךְ Hb 2.8; תְּחָגֻּ֫הוּ Ex 12.14; יְבָ֫זּוּם Zeph 2.9; where all except the first case of which have *u* following the *o* vowel, suggesting the possibility of dis-similation.

h **Aramaising forms.** In addition to Hebrew forms proper whose second root-consonant is long (geminated), there are other forms, termed *Ara-maising*, in which the first consonant is geminated. In Aramaising forms, the doubling of the second consonant is sometimes preserved and sometimes omitted. These forms are called *Aramaising* because they are normal in Aramaic, e.g. in Biblical Aramaic תַּדִּק *it shall break in pieces* Dn 2.40 (Hafel of the verb דקק), in Syriac *nebboz he will plunder* (verb *bzz*). In Hebrew these forms are probably due to the influence of Aramaic; in some cases the analogy of פ"ן verbs may have encouraged their use. The Aramaising forms are found in the future Qal, Hifil, and Hofal, e.g. Qal יִסֹּב(1), יִסְּבוּ; Hifil יַסֵּב, יַסֵּבוּ, יַסֵּ֫בּוּ; Hofal יֻסַּב.

Examples(2). In the case of the stative verb תַּם *to be perfect, complete, finished, consumed* there is a future in *a*, יִתַּם, and a future in *o*, יִתֹּם, which really seem to be synonymous. Since the verb is stative, the future in *a* is normal. The Aramaising gemination is found everywhere in this verb (except Ps 19.14, a doubtful form). In the 3rd person plural the form יִתַּ֫מּוּ with gemination of the second radical is found five times, the form יִתַּמּוּ only once(3).

The verb סָבַב presents special difficulties. The Qal סָבַב has an active transitive sense, namely *to surround, to go around*, and a reflexive sense, namely *to turn (oneself), to turn about*, hence simply *to pass to, to go, to come*. Consequently there seems to be no need for a Nifal; and indeed the Nifal is rather rare and seems secondary. In every instance of the Nifal the Qal could be used, and one would even expect it in those cases where the meaning is *to surround*, e.g. Gn 19. 4; Jdg 19.22 (comp. 20.5 יָסֹ֫בּוּ); Josh 7.9. The future יִסַּב *to turn oneself, to turn round*, is only used in Ezekiel (who also uses the pf. נָסַב) and is Nifal. The frequent future form יִסֹּב, which is only used in a reflexive sense, is originally Qal (evident in 1Sm 22.18, after סֹב). Since the future form יָסֹב is only used in an active transitive sense (except in Jer 41.14), the future יִסֹּב could, at some stage, have easily been felt to be Nifal, and this could have brought about the creation of a corresponding perfect נָסַב; comp., in a similar context, יִסֹּב Nu 36.7 and נָסַב Jer 6.12.

The stative verb שַׁם* (f. שָׁמְמָה) *to be appalled, awestruck (*speaking of a person), *to be desolated (*of a land etc.) has a normal future יֵשַׁם*, which is rare (Gn 47.19; Ez 12.19; 19.7; cf. 6.6). The future יִשֹּׁם is Qal; it is perhaps from this future regarded as a Nifal that the perfect Nifal נָשַׁם* was created; this perfect lacks a corresponding future and has the same meaning as the perfect Qal.

Other Qal future forms in *ọ*: יִדֹּם *to become silent* (but יִדַּם *to be made silent* i.e. *to be destroyed* is Nifal); יִקֹּב *to curse*, יִקֹּד *to bow down.*

Other Qal future forms in *a*: יֵדַל *to be weak*; probably יָשַׁח *to bend.*

(1) The Aramaising Qal futures of the types יִסֹּב and יִסַּב are similar to Nifal, § *c*. Moreover, these forms are similar to the Qal of פ"ן verbs: יִפֹּל, יִגַּשׁ.

(2) Every example can be found in E. Kautzsch, "Die sogenannten aramaisierenden Formen der Verba ע"ע im Hebräischen," in C. Bezold (ed.), *Orientalische Studien Th. Nöldeke ... gewidmet* (Giessen, 1906), vol. 2, pp. 771-80. Kautzsch has toned down the conclusions of that study in the last (28th) edition of his *Grammar*, § 67 *g*.

(3) On the lighter form (יִתְּמוּ), see also יִדְּמוּ Ex 15.16, Job 29.21; וַיַּכְּתוּם Nu 14.45; וַיַּכְּתוּ Dt 1.44.

i Instances of **Hifil** (and **Hofal**): Future: Besides the usual יָחֵל *to begin*, we find יַחֵל *to violate* Nu 30.3, אַחֵל *I will violate* Ez 39.7 (but perhaps read Piel יְחַלֵּל); יַכֵּת* *to crush by beating* Dt 1.44; Nu 14.45. Hofal (or passive of Qal) יֻכַּת Is 24.12 etc.; יַסֵּב, frequent form, e.g. Ex 13.18; Hofal (or passive of Qal) יֻסַּב *to be turned.*

Some Aramaising forms are found outside the future Qal and Hifil, e.g. **perfect Nifal** נִחַל *to be defiled* Ez 7.24; 22.16; 25.3; נִחַר *to be burned, to be parched* Ps 69.4; 102.4; נֵאָרִים *to be cursed* Mal 3.9; נֵחַנְתְּ *you were pitied* (?) Jer 22.23. All these forms are confined to roots whose R1 is a guttural.

j **Forms without a linking vowel** (cf. § *f*). Sometimes there is no linking vowel; the normal state of the root, which had been preserved by the linking vowel, changed to the **reduced state**. Examples: Qal: תַּמְנוּ (for תַּמּוֹנוּ) Nu 17.28; Jer 44.18 (form similar to קַמְנוּ); Hifil: הֵחַלְתָּ Jdg 16.10 (for הֲתִלּוֹתָ); וְהֵפַרְתָּ 2Sm 15.34. The **reduced state** is also found in other cases. e.g. Qal: נָבֹזָה 1Sm 14.36 (for נָבֹזָּה); נָבְלָה Gn 11.7 (for נָבֹלָּה); יָזְמוּ 11.6 (for יָזֹמּוּ. Nifal: נָסְבָה Ez 41.7 for נָסַבָּה).

k **Dissociated state and non-dissociated state**(1)

In the **Inf. cst.** (§ *b*), besides the normal form סֹב (comp. future יָסֹב), we sometimes find, especially with לְ, the dissociated state סְבֹב (like קְטֹל), e.g. סֹב (attested once) Dt 2.3, לִסְבֹב (attested once) Nu 21.4; לִשְׁדוֹד Jer 47.4; בִּגְזֹז 1 Sm 25.2, לִגְזֹז Gn 31.19, but לָגֹז 38.13; always (Is 10.6; Ez 38.12,13) לִשְׁלֹל שָׁלָל, but (ibid.) וְלָבֹז בַּז (assonance).

In the **perfect Qal** of **action** verbs we usually find the dissociated state: סָבַב, סָבֲבָה, סָבֲבוּ. With the suffixes, writers sometimes prefer to use the normal state, which is shorter, e.g. סַבּוּנִי (4 times; סְבָבוּנִי 8

times). Besides the regular בַּזּוֹנוּ Dt 3.7 we find the dissociated state בָּזַזְנוּ 2.35.

In the perfect Qal of **stative** verbs we usually find the following types: קַל, קַלָּה, קַלּוּ; but there are exceptions, e.g. דָּלְלוּ Is 19.6 besides דַּלּוּ 38.14; Job 28.4; עֲשָׁשָׁה, עָשֵׁשׁוּ; שָׁחֲחוּ Job 9.13 as against שַׁחוּ Hb 3.6. In the stative verb שַׁם we always find שָׁמֵמוּ, שָׁמֵמוּ.

The stative future Qal in the dissociated state; יֶחֱנַן Am 5.15 *he will favour* stands for יֵחַן* or יִחַן*, and is the only stative form of this verb the original meaning of which is *to be gracious*. The frequent sense of *to be gracious to somebody* has brought about transitivity (cf. Brock., *GvG*, II, p. 286) and the forms חָנַן, יָחֹן which are typical of an action verb.

In the Hifil the dissociated state is found with the following: the inf. הַשְׁמֵם Mi 6.13; the ptc. מַשְׁמִים Ez 3.15; all the forms of the verb רנן, e.g. הַרְנִינוּ, אַרְנִין *to cause to ring out*.

(1) Comp. in Fr. *j'acquerrai* and the old *j'acquérerai* (Corneille).

Further observations about various conjugations *l*

Qal: Perfects in *ọ*: זֹרוּ Is 1,6 *they have been pressed* is a Qal passive; probably also רֹמּוּ Job 24.24 *they were exalted* (contrasts with the passive הֻמְּכוּ); but רֹבּוּ Gn 49.23 *they shot* (?) is difficult to explain (the active meaning rules out the possibility of a stative form).

Future forms in *u* (through contamination by the ע"ו verbs), e.g. יָרוּן Pr 29.6.

There is, likewise, an **inf. cst.** with *u*: בּוּר Ec 9.1; בְּחוּקוֹ Pr 8.27. The inf. cst. in *a*, which has been replaced by the inf. in *ọ* in the stative verbs (§ *b*), is found, strangely enough, in some action verbs (perhaps incorrectly): לְבָרָם Ec 3.18 *to test them* (comp. בּוּר 9.1); לְרַד Is 45.1 *to subdue*; כְּשַׁךְ Jer 5.26 *like a bending*.

The **imperative** גַּל Ps 119.22 (besides גֹּל) is perhaps a shortened form of גֵּל* (cf. § *b*, n., according to Barth).

In Nu 22.11,17, instead of קָבָּה־לִּי* we find קָבָה־לִּי *qọvå-lli*(1), no doubt to avoid two instances of gemination one after another. Compare the qameṣ in an open syllable corresponding to the origial short *u* in קָדָשִׁים. Likewise in 22.6 and 23.7 we find אָרָה־לִּי *'ọrå-lli* for *'ur(r)å-lli*. In Nu 23.13 the form קָבְנוֹ (for *quvnọ* or *qubbẹnnu*) has an epenthetic נ (comp. יְשֻׁנּוֹ, § 102 *k*), as is highly frequent in Ugr. (Gordon, *UT*, § 6.16,17).

(1) Since the second qameṣ also has the quality *ọ* (§ 18 *i*) the form sounds like *qọvọ-lli* in the Tiberian pronunciation.

m **Nifal.** As we said in § *c*, the perfect Nifal נָסַב came to be regarded as the Qal of a פ"ן verb and stative perfects in *ẹ* were created by analogy, e.g. נָמֵס *to melt*, fut. יִמַּס. There is also נָקֵל (4 times; used rather as a verbal adjective than as a perfect) besides נָקַל. We have a stative perfect נָגֹל *to be rolled* or *to roll* (intransitive) in נָגֹלּוּ Is 34.4, because the future is in *a*: יִגַּל Am 5.24. On the other hand, there are perfects in *ọ* which correspond to futures in *ọ* and which therefore are of the נָקוֹם, יִקּוֹם type (contamination by the ע"ו verbs), e.g. נָבֹזּוּ Am 3.11 (fut. תִּבּוֹז Is 24.3, with וֹ); נָרֹץ Ec 12.6 (fut. תֵּרוֹץ Ez 29.7, for *tirrọṣ*). Furthermore, from the future forms תִּבּוֹק Is 24.3 and יֵרוֹעַ Pr 11.15 and 13.20, we can reconstruct the corresponding perfect forms נָבֹק* and נָרֹעַ*(1).

In תֵּחֵל Lv 21.9 *she will defile herself*, we may have a unique case of a future Nifal with *ẹ* as second vowel. This *ẹ*, if authentic, could have arisen on the analogy of the *ẹ* of יִקָּטֵל (just as the *ẹ* of the inf. cst. הֵחֵל and הִמֵּס arose on the analogy of הִקָּטֵל); but here the *ẹ* is very suspect, because elsewhere we find the vowel *a*: וָאֵחַל Ez 22.26; יֵחָל Is 48.11.

A future in the dissociated state is found in Job 11.12 יִלָּבֵב.

(1) In view of all this the existence of ע"ע Nifal futures with medium *ọ* seems doubtful.

n **Hifil.** There are some forms with *i* (contamination by the ע"ו verbs): הֵפִיר Ez 17.19; Ps 33.10 (cf. 89.34); הֵשִׂיר Ho 8.4; Jer 49.20 (with Aramaising gemination).

The vowel of ה. In anteprestress position ָ is not maintained; it usually becomes ֲ, e.g. הֲסִבּוֹתָ. Before a guttural ֲ is lengthened to ַ; the only examples are הַחִלֹּתָ and הַחִלֹּתִי *to begin* in Dt 2.31; 3.24; 1Sm 22.15; Esth 6.13 (comp. inf. הַחִלָּם Gn 11.6) and הַחִתֹּתָ in Is 9.3. (comp. same phenomenon in ע"ו verbs, § 80 *m*, e.g. הַעִידֹתִי. Since, quite probably, there is no virtual doubling before this ע, there probably is none before ח either).

The vowel ֵ following R1 changes to ֶ when the stress recedes as in וַיָּחֶל and וַיָּסֶךְ (but וַתָּרַע and וַיָּצַר where R2/3 is a guttural or Resh, though וַיָּפֶר), and to ֲ where the stress advances as in וַהֲדִיקוֹתָ and וַתְּחִלֶּינָה, but we find הֲרֵעֹתָ and יְפֵרְנוּ when R2/3 is a guttural or Resh; more examples in Berg., II, § 27 *l*.

Contamination of the ע"ע verbs by the ע"ו verbs. Just as there are, in the ע"ו verbs, many forms contaminated by the ע"ע verbs (80 *o*), so there are also many ע"ע forms contaminated by ע"ו forms. Several were quoted in §§ *l*, *m*, *n*; many more will be found in dictionaries or concordances. The Hebrew verb meaning *to murmur*, vocalised by the Naqdanim as if from a root לון, probably originated as a ע"ע verb, namely לנן (cf. the derived noun תְּלֻנּוֹת *murmurings*), which was then entirely contaminated by the ע"ו verbs(1): i.e., Nifal נָלוֹן*, תִּלּוֹנוּ; Hifil וַיָּלֶן, תַּלִּינוּ, הֲלִינֹתֶם. Besides משׁשׁ *to feel by touching*, *to grope*, which seems to be the original root, there is probably in Hebrew (and in Aramaic) a secondary root מושׁ attested by a few forms, e.g. Gn 27.21; Jdg 16.26; Ps 115.7. o

(1) Cf. P. Joüon, *Bib* 1 (1920) 361.

Comparison with the nominal forms (cf. § *a*) p

Apart from the participles סֹבֵב, סָבוּב and the inf. abs. סָבוֹב, the dissociated state is rather rare in the nominal forms, e.g. שָׁמֵם *devastated*, הֲרָרִים, a poetic form besides הָרִים *mountains*; instead of עַמִּים *peoples*, עֲמָמִים (cf. BA עַמְמַיָּא) is found, but very rarely.

The normal state and the reduced state are found under the same conditions as in the verb: the *qatl* type: עַם *people* (and עָם), עַמִּי; *qitl*: חֵן *favour*, *grace*, חִנִּי; *qutl*: חֹק *statute*, חֻקִּי: the *qatl* type with ר: שַׂר *prince*, plural שָׂרִים, שָׂרֵי (for *śarre*; ֵ in this position is maintained). Comp. קָם, קָמִים, קָמֵי (§ 80 *d*), and contrast, for example, שָׁנָה *year*, pl. שָׁנִים, שְׁנֵי. The *taqtila* type: תְּחִלָּה *beginning* (corresponds to the Hifil הֵחֵל *to begin*); the *maqtal* type: מָסָךְ *covering*, *protection*, מַשָּׁק action of *penetration* ? (with Aramaising gemination).

§ 83. Comparison of the various verb classes (Paradigm 16)

The student will find here a synopsis of the conjugations of various a types of verbs which will help him to determine the relevant roots. He may add to it as his knowledge increases.

b **Preformative in open syllable.**

Verb class	Examples			
1) ע"ו Qal	יָקוּם, יֵבוֹשׁ;	Nif. נָקוֹם;	Hif. הֵקִים, יָקִים;	Hof. הוּקַם.
2) ע"ע Qal	יָסֹב, יֵקַל;	Nif. נָסַב;	Hif. הֵסֵב, יָסֵב;	Hof. הוּסַב.
3) פ"י Qal	יֵשֵׁב, יִירַשׁ;	Nif. נוֹשַׁב;	Hif. הוֹשִׁיב, יוֹשִׁיב;	Hof. הוּשַׁב.

c **Geminated consonant after preformative.**

1) In the Nifal (future etc.) of all the verbs (except first-guttural verbs), e.g. יִקָּטֵל, יִקּוֹם, יִסַּב.
2) Regularly in the פ"ן verbs, e.g. fut. יִגַּשׁ, יַגִּישׁ.
3) In the פ"יצ verbs, e.g. יַצִּיעַ.
4) In the Aramaising forms of the ע"ע verbs, e.g. fut. יִסֹּב, יִדַּל; יַסֵּב.
5) In the Aramaising forms of the ע"ו verbs, e.g. הִנִּיחַ, יַנִּיחַ § 80 *p*.

d **Final vowel ◌ֵ in the future:**

1) Generally in the Piel and Hitpael: יְקַטֵּל, יִתְקַטֵּל.
2) In the Nifal: יִקָּטֵל.
3) In the Qal of active פ"ו verbs: יֵשֵׁב.
   of some other verbs, e.g. יִתֵּן.
   of פ"א verbs in pause(1): יֹאכֵל, יֹאבֵד, תֹּאמֵר.
4) In the jussive Hifil in general, e.g. יַקְטֵל, יָקֵם.
5) In the indicative Hifil of ע"ע verbs: יָסֵב, יַסֵּב.

(1) But here *ẹ* is of secondary origin, § 73 *e*.

e **First vowel ◌ֵ in the future:**

1) In the Qal of active פ"ו verbs: יֵשֵׁב.
   of stative ע"ע verbs: יֵקַל.
2) In the Hifil of פ"י verbs: יֵיטִיב.

§ 84. Relation of the weak verbs to one another

a The mark of a weak verb is the presence in it of a weak element side by side with strong elements: the weak element can often vary and yet the idea expressed by the verb as a whole remains the same. Thus to express the verbal notion *to lay snares* Hebrew has augmented the stable core קשׁ with an initial weak element, either י or נ, to give יָקֹשׁ and נָקֹשׁ. Likewise to express the verbal notion *to be alienated* Hebrew has produced both נקע and יקע. In the case of verbs whose forms are poorly attested in the Bible, it is sometimes difficult to tell whether or not we are actually dealing with two related roots: this applies in particular to certain ע"ו and ע"ע verbs. A phonetic accident in a given form can cause a metaplasm(1). An isolated form cannot be used to postulate the existence of a root; thus we cannot argue from the Hitpael form הִתְיַצֵּב (§ 77 *b*) that there is in Hebrew a root יצב alongside נצב, nor can we argue, from the future יֵלֵךְ, that there is a root ילך alongside הָלַךְ (§ 75 *g*).

(1) Thus, in Syrian Arabic *waqada* "to light" becomes *qād*, fut. *yaqid*, via the imperative *qid* pronounced *qid* (cf. C. von Landberg, *Proverbes et dictons de la province de Syrie. Section de Saydâ* [Leiden, 1883], p. 290).

Examples of a core used with various weak elements: *to crush*: דכךְ, דוךְ, דכא; *to be numerous*: רבב and רבה; *to be silent*: דום, דמם, דמה; *to despise*: בוז and בזה; *to meet*: קרא and קרה. b

For other examples in the case of defective verbs see § 85.

§ 85. Defective verbs

a Sometimes in order to express the same verbal notion, some of the forms (conjugations, tenses) are borrowed from one root and the rest from another. Each of the two verbs is said to be *defective*. Here are the most common defective verbs:

to be ashamed: בּוֹשׁ*(§ 80 *q*) and יבשׁ (§ 76 *d*).

to be good: טוֹב (§ 80 *q*) and יטב (§ 76 *d*).

to wake up (intransitive): יקץ (§ 76 *d*) and קיץ.

to dread: יָגֹר (§ 75 *i*) and גּוּר (cf. § 41 *f*, n.).

to drink: שָׁתָה; *cause to drink water, give to drink* הִשְׁקָה (a remote etymological link between the two verbs is doubtful).

b Other verbs are defective, or suppletive (as they are sometimes called), as far as the conjugations are concerned, some tenses being borrowed from one conjugation, the rest from another:

יָסַף *to add* is quasi-defective, § 75 *f*: Pf. (Qal) יָסַף; fut. (Hif.) הוֹסִיף.

יצת *to burn* (intransitive): Pf. (Nif.) נִצַּת; fut. (Qal) יִצַּת (§ 77 *b*).

כשל *to stumble*: Pf. (Qal) כָּשַׁל (rarely נִכְשַׁל); fut. (Nif.) יִכָּשֵׁל, ptc. (Nif.) נִכְשָׁל.

לאה *to be weary*: Pf. (Nif.) נִלְאָה; f. (Qal) יִלְאֶה.

מוג *to melt*: Pf. ptc. (Nif.) נָמוֹג; f., inf.cst. (Qal) תָּמוֹג, מוּג.

נגשׁ *to approach*: Pf. (Nif.) נִגַּשׁ; fut. (Qal) יִגַּשׁ, impv. (Qal) גַּשׁ (§ 72 *g*).

נחה *to lead*: Pf. (Qal) נָחָה; fut. (Hif.) יַנְחֶה.

נתך *to pour forth* (intransitive): Pf. (Nif.) נִתַּךְ; fut. (Qal) יִתַּךְ.

פוץ *to be scattered*: Pf. (Nif.) נָפוֹץ; fut. (Qal) יָפוּץ.

Note that in several instances (יצת, נגשׁ, נתך) we have a perfect Nifal and a future Qal, and that the two forms resemble each other(1).

(1) Cf. M. Lambert, *RÉJ* 41 (1900) 212. There is also a certain resemblance in the case of נפוֹץ, יפוּץ; יגר, יגוּר, § *a*.

c For the *participium tantum*, in the Qal, cf. § 50 *d*.

CHAPTER III: THE NOUN

§ 86. General observations

The *noun* in Hebrew and Semitic grammar includes not only the substantive but also the adjective(1), for in its formation and inflection the adjective does not differ from the substantive(2). Because the Hebrew noun has lost the final vowels which indicated *cases* (nominative, accusative, genitive, § 93 *b*), there is no declension properly speaking. The logical relations expressed by the nominative, the accusative, and the genitive are shown by the position of the noun in the sentence. For the genitive, however, the first noun (*nomen regens*), which *governs* the second noun (*nomen rectum*), often has a special form called the *construct state*, as opposed to the ordinary form which is called the *absolute state* (§ 92 *a*). The changes in the vocalisation of the noun in the construct state and those changes which occur when a noun is lengthened by the addition of the plural, dual, and feminine endings and of the suffixes are due to stress shift. All these changes in the vocalisation constitute the *inflection* of the noun, § 95 *a*. This inflection, which is very subtle and less regular than that of the verb, requires, in order to be understood, a knowledge not only of phonetic laws but also of the primitive forms of the various Hebrew nouns.

(1) In its broad sense, the noun also includes the verbal adjectives, namely the infinitives and the participles.

(2) But adjectives do not have all the forms of substantives (cf. § 87 *c*).

§ 87. Noun formation

Nouns are either *primitive*, like אָב *father*, אֵם *mother*, רֹאשׁ *head*, רֶ֫גֶל *foot*, or *derivative*. Nouns are derived either from another noun, e.g. pl. מַרְגְּלוֹת *place of the feet* (from רֶ֫גֶל), שֹׁעֵר *porter* (from שַׁ֫עַר *gate*) or from a verb. The latter are very numerous, but it is unfounded to suppose that every noun is derived from a verb. Actually many verbs are derived from a noun (*denominative* verbs). In the case of many roots it is impossible to determine which came first, the noun or the verb. a

Certain noun forms are associated with certain verb forms, e.g. גִּדּוּף *insult* is associated with the Piel גִּדֵּף *to insult*, תְּהִלָּה *praise* with the Piel הִלֵּל *to praise*. On the other hand, the attempts which have been made to link the majority of nominal forms to the tenses (perfect and imperative according to de Lagarde(1), perfect and future according to Barth)(2), are not conclusive.

(1) P. de Lagarde, *Übersicht über die im Aramäischen, Arabischen und Hebräischen übliche Bildung der Nomina* (Göttingen, 1891).
(2) *Nominalbildung*.

b Whereas verbal forms (*conjugations* § 40 *a*) are few in number, nominal forms are many and varied. Each verbal form expresses scarcely more than one notion (e.g. the Piel: on the various notions associated with Piel, see § 52 *d*). Many nominal forms, on the other hand, are linked with more than one particular notion. However, one may say that, generally speaking, Hebrew (like other Semitic languages) tends to cast in the same morphological mould nouns designating similar things. Thus the form קִטֵּל is commonly associated with adjectives denoting a physical or mental defect, e.g. עִוֵּר *blind* (§ 88 H *b*); the form קַטָּל with *nomina opificum* [= nouns of occupations], e.g. דַּיָּן *judge* (§ 88 H *a*); the form קָטֵל with names of limbs, e.g. כָּתֵף *shoulder* (§ 88 D *b*); the form קָטִיל with names of agricultural activities, e.g. קָצִיר *harvest* (§ 88 E *b*).

c Concrete nouns as well as abstract nouns are used in certain forms only.

Adjectives are used in certain forms only(1). Generally speaking, (primitive) forms with one vowel and those with a preformative are not used for adjectives in Hebrew. The forms which we find used for adjectives are the simple forms with two primitive short vowels קָטָל, קָטֵל, קָטֹל, with an etymologically short first vowel and an etymologically long second vowel קָטוֹל, קָטִיל, קָטוּל; the forms with doubling of the second consonant קַטָּל, קַטֵּל, קַטִּיל, קַטּוּל; the form with afformative ִי-, and some rarer forms like קְטַלְטַל.

Compound nouns are frequently used as proper nouns, e.g. גַּבְרִיאֵל = *man of God* (§ 93 *m*); on the other hand they are very rarely used as common nouns: בְּלִיַּעַל *good-for-nothing*, *base*, composed of the negation בְּלִי and of an element whose meaning is still debated, and the noun is indeclinable; perhaps צַלְמָוֶת, interpreted as צֵל מָוֶת as far back as the

LXX σκιὰ θανάτου (but the vocalisation is suspect; it has been suggested that it be read צַלְמוּת or צַלְמוֹת which would mean *darkness*).

(1) Cf. F. Werner, *Die Wortbildung der hebräischen Adjektiva* (Wiesbaden, 1983).

§ 88. Nominal forms

Because of its length this paragraph is subdivided into several shorter paragraphs (which are indicated by capital letters A, B, C, etc.) as follows:

§ 88 A) Forms with only one consonant; B) with two consonants; C-G) with three consonants; H-I) with three consonants the second of which is doubled; J) with repeated consonant; K) with four consonants; L) with preformative; M) with afformative. The aim of the following lists is to give a selection of forms about whose classification there is universal agreement. The reader will find relatively complete lists in Bauer and Leander(1), often with the reasons justifying the attribution of such and such a noun to such and such a form. Brockelmann gives the Hebrew forms within the framework of noun formation in all Semitic languages, which greatly helps the reader to understand them. In spite of all the work done up till now, the primitive form of a large number of nouns remains unclear.

(1) § 61 (pp. 448-506). This section of the grammar of Bauer and Leander is excellent; we have benefitted much from its use.

§ 88 A. FORMS WITH ONLY ONE CONSONANT

Forms which have (on the surface at least) only one consonant are very rare: אִי, plural אִיִּים I *island*, II *jackal*; צִי I pl. צִיִּים and צִים *ship*; צִי* II pl. צִיִּים *an unidentified desert animal*.

§ 88 B. FORMS WITH TWO CONSONANTS

Qal. With the primitive **short vowel** *a*, which has usually become a
å(1): יָד *hand* (§ 96 E *a*), דָּם *blood* (§ 96 E *a*), שָׁד *female breast*, וָו *hook* (§ 26 *f*), דָּג *fish*, תָּו *mark*. Nouns of kinship (§ 98 *b*): אָב *father*, אָח *brother*, חָם *husband's father*.

With feminine ending: שָׁנָה *year*, שָׂפָה *lip*, אָמָה *handmaid* (§ 98 *d*); דֶּלֶת *door*, קֶשֶׁת *bow*. Compare the aphaeretic infinitives like גֶּשֶׁת (§ 72 *c*) (from נגשׁ), דַּעַת (§ 75 *g*) (from יָדַע).

(1) For several of these nouns, the primitive state of the root is the object of debate; likewise for **Qil**.

b **Qil** (Inflection, § 96 E *b*). With the primitive short vowel *i*, which has usually become ẹ: עֵץ *wood*, אֵל *god*; בֵּן *son* (§ 98 *c*), שֵׁם *name*, שֵׁת *base*.

With feminine ending: מֵאָה *hundred*, פֵּאָה *side, angle*. Compare the aphaeretic substantives of פ"ו verbs such as לֵדָה *the bringing forth of children* (also infinitive) listed in § 75 *m*, and the infinitives like לֶדֶת, שֶׁבֶת (§ 75 *a*).

c **Qul**. With the primitive short vowel *u*, which has usually become ọ: perhaps תּוֹר *turtle-dove* (the *plene* ו could be improper).

d **Qāl**. With the primitive **long vowel** ā, which has usually become ọ(1): דּוֹד *beloved*, חוֹף *shore*, טוֹב *good* (probably).

(1) Nouns of the קוֹל type are sometimes of doubtful origin; ọ may come from the contraction of *aw*.

e **Qīl**. With the primitive long vowel ī, which has been preserved in Hebrew(1): גִּיד *sinew*, טִיט *clay, mud*, מִין *kind*, סִיג *dross*, סִיר *pot*, עִיר *city*, קִיר *wall*, רִיר *spittle*, שִׂיחַ *shrub*.

The infinitive of ע"י verbs can be a substantive and it also has the form *qil*, e.g. דִּין *to judge* and *a judgment*, רִיב *to quarrel* and *a quarrel*, שִׁיר *to sing* and *a song*.

With feminine ending: בִּינָה *understanding*, קִינָה *dirge*, טִירָה *encampment*.

(1) See what was said about the root of ע"ו verbs (§ 80 *a*) and ע"י verbs (§ 81 *a*).

f **Qūl**. With the primitive long vowel ū, which has been preserved in Hebrew(1): דּוּד *basket*, חוּט *thread*, חוּץ *the outside, street*, טוּב *goodness*, לוּחַ *table*, צוּר *rock*, רוּחַ *breath*, שׁוּק *street*, שׁוּר *wall*.

With feminine ending: שׁוּרָה *row*, פּוּרָה *wine-press*.

(1) See what was said about the root of ע"ו verbs (§ 80 *a*) and ע"י verbs (§ 81 *a*).

g Forms with **long (doubled) 2nd consonant**(1)

Qall (Inflection, § 96 A, *n*). With the primitive short vowel *a*, which has usually become ַ because of the tendency towards doubling. Before the labial *m* the vowel is labialized to *ǫ* (å)(2): יָם, עָם (usually with disjunctive accent; otherwise עַם); adj. חָם, תָּם.

Substantives(3): עַם and עָם; pl. עַמִּים *people*; הַר, הָהָר *mountain*; פַּר, הַפָּר *young bull*, שַׂר *prince*, כַּף *palm of the hand*; יָם *sea*.

With feminine ending: אַמָּה *cubit*, שָׂרָה *princess* (for *śarra*).

Adjectives(4): דַּל *weak*, דַּק *thin*, חַי *living*, מַר *bitter*, עַז *strong*, צַר *enemy*, קַל *light*, רַב *great*, רַךְ *tender*, רַק *thin*, רַע *bad*, חָם *hot*, תָּם *perfect*.

With feminine ending: חַמָּה (poetic) *sun*, צָרָה *female rival* (for *ṣarra*), חַיָּה *animal*.

(1) See what was said about the root of ע"ע verbs in § 82 *a*.

(2) This phenomenon presupposes that the ָ has the sound *ǫ*. Comp. the מָוֶת type (§ C *f*). On this question, see also a study by E.J. Revell, *HAR* 5 (1981) 84-99.

(3) Substantives of the עַם type correspond to the *qatl* form of triliteral roots.

(4) Adjectives of the קַל type probably correspond to the *qatil* form of triliteral roots; it is likely that here *qall* is a reduction of *qalil* (cf. P. Joüon in *MUSJ* 5 [1911] 402). Cf. § D *b*.

Qill (Inflection, §96 A *o*). With the primitive vowel *i*, which has usually been retained, except in final position where it has become *ẹ*: h

אֵם, suff. אִמִּי *mother*, אֵשׁ *fire*(1), לֵב, suf. לִבִּי *heart*, צֵל *shadow*, קֵן pl. קִנִּים *nest*, חֵן, suff. חִנּוֹ *grace*.

With feminine ending: פִּנָּה *angle*, צִנָּה *shield*, גֵּרָה *cud*.

(1) Diachronically אֵשׁ (with its אִשּׁוֹ) may go back to a biliteral form /*'iš/; J. Blau, *IOS* 2 (1972) 62-65 and Baumgartner, *Lexikon*, s.v.

Qull (Inflection, §96 A *p*). With the primitive vowel *u*, which has been retained, except in final position where it has become *ọ*: i

חֹק, suff. חֻקִּי *statute*, כֹּל *the whole, all*, חֹר *free man, noble*. The *qull* form is often used to form abstract nouns which correspond to the adjectives of the type *qall* (§ g): חֹם *heat*, עֹז *strength*, רֹב *multitude*, רֹךְ *tenderness*, רֹעַ *wickedness*, תֹּם *perfection*(1).

With feminine ending: חֻקָּה *decree*, סֻכָּה *booth* (properly *covering*)(2).

(1) Analogously, many *qutl* nouns are abstract nouns (§ 88 C *j*).

(2) Despite the pl. עֻמּוֹת (once only in Ez 45.7), עֻמַּת (usually with -לְ) may not belong here, but rather the final Taw may be radical. Cf. Ben-Ḥayyim, *LOT*, vol. 5, p. 243.

[§§ 88 C-G. FORMS WITH THREE CONSONANTS]

§ 88 C. FORMS WITH ONLY ONE VOWEL

*a** A substantial number of Hebrew nouns are derived from the primitive pattern CVCC and its derivative CCVC (relatively few) in which the vowel was short. However, since the Hebrew phonology in the Tiberian tradition does not normally allow word-final consonantal clusters (§§ 18 *l*, 27 *db*), the pattern CVCC is actualised as CVCVC in the basic form, namely the singular form without a pronominal suffix. The extra vowel, termed epenthetic or anaptyptic because added on, is seghol. Hence the designation of these nouns as segholates. This seghol changes to pataḥ when R2 or R3 is a guttural including pronounced ה (exceptions: לֶ֫חֶם and רֶ֫חֶם, §§ *c* and 96 A *i*). It is important to note that all segholate nouns are stressed on the penultimate syllable(1), and this is the only group of polysyllabic nouns so stressed. The reason why these segholate nouns are classified as having only one vowel is twofold. (1) In their inflected forms the one-vowel pattern can still be observed: for instance, from עֵ֫גֶל *calf* we find עֶגְלְךָ *your c.*, pl. cst. עֶגְלֵי, and fem. עֶגְלָה *heifer*. (2) Their analogues in cognate languages attest to the same basic pattern: Syr. *ʿeglå*, Arb. *ʿijl*, both meaning *calf*. It is for these reasons that one often discusses segholate nouns in terms of **qatl**, **qitl**, and **qutl** patterns. A number of factors, however, complicate the task of establishing the correlation between these three primitive segholate types and the forms actually attested in Hebrew.

1. Hebrew segholate nouns can have one of *four* vowels in their first syllable, namely pataḥ, seghol, ṣeré, and ḥolem.

2. Most segholates with pataḥ and ḥolem in the first syllable can be safely considered as reflecting, respectively, the primitive qatl and qutl patterns: e.g. נַ֫עַל *shoe*, cf. Arb. *naʿl* and Syr. *naʿlå*; קֹ֫דֶשׁ *sanctity*, cf. Arb. *quds* and Syr. *qud̲šå*.

3. The Hebrew data are sometimes equivocal. For example, the fem. form of כֶּ֫בֶשׂ *lamb* is either כִּבְשָׂה or כַּבְשָׂה. אֹמֶר *utterance* is inflected as אִמְרוֹ *his u.*, and pl.cst. אִמְרֵי, unless we postulate a variant singular form אֵ֫מֶר or אֶ֫מֶר, cf. אִמְרָתִי from the synonymous אִמְרָה*. Likewise שִׂמְלָה vs. שַׂלְמָה (with metathesis) *garment*. Note also slightly different

fluctuations: נֶ֫בֶל / נֵ֫בֶל *some sort of musical instrument*; נֶ֫דֶר / נֵ֫דֶר *vow*; הֶ֫פֶךְ / הֵ֫פֶךְ (the latter with silluq and both within a single verse, Ez 16.34). Cf. § 96 A *f*.

4. Non-Tiberian traditions also attest to fluctuation: מֶ֫לֶךְ vs. *melchechem* your (pl.) king in Jerome ad Am 5.26 מַלְכְּכֶם, and Bab. /milkiyyå/ (MT מַלְכְּיָה)(2) alongside λαμαλαχη in the Secunda at Ps 89.28.

5. The evidence of cognate languages is sometimes equivocal. For instance, בֶּ֫רֶךְ, בִּרְכַּ֫יִם *knee*, but Syr. *burkå*; מֶ֫לֶךְ, מַלְכֵּי, but Arb. *malik*; אֹ֫זֶן, but Syr. *'ednå*; כֶּ֫סֶף, כַּסְפּוֹ, but BA כַּסְפָּא; Syr. *kespå*.

6. The vowel following the first radical in the pausal form does not always clinch the matter. Whilst the pausal form בָּטֶן from בֶּ֫טֶן *belly* may help assign the word to the primitive qatl pattern despite its inflection בִּטְנִי and the like, forms on the other hand such as שָׁ֫בֶט *staff* (alongside שִׁבְטוֹ from שֵׁ֫בֶט), סָתֶר *hiding-place* (alongside סִתְרִי from סֵ֫תֶר), all with qameṣ in contrast to סֵ֫פֶר (a qitl segholate without a doubt), and אָ֫רֶץ (a qatl segholate) on the other, highlight the complexity of the problem.

The difficulty is felt most acutely with the קֶ֫טֶל pattern (§ 96 A *f*). Obviously not every קֶ֫טֶל segholate is derived from the primitive qatl pattern. For a synchronic classification of Hebrew segholates, it seems best to us to rely on their inflection pattern as the principal criterion, though the required data are not always available due to the accident of insufficient attestation(3). Accordingly, בֶּ֫טֶן would be classified as an *i*-segholate in spite of Arb. *baṭn*(4). Likewise שֶׁ֫מֶשׁ on account of שִׁמְשָׁהּ in spite of שָׁ֫מֶשׁ and χασαμς in the Hexapla at Ps 89.37 (MT כַּשֶּׁ֫מֶשׁ), and Akk. *šamšu* and Arb. *šams*.

(1) Except those derived from some weak roots, e.g. בְּכִי alongside בֶּ֫כֶה *weeping*. In this respect the place-name בָּבֶל with mil'ra stress is striking.

(2) See Yeivin, *Babylonian Tradition*, p. 1092.

(3) Pedagogically speaking, it may be helpful to establish a fourth pattern, i.e. qetl segholate, which would comprise nouns such as נֶ֫גֶד *opposite* (cf. נֶגְדִּי, נֶגְדּוֹ etc.), חֵ֫לֶק *portion* (cf. חֶלְקִי), עֵ֫זֶר *aid* (cf. עֶזְרִי).

(4) So in the Babylonian tradition; see Yeivin, op. cit., p. 837.

Qatl. With the primitive vowel *a*. The form is usually segholised (§ 96 A *b*): קֶ֫טֶל. Sometimes the form becomes קְטַל with the vowel *a* at the end (§ *g*). Some *qatl* nouns can be of secondary origin, e.g. *bint > *bant > בַּת *daughter* (Philippi's law, § 29 *aa*) or a reduction of the *a* *qatil* or *qatal* forms (compare מֶ֫לֶךְ *king* with the Arabic *ma'lik* and יֶ֫לֶד *child* with the Arabic *wa'lad*). The nouns of the *qatl* form are by far the most numerous nouns.

b Strong roots: מֶ֫לֶךְ, suff. מַלְכִּי *king* (§ 96 A *c*), אֶ֫בֶן *stone*, אֶ֫רֶץ, הָאָ֫רֶץ *earth*, כֶּ֫לֶב *dog*, כֶּ֫רֶם *vineyard*, שֶׁ֫מֶן *oil*.

With feminine ending (Inflection, § 97 A *b*): מַלְכָּה *queen*, עַלְמָה *young woman*.

c Roots with the guttural א as second radical: *ra'š* > *rā(')š* > *rō'š* > *rọ(')š* = רֹאשׁ (with a purely graphic etymological א); likewise צֹאן *small cattle* (comp. Arb. *ḍa'n*); cf. § 24 *d*.

Roots with the gutturals ה, ח, ע as second radical. The guttural almost always brings about the vocalisation ַ ַ: לַ֫הַב *flame*, נַ֫חַל *valley*, פַּ֫חַד *fear*, נַ֫עַל *sandal*, נַ֫עַר *young man*, שַׁ֫עַר *gate*. However we find with ח the two words לֶ֫חֶם *bread* and רֶ֫חֶם *womb, breast*; cf. § 96 A *i*.

d Roots with א as third radical(1): פֶּ֫רֶא *wild ass*, גֶּ֫בֶא *pool*, טֶ֫נֶא *vase*.

Roots with the gutturals ה, ח, ע as third radical. The guttural brings about the vocalisation ֶ ַ: זֶ֫רַע *seed*, סֶ֫לַע *rock*.

(1) Since the Alef is not pronounced, it does not change the usual vocalisation of the מֶ֫לֶךְ type. For similar forms derived from *qitl*, see § *h*.

e ל"י roots (Inflection, § 96 A *q*). The primitive form *qaty* has changed into the two forms קֶ֫טֶה and קְטִי, קֶ֫טִי (for a detailed explanation cf. § 96 A *q*): צְבִי *gazelle*, גְּדִי *kid*.

With feminine ending: צְבִיָּה *gazelle*.

ל"ו roots. שָׂחוּ (Ez 47.5)(1) *swimming*. With feminine ending: שַׁלְוָה *tranquillity*.

(1) The ָ for ַ is probably due to the zaqef accent; cf. P. Joüon in *Bib* 1 (1920) 367, n.

f ע"ו roots. With consonantal ו. *a* has been labialised to *ọ* (*å*) before the ו (cf. § B *g*): מָ֫וֶת, cst. מוֹת *death* (§ 96 A *l*), אָ֫וֶן *wickedness*, עָ֫וֶל *injustice*, תָּ֫וֶךְ *middle*. Instead of שָׁ֫וֶא* we find the shortened form שָׁוְא *nothingness* and (once) even שָׁו (Job 15.31K). With contraction: יוֹם *day*, צוֹם *fast*, שׁוֹר *head of cattle*, שׁוֹט *whip*.

With feminine ending: עַוְלָה, pl. עוֹלֹת *injustice*.

ע"י roots. With consonantal י. The י has brought about the auxiliary vowel *i*: בַּ֫יִת, cst. בֵּית *house*, עַ֫יִן *eye*, חַ֫יִל *strength*, זַ֫יִת *oil* (§ 96 A *l*), יַ֫יִן *wine*, צַ֫יִד *hunt*. With contraction(1): חֵיל *rampart*, חֵיק *breast*.

With feminine ending: אֵימָה *terror*, צֵידָה *provision for journey*, שֵׂיבָה *hoary head*.

N.B. The form *qall* in the ע"ע roots corresponds to the form *qatl*, § B *g*.

(1) Whereas contracted forms are numerous in ע"ו verbs, they are rare in ע"י verbs. The two examples quoted could originally have been *qatil*, according to BL, p. 457.

Qtal(1). In some nouns the vowel has shifted to the end of the word, as in Aramaic (several of these words are also found in Aramaic): דְּבַשׁ, suf. דִּבְשִׁי *honey* (Arm), זְמָן*, suf. זְמַנָּם *time* (Arm), סְבַךְ* *thicket* (Arm) אֲגַם, pl. אֲגַמִּים *marsh* (Arm), הֲדַס, pl. הֲדַסִּים *myrtle* (Arm), חֲשַׁשׁ *chaff*, חֲתַת *terror*, סְתָו *winter* (Arm). g

The feminine form **qtalla**, with secondary doubling, is very rare and is found in the Jewish name of Esther הֲדַסָּה *myrtle*, and in סְעַפָּה* *branch*.

(1) The vocalisation *qtal* is sometimes found in the cst. state, e.g. נֶטַע*, cst. נְטַע *plantation* (§ 96 A *c*).

Qitl. With the primitive vowel *i*. The form has usually been segholised to קֵטֶל (§96 A *b*), sometimes to קֶטֶל (it is then identical with *qatl*)(1). In roots with א as second radical, the vowel has shifted to the end of the word: קְטַל (§ *i*). h

Strong roots: סֵפֶר, suff. סִפְרִי *book* (§ 96 A *e*), עֵגֶל *calf*, סֵתֶר *secret, shelter*, חֵפֶץ *love, will*; with a guttural as third radical שֵׁמַע *hearing*, תֵּשַׁע *nine*. Some nouns with seghol after the first radical also belong here (see above under § *a**): e.g. בֶּטֶן *belly*, קֶבֶר *grave*, זֶבַח *sacrifice*, נֶגַע *blow*. With feminine ending: תִּשְׁעָה *nine*, סִתְרָה *protection*, בִּקְעָה *valley*; with ◌ֶ◌ָ: עֶגְלָה *heifer*.

ל"א roots: Instead of חֵטֶא* we have the shortened form חֵטְא *sin* (comp. שָׁוְא, § *f*). The following words are probably *qitl* in origin: דֶּשֶׁא *grass*, פֶּלֶא *wonder*, כֶּלֶא *prison*.

ל"י roots: *ḥiṣy* has become חֵצִי *half* in pause and חֲצִי in context; cf. § 96 A *r*. Also belong here בֶּכֶה *weeping*, קֵצֶה *end*; בְּכִי (other form of בֶּכֶה), שְׁבִי *captivity*, פְּרִי *fruit*. With feminine ending: שִׁבְיָה *captivity*.

N.B. The form *qill* in the ע"ע roots corresponds to the form *qitl*, § B *h*.

(1) According to I. Ben-David there is a complementary distribution, the pattern with ṣeré being the rule at the beginning of a phrase, and that with seghol at the end of

it: *Leš* 47 (1983) 232-47.

i **Qtil.** In nouns with א as second radical the vowel ֵ had shifted to the end of the word: בְּאֵר *well*, זְאֵב, pl. זְאֵבִים *wolf*, כְּאֵב *pain*, רְאֵם *wild ox*, שְׁאֵר *flesh*; תְּאֵנָה *fig*(1).

The form qtilla with secondary doubling is rare: שְׁמִטָּה *release*, כְּלִמָּה *embarrassment*, קְהִלָּה *assembly*. This form seems to be the fem. of an infinitive *qtil* > קְטֵל, corresponding to the future in *i*(2), just as the form *qtulla* is the fem. of the inf. *qtul* > קְטֹל, § *k*. Instead of the expected form קְטֵלָה we find קְטִלָּה with a secondary doubling, perhaps by analogy with קְטֻלָּה where the doubling is phonetically necessary (§ *k*).

(1) For an attempt to reconstruct the evolution of forms such as בְּאֵר, זְאֵב, see J. Blau, *IOS* 7 (1977) 17-23. From these nouns must be distinguished זְעֵיר *a little* and פְּלֵיטָה *fugitives*, which are related to the diminutive pattern *qutayl* so common in Classical Arabic. Note that both words are almost always (three exceptions for the latter in BHS) spelled *plene*. Cf. Barr, *Spellings*, pp. 141, 147.

(2) Cf. Barth, *Nominalbildung*, § 96.

j **Qutl.** With the primitive vowel *u*. The form has generally been segholised to קֹטֶל (§ 96 A *b*). In some rare instances the vowel *ọ* has shifted to the end: קְטֹל (§ *k*).

Strong roots (Inflection, § 96 A *g*): אֹזֶן *ear*, עֹרֶף *back of neck*; with ה as second radical: אֹהֶל *tent*, בֹּהֶן *thumb*; with ע as second radical: פֹּעַל *work*; with a guttural as third guttural: גֹּבַהּ *height*. Many abstract nouns: גֹּבַהּ, עֹמֶק *depth*, אֹרֶךְ *length*, רֹחַב *breadth*, גֹּדֶל *greatness*, עֹצֶם *strength*, עֹשֶׁר *wealth*, חֹשֶׁךְ *darkness*.

With feminine ending: קׇרְחָה *bald spot*, חׇרְבָּה *ruin*, עׇרְלָה *foreskin*, חׇכְמָה *wisdom*, עׇרְמָה *cunning*, טׇהֳרָה *purity*, טֻמְאָה *impurity* (with *u* retained before the labial *m*), בׇּאְשָׁה *weed*.

ל״י roots (Inflection, § 96 A *s*): אֳנִי *fleet*, fem. (name of unit) אֳנִיָּה *ship*; עֳנִי, עׇנְיִ *affliction*; חֳלִי, חׇלְיִ *sickness*; *יֳפִי, יׇפְיִ *beauty*.

ל״ו roots: בֹּהוּ *emptiness*, תֹּהוּ *emptiness*.

N.B. The form *qull* in the ע״ע roots corresponds to the form *qutl*, § B *i*.

k **Qtul.** The vowel *ọ* has shifted to the end of the word in some nouns, especially in those with א as second radical, בְּאֹשׁ *stench*, לְאֹם pl. לְאֻמִּים *people*, שְׁאָט־ (doubtful meaning), סְבָךְ־ *thicket* (comp. סְבַךְ,

§ *g*).

The form **qtulla** with secondary doubling is fairly frequent. In most cases this form seems to be the feminine of the inf. *qtul* > קְטֹל. The spontaneous doubling of a non-final consonant after the vowel *u* is constant, § 18 *e*. E.g. אֲחֻזָּה *possession*, יְרֻשָּׁה *possession*, סְגֻלָּה *property*; פְּקֻדָּה *inspection* etc., גְּאֻלָּה *liberation*, חֲנֻכָּה *consecration*, אֲלֻמָּה *sheaf*, כְּהֻנָּה *priesthood*(1).

(1) On this formation, see T.N.D. Mettinger, "The nominal pattern *qətullā* in BH," *JSS* 16 (1971) 2-14. Most of these nouns, which are common in late books, are legal or technical terms.

§ 88 D. FORMS WITH TWO SHORT VOWELS

Qatal (Inflection, § 96 B *b*). With two primitive short *a* which have usually become *å*. This form is frequent both as substantive and adjective. *a*

Substantives: דָּבָר *word*, אָדָם *man*, פָּרָשׁ *horse*, בָּקָר *large cattle*, שָׂכָר *wages*, רָעָב *hunger*, צָמָא *thirst*.

Adjectives: חָכָם *wise*, חָדָשׁ *new*, יָשָׁר *upright*, רָחָב *wide*, חָזָק *strong*, קָטָן, fem. קְטַנָּה *small* (with spontaneous doubling, § 18 *f*), אֶחָד *one* (from *'aḥad*, with spontaneous virtual doubling, § 20 *c*).

ל"י roots (Inflection, § 96 B *f*): שָׂדֶה *field* and (poetic) שָׂדַי, קָנֶה *reed*, מָנֶה *mina*. ל"ו roots: עָנָו *humble*.

ע"ע roots: בָּדָד *isolated*, חָלָל *pierced*, *fatally wounded*. With feminine ending (Inflection, § 97 B *b*): the form *qatalat* has usually become קְטָלָה. This form is frequent with abstract nouns: צְדָקָה *justice*, נְבָלָה *infamy*, and expressions for giving out a loud noise: זְעָקָה, צְעָקָה and צְוָחָה *cry*, שְׁאָגָה *roaring*, אֲנָחָה *sigh*. Does בְּרָכָה *blessing* also belong here?

Qatil (Inflection, § 96 B *d*). The primitive form has normally become קָטֵל. This form is frequent with adjectives: it is the form which has supplied the stative perfect of the first group, § 41 *b*. It is fairly frequent with substantives, in particular with names of limbs (which are in part substantivised adjectives). *b*

Adjectives: כָּבֵד *heavy*, זָקֵן *old*, יָבֵשׁ *dry*, מָלֵא *full*, דָּשֵׁן *fat*, עָרֵל *uncircumcised*.

Substantives: רָחֵל *ewe*, גָּדֵר *wall*, חָצֵר *court*. Limbs of the body: כָּבֵד *liver* (i.e. *the heavy one*), כָּתֵף *shoulder* (probably *flat* or *large*), יָרֵךְ *thigh*, עָקֵב *heel*, כָּרֵשׂ* *belly*, probably חָזֶה *breast* (perhaps *that which faces, that which is opposite*). With an abstract meaning there is only גָּזֵל *robbery* (associated with עֹשֶׁק *gain of extortion, act of extortion*).

ל״י roots (Inflection, § 96 B *f*): דָּוֶה *ill*, יָפֶה *beautiful*, קָשֶׁה *hard*.

ל״ו roots: שָׁלֵו *quiet*.

ע״ע roots: adjectives of the type קַל *light*; שָׁמֵם *desolate* (cf. § B *g*, n.).

With feminine ending (Inflection, § 97 B *d*): בְּרֵכָה *pool*, בְּהֵמָה *beast*, גְּדֵרָה *wall*, לְבֵנָה *brick*; rarely in abstract nouns: מְהֵרָה *haste*. In some words the meaning has a passive nuance: טְרֵפָה *animal torn (by wild beasts)*, אֲבֵדָה *lost object*, גְּנֵבָה and גְּזֵלָה *stolen object*.

To this *qatilat* form also belong the aphaeretic forms of the פ״ו verbs, like לֵדָה *the bringing forth* (*of children*), which are quoted in § 75 *m*.

c **Qatul** (Inflection, § 96 B *e*). The primitive form has usually become קָטֹל. This form is frequent in adjectives: it is the form which has supplied the stative perfect of the second type, § 41 *b*. It is not used in Hebrew for substantives. The *u* reappears in the course of inflection, e.g. עֲגֻלָּה (§ 18 *e*).

Adjectives of space: אָרֹךְ *long*, עָמֹק *deep*, גָּבֹהַּ *high*, קָטֹן *small* (besides קָטָן); נָכֹחַ *straight*, עָגֹל *round*.

Adjectives of colour: אָדֹם, suf. אֲדֻמָּה *red*, יָרוֹק *green*, צָהֹב *golden*, צָחֹר *brilliant white* (?), שָׂרֹק *red*, שָׁחֹר *black*, בָּרֹד and נָקֹד *spotted*.

In the following adjectives, which also belong to the form *qatul* > קָטֹל, the *o̩* does not get deleted: גָּדוֹל *great*, טָהוֹר *pure*, קָדוֹשׁ *holy*, קָרוֹב *ne̩ar*, רָחוֹק *far* (cf. § 18 e, n.)(1).

(1) Cf. P. Joüon in *MUSJ* 5 (1911) 397ff.; BL, p. 467.

d **Qital.** (Inflection, § 96 B *c*). The primitive form has normally become קֵטָל. This rather rare form is found only with substantives, almost all of them concrete: עֵנָב *grapes*, שֵׁכָר *intoxicating drink*; צֵלָע *rib*, לֵבָב *heart* (extended form of לֵב which is far more frequent), חֵמָר *bitumen*, שֵׂעָר *hair*, שֵׁגָל *queen-consort*; מֵעֶה*, pl. מֵעַיִם* *internal organs*; נֵכָר *foreignness*. It seems that some of these nouns were originally *qitl* (cf. § 96 B *c*).

§ 88 E. FORMS WITH A SHORT FIRST VOWEL AND A LONG SECOND VOWEL

Qaṭāl. The primitive form has usually become קָטוֹל. a

Substantives: אָתוֹן *female donkey*, עָרוֹד *wild ass*; שָׁלוֹם *peace*, כָּבוֹד *glory*, שָׁלֹשׁ *three*, אָחוֹר *back part*; אָמוֹן *builder*, עָשׁוֹק *oppressor*(1).

As an action noun, קָטוֹל is used in the infinitive absolute, § 49 a. Genuine adjectives of the קָטוֹל type are usually *qatul* > קָטֹל, cf. § D *c*(2).

(1) In MH and Late Aramaic קָטוֹל is frequent for nouns for professions (*nomina opificum*), e.g. טָחוֹן *miller*, and for names of instruments, e.g. דָּקוֹר *perforator*. This tendency is already noticeable in LBH: Jer 22.3 עָשׁוֹק //21.12 עוֹשֵׁק; Jer 3.7-11 בָּגוֹדָה //בֹּגֵדָה. See M. Bar-Asher in *Leš* 41 (1977) 95-102.

(2) The spelling differentiation can hardly be a factor. If one includes words belonging to either category (qatul or qatāl), the statistics are: 2643 defectives vs. 4002 plenes. See AF, p. 198.

Qaṭīl (§ 96 D *b*). The primitive form has usually become קָטִיל. It is an extended form of *qatil*, § D *b*. With this form are found adjectives, sometimes substantivised, adjectives with a passive meaning(1), action nouns, for agricultural activities in particular: צָעִיר *small*, *young*, נָעִים *pleasant*, חָסִיד *pious*, נָקִי *clean*, עָנִי *afflicted* (§ 96 D *c*), כָּלִיל *entire* and *entirety*, אָסִיר *prisoner*, מָשִׁיחַ *anointed* (*Messiah*), נָשִׂיא *prince*, נָזִיר *consecrated*, *Nazirite*, פָּקִיד *overseer*, שָׂכִיר *mercenary*; חָלִיל (*pierced*) *flute*; יָמִין *right-hand side* (substantive), קָדִים *the East*, *the Orient* (substantive). Action nouns: agricultural operations: זָמִיר *pruning of the vine*, קָצִיר *harvest*, בָּצִיר *vintage*, אָסִיף *ingathering*, *harvest*, חָרִישׁ *ploughing*(2); utterance of a sound: זָמִיר *song*, הָגִיג *whisper*. b

With feminine ending. Action nouns: הֲלִיכָה *march*, חֲלִיפָה *change*, סְלִיחָה *forgiveness*(3).

(1) In Ugaritic and Aramaic *qatīl* (> קְטִיל in the latter) is the passive participle of the Qal conjugation.

(2) Some of these words and a couple of others not attested in the Bible occur in the 10th century Gezer calendar.

(3) In MH קְטִילָה can be used for the action noun of any verb.

Qaṭūl. The primitive form has usually become קָטוּל. It is an extended form of *qatul* (§ D *c*), just as *qatīl* is an extended form of *qatil*. We find adjectives, participles, and action nouns of this form. c

Adjectives: עָצוּם *mighty*, *numerous*, עָרוּם *shrewd*, בָּצוּר *fortified*. This קָטוּל form is the passive participle of the Qal conjugation (§ 50 *c*); sometimes the sense is virtually active, e.g. אָחוּז *holding* (§ 50 *e*).

Action nouns (rarely): שָׁבוּר *breaking* and חָרוּץ *mutilation* (Lv 22.22). With feminine ending: Abstract nouns: אֱמוּנָה *fidelity*, גְּבוּרָה *strength*, מְלוּכָה *kingship*. Action nouns: קְבוּרָה *burial*, שְׁבוּעָה *oath*, יְשׁוּעָה *effective help, victory*.

d **Qitāl.** The primitive form has usually become קְטוֹל: the primitive short vowel *i* is dropped, § 30 *d*: זְרוֹעַ *arm*, חֲמוֹר *donkey* (§ 21 *g*), אֱלוֹהַּ *god*; nouns of instruments, bonds, and receptacles: חֲגוֹר *belt*, f. חֲגוֹרָה, אֵזוֹר *belt* (א, § 21 *h*), שְׂרוֹךְ *sandal-thong*, צְרוֹר *bag*. For אִסָּר (with *å*, § *f*), cf. § 18 *g*.

With feminine ending: עֲבֹדָה *work*, בְּשֹׂרָה *good news* (*gospel*).

e **Qutāl.** The primitive form usually becomes קְטוֹל: the primitive short vowel *u* is dropped, § 30 *d*: רְחוֹב *broad place*, אֱנוֹשׁ *man* (§ 21 *h*). In some words, as is often the case in Arabic, this form has a pejorative nuance, e.g. for waste products, rubbish: נְעֹרֶת *tow*, בְּלוֹי *rag*, probably קְטֹרֶת *smoke*(1).

(1) Alongside קְטוֹרָה (1 x). The form *qutāl* is found in the Arabic *'uṭān* "smoke." According to BL, p. 469 קְטֹרֶת is a *qutul*.

f קְטָל (§ 96 D *d*). The Aramaic form קְטָל (*qṭål*) with originally long *å*(1) (instead of Hebrew *ọ*) is found in some nouns. The lost first vowel may have been *a*, *i* or *u*: כְּתָב *something written, book* (hence Arb. *kitāb*), קְרָב *battle*, סְפָר *numbering*, יְקָר *honour*, שְׁאָר *rest* (probably *qutāl*), מְצָר *stronghold*.

(1) This ָ must have been originally long in Hebrew also, in spite of the tendency to shorten it in the construct state (§ 96 D *d*).

g The Hebrew form קְטִיל may come from a hypothetical primitive form *qitīl*. In fact קְטִיל seems to be a reduction of *qatīl*, in which case the *a* would have been lost for abnormal and unknown causes, perhaps under Aramaic influence. Hardly anything but substantives are found in this form, and most of them seem to be of foreign origin: גְּבִיר *lord* (f. גְּבִירָה *lady*, absolute and cst. גְּבֶרֶת, § 97 F *b*), אֱוִיל *mad* (subst. and adj.), כְּסִיל *stupid*, *mad*, אֱלִיל *nothingness*, *idol*, יְגִיעַ *weariness*, בְּדִיל *lead*, בְּרִיחַ *bolt*, *bar*, דְּבִיר *hindmost chamber (of the temple)*, כְּפִיר *young lion*, מְחִיר *dowry* (Akkadian word); cf. BL, p. 471 and W.R. Garr, *VT* 37

(1987) 136.

The Hebrew form קְטוּל is found in some substantives, several of which are collective nouns. Quite normally the lost first vowel may be *i* or *u* or, abnormally, it may be *a* as in Aramaic. h

Perhaps belonging to *qitūl*: כְּלוּב *cage* (Tell el Amarna: *kilubi*).

Probably belonging to *qutūl* are the following collective nouns: זְכוּר *males*, רְכוּשׁ *movable possessions*, יְקוּם *the living* (for *qyūm*), all three without a plural; גְּבוּל *border* (collective and sg.), לְבוּשׁ *garment* (coll. and sg.).

Other nouns: גְּדוּד *band (of plunderers)*, זְבֻל *habitation*, גְּמוּל *deed* (fem., גְּמוּלָה), יְבוּל *produce*.

With first א (§ 21 *h*): אֵבוּס *crib, manger*, אֵטוּן *thread*, אֵמוּן *fidelity*. Judging from its meaning, אֵסוּר *bond, tie* is probably *qitāl*, § *d*; אֵסוֹר* seems to have become אֵסוּר by phonetic accident or analogy (cf. § 29 *b*).

§ 88 F. FORMS WITH LONG FIRST VOWEL AND SHORT SECOND VOWEL

Qātal > קוֹטָל (Inflection, § 96 C *b*). The primitive form *qātal* is very rare: perhaps עוֹלָם *aeon*(1), חוֹתָם *seal* (an Egyptian word), חֹתֶמֶת probably being its feminine form; כֹּתֶרֶת *capital of a column* (because of the pl. כֹּתָרוֹת), עֹפֶרֶת *lead*. a

The other words found in the קוֹטָל form come from *qawtal*; cf. § K *a*. According to § 26 *g*, עוֹלָל probably does not belong here, but rather to the pattern Qattal (§ 88 H *a*).

(1) But *-ām* here may be the accusative ending (Brock., *GvG*, I, p. 474).

Qātil > קוֹטֵל, קֹטֵל (Inflection, § 96 C *c*). Like *qatīl* (§ E *b*), it is an extended form of *qatil*. It is the form of the active participle of the Qal conjugation. b

Its use as a substantival participle is frequent: אוֹיֵב *enemy*, אֹהֵב *friend (loving* and also, e.g. 2Ch 20.7 *loved)*, קֹרֵא *partridge (which cries)*. Rather frequent as *nomen opificis:* רֹעֶה *shepherd*, צֹרֵף *jeweller* (properly speaking *smelter*), כּוֹבֵס *fuller* (participium tantum), שֹׁפֵט *judge*, סוֹפֵר *scribe*; sometimes denominative: שֹׁעֵר *doorkeeper* (from שַׁעַר *gate*), בּוֹקֵר *herdsman* (< בָּקָר), קֹהֶלֶת *man of assembly* (קָהָל); § 89 *b*.

With feminine ending: חוֹמָה *(protecting) wall* of a city, עוֹלָה *holocaust,* קוֹרָה *beam.* In two Aramaic-looking words ā has become ◌ָ (stable and probably long): דָּלִית* *branch,* pl. דָּלִיּוֹת; זָוִית* *angle,* pl. זָוִיּוֹת (cf. BL, p. 505).

According to § 26 *g*, עוֹלֵל probably does not belong here, but rather to the pattern Qattil (§ 88 H *c*). This pattern sometimes occurs side by side with the Qattal pattern (§ 88 H *a*): חֹרֵשׁ vs. חָרָשׁ, חֹבֵר vs. חַבָּר.

(1) Some *qātil* forms have become mere verbal nouns: e.g. Nu 24.20 אֹבֵד *destruction;* Jer 29.16 גּוֹלָה *exile;* 1Kg 10.5 עוֹלָתוֹ *his ascent* (// 2Ch 9.4 עֲלִיָּתוֹ). Originally, they were most likely genuine participles. Cf. P. Wernberg-Møller in *ZAW* 30 (1959) 54-67.

c **Qūtal.** Very rare form: שׁוּשַׁן *lily* (alongside שׁוֹשָׁן), סוּגַר *cage*(?).

§ 88 G. FORMS WITH TWO LONG VOWELS

Hebrew form קִיטוֹל, rather rare: נִיחֹחַ *pleasantness, satisfaction,* כִּידוֹר and נִיצוֹץ *spark,* תִּירוֹשׁ *must,* קִיטוֹר *smoke,* צִינֹק *pillory* (probably *qitāl* form with abnormal lengthening of the *ī*).

[§§ 88 H-I. FORMS WITH DOUBLED SECOND CONSONANT]

§ 88 H. FORMS WITH TWO SHORT VOWELS

a **Qattal** > קַטָּל. In Hebrew many nouns such as some *nomina opificum,* which in other Semitic languages are *qattāl,* have the form קַטָּל, e.g. טַבָּח *butcher.* Nevertheless the *å* here does not seem to be etymologically long[1]. Examples: Adjectives: קַנָּא *jealous* (5 times; קַנּוֹא twice), דַּוָּי *sick,* חַטָּא *sinner.* Substantives: גַּנָּב *thief,* דַּיָּן *judge,* רַכָּב *charioteer,* פָּרָשׁ *horseman* (for *parraš*), חָרָשׁ *workman* (for *ḥarraš*).

With feminine ending: קַטָּלָה or קַטֶּלֶת. The form קַטָּלָה is found in לֶהָבָה *flame,* cstr. לַהֶבֶת, חֲרָבָה *dryness,* יַבָּשָׁה (also יַבֶּשֶׁת, not cst.st.) same meaning. In some cases קַטָּלָה corresponds to the Aramaic Pael infinitive, where the ◌ָ is etymologically long[2]: בַּקָּרָה *care,* בַּקָּשָׁה *request,* בֶּהָלָה *suddenness,* נֶאָצָה *outrage,* נֶחָמָה *consolation.*

The form קַטֶּלֶת is frequent in nouns corresponding to the קִטֵּל adjectives of infirmities or of physical peculiarities, § *b*: עַוֶּרֶת *blindness* (עִוֵּר *blind*), קָרַחַת and גַּבַּחַת *baldness* (קֵרֵחַ and גִּבֵּחַ *bald*), דַּלֶּקֶת and

קַדַּחַת *burning fever;* אִוֶּלֶת *madness* (with attenuation of *a* to *i*). Some nouns of vessels: צַלַּחַת *deep vase,* צַפַּחַת *jug,* קַלַּחַת *kettle.*

(1) Same problem with the *å* of the afformative *ån*, § M *a*. In both cases we can hardly think in terms of borrowings from Aramaic, as for קָטָל (§ E *f*). The cst. state in ַ indicates that the *å* is not etymologically long: דַּיַּן, חָרָשׁ, פָּרָשׁ. The retention of qameṣ in the cst. pl. is no proof to the contrary: חָרָשֵׁי, חַטָּאֵי (comp. חַטָּאֵי, § 96 A *e*), מַלָּחֵיהֶם. For a diachronic analysis, cf. O. Loretz, "Die hebräische Nominalform *qattāl*," *Bib* 41 (1960) 411-16. See also K. Aartun in *JNWSL* 4 (1975) 1-8.

(2) If these Hebrew nouns have been influenced by Aramaic, the ָ can be regarded as long. See the Aramaic form of the causative הַקְטָלָה, § 88 L *b*.

The form קִטֵּל, a genuine Hebrew form, is found in adjectives of infirmities or of physical peculiarities: עִוֵּר *blind,* אִלֵּם *dumb,* פִּסֵּחַ *lame,* גִּבֵּן *hunchback,* עִקֵּשׁ *crooked,* חֵרֵשׁ *deaf* (for *ḥirreš*), כֵּהֶה *darkened,* צִחֶה *dry*. We also have גֵּאֶה *proud,* פִּקֵּחַ *seeing* (antonym of עִוֵּר), שִׁלֵּשׁ and רִבֵּעַ *of the third* and *forth generation* respectively; on the last two, see § 96 C *c*(1). b

(1) Tur-Sinai argues that this pattern is related to the Piel passive participle: N.H. Tur-Sinai, *The Language and the Book*, the *Language* vol. [Heb] (Jerusalem, 1954), pp. 265-67.

Qattil > קַטֵּל is the infinitive construct of the Piel conjugation in the active voice, § 52 *a*. c

Quttal > קֻטָּל (rare): סֻלָּם *ladder;* קֻבַּעַת *chalice.* d

§ 88 I. FORMS WITH LONG SECOND VOWEL

Qattāl > קַטּוֹל (rare): קַנּוֹא *jealous* (twice; five times קַנָּא, § H *a*). a

Qattīl > קַטִּיל. An intensive form of *qatīl:* אַבִּיר *strong,* אַדִּיר *powerful,* אַמִּיץ *firm,* כַּבִּיר *great,* שַׁלִּיט *ruler,* צַדִּיק *righteous,* עַלִּיז *joyful,* עַתִּיק *ancient;* בָּרִיחַ *swift* (for *barrīḥ*), עָרִיץ *violent,* פָּרִיץ *burglar, wall breaker.* b

Qattūl > קַטּוּל. An intensive form of *qatūl:* חַנּוּן *gracious,* רַחוּם *merciful,* שַׁכּוּל *childless,* קַשּׁוּב *attentive.* Substantives: עַמּוּד *column,* אַשֻּׁר *step.* With feminine ending: חַבּוּרָה *bruise,* בַּטֻּחוֹת *security.* c

קַטּוֹל represents various primitive forms which are not always easy to distinguish. The ַ could be an attenuated *a*. The *o* comes from either *ā* or *u*. Examples: גִּבּוֹר *hero* (probably from *gabbār*), שִׁכּוֹר *drunkard* (*šakkār* d or *šikkār)*, צִפּוֹר *bird* (from *ṣuppur*; *i* for *u* by dissimilation, cf. § 29 *h*); רִמּוֹן *pomegranate* (from *rummān* > *rummọn*; *i* by dissimilation).

e קִטּוּל may come from *quttūl* (by dissimilation) or from *qattūl* (by attenuation of *a* to *i*). This form is mainly used, as in MH, in action nouns corresponding to the Piel conjugation: צִפּוּי *coating*, שִׁלּוּם *retribution*, שִׁקּוּץ *horror*, שִׁקּוּי *drink*; with concrete meaning: לִמּוּד *disciple* (properly speaking *teaching*), עִזּוּז *strong* (strictly speaking, *strength*). Quite often in the masc. plural: גִּדּוּפִים *insult*, מִלּוּאִים *filling*, *consecration*, נִחֻמִים *consolation*, *compassion*, שִׁכֻּלִים *childlessness*, שִׁלּוּחִים *repudiation*(1).

(1) *Pace* L. Gulkowitsch, *Die Bildung von Abstraktbegriffen in der hebr. Sprachgeschichte* (Leipzig, 1931), p. 22, n. 7, this pattern is a rather productive one in MH: see J. Elizur, "The *qittul* pattern in Mishnaic Hebrew," M. Bar-Asher (ed.), *Meḥqarim balašon II-III* [Heb] (Jerusalem, 1987), pp. 67-93.

§ 88 J. FORMS WITH REPEATED CONSONANT

a Repetition of the third consonant:

Qatlal. Adjective שַׁאֲנָן *quiet* (pl. שַׁאֲנַנִּים) and רַעֲנָן *green* (pl. רַעֲנַנִּים); see the corresponding perfects, § 59 *b*.

Qutlal: Adjective אֻמְלָל* *feeble*; see the corresponding perfect, § 59 *b*.

Qatlīl: סַגְרִיר *rain (continuous* or *intermittent)* Pr 27.15†; עַבְטִיט *heavy debt*.

Qatlūl: נַעֲצוּץ *thorn-bush*, נַאֲפוּפִים *adulterers*, שַׁעֲרוּר *horrible*(1).

(1) Perh. also זְנוּנִים *prostitution* (*zanūn* for *zanwūw*); cf. P. Joüon in *Bib* 1 (1920) 366. Cf. also נַהֲלֹלִים *pasture*.

b Repetition of the second and third consonants:

Qataltal: Two diminutive colour adjectives: אֲדַמְדָּם *reddish* (from אָדֹם) and יְרַקְרַק *greenish* (from יָרוֹק). Other adjectives: הֲפַכְפַּךְ *tortuous*, חֲלַקְלַק* *slippery*, עֲקַלְקַל* *tortuous*.

Qataltul: One diminutive colour adjective: fem. שְׁחַרְחֹרֶת *blackish* (from שָׁחֹר). Another adjective: פְּתַלְתֹּל *tortuous*.

Qataltūl: אֲסַפְסֻף *mixed multitude* Nu 11.4 † (from אָסוּף *gathered*).

c Repetition of the (biliteral) root, namely ע"ע or ע"ו:

Qalqal: גַּלְגַּל *wheel,* דַּרְדַּר *thorns,* עַפְעַפַּיִם *eyelids.* Also belonging to this form: כּוֹכָב *star (*kabkab > *kawkab > koḫåv),* כִּכָּר *disk, talent (*karkar > kirkar > kikkar),* and probably טוֹטָפוֹת *frontlet bands (*ṭafṭaf).*

Qulqul: קָדְקֹד *top of the head,* גֻּלְגֹּלֶת *skull.*

Qalqūl: בַּקְבֻּק *jug,* חַרְחֻר *burning fever*; in the plural: שַׁעֲשֻׁעִים *delights,* תַּעְתֻּעִים *jokes.*

§ 88 K. QUADRILITERAL FORMS

Forms with four radicals are relatively few. In some, one of the consonants may be of secondary origin. We shall here conventionally designate the fourth radical by the fourth letter of the alphabet: ד = *d*.

Qatlad is the most frequent: עַקְרָב *scorpion,* עַכְבָּר *mouse,* קַרְקַע *bottom,* חַשְׁמַל *electrum (?),* גּוֹזָל *young bird* (from *gawzal) (cf. § F *a*), גּוֹרָל *lot* (from *gawral); זַלְעָפָה *violence* etc. (secondary ל). With א as first radical: אַלְמָנָה *widow,* אַמְתַּחַת *bag,* אַרְנֶבֶת *hare.* In שַׁלְהֶבֶת *flame* (alongside לַהַב) the שׁ is probably secondary (preformative שׁ of the causative in Aramaic)(1). a

(1) For a possible pattern *qatyal* or *qityal*, see A. van Selms, "Pa'yal formations in Ugaritic and Hebrew nouns," *JNES* 26 (1967) 289-95.

Qatlud: כַּרְכֹּב *margin,* כַּרְכֹּם *saffron,* חַרְגֹּל species of *locust,* פַּרְעֹשׁ *flea,* קַרְדֹּם *axe,* קַרְסֹל *ankle;* חַרְצֻבּוֹת *fetters.* b

Qatlīd: שַׁרְבִיט *scepter* (secondary ר), זַרְזִיף *shower.* c

Qatlūd גַּלְמוּד *barren* (ל is perhaps secondary), עַכְשׁוּב *viper(?),* שַׁבְּלוּל *snail* (dagesh dirimens, § 18 *k*). d

Forms with **three vowels:** סְמָדַר *blossoming,* עַכָּבִישׁ *spider,* חַלָּמִישׁ *granite,* cst. חַלְמִישׁ, § 96 D *b*, n. e

Quinqueliteral forms are very rare: צְפַרְדֵּעַ *frog;* שַׁעַטְנֵז *mixed stuff.* f

§ 88 L. FORMS WITH PREFORMATIVES

The preformatives א, ה and י are rather uncommon; מ and ת, on the other hand, are very frequent.

א is prosthetic (§ 17 *a*) in a few nouns: אֶזְרוֹעַ *arm* (twice) alongside a the usual זְרוֹעַ, אֶצְבַּע *finger* (Ar. *'iṣba'*; Syr. *ṣev'â*), אֶצְעָדָה *bracelet*, אֶזְרָח *indigenous*, אַשְׁמוּרָה, cst. אַשְׁמֹרֶת *night-watch*. With א forming an open semi-syllable: אֲבַטִּחִים *melons*, אֲבַעְבֻּעֹת *pustules*, אֱגוֹז *nut*.

Three words in the *'aqtal* form seem to correspond to the Arabic *'aqtal* form (used as elative, as adjective for colours and certain physical peculiarities): אַכְזָב *deceptive (torrent)*, אֵיתָן (*'aytan*) *perennial (torrent)*, אַכְזָר (poet.) *cruel, executioner*(1). For אַזְכָּרָה, cf. § *b*.

In other words the initial Alef seems to be a radical, § K *a*.

(1) The number אַרְבַּע *four* (§ 100 *d*) also has this form. Note that in these forms we have אַ and not אֲ.

b ה is only found in הַקְטָלָה, which is the form of the Aramaic causative infinitive(1). We only find the infinitive הֲנָפָה in Is 30.28† *the act of winnowing* (from נוף, probably for assonance with נָפַת). We find substantives הֲנָחָה Esth 2.18† *unburdening* (from נוח), הַכָּרָה Is 3.9† *bias* (*for a person*), הַצָּלָה Esth 4.14† *deliverance*.

With א for ה: אַזְכָּרָה *memorial*.

(1) Note קַטָּלָה as infinitive of the Aramaic Pael conjugation (§ 88 H *a*).

c ' is found in some nouns which perhaps originally were futures in the 3 p.m.sg., as several proper nouns are, e.g., יִצְחָק *he laughs*, יַעֲקֹב *he trips*(1).

Examples: יִצְהָר *exquisite oil* (perhaps *it is bright*); יַלְקוּט *pocket* (perhaps *it collects*), יַחְמוּר *species of antelope*, יָרִיב *adversary*; יְקוּם *substance*; יַנְשׁוּף *owl*; also יהוה?

(1) Many cognate languages display similar "sentence-names." Cf. D. Cohen, *Études* [§ 34a, n. 2], p. 34. M. Noth, *Die israelitischen Personennamen im Rahmen der gemeinsemitischen Namengebung* (Stuttgart, 1928). For an attempted morphological classification, see L. Koehler, "Jod als hebräisches Nominalpräfix," *Die Welt des Orients*, 1 (1947-52) 404f.

d מ is very frequently used as a preformative. The two primitive vowels of preformative מ are *a* and *i*, which normally become ָ and ֵ in an open syllable. In a closed syllable *a* can be maintained or it can be weakened to ַ or ֶ; *i* is maintained except before a guttural where it becomes ֶ (§ 29 *e*, n.). As we can see, it is difficult to identify the primitive vowel of preformative מ. That is why the Hebrew forms will be given here(1).

Nouns with preformative מ are mainly abstract nouns(2), nouns of place and nouns of instrument. As nouns of place we mainly find the form מַקְטָל, then מִקְטָל; as nouns of instrument mainly מַקְטֵל.

(1) In the tradition lying behind the Secunda and Jerome's transliterations, *ma-* predominates, *mi-* or *me-* being largely confined to cases where R1 is a sibilant: e.g. Ps 35.20 מִרְמוֹת μαρμωθ; 46.10 מִלְחָמוֹת μαλαμωθ, but 46.8 מִשְׂגָּב μισγαβ. See Brønno, *Studien*, pp. 172-81, and Sperber, *Hist. Gram.*, pp. 206f. This tendency is observable in the Babylonian and Samaritan traditions of Hebrew pronunciation as well: see Yeivin, *Babylonian Tradition*, pp. 995f., and Ben-Ḥayyim, *LOT*, vol. 5, pp. 206f. For a recent, fresh study of the question, see Lambdin, art. cit. [§ 29 *aa*, n.], esp. p. 138.

(2) Compare the rare infinitive forms in מַ, § 49 *e*.

מַקְטָל[1]. Strong roots: מַלְאָךְ *envoy, angel*[2], מַאֲכָל *food*, מַמְלָכָה *kingdom*, מְלָאכָה *business* (for מַלְאָכָה*, § 24 *f*), מַאֲרָב *ambush*, מַעֲרָב *west*, מַעְבָּרָה *ford*, מַעֲמָק* *deep place*. e

פ״ן roots: מַתָּן *gift*, מַטָּע *plantation* (and the plants themselves, Is 61.3), מַסָּע* *decampment* (cf. § 49 e), מַשָּׂא *weight, burden*, מַשָּׁא *debt*. From יָדַע we have the Aramaising and late form מַדָּע *knowledge*; from יצע we have †מַצָּע *couch* (§ 77 *b*).

פ״ו roots: מוֹשָׁב *dwelling-place* (from *mawšab*), מוֹצָא *exit*, מוֹרָא *fear*, מֹדָע *relative*[3], מוֹרָשָׁה *inheritance* (in the locative meaning), probably מוֹלֶדֶת *birth place* (but *maqtil* is possible). In some nouns the ọ, for some peculiar reason, has been weakened to *u* (cf. § 29 *b*); מוּסָר *correction* (*maw* > *mọ* > *mu*), מוּצָק *fusion*, מוּעָדָה *convention*[4].

פ״י roots: מֵיטָב *good thing* (from *mayṭab*), מֵיתָר *cord*, מֵישָׁרִים *rectitude*.

ל״ה roots[5]: מַרְאֶה *aspect* (from *mar'ay*), מַעֲשֶׂה *deed*, מַעֲלֶה *ascent*, מַעֲנֶה *intention*, מַטֶּה *stick*; feminine מַכָּה *stroke*; with apocope: מַ֫עַל *above*, לְמַ֫עַן *because of*.

ע״ו and ע״י roots: מָקוֹם *place* (from *maqām*), מָבוֹא *entrance*, מָדוֹן *quarrel* (root דין); with consonantal י: מַעְיָן *source*; מְנוֹרָה *candlestick*. In nouns of the type מְנוּחָה *rest* (alongside מָנוֹחַ) the *u* is usually for ọ (§ 29 *b*); but in some nouns the *u* may be primitive. The noun מָעוֹז (with וֹ) *place of refuge*, is *maqtal* from עוז *to take refuge* (cf. Arb. *maʿāḏ*). The doubling of ז in the inflection (e.g. מָעֻזִּי, מָעוּזִּי) is due to the contamination of the root עזז *to be strong*, caused by closeness of meaning (*place of refuge, stronghold*). The sibilant has also contributed to the doubling. The intermediate ָ is stable; likewise in מָגֵן

(§ *h*).

ע"ע roots: מָסָךְ *cover, protection,* מַשָּׁק* act of *penetrating* ? (Aramaic doubling); in the dissociated state: מַעֲלָל *action.* The abnormal form מֶמֶר *bitterness, grief* (Pr 17.25†) is probably a *maqtal* recast as a *qatl* (**mamarr* > *mamar* > *mamr*); comp. מֹרֶךְ, § *j*, and תֶּמֶס, § *v*.

N.B. In מַשָּׁאוֹן *deceit* (root נשׁא) the form *maqtal* has the afformative *ān*, as in Aramaic (cf. Brock., *GvG*, I, p. 391).

(1) For the inflection of מַקְטָל as well as of מִקְטָל, מֶקְטָל cf. § 96 C *b*.

(2) The primary meaning is doubtless abstract: *sending, mission.* Comp. Arb. *mal'ak* "message" and "messenger"; likewise, in Latin, *nuntius*.

(3) The primary meaning is doubtless abstract: *knowledge*, hence the concrete meaning, *an acquaintance*, and, consequently, *relation* (*by marriage*). Irregular pataḥ.

(4) These forms look like Hofal participles.

(5) Since ־ָה can also come from *iy*, there may be some doubt about the primitive form.

f מִקְטָל. Strong roots: מִגְדָּל *tower,* מִבְטָח *trust,* מִשְׁפָּט *judgement,* מִלְחָמָה *war,* מִבְחָר* *excellence* (less frequent than מִבְחוֹר), מִשְׁקָל *weight* (more frequent than מִשְׁקוֹל). Cf. infinitive מִקְטַל, § 49 *e*.

ל"ה roots: מִקְנֶה *possession,* מִקְוֶה *hope;* fem. מִרְמָה *deceit,* מִצְוָה *precept.*

ע"ו roots: מֵרוֹץ *race* Ec 9.11†.

ע"ע roots: מֵסַב *that which surrounds,* מֵצַר *narrow spot, anxiety.*

g מֶקְטָל(1): מֶרְכָּב *chariot*: fem. מֶרְכָּבָה, cst. מִרְכֶּבֶת, pl. מַרְכָּבוֹת; מֶרְחָב *large place;* מֶרְחָק *distant place;* מֶלְקָחַיִם *tongs,* suf. מַלְקָחֶיהָ; מֶמְשָׁלָה *domination,* suf. מַמְשְׁלוֹתָיו. Before a guttural: מֶחֱזָה *window,* מֶחֱצָה *half,* מֶחְקָר *secret place.*

(1) The use of the מֶקְטָל must have been influenced by a fondness for the vocalic sequence ę - ǫ, § 29 *f*. For the primitive form cf. § 29 *e* 2.

h מַקְטֵל (cst. מִקְטַל § 96 C *c*). Strong roots: מַרְבֵּץ *resting-place (of animals),* מַשְׁעֵן *support,* מַרְזֵחַ *cries,* מַשְׁבֵּר *mouth of the womb* (?), מַשְׁעֵנָה *support, staff,* מַהְפֵּכָה *catastrophe.*

פ"ן roots: מַפֵּץ *war-club;* מַצֵּבָה *stele,* מַסֵּכָה *fusion,* מַגֵּפָה *blow, defeat.*

פ"י roots: מוֹעֵד (for *maw'id*) *appointed place,* מוֹקֵשׁ *snare.*

פ"א roots: likewise we find מֹאזְנַיִם *pair of scales* (in Arabic root *wazana*), מוֹסֵר *bond,* from *ma'sir* (with א omitted in the spelling); cf. § 24 *d*.

ע"י roots: מְרִיבָה *contestation,* מְלִיצָה *riddle,* מְדִינָה *province.*

ע"ע roots: מָגֵן *shield* (with stable ־ָ, § 96 C *c*: מָגִנֵּי, מָגִנַּי); feminine

מְגִלָּה *roll*, מְזִמָּה *purpose*, מְסִלָּה *highway*, מְאֵרָה *malediction, misery* (for *m'ir-ra*), מְגֵרָה *plane*(?).

מִקְטֵל (§ 96 C *c*) is a very rare form for *maqtil*; it is only found in מִזְבֵּחַ *altar* and מִסְפֵּד *act of lamenting* (under the influence of the sibilant, Brock., *GvG*, I, p. 381). i

מַקְטֹל (from *maqtul*) cannot always be distinguished with certainty from מַקְטוֹל (from *maqtāl*), § *k*. The feminine form מַקְטֹלֶת *may* come from *maqtulat* or from *maqtālat*; in fact every instance seems to be *maqtulat*. j

Strong roots: מַחְשֹׂף *peeling off*, מַעֲרֻמִּים *nudity*. With feminine ending: מַאֲכֹלֶת *food*, מַשְׂכֹּרֶת *reward*, מַחֲלֹקֶת *division*, מַתְכֹּנֶת *exact measure*, מַחֲגֹרֶת *act of girding* , מַלְכֹּדֶת *snare*, מַרְכֹּלֶת *market*.

ע"ו roots. In a מְקוּלָה form the *u* may be primitive or come from *ọ* (cf. § 29 *b*)(1). When there is a doublet, *u* is an attenuation of *ọ*, e.g., מְנוּחָה *rest*, alongside מָנוֹחַ. Otherwise the primitive form is doubtful, e.g. מְהוּמָה *trouble, disorder*, מְשׁוּבָה *apostasy*.

ע"ע roots. The expected form *maqull* > מָקֹל is not attested. We only find the two abnormal forms מְתֹם *integrity* (**matumm* > *mutumm* > *mtumm*) and מֹרֶךְ *fear* (**murukk* > *muruk* > *murk*), cf. Brock., *GvG*, I, p. 381(2).

(1) Likewise for the form תְּקוּלָה (§ *s*).
(2) Compare the irregular form תֹּאַר (§ *v*).

מַקְטוֹל (from *maqtāl*) [contrast מַקְטֹל (from *maqtul*, § *j*)]: מַחְסוֹר *lack*(1), מַלְקוֹחַ *booty*, מַטְמוֹן *hidden treasure*, מַכְאוֹב *pain*, מַלְקוֹשׁ *last rains*, מַשְׁקוֹף *upper beam of a door*, מַשּׂוֹר *saw* (from נשׂר). k

There are no feminine endings (cf. § *j*).

(1) a *maqtul*, according to BL, p. 493.

מִקְטוֹל: מִבְחוֹר *excellence* (more frequent than מִבְחָר*), מִשְׁקוֹל *weight* (less frequent than מִשְׁקָל), מִזְמוֹר *psalm*, מִכְשׁוֹל *stumbling*, מִקְצוֹעַ *corner*, מִכְלוֹל *perfection*, מִישׁוֹר *plain* (from ישׁר). Feminine forms: מִשְׁקֹלֶת *plummet*, מִכְמֹרֶת *fillet*. l

מַקְטִיל, which is the form of the Hifil participle, is rarely used for substantives: מַשְׁחִית *perdition, ruin*, מַכְבִּיר *abundance*. m

מַקְטוּל. Whereas *maqtūl*, in Arabic, is the passive participle of the first conjugation, מַקְטוּל forms concrete nouns, e.g. nouns of instruments. Thus we can suspect that *u* sometimes stands for *ọ*. Examples: מַפּוּחַ *bellows* (Dalman: MH מַפּוֹחַ), plural מַקְצוּעוֹת *planes* (?) (Dalman: n

MH מַקְצוֹעוֹת), מַנְעוּל *lock*, מַאֲבוּס *cattle-shed* (?), מַמְּגֻרָה *granary* (dagesh dirimens, § 18 *k*); מַבּוּעַ *source* (Syr. *mabbo'å*); מַבּוּל *deluge* (cf. Syr. *måmolå*). The following words perhaps had a participial sense, as in Arabic: מַלְבּוּשׁ *garment* (Arb. *malbūs*, i.e. *that which is donned*), מַסְלוּל *road* (perhaps *something heaped up*), מַצְפּוּנִים *hidden things*, מַחֲלֻיִים *illnesses*.

o ת, though less often used than מ as a preformative, is nonetheless very common. The vowel of preformative ת is almost always *a*; *i* is only found in the form תִּקְטָל where it may not be primitive. Here too we shall give the Hebrew forms. Forms with a feminine ending are by far the more common(1). Thus there is only one instance of the form תַּקְטֵל in the masculine, and none of תִּקְטָל and תַּקְטֹל.

The majority of nouns with ת preformative are verbal substantives, e.g. תְּעוּדָה *testimony*. These forms are found mainly in the ע"ו roots, but also in the פ"ו and ע"ע roots. According to their meaning, verbal substantives can be associated with any conjugation. In fact they are mainly associated with Hifil, less often with Piel, Hitpael and Qal, rarely with Nifal. The same verbal substantive can, depending on its meaning, be associated with several conjugations. Thus תְּשׁוּבָה (root שׁוּב) with the usual meaning of *return* is associated with the Qal, whilst with the rare meaning of *answer* it is associated with Hifil; תְּחִנָּה (root חנן) in the sense of *prayer* is associated with Hitpael, in the rare sense of *grace* it is associated with Qal. Examples: **Qal:** תְּמוּתָה *death*; **Nifal:** תַּרְדֵּמָה *deep sleep*; **Piel:** תְּהִלָּה *praise*, תַּנְחוּמִים *consolations*; **Hifil:** תְּחִלָּה *beginning*, תְּעוּדָה *testimony*, תּוֹלֵדָה *generation*, תְּשׁוּעָה *effective help, victory*, § *s*; **Hitpael:** תַּחֲנוּנִים *supplications*, תְּפִלָּה *prayer*.

(1) Is this pure coincidence, or has ת, a letter associated with the feminine gender, influenced the use of the feminine ending?

p תַּקְטֵל: תֵּימָן *south*, probably תּוֹשָׁב *resident alien* (cst. תּוֹשַׁב, but pl. cst. תֹּשָׁבֵי, § 96 C *b*). Feminine forms: תּוֹצָאוֹת *issues*, תּוֹעָפוֹת *masses*(?).

The feminine forms of the ל"ה roots, e.g. תַּאֲוָה *desire*, are ambiguous; they can come either from *taqtalat* or from *taqtilat*. The lack of sufficient data often makes it impossible to decide which. תּוֹדָה *praise* seems to be *taqtilat* (Syr. *tawditå*); תּוֹרָה *law* seems to be *taqtalat* (comp. Arm. אוֹרָיְתָא).

q תִּקְטָל. Feminine forms: תִּפְאָרָה (twice) and תִּפְאֶרֶת *ornament*, תִּפְלֶצֶת

fear(?). For the feminine forms of ל"ה roots, cf. § *p*: תִּקְוָה *hope*.

r תַּקְטֵל: תַּשְׁבֵּץ *cloth*. All the other nouns have the feminine ending: תַּרְדֵּמָה *deep sleep*, תַּרְעֵלָה *reeling*, תּוֹכֵחָה and (more commonly) תּוֹכַחַת *correction*, תּוֹלֵדָה *generation*. In the ע"ע roots the first vowel *a* is dropped: תְּחִלָּה *beginning*, תְּחִנָּה *prayer, grace*, § *o*, תְּפִלָּה *prayer*. In the ל"ה roots, with the ending ־ָה, the form *taqtilat* cannot be distinguished from the form *taqtalat* (§ *p*). With the endings ־ִיָּה and ־ִית the form is *taqtilat*: תַּאֲנִיָּה *sadness*, תּוּשִׁיָּה *advice, purpose*(1) (with *u* for *ọ*); תַּרְבִּית *profit*, תַּרְמִית *deceit*, תַּעֲנִית *fasting (humiliation)*, תַּבְנִית *form*, תַּכְלִית *completion*.

(1) Cf. P. Joüon in *MUSJ* 3(190-09) 326.

s תַּקְטֹל (from *taqtul*). No instance of masculine nouns.

In the ע"ו verbs the feminine form is תְּקוּלָה, in which *u* may either be primitive or come from *ọ* (cf. § 29 *b*)(1). Only rarely can the origin of this *u* be determined. Examples: תְּקוּמָה *resistance*, תְּמוּתָה *death*, תְּבוּסָה *act of trampling underfoot*, תְּמוּרָה *exchange*, תְּשׁוּבָה *return, answer*, § *o*, תְּבוּאָה *entrance, produce*, תְּעוּדָה *testimony*; תְּבוּנָה *intelligence* (from בין).

The form תְּקוּלָה has spread beyond the ע"ו roots: תְּקוּפָה *circuit* (root נקף), תְּרוּפָה *remedy* (root רפא), תְּשׁוּעָה *effective help, victory* (root ישׁע, perhaps under the influence of the synonym יְשׁוּעָה).

(1) Likewise for the form מְקוּלָה, § *j*. Cf. P. Joüon in *Bib* 1 (1920) 369. According to Brock., *GvG*, I, p. 359, the form would be a substitute for *qutūl*.

t תַּקְטִיל. Very rare and of Aramaic origin: תַּלְמִיד *disciple*, תַּכְרִיךְ *mantle*.

u תַּקְטוּל: תַּגְמוּל *kindness*, תַּעֲנוּג *delights*, תַּחֲנוּנִים *supplications*, תַּמְרוּרִים *bitterness*. Feminine forms: תַּהֲלוּכָה *procession*, תַּהְפּוּכָה *reversal, perverseness*, תַּעֲלוּמָה *mystery*(1).

(1) Cf. W. von Soden, "Die Nomialform *taqtûl* im Hebräischen und Aramäischen," *ZAH* 2 (1989) 77-85, where the author argues that this pattern comprises emotionally charged nouns.

v Moreover a secondary ת, the origin of which is obscure, is found in certain forms: תֶּ֫מֶס *liquefaction* probably comes from **tamass* > *tamas* > *tams* (comp. מֶ֫מֶר, § *e*); likewise probably תֶּ֫בֶל *pollution, infamy* (בלל). The word תַּ֫עַר *razor* is associated with the root ערה, תְּעָלָה *healing* to

עָלָה. The word תֹּאַר *aspect* seems to come from ראה with metathesis (cp. מֹרֶךְ, § *j*): it would then be a *taqtul* word reshaped into a *qutlat*.

§ 88 M. FORMS WITH AFFORMATIVES

a The afformative **ān* usually becomes *ọn* וֹן. In a certain number of nouns which in other Semitic languages have *ān*, we find ָן in Hebrew, e.g. קָרְבָּן *offering*. However the *å* does not seem to be etymologically long here(1). For the ending ָן in place names, cf. § 91 *h*.

(1) Same problem with the *å* of the form *qattål*, § H *a*. One might hesitate in the case of a noun which would be a pure borrowing from Aramaic. But even with עִנְיָן *affair* (only in Ecclesiastes) the cst. state עִנְיַן indicates that Hebrew has shortened the primitive long *ā*. The cst. state in ַ is also found with קִנְיָן, שֻׁלְחָן, קָרְבָּן, אָבְדָן.

b **Qatalān** is made up of *qatal* + *ān*. This form of abstract noun, as expected, becomes קְטָלוֹן in Hebrew, which is only found in רְעָבוֹן *famine*(?). Elsewhere *qatalān* has a doubling of the second consonant. This secondary doubling was perhaps due to the need to preserve the three vowels which give the form a characteristic aspect. This doubling may also have originated in certain nouns for some phonetic reason and then spread to the others(1). The primitive first vowel *a* has only been preserved in שַׁבָּתוֹן *abstention from work, rest*, probably under the influence of שַׁבָּת (same meaning). (Compare the name of the city Ἀκκαρών [Akk. *Amqarrūna*] with עֶקְרוֹן). Everywhere else the *a* is weakened to *i* (*qittålọn*), probably because it is far from the stressed long syllable *ọn*(2). In the cst. state or with a suffix, the form is קִטְלוֹן, without doubling (usually)(3), but with seghol instead of ḥireq (but עִזְבוֹנַיִךְ Ez 27.27) when the first radical is guttural הִגָּיוֹן, cst. הֶגְיוֹן *musing*, עִשָּׂרוֹן, pl. עֶשְׂרוֹנִים *tenth part*. Examples: זִכָּרוֹן, cst. זִכְרוֹן, pl. זִכְרֹנִים *remembrance*, שִׁבָּרוֹן *breaking*, פִּקָּדוֹן *deposit*, עִצָּבוֹן *hard work*, צִמָּאוֹן *arid land*, חִפָּזוֹן *hasty flight*, בִּטָּחוֹן *confidence*, שִׁמָּמוֹן *desolation*; before ר, which cannot be doubled: עֵרָבוֹן *pledge*(4), דֵּרָאוֹן *horror*. In ל"ה verbs we find likewise חִזָּיוֹן *vision* (9 times; but 36 times חָזוֹן, cf. below), שִׁגָּיוֹן, הִגָּיוֹן a kind of *song*, גִּלָּיוֹן *polished plate*, נִקָּיוֹן *purity*, כִּלָּיוֹן *annihilation*; before ר: הֵרָיוֹן *pregnancy*. But alongside these forms in which י is found there are some syncopated forms: חָזוֹן *vision*, עָוֹן *iniquity*, רָצוֹן *good will*, גָּאוֹן *highness*, הָמוֹן *tumult*, רָזוֹן *leanness*, חָרוֹן *anger*.

In the ע"י verbs the form is very much the same as the preceding one, e.g. שָׂשׂוֹן *joy* (root שׂישׂ, inf. שׂוּשׂ): *śaś* + *ān*, on the analogy of *qatal* + *ān*, just as קָם and דָּן are formed on the analogy of *qatal*; זָדוֹן *pride*, לָצוֹן *insolence*(5).

Abnormal forms: in אֲבַדּוֹן *perdition,* the third radical is doubled (cf. Revelation 9.11 'Ἀβαδδών). In Esth 9.5 we have the Aramaic form אַבְדָן.

In Gn 3.16 הֵרֹנֵךְ the form seems to be incorrect (read הֵרְיוֹנֵךְ); the (unattested) syncopated form would be הֵרוֹנֵךְ*.

(1) Thus עִוָּרוֹן *blindness* is perh. due to analogy with the adj. עִוֵּר and with Piel (the only conjugation attested of the root); עִשָּׂרוֹן *a tenth part* on the analogy of Piel *to tithe.*

(2) Compare **qaṭṭaltem*, which has become *qiṭṭạltẹm*, § 52 *a*, n.

(3) This form has merged with the form קִטְלוֹן (from *qitlān*), § *c*. Alongside the forms *qitlān* and *qutlān*, there is no form *qatlān*; but *qatalān* seems to be an extended form of *qatlān*. The cst. state קִטְלוֹן may come from this *qatlān*. According to A. Hurvitz, the pattern קִטְלוֹן began to be favoured in LBH: *Leš* 33 (1969) 18-24.

(4) Cf. F. Blass/A. Debrunner/F. Rehkopf, *Grammatik des neutestamentlichen Griechisch* (Göttingen, [14]1976), § 40, and also the article by A. Hurvitz mentioned in the foregoing note.

(5) But in these forms the qameṣ is not stable; in the construct state we have e.g. שְׂשׂוֹן, doubtless on the analogy of the ל"ה forms, e.g. cst. רְצוֹן.

Form of abstract nouns **qitlān** > קִטְלוֹן and קִטְלָן. *c*

The normal Hebrew form is קִטָּלוֹן: כִּשְׁרוֹן *success*, יִתְרוֹן *advantage*; חֶסְרוֹן *lack*. The קִטְלוֹן forms, which are only found in the cst. state, could come from *qitlān* or from *qatalān*, § *b*; e.g. פִּדְיוֹן *redemption*, פִּתְרוֹן *explanation*, רִפְיוֹן *slackness*(1).

The abnormal Hebrew form is קִטְלָן: קִנְיָן *acquisition* (cst. =), בִּנְיָן *building* (cst. state not attested), עִנְיָן *business* (cst. =), only in Ecclesiastes (Aramaism).

(1) The pattern קִטְלוֹן is esp. common in Ecclesiastes. See S.J. du Plessis, "Aspects of morphological peculiarities of the language of Qoheleth" in I.H. Eybers et al. (eds), *De fructu oris sui* [Fschr. A. van Selms] (Leiden, 1971), pp. 164-67.

The form **qutlān** has become קֻטְלָן (cst. =) and not קֻטְלוֹן*, probably to avoid the sequence of the two vowels *u*-*ọ*, which are too similar (cf. Brock., *GvG*, I, p. 255): שֻׁלְחָן *table* (cst. =), קָרְבָּן *offering* (cst. =), אָבְדָן* *loss* (cst. =). *d* e **Adjectival** afformative *ān > וֹן. Hebrew forms adjectives by adding וֹן to certain nouns, especially monosyllables: קַדְמוֹן (1 x) *eastern* (from *qadm*, קֶדֶם), אַחֲרוֹן *last* (from אַחַר *behind*), רִאשׁוֹן *first* (dissimilation of רֹאשׁוֹן*, § 29 *h*), whence by analogy קִיצוֹן *extreme* (from קֵץ, root קצץ), חִיצוֹן *outer* (from חוּץ), תִּיכוֹן *middle* (from cst. תּוֹךְ); תַּחְתּוֹן *lower, inferior*, עֶלְיוֹן *of above, superior, Most High*. The afformative *ān is added to the feminine ending, as in Aramaic, in עֲקַלָּתוֹן *tortuous*, and (changed to ָן) in לִוְיָתָן *serpent*, נְחֻשְׁתָּן *serpent*.

f **Diminutive** afformative וֹן (probably coming from ān): אִישׁוֹן *pupil of the eye (little man)*, שַׂהֲרֹנִים *little moons* or *crescents*; perhaps the names of serpents שְׁפִיפוֹן *horned snake*, צִפְעֹנִי *basilisk*, § *g* (alongside צֶפַע; Dalman: MH צִפְעוֹן).

g **Adjectival** afformative i(1). Hebrew forms some adjectives with the afformative ִי, in particular ordinal, gentilic and patronymic adjectives: שִׁשִּׁי *sixth* (from שֵׁשׁ, § 101 *a*), מוֹאָבִי *Moabite* (from מוֹאָב), עִבְרִי *Hebrew*, כְּנַעֲנִי *Canaanite*, צִידֹנִי *Sidonian*, יִשְׂרְאֵלִי *Israelite* (very rare; only Lv 24.10-11, for a special reason, and 2Sm 17.25 in a proper noun); אַכְזָרִי *cruel* (from אַכְזָר, § L *a*), נָכְרִי *foreign* (from an unattested form נֹכֶר*), תַּחְתִּי *inferior* (from תַּחַת), פְּנִימִי *interior* (from the plural פָּנִים *face*), רַגְלִי *pedestrian, foot-soldier* (from *ragl*, רֶגֶל), חָפְשִׁי *freed*; with modified vocalisation: שְׂמָאלִי *left* (from שְׂמֹאל *left-hand side*), יְמָנִי *right* (from יָמִין *right-hand side*; on the analogy of שְׂמָאלִי).

Sometimes the afformative *i* is added to the afformative *ọn*: קַדְמוֹנִי *oriental*, אַדְמוֹנִי *reddish*, צִפְעֹנִי *basilisk* (§ *f*), יִדְּעֹנִי *soothsayer* (from an unattested form יִדָּעוֹן* *science* or *high science*); with ָנִי: רַחֲמָנִי* *merciful*.

Proper nouns ending in וֹ or ה־ have their corresponding adjectives ending in נִי: שִׁילוֹ, שִׁלֹה: שִׁילֹנִי; גִּלֹה: גִּילֹנִי. Likewise we find שֵׁלָה: שֵׁלָנִי.

The feminine ending can either be preserved: פְּלִשְׁתִּי *Philistine* (from פְּלֶשֶׁת), עַזָּתִי *of Gaza* (עַזָּה), or dropped: יְהוּדִי *Judaean, Jew* (from יְהוּדָה), תִּמְנִי *of Timna* (תִּמְנָה).

The adjective of בִּנְיָמִין is בֶּן־יְמִינִי (with the article בֶּן־הַיְמִינִי) or simply יְמִינִי; the adjective of בֵּית לֶחֶם is (with the article) בֵּית הַלַּחְמִי (cf. § 139 *d*).

The afformative ִי becomes in the feminine ִיָּה (§ 89*e*) or ִית (§ 89

f): תַּחְתִּית (7 x), תַּחְתִּיָּה once; מוֹאָבִיָּה (6 x), מוֹאָבִית (1 x); עִבְרִיָּה always (2 x), מִצְרִית always (2 x).

(1) The afformative Yod was originally not a vowel letter; in Phoen. it is still consonantal, and so it is in Heb. f. ־יָּה (see below).

h It is not always easy to distinguish between the afformative *ay* and the radical *ay*. As afformative, *ay* is found in the form of ־ֶה, in אַרְבֶּה *locust swarm*, לִבְנֶה *poplar*; in the form of ־ֵה in עֶשְׂרֵה *ten*, § 100 *e*.

i Afformative **it**. In the ל״י roots the *t* of the feminine, when added to the *i* of the root, gave the ending *it*, e.g. *bki* + *t* > בְּכִית *weeping*. This *it* ending became an afformative of the abstract in other roots: רֵאשִׁית *beginning*, אַחֲרִית *end*, שְׁאֵרִית *rest*, חִתִּית *terror*, תָּכְנִית *measure*. Concrete nouns are very rare: חֲנִית *spear*, זְכוֹכִית *glass*.

j Afformative **ut**. In the ל״ו roots the *t* of the feminine, when added to the *u* of the root, gave the ending *ut*, e.g. *ksu* + *t* > כְּסוּת *covering*. This ending became an afformative of the abstract in other roots: מַלְכוּת *kingship*, יַלְדוּת *youth*, עַבְדוּת *servitude*; מִסְכֵּנוּת *poverty*, עֵדוּת *precept* (pl. עֵדְוֹת* *'edwot*, § 97 G *b*), גֵּאוּת *highness, pride*. The afformative *ut* is even found in ל״י roots: פְּדוּת *deliverance*; בָּכוּת *weeping*, alongside בְּכִית.

The afformative *ut* of the Aramaic infinitive is found in לְהַשְׁמָעוּת Ez 24.26 (§ 54 *c*), הִתְחַבְּרוּת Dn 11.23 (§ 53 *f*).

In words such as גָּלוּת *exile*, חָזוּת *vision*, בָּרוּת *food*, בָּכוּת *weeping*, the ָ is stable and probably etymologically long. This *å* could be explained by the fact that these nouns were perhaps modelled on the Aramaic participle (e.g. *gåle*); thus רָמוּת *height* is modelled on the participle רָם(1).

(1) According to BL, p. 506. If these nouns are not directly formed on the participle, they could be due to the analogy of the parallel forms דָּלִית, זָוִית, which are feminine participles (§ F *b*).

Abstract nouns with the afformative וּת are extremely numerous in MH, probably due to Aramaic influence, and the subsequent phases of Hebrew, though it is not correct to say that such BH nouns mostly occur in late books. See L. Gulkowitsch, op. cit. [§ 88I *e*, n.], pp. 97ff., and A. Hurvitz, *The Transition Period in BH* [Heb] (Jerusalem, 1972), pp. 79-82.

k An afformative וֹת, distinct from the plural ending, is doubtful. The word חָכְמוֹת *Wisdom*, treated as a singular in Pr 1.20, 9.1, seems to be some kind of plural of majesty (cf. § 136 *d*); instead of the normal plural, which should be חֲכָמוֹת*, the word was vocalised *ḥọḵ*- on the analogy of the singular חָכְמָה(1). The word הוֹלֵלוֹת *madness* (Ec 1.17; 2.12; 7.25; 9.3) alongside הוֹלֵלוּת (10.13) is suspect; if the vocalisation וֹת is authentic, it could have arisen on the analogy of חָכְמוֹת.

(1) Compare the rare plurals of the type שִׁקְמָה, שִׁקְמִים *sycamore*, § 96 A *b*.

l According to some grammarians, the ם, which is found in a few words could be an afformative; according to others, it could be a residue of *mimation* in the old declension (cf. § 102 *b*).

On final ָם in place names, cf. § 91 *h*.

m The existence of ל as afformative is doubtful: כַּרְמֶל *cultivated fields* (*for cereals*) (compare כֶּרֶם *vineyard*); גִּבְעֹל *flower*(?) (compare גָּבִיעַ *cup*). Also עֲרָפֶל *cloud* (?). Cf. Akk. *urpatu* "cloud."

§ 89. Noun gender: masculine and feminine endings

a A noun is either masculine or femine; sometimes it has both genders. One must carefully distinguish between gender and **gender endings.** A masculine ending is an ending which is always found in masculine adjectives(1) and often in masculine substantives; a feminine ending is an ending which is always found in feminine adjectives and often in feminine substantives. Thus the singular ending ָה is a feminine ending because it is found only in feminine adjectives and in many feminine substantives. Likewise in the plural, ִים is a masculine ending, וֹת a feminine ending, § 90 *b, d*.

The gender of substantives is known to us mainly through their agreement with adjectives(2). Also a feminine verb form can indicate that the subject noun is feminine, but nothing certain can be inferred from a masculine form(§ 150 *b*). Furthermore, the demonstrative pronoun used attributively can provide a reliable clue in this respect.

(1) Including the verbal adjective and the participle.

(2) Another fairly reliable way of telling the gender of substantives is the use of the cardinal numerals 3-10 (feminine with masculine nouns and masc. with feminine nouns!, § 100 *d*). Thus the plural לֵילוֹת *nights* is masculine like the pl. יָמִים *days*, for we have שְׁלֹשָׁה יָמִים וּשְׁלֹשָׁה לֵילוֹת 1Sm 30.12.

b In the singular, **masculine** nouns usually have no ending. A very small number have a feminine ending, e.g. קֹהֶלֶת *man of an assembly*, *ec*-

clesiastes. Here the feminine ending has an intensive nuance, just as it has in such Arabic forms as *rāwiyat* "a (great) narrator," alongside the simple form *rāwiⁿ* "narrator"(1). Likewise in men's names סֹפֶ֫רֶת *Scribe*, פֹּכֶ֫רֶת הַצְּבָיִים *Catcher*(?) *of gazelles*. Alongside מוֹדָע *kinsman* (Ru 2.1) מוֹדַ֫עַת (3.2) seems to mean *close relative* (probably masculine, speaking of a man). In a few masculine nouns ־ָה is not the feminine ending: מוֹרָה *razor* (for *mọra[y]*), פֶּחָה *governor* (Akkadian word). In nouns from ל״י roots, the ־ֶה is a radical, e.g. שָׂדֶה *field* (alongside שָׂדַי poet.). In fact these nouns are masculine, e.g. מַעֲלֶה *ascent* (comp. fem. מַעֲלָה *degree*)(2).

(1) Cf. Wright, *Arabic Grammar* I, § 233, Rem. *c*.

(2) מַחֲנֶה *camp, army* in Gn 32.9*a* and Ps 27.3† appears to be treated as feminine; but the Massoretic text is doubtful (prob. read האחד and יחנה). Cf. Phoen. רבת מאת *centurion*, if not a misspelling for רב.

In the singular a fair number of **feminine** nouns have no feminine ending, e.g. nouns of female beings: אֵם *mother*, אָתוֹן *she-ass*, עֵז *goat*, רָחֵל *ewe*; and other nouns: אֶ֫בֶן *stone*, עִיר *city*, חֶ֫רֶב *sword*, אֶ֫רֶץ *land*, יָד *hand*. But most feminine nouns, in the singular, have a feminine ending(1). For details, cf. § 134. c

(1) Since the feminine ending is very rare in masculine nouns (§ *b*), it may be said that in the singular the feminine ending almost always indicates a feminine noun.

The main (and perhaps only) feminine ending of the Hebrew noun is primitively *at*, which has been preserved in the construct state(1). In the absolute state the primitive form has become (stressed) ־ָה, or the segholate forms ־ֶ֫־ֶת, ־ַ֫־ַת, ־ֶ֫־ְת, or simple ת. The segholate forms, which are numerous in the construct state, probably arose in the cst. state and in some cases have spread to the absolute state. d

(1) Gelb thinks that /t/ was originally a glide: I.J. Gelb, *Sequential Reconstruction of Proto-Akkadian* (Chicago, 1969), pp. 34f.

The ending ־ָה is by far the most common, and in some forms the only one possible, e.g. סוּסָה *mare*. In certain nouns the segholate form is found alongside ־ָה. In nouns ending in ־ִי, e.g. מוֹאָבִי, alongside the form in ־ָה (מוֹאָבִיָּה) the form in ת, מוֹאָבִית, can occur (§ 88 M *g*). e

Simple ת is mainly found with nouns in ־ִי, as we have just said, e.g. תַּחְתִּית *lower* (§ 88 M *g*); cf. בְּכִית *weeping* (§ 88 M *i*) and כְּסוּת *covering* (§ 88 M *j*)(1). f

(1) See also the three infinitives with a simplified form תֵּת (§ 72 *i*), צֵאת (§ 75 *g*), שְׂאֵת (§ 78 *l*); the adjective אַחַת *one* (for *'aḥadt*, § 100 *b*, and in Ugr. *aḥt*).

The fem. morpheme /-t/ (as against /-at/) is attested in Ugr. as in syllabically spelled words such as *mar-kab-te* "chariot." More examples in Huehnergard, *Ugr. Vocabulary*, pp. 295f. So also AC *mi-te kaspu* "200 pieces of silver" (Sivan, p. 130). Likewise בַּת (Arb. *bintu*), Moabite and Northern Israelite שת *year* on Samaria ostraca and fem. segholate nouns such as שֶׁבֶת, דַּעַת, hence w. suf., שִׁבְתּוֹ etc. Cf. also Sivan, pp. 105-7.

g Of the *segholate endings*, the most common by far is ֶ ֶת. First it is found in nouns with the vowel *a*: *niqtal + t > niqtalt >* נִקְטֶלֶת; then in nouns with the vowel *i*: *qātil + t > qātilt >* קֹטֶלֶת; and finally, by extension, in nouns with the originally long vowel *ī*: מַקְטִיל, מַקְטֶלֶת. (For these examples of participles, cf. § 50 *g*). Other examples: Nouns with the vowel *a*: יַבֶּשֶׁת *dry land* (2 x, alongside יַבָּשָׁה); cst. מַמְלֶכֶת (from מַמְלָכָה *kingdom*). Nouns with the vowel *i*: מַצֶּבֶת abs. and cst. (from מַצֵּבָה *stele*), אַחֶרֶת (m. אַחֵר *other*). Nouns with the originally long vowel *ī*; cst. and abs. גְּבֶרֶת (from גְּבִירָה *lady*); שַׁלֶּטֶת (m. שַׁלִּיט *ruler*); cf. § 97 F *b*.

h The segholate ending ֵ ֶת is very rare. It has usually been replaced by ֶ ֶת, e.g. in the infinitives of the type לֶדֶת (alongside לֵדָה, § 75 a). The ֵ, which comes from *i*, has been preserved in the following constructs: חֲמֵשֶׁת (from חֲמִשָּׁה *five*), שֵׁשֶׁת (from שִׁשָּׁה *six*), אֵשֶׁת (from אִשָּׁה *woman*)(1).

(1) Note that with these three nouns in the abs. state there is doubling: by assimilation in אִשָּׁה (§ 99 *c*) and שִׁשָּׁה (§ 100 *d*); in חֲמִשָּׁה on the analogy of שִׁשָּׁה (§ 100 *d*).

i The segholate ending ֹ ֶת corresponds to the masculine form in ֹ, which comes from either *u* or *ā*. Unfortunately it is often difficult to determine the origin of this ֹ. In ֹ ֶת the ֹ is always changeable, even when the ֹ of the masculine is definitely etymologically long; thus **šalāš >* שָׁלֹשׁ *three*; fem. שְׁלֹשָׁה, cst. שְׁלֹשֶׁת (with *ọ*; comp. שְׁלָשְׁתָּם). Likewise, קְטֹרֶת *smoke* (probably *qutāl*, § 88 E *e*) becomes קְטָרְתִּי(1).

Nouns with the segholate ending ֹ ֶת are rather frequent: In the form קְטֹלֶת: נְחֹשֶׁת *bronze*, cst. כְּתֹבֶת *writing*, cst. חֲרֹשֶׁת *work*, נְעֹרֶת *tow*; the two infinitives יְכֹלֶת (§ 75 *i*), יְבֹשֶׁת (§ 76 *d*). In the form קַטֹּלֶת: בַּצֹּרֶת *dryness*, כַּפֹּרֶת *propitiatory*, פָּרֹכֶת *curtain* (of the temple). In the form קִטֹּלֶת: שִׁבֹּלֶת *ear (of corn)*, בִּקֹּרֶת (of doubtful meaning). In the form מַקְטֶלֶת: מַאֲכֶלֶת *food*, etc. (cf. § 88 L *j*). In the form מִקְטֶלֶת, § 88 L *l*. In other forms: בֹּשֶׁת *shame* (root בושׁ), גֻּלְגֹּלֶת *skull*, שְׁחַרְחֹרֶת *blackish*. For the inflection of segholate endings, cf. § 97 F.

(1) Compare the parallel reduction of גְּבִירָה, גְּבֶרֶת, גְּבִרְתִּי (cf. § *f*).

j A few more or less suspect participial forms lack the expected segholisation: Jer 22.23Q יֹשַׁבְתְּ (K. יֹשַׁבְתִּי with ḥireq compaginis, § 93 *o*); cf. 51.13. Three times (Gn 16.11, Jdg 13.5,7) we find הִנָּךְ הָרָה וְיֹלַדְתְּ בֵּן *behold you are pregnant and you will bear a son*. Here we may have a lectio mixta (§ 16 *g*) giving a choice between the participle וְיֹלֶדֶת (as in Is 7.14) and the inverted perfect וְיָלַדְתְּ, which would be more usual.

k **Rare feminine endings:**

◌ָא, Aramaic spelling for ◌ָה: שֵׁנָא *sleep* Ps 127.2; מַטָּרָא *prison* Lam 3.12; מָרָא *bitter* Ru 1.20.

l The feminine ending *ay* is found in עֶשְׂרֵה *ten*; probably also in אַשְׁרֵי[1] *beatitude of*, the absolute state of which would be אַשְׁרַי*[2]; in the proper noun שָׂרַי (alongside שָׂרָה).

(1) There is also אַשְׁרֵי without metheg, or with the metheg of the shewa only, which indicates that it should not be ignored in pronunciation.

(2) Prob. to be read in Gn 30.13: בְּאַשְׁרַי *with beatitude*; comp. vs. 11 בְּגָד* *with happiness* (cf. Ehrlich *ad loc*.). For Ugaritic parallels illustrating the same morpheme, see Gordon, *UT*, § 8.54.

m The primitive ending *at*[1] is found in a few words, either with the vowel ◌ָ, which is normal in a final stressed closed syllable in nouns, or with the vowel ◌ֶ.

(1) It is also found in the Mēša‘ inscription, in Phoenician and Ammonite inscriptions.

n With ◌ָת, only one common word is found, i.e. מָחֳרָת *(mǫḥǫ̊rå̄ṯ)*[1] *tomorrow* (the formation of which is not clear). Other examples: קָאָת *pelican* (var. קָאַת); שְׁנָת *sleep* Ps 132.4 (for שֵׁנָה); פֹּרָת *fruitful plant* or *fruitful vine* (cf. Is 32.12; Ps 128.3) Gn 49.22 (poet.), substantivised participle (comp. פֹּרִיָּה); יִתְרָת *abundance* (var. ◌ֶ) Jer 48.36 (יִתְרַת עָשָׂה; but Is 15.7 יִתְרָה עָשָׂה); עֶזְרָת *help* Ps 60.13 (perhaps to be vocalised עֶזְרָתָ = עֶזְרָתָה Ps 44.27); נַחֲלָת *inheritance* Ps 16.6 (perhaps wrong); עָזִּי וְזִמְרָת יָהּ *Jehovah is my power and (my) strength*[2]. In some cases ◌ָת can be an abbreviated form of ◌ָתָה, feminine ending with the old *a* of the accusative (§ 93 *c*); likewise in עֶזְרָת, מָחֳרָת.

תָ- is also found in some place-names: בַּעֲלָת, חֶלְקָת, and in some personal names: שִׁמְעָת, גָּלְיָת (female). Alongside the usual אֶפְרָתָה *Ephrata* we have אֶפְרָת in Gn 48.7†, where it is probably a mistake (haplography), § 93 *f*.

(1) *Pace* Brock., *GvG*, I, p. 409, who takes the form as cst. Note the Akkadian indeclinable st. abs. (as distinct from st. rectus) used adverbially; W. v. Soden, *Grundriss der akkadischen Grammatik* (Rome, [2]1969), § 62.3. So the word should, perhaps, belong to § 102 *c*.
(2) Cf. P. Joüon in *MUSJ* 3(1908-09) 335.

o No sure example of common nouns with the ending תֶ- can be found (two variants mentioned in § *n*). The word בָּרֶקֶת (alongside בָּרְקַת) *a precious stone* looks foreign. On the other hand תֶ- is found in several place-names: צָרְפַת *Sarepta*, גִּבְעַת, אֵילַת (alongside אֵילוֹת), and in several personal names: אֲחֻזַּת, בְּכוֹרַת, גִּינַת.

N.B. The ת of the feminine is sometimes regarded as being part of the root: דֶּלֶת *door*, pl. דְּלָתוֹת, du. דְּלָתַיִם; קֶשֶׁת *bow*, pl. קְשָׁתוֹת; שֹׁקֶת *watering-trough*, cst. pl. שִׁקְתוֹת Gn 30.38 (for the *i*, cf. § 96 A *g*); שָׂפָה *lip*, cst. pl. שִׂפְתוֹת; חֲנִית *spear*, pl. חֲנִיתוֹת and חֲנִיתִים.

§ 90. **Plural**

a In the plural, as in the singular (§ 89 *a*), one must carefully distinguish between gender and gender endings. The gender of a noun is usually the same in the singular and in the plural (or dual)(1).

(1) According to A. Cohen, "The plural endings in Biblical Hebrew," *Lš* 2 (1929-30) 282-86, BH has 490 masc. nouns with the plural ending *im*, 80 with *ot*, and 312 fem. nouns with the pl. ending *ot* and 40 with *im*. Nouns of hollow roots (ע"וי) as well as those with the *-on* suffix tend to show the *ot* ending, whilst nouns of *Qittul* and *Qattul* types form their plurals solely with *im*. Furthermore, nouns for a wide range of flora and fauna display the *ot* pl. ending (cf. § 136 *b*).

b The usual masculine ending is ִ-ים; it is found in all masculine adjectives, in many masculine substantives, and in a certain number of feminine substantives. Examples of feminine substantives with ִ-ים: שָׁנָה *year*, usual plural שָׁנִים (a rare and poetic plural שָׁנוֹת* is attested only in the cst. and with suff.); רָחֵל *ewe*, pl. רְחֵלִים; אֶבֶן *stone*, pl. אֲבָנִים(1); פִּילֶגֶשׁ *concubine*, pl. פִּילַגְשִׁים; שִׁבֹּלֶת *ear of corn*, pl. שִׁבֳּלִים;

חִטָּה *wheat* (as a species), pl. חִטִּים *grains of wheat* (grains or stalks) in the collective sense; and likewise שְׂעוֹרָה *barley*, pl. שְׂעוֹרִים.

In nouns in ־ִי the masculine plural is ־ִיִּים, e.g. נְקִיִּים *pure* (sing. נָקִי) or, more often, by contraction, ־ִים, e.g. עִבְרִים *Hebrews* (once: עִבְרִיִּים Ex 3.18).

(1) Thus with an adjective we say, e.g. אֲבָנִים גְּדוֹלוֹת, as one says in the sing. אֶבֶן גְּדוֹלָה.

c Occasionally we have the Aramaic ending ־ִין (very frequent in MH, and the rule in Moabite): מְלָכִין *kings* (or *counsellors* as in Aramaic; cf. Dn 4.24) Pr 31.3; צִדֹנִין *Sidonians* 1Kg 11.33; רָצִין *runners* 2Kg 11.13; חִטִּין *wheat* Ez 4.9; אִיִּן *islands* Ez 26.18; יָמִין *days* Dn 12.13; מִדִּין *carpet(?)* Jdg 5.10 (poet.); עִיִּין *hills of ruins* Mi 3.12; in Job, מִלִּין *words* (Aramaic word) is found 13 times alongside מִלִּים (10 x).

d The feminine ending is וֹת; it is found in all feminine adjectives, in many feminine substantives, and in a fair number of masculine substantives(1).

Examples of masculine substantives with וֹת: אָב *father*, pl. אָבוֹת; אוֹב* *skin-bottle*, אֹבוֹת חֲדָשִׁים *new skin-bottles* Job 32.19; דּוֹר *generation*, pl. דֹּרוֹת (־ִים only in the phrase דּוֹר דּוֹרִים *generation of generations* [3 x]); שָׁבוּעַ *week*, pl. שָׁבֻעוֹת, § 96 D *b*; לַיְלָה *night*, § 93 *g* (3 x לַיִל), pl. לֵילוֹת. Several nouns in ־ֶה have וֹת in the plural: מַטֶּה *rod, tribe*, מַחֲנֶה *camp, army*, שָׂדֶה *field* (and ־ִים, § *e*).

In nouns with ־ִי the feminine plural is ־ִיּוֹת (cf. the sing. ־ִיָּה, § 89 *e*): עִבְרִי, עִבְרִיָּה, עִבְרִיּוֹת; מִצְרִי, מִצְרִית, מִצְרִיּוֹת.

(1) In well-nigh 30% of cases the f.pl. is spelled defectively: AF, p. 197.

da The ancient pl. ending /ān/ can be identified in Jdg 5.7 חָדְלוּ פְּרָזוֹן (פְּרָזוֹן < *פְּרָזָן); with the otiose /im/ added after the primitive ending it had become unidentifiable as such—נְצָנִים, עִזְבֹנִים, and קִמְּשֹׂנִים; cf. Brock., *GvG*, I, p. 451, and H. Bauer, who includes here אַיָּלוֹן and שֹׁמְרוֹן in שֹׁמְרוֹן *the mount of watchers* (*ZAW* NF 7 [1930] 76f.).

e Some nouns have both plural endings; but often only one is used frequently, the other being reserved for special or poetic usages, e.g. עָב *cloud*, normal pl. עָבִים, pl. עָבוֹת only twice, in texts of high poetry: 2Sm 23.4; Ps 77.18; עֲבֹת *rope, bond*, normal pl. עֲבֹתִים, but עֲבֹתֹת for the *bonds of love* Ho 11.4 and for artistic cords, *cordage-work* Ex 28.14, etc. See also שָׁנָה, § *b*, דּוֹר § *d*.

The noun שָׂדֶה *field* has two plurals: שָׂדִים* *fields, countryside*, שָׂדוֹת *individual fields, individual farms*(1). From אֲלֻמָּה* *sheaf* we have the plural אֲלֻמִּים for *sheaves* in general Gn 37.7*a*, and אֲלֻמּוֹת for *individual sheaves* 7*b* and Ps 126.6(2). From כִּכָּר *disk, round* we have כִּכְּרֵי כֶסֶף *disks (coins) of silver*, and כִּכְּרוֹת לֶחֶם *loaves of bread* (the feminine form for the object of lesser value; comp. נַעַל, נְעָלִים *sandals*, but נְעָלוֹת Josh 9.5† in the case of *old shoes*). From צֵלָע *rib* we have צְלָעִים (masc.; 1Kg 6.34†) *leaves of a door* and צְלָעוֹת (fem.) *side-chambers*.

(1) Cf. P. Joüon in *MUSJ* 6 (1913) 140.

(2) *Ibid.*, 141.

f **Plurale tantum.** Some words are only used in the plural. Most of these are abstract and singular in meaning, e.g. סַנְוֵרִים *blindness, false vision* (cf. § 136). There are a few concrete nouns: מַ֫יִם *water, waters*, שָׁמַ֫יִם *sky, skies*, מֵעַ֫יִם* *entrails*, פָּנִים *face* (and *faces* Ez 1.6), מְתִים *men* (the sing. is found in the form of מְתוּ [§ 93 *s*] in a few proper nouns, cf. Ugr. *mt* and Akk. *mutu* "man").

§ 91. Dual(1)

a In the case of things which go in pairs, such as the *eyes* and the *ears*, the dual is used instead of the plural. In Biblical Hebrew the use of the dual is rather restricted(2); it is found only with a few substantives (§ *c*), never with adjectives, verbs or pronouns.

(1) See C. Fontinoy, *Le duel dans les langues sémitiques* (Paris, 1969).

(2) In Archaic Hebrew the use of the dual appears to have been less restricted, as in Ugaritic and Classical Arabic: see Jdg 5.30 רַחֲמָתַ֫יִם *two wenches*; ib. רִקְמָתַ֫יִם *two pieces of embroidery*. Cf. F.M. Cross and D.N. Freedman, *Studies in Ancient Yahwistic Poetry* (Missoula, 1975), p. 19.

b The dual ending is ַ֫יִם. In words without a feminine ending, the form of the word is that of the singular, modified, if needs be, according to the phonetic laws: יָד *hand*, יָדַ֫יִם; רֶ֫גֶל *foot*, רַגְלַ֫יִם (from primitive **ragl*); עַ֫יִן *eye*, עֵינַ֫יִם (comp. זַ֫יִת *olive*, plural זֵיתִים); שֵׁן *tooth*, שִׁנַּ֫יִם (from primitive **šinn*); כָּנָף *wing*, כְּנָפַ֫יִם; יָרֵךְ *thigh* יְרֵכַ֫יִם(1).

In nouns with the singular feminine ending ָה the ת is maintained before the dual ending: שָׂפָה *lip*, שְׂפָתַ֫יִם. In a noun with a segholate ending נְחֹשֶׁת *bronze*, the dual is נְחֻשְׁתַּ֫יִם *fetters* (compare Engl. *irons*). In the word חוֹמָה *wall* the dual ending is added to the plural ending in בֵּין הַחֹמֹתַיִם *between two walls* (4 x). Likewise we have גְּדֵרֹתַיִם *Double-Wall* (name of a city, Josh 15.36†), and לוּחֹתַיִם from לוּחַ *tablet*.

Alongside the regular קַרְנַיִם *horns* we have (in Daniel) קְרָנַיִם, with the prestress ָ of the plural of segholate nouns (comp. pl. קְרָנוֹת), probably on the analogy of the plural. Likewise we have לְחָיַיִם *jaws* (instead of לֶחְיַיִם*, from לְחִי, לֶחִי), דְּלָתַיִם *double door*, דְּרָכַיִם *double way*.

In 1Kg 16.24; 2Kg 5.23 כִּכְּרַיִם כֶּסֶף *two silver kikkar* there is probably a *lectio mixta* (§ 16 *g*) giving the choice between כִּכְּרֵי (genitive construction) and כִּכָּרַיִם (with apposition or accusative)(2).

(1) Names of double members are generally feminine, § 134 *j*.

(2) Alternatively this may be a sandhi effect, the two words being felt to be a close semantic and phonetic unit; see W.R. Garr, *VT* 37 (1987) 135.

The dual is found in numerals: 2 שְׁנַיִם, 200 מָאתַיִם, 2000 אַלְפַּיִם; *c*
in nouns of two countables, when they are regarded as forming a unit: יוֹמַיִם *two consecutive days* (Lat. *biduum*), שְׁנָתַיִם *two consecutive years*, שְׁבֻעַיִם (once) *two consecutive weeks*, פַּעֲמַיִם *twice*, perh. רִבּוֹתַיִם *two myriads*, אַמָּתַיִם *two cubits*, כִּכָּרַיִם *two kikkar*. The dual is also found with things that go in pairs, either in nature or in art: יָדַיִם *hands, arms* (cf. § *b*), אָזְנַיִם *ears*, בִּרְכַּיִם *knees*, כַּפַּיִם *palms* (of hands), כְּתֵפַיִם *shoulders*, מָתְנַיִם *loins*, צִפָּרְנַיִם* *finger-nails*, שָׁדַיִם *breasts*, שׁוֹקַיִם *thighs*, מֹאזְנַיִם *scales*. זְרוֹעַ *arm* usually has the plural form זְרוֹעוֹת (e.g. Jdg 15.14 the [two] *arms* of Samson); we probably have the dual in 2Kg 9.24 בֵּין זְרֹעָיו *between his shoulders*, and perhaps in Gn 49.24 and Is 51.5 where its interpretation is not certain. From נַעַל we have the plural form נְעָלִים, except in Am 2.6 and 8.6 where, as a matter of fact, a *pair of sandals* is referred to: נַעֲלַיִם. Note that in כְּלָיוֹת *kidneys* (sg. כִּלְיָה*) the plural is used, not the dual.

Nouns which in their proper sense are found in the dual are put in *d*
the plural when used in a figurative sense; this is particularly so in the case of manufactured objects: עֲיָנוֹת *sources*, כַּפּוֹת *fistfuls, palms, cups*, כְּנָפוֹת *corners, extremities*, קְרָנוֹת *horns (of the altar)*, יָדוֹת *tenons, axles* and even with the sense of *arm-rests* (of Samuel's throne 1K 10.19), רְגָלִים (fem.) *times*. Note that most of these feminine plurals

are in וֹת (cf. § 134 *q*).

e Several nouns used in the dual have no plural form, whether used figuratively or not; then the dual is used for the plural: אַרְבַּע רַגְלַיִם *4 feet* Lv 11.23; שֵׁשׁ כְּנָפַיִם *6 wings* Is 6.2; Ez 1.6; שִׁבְעָה עֵינַיִם *7 eyes (of a stone*, Zech 3.9; עַיִן is masc. here, § 134 a, n.); שְׁלֹשׁ שִׁנַּיִם *3 prongs (of a fork*, 1Sm 2.13); כָּל־בִּרְכַּיִם *all the knees* Ez 7.17; כָּל־יָדַיִם *all the hands* 21.12; מְצִלְתַּיִם *(several) cymbals* Ne 12.27; שְׁפַתַּיִם *(several) double hooks* Ez 40.43.

ea One may classify Hebrew nouns into three groups:

1) Those which have three distinct forms, the sg. for one of the entities denoted, the du. for two of them, and the pl. for three or more of them. These are comprised mostly by numerals and nouns indicating varying lengths of time or measures: מֵאָה *one hundred* - מָאתַיִם *two hundred* - שְׁלֹשׁ מֵאוֹת *three hundred*; (אֶחָד) יוֹם *one day* - יוֹמַיִם *two days* - אַרְבָּעָה יָמִים *four days*; (אַחַת) אַמָּה *one cubit* - אַמָּתַיִם *two cubits* - חָמֵשׁ אַמּוֹת *five cubits*(1).

2) Those which have two distinct forms, the sg. and the du., the latter doubling for 'three or more': e.g. רֶגֶל *one leg* - רַגְלַיִם *both legs*, but also Lv 11.23 אַרְבַּע רַגְלַיִם *four legs*. The group is comprised mostly of nouns indicating parts of the body(2).

3) Those which are used only in the dual, indicating tools consisting of two parts: e.g. מֹאזְנַיִם *scales*; מְצִלְתַּיִם *cymbals* מֶלְקָחַיִם *tongs*. The dual of these nouns can indicate either one object or more: sg. in Ben Sirah 45.8 מכנסים *breeches* parallel to מעיל.

(1) Only exceptionally is the numeral for 'two' used with a distinct plural noun: e.g. Ez 40.9 שְׁתַּיִם אַמּוֹת; 2Sm 1.1 יָמִים שְׁנַיִם; 1Sm 13.1 שְׁתֵּי שָׁנִים.

(2) Some of these nouns do possess a distinct pl. form, but with a different sense: thus אַרְבַּע רְגָלִים *four times* (§ *d* above). Where the numeral for 'two' is used with a distinct dual noun, there is usually some emphasis on the notion of twoness: e.g. Jdg 16.28 "so that I may be avenged on the Philistines for one of my two eyes (מִשְּׁתֵּי עֵינַי)."

f **Apparent dual endings.** What we have in מַיִם *water, waters* and שָׁמַיִם *sky, skies* is not a dual, but an abnormal plural. In these two words the original plural ending *-īm* has been reduced to *-im* under the influence of the stress. This may be compared with the Biblical Aram. plural participle of the type בָּנַיִן *building* (for *bånay* + *īn*) of ל״י verbs. Likewise in Arabic a noun like **muṣṭafa(y)* becomes in the (genitiveaccus.) plural *muṣṭafáyna* with shortening of the ending *īna*; the future *yarḍa(y)* becomes in the 2nd pers. f. sg. *tarḍáyna*, with shortening of the ending *īna*.

g The word עַרְבַּ֫יִם in the phrase בֵּין הָעַרְבַּ֫יִם can only be a dual: *between the two evenings*(1). Reference is probably made here to the two extreme parts of the period called עֶ֫רֶב(2). In צָהֳרַ֫יִם *noon* the dual could perhaps be explained as reflecting the convergence of two time lines at noon; but *-*ạym* seems more likely to be the dissociation of an ending *-*ām* (the place or time[3] of noon), but in view of Moabite צהרם (Mesha 15) the Heb. form, if cognate, can scarcely be a genuine dual, for in Moabite both the plural and dual endings show /-n/. The ending of נַהֲרַ֫יִם *Mesopotamia*(?) is variously explained(4), as is that of מִצְרַ֫יִם *Egypt*.

(1) Cf. Nöldeke, *ZA* 30 (1916) 168, but see Brock., *Heb. Synt.*, § 18 *b*.

(2) Compare § 136 *b*.

(3) Comp. perh. יוֹמָם, § 102 *b*.

(4) See J.J. Finkelstein in *JNES* 21 (1962) 73-92.

h The endings *-a'yim*, *-åm*; *-a'yin*, *-ån* of place-names can in some cases represent a dual. But in a case where the notion of duality is not justified the ending is a locative ending(1), *ay* being dissociated from ā. Examples דֹּתַ֫יִן Gn 37.17 and דֹּתָן 2K 6.13; עֵינַ֫יִם Gn 38.21 and הָעֵינָם Josh 15.34; יְרוּשָׁלַ֫ם (Qre, but in late books spelt fully with Yod)(2). Comp. the adverbial ending of, for example, אַרְבַּעְתַּ֫יִם *fourfold* (§ 100 *o*). For the dual in the construct state, cf. § 92 *g*.

(1) As the original form of ירושלם is most likely to have ended with /em/ (cf. the cuneiform spelling *urusalim* and Syr. *'orišlem*, Gk. Ιερουσαλημ), these /-ayim/ or /-ayin/ may go back to /-em/ or /-en/.

(2) See Brock., *GvG*, I, p. 393, and N.H. Torczyner, *Die Entstehung des semitischen Sprachtypus*, vol. 1 (Wien, 1916), pp. 67-72. Cf. also Ch. Fontinoy, "Les noms de lieux en *-ayim* dans la Bible," *UF* 3 (1971) 33-40, and Driver, *Notes* ad 1Sm 1.1.

§ 92. Construct state

a A noun can be used in close conjunction with another noun to express a notion of possession, of belonging etc., as in the Latin construction with the genitive e.g. *equus Pharaonis* "the horse *of* Pharaoh." This relation is expressed in Hebrew by the simple close union of the two nouns: סוּס פַּרְעֹה. The two nouns form a phonetic unit resulting from the logical unit. The first noun is called the *governing noun (nomen regens)*, the second the *governed noun (nomen rectum)*. The first noun is said to be in the *construct state* because it rests phonetically on the second as a building rests on its foundations. The opposite of the construct state is the *absolute state*; thus in אִישׁ רֹכֵב עַל־סוּס אָדֹם *a man riding on a red horse* (Zech 1.8), אִישׁ and סוּס are in the absolute state (רכב and אדם are appositions, also in the absolute state).

b From a phonetic point of view the first noun, resting on the second, always loses something of its stress. The stress can become secondary when the union is made closer still by maqqef (§ 13), e.g. פַּחַת־יְהוּדָה *governor of Judah* (Hg 2.21). It can even disappear altogether, e.g. בֶּן־אָדָם *son of man* (Ez 2.1).

c One of the effects of the weakening of the stress is vowel deletion: some vowels were dropped, others were shortened. The tendency towards deletion is even stronger in the case of maqqef (§ 13 *c*). A detailed description of the vocalisation of the construct state will be given in the study of nominal inflection. Here a few examples of construct states with deleted and non-deleted vocalisation will suffice:

Sing.: abs. דָּבָר, cst. דְּבַר *word;* זָקֵן, זְקַן *old man*. But abs. and cst. אֹיֵב *enemy*, אֵם *mother*, שֵׁם *name*, יָם־ *sea* (§13 *c*), אֵפוֹד *ephod*, אֵבוּס *crib* (§ 21 *h*).

Plur.: דְּבָרִים, דִּבְרֵי *words*; שָׁנִים, שְׁנֵי *years*; שֵׁמוֹת, שְׁמוֹת *nouns*. But in the ע"ו roots we have קָמִים, קָמֵי, § 80 *d*; מֵתִים, מֵתֵי; in the ע"ע roots: שָׂרִים, שָׂרֵי *princes*, § 82 *p*.

Dual: יָדַיִם, יְדֵי *hands*; בִּרְכַּיִם, בִּרְכֵּי *knees*; כְּנָפַיִם, כַּנְפֵי *wings*; שְׂפָתַיִם, שִׂפְתֵי *lips*.

N.B. Sometimes in the plural (and dual) construct the vowel of the absolute is wrongly used, e.g. חֲטָאֵי (§ 96 A *e*), גְּדָיֵי (§ 96 A *q*), מִקְרָאֵי (§ 96 C *b*), שְׁבָחֵי (§ 96 B *d*).

d In nouns in ־ֶה the vowel becomes ־ֵה: שָׂדֶה, שְׂדֵה *field* (cf. § 79 *f*, n).

e In nouns with the primitive feminine ending *at*, which has become ־ָה in the absolute, both the primitive *t* and the short *a* are retained: abs. מַלְכָּה, cst. מַלְכַּת *queen*. The other feminine endings remain unchanged.

In the plural, the feminine ending וֹת with etymologically long *ọ* remains unchanged.

f Nouns with the masculine plural ending ־ִים have in the construct state the ending ־ֵי: סוּסִים, סוּסֵי. The origin of this ending, which has no relation whatsoever with the ending ־ִים, is still an unresolved question. Some see in it the ־ֵי of the construct dual, others an abstract ending used as a plural ending. This ẹ seems to us to be the contraction of the *ay* of nouns from the ל״י roots. A noun like **śaday*, שָׂדַי (poet.), שָׂדֶה becomes in the plural with suffixes, e.g. *śadaynu* > שָׂדֵ֫ינוּ *our fields*, whence the cst. pl. שְׂדֵי. This ־ֵי, found originally in nouns of ל״י roots, would then have spread to the nouns formed from the other roots(1).

(1) This explanation is supported by the fact that the vowel *e*, which is found in the types יְקַטְּלֵ֫הוּ § 61 *d*, תְּקוּמֶ֫ינָה § 80 *b*, סוּסֵ֫נוּ, סוּסֶ֫ךָ § 94 *b* and n. there, comes from the ל״י roots.

The dual ending *-*aym* > -*a'yim* becomes -ẹ in the construct, by the contraction of *ay* to ẹ and the dropping of the final consonant: יָדַ֫יִם, יְדֵי *hands*. As we can see in the construct (and also with the suffixes) the form of the dual is not different from that of the plural. It is only in words with a *begadkefat* third radical that a dual form (without aspiration, e.g. בִּרְכֵּי *knees*, בִּרְכֵּיכֶם) can be distinguished from a plural form (with aspiration, e.g. מַלְכֵי, מַלְכֵיכֶם). (Here with a *heavy* suffix, but elsewhere with a *light* suffix, e.g. בִּרְכֶּ֫יךָ, מְלָכֶ֫יךָ). g

In the cst. state we sometimes find the paragogic vowels ־ִי (§ 93 *l*) and וֹ (§ 93 *r*). h

See also the cst. forms אֲבִי, אֲחִי (§§ 93 *b*, 98 *b*).

§ 93. **Paragogic vowels ־ָה, ־ִי, וֹ, ־וּ in nouns**

Certain **paragogic** (= *added*) vowels are found in nouns, especially unstressed ־ָ֫ה- (comp. the stressed paragogic ־ָה of the cohortative, § 45), then the rather frequent vowel ־ִי, and finally וֹ and וּ, both very rare. In order to explain the origin of these vowels (as well as that of some others [§ 94 *b*, *c*; 102 *b*]) it is necessary to know the old Semitic declension, as it still exists in Classical Arabic, and as it must have existed, at some stage, in Hebrew(1). a

(1) The final vowels *u*, *i*, *a* are found in the Canaanite glosses of Tell El Amarna, Ugaritic, and Early Phoenician as in Akkadian. Cf. S.C. Layton, *Archaic Features of Canaanite Personal Names in the Hebrew Bible* (Atlanta, 1990), pp. 37-154.

The complete Semitic **declension** had three cases corresponding to the b

Latin nominative, genitive and accusative. When the noun was indeterminate, *m* was added to the case vowel (mimation)(1). This *m* became *n* in Arabic (nunation). The declension of the word *yawm* > יוֹם *day* was as follows:

	Nominative	Genitive	Accusative
Determinate	*yáwmu*	*yáwmi*	*yáwma*
Indeterminate	*yáwmum*	*yáwmim*	*yáwmam*

In some biliteral nouns of kinship *'ab* "father," *'aḥ* "brother," *ḥam* "husband's father" (§ 98 *b*), the declension in the construct state (and before the suffixes) had a long vowel, e. g.:

Nom. *'abū* **Gen.** *'abī* **Acc.** *'abā*

(1) As the mimation (or nunation) is not evidenced in El Amarna glosses or Ugaritic, it probably did not exist in Early Hebrew.

c **Paragogic vowel ָה -.** This unstressed vowel, formerly thought to be a vestige of the old determinate accusative, is no longer so considered in the light of Ugaritic, which also attests to a form such as *arṣh* "to the ground," where the final letter is not a *mater lectionis*, but a consonant(1). It is mainly used to indicate direction towards, or destination to, a place (§ 125 *n*), hence the designation: ָה *of direction, local* ָה (He *locale*). A noun with paragogic ָה is usually determinate, either by itself or by virtue of the article attached to it. The vocalisation of the word remains unchanged, as far as possible. In nouns with the feminine ending ָה the primitive ת reappears, e.g. תִּרְצָה, תִּרְצָתָה *to Tirṣa*. Short vowels are maintained in open syllables, e.g. מִדְבַּרָה דַמֶּשֶׂק *to the desert of Damascus* 1Kg 19.15 (מִדְבָּר, cst. ־בַּ, but מִדְבָּרָה if not cst.); פַּדֶּנָה אֲרָם *to* פַּדַּן־אֲרָם Gn 28. 2 (vowel sequence ȩ—ǫ, § 29 *f*); הֶרָה *to the mountain* Gn 14.10† (from הַר; instead of הַרָה*, vowel sequence ȩ—ǫ); כַּרְמֶלָה 1Sm 25.5 (from כַּרְמֶל); בָּבֶלָה (from בָּבֶל); גַּתָה 1Kg 2.40 (from גַּת); צְפַתָה 2Ch 14.9 (from צְפַת); צָרְפַתָה 1Kg 17.9 (from צָרְפַת); צָרְתַנָה 4.12 (from צָרְתָן).

Quite often in the segholate nouns, ָה is not added to the primitive form the way suffixes are, but to the Hebrew form which is modified only when necessary. Thus we have בַּיְתָה *to (in) the house* (with ת rafé) from בַּיִת; comp. cst. בֵּיתָה *to the house of*, בֵּיתָהּ *her house*, מַלְכָּהּ *her king*. Likewise אֹ֫הֱלָה is formed from אֹ֫הֶל, and comp. אָהֳלָהּ *her tent*; גֹּ֫רְנָה from גֹּ֫רֶן. From יָם is formed הַיָּ֫מָּה *towards the sea*; comp. יַמָּהּ *her sea*(2). From נֶ֫גֶב is formed נֶ֫גְבָּה *towards the south* (with "quiescent" shewa, but cf. נֶ֫גְדָה Ps 116.14,18 *before*). But derived from the primitive form we find אַ֫רְצָה *to the earth* (אֶ֫רֶץ); הַחַ֫דְרָה *(in)to the room* (חֶ֫דֶר).

The ה ָ has, abnormally and for no apparent reason, become ֶ in נֹ֫בֶה *towards Nob* 1Sm 21.2; 22.9† (before אֶל־); דְּדָ֫נֶה *towards Dedan* Ez 25.13†; אָ֫נֶה וָאָ֫נָה *anywhere* 1Kg 2.36,42; 2Kg 5.25†.

The ה ָ is stressed in מִזְרְחָה שָׁמֶשׁ *towards the rising of the sun* Dt 4.41 (instead of מִזְרָ֫חָה, probably because of the pause) and in the two proper nouns גִּתָּה חֵפֶר and עִתָּה קָצִין Josh 19.13. Comp. עַ֫תָּה, § *g*.

(1) The originally consonantal character of *h* is assured in view of the corresponding Akkadian morpheme *š*, a sound which, when used as grammatical morpheme, often corresponds to *h* in Canaanite. However, the beginning of the loss of the consonantal value of *h* is already attested in Ugr.: Gordon, *UT*, § 5.39.

(2) Comp. שָׁ֫מָּה with the qameṣ of שָׁם.

d The ה ָ is mainly used when there is a notion of direction, of motion *towards* or *to* something(1): קֵ֫דְמָה *towards the east* (but קֶ֫דֶם, § 96 A *f*); הָהָ֫רָה *to the mountain* (13 times; once without the article הֶ֫רָה, § *c*[2] Gn 14.10); הַחוּ֫צָה *towards the outside* (19 times; 8 times חוּ֫צָה with the same meaning); הַיָּ֫מָּה *towards the sea*, but יָ֫מָּה *towards the west*(3); הַבַּ֫יְתָה *(in)to the house*, but בַּ֫יְתָה *(in)to the inside*. In the construct state: בֵּ֫יתָה יוֹסֵף *(in)to the house of Joseph* Gn 43.17,24; אַ֫רְצָה מִצְרַ֫יִם *towards the land of Egypt* Ex 4.20. With a plural: הַשָּׁמַ֫יְמָה *towards the skies*, כַּשְׂדִּ֫ימָה *towards the Chaldeans = towards Chaldea* Ez 11.24, 16.29, 23.16; מִיָּמִים יָמִ֫ימָה *from year to year* (motion applied to time).

(1) The noun in the accusative without ה ָ (§ 125 *n*) can also be found. Cf. J. Hoftijzer, *A Search for the Method. A Study in the Syntactic Use of the H-Locale in Classical Heb.* (Leiden, 1981).

(2) Like הֶ֫רָה we have סֶ֫לָה, an unexplained word (Hab 3.3,9,13; Ps 3.3 etc.).

(3) Likewise, usually הַיָּם *the sea*, יָם *the west*. Cf. § 137 *q*.

e The notion of direction or of motion *towards* (Latin: *ad, in* with acc.) can become weaker and, in some cases, it can even disappear. הַמִּזְבֵּ֫חָה properly *at the altar* is quite frequently found in the ritual for sacrifices, mainly in conjunction with הִקְטִיר *to make (sacrifices) smoke* (Ex 29.13,25 etc.), also with הֶעֱלָה *cause to ascend* (Lv 14.20), זָרַק *toss* or *throw (in a volume), scatter abundantly* (2Ch 29.22). Yet with all these verbs we also find עַל הַמִּזְבֵּחַ; the two expressions are thus practically synonymous. In Jer 29.15 בָּבֶ֫לָה (if authentic) would mean *in Babylon* (without motion). Note also שָׁ֫מָּה *there*, not *thither* 2Kg 23.8; Jer 18.2 etc.

It is probably due to the analogy of the use of ־ָה with nouns and without ־ָה that שָׁ֫מָּה *thither* is used mainly when there is motion, and שָׁם mainly when there is no motion, § 102 *h*.

f The ־ָה of direction is sometimes found, redundantly, after prepositions which already express the idea of motion *towards*: אֶל־הַצָּפ֫וֹנָה *towards the north* Ez 8.14† (like צָפ֫וֹנָה 40.40), לִשְׁא֫וֹלָה *to Sheol* Ps 9.18† (like the usual שְׁא֫וֹלָה). The ־ָה can lose its primary meaning to such an extent that it is used with prepositions without any notion of movement: לְמַ֫עְלָה(1) *above, upwards* (with or without movement), מִלְמַ֫עְלָה *from above, above* (without movement); לְמַ֫טָּה *below* (with or without movement), מִלְמַ֫טָּה *from below, below* (without movement); בַּנֶּ֫גְבָּה *in the south* Josh 15.21 (probably because נֶ֫גְבָּה is quite common); מִצָּפ֫וֹנָה *from the north* Josh 15.10; cf. Jdg 21.19† (prob. because צָפ֫וֹנָה is quite common). With names of cities ־ָה sometimes even becomes an integral part of the word. Thus alongside תִּמְנָה we have עַד־כַּרְמֵי תִמְנָ֫תָה *to the vineyards of Timna* Jdg 14.5, בְּתִמְנָ֫תָה vs. 2; we always have אֶפְרָ֫תָה (7 times; once אֶפְרָת Gn 48.7*b*, prob. incorrect: haplography, § 89 *n*); see also הַגֻּדְגֹּ֫דָה Dt 10.7*b*, קְהֵלָ֫תָה Nu 33.23; יָטְבָ֫תָה vs. 33. This phenomenon is probably best explained by the fact that names of cities lent themselves quite naturally to a frequent use of the accusative of direction, e.g. "I am going to Ephrata"(2).

(1) Note the absence of auxiliary ḥaṭef after the stressed vowel; contr. מַעְלָה, מַעֲלָה (cf. § 22 *b* 1).

(2) Thus *Stamboul* comes from εἰς τὴν πόλιν, *Isnik* from εἰς Νίκαια, *Stanco* from εἰς τὴν Κῶ, etc.

g The *a* of the accusative(1) is probably found in the masc. substantive לַ֫יְלָה *night*(2). The word has remained fossilised in the determinate accusative of time, probably because הַלַּ֫יְלָה was often used for, e.g., "tonight": הַלַּ֫יְלָה (cf. § 126 *i*).

The adverb עַתָּה, mil'ra in context but mil'el in pause (עָ֫תָּה, עַתָּה § 32 *f*), is probably also the determinate accusative of עֵת *time*: "at this time" hence *now*; cf. Brock., *GvG*, I, p. 464(3).

(1) This ending appears to be distinct from the locative ־ָה (§ *f* above). So does עַתָּה;

cf. AC *at-ta* "now" (Sivan, p. 131). Note the frequent and regular defective (?) spelling עת in the Arad inscriptions.
(2) 3 times only לֵיל, cst. לֵיל; pl. לֵילוֹת. The primitive form *laylay* has been, in Hebrew (and in Arabic), reduced to *layl*; cf. Brock., *GvG*, I, pp. 260, 464. In לַ֫יְלָה the contraction of *ay* to *ẹ* does not take place (cf. § 26 *ç*, n.; a tendency to alter vocalisation as little as possible, § 93 *c*); contr. לֵילוֹת. See also J. Blau in M. Bar-Asher et al. (eds), *Hebrew Language Studies* [Heb] [Fschr. Z. Ben-Ḥayyim] (Jerusalem, 1983), p. 79.
(3) An archaic(?) spelling עֵתָ occurs in Ez 23.43 and Ps 74.6 as in Lachish ostracon 4.2 and very often in the Arad ostraca, e.g. 1.2.

The *a* of the accusative is also found in some words with other nuances. In חָלִ֫ילָה, which is generally translated as *ad profanum!*, *Heaven forbid!*, the accusative is rather one of wish, as in some corresponding Arabic phrases (cf. § 105 *f*). In מְא֫וּמָה *something, anything*, the accusative can come from cases where the meaning is *as far as something is concerned*, as in 1Sm 21.3. אָמְנָה *in truth* Gn 20.12, Josh 7.20†, synonymous with אָמְנָם *verily* (§ 102 *b*), could be the accusative of אֹמֶן. h

Sometimes the ָה no longer has its original force; its use is purely rhythmic. In poetry sometimes it could have been used out of metrical necessity: הַחַשְׁמַ֫לָה *electrum* Ez 8.2 (in pause, in a grand description), נַ֫חְלָה *brook* Ps 124.4, הַמָּ֫וְתָה ? *death* Ps 116.15(1), אַ֫רְצָה ? *the earth* Job 37.12. i

(1) Starting from a discussion of this instance, P.C.H. Wernberg-Møller attempts to demonstrate occasional residues of the genuine accusative as distinct from the directional He as in Is 8.23 הֵקַל אַ֫רְצָה זְבֻלוּן and Ho 8.7 סוּפָ֫תָה יִקְצֹרוּ: see *JSS* 33 (1988) 161.

This is rather frequent in the feminine, where we have the ending ָ֫תָה (for ָ֫ה)(1). In some cases this form seems to have been chosen to avoid the contact of two stressed syllables: אֵין יְשׁוּעָ֫תָה לּוֹ *no salvation for him* Ps 3.3(2); קוּמָ֫ה עֶזְרָ֫תָה לָּ֫נוּ *arise for our help* 44.27 (comp. לְעֶזְרָה לוֹ 2Ch 28.21); לֹא עַוְלָ֫תָה בּוֹ Ps 92.16. Other examples: בְּעַוְלָ֫תָה יְדֵיהֶם 125.3; אֵימָ֫תָה וָפַ֫חַד Ex 15.16; בַּצָּרָ֫תָה לִּי *when I was in distress* Ps 120.1; עֹלָ֫תָה קָ֫פְצָה פִּיהָ *iniquity stops her mouth* Job 5.16; אֶ֫רֶץ עֵיפָ֫תָה *a land of gloom* 10.22. All these forms occur only in poetry(3). j

(1) Hurvitz points out that, in the cases discussed here and also under the paragogic vowels, the definite article is significantly absent except in late books such as Ezekiel, another indication of the antiquity of the phenomenon, though not in every such case would the article be required in the first place: A. Hurvitz, in A. Kort

and S. Morschauser (eds), *Biblical and Related Studies* [Fschr. S. Iwry] (Winona Lake, 1985), pp. 116-19.

(2) Cf. Ch.A. and E.G. Briggs *ad loc.* (*ICC*).

(3) See M. Tsevat, *A Study of the Language of the Biblical Psalms* (Philadelphia, 1955), pp. 21f.

k Finally, unstressed הָ‑, which therefore cannot be the feminine ending, is found in some dubious or incorrect examples: הָרָחָמָה ? *the carrion-vulture* Dt 14.17; תַּנּוּר בֹּעֵרָה ? *burning oven* Ho 7.4; הַשַּׁעַר הַתַּחְתּוֹנָה? *the lower gate* Ez 40.19; גָּלִילָה? 2Kg 15.29 (read גליל ו); הַחִיצוֹנָה? 16.18 (dittographic ה).

l **The paragogic vowel** ִי‑. This vowel is called *ḥireq compaginis* (linking *i*) because it is usually found in nouns in the cst. state, and therefore in close link with other nouns(1). Because of its ordinary use and of its origin this ִי‑ can be called *i of the construct state.* It is the ִי‑ which is found in the cst. state of the biliteral nouns of kinship אֲבִי, אֲחִי, חֲמִי* (§ 98 *b*)(2). This ִי‑ was used in poetry in nouns, adjectives and especially participles, at first to express the construct state in the strict sense or in the loose sense, then as a purely rhythmic vowel. In some particles it has become an integral part of the word (§ *q*).

(1) Cf. C. Rabin in *Proceedings*, pp. 194f., and also M. Noth, *Die israelitischen Personennamen* [§ 88 L *c*, n.], pp. 33f.

(2) The *i* of the type אבי, unique to Hebrew, seems to be the old *i* of the genitive **'abī* (§ *b*), to which a new function was assigned after the loss of the cases (cf. § 98 *b*). G.R. Driver mentions a similar *i* as a helping vowel in Old Babylonian attached to a word-final consonantal cluster (*JThSt* 26 [1925] 76f.). Only part of the Hebrew examples adduced lend themselves to such an explanation.

m **In Substantives.** In some compound proper nouns the first substantive of which is in the construct state in relation to the second: מַלְכִּי־צֶדֶק *king of justice*, גַּבְרִיאֵל *man of God*, עַבְדִּיאֵל *servant of God*, חַנִּיאֵל *grace of God* (cp. Phoen. *Hannibal* = חַנִּיבַעַל). Also בְּנִי אֲתֹנוֹ *his ass's colt* (*the son of his she-ass*) Gn 49.11; עַל־דִּבְרָתִי מַלְכִּי־צֶדֶק *after the manner of M.* Ps 110.4; before a preposition רַבָּתִי בַגּוֹיִם *the Great One among the nations* and שָׂרָתִי בַּמְּדִינוֹת *the Princess among the provinces* Lam 1.1(1).

In **adjectives:** רַבָּתִי עָם *populous* (*numerous of people*) Lam 1.1; מְלֵאֲתִי מִשְׁפָּט *full of justice* Is 1.21.

(1) The mil'el stress in these two examples is perh. due to רַבָּתִי עָם, which comes before (where there is nsiga).

In **participles** the ִ-י of the cst. state is rather frequent. This is because on the one hand a participle preceding a substantive is often put in the cst. (§ 121 *l*), on the other hand because a participle, for example, קֹטֵל, usually retains ֵ in the cst. state: a form such as קֹטְלִי had thus the advantage of expressing the cst. state clearly. *n*

In the genitive: עֹזְבִי הַצֹּאן *forsaking the flock (forsaker of the flock)* Zech 11.17 (רֹעִי הָאֱלִיל *shepherd of nothingness* for רֹעֶה is strange; perhaps for assonance); שֹׁכְנִי סְנֶה *inhabitant of the bush* Dt 33.16.

By extension, in a construction where there is a construct state (before a preposition): שֹׁכְנִי בְּחַגְוֵי הַסֶּלַע *dwelling in the retreats of the rock* Jer 49.16(1). Then by extension of this construction : חֹצְבִי מָרוֹם קִבְרוֹ *hewing out in a high place his sepulchre* Is 22.16; שֹׁכְנִי לְבָדָד יַעַר *inhabiting solitarily a wood* Mi 7.14; Ps 101.5; 113.7; Gn 49.11.

Finally there are cases with no notion, even remote, of cst. state. The vowel ִ-י, as was the case for ָ-ה (§§ *i-k*), has now only a rhythmic value: אֹהַבְתִּי לָדוּשׁ *loving to tread out (the corn)* Ho 10.11; Ps 113.5,6; 114.8; 123.1.

(1) Comp. the construction of the type יֹשְׁבֵי בְּאֶרֶץ צַלְמָוֶת Is 9.1 (§ 129 *m*).

The archaic form in ִ-י has, in some cases, been corrected by the Qre: Jer 10.17: K. יוֹשַׁבְתִּי, Q. יוֹשֶׁבֶת; Lam 4.21, Ez 27.3. In Jer 22.23 the Qre strangely requires יוֹשַׁבְתְּ (§ 89 *j*) and likewise (*ibid.*) מְקֻנַּנְתְּ; 51.13 שֹׁכַנְתְּ. In all these examples the form in ִ-י is justified and may be regarded as authentic. On the contrary in 2Kg 4.23, K. הֹלַכְתִּי is probably incorrect in this text which is written in a very simple prose; the ִ-י could be due to the analogy of אַתִּי. *o*

There is a probable example of the passive participle(1) in Gn 31.39 גְּנֻבְתִי יוֹם וּגְנֻבְתִי לָיְלָה *stolen by day and stolen by night*: this probably is the only example of paragogic ִ-י in prose.

(1) However this form could be a qatāl > קָטוֹל with reduction of ǭ (comp. שְׁלֹשׁ, שְׁלָשְׁתָּם); Brock., *GvG*, II, p. 251. translates *Diebstahl*.

The ִ-י is simply incorrect in Ps 113.8 לְהוֹשִׁיבִי (ִ-י brought about by the preceding and following paragogic ִ-י); it is suspect in Ps 116.1 קוֹלִי תַּחֲנוּנָי, because elsewhere we always (5 times) find קוֹל ת׳. *p* q Paragogic ִי is always found in the negative **particle** בִּלְתִּי (§ 160 *m*), לְבִלְתִּי (160 *l*), which presupposes a form *בֶּלֶת or *בֶּלֶת (root בלה) *wear (and tear), consumption*, hence *deficiency, non-existence*; always (6 times) in זוּלָתִי *with the exception of* (thus the only זוּלַת in 2Kg 24.14 is suspect). We often find the poetic form מִנִּי for מִן, § 103 *d*. In the locution אֲנִי וְאַפְסִי עוֹד *I and I only* ִי is the suffix of the first person rather than paragogic ִי (§ 160 *n*).

r **Paragogic vowel** וֹ. This vowel is found only in a few nouns in the construct state, notably חַיָּה *animal*. Just as the ִי of the cst. state comes from the ִי of the type אֲבִי (which itself probably comes from the Semitic *'abī*, § *l*), the וֹ probably comes from the *ā* of the accusative of the type *'abā* § *b*. It is used in some cases in the cst. state instead of ִי for reasons unknown. Instead of בְּנִי Gn 49.11 (§ *m*) we find בְּנוֹ צִפֹּר *son of Z.* Nu 23.18, בְּנוֹ בְעֹר *son of B.* 24.3,15 (poetic and archaic texts). Instead of לְמַעְיְנוֹ־מָיִם Ps 114.8 one should perhaps read the plural לְמַעְיְנֵי (cf. LXX, Pesh., Vulg.). Finally we find חַיְתוֹ 7 times (one of which occurs in a prose passage). In Gn 1.24 חַיְתוֹ־אֶרֶץ *wild animals* (literally: *animals of the earth*) the poetic form may have been chosen to avoid *חַיַּת־אֶרֶץ, which may have been thought too harsh (but vs. 25: חַיַּת הָאָרֶץ with the article); cf. Ps 79.2 לְחַיְתוֹ־אָרֶץ. Other examples: חַיְתוֹ שָׂדָי Is 56.9; Ps 104.11; חַיְתוֹ־יָעַר 50.10; 104.20; חַיְתוֹ־גוֹי Zeph 2.14.

s **Paragogic vowel** וּ. This vowel וּ is only found in a few compound proper nouns the first of which is built on the second. Thus it has the same function as the vowel ִי in proper nouns (§ *m*). Just as ִי and וֹ ultimately come from the types *'abī*, *'abā*, this וּ probably comes from the nominative of the type *'abū* (§ *b*)(1). In the examples, which by the way are rare, one must not exclude the possibility of a radical *w* which could have become *u*(2). Moreover, according to Prätorius(3), there could be in some nouns a form of endearment *qatūl*. Examples: פְּנוּאֵל *face of God* Gn 32.32 (vs. 31 פְּנִיאֵל)(4), רְעוּאֵל *friend of God*(?) 36.4(5); שְׁמוּאֵל *name of God*(?); גְּאוּאֵל *majesty of God*(?) (perhaps from a form **ga'w*). With מְתוּ *man*, the proper form of which is not known, מְתוּשָׁאֵל, מְתוּשֶׁלַח (cf. Phoenician *Metuastart* "man of Astarte" and Akk. *mutu* "man").

Apart from these compound nouns the וּ of the nominative may be found in some names: מְלִיכוּ ,בִּכְרוּ Ne 12.14 Qre, גַּשְׁמוּ 6.6 (name of an Arab; cf.

vs. 1 גֶּשֶׁם).

(1) In Arabic dialects, where the cases of old Arabic have almost disappeared, *'abu* is the normal form in the cst. st., and *'abū* with suffixes: *'Abu Bekr*, *'Abu Nāder*; *'abūna* "our father" (some people affectedly say *'abina*).

(2) Comp. Arabic *ǧazw* "foray" pronounced *ǧazū*; Hebrew **waiyyištaḥw*, which has become וַיִּשְׁתַּחוּ, § 79 *t*.

(3) *ZDMG* 57 (1903) 777ff.

(4) In view of the use of the word as plurale tantum, we may be dealing with vestiges of the archaic plural case endings: *-ū* (nominative case) and *-i* (oblique case).

(5) Cf. M. Noth, op. cit. [§ *l*, n. 1], p. 153, n. 2, and S.C. Layton, op. cit. [§ 93 *a*,n].

§ 94. Nouns with suffixes
(Paradigm 20)

Like a noun, a pronoun which depends on a noun is in the genitive, e.g. אָבִי, which properly speaking means ὁ πατήρ μου "the father *of* me." The suffixes are, in principle, added to the cst. form (the vocalisation of which is sometimes modified). The suffixes which are used with nouns will be found in Paradigm 1; the forms taken by nouns with suffixes in Paradigm 20. As was the case with the corresponding suffixes which were added to verbs, the suffixes כֶם, כֶן, הֶם, הֶן, which are added to nouns, are termed *heavy*: they modify the vocalisation of the word more strongly than the other (*light*) suffixes; cf. § 96 A *b*. *a*

Suffixes beginning with a consonant are linked to nominal forms ending in a consonant by a **linking vowel**. As in the verbs (§ 61 *d*), the two linking vowels *a* and *e* are used. We find ָ in ָם, ָן, and also in **ahu* > וֹ. This *a* is probably the *a* of the old accusative (§ *b*). We find *e* in ֶךָ, ֵךְ; (ֵהוּ § *h*), ֶהָ, ֵנוּ. This *e* probably comes from the nouns of the ל"ה root, e.g. סוּסֵנוּ from שָׂדֵנוּ (1). *b*

(1) For the present inflection of nouns in ֶה, cf. § 96 B *f*. There is nothing surprising in the fact that ל"י (and ל"ו) roots have so often supplied the linking vowel in verbs and in nouns, for indeed only those roots have forms with an originally long stressed vowel after the 2nd radical. Comp. the *ẹ̄* of תַּחְתֵּינוּ, בֵּינֵינוּ § 103, *n*. Cf. §§ 61 *d*, *f*; 78 *b*, *c*; 80 *b*, *i*; 82 *f*; 92 *f*.

Suffixes with singular nouns. [For the sake of clarity the suffixes will be given here joined to a noun. The noun סוּס *horse* has been chosen *c* because it has an unchangeable vowel: thus the form of the cst. is the same as that of the absolute; see Paradigm 20].

Sing. 1st *c.* סוּסִי: primitive form: *sūsiya*; - *(my horse).*
2nd *m.* סוּסְךָ: contextual form, reduced from סוּסֶךָ(1).
2nd *f.* סוּסֵךְ: on the analogy of שָׂדֵךְ(2).
3rd *m.* סוּסוֹ: from *sūsahu*, with the *a* of the old accusative.
3rd *f.* סוּסָהּ: from *sūsaha*, with the *a* of the old accusative.
Plur. 1st *c.* סוּסֵנוּ: on the analogy of שָׂדֵנוּ; - *(our horse).*
2nd *m.* סוּסְכֶם: before the heavy suffix כֶם the primitive vowel, probably also *e*, was dropped(3).
2nd *f.* סוּסְכֶן: (as above).
3rd *m.* סוּסָם: for *sūsahęm*, with the *a* of the old accusative(4).
3rd *f.* סוּסָן: for *sūsahęn*, with the *a* of the old accusative.

(1) The pausal form סוּסֶךָ comes from the ל"ה nouns, e.g. שָׂדֶךָ, form preserved only in pause, § 96 B *f* (comp. קְטָלֶךָ, יִקְטְלֶךָ § 61 *d*); for the vowel sequence *ę-ǫ*, cf. § 29 *f*. These forms illustrate the principle whereby the 2m.sg. suffix ךָ is unstressed when attached to a form ending in a vowel, but stressed when it follows a consonant.

(2) According to Brock., *GvG*, I, p. 478, the ֵ would represent the old *i* of the genitive, § 93 *b*. The original ending *-ki* could also have influenced its emergence.

(3) Primitive forms of the 2 pl. suff.: m. **kumu*, f. **kinna*. The *ę* of the masc. is explained as in the independent pronoun אַתֶּם, § 39 *a* (cf. Brock., *GvG*, I, p. 310). QH as well as SH attests to the long morpheme, -כמה, -המה, *-kimma*, *-imma*, *-inna*: see Qimron, *Hebrew of DSS*, pp. 62f. and Ben-Ḥayyim, *LOT*, vol. 5, pp. 172f.

(4) Primitive forms of the 3 pl. suff.: m. **humu*, f. **šinna*, like the independent pronoun, § 39 *a* (cf. Brock., *GvG*, I, p. 312). See also the preceding note. Cf. AC *ta-aḫ-ta-mu* "under them."

d Suffixes with **plural (and dual) nouns**. The suffixes are added to the primitive ending *ay* of plural (and dual) nouns in the cst. state.

Sing. 1st *c.* סוּסַי, סוּסָי: primitive form: *sūsayya*; - *(my horses)*(1).
2nd *m.* סוּסֶיךָ: from *sūsayka*. For the vowel sequence *ę-ǫ*, cf. § 29 *f*.
2nd *f.* סוּסַיִךְ: from *sūsayki*.
3rd *m.* סוּסָיו: from *sūsayhu*. Here the י is purely graphic(2).
3rd *f.* סוּסֶיהָ: from *sūsayha*. For the vowel sequence *ę-ǫ*, cf. § 29 *f*.

Plur. 1st *c.* סוּסֵ֫ינוּ: from *sūsaynu*; - *(our horses).*
2nd *m.* סוּסֵיכֶם: from *sūsaykẹm.*
2nd *f.* סוּסֵיכֶן: from *sūsaykẹn.*
3rd *m.* סוּסֵיהֶם: from *sūsayhẹm.*
3rd *f.* סוּסֵיהֶן: from *sūsayhẹn.*

(1) Cf. AC *ḫe-na-ya* "my eyes."

(2) It is quite often omitted by the Ktiv, thus bearing witness to the actual pronunciation *sūsåw,* but almost always required by the Qre, e.g. K. רַחֲמָו, Q. רחמיו 2Sm 24.14. For יַחְדָּו *together,* cf. § 102 *d.*

The defective spelling without Yod is what one finds in early Hebrew inscriptions, e.g. אנשו *his men* (Lachish 3:18) and אלו *to him* (Yavneh-Yam, line 13), thus indicating its antiquity. Andersen and Forbes (AF, pp. 324-26) maintain that the standard spelling יו resulted from a spelling reform artificially introduced in the interest of the graphic distinction between, say, בנו *his son* and בניו *his sons.* On the other hand, the well-nigh exclusive attestation of the prepositions אֱלֵי, עֲלֵי, and עֲדֵי in poetic sections of the OT as well as the comparative Semitic data (Arb. *'ilā(y);* Arb. *'alā(y),* Akk. *eli;* Ugr. *'ly;* Akk. *adi*) speak for the originality of the final Yod, whether these prepositions are to be considered originally plural nouns or not; but on Old South Arabic, see A.F.L. Beeston, *Sabaic Gram.* (Manchester, 1984), § 33:3. אַחַר and תַּחַת are liable to analogical development (as against לִפְנֵי and עַל respectively; § 103 *n*), whereas the occasional pseudo-plural use of בֵּין and סָבִיב is easily understandable in terms of their semantics. Thus there is no doubting that /y/ as part of the pl.cst. morpheme /ay/ was a reality at one stage of the evolution of this complex. Whatever explanation is to be sought for the development **ayhu > åw,* the spelling attested by inscriptions can be said to reflect this *phonetic* shape, and thus the form אנשו mentioned above, for instance, can represent basically the same phonetic reality as that of the Massoretic אנשיו: for a different view of the phonetic development, see F.M. Cross and D.N. Freedman, *Early Hebrew Orthography: A Study of the Epigraphic Evidence* (New Haven, 1952), pp. 68f., where a case is put forward for /ēw/ as a dialectal form. See also H.M. Orlinsky, *HUCA* 17 (1942-43) 288-92, and Meyer, II, pp. 56f. It is not impossible that the /åw/ eventually goes back to /aw/, which is paralleled by the corresponding Aramaic form /awhi/ (> /ōhi/) and is explained by some as a result of vowel dissimilation, namely /*ayhu/> /*awhi/. The change /a/ to /å/ would be rather late, due to the influence of the labial /w/, to which the vowel /å/ is akin.

Nouns with the **feminine ending** ָה, e.g. סוּסָה *mare.* The suffixes are added to the cst. form סוּסַת, the ַ of which is retained in סוּסַתְכֶם, סוּסַתְכֶן (shewa "medium"), but everywhere else becomes ָ, e.g. סוּסָתִי, סוּסָתְךָ. e

Nouns with the **feminine pl. ending** וֹת, e.g. סוּסוֹת *mares.* Here Hebrew presents a particular phenomenon: the suffixes are not added directly f to the cst. סוּסוֹת, but come after a syllable *ay, which is none other than the plural (and dual) ending of masculine nouns in the cst. state, e.g. סוּסוֹתֶ֫יךָ, with ־ֵי (= *ay) of סוּסֶ֫יךָ. These forms thus contain a double plural marker: feminine וֹת and masculine *ay.

g However, examples without *ay can be found. They are common only with the 3rd pers. pl. suffix: instead of the type סוּסוֹתֵיהֶם we often find the type סוּסוֹתָם, which is older; the longer pattern is less economical in giving twofold expression to the category of plurarity. Thus אֲבוֹתָם *their fathers* is more frequent than אֲבֹתֵיהֶם(1), which is only found in the later books of Ezra, Nehemiah, and Chronicles; also in Jeremiah and 1Kg 14.15; note 2Sm 22.46 מִסְגְּרוֹתָם as against its parallel Ps 18.46 מִסְגְּרוֹתֵיהֶם(2). We always have אִמֹּתָם (twice) *their mothers,* שְׁמוֹתָם and שְׁמוֹתָן *their names,* דּוֹרוֹתָם *their generations*(3). Euphony sometimes seems to have influenced the choice of a form in some nouns which can be found with both suffixes; thus, for מִזְבְּחוֹת comp. Dt 7.5 with 12.3 (־ָם to avoid a triple repetition of ־ֵם); for מַצֵּבוֹת Ex 34.13 with 23.24 (־ֵיהֶם in pause).

Apart from the suffix ־ָם and ־ָן, examples are rare and dubious: עֵדֹתַי Ps 132.12 (dubious form: the sing. would be עֵדְתִי, the pl. עֵדְוֹתַי *'ed̲wọṯạy*; the absence of ו is probably incorrect); מַכֹּתְךָ Dt 28.59 (the absence of י prob. incorrect); אֲחִיוֹתֵךְ Ez 16.52 (the absence of י prob. incorrect; contr. vs. 51).

(1) 106 : 33. Compare the particle of the accusative אֵת: אֹתָם more common than אֶתְהֶם (§ 103 *k*).

(2) Qimron (*Hebrew of DSS*, p. 63, n. 80) mentions occasional corrections in QH of דורותמה to דורותיהמה. In *Leš* 51 (1987) 237f. he notes that the short form is the dominant one in BH, and that earlier books prefer it.

(3) Böttcher(2.42) quotes 56 nouns in וֹת which always have the suffix ־ָם. One finds another 35 nouns which show the extended form only, and many of these are confined to exilic or post-exilic books. On the other hand, 22 nouns are attested in both the long and the short form, the great majority of which tend to the short form, the notable exception being בַּת (בְּנוֹתָם only once in Gn 34.21, but בְּנוֹתֵיהֶם 20 x).

h **Rare suffix forms in singular nouns**(1).

Sing. 2nd m. Rare spelling ־ְכָה, e.g. Ps 139.5; Pr 24.10(2).

2nd f. Rare (Aramaising)(3) form ־ֵכִי: Jer 11.15; Ps 103.3; 116.19; 135.9, all in poetry except 2Kg 4.2.

Rare form ־ָךְ (usual with particles): participle (§ 66) נֹתְנָךְ Ez 23.28;

25.4. As for כֹּל, we find כֻּלָּךְ 2 x (Is 22.1; Ct 4.7) and the (normal) form כֻּלֵּךְ, 2 x in pause (Is 14.29,31) (cf. below, plural 1st c. כֻּלָּנוּ).

3rd m. The spelling הֹ is fairly common and is normal in early Hebrew inscriptions; the ה represents the *h* of the primitive form *ahu* (cf. § 7 *b*, and above at § *d*, n. 2). Especially noteworthy is כֻּלֹּה, a spelling as common as כֻּלּוֹ. The other examples are rather rare, and the Qre sometimes prescribes וֹ, e.g. for אָהֳלֹה Gn 9.21; 12.8; 13.3; 35.21. The suffix ־ֵהוּ of ל"ה nouns (שָׂדֵהוּ) was introduced in some nouns. Except in Jer 6.21 רֵעוֹ (cf. רעו in the Siloam inscription) we always find רֵעֵהוּ, which comes from the usual form רֵעַ *companion*, not from the rare רֵעֶה *(royal) friend*. Other examples: לְמִינֵהוּ Gn 1.12,21,25 (but לְמִינוֹ vs. 11) (the fuller form לְמִינֵהוּ seems more common in pause); אוֹרֵהוּ Job 25.3.

3rd f. ־ָה (without mappiq, § 25 *a*) is sometimes found, especially before certain consonants, mainly the *begadkefat*; before ב: Nu 15.28, 31; Ez 16.44; 24.6; before פ: Ps 48.14; before ת: Ez 47.10; Job 31.22; before ו; Na 3.9; before א: 2Kg 8.6; Pr 12.28; before ה: Is 21.2; Jer 20.17; before ע: Lv 6.2. In pause: Lv 12.4,5; Is 23.17; 45.6; Pr 21.22. ־ָא is found once Ez 36.5 (probably incorrect).

Plur. 1st c. Rare form ־ָנוּ (usual with the particles, § 103 *e*). We always find כֻּלָּנוּ (cf. *above*, 2nd f. כֻּלָּךְ), perhaps on the analogy of לָנוּ, בָּנוּ, אִתָּנוּ. Apart from these cases only one example is found: מֹדַעְתָּנוּ Ru 3.2 (perhaps because of zaqef and because the word is a predicate).

2nd f. כֵּנָה Ez 23.48,49.

3rd m. ־ָמוֹ Ps 17.10; מוֹ Ps 17.10; 58.7; a form found only once כֻּלָּהַם 2Sm 23.6 (cf. Driver, *Notes* ad loc.).

3rd f. ־ָנָה generally in great pause: Gn 21.29; 42.36; Jer 8.7; Pr 31.29; Job 39.2; in Ru 1.19 probably for assonance; ־ֶנָה Gn 41.21 (with rvia' and zaqef); ־ָהְנָה 1Kg 7.37; Ez 16.53.

The suffix הֶן (without linking vowel) is sometimes found after a noun ending in a consonant (instead of ־ָן): חֶלְבְּהֶן Lv 8.16,25 (but perhaps read the pl. חֶלְבֵּהֶן *defective*; cf. Gn 4.4; comp. לְמִינֵהֶם 1.21 *defective*).

(1) Compare the rare forms of suffixes with verbs § 61 *i*.

(2) The plene spelling כה- is by far the more frequent one in Qumran Hebrew; see Qimron, *Hebrew of DSS*, pp. 58f. On a debate originating with E. Sievers, *Metrische Studien, I. Studien zur hebr. Metrik* (Leipzig, 1901-19) and P.E. Kahle's proposal to

see -*ḫâ* as an unauthentic ending artificially introduced by Naqdanim under Arabic influence, though later, confronted by literally hundreds of forms spelled plene in Dead Sea Hebrew documents, he conceded that such did exist historically (*The Cairo Genizah* [Oxford, [2]1959], p. 174), see Z. Ben-Ḥayyim, "The form of the suffixal pronouns ־ךָ, ־תָ, ־הָ in the traditions of the Hebrew language" [Heb] in *Sefer Simḥa Asaf* (Jerusalem, 1953), pp. 66-99; idem, *Studies in the Traditions of the Heb. Language*, (Madrid/Barcelona, 1954), pp. 22-39, 51-64; Kutscher, *Isaiah*, pp. 446-51; Qimron, op. cit., pp. 58f. Kahle also put forward a similar thesis regarding the pf. 2m.sg. ending. See also H. Yalon, *Studies in the Dead Sea Scrolls. Philological Essays* [in Heb] (Jerusalem, 1967), pp. 16-21. On the other hand, nobody would deny that -*âḫ* is equally genuine and authentic, as is indicated by the pausal form, Mishnaic Hebrew, and transliterations in the Hexapla and Jerome. Cf. Kutscher, *History*, § 46. The form -*âḫ* is regular with some prepositions (e.g. בָּךְ, לָךְ) and the 3 m.sg. pf. of ל"ה verbs such as עָנָךְ *he will answer you*).

(3) See Kutscher, *Isaiah*, pp. 210-13.

i **Rare suffix forms in plural nouns**

Sing. 2nd f. Rare (Aramaising) form ־ֵ֫יְכִי, ־ָ֫יְכִי: 2Kg 4.3;7 (Ktiv), all in a passage evidencing some influence of the northern dialect, likewise 2Kg 4.2 לָכִי, and 16,23 אַתִּי; Ps 103.3-5; 116.7, mostly in poetry.

3rd m. ־ֵ֫יהוּ Hb 3.10; Job 24.23; and *defective* ־ֵ֫הוּ (which has the appearance of a sing.) 1Sm 14.48 (probably); 30.26; Ez 43.17; Na 2.4. The Aramaic suffix וֹהִי is (prob. incorrectly) found in Ps 116.12.

3rd f. ־ֶ֫יהָא Ez 41.15 (prob. incorrect).

Plur. 2nd f. ־ֵיכֶ֫נָה Ez 13.20; 3rd m. ־ֵיהֶ֫מָה Ez 40.16(1); ־ֵיהֶ֫נָה 1.11.

3rd m. ־ֵ֫ימוֹ, very rarely with the sense of *his* as in Ps 11.7 and Job 27.23 (עָלֵ֫ימוֹ); cf. § 103 *m*.

(1) The ending יהמה is highly frequent in QH alongside the standard BH יהם: see Qimron, *Hebrew of DSS*, pp. 62f.

j **Resemblances and confusions in the suffixes of sing. and plural nouns.** Confusions easily arose both graphically and phonetically. In plural nouns the omission of י, whether by design or by error, can produce an ambiguous consonantal group. Thus דְּרָכֶ֫ךָ, vocalised as plural, *your ways* Ex 33.13; Josh 1.8; Ps 119.37, could be vocalised as singular דַּרְכְּךָ, דַּרְכֶּ֫ךָ. In such cases one hesitates between the singular and the plural(1).

The suffixes of plural nouns, longer and more resonant, have sometimes been introduced in singular nouns, especially in nouns in וּת(2):

זְנוּתֵיכֶם Nu 14.33; אַלְמְנוּתַ֫יִךְ Is 54.4 (perhaps for assonance with עֲלוּמַ֫יִךְ); תַּזְנוּתַ֫יִךְ Ez 16.15,20 (Qre); תַּזְנוּתֶ֫יהָ 23.7; שְׁבוּתֵיכֶם Zeph 3.20; in some nouns in *a*ṯ(3): עֲצָתָ֫יִךְ Is 47.13; Ez 35.11; Ps 9.15; Ezr 9.15.

(1) On the likelihood that no phonetic distinction was intended by the Naqdanim between pairs such as ־ֶ֫ךָ, ־ֶ֫יךָ; ־ֵ֫הוּ, ־ֵ֫יהוּ; ־ֶ֫הָ, ־ֶ֫יהָ; ־ֵ֫נוּ, ־ֵ֫ינוּ, see above § 6 *d*, n. 2. A scribe writing from dictation could easily have added or omitted a י. For the apparent plurals in nouns in ־ָה, cf. § 96 C *e*. For a listing of probable defective spellings like חֶלְבֵהֶן Gn 4.4 (§ *h*), see AF, pp. 137f.

(2) According to König, *Syntax*, § 258 *f*., however, a true plural is not absolutely impossible.

(3) But we should perh. vocalise in the plural, e.g. עֲצֹתָ֫יִךְ.

§ 95. Noun inflection

When a noun passes from the *absolute state* to the *construct state*, when it takes the *plural* or the *dual* endings and when it takes the *suffixes*, it usually undergoes some changes in its vocalisation. The sum of such changes in a noun constitutes its *inflection*. These changes are caused by a shifting, weakening or suppression of the stress. They are subject to the laws set forth in the section of this book on phonetics; their application as well as the anomalies will be indicated when we discuss the various *paradigms*. a

We shall see that, in several types of inflection, the vocalisation with the *heavy* suffixes ־ְכֶם, ־ְכֶן, ־הֶם, and ־הֶן is not the same with the *light* suffixes; nouns have one *stem* when used with the heavy suffixes and another when used with the light suffixes. The stem with the heavy suffixes is generally the construct state, and the stem with the light suffixes is the absolute state, e.g.: cst. מַלְכֵי, מַלְכֵיכֶם; abs. מְלָכִים, מְלָכַי (cf. § 96 A *b*, n.). The stem with the light suffixes is often less reduced than the construct state (so in the example given above); sometimes the stem with the heavy suffixes is actually less reduced than the cst. state, e.g. plural abs. מַצֵּבוֹת *stelae*, cst. מַצְּבוֹת, מַצֵּבוֹתֵיהֶם (and מַצֵּבֹתָם). b

As for vowel distribution, note that there is a great difference between **nouns** without suffixes and the **perfect** without suffixes. Of two vowels which can be dropped, it is the first in nouns, the second in c the perfect (§ 30 *e*), e.g.:

NOUNS: דָּבָר, דְּבָרִים; זָקֵן, זְקֵנָה, זְקֵנִים.

PERFECT: קָטַל, קָטְלָה, קָטְלוּ; כָּבֵד, כָּֽבְדָה, כָּֽבְדוּ.

But in the perfect with suffixes, vowel distribution is the same as in nouns, e.g.:

NOUNS: דְּבָרְךָ, דְּבָרֵךְ.

PERFECT: קְטָלְךָ, קְטָלֵךְ.

d There is a noteworthy difference between nouns and verbs in the treatment of stressed *a* in final closed syllables. In the verb ַ is a contextual vowel, ָ a pausal vowel: קָטַל, קָטָֽל. In nouns ָ is generally found in the absolute state (in context and in pause), and ַ in the construct state: דָּבָר, דָּבָֽר; cst. דְּבַר. Thus in Nifal we have נִקְטַל in the perfect and נִקְטָל in the participle (nominal form). In the infinitive we have the vowel ַ (perhaps on the analogy of the future): שְׁכַב, § 49 *c*, הַגֵּשׁ(1). When used as a proper noun the future יִצְחַק *he will laugh* becomes יִצְחָק *Isaac*. In nouns, since ַ was essential for the cst. state, ָ had to be used in the absolute state, not only in pause, but also in context. In verbs, on the contrary, the alternation of ַ and ָ was used to distinguish the contextual form from the pausal form (§ 42 *b*).

(1) Cf. מַסַּע, § 49 *c*.

§ 96. Inflection of masculine nouns
(Paradigm 17)

What is meant here by masculine nouns are nouns which in the singular have no feminine ending, and which in the plural have the masculine ending ־ִים (§ 89 *a*).

Because of its length, this paragraph is subdivided into several shorter paragraphs (which are indicated by the capital letters A, B, C, D, and E) as follows: § 96 (A) Inflection of segholate nouns (with one primitive vowel); (B) nouns with two primitive short vowels; (C) nouns with an unchangeable first vowel and an etymologically short second vowel; (D) nouns with a primitive short first vowel and an etymologically long second vowel; (E) nouns with two consonants and a primitive short vowel.

Nouns which do not belong to any of these types of inflection present no difficulty: i.e. monosyllables with an etymologically long vowel like סוּס (§ 94 *c*), dissyllables with two etymologically long vowels like קִיטוֹר *smoke*, or with an etymologically short first vowel in a closed syllable and an etymologically long second vowel like מַטְמוֹן *hidden treasure*.

§ 96 A. INFLECTION OF SEGHOLATE NOUNS

a Included in this category of inflection are all the nouns with one primitive short vowel, namely the nouns from strong roots or weak roots which have taken an auxiliary vowel (usually seghol, hence the designation: *segholate nouns*) between R2 and R3, and also those which have no auxiliary vowel(1). The paradigms are set out in the following order: 1) segholate nouns from strong roots without guttural, § *b*: *qatl* מֶ֫לֶךְ (§ *c*), *qitl* סֵ֫פֶר (§ *e*), *qutl* קֹ֫דֶשׁ (§ *g*); 2) with a guttural: *qatl* נַ֫עַר (§ *i*), *qutl* פֹּ֫עַל (§ *j*); 3) from ע"ו roots: מָ֫וֶת (§ *l*); from ע"י roots: זַ֫יִת (§ *m*); 4) nouns from ע"ע roots: *qatl* עַם (§ *n*), *qitl* עֵז (§ *o*), *qutl* חֹק (§ *p*); 5) *qatl* from ל"ה roots: גְּדִי (§ *q*).

(1) These primitive forms, which occur only sporadically in the MT, e.g. חֵטְא, נֵרְדְּ, קֹשְׁטְ, are those preserved in the tradition underlying the second column of the Hexapla: e.g. αρς = אֶ֫רֶץ; γαβρ = גֶּ֫בֶר. See Brønno, *Studien*, pp. 123-50. This does not mean, however, that the familiar segholate pattern came into being only after Origen (3rd century); see Kutscher, *Isaiah*, pp. 109-11, 502-4. The structure without an epenthetic vowel between R2 and R3 is still largely preserved in Phoen.; Friedrich—Röllig, §§ 193, 194.

Segholate noun from strong roots: מֶ֫לֶךְ *king*, סֵ֫פֶר *book*, קֹ֫דֶשׁ(1) *holiness*. **General discussion.** Three questions arise in relation to these three types; 1) Why is ֶ uniformly found as auxiliary vowel? 2) Why is a prestress qameṣ uniformly found in the plural absolute? 3) Why is a *begadkefat* third radical fricative in the plural cst.? Various explanations have been put forward. Here is the one which to us seems to be the most satisfactory(2). b

Singular. (The explanation must begin with the type **sifr*). The primitive form **sifr* first became **sẹfr*, then took the auxiliary vowel ę, which is close to ẹ: סֵ֫פֶר(3). This auxiliary seghol spread to the type

**malk* and to the type **qudš*.

Under the influence of the auxiliary vowel ẹ of the type סֵפֶר, the primitive form **mạlk* became *mạlᵃ̈k*, with the auxiliary vowel ᵃ̈, which is very open (= ẹ). Then the main vowel ạ became ä under the influence of the auxiliary vowel ä(4), hence *mälᵃ̈ḇ* = מֶ֫לֶךְ.

The primitive form **qudš* became **qọdš*, and took the auxiliary vowel ẹ on the analogy of סֵ֫פֶר and מֶ֫לֶךְ, hence קֹ֫דֶשׁ(5).

Plural. There are in Hebrew two types of plural. The first, which is older and has become very rare, is formed on the primitive form of the singular: **raḥm*, pl. רַחֲמִים *the bowels*; **šiqm* (שִׁקְמָה), pl. שִׁקְמִים *sycamore trees*; comp. חָכְמוֹת *Wisdom*, a kind of plural of majesty formed on the singular חָכְמָה (§ 136 *d*); probably also פִּשְׁתָּה*, pl. פִּשְׁתִּים *flax*. The second type is a new plural, no longer built on the old, but on the new singular, i.e. on the segholised form. Thus the auxiliary vowel ֶ, regarded as ä, first in *mäläk*, then in the two other types, has become *å* in open syllables: *mlåḇīm*. The prestress qameṣ, which is found in the three plurals מְלָכִים, סְפָרִים, and קֳדָשִׁים, comes from the auxiliary seghol of the three singulars(6).

However, a more plausible explanation of the origin of the qameṣ appears to be that it has resulted from later lengthening of the original short /a/ as is attested in Ugr., e.g. /ḫabalīma/, pl. oblique of /ḫablu/ "rope"(7). In other words, one postulates an alternative plural base, *qVtal* comparable with the "broken" plural of Arabic and Ethiopic, to which the regular pl. ending was further added: thus **malak* > **malakīm* > *malākīm* > מְלָכִים(8).

The construct state, e.g. מַלְכֵי, comes from the full form of the absolute state **målåḇīm*. The shewa is a relic of the prestress qameṣ. Alternatively, if we are to adopt the alternative explanation of the qameṣ in the plural as outlined above, /malḇẹ/ can be easily derived from /malaḇẹ/, in which case the rule governing the spirantisation of Begadkefat must have ceased operating prior to the elision of the short /a/ between the last two radicals.

The light form of the construct state is used with the heavy suffixes, e.g. מַלְכֵיכֶם; conversely the heavy stem מְלָכ of the absolute state מְלָכִים is used with the light suffixes, e.g. מְלָכַי, מְלָכֶ֫יךָ(9).

The **dual** is formed on the primitive form of the singular, like the old plural: **ragl*, רֶ֫גֶל *foot*, רַגְלַ֫יִם; **birk*, בֶּ֫רֶךְ *knee*, בִּרְכַּ֫יִם, בִּרְכֵּי (without spirantisation, § 92 *g*). See § 91 *b* for some irregular dual forms with prestress qameṣ.

(1) The usual paradigm קֹ֫דֶשׁ has been retained, in spite of a small anomaly displayed by this noun in the absolute plural: קֳדָשִׁים or 'קֳ instead of 'קְ (contr. בֹּ֫קֶר *morning*, בְּקָרִים).

(2) Cf. P. Joüon in *MUSJ* 5 (1911) 375ff.

(3) Compare, in the apocopated Qal future of ל״ה verbs, the forms יִגֶל, יִגְּל, יִ֫גֶל; the most usual form יִ֫גֶל is not found in nouns, any more than יִגֶל (cf. § 79 *i*).

(4) Cf. Brock., *GvG*, I, p. 184.

(5) There was probably an intermediate stage *qọdọš*, judging from certain transcriptions of the LXX, e.g., Γοσόν = גֹּ֫שֶׁן, Τοφόλ = תֹּ֫פֶל, Βοόζ = בֹּ֫עַז, Βοόν = בֹּ֫הַן, and QH spellings such as פועל = פֹּ֫עַל or שוחד = שֹׁ֫חַד ; cf. P. de Lagarde, *Übersicht über die im Aramäischen und Hebräischen übliche Bildung der Nomina* (Göttingen, 1889), pp. 52-7, and Kutscher, *Isaiah*, pp. 502-4.

Alternatively the sg. מֶ֫לֶךְ etc. may also be explained as backformation of */malak/ derived from the postulated broken plural (n. below) and as a neutral realisation of pataḥ as seghol. Likewise */sẹfar/ > /sẹfẹr/, and */qọdaš/ > /qọdẹš/. Cf. also I. Yeivin, *Leš* 44 (1980) 184, W.R. Garr, "The *seghol* and segholation in Heb.," *JNES* 48 (1989) 109-16, and R.L. Goerwitz, "Tiberian Heb. segol—a reappraisal," *ZAH* 3 (1990) 3-10.

(6) See § 97 A *b*, n.

(7) Huehnergard, *Ugr. Vocabulary*, pp. 304-307.

(8) Cf. Arb. /'arḍun/ *earth*, but pl. /'araḍūna/; Eth. /ḥelqat/ *ring*, but pl. /ḥelaqāt/. However, the general preponderance of the "broken" plural in these languages may suggest that, at least in these, the suffixal plural morpheme was not a secondary feature: cf. Blau, *Heb. Phonology and Morphology*, p. 208.

The pl. forms such as פְּסִילִים, sg. פֶּ֫סֶל *idol* (§ 99 *f*), שְׁחִיתוֹת, sg. שַׁ֫חַת *pit* (§ 99 *f*), and בְּהֹנוֹת sg., בֹּ֫הֶן *great toe* or *thumb* (cf. Arb. sg. *'ibhām*; § 96 A *j*) can only be accounted for by either postulating a variant singular form or a pseudo-broken plural. Cf. N.H. Tur-Sinai, *The Language and the Book*, the *Language* vol. [Heb] (Jerusalem, 1954), pp. 247f.

(9) There is here a sort of a law of balance. The double stem is also found in the plurals of the masc. types with two primitive short vowels דָּבָר (§ B *b*) and זָקֵן (§ B *d*). Similarly we have כְּ with the heavy suffixes כָּכֶם, כָּהֶם, and כְּמוֹ with the light suffixes כָּמוֹנִי, כָּמ֫וֹךָ (§ 103 *g*); אֵת with heavy suffixes אֶתְכֶם, אֶתְהֶם; and אוֹת with light suff. אֹתִי, אֹתְךָ (§ 103 *k*). Note that a form like *מְלָכֵיכֶם would be quite abnormal: the qameṣ would then find itself in an ante-prestress syllable as in an equally anomalous שְׁבוּעוֹת.

Inflection of 1. מֶ֫לֶךְ *king*. The *a* of the primitive form *malk* reappears in the sing. with suffixes: מַלְכִּי, מַלְכְּכֶם. The *a* reappears also in pause as ָ, but not in every noun. Thus we find כֶּ֫רֶם *vineyard*, אֶ֫רֶץ (cf. הָאָ֫רֶץ, § 35 *f*), but מֶ֫לֶךְ. ָ is usually found in nouns which were origi- c nally *qitl* but passed to the type מֶ֫לֶךְ, e.g. probably צֶ֫דֶק *righteousness*, קֶ֫דֶם *the East*, דֶּ֫שֶׁא *grass*, פֶּ֫לֶא *wonder*, כֶּ֫לֶא *prison*.

But primitive *a* is often weakened to *i* in inflected forms, and thus the form *qatl* merges with the form *qitl*(1): בֶּ֫טֶן *belly*, בִּטְנִי; בֶּ֫גֶד *garment* בִּגְדִי (with fricative ד !), בִּגְדֵי; קֶ֫בֶר *grave*, cst. קִבְרֵי (and קִבְרוֹת). The vowel ẹ is occasionally found: נֶ֫גֶד (prep.) *in front of*, נֶגְדִּי(2); נֶ֫כֶד *posterity*, נֶכְדִּי(3); חֶ֫לֶד *life*, חֶלְדִּי.

As a rule the construct does not differ from the absolute state: מֶ֫לֶךְ. Sometimes, however, the cst. state has the form קְטַל, e.g. חֶ֫דֶר *room*, cst. חֲדַר (חֶ֫דֶר Ct 3.4†); שֶׁ֫גֶר *litter, young (of beasts)*, cst. שְׁגַר (שֶׁ֫גֶר Ex 13.12†). Comp. the form קְטַל, § 88 C *g*.

(1) Cf. E.J. Revell, "The vowelling of '*i*-type' segholates in Tiberian Hebrew," *JNES* 44 (1985) 319-28.

(2-3) Cf. Brock., *GvG*, I, p. 198: under the influence of the following palatal.

d **Plural.** The paradigm, like all the other paradigms of masculine nouns, only gives the plural with the masculine ending ־ִים; but the plural in וֹת can of course be found. Thus we have the plural in וֹת in the nouns of feminine gender אֶ֫רֶץ, אֲרָצוֹת; נֶ֫פֶשׁ *soul*, נְפָשׁוֹת and in the masculine noun קֶ֫בֶר *grave*, קְבָרוֹת (alongside קְבָרִים). For the type קְטָלִים, cf. § *b*.

In the cst. state of the pattern מַלְכֵי, the spirantisation sometimes disappears. In several cases this is due to the influence of a sibilant(1): כַּסְפֵּיהֶם Gn 42.25,35; נִסְכֵּיהֶם Is 41.29 etc.; רִשְׁפֵּי Ct 8.6 (but רִשְׁפֵי Ps 76.4); אַסְפֵּי Mi 7.1; טַרְפֵּי Ez 17.9; צִמְדֵּי Is 5.10. For the weakening of *a* to *i*, cf. § *c*. **Dual**: cf. § *b* (end).

(1) See Th. Nöldeke in *ZA* 18 (1904-05) 72.

e **Inflection of 2.** סֵ֫פֶר *book*. It is parallel to that of מֶ֫לֶךְ. The *i* of the primitive form *sifr* reappears in the singular with suffixes: סִפְרִי, and in the cst. plural סִפְרֵי. But after a 1st guttural, *i* becomes ẹ (§ 21 *e*): חֵ֫לֶק *part*, חֶלְקִי, חֶלְקֵיהֶם (comp. fem. doublet חֶלְקָה); עֵ֫זֶר *help*, עֶזְרִי (comp. fem. doublet עֶזְרָה); עֵ֫גֶל *calf*, עֶגְלִי, עֶגְלֵךְ (comp. f. עֶגְלָה), but חִקְרֵי, עִמְקֵי. In pause we normally find סֵ֫פֶר; sometimes we find, e.g., שָׁ֫בֶט *stick*, סָ֫תֶר *hiding place*, נָ֫צַח *eternity*, יָ֫שַׁע *help*, חָ֫רֶם *anathema*, under the influence of the type *qatl*, which has often contaminated *qitl* (§ *f*). Generally speaking, the construct state does not differ from the absolute state. The cst. הֲבֵל *breath* (as well as הֶבְלֵי) presupposes an abs. הֵ֫בֶל* alongside (or supplanted by) הֶ֫בֶל(1).

Plural. The old plural type (§ *b*) is found in שִׁקְמִים *sycamore-trees*, פִּשְׁתִּים *flax*, and the tens עֶשְׂרִים, שִׁבְעִים, תִּשְׁעִים. The sing. חֵטְא *sin* (without auxiliary vowel) has חֲטָאֵי in the cst. pl., with the qameṣ of חֲטָאִים (comp. גְּדִי, גְּדָיִים, גְּדָיֵי, § *q*; מִקְרָאֵי, § C *b*).

(1) The nature of the vowel following the first radical appears to be, to a large extent, a function of the latter; for details, see E.J. Revell, art. cit. [§ *c*, n. 2] 320-22.

Contamination of *qatl* and *qitl* forms. A considerable number of primitive *qitl* forms have become *qatl* in Hebrew as far as the first vowel is concerned; see § 88 C *a**. The transition from the one type to the other was facilitated by the similarity of forms in inflection: thus the forms קִטְלִי, קְטָלִים(1), קִטְלֵי(2) may come either from *qatl* or from *qitl*. The segholate form קֵ֫טֶל tends to become קֶ֫טֶל, a more resonant form (cf. infinitive שֶׁ֫בֶת, § 75 *a*). In one and the same noun we may find some forms which presuppose a *qatl* and others which presuppose a *qitl*; consequently it is sometimes difficult or even impossible to tell whether a noun was originally a *qatl* or a *qitl*, or if both forms existed simultaneously. Example: the form קֵ֫דְמָה *eastward* (§ 93*d*) presupposes a form *qidm*, whilst קֶ֫דֶם, קַדְמֵי and קַדְמוֹן presuppose a form *qadm*; but probably only the *qidm* form is primitive. f

(1) The form קְטָלִים of the three segholate types is also the pl. of the type דָּבָר, § B *b*.

(2) The form קִטְלֵי is one of the most ambiguous; besides being the constant plural of קֶ֫טֶל, קְטָל, and the ordinary plural of קָטֵל, קָטָל, it is sometimes found as the plural of קֶ֫טֶל, and even of קֹ֫טֶל.

Inflection of 3. קֹ֫דֶשׁ *holiness*. It is parallel to the inflection of מֶ֫לֶךְ and of סֵ֫פֶר (cf. § *b*). However, the primitive vowel *u* reappears in inflection only rarely: e.g. גֻּדְלוֹ Ps 150.2† (everywhere else גָּדְלוֹ etc.). *ǫ* is found almost everywhere; e.g. קָדְשִׁי(1). The vowel *i* is found in בֹּ֫סֶר *verjuice*, בִּסְרוֹ; אֹ֫מֶר *word*, אִמְרוֹ, אִמְרֵי etc.; שֹׁ֫קֶת *canal*, cst. pl. שִׁקֲתוֹת (§ 89 *p*) (its presence there is difficult to explain). g

Plural. The ordinary plural has the same form קְטָלִים as the plural of the מֶ֫לֶךְ and סֵ֫פֶר types, e.g. בְּקָרִים *mornings*. With a 1st-guttural we have חֳדָשִׁים *months*, עֳפָרִים *gazelles*. This same very short *ǫ* is found in

הַגֳּרָנוֹת *the threshing floors* (1Sm 23.1; Jl 2.24), קֳדָשִׁים *holy things*. It is lengthened to ǫ in the doublet קָדָשִׁים *qǫ-ḏåšîm* and in שָׁרָשִׁים *roots* (cf. § 6 *l*). In all these words ǫ instead of shewa is due to the influence of the preceding consonant(2). The old plural type (§ *b*) is found in בָּטְנִים *pistachio nuts* (from בֹּטֶן* or בָּטְנָה*). **Dual:** e.g. מָתְנַ֫יִם *loins, hips* (from **mutn* > מֹתֶן*); cf. § *b* (end).

(1) Likewise in the feminine forms, e.g. חָכְמָה, § 88 C *j*; 97 A *a*.

(2) For ג and ק, compare the preservation of *ŭ* with the labialised consonants *g, q, k, ḫ* in Ethiopic.

h **Segholate nouns with gutturals.** A guttural R2 or R3 usually attracts ַ instead of ֶ. The characteristics of the gutturals as described in the section of this book on phonetics find their application here. With a guttural R3 we find the types זֶ֫רַע *seed*, נֵ֫צַח *eternity*, which present no difficulty, and the type רֹ֫מַח *lance*, which is identical with the type פֹּ֫עַל *work* with a guttural R2. With a guttural R2 we have the type פֹּ֫עַל for *qutl* and נַ֫עַר *boy* for *qatl*. There is no *qitl* form with a guttural R2, or if there is, it probably also belongs to the נַ֫עַר type, and therefore is indistinguishable from it (cf. שֵׂעָר § B *c*).

i **Inflection of 4.** נַ֫עַר *boy*. After the guttural we often find an auxiliary vowel, namely ֲ, or the full vowel ַ when the word is lengthened, e.g. נַעַרְךָ, נַעֲרִי (§ 22 *b-c*). The vocalisation ֶ ֶ has become usual in two words ending in חם, a phenomenon which is difficult to explain(1): לֶ֫חֶם *bread*, רֶ֫חֶם *womb, breast* (but רַ֫חַם in the sense of *woman* or *young woman* in the archaic and poetic text of Jdg 5,30†); in pause לָ֫חֶם, רָ֫חֶם. For the plural of the old type רַחֲמִים, cf. § *b*.

(1) Perh. due to influence of the nasal; likewise בֹּ֫הֶן, § *j*.

j **Inflection of 5.** פֹּ֫עַל *work*. Here, too, an auxiliary vowel is often found after the guttural, namely ֳ, or, when the word is lengthened, the full vowel ָ: פָּעֳלִי, פָּעָלְךָ (§ 22 *b-c*). The same auxiliary vowel ָ is found, without a guttural, in קָטָבְךָ (comp. קָרָבְכֶם, § 65 *c*). Instead of the normal form פָּעֳלוֹ the following forms may be found: פָּעֳלוֹ in Is 1.31; Jer 22.13 (with ọ in an open syllable and ֳ normal under ע); תֹּאֲרוֹ in Is 52.14 (but תָּאֳרוֹ 1Sm 28.14); compare with the similar phenomenon in verbs, § 68 *f*).

In אֹ֫הֶל *tent*, the initial א always has a full vowel, either ǫ or ọ: אָהֳלִי, אָהָלְךָ etc.; אֹהָלִים, אָהֳלֵי etc.; for הָאֹ֫הֱלָה, cf. § 93 *c*. ọ is also found in אֹרְחוֹתֶ֫יךָ *your ways*, אֹרְחוֹתָם, אֹרְחֹתָיו (but אָרְחֹתַי, אָרְחֹתֵיהֶם). The word בֹּ֫הֶן *thumb* has ֶ despite the guttural(1); the cst. pl. בְּהֹנוֹת with ọ presupposes sing. בְּהוֹן* (read thus everywhere in the Samaritan Pentateuch).

(1) See § *i*, n., and above at § *b*, n. 8.

Inflection of monosyllabic nouns with the vowel at the end: קְטַל, קְטֵל, קְטֹל (cf. § 88 C *g*, *i*, *k*). In קְטַל nouns there usually is spontaneous doubling before the afformatives, e.g. מְעַט *little*, מְעַטִּים(1). With suffixes: e.g. דְּבַשׁ *honey*, דִּבְשִׁי; שְׁכֶם(2) *back*, שִׁכְמוֹ. The instances of קְטֵל which we have are ע"א, e.g. בְּאֵר *well*, pl. בְּאֵרוֹת, cst. בְּאֵרוֹת; זְאֵב *wolf*, pl. זְאֵבִים, זְאֵבֵי. קְטֹל words necessarily have virtual doubling (§ 18 *e*): לְאֹם *people*, לְאֻמִּים. With a suffix we find בְּאֹשׁ *stench*, בָּאְשׁוֹ. For the infinitive form קְטֹל with suffixes, cf. § 65 *b*. These CCVC forms most likely originated in the construct forms, with relatively weak stress, as in גְּבֹהַּ 1Sm 16.7; בִּגְדֹל Ex 15.16; קְדֹשׁ Ps 46.5. Cf. also שְׁבַע and תְּשַׁע used with tens and hundreds. This supposition is reinforced by Qumran Hebrew, in which forms of *qotol* type are almost entirely confined to the cst.(3). *k*

(1) Comp. the plural גְּמַלִּים of גָּמָל, § B *b*.

(2) Only form with ֶ. The primitive form probably was *šakm* (BL, p. 456, quote *ša-ak-mi* from the Tell el Amarna letters). But שְׁכֶם could also be a *qitl* or even the cst. state of some *qatil* form (fairly common for names of parts of the body, § 88 D *b*), which could have become an absolute state.

(3) See Qimron, *Hebrew of DSS*, pp. 36-8.

Inflection of 6. מָ֫וֶת *death*. *Qatl* forms from ע"ו roots (§ 88 C *f*) have consonantal ו. Primitive form *mawt*: the *a* was labialised to *å* (ọ) before ו; the auxiliary vowel ֶ was introduced on the analogy of the segholates from strong roots. Only the word רֶ֫וַח *space* is entirely similar to a segholate from a strong root, e.g. זֶ֫רַע. For more examples, see § 88 C *f*. In the cst. state the form is contracted: *mawt* > *mōṯ* מוֹת; this form is kept throughout the inflection. *l*

In some words the contraction takes place even in the absolute state: שׁוֹט *whip*, יוֹם *day*, צוֹם *fast*, etc.; or rather the cst. state is used instead of the absolute state.

Instead of a normal plural form like שׁוֹטִים, the form שְׁוָרִים (from שׁוֹר *ox*) is found in Ho 12.12†. Comp. in the *qūl* form: שׁוּק *street*, שְׁוָקִים;

דּוּד, דְּוָדִים in the sense of *pots* 2Ch 35.13† (but דּוּדִים in the sense of *baskets* 2Kg 10.7†).

m **Inflection of 7.** זַ֫יִת *olive*. The *qatl* forms from ע״י roots have consonantal י. The primitive form *zayt* becomes זַ֫יִת with auxiliary *i* due to the preceding *y*. In the cst. state the form is contracted: *zayt* > *zēṯ* זֵית; this form is kept throughout the inflection.

In some rare words the contraction takes place even in the absolute state: חֵיק *breast*, חֵיל *rampart* (לֵיל *night* Is 21.11†); or rather the construct state is used instead of the absolute state.

Instead of a normal plural form like זֵיתִים, the plural of חַ֫יִל *army* is חֲיָלִים; תַּ֫יִשׁ *he-goat*, תְּיָשִׁים; עַ֫יִר *young ass*, עֲיָרִים; עַ֫יִן *spring (of water)*, עֲיָנוֹת.

The word גַּ֫יְא *valley* presents several anomalies. In the singular the א, which is not pronounced, is sometimes omitted in writing: גַּי, cst. גֵּי. In the plural, Q. is גֵּאָיוֹת (irregular!) and K. גֵּיאָוֹת or גֵּיאוֹת.

n **Inflection of 8.** עַם *people*. *Qatl* forms from ע״ע roots (cf. § 88 B *g*). Some words present peculiarities. With a disjunctive accent and the article, עָם is found instead of עַם. יָם *sea* is used even in the construct state (even with maqqef) except in יַם־סוּף *sea of reeds, Red Sea* (§ 13 *c*). Before a guttural, genuine doubling of which is impossible, there is only virtual doubling, e.g. פַּחִים *traps*, or total absence of doubling, hence ָ in an open syllable, e.g. שָׂרִים *princes* (for *śarrim*). This ָ is a stable vowel: cst. שָׂרֵי, מָרֵי, רָעֵי. Rarely does *a* weaken to *i* in inflection: פַּת *bit*, פִּתִּי (comp. בַּת *daughter*, בִּתִּי, § 98 *d*); מַס — מִסִּים; צַר — צִדּוֹ; and cf. Ps 30.12 σεκκι in Origen's Hexapla for MT שַׂקִּי; סַף *threshold*, סִפִּים; סַף *cup* סִפּוֹת (and סַפּוֹת 2Sm 17.28). Forms in the dissociated state (cf. § 82 *a*) are very rare: עֲמָמִים alongside the usual עַמִּים; הֲרָרֵי, cst. pl. הַרְרֵי. The word אַף *nose*, from the root אנף, is inflected like a noun of the type עַם: אַפִּי, dual אַפַּ֫יִם *face*.

o **Inflection of 9.** עֵז *goat* (אֵם *mother*). [עֵז has been chosen for the paradigm because of its plural in ים־ִ, even though its root is ענז and not עזז]. *Qitl* forms from ע״ע roots (§ 88 B *h*). The primitive *i* is retained in acute syllables: עִזִּי, אִמִּי; dual שִׁנַּ֫יִם *teeth*. Forms in the dissociated state: צֵל *shadow*, צְלָלִים; חֵץ *arrow*, חֲצָצֶ֫יךָ Ps 77.18 (alongside the usual חִצִּים). As with עֵז, the 2nd radical נ of חֵךְ *palate* and זֵק*, זִקִּים *chains* has been assimilated.

p **Inflection of 10.** חֹק *statute*. *Qutl* forms from ע״ע roots (cf. § 88

B *i*). The primitive *u* is generally retained in acute syllables: חֻקִּי, עֻזִּי; ָ is found only rarely: עָזִּי. But ָ is found if the doubling is omitted: חָקְכֶם, חָקְךָ. In the cst. state the forms חֹק and כֹּל are found, but with maqqef they become ־חָק and ־כָּל (cf. § 13 *b*). In the dissociated state, the form חִקְקֵי Jdg 5.15 (poetic and archaic), Is 10.1† probably does not come from חֹק (in spite of cases like אֹמֶר, אִמְרֵי § *g*), but from חֵק*.

Inflection of 11. גְּדִי *kid*. *Qatl* forms from ל"ה roots (cf. § 88 C *e*). q
The primitive form *qaty* usually becomes קְטִי, less often קֶטֶה; thus the doublet בְּכִי and בֶּכֶה *weeping* Ezr 10.1† developed from **baky*. This double form can be explained thus: the primitive form **baky* became בֶּכֶה in the absolute state on the analogy of מֶלֶךְ and כֶּלֶא; in the cst. the vowel *a* was dropped and the *y* became vocalic: בְּכִי; and this form was used in the absolute state as well. In pause ֶ is used in the form בֶּכִי, probably by analogy with בֶּכֶה. Formed like בֶּכֶה are הֶגֶה *whisper* and קֶצֶה *end*; like בְּכִי: פְּרִי, שְׁבִי *captivity*, צְבִי I *ornament*, II *gazelle*, גְּדִי *kid*, לְחִי *cheek*. In the course of inflection the *a* of *pary* is usually weakened to *i*: פִּרְיִי; but *ẹ* is sometimes found, e.g. פֶּרְיְךָ (vowel sequence *ẹ—ọ*, § 29 *f*), פֶּרְיְכֶם. Some forms are found with the stem פְּרִי, e.g., פְּרִיהֶם, פְּרִיהֶן alongside פִּרְיָם, פִּרְיָן. By analogy with מְלָכִים and כְּלָאִים the following forms are found in the plural: גְּדָיִים (cst. גְּדָיֵי with ָ retained; cp. חֲטָאֵי, § *e*), אֲרָיִים, אֲרָיוֹת *lions* once (from אֲרִי; אַרְיֵה is the more usual doublet), חֲלָאִים *rings* (from חֲלִי; א for י). Instead of the expected forms צְבָאִים* and פְּתָאִים* the massorah requires צְבָאִים and פְּתָאִים (from צְבִי *gazelle* and פֶּתִי *simple-minded* [only instance of a pausal form used as a contextual form]). Likewise in the dual לְחָיַיִם, cst. לְחָיֵי. (Cp. cst. plurals with ֲ as penultimate vowel, § B *d*).

Inflection of חֲצִי *half*. *Qitl* form from ל"ה root (cf. § 88 C *h*). The r
primitive form *ḥiṣy* becomes חֲצִי in cst. and abs., in pause חֵצִי; with suf. חֶצְיוֹ (ֶ after the guttural; cf. § *e*).

Inflection of חֳלִי *sickness*. *Qutl* forms from ל"ה root (cf. § 88 C s
j). The primitive form *ḥuly* becomes חֳלִי in cst. and abs., in pause חֹלִי; with suf. חָלְיוֹ. As a remnant of the characteristic vowel of the form, ֳ is usually found instead of shewa (or, after a guttural, instead of ḥaṭef pataḥ). However ְ is found occasionally: בִּדְמִי (cst., alongside דֳּמִי) Is 38.10; יְפִי (cst.) Ez 28.7; וּצְרִי Gn 37.25.

§ 96 B. INFLECTION OF NOUNS WITH TWO PRIMITIVE SHORT VOWELS

a Included in this category are the forms *qatal*, *qital*, *qatil*, and *qatul*. They will be dealt with in that order, except for the *qatal* form of ל"ה nouns, which will be treated last (§ *f*).

b **Inflection of** 12. דָּבָר *word*. *Qatal* form (cf. § 88 D *a*). The primitive form *dabar* usually becomes דָּבָר in the abs. state and דְּבַר in the cst. state. The heavy stem דְּבָר is used with the light suffixes: דְּבָרִי, דְּבָרְךָ etc., the light stem דְּבַר with the heavy suffixes: דְּבַרְכֶם. Plural: the primitive form *dabarīm* usually becomes דְּבָרִים in the absolute state, *davrẹ̄*(1) in the cst. state, hence, in general, with weakening of *a* to *i* (§ 29 *g*): דִּבְרֵי. The shewa in דִּבְרֵי, having resulted from the deletion of a primitive short vowel, occasions the spirantisation of the following begadkefat; cf. כִּזְבֵיהֶם *their lies* (but*עַנְפֵיהֶם *their branches*). The heavy stem דְּבָר of the absolute state דְּבָרִים is used with the light suffixes: דְּבָרַי, the light stem דִּבְר of the cst. state דִּבְרֵי with the heavy suffixes: דִּבְרֵיכֶם. The primitive form of the dual **kanafa'yim* usually becomes abs. כְּנָפַ֫יִם *wings*, cst. כַּנְפֵי (with fricative /f/; comp. שִׂפְתֵי *lips*, § 97 E *b* end); with suf.: כְּנָפַי, כַּנְפֵיכֶם.

Spontaneous doubling occurs in a few plural forms (§ 18 *f*): גְּמַלִּים *camels*, קְטַנִּים *small ones*(2). In the pl. cst. the *a* of the primitive form *davrẹ* is preserved in a few words: זַנְבוֹת *tails*, כַּנְפוֹת *wings* and dual כַּנְפֵי (*supra*), mainly after a guttural: חַכְמֵי *wise men*, עַנְוֵי *humble men*; of course before a guttural: נַהֲרֵי *rivers*.

Irregular nouns: the plural of פָּרָשׁ *horse* is פָּרָשִׁים instead of *פְּרָשִׁים(3). This form has the same vocalisation as פָּרָשִׁים from פָּרָשׁ *horseman* (*parraš* form). The two words being similar in the singular, the similarity (and therefore the ambiguity) was mechanically extended to the plural. The cst. state of לָבָן *white* is found as לְבֶן־ Gn 49.12† in לְבֶן־שִׁנַּ֫יִם *white of teeth*; *ẹ* is used here instead of *ạ* probably for the sake of euphony. The cst. of חָלָב *milk* is חֲלֵב, a form which is difficult to explain. As one would expect, the cst. of עָשָׁן *smoke* is עֲשַׁן Josh 8.20, 21†; yet the form עֶ֫שֶׁן Ex 19.18† is found in עֶ֫שֶׁן הַכִּבְשָׁן *the smoke of a furnace*; the vowel *a* of עֲשַׁן has been thrown backwards to the beginning of the word, hence *'ašn*, segholised to עֶ֫שֶׁן. This shifting of *a*, rather common in the *qatil* form (§ *d*), is perhaps found in the *qatal* form only in עֶשֶׂן and probably also in שֶׂכֶר *wages* Pr 11.18. For אֶחָד *one*, cf. § 20 *c* and 100 *b*; for אַחֵר, § 20 *c*.

(1) It so happens that we have the transcription δαβρη in the Hexapla Ps 34.20. Besides, the stage *davrẹ* is confirmed by examples such as זַנְבוֹת (see below).

(2) The plurals of the form קְטַל are identical (§ A *k*), e.g. מַעֲשִׂים; hence our ignorance of the singular of some plurals of this form, the singular of which is not found in the Bible: עֲצַבִּים *idols*, שְׁלַבִּים *rungs* (?), חֲרַכִּים *trellis*.

(3) Other examples of ante-prestress ָ in § 96 D *b*, 88 M *j*; 88 L *e*; forms of מָעוֹז, *h* מָגֵן; cf. § 30 *e*. The Secunda displays the pattern χαθαβιμ and χαθαβωθ: e.g. Ps 18.48 נְקָמוֹת νακαμωθ; 46.8,12 צְבָאוֹת σαβαωθ, and cf. 35.20 דִּבְרֵי δαβρη; 18.43 פְּנֵי φανη. See Brønno, *Studien*, p. 151.

Inflection of the קְטָל form, primitively *qital* (cf. § 88 D *d*). The inflection is similar to that of קָטָל; the ֵ is dropped under the same conditions as the ָ. Most of these words, which incidentally are not very numerous, present some anomalies. From שֵׂעָר *hair* some forms are found which presuppose the existence of a doublet שַׂעַר*: cst. וְשַׂעַר Is 7.20; שַׂעְרֵךְ Ct 4.1; 6.5; fem. הַשַּׂעֲרָה. The primitive Hebrew form was probably *śi'r*, which on the one hand developed into *śa'r* > שַׂעַר and on the other hand, retaining the primitive vowel, into *śi'ᵉar* with *a* as auxiliary vowel, hence *śẹ'ᵉar*; then the auxiliary *a* must have become the main vowel and carried the stress: *śẹ'a'r* > שֵׂעָר (cf. § A *h*); the usual cst. state is שְׂעַר. צֵלָע *side* only has צֶלַע or צֵלַע in the cst. state, with suf. צַלְעוֹ, pl. cst. צַלְעוֹת; here too the primitive form is probably *ṣil'* (in Arabic *ḍil'* is found alongside the more common *ḍila'*). נֵכָר *stranger* (in an abstract sense) becomes נֵכַר Dt 31.16† in the cst. state. The primitive form may have been *nikr*; the *qital* form does not appear to be attested by any other abstract noun. c

Inflection of 13. זָקֵן *old, old man* (כָּתֵף *shoulder*). *Qatil* form (cf. § 88 D *b*). The primitive form *zaqin* usually becomes זָקֵן. In the cst. state the ֵ changes to ַ: זְקַן (Philippi's law, § 29 *aa*). This is the form of the cst. state in most words. But in some words the vowel of this קָטֵל form passes to the 1st consonant, hence *qatl*, which, in turn, becomes קֶטֶל or קֵטֶל by segholisation. Thus cst. כֶּתֶף *shoulder*, יֶרֶךְ *thigh*, גֶּדֶר *wall*, עֶרֶל *uncircumcised* alongside עֲרַל, כֶּבֶד *heavy* 1 x alongside כְּבַד 1 x; גֶּזֶל *robbery*. (In the case of these doublets, harmony probably dictates which form is to be used)(1). Irregular forms: ֵ is retained in חֲמֵשׁ *five* (cf. fem. חֲמִשָּׁה, § 100 *d*), in בַּעֲקֵב עֵשָׂו Gn 25.26†, and יְרֵא; on d the other hand it is reduced to ֶ in כַּאֲבֶל־אֵם Ps 35.14† (comp. the cst. forms לְבֶן־ and חֲלֵב, § *b*). With suffixes, forms normally found are, e.g. כְּתֵפִי, זְקֵנִי, with prestress ֶ.

Plural: abs. זְקֵנִים with prestress ֵ; cst. זִקְנֵי (like דִּבְרֵי), but with guttural R1: חַבְרֵי *companions*, חַנְפֵי *profane*, חַצְרֵי *courts*, עַרְלֵי *uncircumcised*. The heavy stem זְקֵנ of the abs. form זְקֵנִים is used with the light suffixes: זְקֵנַי, the light stem זִקְנ of the cst. form זִקְנֵי with the heavy suffixes: זִקְנֵיכֶם.

ֵ is found as the penultimate vowel in the pl. cst. of the following verbal adjectives: שְׁכֵחֵי 1 x, שְׂמֵחֵי 1 x alongside שִׂמְחֵי 1 x, אֲבֵלֵי 1 x, יְשֵׁנֵי 1 x, חֲפֵצֵי 1 x (comp. the added ֵ in, e.g. גְּדָיֵי, § A *q*). But יָרֵא *fearing* has a regular form: יִרְאֵי and יִרְאַת. The ֵ of the pl. of יָתֵד *peg* with suff., יְתֵדֹתָיו, etc. is irregular (cst. יִתְדֹת); cf. § 97 B *e*, n.

For אַחֵר, cf. 20 *c*.

(1) With this double form of cst. state compare the double form of cst. state of the aphaeretic forms of פ"ו nouns (§ 75 *m*), e.g. **lidat* > לֵדָה, abs. and cst. לֶדֶת, *šinat* > שֵׁנָה, cst. שְׁנַת.

e **Inflection of the קָטֹל form,** primitively *qatul* (cf. § 88 D *c*). The cst. form of קָטֹל is קְטֹל (like that of קָטֵל and of קָטָל): גְּבַהּ *high*(1) (absolute גָּבֹהַּ). As in the cst. state of זָקֵן (§ *d*), the vowel passes to the 1st consonant, giving *qatl*, which becomes קֶטֶל by segholisation: אֶרֶךְ *long*(2) (abs. אָרֹךְ), e.g. in אֶרֶךְ אַפַּיִם *longanimis (slow to anger)*. With the addition of an inflectional ending, spontaneous doubling takes place(3): עֲגֻלִּים *round*, אֲדֻמִּים *red*; עֲמֻקָּה *deep*, except before a guttural: גְּבֹהִים; cf. § 18 *e*; and elsewhere also, e.g. מְתוּקָה *sweet*.

(1) The only and, because of the guttural, unconvincing example.

(2) Only example. Note that there is no form אָרֵךְ*, from which אֶרֶךְ could come; cf. N. H. Torczyner, *ZDMG* 64 (1911) 273.

(3) Is גְּדֻלָּה *greatness* possibly a lexically specialised use of a variant of גְּדֹלָה?

f **Inflection of** 14. **שָׂדֶה** *field*. Most nouns from ל"ה roots with the vocalisation ָ ֶה are *qatal* (cf. § 88 D *a*); a few are *qatil* (§ 88 D *b*), e.g. חָזֶה *breast* (probably). Whatever the primitive form may have been, the inflection of the *qatil* forms is similar to that of the *qatal*. In the word שָׂדֶה the primitive form *śaday* is preserved in the rare and poetic form שָׂדַי. The ditphthong *ay* was contracted to ē, which appears in two different forms: as ę in the abs. state שָׂדֶה, as ẹ in the cst. state

שְׂדֵה(1). Before certain suffixes (see Paradigm 20) the ē is retained, either as ֵ or (before ָ, cf. § 29 *f*) as ֶ: שָׂדֶךָ (pausal form, hence the pausal form in nouns from other roots: סוּסֶךָ § 94 *c*), שָׂדֵךְ (hence סוּסֵךְ), שָׂדֵהוּ, שָׂדֶהָ, שָׂדֵנוּ (hence סוּסֵנוּ). Before the other suffixes the form is syncopated: שָׂדִי, שָׂדְךָ, שָׂדָם on the analogy of סוּסִי, סוּסְךָ, סוּסָם; likewise the rare forms of the 3rd pers. שָׂדוֹ, שָׂדָה(2). (Comp. the verbal forms in ֶה with suffixes, § 79 *k*). The form is also syncopated before the plural ending: שָׂדִים*, שָׂדוֹת; plurale tantum פָּנִים *face*. For the apparent plurals, cf. § C *e*.

(1) Compare the differentiation of יִגְלֶה from impv. גְּלֵה, § 79 *e*, *f*, and cf. the observation about the real quality of the vowel, § 79 *e* Obs. 2.

(2) It is obvious that there is a mutual influence of the ל"ה noun on the ordinary noun and of the ordinary noun on the ל"ה noun.

§ 96 C. INFLECTION OF NOUNS WITH A STABLE 1st VOWEL AND A 2nd SHORT PRIMITIVE VOWEL

This category contains nouns with a primitive long (in open syllables) or short (in closed syllables) 1st vowel and a primitive short 2nd vowel, e.g. the forms *qātal* and *maqtal*, *qātil* and *maqtil*(1). The peculiarities of the inflection are usually shown by the 2nd vowel only (one exception, § *c*). The paradigms include one *qātal*, one *qātil* and one *qātal* — *qātil* from a ל"ה root. *a*

(1) In the case of words of more than two syllables one should speak of penultimate vowel and last vowel rather than the 1st and 2nd.

Inflection of 15. עוֹלָם *eternity* (*qātal* form, § 88F *a*) and other nouns with an etymologically long 1st vowel in an open syllable or short 2nd vowel *a* in a closed syllable (e.g. מַקְטָל). The inflection of these nouns is very simple. The 1st vowel is stable; the 2nd vowel *a* is treated like the 2nd vowel of דָּבָר, § B *b*. Abnormal constructs: אוּלָם; מִבְטָח Ps 65.6, Pr 25.19; מַתָּן Pr 18.16. *b*

In the Nifal participles of ל"א verbs (type נִמְצָא), instead of the usual type נִמְצָאִים (with prestress ָ as in עוֹלָמִים, דְּבָרִים) the type נִמְצְאִים is often found; for instance, we almost always find נִמְצְאִים and נִבְּאִים (§ 78 *h*)(1). On the other hand the cst. state of מִקְרָאִים *convocations* has an irregular ָ as penultimate vowel: מִקְרָאֵי(2) (comp. חֲטָאֵי,

§ A e, גְּדָיֵי, § A q).

Several nouns of the form מַקְטָל have spontaneous doubling in the plural (§ 18 f), e.g. מַעֲמַקִּים *deep places*, מַחֲמַדִּים *beautiful things*, מַרְבַדִּים *carpet*, מַטְעַמִּים *stew*, מַעֲדַנִּים *delights*; of the form מִקְטָל, e.g. מִשְׁמַנִּים *succulent dishes*, מִכְמַנִּים *treasures* (with virtual doubling we find, with suf., מִבְטַחִי etc., § 20 c). Nouns of other forms: עַקְרַבִּים *scorpions*, אַשְׁמַנִּים (meaning uncertain). נִכְבַּדֵּי־ (but נִכְבָּדִים) *honoured*. Apparently the fact that the 1st syllable is closed caused the 2nd syllable to become closed as well. The plural of מוֹרַג (var. ־ָ) Is 41.15† is מוֹרִגִּים, with weakening of *a* to *i*(3).

(1) In these two words the pronunciation is rapid and, as if neglected, perh. because they are frequently used. In most cases with shewa one finds a conjunctive accent, important exceptions being 1Sm 19.20, Ez 13.16, 38.17, 1Ch 25.1Q, esp. Ez 20.30 נִטְמְאִים with atnaḥ; cf. W.R. Garr, *VT* 37 (1987) 134f.

(2) The odd תֹּשָׁבֵי *settlers* in 1Kg 17.1† is doubtful (cf. LXX).

(3) Many plurals with a doubled 3rd radical carry a certain strong emotional overtone, according to W. von Soden, *ZAH* 1 (1988) 38-41.

c **Inflection of 16.** אֹיֵב *enemy* (*qātil* form, § 88 F *b*) and other nouns with a 1st vowel etymologically long in an open syllable or short in a closed syllable and an etymologically short 2nd vowel *i* > ֵ (e.g. מִקְטֵל, מַקְטֵל). The 1st vowel is stable; the 2nd vowel ֵ is not treated like the 2nd vowel ֵ of זָקֵן, § B *d*.

Whereas in זָקֵן the ֵ is not retained in the cst. state but is retained in an open syllable (זְקֵנִים, זִקְנֵי), in אֹיֵב (and also in most other forms) the ֵ is generally retained in the cst. state, but not in an open syllable (אֹיְבִים, אֹיְבֵי).

The cst. state usually has ֵ: thus the participles קֹטֵל, מְקַטֵּל, מִתְקַטֵּל, e.g. שֹׁפֵךְ Gn 9.6; חֹלֵם Dt 13.6; subst., כֹּהֵן *priest*, חֹתֵן *wife's father* (the form קֹטַל is rare: אֹבַד Dt 32.28† [poetic], proper noun עֹבַדְיָה; נֹטַע Ps 94.9; also, e.g., תֵּבֵל *orb*, מָגֵן *shield* (both these words with a stable 1st vowel), עִקֵּשׁ *perverted*, מַקֵּל *rod* (1 x מַקַּל). But the form מַקְטֵל (§ 88 L *g*) has the cst. form מַקְטַל(1) (with ַ for ֵ by dissimilation; cf. Brock., *GvG*, I, p. 147): מַרְבֵּץ *resting-place*, cst. מַרְבַּץ; and likewise מַשְׁעֵן, מִשְׁעַן *support*, מַשְׁבֵּר, מִשְׁבַּר *mouth of womb* (?), מַרְזֵחַ, מִרְזַח *cries*. Likewise the form מִקְטֵל (for מַקְטֵל, § 88 L *i*): מִסְפֵּד, מִסְפַּד *act of wailing*, מִזְבֵּחַ, מִזְבַּח *altar*.

The vowel ◌ֵ in an open syllable is retained in a few words: thus in the form קִטֵּל (§ 88 H *b*) only שִׁלֵּשִׁים *of the 3rd generation* and רִבֵּעִים *of the 4th generation*; מַקְהֵלִים, מַקְהֵלוֹת *assemblies*, מַחֲרֵשׁוֹת *ploughshares*, מַצֵּבוֹת *pillars*, מַסֵּכוֹת *molten images*, מוֹעֵצוֹת *counsels*, מוֹסֵרוֹת *bands*, סַנְוֵרִים *sudden blindness, false vision*, פַּרְדֵּסִים *gardens*. In participial forms ◌ֵ is very rarely retained, e.g. שׁוֹמֵמִין Lam 1.4; שׁוֹמֵמִים 1.16 (comp. for the feminine § 97 C *a*)([2]).

In a semi-closed syllable, namely before ךָ, כֶם we find ◌ֶ or ◌ִ, but ◌ַ with a guttural R1: יֹצֶרְךָ, אֹיִבְךָ, אֹסִפְךָ, גֹּאַלְךָ, אֹהַבְךָ. With a guttural R3 both the type בֹּרַאֲךָ and the type שֹׁלֵחֲךָ are found. The word מָגֵן *shield* (root גנן) has a stable ◌ָ: cst. מָגֵן *(see above)*, מָגִנִּי, מָגִנִּים, מָגִנֵּי, § 88 L *h*.

(1) Therefore a מִקְטֵל form is ambiguous: it may come from מִקְטָל, from מַקְטֵל or from מִקְטֵל (see below).

(2) See a discussion by W.R. Garr, *VT* 37 (1987) 147.

Inflection of noun with a stable 1st vowel and a 2nd vowel *u* > ◌ֹ. *d*
The ◌ֹ is treated like that of the type קָטֹל (§ B *e*), e.g. עֵירֹם *naked*, עֵירֻמִּים; קַרְדֹּם *axe*, קַרְדֻּמּוֹ, קַרְדֻּמּוֹת. For מָעוֹז, cf. § 88 L *e*.

Inflection of 17. חֹזֶה *seer* (*qātal* and *qātil* forms of ל"ה roots and *e*
of nouns with an etymologically short 1st vowel in a closed syllable, e.g. מַעֲלֶה Hifil ptc. *cause to ascend* and subst. *ascent*)([1]). The first vowel, which is long, etymologically speaking, in an open syllable and short in a closed syllable, is stable; the ◌ֶה is treated as in שָׂדֶה, § B *f*.

◌ֵה is found in the abs. state instead of ◌ֶה in הָעֹשֵׂה Ez 17.15; conversely ◌ֶה is found in the cst. state instead of ◌ֵה in חֹזֶה 2Sm 24.11 (BHS ◌ֵ); רֵעֶה 2Sm 15.37; 16.16; 1Kg 4.5†. All these anomalies are suspect.

Apparent plurals (cf. § 94 *j*) in nouns in ◌ֶה (of every form). Some suffixes have forms which seem to be plural in pronunciation and, usually, even in the spelling, but which in fact are singular. In these forms the ending *ay* has been contracted to *ẹ*, which has usually been written ◌ֵי, with a י as in the plural. Forms without י; נְוֵהֶם *their pasture* Jer 49.20; Ez 34.14; אֹפֵהֶם *their baker* Ho 7.6. Forms with י: מַרְאֵיהֶם *their aspect* Dn 1.15, מַרְאֵיהֶן Gn 41.21; Na 2.5; נוֹטֵיהֶם *he who stretches* *them out* Is 42.5 (cf. § 136 *e*, n.); מַחֲנֶ֫יךָ *your camp* Dt 23.15 (after מַחֲנֶךָ), שָׂדֶ֫יךָ *your field* 1Kg 2.26; מִקְנֶ֫יךָ *your cattle* Is 30.23.

(1) The participle is prob. a *maqtil* and the substantive prob. a *maqtal*.

§ 96 D. INFLECTION OF NOUNS WITH A PRIMITIVE SHORT 1st VOWEL AND A PRIMITIVE LONG 2nd VOWEL

a The 2nd vowel of these nouns is etymologically long and is therefore retained; the 1st vowel, primitively short, is liable to deletion; in some forms such as כְּתָב and שְׁאָר the primitive vowel has even disappeared. The paradigm פָּקִיד gives an example of *qatīl* form of strong root, עָנִי from a ל"ה root; finally, כְּתָב an example of *qitāl* or *qutāl*.

b **Inflection of 18.** פָּקִיד *commissioner* and other nouns with a primitive short *a* as 1st vowel and with a primitive long 2nd vowel, e.g. קָטוֹל, גָּדוֹל (with non-deletable ọ, § 88 D *c*)(1), שָׁלוֹם, מָקוֹם.

The primitive short *a* becomes ָ in prestress position. It is usually dropped in ante-prestress position, as also in the cst. state. **Exceptions**(2): שָׁלִישׁ *adjutant*, cst. unattested, שָׁלִישׁוֹ; pl. שָׁלִישִׁים, cst. unattested, שָׁלִישָׁיו. [In סָרִיס *eunuch* some forms presuppose a *qatīl*, others a *qattīl*: cst. סְרִיס; pl. סָרִסִים, cst. סָרִיסֵי (1 x סְ), סָרִיסָיו etc. Likewise for פָּרִיץ *one who makes a breach in a wall*: cst. פְּרִיץ; pl. פָּרִיצִים, cst. פָּרִיצֵי]. שָׁבוּעַ *week* has the following plural forms: שָׁבֻעִים, שָׁבֻעוֹת, cst. שְׁבֻעוֹת (שְׁבֻעֹתֵיכֶם, § 14 *c* 2); but dual שְׁבֻעַ֫יִם Lv 12.5† (comp. the absolute שְׁבֻעוֹת *oaths* Ez 21.28, from שְׁבוּעָה).

For the inflection of the form *qatalān*, e.g. זִכָּרוֹן, cst. זִכְרוֹן(3), plural זִכְרֹנִים, cf. § 88 M *b*.

(1) Cst. state גְּדוֹל־ and גְּדָל־; and likewise טְהוֹר־ and טְהָר־.

(2) Other examples of abnormally stable ָ: פָּרָשִׁים (§ B *b*), מָגֵן (§ C *c*), מָעוֹז (§ 88 L *e*); fem., § 97 D *b*, E *b*, G *b*.

(3) Same relation between the abs. state and the cst. state in חַלָּמִישׁ, cst. חַלְּמִישׁ *granite*.

c **Inflection of 19.** עָנִי *afflicted* (*qatīl* form from ל"ה, § 88 E *b*). The 1st vowel ָ is treated like that of פָּקִיד (§ *b*). In the plural, *ʿanīyīm* becomes *ʿaniyyīm* > עֲנִיִּים (comp. the formation of the fem. עֲנִיָּה); with contraction: שָׁנִי *scarlet*, plural שָׁנִים (cf. § 90 *b*).

d **Inflection of 20.** כְּתָב *writing, book* (§ 88 E *f*). In this noun the primitive 1st vowel is probably *i* (cf. Arb. *kitāb* "book"); in other words it may be *u* or even *a*. The ָ, here representing a primitive long ā, is retained throughout the inflection, but exceptionally חֲמַת רַבָּה Am 6.2†. Compare the forms קָטָל (§ 88 H *a*) and the forms in ָן (§ 88 M *a*), with cst. state in ַ. Example of construct state pl.: מְצָדוֹת *stronghold* 1Sm 24.1; Is 33.16 (sing. מְצָד; compare תְּעָלָה, § 97 D *b*).

§ 96 E. INFLECTION OF NOUNS WITH TWO CONSONANTS AND A PRIMITIVE SHORT VOWEL

a **Form qal** > קָל (§ 88 B *a*). The ָ is treated like the final ָ of דָּבָר (§ 96 B *b*), except for some slight peculiarities, e.g. יָד *hand*, cst. יַד, יָדִי, but יֶדְכֶם (§ 29 *e*); pl. יָדוֹת, יְדוֹת; dual יָדַיִם, יְדֵי, יָדַי, יְדֵיכֶם; דָּם *blood*, cst. דַּם, דָּמִי, but דִּמְכֶם (§ 29 *g*); pl. דָּמִים, דְּמֵי. In the participle קָם the ָ is stable: pl. cst. קָמֵי (§ 80 *d*).

For the irregular nouns אָב, אָח, חָם, cf. § 98 *b*.

b **Form qil** > קֵל (§ 88 B b). The ֵ is not treated like that of זָקֵן (§ 96 B *d*). It is usually maintained in the cst. state, e.g.: cst. אֵל *god*, עֵץ *wood*, שֵׁם (6 x only שֶׁם־), but בֶּן־ (almost always with maqqef)(1). Examples of inflected forms: עֵצוֹ, עֵצְךָ; עֵצִים, עֲצֵי, עֵצֵינוּ; (likewise אֵל, אֵלִי, אֵלִים); but שְׁמוֹ, שִׁמְךָ, שְׁמֶךָ, שִׁמְכֶם (and likewise בְּנוֹ etc.); pl. שֵׁמוֹת, cst. שְׁמוֹת. In the participle מֵת the ֵ is stable: pl. cst. מֵתֵי (§ 80 *d*).

For the irregular noun בֵּן, cf. § 98 *c*. Nouns of the types *qall* עַם, *qill* אֵם, *qull* חֹק do not fall into this category; cf. § 96 A *n, o, p*.

(1) Compare the treatment of the ֵ of the אֵיבָ inflection (§96 C *c*).

§ 97. **Inflection of feminine nouns**
(Paradigm 18)

Feminine nouns are those nouns which, in the singular or in the plural, have a feminine ending (§ 89 *a*). A feminine noun is formed from the corresponding (real or hypothetical) masculine noun with the addition of one of the feminine endings ָה, ת (ֶ ֶת, ַ ַת, ֶ ֶת, ַ ַת) (§ 89 *d-j*). The modifications which can affect the masculine form will be given when we deal with each particular inflection.

This paragraph is subdivided into several subparagraphs which are indicated by the capital letters A, B, C, D, E, F, and G; these correspond to the subdivisions of § 96: (A) Inflection of nouns with only one primitive vowel; (B) nouns with two primitive short vowels; (C) nouns with a stable first vowel and a primitive short second vowel; (D) nouns with a primitive short first vowel and an etymologically long second vowel; (E) nouns with two consonants and a primitive short vowel; and in addition, (F) inflection of segholate endings; (G) inflection of nouns in ִית, וּת, and ָת.

§ 97 A. INFLECTION OF NOUNS WITH ONLY ONE PRIMITIVE VOWEL

a This category includes the feminine nouns of the patterns *qatl*, *qitl*, and *qutl*, the corresponding masculines of which have for the most part been segholised. To form the feminine noun, *at* > *å* is added to the primitive form, hence *qatlat*, *qitlat*, and *qutlat*, e.g. מַלְכָּה *queen*, סִתְרָה *protection*, טֻמְאָה *impurity*. Sometimes the primitive vowel is altered, as it is in the masculine nouns with the suffixes. Thus **kabś* (כֶּ֫בֶשׂ *lamb*) has the feminine form כִּבְשָׂה *ewe-lamb*, alongside כַּבְשָׂה (§ 88 C *b*); **raš‘* (רֶ֫שַׁע, רֶ֫שַׁע *impiety*) has the (synonymous) fem. רִשְׁעָה with *i* as in רִשְׁעוֹ (comp. forms such as בִּטְנִי alongside מַלְכִּי, § 96 A *c*)(1). In the *qitl* form ֶ is used after a guttural R1 (§ 21 *e*), e.g. **ḥilq* (חֵ֫לֶק *part*) חֶלְקָה as we have חֶלְקִי (§ 96 A *e*); likewise עֵ֫גֶל *calf*, עֶגְלָה *heifer* as we have עֶגְלְךָ, עֵ֫זֶר *help*, עֶזְרָה as we have עֶזְרִי. In the *qutl* form the *u* almost always becomes ָ just as in the masculine inflection, e.g., קָרְחָה *bald spot*, as we have קָדְשִׁי, § 96 A *g* (cf. § 88 C *j*). The primitive *u* has been preserved in טֻמְאָה *impurity* (before the labial), in the feminine proper noun חֻלְדָּה (comp. חֹ֫לֶד *weasel*, or *mole*).

With guttural R2: נַ֫עַר *boy*, fem. נַעֲרָה *young woman* (comp. נַעֲרִי); טָהֳרָה *purity* (comp. פָּעֳלִי), בָּאְשָׁה *weed* (comp. בָּאְשׁוֹ from בְּאֹשׁ *stench*, § 96 A *k*).

ע"ע roots: רַב *numerous*, fem. רַבָּה; (with guttural) רַע *bad*, רָעָה; חֹק *due, decree*, חֻקָּה *decree* (comp. חֻקִּי).

ל"ה roots: אַלְיָה *fat tail* (from **'aly*, comp. פִּרְיִ from **pary*); שִׁבְיָה *captivity* (from *šaby*, hence שִׁבְיִ) with weakening of *a* to *i* (comp. שִׁבְיוֹ).

From the secondary forms גְּדִי *kid*, אֳנִי *fleet* the following fem. nouns were formed: גְּדִיָּה *young she-goat*, אֳנִיָּה *ship*.

(1) *Qatlat* may also become קְטָלָה, but there is no sure example.

Inflection of 21. מַלְכָּה *queen* (*qatlat* pattern, § 88 C *b*). The ָ is treated like the final ָ of דָּבָר: מַלְכָּתִי, מַלְכָּתְךָ, but with heavy suffix: מַלְכַּתְכֶם. Plural: abs. state מְלָכוֹת with prestress qameṣ, on the analogy of the prestress qameṣ of the masculine type מְלָכִים, § 96 A *b* (where the qameṣ possibly comes from the auxiliary vowel of the singular)(1). Cst. state: מַלְכוֹת (with fricative כ, like מַלְכֵי). Note that the stem of the cst. state is used with all the suffixes. (Comp. the double stem of the plural in the masc. segholates and in the types דָּבָר and זָקֵן). A form such as מְלָכוֹתַי* would be quite abnormal, since the qameṣ would be in an ante-prestress syllable (comp. the impossibility of מְלָכֵיכֶם*, § 96 A *c*, n.). *b*

For the dual, cf. § 91 *b*.

(1) So besides the category of the segholate nouns, there is no prestress qameṣ, e.g. מִרְמָה *fraud*, pl. מִרְמוֹת (and not מְרָמוֹת*); מִצְוָה, pl. מִצְוֹת (מִקְטָלָה forms, § 88 L *f*).

Inflection of the *qitlat* (§ 88 C *h*) **and *qutlat* patterns** (§ 88 C *j*). *c*
The inflection of these forms קִטְלָה (קְטָלָה) and קֻטְלָה (קָטְלָה) and that of קַטְלָה are perfectly symmetrical. Thus from שִׁפְחָה *maid-servant* are formed the following: pl. abs. שְׁפָחוֹת, cst. שִׁפְחוֹת; from חָרְבָּה *ruin*, pl. abs. חֳרָבוֹת, cst. חָרְבוֹת (comp. קֳדָשִׁים, חֳדָשִׁים, § 96 A *g*); but from עָרְלָה *foreskin* are formed הָעֲרָלוֹת Josh 5.3†, cst. עָרְלוֹת(1).

In the inflection of תְּאֵנָה *fig* (*qtil* form, § 88 C *i*) the ֵ is retained: תְּאֵנָתִי, תְּאֵנִים, תְּאֵנֵי (comp. בְּרֵכָה, § 97 B *b*).

(1) About the form חָכְמוֹת *Wisdom*, cf. § 96 A *b*.

§ 97 B. INFLECTION OF NOUNS WITH TWO PRIMITIVE SHORT VOWELS

This category includes the feminine nouns with two primitive short vowels (§ 88 D), notably *qatal, qatil, qatul*. *a*

Inflection of 22. צְדָקָה *justice* (*qatalat* pattern). The primitive form **ṣadaqat* becomes צְדָקָה in the abs. state; the 1st vowel in ante-prestress syllable is dropped. In the cst. state, **ṣadqat* becomes צִדְקַת, *b* with weakening of *a* to *i* (§ 29 *g*); the shewa is "medium," hence a begadkefat as R3 will become fricative. With suffixes: צִדְקָתִי, צִדְקָתְךָ, but צִדְקַתְכֶם. In the plural, *ṣadaqāt* becomes צְדָקוֹת in the absolute state, whilst in the cst. state *ṣadqāt* becomes צִדְקוֹת (with shewa "medium"). Note that the stem of the cst. state is used with all the suffixes (like מַלְכוּת, § A *b*).

c In the cst. state צִדְקַת a begadkefat as R3 is pronounced as a fricative in, e.g. נִדְבַת *generosity*; it becomes a plosive in חֶרְדַּת *terror* (from חֲרָדָה), בִּרְכַּת *blessing* (but בְּרָכוֹת, בִּרְכָתִי). The *a* of the 1st syllable of *ṣadqat* is retained in אַדְמַת *earth*. Otherwise, after a guttural, the secondary *i* becomes *ẹ*: חֶרְדַּת, עֶגְלָתוֹ (from עֲגָלָה *cart*). From עֲטָרָה *crown* the cst. state is segholised: עֲטֶרֶת. From עֲצָרָה (4 x) *abstention* is formed עֲצֶרֶת, not only as the cst. state Jer 9.1, but also as the absolute state (4 x); in pause עֲצָרֶת 2Ch 7.9. The forms with suffixes יְבִמְתֵּךְ, יְבִמְתּוֹ *sister-in-law* are derived from a segholate form *יְבֶמֶת; (the *i* has been weakened from *a*); the abs. state is not attested in the Bible (יְבָמָה in the Mishna).

d **Inflection of the pattern *qatilat* > קְטֵלָה**(1). The inflection of nouns of the *qatilat* form shows a remarkable anomaly: the ֵ tends to be retained, while the corresponding ָ of the קְטָלָה type is dropped. Most nouns of this category have some peculiarity or other. Nouns of the קְטֵלָה form may be divided into two groups: some nouns keep the ֵ when inflected (like תְּאֵנָה, *qtil* form, § 97 A *c*), the others do not.

ֵ is retained in the following nouns: בְּרֵכָה *pool*, cst. בְּרֵכַת(2), plural בְּרֵכוֹת (abs. and cst.); גְּזֵלָה, גְּזֵלַת *rapine*; טְמֵאָה, טְמֵאַת *impure*, מְלֵאָה, מְלֵאַתִי *full of* (ḥireq compaginis, § 93 *m*); שְׁאֵלָה *request*, שְׁאֵלָתִי etc., but שֶׁאֱלָתִי Job 6.8, שֶׁאֱלָתָם Ps 106.15.

On the other hand we find the following forms: נְבֵלָה, נִבְלַת *corpse*(3); בְּהֵמָה *beast*, בֶּהֱמַת (*ẹ* for *i* before a guttural), pl. cst. בַּהֲמוֹת, but the sg. forms with suffixes, e.g. בְּהֶמְתֵּנוּ, presuppose a segholate doublet *בְּהֶמֶת; חֲשֵׁכָה *darkness*, חֶשְׁכַת (*ẹ* for *i* after a guttural).

The word *ירכה *side* has the forms יַרְכְּתֵי, יַרְכָּתַיִם, יַרְכָתוֹ. The spirantisation of the כ presupposes a form *יְרֵכָה (fem. of יָרֵךְ *hip, thigh*). The origin of the vowel ַ, which would suggest a form *יַרְכָּה, is unknown.

(1) On the basis of its dominantly plene spelling, Barr (*Spellings*, p. 141) holds that פְּלֵיטָה is of the diminutive *qutailat* pattern, although this pattern, contrary to

the case in Arabic, is extremely rare in Hebrew: cf. Barth, *Nominalbildung*, § 192d, and Brock., *GvG*, I, § 137 a.
(2) Contr. בִּרְכַּת from בְּרָכָה *blessing* (§ *c*).
(3) Contr. נְבָלָה *infamy*, with no construct state.

The *qatilt* form becomes קְטֶלֶת by segholisation (like *qatalt*, § *c*); *e*
thus גָּדֵר *wall*, גְּדֵרָה* (cf. Ps 62.4), גְּדֶרֶת(1); חָבֵר *companion*, חֲבֶרֶת*. In אֱמֶת (אֱמֶת Ps 19.10, אֲמִתּוֹ) the primitive form *'amint* became *'ạmẹ'nẹt*, *'ạmẹtt*, and by assimilation of the (very short and unstressed) 1st vowel to the stressed vowel: *'ẹmẹtt*, אֱמֶת(2).

(1) Plural with suf. גְּדֵרֹתָיו (cf. § *d*) despite cst. גִּדְרוֹת. Cp. יָתֵד, יְתֵדֹתָיו despite cst. יִתְדֹת (§ 96 B *d*); מַצֵּבָה, מַצְּבוֹתֶיךָ despite cst. מַצְּבוֹת (§ 97 C *b*).
(2) Alternatively one could postulate *'*imint* as the primitive form; W.R. Garr, *VT* 37 (1987) 137.

The inflection of the pattern *qatulat*, which in Hebrew becomes קְטֻלָּה *f*
(cf. § 18 *d*, § 96 B *e*), presents no difficulty, the vowel *u* being in a closed syllable.

§ 97 C. INFLECTION OF NOUNS WITH A STABLE 1st VOWEL AND A PRIMITIVE SHORT 2nd VOWEL

The forms קֹטֵל, מְקַטֵּל, מִתְקַטֵּל can have a triple form in the fem. sg., *a*
e.g., קֹטְלָה, קֹטֵלָה and especially קֹטֶלֶת. Before ָה, as also before the endings in וֹת (and ִים, § 96 C *c*) of the plural, the ֵ is sometimes retained, sometimes dropped, but not according to any clear rule. Generally speaking it may be said that the ֵ tends to be dropped, and that in order for it to be retained a pause or the influence of certain consonants, or the repetition of a consonant must be present. It also seems that the ֵ is more likely to be retained before ָה than before the syllables וֹת and ִים with their primitive long vowels. Examples: אֹכְלָה, but אוֹכֵלָה Is 29.6; 30.30; 33.14; יוֹלֵדָה even in context, but הַיּוֹלְדוֹת (1 x); בֹּגֵדָה, but בֹּגְדוֹת Zeph 3.4 (despite the pause); נֹטֵרָה *guardian* Ct 1.6, but נֹטְרִים *guardians* 8.11,12; with repetition of a consonant: שׁוֹמֵמָה.

For the inflection of the segholate ending, cf. § 97 F *b*.

For the feminine of the גֹּלָה type, cf. § 79 *p*.

Apart from these forms the ֵ is retained in the absolute state, *b* e.g., מַצֵּבָה *stele*, abs. and cst. מַצֶּבֶת, cst. מַצְּבַת; pl. מַצֵּבוֹת, מַצְּבוֹתֶיךָ despite cst. מַצְּבוֹת (cf. § 97 B *e*, n.). In מַהְפֵּכָה* *catastrophe*, תַּרְדֵּמָה *deep sleep*, the ֲ is maintained in the cst. state: מַהְפֵּכַת, תַּרְדֵּמַת (cf. זֵעַת, § E *b*).

§ 97 D. INFLECTION OF NOUNS WITH A PRIMITIVE SHORT 1st VOWEL AND A LONG 2nd VOWEL

a With the addition of the ending ָה, the primitive short 1st vowel finds itself in an ante-prestress syllable and is therefore dropped, e.g. קָטוּל, קְטוּלָה. The inflection of these words presents no difficulty whatsoever. Likewise for forms like מְגִלָּה *scroll*, תְּהִלָּה *praise*, where the short vowel is in a closed syllable. (Comp. § B *f*, קְטֻלָּה form).

b In the word תְּעָלָה *canal* the qameṣ is stable (like that of כְּתָב, מְצָד, § 96 D *d*): cst. תְּעָלַת; pl. with suff. תְּעָלֹתֶיהָ. Therefore this ָ is probably long, etymologically speaking. (Comp. e.g., סְעָרָה *tempest*, cst. סַעֲרַת). Likewise, the qameṣ of מְעָרָה *cave* is stable; cst. מְעָרַת, pl. abs. and cst. מְעָרוֹת. But here the qameṣ (from the original form *ma'arrat*) was protected by the primitively doubled consonant (comp. שָׂרֵי etc., § 96 A *n*).

§ 97 E. INFLECTION OF NOUNS WITH TWO CONSONANTS WITH A SHORT PRIMITIVE VOWEL

a The short primitive vowel (*a*, *i*) is treated like the 1st vowel of the forms קָטָל and קְטָל, § 96 B *b*, *c*.

b **The inflection of 23.** שָׁנָה *year* (root שׁנה) and of שֵׁנָה *sleep* (root ישׁן) therefore presents no difficulty whatsoever. The forms of the two words coincide when the vowel is dropped, e.g. שְׁנַת, שְׁנָתוֹ; pl. cst. שְׁנוֹת (cf. § 90 *b*).

Nouns from ע"ו roots (קָמָה and מֵתָה types) have a stable 1st vowel (§ 80 *d*). Thus עֵדָה *testimony* (root עוד) would give *עֵדָתִי, whereas עֵדָה *rendezvous, assembly* (root יעד, § 75 *m*) gives עֲדָתִי. רָמָה *height* (root רום) gives רָמָתֵךְ, רָמֹתַיִךְ.

ֲ is retained in cst. זֵעַת *sweat* (root יזע); comp. מַהְפֵּכַת etc., § C *b*. So also עֵצָה in the tradition represented by Secunda: Ps 1.1 βησαθ for MT בַּעֲצַת.

In the word בָּמָה *height, high-place*, the origin(1) and the form of which are obscure, the qameṣ is stable (comp. רָמֹתֶ֫יךָ with qameṣ): cst. בָּמוֹת, בָּמוֹתֵי. In בָּמֳתֵי *bâm^{o}ṯẹ*, another cst. form found 6 times, the *ọ* of the plural has been, strangely enough, shortened to very short ^{o}: the cst. ending of the masc. pl. ־ֵי has been added to the ending of the cst. state of the fem. plural(2), as if to compensate for the shortening of the *ọ*. This form is only found in the poetic books: בָּמֳתֵי עָב Is 14.14; בּ' יָם Job 9.8; בּ' אָרֶץ Am 4.13 and, as Qre (against Ktiv בָּמוֹתֵי) Dt 32.13; Is 58.14; Mi 1.3; therefore always before a stressed syllable in major pause. (But cf. בָּמוֹת יָעַר Jer 26.18; Mi 3.12; בָּמוֹת אָ֫וֶן Ho 10.8.

In the word אָלָה *imprecation, oath* (root אלה) the qameṣ is stable; אָלָתִי, pl. cst. (and abs.) אָלוֹת.

Dual: Example: שָׂפָה *lip*: שְׂפָתַ֫יִם, שִׂפְתֵי; comp. כַּנְפֵי, § 96 B *b*.

(1) A. Cuny, in "Les mots du fond préhellénique en grec, latin et sémitique occidental," (*Revue des Études anciennes* 12 [1910] 154-64), compares βωμός *platform, altar*.

(2) Comp. the ־ֵי placed before the plural suffixes in וֹת, § 94 *f*.

§ 97 F. INFLECTION OF SEGHOLATE ENDINGS

That which pertains to the inflection of the segholate endings will be brought together here, regardless of the form of the nouns. *a*

It seems that the segholisation(1) of the feminine ending arose in the construct state (§ 89 *d*). Sometimes it is found only in the construct state, sometimes it has spread to the absolute state(2).

Nouns with segholate ending in the cst. state: עֲטָרָה, cst. עֲטֶ֫רֶת *crown*; לֶהָבָה, cst. לַהֶ֫בֶת *flame*; several nouns with the preformative מ, e.g. מַמְלָכָה, cst. מַמְלֶ֫כֶת *kingdom*, מִשְׁפָּחָה, cst. מִשְׁפַּ֫חַת *clan*; מֶרְכָּבָה *chariot*, cst. מִרְכֶּ֫בֶת, מֶרְכַּבְתּוֹ; pl. מַרְכָּבוֹת, cst. מַרְכְּבוֹת.

Nouns with the segholate form, alongside the form in ־ָה, in the absolute state: עֲצָרָה and עֲצֶ֫רֶת, עֲצָרֶת *abstention*; תִּפְאָרָה and more often תִּפְאֶ֫רֶת, תִּפְאָרֶת *ornament, glory*; מַחֲשָׁבָה and מַחֲשֶׁ֫בֶת, מַחֲשָׁבֶת *design*(3).

Some nouns only have the segholate form, e.g. מִשְׁמֶ֫רֶת *observance*, יוֹנֶ֫קֶת *young shoot, twig*, כֹּתֶ֫רֶת *capital (of column)*.

(1) The process is extended to some numerals: שְׁלֹ֫שֶׁת, אַרְבַּ֫עַת, חֲמֵ֫שֶׁת, שֵׁ֫שֶׁת, עֲשֶׂ֫רֶת.

(2) We have seen examples of the cst. state of masc. nouns adopted as absolute state, e.g., § 96 A *l, m, q*; with fem. nouns, § 97 B *c*, C *b*.

(3) Note that in the case of a doublet the segholate form is used. Note too that in cases like עֲצֶרֶת there is no prestress qameṣ even when the word is used in the absolute state, and even in pause (עֲצָרֶת). The absence of prestress qameṣ indeed seems to indicate that the form was originally a construct state (cf. § 89 *d*).

b **Inflection of the ending** ־ֶ ֶלֶת(1), § 89 *g*. When ־ֶ ֶלֶת comes from *alt*, ־ַ is normally used in the inflection, in a closed syllable, just as מֶלֶךְ (from **malk*) becomes מַלְכִּי etc.; e.g. אִוַּלְתִּי from אִוֶּלֶת *madness* (*qittal* for *qattal*, § 88 H a); מַמְלַכְתּוֹ, מַחֲשַׁבְתּוֹ. Exception: יְבִמְתֵּךְ, § B *c*. The infinitive גֶּשֶׁת (§ 72 *d*) becomes גִּשְׁתּוֹ, like שִׁבְתּוֹ. When the ending ־ֶ ֶלֶת comes from *ilt*, ־ִ is sometimes used, but sometimes also ־ַ. We get ־ִ in the שֶׁבֶת type of inf. cst.: רִדְתִּי, לִדְתִּי, שִׁבְתִּי (cf. § 75 *m*); in nouns with etymologically long *ī* in the absolute: גְּבִירָה (§ 88 E *g*), *mistress*, **gbirt*, גְּבֶרֶת, גְּבִרְתִּי; מֵינִיקָה*, *nurse*, /*mēniqt/, מֵינֶקֶת, מֵינִקְתּוֹ. In foms such as חֲבֶרְתֵּךְ (masc. חָבֵר *companion*) and בְּהֶמְתֵּנוּ (from בְּהֵמָה, § B *d*), ־ֶ probably stands for ־ִ.

On the other hand ־ַ is found in words of the קֹטֶלֶת type (cf. Paradigm of 24 יוֹנֶקֶת *young shoot, twig*): יוֹנַקְתּוֹ, יוֹלַדְתּוֹ *mother*, אֹמַנְתּוֹ *nurse*, חֹתַנְתּוֹ *wife's mother*, אֹיַבְתִּי Mi 7.8,10 (cp. the ־ַ of אוֹיִבְךָ, § 96 C*c*).

Observation. ־ֶ ֶאת gets simplified to ־ֵאת in the inf. צֵאת (§ 75 *g*) and in the participles of the ל"א verbs: מֹצֵאת, נִפְלֵאת (§ 78 *h*).

(1) The ל here designates the last consonant of the word.

c The inflection of the very rare ending ־ֶ ֶלֶת (§ 89 *h*), from *ilt*, has ־ִ in אִשָּׁה *woman*, cst. אֵשֶׁת, אִשְׁתִּי etc. (§ 99 *c*).

d In the inflection of the ending ־ֹ ֶלֶת (§ 89 *i*) either ־ֻ or ־ָ is found: the choice of the vowel seems to depend on the nature of the consonants (comp. the inflection of קֹדֶשׁ, § 96 A *g*). Forms with ־ֻ: מַשְׂכֻּרְתִּי *reward*, מַחֲלֻקְתּוֹ *division*, מַתְכֻּנְתּוֹ *exact measure*, מַלְכֻּדְתּוֹ *trap*, מַרְכֻּלְתֵּךְ *market-place* (all *maqtul* forms, § 88 L *j*). In נְחֹשֶׁת *bronze*, ־ֻ is almost always used(1)(1 x ־ָ: נְחָשְׁתִּי Lam 3.7). Forms with ־ָ: גֻּלְגָּלְתּוֹ *skull* (*qulqul* pattern, § 88 J *c*), קְטָרְתִּי *smoke* (prob. *qutāl*, § 88 E *e*), שְׁלָשְׁתָּם *three* (*qatāl* pattern, § 88 E *a*), בָּשְׁתִּי *shame* (perh. בֹּשֶׁת was formed on בּוּשָׁה), כֻּתָּנְתִּי *tunic* (from כֻּתֹּנֶת.; prob. *quttāl* pattern: comp. Arb. *kattān* "flax, linen cloth," Arm. *kittånå*, Syr. *kettånå*). This word is rather irregular: cst. כְּתֹנֶת; pl. כֻּתָּנוֹת, cst. כָּתְנוֹת(2).

(1) The reason for the persistence of *u* is probably that נְחֹשֶׁת is formed on נְחוּשָׁה, as גְּבֶרֶת on גְּבִירָה (§ *b*). Contr. (likewise before שׁ) בָּשְׁתִּי, שְׁלָשְׁתָּם.

(2) The absence of doubling in the cst. state forms perh. indicates that the doubling in כֻּתֹּ֫נֶת is secondary, as it is in the type זִכָּרוֹן, cst. זִכְרוֹן (§ 88 M *b*); comp. χιτών.

Observation. In the absolute plural, nouns the last vowel of which e
was primitive *a* always have prestress ־ָ, e.g. מִשְׁמֶ֫רֶת *observance*, מִשְׁמָרוֹת. Therefore a plural abs. in ־ְלוֹת can only come from a form in *ilt* or *ult*; e.g., אִגֶּ֫רֶת, pl. abs. אִגְּרוֹת, is from the form *'iggirt* (cf. Akk. *egirtu*). On the other hand, a plural like כּוֹתָרוֹת indicates that כּוֹתֶ֫רֶת *capital* (*of a column*) comes from the form *kātart* and not *kātirt*.

The usual form חַטָּאת *sin*, alongside the very rare חַטָּאָה (2 x in major f
pause), stands for חַטַּ֫את*; the cst. state חַטַּאת is secondarily formed on the absolute חַטָּאת. Plural abs. חַטָּאוֹת, cst. חַטֹּאת(1).

(1) Suffixed forms such as שַׁבַּתּוֹ and שַׁבַּתָּהּ with תּ (not ת) and בַּ (not בְּ as in שַׁבְּתוֹת pl. cst.) led Ibn Ezra to believe that the basic form is שַׁבֶּ֫תֶת: see his ספר צחות ed. C. del Valle Rodriguez (Salamanca, 1977), p. 92 (281), and also on Ho 2.13.

§ 97 G. INFLECTION OF NOUNS IN ־ִית, ־וּת AND ־ָת

Nouns in ־ִית. Adjectives of the type מוֹאָבִית (alongside מוֹאֲבִיָּה; masc. a
מוֹאָבִי) become, for example, מוֹאֲבִיּוֹת in the plural (cf. § 89 *e*). Substantives in ־ִית, most of them being abstract (§ 88 M *i*), are not found in the plural. For the plural of the concrete substantives חֲנִית *lance*, cf. § 89 *p*; דָּלִית and זָוִית (§ 88 F *b*).

Nouns in ־וּת (cf. § 88 M *j*). Some nouns like גָּלוּת have a stable ־ָ b
(cf. *ibid.*). Forms found in the plural: מַלְכוּת(1) *royalty*, pl. מַלְכֻיוֹת Dn 8.22† for *mąlḵuwwọṯ* (comp. BA מַלְכוּתָא, pl. מַלְכְוָתָא); חָנוּת* *vault*, pl. חֲנֻיוֹת Jer 37.16; abs. and cst. עֵדוּת *ordinance* (with stable ־ֵ, for root עוד), pl. עֵדְוֹת* *'ẹḏwọṯ*, עֵדְוֹתֶ֫יךָ, etc. For the apparent plurals (with suffixes) of the type זְנוּתֵיכֶם, cf. § 94 *j*.

(1) With aspiration as in the cst. state types מַלְכֵי (§ 96 A *b*), מַלְכוֹת (§ 97 A *b*).

Nouns in ־ָת. In the word מְנָת *part* (root מנה), borrowed from c
Aramaic, the ־ָ is etymologically long, as it is in that language: cst. מְנָת; pl. cst. מְנָיוֹת and מְנָאוֹת. Likewise in קְצָת, Aramaising doublet of קְצוֹת *extremity* (root קצה), the cst. is קְצָת, the pl. קְצָוֹת; comp. כְּנָוֺתָיו Ezr 4.7 (from Arm. כְּנָת *companion*, pl. כְּנָוָתָא). With these cst. forms in ־ָת comp., e.g., מָחֳרָת (§ 89 *n*), cst. ־ֳרַת; חַטָּאת (§ 97 F *f*), cst. ־ַאת.

§ 98. **Irregular nouns**
(Paradigm 19)

a The nouns brought together here are particularly irregular and may, for the sake of convenience, be divided into three categories: I) Nouns with two strong consonants; II) nouns with one or two consonants from ל״י roots; III) nouns with a weak 2nd radical א, ו, or י.

b **I) Nouns with two strong consonants** (mostly nouns of kinship). The first three nouns, of קָל form (§ 88 B *a*), have ִי— in the cst. state and before the suffixes (cf. § 93 *l*):

1. אָב *father*, cst. אֲבִי; with suffixes אָבִי etc. (prestress qameṣ). The plural אָבוֹת is in וֹת, perhaps on the analogy of אִמּוֹת *mothers*; cst. אֲבוֹת, with suf. אֲבוֹתַי etc.; with 3rd pl. suf. אֲבוֹתָם is more frequent than אֲבוֹתֵיהֶם (§ 94 *g*). The cst. state אַב is found in proper nouns like אַבְשָׁלוֹם (possibly a defective spelling for אֲבִישָׁלוֹם, which also occurs once), אַבְרָהָם (and in the etymology of this name, Gn 17.4,5 אַב הֲמוֹן־).

2. אָח *brother*, cst. אֲחִי; with suf. אָחִי etc. (prestress qameṣ). In the plural there is virtual spontaneous doubling in the absolute state(1) and with the light suffixes: אַחִים, אַחַי etc. (§ 20 *c*); before ָיו: אֶחָיו, אֶחָי (§ 29 *f*).

3. חָם *husband's father*, cst. חֲמִי*; with suff. חָמִיךְ, חָמִ֫יהָ†.

(1) Cf. Akk. pl. *aḫḫū*.

c One noun of קֵל form (§ 96 E *b*):

4. בֵּן *son*, cst. usually בֶּן־ (almost always with maqqef), rarely בִּן־ (always in בִּן־נוּן, in the proper nouns בִּן־יָקֶה Pr 30.1, בִּנְיָמִין but בֶּן־יְמִינִי), once בְּנִי (§ 93 *m*), once בְּנוֹ (§ 93 *r*). The irregular plural בָּנִים is difficult to explain (according to Brock., *GvG*, I, p. 322, dissimilation of **binīm*).

d Four feminine nouns:

5. בַּת *daughter*, for **bant* (from **bint*); with suf. בִּתִּי etc. (weakening of *a* to *i* (§ 29 *g*)(1); pl. בָּנוֹת on the analogy of בָּנִים.

6. אָמָה *handmaid*. In the plural אֲמָהוֹת, cst. אַמְהוֹת, a ה appears as in the corresponding Aramaic word אַמְהָתָא (and in אֲבָהָתָא *the fathers*, and MH אִמָּהוֹת *mothers*).

7. אָחוֹת *sister*, from a form **'aḥāt* (so in Akk.), which is variously explained; cst. אֲחוֹת, with suf. אֲחוֹתִי etc, once וּלְאַחֹתוֹ Nu 6.7, with

virtual doubling as in אַחִים, but for no apparent reason (comp. וְלַאֲחֹתוֹ Lv 21.3). The pl. אֲחָיוֹת*, cst. אַחְיוֹת*, which is not found in the Bible, is difficult to explain; with suf., אַחְיוֹתַי etc; the rare forms such as אַחוֹתַי Josh 2.13K are abnormal or incorrect.

8. חָמוֹת* *husband's mother*; same form as אָחוֹת (comp. Arb. *ḥamāt*, pl. *ḥamawāt*); with suf. חֲמוֹתֵךְ, חֲמוֹתָהּ.

(1) Synchronically, but diachronically the change *i* > *a* is an effect of Philippi's law (§ 29 *aa*).

II) Nouns with one or two consonants, from ל"י roots: e

9. שֶׂה *a head of small cattle* (noun of unit of צֹאן *small cattle*, § 135 *b*), from **śay*, cst. שֵׂה; suff. שֵׂיוֹ Dt 22.1†, שֵׂיֵהוּ 1Sm 14.34†.

10. פֶּה *mouth*, probably from **piy*, cst. פִּי; with suf., פִּי, פִּיךָ, פִּיו (more common than פִּיהוּ), פִּיהָ etc. Pl. פִּיוֹת with the meaning of *cutting edges* Pr 5.4†, פִּיוֹת Jdg 3.16† (as if from **pay*)(1). Plural, with repetition of the root, פִּיפִיּוֹת Is 41.15; Ps 149.6 (comp. the forms with repetition מֵימֵי, מֵימַי etc. from מַיִם *infra*, 11).

11. מַיִם *water*, *waters*, irregular plural (cf. § 91 *f*) of sing. **may*; cst. מֵי, rather rarely (13 x) מֵימֵי; but the form with repetition is always used with the suffixes: מֵימַי etc.

12. שָׁמַיִם *sky*, *skies*, irregular plural (cf. § 91 *f*) of singular **šamay*, construct שְׁמֵי, with suf., שָׁמֶיךָ etc.

13. כְּלִי *vessel*, כֶּלְיִ, כֶּלְיְךָ. These forms, which are similar to פְּרִי, פֶּרְיִ, פֶּרְיְךָ (§ 96 A *q*), allow us to postulate a primitive sing. form *kaly*. But the relation of the sing. to the pl. כֵּלִים, כְּלֵי is obscure; here the ִ is deletable, whereas it is not in the forms of MH פֵּירוֹת *fruit* (pl. of פְּרִי) and of Aramaic פֵּירָא, pl. פֵּירִין, with which it would be tempting to assume a close link.

(1) In 1Sm 13.21 פִּים (vocalisation ?) is not the plural of פֶּה, but probably the name of the *weight* פים, read on a weight by Macalister; cf. S. Moscati, *L'epigrafia ebraica antica 1935-50* (Rome, 1951), pp. 99-101, 102f.

III) Nouns with a weak 2nd radical: R2 א - רֹאשׁ; R2 ו - יוֹם; R2 י - בַּיִת, עִיר. Plural in ָ-ִים: f

14. רֹאשׁ *head*, pl. רָאשִׁים, cst. רָאשֵׁי. In the monosyllabic noun **ra'š*, the *a* became long because of the quiescence of the Alef: *rāš*, hence רֹאשׁ, while in the plural **ra'šīm* the *a* was also lengthened, but

unstressed: hence רָאשִׁים(1). See also שְׂמֹאל *left-hand side*, adjective שְׂמָאלִי *left* (cf. § 24 *d*).

15. יוֹם *day*, pl. יָמִים, cst. יְמֵי. By contraction the primitive form *yawm* has become יוֹם; dual יוֹמַ֫יִם In the plural, instead of the expected forms יוֹמִים*, יוֹמֵי* the forms יָמִים, יְמֵי are used, probably on the analogy of שָׁנִים, שְׁנֵי(2). Poet. pl. cst. יְמוֹת Dt 32.7; Ps 90.15† (in both cases with שְׁנוֹת, poet. pl.cst., § 90 *b*).

16. עִיר *city*, pl. עָרִים, cst. עָרֵי. The relation between singular and plural is obscure. The plural may have been formed from a singular form עַר*, which is still found e.g. in עַר־מוֹאָב. For the alternation ī / å, comp. יָמִין *right-hand side*, adj. יְמָנִי *right* (where the ָ is due to the analogy of שְׂמָאלִי *left*).

17. בַּ֫יִת *house*, cst. בֵּית; pl. בָּתִּים, cst. בָּתֵּי. The plural, which is very irregular, has not yet been explained in a fully satisfactory way. Some scholars go so far as to reject the pronunciation *båttim* and they pronounce *båtīm*, mistakenly in our opinion. The sound *å* is found in the same position in Biblical Aramaic תְּלָתְּהוֹן *the three of them* (Dn 3.23) *tlåttẹhọn*, Syr. *tlåttayhon*(3). For the abnormal alternation *ay*, *å*, comp. אַ֫יִן and אָן *where?* and the endings of place names ַ֫יִם, ָם; ַ֫יִן, ָן (§ 91 *h*).

(1) Contr. רָשׁ, רָשִׁים *poor* (root רושׁ). These two plurals differ from each other in spelling only.

(2) Cf. J. Barth, "Formangleichung bei begrifflichen Korrespondenzen," in C. Bezold (ed.), *Orientalistische Studien Theodor Nöldeke zum 70. Geburtstag gewidmet* etc. (Giessen, 1906), vol. 2, p. 791. The pl. may indeed have been influenced by שָׁנִים, but the Siloam inscription, other early Hebrew epigraphic materials, Phoen. and Ugr. show that there existed a by-form ים (even in the singular). ESA attests to *ym* alongside *ywm*. Thus the two alternative forms may have existed side by side.

(3) On these forms, see T. Muraoka, *Classical Syriac for Hebraists* (Wiesbaden, 1987), p. 49, n. 98.

§ 99. Defective nouns

a In the preceding paragraphs (§§ 96-98), the reader's attention was drawn to certain nouns which, in the plural, have (or can have) a form different from the form they have in the singular, e.g. עִיר *city*, pl. עָרִים (§ 98 *f* 16). In this paragraph the reader will find a few defective nouns of particular interest, beginning with the nouns for *man* and *woman*, which have different roots in the singular and in the plural.

For *man* (Latin *vir*), as opposed to *woman*, אִישׁ is used in the singular. This noun probably comes from a root אישׁ or אושׁ (perh. with the sense of *strength*). In the plur. the word used is אֲנָשִׁים(1) the primary meaning of which does not seem to be *viri* "males," but *homines* "people" (as opposed to *animals*); the root is אנשׁ, which is found in the poetic noun אֱנוֹשׁ (synonymous with אָדָם) *homo*, *Man* (cf. Arb. *'unās* "men"). Cf. Paradigm 19.18. b

(1) Three times אִישִׁים Is 53.3; Ps 141.4; Pr 8.4.

For *woman* we find אִשָּׁה in the singular, cst. אֵשֶׁת (§ 97 F *c*), אִשְׁתִּי etc.(1) (comp. חֲמִשָּׁה, חֲמֵשֶׁת). The word is derived from another root אנשׁ, which corresponds to the Arabic root *'nṯ* (cf. *'unṯā* "female"). The primary meaning of אִשָּׁה therefore would be *female*. The plural נָשִׁים, נְשֵׁי, the proper meaning of which is *women*, comes from a root נשׁו or נשׁי (cf. Arb. *niswat* "women"). The plural is perhaps due to the analogy of אֲנָשִׁים (cf. e.g., Jdg 9.51 הָאֲנָשִׁים וְהַנָּשִׁים). Cf. Paradigm 19.19. c

(1) Instead of the normal and usual אִשְׁתְּךָ we have אֶשְׁתְּךָ Ps 128.3† for no apparent reason.

For *small*, both קָטֹן and קָטָן are used in the masculine singular; in the feminine and in the plural there is only קְטַנָּה, קְטַנִּים, קְטַנּוֹת (§ 18 *f*). d

For *water*, the form with repetition (cf. מֵימֵי, מֵימַי) is not used in the abs. state, and the simple form is not used with the suffixes; cf. § 98 *e*. e

For *idol* the sg. form פֶּסֶל and the pl. form פְּסִילִים (from unattested פָּסִיל*) are used; for *pit*, sg. שַׁחַת, pl. שְׁחִיתוֹת (2 x); and perh. נְטִעִים for נֶטַע Ps 144.12(1); for *supplication* we always(2) find in the sg. תְּחִנָּה, in the pl. תַּחֲנוּנִים. Cf. also צְנִנִים alongside צִנִּים, pl. of צֵן or צִנָּה *thorn*; MH נְזִקִין (< נֶזֶק *damage*); QH נגיעין(?) (< נֶגַע *stroke*). f

(1) See A. Hurvitz, op. cit. [§ 88 M *j*, n.], p. 167.
(2) The plural at 2Ch 6.39 is suspect; the parallel text at 1Kg 8.49 has the singular.

Some nouns have such different forms in the sing. and in the plural that one wonders whether these plural forms are simply irregular or g whether they come from singular doublet, e.g. צֵלָחַת *vase*, pl. צְלָחוֹת; יַעֲנָה *ostrich*, pl. יְעֵנִים; יַעֲלָה *antelope*, pl. יְעֵלִים(1).

(1) Cf. M. Lambert, *RÉJ* 43 (1901) 213.

§ 100. Number nouns: cardinal numerals

a The nouns of number are in origin either substantives or adjectives, but all of them, to different degrees, now possess a mixed character, partly substantival and partly adjectival.

The first two numerals 1 and 2, which have a more adjectival character than all the others, must be considered separately. The numerals 3 to 10 form a homogeneous group of collective substantives. The numerals 11 to 19, composed of two closely knit nouns, the first of which expresses the unit and the second the number 10, form a group in which 11 and 12 (like 1 and 2) present some peculiarities. The numerals expressing tens from 20 to 90 form a special group.

b **Numeral 1**: Masc.: abs. אֶחָד, cst. אַחַד; fem. abs. and cst. אַחַת. The primitive form is *'aḥad* (comp. Arb. *'aḥad*, Ugr. *aḥd*). In the sing. there is spontaneous gemination of ח, § 20 *c*. For the ֶ of אֶחָד, cf. § 29 *f*. The primitive form of the feminine *'aḥadt* has, by assimilation of *d* to *t*, become *'aḥatt* > אַחַת (§ 17 *g*), with final ַ preserved by the earlier gemination; in pause אֶחָת. Plural: אֲחָדִים *several*, etc., of which the feminine form is lacking in the Bible. The form of the cst. st. אַחַד is also used for the abs. st. as a light form, e.g. in the numeral 11 אַחַד עָשָׂר (cf. § 129 *m*)(1).

(1) The aphaeretic form חַד of Ez 33.30† is suspect; it is the normal Aramaic form.

c **Numeral 2**: Masc.: abs. שְׁנַיִם (a light, contracted form שְׁנֵים[1] in the numeral 12 שְׁנֵים עָשָׂר), cst. שְׁנֵי; fem. שְׁתַּיִם (a light form שְׁתֵּים in שְׁתֵּים עֶשְׂרֵה), cst. שְׁתֵּי. The numeral 2 has the form of a dual, which is natural. The primitive form of the masc. is probably *šinayim*. The fem. שְׁתַּיִם must be pronounced *štạyim* with the plosive תּ, despite the preceding shewa (§ 19 *f*). The primitive form **šintayim* has become **šittayim*; then, by the analogy of שְׁנַיִם (with initial simple shewa) it came to be pronounced as שְׁתַּיִם with shewa, but retaining the plosive articulation *t*, which must have been used in the form **šittayim*. The anomalous form

שְׁתַּ֫יִם is therefore a hybrid form: of *šittayim it has retained the plosive character of *t* (but without its length), and of שְׁנַ֫יִם it has received the shewa(2). Of course, the תּ remains plosive in combinations such as בִּשְׁתַּ֫יִם, בִּשְׁתֵּי.

(1) Comp. אַ֫יִן and the light form אֵין, § 160 *g*. Syriac differentiates *l'aynaw(hy)* "to his eyes" and *l'ēnaw(hy)* "before him."

(2) If one should take Arb. m. *'iṯnāni* / f. *ṯintāni* as affiliated to the Heb. forms rather than Akk. *šina* / *šitta*, then the m. form would have had an exceptional initial consonantal cluster. Hoberman also argues for *štayim*, i.e. without shewa mobile, as the genuine, original shape of the numeral: *JNES* 48 (1989) 25-29. Tiberian Massoretic scholars read the form as /'ištayim/ etc.: Kimhi, מכלול, p. 140a, where the absence of dagesh in the Shin in Jon 4.11 מִשְׁתֵּים־עֶשְׂרֵה is noted; and K. Levy, op. cit. [§ 1 *a*, n.], pp. 8f. This prosthetic Alef is also attested occasionally in Phoen. The original f. form /ṯintay(m-)/ is preserved only in SH /šittəm/: Ben-Ḥayyim, *LOT*, vol. 5, p. 231.

Numerals 3-10: The nouns for 3-10 are collective substantives. Each numeral has a double form, masculine and feminine, which one may compare with the French collectives, *un sixain, une dizaine*. A most remarkable peculiarity of the numerals 3-10, which goes back to Common Semitic, is that the feminine collective is used with masculine nouns and the masculine collective with feminine nouns(1). *d*

3: masc.: abs. שָׁלֹשׁ, cst. שְׁלֹשׁ; fem. שְׁלֹשָׁה, cst. שְׁלֹ֫שֶׁת. Primitive Heb. form. *šalāš*: the *ọ*, though etymologically long, is usually written *defectively*, § 7 *c*. The primitive *ō̦* of שְׁלֹשָׁה becomes, via the segholised form שְׁלֹ֫שֶׁת(2), *ọ* in the inflection: שְׁלָשְׁתָּם, § 97 F *d*. With maqqef one finds שְׁלֹשׁ־ and שְׁלָשׁ־.

4: masc.: abs. and cst. אַרְבַּע; fem. אַרְבָּעָה, cst. אַרְבַּ֫עַת. Primitive form *'arba'* (cf. § 88 L *a*).

5: masc.: abs. חָמֵשׁ, cst. חֲמֵשׁ; fem. חֲמִשָּׁה, cst. חֲמֵ֫שֶׁת. Primitive Heb. form *ḥamiš*. The form חֲמִשָּׁה, with gemination of the שׁ, instead of the expected form חֲמֵשָׁה*, is probably due to the analogy of the following numeral שִׁשָּׁה. For the segholised ending ֶ֫ ֶת, cf. § 89 *h*.

6: masc.: abs. and cst. שֵׁשׁ; fem. שִׁשָּׁה, cst. שֵׁ֫שֶׁת. Primitive Heb. form *šidš*(3), hence, by assimilation, *šišš* > שֵׁשׁ. For the segholised ending ֶ֫ ֶת, cf. § 89 *h*.

7: masc.: abs. and cst. שֶׁ֫בַע; fem. שִׁבְעָה, cst. שִׁבְעַת. Primitive form *šab'*. In, e.g., שֶׁ֫בַע הַפָּרוֹת *the seven cows* Gn 41.20, שֶׁ֫בַע can be in the cst. state; but it can also be in the abs. state. (Cf. עֲשָׂרָה הַשְּׁבָטִים *the ten tribes*, 1Kg 11.31). The form שְׁבַע occurs only before מֵאוֹת where it is probably cst. state (cf. שִׁבְעַת אֲלָפִים) and before עֶשְׂרֵה where it is prob. abs. st.([4])(cf. שִׁבְעָה עָשָׂר). The same is true of the form תְּשַׁע (alongside תֵּשַׁע), which occurs only in תְּשַׁע מֵאוֹת and תְּשַׁע עֶשְׂרֵה.

8: masc.: abs. and cst. שְׁמֹנֶה; fem. שְׁמֹנָה, cst. שְׁמֹנַת. Primitive Heb. form *šamāniy* (comp. Arb. *ṯamān*^{in}). One always has ֶ, even when the word is prob. in the cst. state as in שְׁמֹנֶה מֵאוֹת. Compare שְׁמֹנַת with the segholised form שְׁלֹשֶׁת.

9: masc.: abs. and cst. תֵּשַׁע, fem. תִּשְׁעָה, cst. תִּשְׁעַת. Primitive Heb. form *tišʿ*. On the form תְּשַׁע, see שְׁבַע (*supra*).

10: masc.: abs. and cst. עֶשֶׂר; fem. עֲשָׂרָה, cst. עֲשֶׂרֶת. The form of the masc. is a *qatl* whilst that of the fem. is a *qatal* (of which the masc. עָשָׂר occurs in the numerals 11-19[5]).

(1) French is said to copy the Semitic usage in expressions such as *une dizaine d'hommes* and *un dizain de femmes*. This peculiar usage has not yet been explained satisfactorily. The phenomenon seems to have something to do with linguistic psychology, and perhaps we should see here mainly an aesthetic tendency towards dissymmetry. This is in essence the reason suggested by Schultens long ago: "non injucunda connubia"! Another explanation of reflex kind is that the language may have wished thus to lay greater emphasis on the substantival character of these numerals (cf. P. Joüon in *MUSJ* 6 [1913] 134ff.). The rule in Hebrew is meticulously observed, so that from the masculine or feminine form of the numeral one can infer the feminine or masculine gender of the noun (cf. § 89 *a*) ! Exceptions are rare (e.g. שְׁלֹשֶׁת נָשִׁים Gn 7.13; שְׁלֹשֶׁת כִּכְּרוֹת לֶחֶם 1Sm 10.3; שְׁלֹשֶׁת אַחְיֹתֵיהֶם Job 1.4) and may be scribal errors. The principal form is the feminine form: it is this that is used, e.g. in Arabic—the reverse in Modern Hebrew—to express the number in an absolute fashion, e.g. in "3 is half of 6" (cf. § *o*); consequently the masculine form can be deduced from it. On the choice of the form in cases of the *neuter*, cf. § 152 *g*.

(2) Contrast this with the non-segholised form שְׁמֹנַת (*infra*, 8).

(3) Cf. Arb. ordinal "6th": *sādis*,

(4) This therefore would be a reduced form. Likewise in the other numerals for 11-19, the first noun with the form of the cst. st., e.g. in שְׁלֹשׁ עֶשְׂרֵה, would be a reduced form, and not a genuine cst. st. form.

(5) In all the other numerals the feminine form is modelled on the masculine.

e **Numerals 11-19.** These numerals are composed of two closely knit nouns, the first of which expresses the unit and the second the numeral 10. Thus 11 is expressed as *one-ten*. In this group there is no subordination (genitive), but co-ordination: *one* (*and*) *ten* exactly as in now obsolete English, e.g. *five and twenty*. The first noun closely linked with the second takes a reduced form, which is often similar to the form of the cst. state. However in the nouns with ָה the reduced form (here similar to the cst. state) is extremely rare, e.g. חֲמֵשֶׁת עָשָׂר Jdg 8.10; 2Sm 19.18; שְׁמֹנַת עָשָׂר Jdg 20.25. The numbers 3-9 used here as first component of 13-19 are treated in the usual manner: the masc. form is used with fem. nouns and the fem. form with masc. nouns. For the numeral 10 one has here two new forms, which are prob. adjectival: masc. עָשָׂר, fem. עֶשְׂרֵה (with ֵ stemming from *ay*(1); comp. שְׁמֹנֶה always with ֶ, e.g. in שְׁמֹנֶה עֶשְׂרֵה בְּרָכוֹת *18 benedictions* [Talmud]). More details below.

(1) In view of some significant differences in morphology and syntax between the Hebrew and Ugaritic numerals, it is probably wrong to conclude that because of the spelling *'šrh* in the latter the He of עֶשְׂרֵה was originally consonantal. Cf. R. Hetzron in *JSS* 22 (1977) 183f.

f **Numeral 11**: Masc.: אַחַד עָשָׂר; fem. אַחַת עֶשְׂרֵה. The adjectives אֶחָד and אַחַת are here light forms, not genuine construct states (§ *b*). We also find the forms: masc.: עַשְׁתֵּי עָשָׂר, fem. עַשְׁתֵּי עֶשְׂרֵה (comp. Akk. *ištēn ešret* or *ištenšeret*)(1). These forms, which are considered by most authorities to be derived from the Akkadian, could, according to Brockelmann (*GvG*, I, p. 490) and others, be early dialectal Hebrew forms. The form עַשְׁתֵּי is an abbreviation of עַשְׁתֵּין* (comp. שְׁנֵים עָשָׂר, שְׁנֵי עָשָׂר).

(1) Cf. also Ugr. *'št 'šr*, and ESA *'št* and *'štnm*.

g **Numeral 12**: masc. שְׁנֵים עָשָׂר; fem. שְׁתֵּים עֶשְׂרֵה. We also find, though rarely: masc. שְׁנֵי עָשָׂר; fem. שְׁתֵּי עֶשְׂרֵה. The forms שְׁנֵים and שְׁתֵּים are light forms in the absolute state preferred here because of the close juncture. The rare forms שְׁנֵי and שְׁתֵּי (perh. influenced by עַשְׁתֵּי) are still further reduced(1).

(1) Certain grammarians wrongly see in שְׁנֵים and שְׁתֵּים a Qre perpetuum: then one would have to read שְׁנֵי and שְׁתֵּי, whilst the Ktiv would have to be vocalised שְׁנַ֫יִם and שְׁתַּ֫יִם respectively (cf. § 16 *f*).

h **Numerals 13-19**: In these numerals the first component (3-9), which is a substantive, has the opposite gender of the noun, whilst the second component (10), which is an adjective, has the same gender as the noun. One can say that the total number, e.g. 13, is masc. or fem., depending on whether the second component is masc. עָשָׂר or fem. עֶשְׂרֵה.

	Masculine numerals	Feminine numerals
13.	שְׁלֹשָׁה עָשָׂר	שְׁלֹשׁ עֶשְׂרֵה
14.	אַרְבָּעָה עָשָׂר	אַרְבַּע עֶשְׂרֵה
15.	חֲמִשָּׁה עָשָׂר	חֲמֵשׁ עֶשְׂרֵה
16.	שִׁשָּׁה עָשָׂר	שֵׁשׁ עֶשְׂרֵה
17.	שִׁבְעָה עָשָׂר	שְׁבַע עֶשְׂרֵה
18.	שְׁמֹנָה עָשָׂר	שְׁמֹנֶה עֶשְׂרֵה
19.	תִּשְׁעָה עָשָׂר	תְּשַׁע עֶשְׂרֵה

Example: with the masc. noun דָּבָר one says שְׁמֹנָה עָשָׂר דְּבָרִים *18 words* (comp. *18 benedictions*, § *e* end).

i **Numerals for the tens 20-90**: 20 עֶשְׂרִים, 30 שְׁלֹשִׁים, 40 אַרְבָּעִים, 50 חֲמִשִּׁים, 60 שִׁשִּׁים, 70 שִׁבְעִים, 80 שְׁמֹנִים, 90 תִּשְׁעִים. These numerals, even 20, have the ending of the plural. The numeral 20 was originally the dual of 10, Heb. עֶשְׂרַ֫יִם*(1); but the ending ִים of the other numerals replaced ַ֫יִם. The other tens, 30 etc., are thought of as the plural of the corresponding unit 3, etc. Segholised forms שֶׁ֫בַע and תֵּ֫שַׁע have not formed שְׁבָעִים* and תְּשָׁעִים*, but שִׁבְעִים and תִּשְׁעִים, probably on the analogy of עֶשְׂרִים.

(1) So also in Akk. (e.g. *ešrā*), ESA, and Eth.; see R. Hetzron, *JSS* 22 (1977) 192-95.

j **Intermediate numerals 21-99.** These numerals are expressed by joining the two components by means of ו *and*. Most often it is the ten that precedes, e.g. עֶשְׂרִים וְאֶחָד; less frequently אֶחָד וְעֶשְׂרִים(1).

(1) For details, see König, 2.215ff.

k **Numeral 100**: מֵאָה (fem.), cst. מְאַת; pl. abs. מֵאוֹת (the cst. state is not attested)(1).

(1) The Ktiv מאיות 2Kg 11.4,9,10,15† is usually read מְאָיוֹת (comp. עֲשָׂרוֹת *decades, groups of ten*); one could equally read מָאיוֹת (comp. מָאתַיִם), König, vol. 2, p. 217 reads מֵאיוֹת.

l **Numeral 200**: מָאתַ֫יִם, dual of מֵאָה, for מְאָתַ֫יִם*.

Numerals for hundreds 300-900: the noun מֵאוֹת being feminine, the nouns for the units 3-9 have the masculine form; they are put in the cst. state, e.g. 300 שְׁלֹשׁ מֵאוֹת. Note the forms שְׁבַע מֵאוֹת, § *d*; שְׁמֹנֶה מֵאוֹת, § *d*; תְּשַׁע מֵאוֹת, § *d*.

Numeral 1,000: אֶ֫לֶף (masc.); pl. אֲלָפִים, cst. אַלְפֵי.

Numeral 2,000: אַלְפַּ֫יִם, dual of אֶ֫לֶף; the cst. state would be *אַלְפֵּי (with plosive פּ).

Numerals for thousands 3,000-9,000: the noun אֲלָפִים being masculine, the nouns for the units 3-9 take the feminine ending; they are put in the cst. state, e.g. שְׁלֹ֫שֶׁת אֲלָפִים.

Intermediate numerals 101-9,999. Examples: 120 is expressed by 100 *and* 20, less frequently by 20 *and* 100; 324 is expressed by 300 *and* 20 *and* 4, less frequently by 4 *and* 20 *and* 300; 1222 is expressed by 1000, 200, 20 *and* 2 (Ezr 2.12). It appears that there is some historical evolution. In the Priestly code (P), Ez and Ch, thousands follow smaller numbers. The tens precede the units in the sources JED, Josh 1-12, Jdg, Sm and Is, whereas the reverse order is observed in Jer, P, Ez and Josh 13-24(1). m

(1) See S. Herner, *Syntax der Zahlwörter im Alten Testament* (Lund, 1893), 73ff.

For 10,000, in addition to the usual עֲשֶׂ֫רֶת אֲלָפִים, there are also special words: רְבָבָה, רִבּוֹ, רִבּוֹא(1). Likewise for **20,000** עֶשְׂרִים אֶ֫לֶף or רִבֹּתַ֫יִם or שְׁתֵּי רִבּוֹת Ne 7.71, שְׁתֵּי רִבּוֹא 7.72; **40,000** אַרְבַּע רִבּוֹא 7.66; **60,000** שֵׁשׁ־רִבֹּאוֹת Ezr 2.69. n

Intermediate numbers, e.g. **18,000** שְׁמוֹנָה עָשָׂר אֶ֫לֶף 2Sm 8.13.

Numeral 100,000: מְאַת אֶ֫לֶף Nu 2.9 etc.; מֵאָה אֶ֫לֶף 2Kg 3.4.

(1) A late form; note also the pleonastic final Alef characteristic of Qumran orthography. Cf. Kutscher, *Isaiah*, pp. 171-75; Qimron, *Hebrew of DSS*, pp. 21f.

Multiplicatives. We find the forms אַרְבַּעְתַּ֫יִם *fourfold* 2Sm 12.6; שִׁבְעָתַ֫יִם *sevenfold* Gn 4.15,24; Is 30.26?; Ps 12.7; 79.12. This is the feminine form (which is the principal form, § *d*, n.) with an ending ־ַ֫יִם, which looks like a dual, but is in fact an adverbial ending (probably dissociated from ־ָם, cf. § 91 *g*, 102 *b*); note also כִּפְלַ֫יִם *double* Is 40.2, Job 11.6. These words correspond rather closely to our *fourfold* and *sevenfold*. The obscure רִבֹּתַ֫יִם Ps 68.18 is perh. formed in the same manner(1). For other modes of expressing the multiplicative idea, cf. § 142 *q*. For the numerals of frequency, cf. § 102 *f*. o

(1) Cf. D.H. Müller, "Die numeralia multiplicativa in den Amarnatafeln und im Hebräischen," *Semitica*, I (1906), Sitzungsberichte der Kais. Akademie der Wissenschaften in Wien, Philosophische-Historische Klasse, Band CLIII, III. Abhandl., pp. 13ff.).

§ 101. Ordinal numerals

a Ordinal adjectives exist only for the first ten numerals; for above *tenth* the cardinal numerals are used (cf. § 142 *o*). **First**(1) is expressed by the adjective רִאשׁוֹן (from רֹאשׁ *head*, § 88 M *e*)(2), **second** by שֵׁנִי (f. שֵׁנִית, pl. שֵׁנִים), which is formed directly from the cardinal numeral; similarly שִׁשִּׁי **6th** is formed directly from שֵׁשׁ. The other numerals show the pattern *qatili* > קְטִילִי, which is composed of the form *qatil* and the adjectival ending ִי: **3rd** שְׁלִישִׁי, **4th** רְבִיעִי (without the Alef of אַרְבַּע), **5th** חֲמִישִׁי (the form חֲמִשִּׁי with gemination on the analogy of חֲמִשָּׁה is suspect), **7th** שְׁבִיעִי, **8th** שְׁמִינִי, **9th** תְּשִׁיעִי, **10th** עֲשִׂירִי.

(1) For vestiges of the archaic expression (as in Ugaritic) of the notion of 'first' without any specific word as in Ex 38.14 אֶל־הַכָּתֵף vs. 15 לַכָּתֵף הַשֵּׁנִית, see J. Blau in *JNWSL* 10 (1982) 5-7.

(2) This appears to be a comparatively late, secondary formation. In the creation account (Gn 1), the first day is called יוֹם אֶחָד, whereas the subsequent days are designated by the appropriate, regular ordinals such as שְׁלִישִׁי, רְבִיעִי. See S.E. Loewenstamm, *Tarbiz* 24 (1954) 249-51.

b The feminine forms end in ִית, e.g. שְׁלִישִׁית *3rd*; we very rarely find the ending ִיָּה: שְׁלִשִׁיָּה Is 19.24; 15.5 = Jer 48.34† and עֲשִׂירִיָּה Is 6.13†. These same forms express **fractions**, e.g. שְׁלִישִׁית *third part, one third*. For fractions there also exist certain special words: **half** חֲצִי, rather rarely מַחֲצִית(1), twice מֶחֱצָה Nu 31.36,43†; **one third** שָׁלִישׁ; **a quarter** רֶבַע, רֹבַע(2); **one fifth** חֹמֶשׁ; **one tenth** עִשָּׂרוֹן, pl. עֶשְׂרֹנִים (*qatalān* pattern, § 88 M *b*); מַעֲשֵׂר *tenth part, tithe*.

For **two thirds** one says פִּי שְׁנַיִם Dt 21.17; 2Kg 2.9; Zech 13.8 (whereas שְׁנַיִם means *double* Ex 22.3,6,8).

For the notion of **how many times**, cf. § 102 *f*.

(1) Ugaritic fractions, except for those for 1/2 (!) and 2/3, show a prefix /m-/ and a suffix /-t/. Note מַעֲשֵׂר.

(2) Though personal names of segholate pattern, שֶׁלֶשׁ and שִׁלְשָׁה may also be noted.

CHAPTER IV: PARTICLES.

We call *particles* any part of speech which is not a noun, pronoun, or verb, namely the adverb, the preposition, the conjunction and the interjection. The demarcation between these diverse categories of particles is often imprecise; the same word can, for instance, be used as an adverb and as a preposition.

§ 102. Adverb.

Certain adverbs are primitive, e.g. לֹא *no, not*, שָׁם *there*, אָז *then*; others are *derived*, e.g. אָמְנָם *truly, in truth* (from אֹ֫מֶן, 1 x); finally numerous adverbs are simply other parts of speech (substantives, adjectives, infinitive absolutes) used in an adverbial role, e.g. הַרְבֵּה *much* (Hifil inf. abs. of רָבָה: *act of making much, in making much*, § 79 *q*). Often the adverbial idea is expressed by a group of two or more words, especially preposition and substantive, e.g. בֶּאֱמֶת *truly, really*, לָ֫מָּה *why?* (לְ and pronoun מָה), מַדּוּעַ *for what reason?* (מָה + יָדוּעַ, *scibile quid?* with weakened יָדוּעַ in the sense of *thing*(1): "what thing?" = *why?*). a

(1) Comp. Jewish Arm. מַדְּעַם from *middā*ʻ + *ma* "scibile quid," *something* (Syr. *meddem*). In the Arabic dialect described by A. Socin, *Diwan aus Centralarabien* (Leipzig, 1900-1), § 63 *d*, *ʻilm* "knowledge" has come to mean "thing," e.g. *weš ʻilm* "why?" P. Joüon argued for a distinction between לָ֫מָּה and מַדּוּעַ in *MUSJ* 10 (1925) 15f., whereas J. Barr holds that there is scarcely any distinction in meaning between the two: *JThSt* 36 (1985) 1-33.

The **derived adverbs** are few and far between. With the ending ָם: אָמְנָם *truly, in truth*, but after the interrogative הֲ: הַאֻמְנָם (from אֹ֫מֶן, 1 x); דּוּמָם *silently*; חִנָּם *in favour, for nothing, gratuitously, in vain, for no reason* (from חֵן *grace*; comp. *gratia* and *gratis*); רֵיקָם *empty, empty-handed, for no reason* (from רֵיק *empty*); יוֹמָם *by day* (Lat. *diu, interdiu*). With the ending ֹם we have only פִּתְאֹם *suddenly* and שִׁלְשׁוֹם (11 x; שִׁלְשֹׁם 12 x) *the day before yesterday*. These endings have been explained in diverse ways. Some writers see in ָם the old ending of the indeterminate accusative (§ 93 *b*)(1), whilst others see in it a special ending(2). For some nouns with ֹם one must first find out if the *ọ* is b etymologically long or not. פִּתְאֹם may be derived from *pit'am* (from פֶּתַע *instant*) > *pit'ām* by attenuation of the ע and compensatory lengthening of the *a*. As regards שִׁלְשׁוֹם, this seems to be a loan from Akkadian *ina šalši ūme* "in three days," in which case the *ọ* would be long. The Akkadian adverbial ending *-u(m)* seems to indicate the derivation ם- < *um*(3). Here also belong הֲלֹם and עֵירֹם.

With the ending *annīṯ* composed of *ann* and the feminine ending *īṯ* (§ *c*) we find the two adverbs of manner אֲחֹרַנִּית *backwards*(4) and קְדֹרַנִּית *lugubriously*.

(1) For example, חִנָּם *gratis* can be compared with Arb. *majjānan* "gratis" in the indeterminate accusative, and Ugr. *šPšm* "at sunset(?)" (Gordon, *UT*, § 11.4,5); also Greek μάτην *in vain*, acc. of μάτη.

(2) In יוֹמָם the radical מ may have been doubled; cf. Syr. *'imâmâ*; or more likely *âm* could be an adverbial ending, here specifically indicating time: "daytime", hence Fr. *la journée*, Ital. *la giornata*. Comp. perhaps צָהֳרַיִם *noon*, § 91 *g*. The latter explanation is more likely in the light of AC *ḫa-ya-ma* "alive" (Sivan, p. 131) and comp. also El Amarna 137.21 *ri-qa-mi* (= רֵיקָם).

(3) See K. Deller in *Or* 34 (1965) 40.

(4) Different from אָחוֹר used adverbially in the sense of "at the back." See P. Joüon in *MUSJ* 10 (1925) 4f.

c **Adverbs of suppletion.** This is the name given to diverse parts of speech which, functioning as adverbs, make up for the lack of adverbs.

Adjectives. Rarely a masculine adjective(1), e.g. רַב sometimes in the sense of *much, quite*; מַר *bitterly* Is 33.7; Zeph 1.14 (poetic); רָחוֹק *far* Ps 22.2; 119.155. Rather rarely a sing. feminine adjective: רִאשֹׁנָה *first, formerly* (9 x; but usually בָּרִאשֹׁנָה 22 x; לְרִ' 2 x)(2); with final ת(3): רַבַּת *much* Ps 120.6; 123.4; 129.1; יְהוּדִית *in a Jewish fashion, in the Jewish language*, and likewise אֲרָמִית, אַשְׁדּוֹדִית; cf. קְדֹרַנִּית, אֲחֹרַנִּית, § *b* (end).

(1) The adjectives טוֹב *good* and רַע *bad* do not appear to be used in the adverbial sense of *well* and *badly* respectively. For *well* we find the inf. abs. הֵיטֵב and for *badly* one could no doubt have used the inf. abs. הָרֵעַ, though it is not found in this sense.

(2) For the antonym we only find בָּאַחֲרֹנָה 6 x and לָאַ' 2 x *then, finally*.

(3) A vestige of the old adverbial use of the status absolutus: see W. von Soden, *Grundriss der akkadischen Grammatik* (Rome, 1952), § 113 *n*, and T. Muraoka, op. cit. [§ 98 *f*, n.], § 60.

d **Substantives:** יַחַד *together* [(*in*) *unison*, (*as*) *a group*, cf. 1Ch 12,17];

יַחְדָּו(1)(very rarely יַחְדָּיו) *together*; סָבִיב *around* (as substantive once in the singular, but rather frequently in the plural סְבִיבִים, סְבִיבוֹת *environs*; cf. § 103 *n*); מְהֵרָה *rapidly*, (*with*) *speed*; בֶּהָלָה *suddenly* Lv 26.16†; אֱמֶת *truly* Jer 10.10; Ps 132.11† (usually בֶּאֱמֶת); פֶּתַע *suddenly* (poetic; also לְפֶתַע, בְּפֶתַע); בֶּטַח *safely* (more often לָבֶטַח); מֵישָׁרִים (*with*) *righteousness, justly*. These substantives, from the syntactical point of view, must be considered as being in the adverbial accusative (cf. § 126 *d*). Several adverbs, whose substantival meaning is not apparent, are originally substantives.

Much more frequently the adverbial notion is expressed by a substantive preceded by a preposition, especially ב and ל (see several examples cited above). Examples: לְבַד *apart* [not necessarily *alone*(2)]; לָרֹב *much*, לְשָׁלוֹם and בְּשָׁלוֹם *peacefully*, בְּמִרְמָה *fraudulently*, etc.

(1) Probably from *yaḥday* with a fem. ending *ay* as in אַשְׁרֵי (rather than pl. ending). The suffix has a vague value: (*in*) *unison with this*, (*in*) *its unity* (cf. § 146 *j*). An alternative proposal by Brockelmann (*ZA* 14 [1899] 344-46) to see here an archaic adverbial ending /ū/ as in Akkadian would make this a unique example of such.
(2) E.g. 1Kg 18.6 לְבַדּוֹ "Ahab went *on his own*," which does not exclude an escort.

e **Infinitive absolute:** Hifil: הֵיטֵב *well*, הַרְבֵּה *much* (§ *a*), הַרְחֵק *far*, הַשְׁכֵּם *early in the morning*, הַעֲרֵב *in the evening* 1Sm 17.16†; Piel: מַהֵר *fast*. These words, strictly speaking, mean: *act of doing well, of doing much, of moving away, of doing something in the morning, the evening, of doing something fast*. The infinitive absolute used adverbially is an extension of the use of the inf. absolute as accusative of internal object after a verb (cf. § 123 *r*).

f **Cardinal numerals** used **adverbially** for **number of times:** אַחַת *once*, *semel* Lv 16.34; שְׁתַּיִם *twice*, *bis* Ne 13.20; שָׁלֹשׁ *thrice*, *ter* Job 33.29, etc. This use can be explained in terms of the ellipsis of the fem. word פַּעַם *time*.

Ordinal numerals used **adverbially** to express **how many times:** שֵׁנִית *for the second time*, *secundo*, *secundum* Gn 22.15; בַּשְּׁבִיעִית *at the seventh time* 1Kg 18.44. The word פַּעַם here also is understood, cf. בַּפַּעַם הַשְּׁבִיעִית Josh 6.16.

g There are some other ways of expressing the **adverbial notion.** Thus, an adverbial Hifil (§ 54 *d*) is equivalent to a verb with a general meaning such as *to do, to act*, accompanied by an adverb, e.g. הֵיטַבְתָּ לִרְאוֹת Jer 1.12, literally "you have done well by looking," which is equivalent to *you have seen well* (cf. § 124 *n*). The verbs יסף and שׁוב contain our adverbial notion of *still, once again* (§ 177 *b*). For the notion of *immediately* we find Piel מִהַר used in the sense of *to act fast*: 1Kg 20.41 וַיְמַהֵר וַיָּסַר *he immediately removed* (probably also 1Sm 28.20: *he fell at once*). This same verb used transitively is equivalent to *to bring quickly* (Gn 18.6; 1Kg 22.9); likewise Hifil הֵרִיץ *to carry quickly* (*running*) (1Sm 17.17; 2Ch 35.13). A sentence such as קִרְאוּ בְקוֹל־גָּדוֹל 1Kg 18.27 "cry in a loud(er) voice" is equivalent to "cry more loudly." The adverbial notion of *very much* is rendered by an adverbial Hifil in, e.g. 2Sm 18.8 וַיֶּרֶב לֶאֱכֹל מִן *et multum egit edendo prae* = "he devoured *more* than ..."

h We shall list below some adverbs which are particularly common or are of particular interest.

Demonstrative adverbs: A) in the strict sense of the term (as the demonstrative proper זֶה, the primary meaning of which is *here*, § 143 *a*) and presupposing the object as present; and B) demonstrative adverbs in a broad sense:

A): פֹּה *here* (without movement, Lat. *hīc*); more common than בָּזֶה; מִזֶּה *from here*; B): שָׁם *there*, more frequent for this sense than שָׁמָּה; מִשָּׁם *from there*.

A): הֵנָּה[1] *hither* (Lat. *hūc*); more frequent than הֲלֹם; B): שָׁמָּה[2] *thither*, more frequent for this sense than שָׁם, § 93 *e*; הָלְאָה *yonder*.

A): עַתָּה *now*, § 32 *f*; B): אָז *then*.

A): כֹּה *thus* (*in this fashion*), e.g. כֹּה אָמַר יהוה "*thus* says Jahweh" (in order to proclaim his words); B): כֵּן *thus* (*in this fashion*), e.g. וַיְהִי כֵן "and it was *thus*"; similarly כָּכָה is *retrospective*, but has an intensive force.

(1) To be distinguished from the pronoun הֵנָּה *they* (fem.).

(2) On the gemination, cf. Arb. *ṯumma*, and Arm. *tammâ(n)*.

i **Interrogative adverbs**: הֲ *is it that? num?* (for the vocalisation, cf. § *l*); הֲלֹא *is it not that ...?, nonne?*; לָמָּה *why?* (and לָמָה § 37 *d*), לָמָּה זֶּה *why then?* (usually without maqqef); מַדּוּעַ *for what reason?* (§ *a*; more precise than לָמָּה); אֵיךְ *how?*, more frequent than אֵיכָה; אַיֵּה *where?* (without movement, Lat. *ubi?*), rarely אֵיפֹה[1]; אָנָה *whither?, where to?* (Lat. *quo?*), more frequent than אָן; מֵאַיִן *where from?*, more frequent than אֵי מִזֶּה. For "*where?, through where?*," we find אֵי־זֶה הַדֶּרֶךְ נַעֲלֶה 2Kg 3.8 "*by which way* shall we go up?," literally "where is the way by which we are going to go up?"; מָתַי *when?*; עַד־מָתַי *until when?*, rarely עַד־אָנָה (compare Lat. *usquequo*, also in the temporal sense).

(1) A distinction must be maintained between אֵיפֹה *where?* and אֵפוֹא, which, in origin, is probably a demonstrative particle, but, in actual usage, a logical particle, *then, therefore*.

Negative adverbs: לֹא *no, not* (35 x[1] לוֹא according to the massorah); אַל *do not* (for prohibition, like *ne* in Latin); אַיִן, אֵין(2) (§ 160 *g*) *there is not, it is not* (adverb of non-existence, opposite of יֵשׁ *there is, it is*, adverb of existence); לְבִלְתִּי (§ 93 *q*), special negative of the infinitive cst. Besides these four common negatives, the use of which will be explained in the Syntax section (§ 160) as well as that of the rare negatives בַּל, בְּלִי, בִּלְתִּי, there are also negatives with the special nuances טֶרֶם *not yet*, אֶפֶס *no more*. *j*

(1) Not counting combinations with proclitic -ה, -ב, and -ו. If these are included, לוא occurs 187 times (out of a total of 5184 x). On a problem of computation involved, see AF, pp. 186f.

The plene spelling is the most common in Jer, and also in books earlier than Jer, but not later: see also Barr, *Spellings*, pp. 154-58. In DSS it far outweighs the defective spelling. The historical evolution appears to have been /la'/> /lā/> /lō/ (cf. § 98 *f*). Hence the final Alef differs in origin from that so typical of DSS. See Brock., *GvG*, I, § 253 A, a, and Qimron, *Hebrew of DSS*, pp. 21f. The Heb. negative, then, would be distinct from Ugr. /l/= most likely /lā/ (Huehnergard, *Ugr. Vocabulary*, pp. 25, 255). In other words, the Alef of the Hebrew negative may originally not have been a vowel letter. Cf. § 7 *b*. If, on the other hand, לא be a rare example of early use of Alef as mater lectionis, it may have been introduced to keep this common word graphically distinct from another equally frequent לה, originally "to him" (§ 94 *h*) as well as "to her."

(2) אִי in Job 22.30 ? and in the proper noun אִי־כָבוֹד 1Sm 4.21; 14.3 is probably a negative form reduced from אין. Phoen. also has negative *'y*.

Adverbs with suffixes (Paradigm 20). Some adverbs can take suffixes. This can be easily understood for an adverb whose substantival force is still apparent, e.g. לְבַד literally *separately, alone*, § *d* (לְבַדִּי, לְבַדְּךָ, לְבַדּוֹ etc.); cf. also יַחְדָּו, § *d*. But some adverbs, which are either primitive or whose substantival force is no longer manifest also take suffixes: the pronoun, logically subject, and which, in consequence, ought to be separated, is attracted by adverbs, which turn it into a suf- *k* fix(1). Thus with הִנֵּה *behold* side by side with הִנֵּה־הוּא (e.g. Ru 3.2) one has הֵנוֹ (3 x; the form הִנֵּהוּ, Ktiv of Jer 18.3 is ?)(2). The use of the suffixes with the form הִנֵּה, אֵין, and עוֹד *still* is rather unique (see Paradigm 20). One should note the suffixes such as ־ֵנִי, ־ֶנִּי similar to those of the future. Their origin is not clear. Perhaps one said הִנְנִי *here I am*, הִנֶּנּוּ *here we are* on the analogy of the impv. *רְאֵנִי and *רְאֶנּוּ(3). Then *ənn* was perhaps extended to the adverb אֵין (which is well-nigh antonymous) and to עוֹד. One may note that עוֹד, which is probably in origin a substantive (*repetition, continuation*), has the form עוֹדִי (4 x) alongside עוֹדֶנִּי. One has הִנְּךָ, עוֹדְךָ with ָ as in the majority of the prepositions; the ֶ of אֵינְךָ is probably due to the influence of the preceding vowel ֵ (comp. מִמְּךָ). Outside of the pause one has הִנְנִי with the omission of the gemination, § 18 *m*; twice only הִנֵּנִי Gn 22.7; 27.18. Besides הִנֶּנּוּ (3 x) we find הִנְנוּ (4 x), although we cannot see the reason for the choice. As for אַיֵּה *where?* we only find אַיֶּכָּה Gn 3.9†, אַיָּם, אַיּוֹ; from יֵשׁ *there is* (יֶשׁ־) only יֶשְׁךָ, יֶשְׁכֶם Gn 24.49†, הֲיִשְׁכֶם Dt 13.4, and the anomalous, though probably authentic, form יֶשְׁנוֹ(4) Dt 29.14; 1Sm 14.39; 23.23; Esth 3.8†, with a נ of analogous origin (comp. קָבְנוֹ Nu 23.13, § 82 *l*).

(1) Cf. Brock., *GvG*, II, pp. 264ff.

(2) < **hinnahu*, which can be postulated as an earlier stage of the form, and it agrees with SH /inna/ and is akin to Arb. /'inna/ of similar function: see Ben-Ḥayyim, *LOT*, vol. 5, p. 242.

(3) The secondary form הִנֵּה, alongside הֵן, is perhaps derived from הִנְנִי (the ֵה of אַיֵּה perhaps has a similar origin). On the unique form הִנֶּה־נָּא, cf. § 18 *i*, n.

(4) Given the distribution of the form יֶשְׁנוֹ, one hesitates to accept the suggestion by J. Blau that the form is due to the analogy of MH אֵינוֹ (*IOS* 2 [1972] 61f.).

l **Vocalisation of the interrogative ה**(1). The primitive Hebrew form is *ha*. Unlike the *a* of the article (§ 35 *b*), of the pronoun *ma* (§ 37 *c*), of *wa* of the type וַיִּקְטֹל (§ 47 *a*), this *a* does not exert any pressure on the following consonant, which as a consequence is not doubled. The primitive short *a* in open syllables is not maintained, but becomes extremely short *ă*, e.g. הֲלֹא *is it not that ...? nonne?* One nevertheless finds some examples of doubled consonant and numerous examples where the short vowel is maintained in an open syllable.

(1) Called by mediaeval Jewish grammarians הֵא הַתְּמִיהָה *He of surprise*, on account of the fact that the sense of this ה is sometimes exclamatory rather than interrogative;

cf. § 161 *a*.

Before shewa (simple or nuanced), as the ḥaṭef pataḥ cannot be retained, we have ַ, e.g. הַבְרָכָה *num benedictio?* (= *[is there] a blessing?*) Gn 27.38; הַמְכַסֶּה *num celans?* (=*[shall I] hide?*) Gn 18.17 (comp. the same form with the article Lv 3.3 LXX: τὸ κατακαλύπτον *that which conceals*, § 35 *c*). With the article there is virtual gemination; with the interrogative ה, which does not require gemination, there can, however be virtual gemination, judging from the cases where there is genuine gemination). In some cases the consonant (even ר) is geminated, e.g. הַלְבֶן *num filio?* (= *to a son?*) Gn 17.17; הַבְּדֶרֶךְ *num in via* ? (= *in the way?*) Ez 20.30; הַכְּתֹנֶת *num tunica?* (= *the tunic?*) Gn 37.32; always הַרְּאִיתֶם *num vidistis?* (= *surely you saw?*) 1Sm 10.24; 17.25; 2Kg 6.32† (cf. § 23 *a*). m

Before a guttural (but not ר) there takes place a slight slowing-down of the pronunciation, which prevents the short *a* from becoming very short: we therefore have ַ in open syllables (§ 28 *b*), e.g. הַאֵלֵךְ *num ibo?* (= *surely I should go?*)(1). If the pataḥ is to be found before a guttural followed by qameṣ, it becomes ֶ (§ 29 *f*), e.g., הֶחָכָם *num sapiens?* (= *is he wise?*) Ec 2.19 (comp. the same form with the article in 2.16*b*: *the wise man*. With the article, virtual gemination takes place; with the interrogative ה it is rather unlikely). The ר, which (is not a guttural at all, § 5 *n*) has here no reason to be treated like the gutturals; it is therefore treated as the other consonants, e.g. הֲרָאִיתָ *num vidisti?* (= *surely you saw?*) (Comp. הַרְאִיתֶם, § *m*). The divine name יהוה is pronounced אֲדֹנָי, § 16 *f*, so that we have הַיהוה *num Dominus?* (= *surely the Lord is ...?*) Jer 8.19†. n

(1) Compare this with ַ, instead of ֲ, before a guttural as in הַעִידֹתִי, § 80 *m* and הַחִלֹּתִי, § 82 *n*.

Comparison with the vocalisation of the article (cf. § 35). The ה of the article has a short *a* which exerts pressure on the following consonant and tends to trigger gemination. Before a guttural, if there is no gemination, the vowel is ָ, which never occurs with the interrogative ה(1); if there is virtual gemination then we have ַ or ֶ. These same vowels also occur with the interrogative ה, but for another reason, namely the slowing-down of pronunciation. o

(1) Contrast, for instance, הָאַף *the nose, the anger* and הַאַף *num etiam?*.

§ 103. Preposition.

a Apart from the monoconsonantal prepositions בְּ, כְּ, and לְ, and some other rather old prepositions of obscure origin, prepositions are old nouns used first as adverbs, which were subsequently used as prepositions, namely before a noun or its equivalent. Thus *'aḥar (Heb. אָחָר*, cst. אַחַר; cf. § n) was originally a substantive meaning *the back*, used afterwards as an adverb in the sense of *at the back, behind* (Gn 22. 13?), and in the temporal sense of *then, afterwards* (Gn 18.5); and finally as a preposition *at the back of sth, behind sth* in the local (Gn 37.17) or temporal (15.1) sense. Likewise עַל originally meant *the high, the height*; it is still used in this sense in Ho 7.16; 11.7, and as an adverb *above* in 2Sm 23.1. A preposition, being originally a noun, is considered as *nomen regens* (§ 92 a) linked to the following noun.

b **Prefixed prepositions** בְּ, כְּ, and לְ. The three monoconsonantal prepositions בְּ *in*, כְּ *like*, and לְ *to* are always prefixed to a noun, hence sometimes called proclitics. Though the primitive form of בְּ was probably *bi, whilst that of כְּ and לְ was probably *ka and *la(1) respectively, בְּ is treated in a manner similar to כְּ and לְ(2). The three prefixed prepositions are usually vocalised *weak* (that is to say, with shewa or its substitutes), though in certain cases special, *strong* (i.e. ◌ַ) vocalisation is applied.

I. **Weak vocalisation.** Usually, and excepting the special cases to be enumerated below, the preposition takes a simple shewa, a vestige of the primitive short vowel, e.g. לְאִישׁ (even in major pause: 1Kg 2.2). Before a shewa the preposition has the vowel *i*; thus with the cst. state דְּבַר we find בִּדְבַר, כִּדְבַר, and לִדְבַר(3). But if the consonant is י, this י becomes quiescent, § 26 b; e.g., with the cst. state pl. יְמֵי (from יוֹם *day*) one has לִימֵי, כִּימֵי, בִּימֵי (and similarly מִימֵי, § d, וַיְמֵי, § 104 c). Before a ḥaṭef (nuanced shewa) we have the short vowel with the nuance of ḥaṭef, e.g. כַּאֲשֶׁר *as*, כַּאֲרִי *like a lion* (§ 35 e); לֶאֱנוֹשׁ *to (the) man*, בָּאֱנִיָּתִי* *in my ship*(4). With the Qal inf. cst., we sometimes find, alongside the normal pattern לַעֲמֹד, the type לַחְפֹּר, § 68 e.

The inf. cst. אֱמֹר with לְ becomes לֵאמֹר *in saying* (for לֶאֱמֹר*, § 24 *e*; 73 *g*), no doubt due to the frequency(5) of this form, for we also find בֶּאֱמֹר (and likewise imperative וֶאֱמֹר, § 104 *c*).

With אֱלֹהִים *god*, no doubt because of the frequency of this word, we find בֵּאלֹהִים, כֵּא', לֵא' (and וֵאלֹהִים, § 104 *c*); however, with the sing. (rather rare and poetic) we find לֶאֱלוֹהַּ (וֶאֱ'), once לֵאלֹהוֹ Hb 1.11 (prob. because the word is longer; comp. BA לֶאֱלָהּ, but לֵאלָהָא, לֵאלָהֵי, לֵאלָהַי etc.).

For the vocalisation before the infinitive of the verbs הָיָה and חָיָה, cf. § 79 *s*, e.g. הֱיוֹת, לִהְיוֹת.

אָדוֹן *lord* with בְּ, כְּ, and לְ (and וְ, § 104 *c*) receives a highly unique treatment. In certain forms with אֲ, this א becomes quiescent (no doubt, as in the preceding cases, because of the frequency of these forms); but the preceding ַ, though it is now found in open syllables, is maintained (comp. בָּארוּמָה for בַּאֲ' Jdg 9.41). The reason for this anomaly may have been a desire to avoid too great a difference with the forms with ֲ ַ. In the singular, א is quiescent with the suffix of the 1st pers. sg. (incidentally, the only form that actually occurs) לַאדֹנִי (without suffix: cst. לַאֲדֹן Mi 4.13†). In the plural, א is not quiescent in the cst. state (e.g. לַאֲדֹנֵי) nor in the forms containing the theme אֲדֹנֵי of the cst. state, namely the forms with plural suffix, לַאֲדֹנֵיכֶם, לַאֲדֹנֵינוּ, לַאֲדֹנֵיהֶם(6). It is quiescent in the other forms, namely in the forms with a singular suffix: לַאדֹנָי, לַאדֹנֶיךָ, לַאדֹנָיו, לַאדֹנֶיהָ(7). The divine name יהוה is pronounced אֲדֹנָי, so that a form like ליהוה must be pronounced לַאדֹנָי.

(1) /li/ in Ugr.: Huehnergard, *Ugr. Vocabulary*, p. 27, but *bi-i* (Sivan, p. 132, and Huehnergard, op. cit., pp. 27,53,112).

(2) The Greek and Latin transliterations make no distinction between these three prepositions, either: see Brønno, *Morphologie*, pp. 216-24; Sperber, *Hist. .Gram.*, pp. 208f.

(3) Compare this with דִּבְרֵי from *dabrē*, § 96 B *b*. But one could equally have said that כִּדְבַר and לִדְבַר have *i* on the analogy of בִּדְבַר. The best synchronic explanation is the traditional one, according to which the first of two simple shewas, which both presuppose a primitive short vowel, changes to *i*.

(4) On the ambiguity of a form such as בַּאֲנִיָּה, cf. § 35 *e*.

(5) Same reason of frequency for לִנְפֹּל alongside of בִּנְפֹל, כִּנְפֹל, § 49 *f*.

(6) It appears that in the form of the st. cst., which is shorter, the longer vocalisation of ֲ and ֵ may have been preferred by way of compensation.

(7) לַאדֹנִים* would probably have been possible also.

c II. **Strong vocalisation,** namely ָ. In בָּ and לָ we have the primitive *a* (but see § *b*, n. 1); כָּ is due to the analogy of בָּ and לָ. This *a* does not exert any pressure on the following consonant, and consequently there is no gemination. (Contrast the *a* of the article **ha*, of the pronoun **ma*, and of the *wa* of the form וַיִּקְטֹל.) The strong vocalisation does not occur except before certain categories of fully or specially stressed monosyllabic words (in the strict or loose sense of the term). The reason for the strong vocalisation is therefore of a rhythmic nature. The following is a list of the cases where this strong vocalisation occurs:

A) Cases common to the three prepositions בּ, כּ, and ל: Before the demonstrative זֶה and זֹאת, and even the dissyllabic אֵלֶּה, e.g. בָּזֶה(1), בָּאֵלֶּה(2). But, when the stress is weak, we find the weak vocalisation, e.g. Gn 2.23 לְזֹאת. Compare the vocalisation with ָ before the heavy suffixes בָּכֶם, כָּכֶם, לָכֶם, בָּהֶם, כָּהֵם (ṣeré ![3]), לָהֶם as opposed to בְּךָ and לְךָ.

B) Special cases with ל: 1) Before the monosyllabic infinitives (in the strict or broad sense): לָשֵׂאת, לָצֵאת, לָתֵת, לָקַחַת, לָשֶׁבֶת, לָקוּם (from שְׂאֵת, § 78 *l*). However, when the stress is weak, we find the weak vocalisation, e.g. Gn 16.3 לְשֶׁבֶת אַבְרָם (in close juncture, as with the genitive, § 124 *g*: *mērḇa* with *ṭifḥa*); 2) before certain specially stressed monosyllables, namely in pause, e.g. לָנֶפֶשׁ in intermediate pause, Lv 19.28; Nu 9.10; לָנָפֶשׁ Nu 5.2; לָטֹרַח Is 1.14; 3) when the group constitutes a locution, e.g. לָבֶטַח *safely*; לָרֹב *abundantly*; לָעַד *for eternity, for ever*; לָנֶצַח *for eternity, for ever* (but לְנֵצַח נְצָחִים). 4) when there is a repetition of the noun, e.g. פֶּה לָפֶה *from one end to the other* 2Kg 10.21; 21.16†; מִדּוֹר לָדוֹר Is 34.10 (not in pause); בֵּין מַיִם לָמָיִם Gn 1.6(4). Comp. the analogous case for וָ, § 104 *d*.

N.B. The special treatment of ל is solely due to the fact that this preposition sometimes takes the strong stress, which is not the case with ב and כ. Thus בְּקוּם is, in fact, always found in close juncture (Ps 76.10; 124.2; Pr 28.12,28†).

On the forms of ב, כ, and ל with the **article**, cf. § 35 *e*, with the **interrogative** pronoun מָה, § 37 *d*(5). On the inflection of ב and ל, see § *f*, and on that of כ, § *g*.

(1) בָּזֶה is generally adverbial: *here*, § 102 *h*; in the sense of *in this* only four

times: 1Sm 16.8,9, Ec 7.18, Esth 2.13†.
(2) In a form like בָּאֵ֫לֶּה, the ָ cannot be that of the article. In fact, a demonstrative can take the article only when it is used as an adjective, namely after a determinate noun, e.g. in כַּמְּלָכִים הָאֵ֫לֶּה *like these kings* (§ 137 *e*). A form compounded from a preposition and the demonstrative therefore cannot take the article. Thus a form such as בָּזֶה* is impossible.
(3) Once כָּהֵם 2Kg 17.15 (with silluq), and כָּהֵן once only (Ez 18.14). Note also that בָּהֵן (not בָּהֵן) is by far the commoner form.
(4) With רַע and רָע there are some peculiar features, e.g. בֵּין טוֹב לָרַע Lv 27.33 (in minor pause), but בֵּין טוֹב לְרָע 1Kg 3.9 (in major pause). It seems that ָ is avoided when it can be taken for that of the article; thus one always finds לְעָם, e.g. Jer 32.38.
(5) One ought to note the difference in vocalisation between, e.g., בַּמֶּה, § 37 *d* and בָּזֶה. Perhaps בַּזֶּה, for example, was avoided because this form would have seemed to have the article (cf. note 2). Compare the vocalisation of the ו in וַיִּקְטֹל, § 104 *c*.

Occasionally prefixed preposition מִן. The preposition מִן־ *from* (Lat. *de, ex, a*) shows a most peculiar treatment which can be summarised by the following two statements: A) generally the ן is assimilated to the following consonant; B) generally this following consonant is doubled. *d*

Details: A) 1) Fairly frequently, irrespective of the nature of the consonant (guttural or not), the intact form מִן־ (always with maqqef, save Ex 2.7 with a disjunctive accent!) is maintained (especially in the book of Chronicles)(1).

2) In particular, before the ה of the article, מִן־ is usually maintained, no doubt for the sake of euphony, e.g. מִן־הָאֲדָמָה Gn 2.7(2).

B) 1) Before a non-guttural, gemination usually takes place, e.g., מִיָּמִים. However, before י gemination hardly ever occurs(3), and the י becomes quiescent; e.g., with the pl. cst. state יְמֵי one finds מִימֵי, as one has בִּימֵי, כִּימֵי, לִימֵי (§ *b*), and probably on the analogy of these forms; with יְהוּדָה we find מִיהוּדָה.

2) With a guttural (even ח) virtual gemination hardly occurs; we therefore find ֵ, in open syllables, e.g. מֵחֹ֫דֶשׁ *since (the) month*. We find virtual gemination with ח in מִחוּץ *outside* (comp. הַחוּץ, הַחוּ֫צָה), מִהְיוֹת (comp. לִהְיוֹת, בִּהְיוֹת, § 79 *s*), מִחוּט Gn 14.23† (comp. הַחוּט *the string*). N.B. The divine name יהוה is pronounced אֲדֹנָי, so that we have מֵיְהוָה = מֵאֲדֹנָי; with יַהְוֶה* we should read מִיַּהְוֶה* (§ 16 *f*).

N.B. We fairly often meet the poetic form מִנִּי (§ 93 *q*), e.g., Jdg 5.14; Is 46.3; especially in Job (19 x) and Psalms (8 x); twice מִנֵּי־ Is

30.11 (why?). Comp. מִנִּי *from me* (with suffix of the 1st pers.), § *h*. On the inflection of מִן, see § *h*.

(1) See Polzin, p. 66, and Qimron, *Hebrew of DSS*, pp. 30f.

(2) For a (possibly full) list of exceptions to the rule that the full form of the preposition מִן is used when followed by the definite article, see A. Sperber in *JBL* 62 (1943) 141-43 [= *Hist. Gram.*, pp. 4f.].

(3) Cp. § 18 *m*: הַיְלָדִים, וַיְקַטֵּל. With doubling: מִיְּשֵׁנֵי Dn 12.2, מִירֻשָּׁתְךָ 2Ch 20.11.

e **Inflection of the prepositions** (Paradigm 20). The prepositions, which are considered as nouns, take the suffixes in analogous fashion(1). The suffixes of the prepositions are generally those of the nouns; however there are a fair number of exceptions, especially with the primitive prepositions. With some of these prepositions, in the 2nd fem. sing. and the 1st pl., we have ◌ָ instead of the ◌ֵ of the noun. In the 2nd feminine sg. we have לָךְ (primitive form *la*, § *b*), which contrasts with סוּסֵךְ and (prob. following לָךְ) בָּךְ, עִמָּךְ, אִתָּךְ, אוֹתָךְ (cf. הִנָּךְ and עוֹדָךְ, § 102 *k*); but we have מִמֵּךְ and בֵּינֵךְ (אֵינֵךְ, § 102 *k*). The pausal form of the 2nd m. takes ◌ָךְ (בָּךְ, לָךְ, עִמָּךְ, אִתָּךְ, אוֹתָךְ) whilst in the noun it takes ◌ֶךָ (on the analogy of ל"ה nouns, § 94 *c*). In the 1st pl., unlike סוּסֵנוּ, we find לָנוּ and (probably following לָנוּ) בָּנוּ, עִמָּנוּ, אִתָּנוּ, אֹתָנוּ; but we also find מִמֶּנּוּ (הִנֵּנוּ, הִנֶּנּוּ, הִנְנוּ). In the 3rd pl. the prepositions generally have the suffix ◌ָם like the nouns (סוּסָם); but a number of prepositions take, some exclusively and some alternatively, the suffix ◌ֶהֶם. We find בָּם, בָּהֶם (both in a single verse, Lv 11.43); לָהֶם; בָּהֵם (ṣeré, § *c*, n. 3); עִמָּהֶם, עִמָּם; אִתְּהֶם occurs less often than אִתָּם(2).

Most prepositions take the suffixes in the manner of the singular noun, some (§ *l*) in the manner of the plural noun.

Among the prepositions which take the suffixes in the manner of the singular noun, those which have a more nominal character do not usually present any irregularity. Thus נֶגֶד *opposite, against* takes suffixes exactly like סוּס: נֶגְדִּי, נֶגְדְּךָ, נֶגְדּוֹ, נֶגְדָּם etc., § 96 A *c*; likewise abs. *בַּעַד (in מִבַּעַד), בְּעַד *against, across, for*: בַּעֲדִי (once בַּעֲדֵנִי), בַּעַדְךָ (compare נַעַרְךָ, § 96 A *i*), בַּעֲדָם etc.(3)

The primitive prepositions, however, present numerous peculiarities. We shall classify these prepositions in the following order: ל and ב, כ; מִן, עִם; אֵת *with*, אֵת as accusative particle.

(1) Rarely in the manner of a verb, e.g. תַּחְתֵּנִי 2Sm 22.37,40,48 (but in the parallel

Ps 18.37,40,48 תַּחְתַּי); תַּחְתֶּ֫נָּה Gn 2.21; בַּעֲדֵ֫נִי Ps 139.11 here not only in pause as in the preceding examples, but also rhyming with יְשׁוּפֵ֫נִי.
(2) אֶתְהֶן, however, far outnumbers אֹתָן — 13 : 1 (besides אוֹתָ֫נָה twice). In addition, forms which are most likely due to analogy, such as אוֹתְכֶם, אוֹתְהֶם, and אוֹתְהֶן, occur once each. Andersen and Forbes (AF, p. 189) hold that more cases of defectively spelled אתכם etc. could conceal the analogical form אֹתְכֶם etc. But given the fact that the force of paradigmatic analogy would have favoured אֹתְכֶם etc., it is striking that the majority of cases are pointed as אֶתְכֶם etc. The latter, therefore, is likely to have preserved an authentic form.
(3) The alternation in vowel pattern between בַּ֫עַד, בְּעַד־, and בַּעַד־ (which is basically *בַּעְדְ־) is analogous to that between חֶ֫דֶר, חֲדַר־, and חַדְרְ־: Blau, *Heb. Phonology and Morphology*, p. 215.

Inflection of לְ and בְּ (Paradigm 20). Although the primitive form of בְּ was most likely **bi*, this preposition almost has the same inflection as לְ, the primitive form of which is *la* (but cf. § *b*). The pausal forms לָךְ and בָּךְ of the masc. are similar to the contextual (and pausal) forms of the feminine. In the plural, the primitive form *la* appears: לָ֫נוּ, לָכֶם, לָהֶם; and probably on the analogy of these forms, we have בָּ֫נוּ, בָּכֶם, בָּהֶם alongside בָּם(1). The poetic form לָ֫מוֹ(2), which is frequent (about 50 times) for לָהֶם, is also used, but very rarely, as a pausal form, for לוֹ: Is 44.15; probably Gn 9.26,27; perh. Dt 33.2; Is 53.8. Rare spellings: לְכָה(3), בְּכָה; we sometimes find לוֹ wrongly spelled לא (and vice versa); instead of לָהּ the massorah prescribes לָה (with ה rafé) in Nu 32.42; Zech 5.11; Ru 2.14 (before a mil'el word in all three cases); cf. § 25 *a*. f

(1) בָּהֶם is appreciably more common in LBH than בָּם. In MH the former far outnumbers the latter.
(2) Compare עָלֵ֫ימוֹ *on him*, § *m*, n.
(3) Similar to לְכָה *come* (impv. לֵךְ with paragogic ה).

Inflection of כְּ (Paradigm 20). The primitive form **ka* (§ *b*) occurs in all the forms. With the heavy suffixes(1) we have the simple **ka*: כָּכֶם, כָּהֶם (ṣeré), כָּהֵ֫נָּה. With the light suffixes, **ka* is augmented by the pronoun **mā* (§ 37 *b*), hence כְּמוֹ, a form which is also often used, without suffixes, in poetry(2). The form כְּמוֹ was no doubt created in order to avoid certain confusions: in the 1st pers. sg. כִּי* could be confused with the conjunction כִּי, in the 3rd pers. sg. כוֹ* with the adverb כֹּה *thus*. The נ of כָּמ֫וֹנִי can probably be explained in terms of the need to g separate the two vowels in *$k\mathring{a}m\bar{\varrho}n$-$\bar{\imath}$: recourse was taken to נ, which occurs in the verbal suffix נִי.

(1) Compare the double theme with light suffixes and heavy suffixes in מַלְכֵיכֶם, מְלָכַי, § 96 A *b*, n.

(2) It is no doubt due to the analogy of the frequent כְּמוֹ (56 x) that the rare poetic forms בְּמוֹ (9 x) and לְמוֹ (4 x) were created. With the poetic כְּמוֹ, which has an extra syllable, compare the forms of French *avecque* and *avecques* used by poets. These מוֹ forms have sometimes been cited as cases of the so-called enclitic Mem, e.g. H.D. Hummel, *JBL* 76 (1957) 96; one serious problem with such a suggestion is the difficulty in identifying the nature of the vowel preceding or following the Mem.

h **Inflexion of** מִן (Paradigm 20). The simple form occurs with the heavy suffixes: מִכֶּם, מֵהֶם, מֵהֵנָּה. With the light suffixes we have a form with repeated מ, e.g. מִמֶּנִּי, מִמֶּךָּ. These forms are variously explained. The most plausible explanation seems to be that the simple form *min* was reinforced by total repetition(1), hence *minmin* > *mimmin*. Before the suffix *hu*, *mimmin* + *hu* became מִמֶּנּוּ(2), hence in the 1st pers. מִמֶּנִּי. Before the suffix *ka*, *mimmin* + *ka* became מִמֶּךָּ, a pausal form from which the contextual form מִמְּךָ was obtained (probably on the analogy of שָׂדֶךָ, שָׂדְךָ; סוּסֶךָ, סוּסְךָ). In the 1st pers. sg. one finds in poetry the rare form (4 x) מִנִּי(3), in pause מֶנִּי (6 x).

(1) The examples of reinforcing through repetition are not rare in languages. In Fr. *dedans* the preposition *de* is found twice, for *dans* comes from *de* + *ans* (*ens*) = Lat. *de* + *intus*. In Old Italian one often finds, e.g., "*in nell*'arca di Noè." Compare the reduplicated form מֵימֵי *waters of*, § 98 *e*.

(2) The "Orientals" vocalise the form differently for "from us": מִמֶּנּוּ. This explanation of the doubled /n/ can apply to such forms as הִנְּנִי, אֵינֶנִּי and עוֹדֶנִּי.

(3) This is exactly the form of Arabic *minni* (with doubling of *n*). We also have the poetic form מִנֵּי for מִן, § *d* (end).

i **Inflection of** עִם *with* (Paradigm 20). There is always gemination of the מ before the suffixes. These suffixes are exactly those of לְ. The vowel ָ in עִמָּנוּ, עִמָּךְ is probably due to the analogy of לָךְ and לָנוּ (§ *e*); likewise for עִמָּכֶם and עִמָּהֶם. Alongside this last form, which occurs especially in the late books (Ezr, Ne, Ch)(1), we find the more usual form עִמָּם. Besides עִמִּי we find the equally frequent form עִמָּדִי, variously explained(2).

(1) עִמָּם is extremely rare in MH, whereas the longer עִמָּהֶם is the usual form in LBH and MH. See Ec 10.9 where both בָּהֶם and בָּם occur for the sake of stylistic variation.

(2) Cf. P. Joüon in *MUSJ* 5 (1911) 395: explained by עִם + יָדִי *next to my side, near*

me, with me.

Inflection of אֵת *with* (Paradigm 20). With maqqef: ־אֶת, § 13 *b*. We always find gemination of the ת before the suffixes. The inflection of את is very similar to that of the synonymous עִם(1); however, against עִמָּכֶם we find אִתְּכֶם with shewa (perh. due to the influence of אֶתְכֶם). Instead of ָ, in the 2nd f.sg., we find ֵ in מֵאִתֵּךְ Is 54.10 (perh. because of the preceding ֵ or the conjunctive accent). j

Instead of the forms of the preposition אֵת *with* we often find forms of the accusative particle אֵת (§ *k*). The confusion(2), which is due to the resemblance of the forms, is an ancient one. One finds forms with אֹת' and אוֹת' especially in the books of Kings (1Kg 20 — 2Kg 8), Jeremiah and Ezekiel, e.g. אוֹתִי *with me* Josh 14.12; אוֹתָם *with them* 2Kg 6.16 (following the correct אִתָּנוּ!); מֵאוֹתוֹ *from* (*with*) *him* 8.8; אוֹתָךְ *with you* 1Kg 22.24 (following the correct אִתָּנוּ!). This erroneous use may have originated with the forms of מֵאֵת in those cases where the value of אֵת is weakened and where מִן alone would have sufficed.

The preposition את *with* is extremely rare in late books such as Esth, Ezr, Dn, and Ch, occurring a mere 13 times in these books out of the over 900 instances in the OT. It has entirely gone out of use in MH. Aramaic influence is most likely, since Aramaic uses only עם in the sense of *with* of association.

(1) For the synonymity of the two prepositions, see Jdg 7.4 זֶה יֵלֵךְ אִתָּךְ ... זֶה לֹא יֵלֵךְ עִמָּךְ; 1Sm 26.6 מִי יֵרֵד אִתִּי ... אֲנִי אֵרֵד עִמָּךְ. More examples in Bendavid, 1.29.

(2) SH and Babylonian Heb. alone keep the two apart: SH—/at/ and /itt-/ *with*, but /it/ and /ūt-/ *nota accusativi* (Ben-Ḥayyim, *LOT*, vol. 5, p. 242); Bab.— /'itt/ or /'ẹt/ and /'itt-/ *with*, but /'ẹt/ and /'ọt-/ or /'eṯhem/ (Yeivin, *Babylonian Tradition*, pp. 1120-25).

The *nota accusativi* for the preposition occurs 61 times in all, only in late books (Kg 17x; Jer 17x; Ez 21x; 2nd Is 2x): Sh. Morag, art. cit. [§ 38, n. 6], p. 129. He further thinks (pp. 138-41) that the usages in Ez and 2nd Is are Akkadianisms, and those in Jer and Kg Aramaisms. Both, of course, can be put down to Aramaisms, if outside influence is to be sought, though the nota acc. is of rather infrequent occurrence in contemporary Aramaic documents.

Sperber (*Hist. Gram.*, pp. 63-65) presents a classification of a large number of plausible examples of confusion of the two prepositions according to verbs and some other phraseological criteria.

Inflection of אֵת, particle of the accusative (Paradigm 20). With maqqef: ־אֶת, § 13 *b*. This particle את, exponent of the accusative (§ 125 *e*), takes the same suffixes as the preposition אֵת. Undoubtedly k this was initially used with the pronouns in order to give them the value of the accusative (§ 61 *a*); subsequently it was used with the nouns. The primitive Hebrew form is *'*āt* with a long ā(1), but it can be shortened(2).

With the long vowel ā, the form becomes אוֹת, written more often אֹת (*defective*)(3). This long form occurs with the light suffixes(4): אֹתִי, אֹתְךָ etc.

Before the heavy suffixes *'*āt* is shortened to *'*at*, which, through another attenuating process becomes '*ęt*, e.g. אֶתְכֶם(5). This same form occurs with maqqef, namely in very close juncture: אֶת־. In less close juncture, the particle is stressed, and as a consequence אֶת־ becomes אֵת(6). The vowel *e* (ֵ, ֶ) may have been influenced by the preposition אֵת, אֶת־ *with*: here the vowel goes back to *e*, cf. Akk. *itti* "with."

In the 3rd pl. we have אֹתָם rather than אֶתְהֶם(7), but אֶתְהֶן is more frequent than אֹתָן (§ *e*, n. 2). The forms of the exponent of the accusative often occur with the sense of the preposition אֵת *with* (cf. § *j*). In contrast, Aquila, identifying the two particles, translates the exponent of the accusative with σύν!(8)

N.B. The origin and the meaning of the particle *'*āt* are controversial(9). It is probably an old substantive with vague meaning. One could postulate the sense of *thing*, and associate the word with the root אוה *to desire*. In Semitic languages many words for *will, desire* take on the meaning of *thing*, e.g. LBH and MH חֵפֶץ, Arb. *šay'*, Syr. *ṣvuṯå*. The word *āt*, having lost its original sense(10), has been turned into a grammatical function word(11).

(1) Compare the long *a* of the parallel form in BA יָת *yåṯ* (Dn 3.12 יָתְהוֹן *them*†) and Targumic Aramaic.

(2) Compare the long form מוֹ and the short forms מָה and מֶה of the pronoun *ma*, § 37*b*.

(3) 1031 cases against 357: AF, pp. 189-91. See also Barr, *Spellings*, pp. 158-61.

(4) Law of equilibrium; cf. § 96 A *b*, n.

(5) Compare the weakening of *a* to *ę* in יֶדְכֶם, § 29 *e*.

(6) This ֵ is therefore found to be derived indirectly from *a*!

(7) Compare, e.g. אֲבוֹתָם rather than אֲבֹתֵיהֶם, § 94 *g*, n. 1.

(8) Since σύν, where Aquila uses it to render the nota accusativi, does not mean "together with," it cannot be defended by the supposition that it is akin to its adverbial use as in Homeric Greek.

(9) On the etymology of the particle, see Muraoka, *Emphatic*, p. 147, n. 116.

(10) The use of אֹתִי etc. with reflexive force (§ 146 *k*) indicates, however, that the original force had not entirely disappeared.

(11) One may compare the often pleonastic use of *šān* "thing" in Egyptian Arabic, e.g. *'alā šān kədā* "because of this, that is why" (comp. עַל־כֵּן), *'alā šān inno* "in order that it ...."

Inflection of the prepositions which take suffixes in the manner of *l*
the **plural noun.** Amongst such prepositions there are those which are genuine plurals like סְבִיבוֹת, בֵּינוֹת, or merely appear to be plural like תַּחַת, תַּחְתֵּי, or their י belongs to the root (עַל, עַד, אֶל)(1). Of these prepositions, which are seven in number, בֵּין is not treated as a plural noun except when it takes the plural suffixes. Since the inflection of these prepositions presents no difficulty, the paradigm gives only the inflection of עַל, עַד (similar to עַל), אֶל (the vowel of which may vary), and בֵּין.

(1) Note Arb. *'ilā* and *'alā* each spelled with a final Yod (Yā') on the one hand, and Akk. *eli* "upon" and *adi* "until" on the other.

A. **Prepositions with ל"י root:** עַל, עַד, אֶל (Paradigm 20). *m*

עַל־ *on* (almost always with maqqef, § 13 *b*). The radical י is preserved in the frequent poetic form עֲלֵי. In prestress open syllables we find, e.g. עָלַי, in ante-prestress syllables, e.g. עֲלֵיכֶם. The poetic form עָלֵימוֹ Dt 32.23 etc. *on them* does seem to be used in the sense of *on him* in Job 20.23; 22.2; 27.23; comp. לָמוֹ for לוֹ, § *f*.

עַד־ *till* (nearly always with maqqef, § 13 *b*)(1). The radical י is preserved in the rare poetic form עֲדֵי. The inflection of עַד is similar to that of עַל(2).

אֶל־ *towards, to* (nearly always with maqqef, § 13 *b*). The radical י is preserved in the extremely rare (4 x) poetic form אֱלֵי. In prestress open syllables we find, e.g. אֵלַי, in ante-prestressed syllables, e.g. אֲלֵיכֶם (not 'אֱ, § 21 *i*)(3).

(1) The force of עַד is often pregnant, e.g. Jdg 19.26 "Then came the woman in the dawning of the day, and fell down at the door ... till it was light," namely "she remained there fallen till ..." or 1Ch 5.26 "he carried them away ... and brought them to Halah ... and the river Gozan to this day," i.e. they are still there.

(2) Two anomalous forms: עֲדֵיכֶם Job 32.12 (instead of 'עָ), עַד־הֵם 2Kg 9.18.

(3) With the heavy suffixes of the 2nd and 3rd pers. pl., defective spellings such as אֲלֵהֶם (but not אֲלֵכֶם) are rather common: 136 out of 419 instances, though far less so in עַל (15/523): AF, pp. 171f., and see also Barr, *Spellings*, pp. 134-37, 179f. In the Pentateuch אֲלֵהֶם etc. are more common (92: 52), also all 15 cases of עֲלֵהֶם are confined

to the Pentateuch. This is striking in view of the extreme rarity (47/7305) of the comparable defective orthography in nouns, as in גּוֹיֵהֶם or יְדֵכֶם.

The usual short form אֶל is due to the process of backformation expressible by the following proportion:

דַּג־ : דָּגֶיךָ = אֵלֶיךָ : x

ergo x = אֶל

The same is true of עַל and עַד.

n **B. Other prepositions: אַחַר, בֵּין, סָבִיב, תַּחַת.**

אַחַר *after, behind*. The form אַחַר (§ 20 *c*) is not used with suffixes; one uses the form אַחֲרֵי, which is probably a pseudo-plural (by analogy with the antonym לִפְנֵי *before*), e.g. אַחֲרַי, אַחֲרֵיכֶם etc.

בֵּין *between, amongst* (Paradigm 20) is the cst. state of a non-existent בַּיִן*, the meaning of which is *distinction, interval*. With the suffixes for the singular we have the form בֵּין: בֵּינִי, בֵּינְךָ, בֵּינֵךְ, בֵּינוֹ (Gn 30.36; Lv 26.46†), instead of which the Qre of Josh 3.4; 8.11† prescribes בֵּינָיו, a form which along with בֵּינֶיךָ Gn 16.5 (hapax) is almost certainly corrupt(1). With the suffixes for the plural we find the form בֵּינֵי, which is probably a pseudo-plural [on the analogy of עֲלֵי etc.(2)] and בֵּינוֹת, which is a genuine plural(3). For בֵּין...לְ, cf. § 133 *d*.

סָבִיב *around*. The sing. סָבִיב is still employed as a substantive in 1Ch 11.8†, as well as the two plurals סְבִיבִים* Jer 32.44; 33.13† and סְבִיבוֹת (frequent). With the suffixes one finds only the two plurals, whether in the sense of the substantive *surroundings* or in the sense of the preposition *around*. Practically speaking, one may say: for *around* with a noun, סְבִיבוֹת (20 x) and סָבִיב לְ (12 x) are favoured, but סְבִיבֵי never occurs. For *around* with a pronoun סְבִיבוֹת is almost always used, very rarely סְבִיבֵי Ps 50.3; 97.2; Lam 1.17†; thrice סָבִיב לָהּ Na 3.8, Ps 125.2, and Ct 3.7.

תַּחַת *under*. With the suffixes the form is always(4) תַּחְתֵּי, which is a pseudo-plural; thus תַּחְתֵּינוּ, for example, on the analogy of the antonym עָלֵינוּ(5). For the rare and anomalous forms with suffixes in the manner of the verb, cf. § e, n.

(1) See H.M. Orlinsky in *HUCA* 17 (1942-43) 278-81.

(2) Comp. the *e* of the suffixes of nouns deriving from ל״י roots, § 94 *b* and the relevant note there.

(3) בֵּינוֹת without suffixes in the absolute state in Ez 10.7 מִבֵּינוֹת לַכְּרוּבִים *between the cherubim*.

For a critique of the commonly held view that בֵּינוֹתֵ֫ינוּ (e.g., Gn 26.28) is inclusive, namely "amongst us", whereas בֵּינֵ֫ינוּ is exclusive, anticipating another group such as "between us and them," see J. Barr, "Some notes on *ben* 'between' in Classic. Heb.," *JSS* 23 (1978) 1-22; and G. Haneman, *Leš* 40 (1975) 44f., where it is shown that בֵּין ... בֵּין is typical of Classical BH, and בֵּין ... לְ- of LBH.

(4) The only exceptions occur with the 3m.pl. suf., תַּחְתָּם (Dt 2.12 and 10 more times) as against תַּחְתֵּיהֶם (5 x), in relation to which note a common preference for the shorter ending (§ 94 *g*, 103 *e*, *k* with n. 7). On four cases of Ktiv תחתו as cases of archaic defective spelling, see H.M. Orlinsky, *HUCA* 17 (1942-43) 269-77.

(5) Cf. בֵּינֵי above, and the preceding note 2.

§ 104. Conjunction.

The simple conjuctions are few in number. The principal ones are: *a*
Coordinating (or: **juxtaposing**): וְ *and* (for the vocalisation, cf. § *c*; it is also used with a subordinating force, as we shall see in the section on the syntax of tenses, § 116); אַף *also*, גַּם *also*; אוֹ *or*.

Subordinating: אֲשֶׁר and שֶׁ, relative conjunctions in a broad sense of *that*, representing a stage before they became relative pronouns proper, §§ 38,145; כִּי *that* and various meanings: *when, if, because, but*; פֶּן *in case, lest*; אִם *if*, לוּ *if* (unreal), לוּלֵי and לוּלֵא *if ... not*, Lat. *nisi*, § 29 *h*.

On the other hand, the subordinating conjuctions compounded with אֲשֶׁר   *b* and כִּי are quite numerous, e.g., יַ֫עַן אֲשֶׁר (32 x) *because* (also יַ֫עַן only, 23 x); לְמַ֫עַן אֲשֶׁר *in order that* (frequent, and, as often, לְמַ֫עַן only); כַּאֲשֶׁר *as, just as, when, because*; אַחֲרֵי אֲשֶׁר *after*, more frequent than אַחַר אֲשֶׁר (very rarely just אַחֲרֵי); עַד אֲשֶׁר *until* and *before* (also just עַד); עֵ֫קֶב אֲשֶׁר, עֵ֫קֶב כִּי (also just עֵ֫קֶב) *as a consequence of* (*recompense for*), *because* (cf. § 129 *p-q*).

It may be seen that a preposition, e.g., עַד, or a prepositional phrase such as לְמַ֫עַן, can become a conjunction. The adverb טֶ֫רֶם *not yet* is also, though rarely, used as a conjuction *before*; but בְּטֶ֫רֶם *before* is often used.

Vocalisation of וְ. The vocalisation of the conjunction וְ is largely   *c* similar to that of the prepositions בְּ, כְּ, and לְ (§ 103 *b-c* where similar cases with ו are mentioned); but the ו, a labial vocalic consonant, has some peculiarities. The primitive form is *wa*. There is a *weak* vocalisation (namely the shewa or its substitutes) and a vocalisation unique to certain cases, which is *strong* (namely וָ). Moreover, in the unique case of the inverted future *wayyiqtọl*, there is a very forceful pronunciation (vowel *a* with doubling, whether real or virtual), which we discussed in § 47(1).

I. **Weak vocalisation.** Usually, and excepting the special cases enumerated below, the ו has a simple shewa, e.g. וְאִישׁ Gn 19.31; וְלֹא (always, except twice, § *d*, n. 1); with the verbal forms: וְקָטַ֫לְתִּי *and I killed*, וְקָטַלְתִּ֫י *and I shall kill*, וְיָקוּם *and he will arise*, וְיָקֹם *and may he arise, so that he may arise*, וְאָק֫וּמָה *and I want to arise, in order that I may arise*, וְקוּם *and arise!*. Before י, the ו takes the vowel *i* and the י becomes quiescent, e.g., with the cst. state pl. יְמֵי we find וִימֵי, with the jussive יְהִי we find וִיהִי, § 79 *s*. Before a ḥaṭef (nuanced shewa) we find the short vowel of the nuance of ḥaṭef, e.g. וַעֲבָדִים, וַחֲלִי *and a ring*, וָחֳלִי *and an ailment*, וֶאֱכֹל *and eat!*, וֶאֱמֹר *and say!* (contr. לֵאמֹר, § 103 *b*)(2). But with אֱלֹהִים we find וֵאלֹהִים (like בֵּאלֹהִים etc., § 103 *b*). With אָדוֹן the treatment of וְ is similar to that of בְּ, כְּ, and לְ, § 103 *b*. For the ו before the forms of the verbs הָיָה and חָיָה, cf. § 79 *s*, e.g. וִהְיִיתֶם, הֱיִיתֶם. Before a consonant followed by shewa (except י) *w*- becomes *u*, e.g. וּדְבַר *and the word of* ...(3). Before the labial consonants (ב, ו[4], מ, and פ; mnemonic word בּוּמַף) *w*- becomes *u*, e.g. **w-mẹ'lẹḵ* > **wᵘmẹ'lẹḵ* > וּמֶ֫לֶךְ. This rule, however, is overridden by the rule on the strong vocalisation of the conjunction (§ *d* below: e.g. וָמֵת, and לֶ֫חֶם וָמַ֫יִם).

(1) Compare the vocalisation of the type בַּמֶּה, § 37 *d*.

(2) In וַעְצֹר Job 4.2 there is secondary suppression of the ḥaṭef, cf. § 22 *d*.

(3) For the special case of the type וּזֲהַב (instead of וּזְהַב*), cf. § 9 *c*.

(4) In fact, no example with ו, which is, moreover, extremely rare as an initial radical (cf. § 26 *f*).

d II. **Strong vocalisation**, namely וָ. This *a*, which is the primitive vowel, does not exert any pressure on the following consonant, and consequently there is no gemination (as opposed to the *a* of the article **ha*, the pronoun **ma* and the form וַיִּקְטֹל). The strong vocalisation is used before the monosyllabic or disyllabic mil'el when they have an especially strong stress, namely in pause (major, and sometimes minor), sometimes in prepause. Examples: וָמֵת Ex 21.12 (at the end of the protasis; here the accent ṭifḥa is a major disjunctive). But if the stress is weak, we find the weak vocalisation, e.g. vs. 20 וּמֵת (in the middle of the protasis; here the accent ṭifḥa is a minor disjunctive as usual). Example with a mil'el disyllable: וָמַ֫תְנוּ 2Kg 7.4 (in the same verse we even find וָמַ֫תְנוּ שָׁ֖ם in minor prepause [zaqef], but at the end of an apodosis)(1). The strong vocalisation is particularly frequent when two analogous words are closely(2) associated and form a group, e.g. תֹ֫הוּ וָבֹ֫הוּ Gn 1.2; always לֶ֫חֶם וָמַ֫יִם and לֶ֫חֶם וָמָ֑יִם; יוֹם וָלַ֫יְלָה Gn 8.22; זָהָב וָבֹהוּ Ex 25.3; כֹּה וָכֹ֫ה Ex 2.12; אִישׁ־וָאִישׁ Esth 1.8, but אִישׁ וָאִישׁ Ps 87.5 in minor pause; in a series of three words: פַּ֫חַד וָפַ֫חַת וָפָ֑ח Is 24.17 (prepause and pause); Ez 2.10; in a sequence of four words: צָפֹ֫נָה וָנֶ֫גְבָּה וָקֵ֫דְמָה וָיָ֑מָּה Gn 13.14 (here probably for the sake of emphasis). In Gn 8.22 eight nouns are grouped into four pairs, each consisting of two nouns, whilst each pair is linked to the next by וָ, and within each pair (except the first) the two constituent nouns are joined by וָ.

One can see that the strong vocalisation of וָ, like that of בָּ, כָּ, and לָ, § 103 c, is of rhythmic nature. Note that before the demonstratives, ו has the weak vocalisation (וְזֶה, וְזֹאת, וְאֵ֫לֶּה) whilst the three prepositions have the strong vocalisation. One should also note that with a word such as קוּם we find וְקוּם and arise!, although לָקוּם occurs.

(1) We always find וַיְ֫שׁ, except once וַיֶ֫שׁ 2Kg 10.15 forming a protasis: "if it is it." We always find וְלֹא except twice וָלֹא 2Sm 13.26; 2Kg 5.17 forming a protasis "since it is not" (§ 167 o).

(2) Not necessarily in a semantic sense; cf. E.R. Revell, *HAR* 5 (1981) 76-84. An amply illustrated and more detailed classification of the conjunction ו vocalised with qameṣ may be found in Sperber, *Hist. Gram.*, pp. 582-86.

§. 105. Interjection

The interjections are words of emotion. The simplest interjections are pure words of emotion, cries or onomatopoeic sounds. The others are words expressing a more or less precise notion with a nuance of emotion. Lastly, any word used with a special nuance of emotion can take on an interjectional value. An imperative can become pure interjection, like Fr. *tiens!* [= *Here (you) are, well!, Hello!*]; such is the case for רְאֵה, § d, הָבָה, § e, לְכָה, § e. Conversely, an interjection addressed to somebody can lose an afformative like the imperative; such is the case for הַס *ssshhh!, Silence!*; pl. הַ֫סּוּ Ne 8.11†, § b.

b **Cry of joy:** הֶאָח *Ah!* (9 x).

Cry of sorrow: אֲהָהּ *Ah!* (13 x)(1); הָהּ Ez 30.2ʔ; אָח Ez 6.11; 21.20†(2).

Cry of intimidation: הוֹי *vae! Woe (to the man who ...)*(50 x); אוֹי (22 x); אוֹיָה Ps 120.5† (אִי Ec 4.10; 10.16 is ʔ); אַלְלַי Mi 7.1; Job 10.15†. Cf. § 162 *d*.

Cry for demanding silence הַס, הָס *ssch!, Silence!*; pl. הַסּוּ Ne 8.11†, § *a* end.

(1) We find the element אָהּ in אָנָּא, § *c*. The interjection אֲהָהּ is generally followed by a vocative, ordinarily אֲדֹנָי יֱהוִה.

(2) אָח is probably present in אַחֲלַי Ps 119.5 (a disjunctive accent) *would that!* and אַחֲלֵי 2Kg 5.3 (a conjunctive accent) *Oh! if*... The second element is probably corrupted from the conjunction לוּ *if*. The word could then be an exclamatory conjunction (cf. § 163 *c*).

c **Entreating** interjection ־נָא. This word, which occurs only after another word, is nearly always preceded by a maqqef, § 13 *b*. It is mostly used for the purpose of adding a usually weak entreating nuance, which is roughly equivalent to a stressed and lengthened *Please* in English(1). One can sometimes render נָא by *I beg (you), For pity's sake!*(2) (which corresponds more to אָנָּא), and sometimes by the emphatic *Do* prefixed to an imperative as in "Do come!"; in certain cases, and notably when it is used in a rather loose fashion, נָא must not be translated. The entreating particle is highly frequent with the volitive moods (imperative, cohortative and jussive). In the cohortative, alongside cases where the entreating sense is evident (because the action willed by the speaker depends on the will of others, e.g. Nu 20.17 נַעְבְּרָה־נָּא "we wish to pass, *if you please*"), there are cases where the נא is used in a rather loose manner and hardly adds anything other than a forceful nuance, e.g. Ex 3.3 אָסֻרָה־נָּא *I wish to go forward*; Nu 16. 26; 20.10(3). In אִם־נָא of a conditional protasis, the entreating nuance, which logically affects the apodosis containing the request, is anticipated(4), e.g., Gn 33.10 "*I beg you*, if I found favour in your eyes, you may care to accept my offering." In the frequent הִנֵּה־נָא *here, look! (I beg you)*, הִנֵּה draws attention to what one is going to say, and נא begs the hearer to pay attention to the thing announced by הִנֵּה and (through anticipation[5]) to look favourably upon the request that follows, which often contains a second נא: e.g., Gn 16.2 roughly means "*Now, look here,*

I beg you," and Gn 19.2 "*Listen, I beg you*" (here הִנֵּה־נָא is immediately followed by the request).

The **reinforced entreating** אָנָּא (7 x), אָנָּה (6 x) *ah!*, *For pity's sake!* is composed of the element אָה*, which we have in אֲהָהּ *ah!* § *b*, and נא. Sometimes the word is mil'ra, but some other times it has two accents (probably because the two elements of the word were still felt as distinct components).

בִּי is an **entreating** interjection in the special sense of *Pardon!*, *Excuse me!* The fact that we find בִּי solely before אֲדֹנִי (7 x) and אֲדֹנָי (5 x) already indicates that this is mainly a term of politeness. It is used with the strong nuance in Nu 12.11 in order to beg forgiveness for an offence; elsewhere always in a weakened sense, like our *Pardon me!*: in order to excuse oneself for doing something as in Ex 4.10,13; Jdg 6.15; in order to excuse oneself for what one is going to say as in Josh 7.8; Jdg 6.13; 13.8; in order to excuse oneself for addressing a person of distinction as in Gn 43.20; 44.18; 1Sm 1.26; 1Kg 3.17,26†(6).

(1) But cf. M. Bar-Magen, "The word נָא in BH" [Heb], *Beth Mikra* 25 (1980) 163-71.

(2) But without characteristic nuance of *politeness*. Thus Eli says עֲלֵה־נָא to his servant 1Kg 18.43, and simply עֲלֵה to the king (v. 41). God uses נָא in speaking to Abraham Gn 13.14; to Moses Ex 4.6, 11.2; to Isaiah Is 7.3.

(3) Rabin holds that the particle was originally identical with the element /-na/ of the second energic in Arabic, /yaqtulanna/: C. Rabin, *The Meanings of the Grammatical Forms in Biblical and Modern Hebrew* [Heb.] (Jerusalem, 1971), p. 28.

(4) Compare the anticipation of אָנָּא Ex 32.31 and particularly Dn 9.4 (the request coming only in vs. 16).

(5) See the immediately preceding note.

(6) בִּי therefore has a sense totally different from אָנָּא. It does not mean: *for pity's sake I beg you*, as it is usually translated. The sense *Pardon!, excuse me!* is in favour of the explanation according to which בִּי would be elliptical for "(the fault is) *upon me*," "I am to blame," which amounts to asking for forgiveness. Note that we never find in Hebrew an expression corresponding to the notion of *begging pardon*; for that one says "I have sinned" (cf. Ehrlich, *Randglossen* ad Ex 9.27).

d In order to attract **attention** one uses the presentative adverb הִנֵּה *Behold!*, *Look!*, often reinforced by the interjection נָא *I beg you*: הִנֵּה־נָא, § *b*. Frequent use is also made of the imperative רְאֵה *look!*, e.g. Gn 27.27; 31.50; 41.41; Ex 7.1; 31.2; 33.12; 2Sm 15.3; even when addressing several people(1)(therefore = *here it is!*) Dt 1.8.

(1) Comp. Fr. *tiens!* even when addressing several people or a person addressed politely with *vous*.

e In order to incite and **encourage** one uses especially the imperative לְכָה *Come!*, *Come on*, e.g. Gn 31.44; 37.13; even when speaking to a woman as in Gn 19.32; in the fem. לְכִי 1Kg 1.12; in the plural לְכוּ Gn 37.20; 1Sm 9.9 (cf. § 177 *f*). In Genesis and Exodus we find five times the imperative הָבָה (from the unused verb יָהַב* *to give*, § 75 *k*) in the interjectional sense of *Come on!* In four examples someone is addressing more than one person (Gn 11.3,4,7; Ex 1.10). In Gn 38.16 we have הָבָה־נָּא in the sense of *Allow me, I beg you*, where a woman is being addressed.

f In order to express a **wish** one uses אַחֲלַי, אַחֲלֵי *ah!*, *if*, La. *utinam* (= *would that!*) (§ *b*, n.), מִי יִתֵּן (cf. § 163 *d*)(1). For a **negative wish** or **rejection** (Lat. *absit*), we find חָלִילָה, § 93 *h*, the primary meaning of which is probably *profanation!* (cf. § 165 *k*).

אָבִי (2 x) seems to be a dialectal form having, like לוּ, the sense of *ah!*, *if* Job 34.36 and of *if* (unreal) 2Kg 5.13.

(1) For the special wish *so be it* one has the verbal adjective אָמֵן *Amen!*, *I wish that it were true!* This word is always used, in the Old Testament, to express wishes; likewise in the rabbinic literature (cf. Dalman, *Grammatik* [§ 29 *g*], p. 243), in the Apocalypse of John (except 3.14), but not in the Gospels.